THE MASTER OUTLINE & SUBJECT INDEX

VOLUME 14

THE PREACHER'S OUTLINE & SERMON BIBLE®

THE MASTER OUTLINE & SUBJECT INDEX

VOLUME 14

THE
PREACHER'S
OUTLINE & SERMON
BIBLE®

NEW TESTAMENT

NEW INTERNATIONAL VERSION

Leadership Ministries Worldwide
PO Box 21310
Chattanooga, TN 37424-0310

Publisher & Distributor

DEDICATED:

To all the men and women of the world
who preach and teach the Gospel of our
Lord Jesus Christ and
To the Mercy and Grace of God.

———————————— *&* ————————————

• Demonstrated to us in Christ Jesus our Lord.

> "In him we have redemption through his blood, the forgiveness
> of sins, in accordance with the riches of God's grace." (Eph. 1:7 NIV)

• Out of the mercy and grace of God His Word has flowed.
Let every person know that God will have mercy upon him,
forgiving and using him to fulfill His glorious plan of salvation.

> "For God so loved the world, that he gave his one and only Son, that
> whosoever believes in him shall not perish, but have eternal life. For
> God did not send his Son into the world to condemn the world, but to
> save the world through him." (Jn 3:16-17 NIV)

> "This is good and pleases God our Saviour; who wants all men to be
> saved and to come to the knowledge of the truth." (I Tim. 2:3-4 NIV)

———————————— *&* ————————————

The Preacher's Outline and Study Bible®-NIV
is written for God's servants to use in their
study, teaching, and preaching of God's Holy Word.

OUR VISION - PASSION - PURPOSE

- To share the Word of God with the world.
- To help the believer, both minister and layman alike, in his understanding,
  preaching, and teaching of God's Word.
- To do everything we possibly can to lead men, women, boys, and girls to
  give their hearts and lives to Jesus Christ and to secure the eternal life
  which He offers.
- To do all we can to minister to the needy of the world.
- To give Jesus Christ His proper place, the place which the Word gives Him.
  Therefore — No work of Leadership Ministries Worldwide will ever be
  personalized.

Sharing

The OUTLINED BIBLE

With the World!

MISCELLANEOUS ABBREVIATIONS

&	=	And
Arg.	=	Argument
Bckgrd.	=	Background
Bc.	=	Because
Circ.	=	Circumstance
Concl.	=	Conclusion
Cp.	=	Compare
Ct.	=	Contrast
Dif.	=	Different
e.g.	=	For example
Et.	=	Eternal
F.	=	Following
Govt.	=	Government
Id.	=	Identity or Identification
Illust.	=	Illustration
K.	=	Kingdom, K. of God, K. of Heaven, etc.
No.	=	Number
N.T.	=	New Testament
O.T.	=	Old Testament
Pt.	=	Point
Quest.	=	Question
Rel.	=	Religion
Resp.	=	Responsibility
Rev.	=	Revelation
Rgt.	=	Righteousness
Thru	=	Through
V.	=	Verse
Vs.	=	Verses
Vs.	=	Versus

Currently Available Materials, with New Volumes Releasing Regularly

- **THE PREACHER'S OUTLINE & SERMON BIBLE® — DELUXE EDITION**

  Volume 1 . . . . St. Matthew I (chapters 1-15)   3-Ring, looseleaf binder
  Volume 2 . . . . St. Matthew II (chapters 16-28)
  Volume 3 . . . . St. Mark
  Volume 4 . . . . St. Luke
  Volume 5 . . . . St. John
  Volume 6 . . . . Acts
  Volume 7 . . . . Romans
  Volume 8 . . . . 1, 2 Corinthians (1 volume)
  Volume 9 . . . . Galatians, Ephesians, Philippians, Colossians (1 volume)
  Volume 10 . . . . 1,2 Thessalonians, 1,2 Timothy, Titus, Philemon (1 volume)
  Volume 11 . . . . Hebrews -James (1 volume)
  Volume 12 . . . . 1,2 Peter, 1,2,3 John, Jude (1 volume)
  Volume 13 . . . . Revelation
  Volume 14 . . . . Master Outline & Subject Index
  FULL SET — 14 Volumes

- **THE PREACHER'S OUTLINE & SERMON BIBLE® — OLD TESTAMENT**

  Volume 1 . . . . Genesis I (chapters 1-11)
  Volume 2 . . . . Genesis II (chapters 12-50)
  Volume 3 . . . . Exodus I (chapters 1-18)
  Volume 4 . . . . Exodus II (chapters 19-40)
  Volume 5 . . . . Leviticus   New volumes release periodically

- **THE PREACHER'S OUTLINE & SERMON BIBLE® — SOFTBOUND EDITION**

  Identical content as Deluxe above. Lightweight, compact, and affordable for overseas & traveling

- **THE PREACHER'S OUTLINE & SERMON BIBLE® — 3 VOL HARDCOVER w/CD**

- **THE PREACHER'S OUTLINE & SERMON BIBLE® — NIV SOFTBOUND EDITION**

- **The Minister's Personal Handbook - What the Bible Says...to the Minister**

  12 Chapters - 127 Subjects - 400 Verses *OUTLINED* - Paperback, Leatherette, 3-ring

- **THE TEACHER'S OUTLINE & STUDY BIBLE™ • New Testament Books •**

  Complete 45 minute lessons - 4 months of studies/book; 200± pages - Student Journal Guides

- **OUTLINE Bible Studies series: 10 Commandments - The Tabernacle**

- **Practical Word Studies: New Testament - 2,000 Key Words Made Easy**

- **CD-ROM: Preacher, Teacher, and Handbook-** (Windows/STEP) - **WORD***Search*

- **Translations of Preacher, Teacher, and Minister's Handbook: <u>Limited Quantities</u>**

  Russian — Spanish — Korean Future: *French, Portuguese, Hindi, Chinese*
  — *Contact us for Specific Language Availability and Prices* —

For quantity orders and information, please contact either:

LEADERSHIP MINISTRIES WORLDWIDE   *Your OUTLINE Bible Bookseller*
PO Box 21310
Chattanooga, TN 37424-0310
(423) 855-2181 (9am - 5pm Eastern) • FAX (423) 855-8616 (24 hours)
E•Mail - outlinebible@compuserve.com.

→ FREE Download Sample Pages — www.outlinebible.org

• *Equipping God's Servants Worldwide with OUTLINE Bible Materials* •
LMW is a nonprofit, international, nondenominational mission agency   9/98

The
Preacher's
Outline
&
Sermon
Bible®

—————

"

*Woe to me if I do not
preach the gospel!*

"
(I Cor. 9:16 NIV)

—————

THE MASTER
OUTLINE & SUBJECT INDEX

AT LAST, ALL THE SUBJECTS OF THE NEW TESTAMENT

ARE INDEXED...

- *AND OUTLINED*
- *AND FULLY DEVELOPED*

Just glance over to the next page to the Subject...

ABIDE - ABIDING

Note two things.

1.   The Subject Abide - Abiding is *ALREADY OUTLINED* for you in the Index. It is ready to be taught. You can teach your people what the Bible has to say about Abide - Abiding. Believers, yea, all people, are to abide--take up residence, live, move, have their being--in Christ.
   ⇒ The Condition for Salvation. Belief and abiding
   ⇒ The Duty of Abiding
   ⇒ The Meaning of Abiding
   ⇒ The Proof that One Abides in God and Christ
   ⇒ The Results of Abiding
   ⇒ The Source of Abiding
   ⇒ Things that are to abide

There are five or six messages here alone--if one desires to teach a series on what the Bible has to say about **Abiding**. Just think! Every subject you could ever want is now outlined for you--ready for you to preach and teach.

But there is MORE, MUCH MORE.

2.   *REMEMBER*: you can look up *any* subject and turn to the Scripture reference, and what you find is the *greatest help imaginable*: the Scripture is *already outlined* for you; and in addition, it is *already fully developed* for you--point by point.

This is the *GREAT VALUE* of **The Preacher's Outline & Sermon Bible®**. You have not only what all other subject indexes give you, that is, a list of all the subjects and their Scripture references, *BUT* you also have...

- Every subject *ALREADY OUTLINED* for you.
- Every subject *ALREADY FULLY DEVELOPED* for you.
- Every subject supported by other Scripture *ALREADY WRITTEN OUT* for you.

DISCOVER THE GREAT VALUE for yourself. Quickly glance below to the very first subject under ABIDE - ABIDING. It is:

ABIDE - ABIDING
Condition for salvation. Belief & **a.**   Jn.8:31

Turn to the reference. Glance at the Scripture and outline of the Scripture, then read the commentary. It will only take a moment. Look up John 8:31. You will immediately see the GREAT VALUE of the INDEX of **The Preacher's Outline & Sermon Bible®**. It is a TOPICAL BIBLE ready to preach, teach, and study--subject by subject--any subject you might want.

_____

THE MASTER OUTLINE AND SUBJECT INDEX

A

AARON
Priesthood of.
    Contrasted with Melchizedek's priesthood. Heb.7:1-24
    Qualifications of. Heb.5:1-4
    Weakness & insufficiency of.
    Heb.7:1-24; 9:1-10

ABADDON
Meaning. Hebrew name for the king of evil spirits. Rev.9:11

ABASE - ABASED
Caused by.
    Selfishness & godless independence.
    Lk.15:14-16
    Self-glory & self-exaltation. Acts 12:20-23
Discussed. Lk.14:11

ABEL
Blood of Christ is superior to Abel.
    Heb.12:24
First righteous man killed upon earth.
    Mt.23:35

ABIDE - ABIDING (See **CONTINUE - CONTINUING**)
Condition for salvation. Belief & **a**. Jn.8:31
Duty.
    To **a**., continue in the teaching of Christ. 2 Jn.9
    To **a**. in the walk and life of Christ.
    1 Jn.2:6; 3:23-24
    To **a**. in Christ. Jn.15:1-8
    To let the Word **a**. or dwell in us.
    Jn.5:38
Meaning. "In" Christ. Ro.8:1
Proof that one **a**. in God & Christ.
    A person's obedience. Jn.15:10
    Faithfulness. 1 Jn.2:17
    How one knows God **a**. within.
    1 Jn.3:24
    Love. 1 Jn.4:12-16
    One has God & Christ **a**. within.
    2 Jn.9
    Righteousness. 1 Jn.2:29
    The new birth. One is born again.
    1 Jn.2:28-29
Results of **a**.
    Answered prayer. Jn.15:7
    Comfort & help. Jn.14:15-26
    Confidence. 1 Jn.2:28-29
    Deliverance from judgment. Jn.15:6
    Discipline and correction. Jn.15:2-3
    Fruit. Jn.15:5-8
    Keeps one from sin. 1 Jn.3:6
    Power. 1 Jn.2:24; 2:27
    Salvation. Jn.8:31
    Unashamedness. 1 Jn.2:28
Reward for **a**. 1 Cor.3:13-15
Source of **a**.
    A Christ-like walk. 1 Jn.2:6
    Christ. Jn.15:1-8
    Christ's love. Jn.15:9-11
    Continuing in the Word & doctrine of Christ. Jn.8:31; 2 Jn.9
    Holy Spirit. Jn.14:16-17; 1 Jn.2:27; 3:24
    Loving one another. 1 Jn.4:12-16

Obedience and discipline. 1 Jn.2:5-6;
    2:17; 3:24
The gospel. 1 Jn.2:27
The truth. 2 Jn.2
Things that are to **a**.
    Christ's priesthood. Heb.7:3
    Faith, hope, and love. 1 Cor.13:13
    God Himself. 2 Tim.2:13
    The believer himself. 1 Cor.3:13-15;
    1 Jn.2:5-6, 17, 24, 28
    The believer's anointing. 1 Jn.2:27
    The believer's works. 1 Cor.3:13-15
    The gospel. 1 Jn.2:24
    The obedient. 1 Jn.2:17
Verses. List of. Jn.8:31; 15:4

ABILITIES (See **GIFTS, SPIRITUAL - TALENTS**)
Duty. To surrender to Christ. Mt.14:18-21

ABOMINATION THAT CAUSES DESOLATION (See **ANTICHRIST-- THE ABOMINATION THAT CAUSES DESOLATION**)
Discussed. Mt.24:15; Mk.13:14-23
Predicted. By Daniel the prophet.
    Mt.24:15; Mk.13:14

ABOUND (See **INCREASING MEASURE**)

ABOVE REPROACH
How to be **a**.
    By being diligent & seeking to be **a**. at the return of Christ. 2 Pt.3:14
    By God keeping us until the end & making us **a**. in the day of Christ.
    1 Cor.1:4, 8
    By not murmuring & arguing. Ph.2:14-15
    By obeying the charges of the Word.
    1 Tim.5:7
    By praying for God to sanctify us.
    1 Th.5:23
Meaning. Eph.1:4; Ph.2:15; 1 Tim.3:2-3;
    Jude 24-25
Who is to be blameless.
    Believers. 1 Cor.1:8; Ph.2:14-15;
    1 Tim.5:7; 2 Pt.3:14
    Bishops, elders, ministers. 1 Tim.3:2;
    Tit.1:6-7
    Deacons. 1 Tim.3:10

ABRAHAM
And history. A type or symbol, a representative man in history. Ro.4:11-12
Call of. Jn.4:22; 8:54-59; Acts 7:2-8;
    Ro.4:1-25
Covenant of. Acts 7:2-8; Ro.4:1-25;
    Gal.3:6-7; 3:15-18
Discussed. Acts 7:2-8; Ro.4:1-25;
    Gal.3:6-7; 3:15-18; 4:22-23
Example of.
    Faith and endurance. Heb.6:12-15
    Faith over works. Justification & righteousness. Ro.4:1-25
    Grace over law. Gal.4:21-31
    Great faith. Pivotal point in history.
    Ro.4:1-25
    Justification by faith. Ro.4:9; 4:17-25;
    Gal.3:6-14
    Superiority of Christ's priesthood.
    Heb.7:4-10

Faith of.
    An obedient, hopeful faith. Heb.11:8-10
    Believed the promises of God.
    Heb.11:17-19
    Offered up Isaac by faith. Heb.11:17-19
    Proved his faith by works or deeds.
    Jas.2:21-24
    Sacrificial faith. Heb.11:17-19
    What he believed. Four things.
    Heb.11:8-10
Offered Isaac as a sacrifice. Discussed.
    Gal.3:8, 16
Paid tithes to Melchisedek. Heb.7:4-10
Place in Jewish history.
    Discussed. Jn.4:22; 8:54-59
    Father of believers. Ro.4:11-12; 4:17-25;
    Gal.3:6-14
    Father of the Jews. Jn.4:22; 8:33, 53
    Founder of the Jewish nation. Jn.4:22;
    Ro.4:1-25; Gal.3:6-7
Promises to. Discussed. Ro.4:1-25
Seed of.
    Christ. Lk.19:9-10; Jn.1:23; Ro.4:1-25;
    Gal.3:7-8, 16, 19, 29, cp. 3:6-29
    Discussed. Gal.3:8, 16; 3:16
    Nations of people. Ro.4:11-12; 4:13;
    4:17; Gal.3:7-8, 29
Testimony of.
    Hoped for the Messiah. Jn.8:56
    Rejoiced to see Jesus' day. Jn.8:54-59
Work of.
    Bearing the promised seed. (See **ABRAHAM**, Seed of)
    Believing. Man fails to follow the belief of Abraham. Jn.8:39-40
    To be the father of believers. Justification by faith. Ro.4:11-12; 4:17-25;
    Gal.3:6-14
    To be the founder of the Jewish nation.
    Jn.4:22; Ro.4:1-25; Gal.3:6-7

ABUNDANCE - ABUNDANT (See **HUNGER, SPIRITUAL; LIFE; SALVATION; SATISFACTION, SPIRITUAL**)
Spiritual **a**.
    Of grace & of all things. 2 Cor.9:8
    Of grace & salvation. Six things.
    Ro.5:15-18
    Of life. Jn.10:10
    Of one's entrance into heaven.
    2 Pt.1:11
    Of power. Eph.3:20
    Of provision for one's needs. Ph.4:19

ABUSE
Physical **a**. (See **INJURY; PERSECUTION**)
Sexual perversions. Ro.1:24-32; 1 Cor.
    6:9-11; Gal.5:19-21; Eph.4:17-19
Spiritual **a**.
    Of authority. 1 Cor.9:18
    Of the Lord's Supper. 1 Cor.11:17-34
    Of the world. 1 Cor.7:31

ABUSIVE; CURSING; GODLESS; SLANDER; SWEARING
Against the Holy Spirit. Mt.12:31-32;
    Mk.3:29-30; Lk.12:4-12

3

Caused by.
    Backsliding - a shipwrecked faith.
      1 Tim.1:19-20
    Claiming deity. 2 Th.2:4
    Covetousness & worldliness. Jas.2:6-7
    False religion. Rev.2:9
    Natural & physical difficulties & cir-
      cumstances. Rev.16:9-11, 21
    Not doing to others as we should.
      1 Tim.6:1
    Not living responsibly & righteously
      before the world. 1 Tim.6:1; Tit.2:1-5,
      esp. 5
    Persecution. Acts 26:11
    Professing Christ, but living a hypo-
      critical life. Ro.2:24, cp. 17-29
    Rejection & hatred of Christ. Jn.8:48-59;
      Acts 18:5-6
    The antichrist. Rev.13:1, 6
    The dragon, Satan. Rev.13:4-6
Charged against. Christ. Mt.9:3; Mk.2:6-7;
  Jn.10:36
Duty.
    Not to speak evil of any person, not a
      single person. Tit.3:2
    To have such a good conscience that
      those who s. will be put to shame.
      1 Pt.3:16, cp. 15
    To know that people watch to find ac-
      cusations. Lk.6:7
    To live a righteous life, not giving the
      world any reason for s. 1 Pt.2:12
    To prepare for the end time: a terrible
      period of world-wide s. 2 Tim.3:1-5,
      esp. 3
    To put away all evil or s. speaking. Eph.4:31
    To put off being a. Col.3:8
    To rejoice & endure s. for the sake of
      Christ. Mt.5:11-12
Is forgiven. Mk.3:28
Meaning. Mt.9:3;Mk.7:22; Ro.1:30;
  Col.3:8-11; 1 Tim.3:11-12; 2 Tim.3:2-4;
  Heb.12:15-17
Sin of.
    Religion can be guilty of a. Rev.2:8-11
    Will be a trait of the last days. 2 Tim.
      3:1-2; Rev.6:9-11, 21
    Will be committed by the antichrist.
      Rev.13:4-8
The promise to believers when slandered. To
  be blessed & greatly rewarded. Mt.5:11-12
Who is often a.
    Believers. 1 Pt.2:12; 3:16; Acts 2:1-13,
      esp. 13; 24:5-6; Rev.2:9
    Christ. (See **JESUS CHRIST**, Ac-
      cused - Accusation against)
    Ministers & church leaders. Lk.7:33;
      Acts 6:13; 3 Jn.9-10
Who it is that is a.
    A whole generation of unbelievers
      who stand against true righteousness.
      Mt.11:16-19
    Corrupt political & religious officials.
      Lk.22:66-71; 23:1-5
    Religious leaders. Acts 6:9-15; 24:1-9
    Some church leaders & members who
      oppose the minister. 3 Jn.9-10
    Some religionists. Mt.9:34
    The average citizen who mocks spiri-
      tual things. Acts 2:1-13, esp. 13

ABYSS
Described.
    As a great smoking furnace. Rev.9:2
    As a prison. Rev.20:7
Meaning. 1 Pt.3:19-20; Rev.9:2

Ruler over. Discussed. Rev.9:1; 9:11
The beast, that is, the antichrist shall
  come from. Rev.11:7; 17:8
The destiny of Satan. Satan shall be cast
  into the a. pit for one thousand years.
  Rev.20:1-3

ACCEPTANCE - ACCEPTABLE
Discussed. Lk.9:49-50
    Receiving and rejecting men. Mt.8:5-13
How one becomes a.
    Discussed. Mk.9:38-41; Ro.2:25-27;
      Gal.2:6
    Repentance. Lk.15:20-21
Who - what is a.
    Children caring for parents.
      1 Tim.5:4-8; 5:16
    Coming to God "now." 2 Cor.6:1-2
    Man's person is not a. Gal.2:6
    Prayer. 1 Tim.2:1-8
    Spiritual sacrifices. 1 Pt.2:5
    Suffering for good. 1 Pt.2:20

ACCESS
Available.
    Into Jesus' presence. Any hour or day.
      Mk.1:33
    Into the grace, the presence of God.
      Ro.5:2; 8:15
Discussed. Eph.2:18
    Old vs. new approach to God.
      Heb.12:18-24
Duty. To approach God boldly. Heb.4:14-16
How man draws near God.
    By a better hope. Heb.7:18-19
    By a new & living faith. Heb.10:19-21;
      10:22-24
Meaning. Eph.2:18
    Drawing near God. Heb.7:18-19;
      10:22-25
Source - Is through.
    A better hope. Heb.7:18-19
    Christ. Jn.14:6
    Christ's high priesthood. Heb.2:17-18;
      4:14-16; 7:25-28
    Justification. Ro.5:1-2
    The blood of Christ. Eph.2:13; 2:18;
      Heb.10:19-21
    The Spirit of God. Eph.2:18
Verses. Ro.5:2

ACCOUNTABLE - ACCOUNTABILITY
Described as.
    A king's day of a. Mt.18:21-35
    A lord's day of a. Mt.25:14-30
    A property owner's a. Mt.21:33-46;
      Mk.12:1-12
Meaning. Mt.18:24
Who is a.
    A king's subjects. Mt.18:21-35
    A servant. Mt.25:14-30
    A tenant. Mt.21:33-46
    Each one - individually. Lk.12:20;
      12:48
    The living and the dead. 1 Pt.4:5-6
    The worldly. 1 Pt.4:3
Why men are a.
    Acting wickedly. Mt.24:48-51
    Are responsible for their gifts. Lk.
      16:1-7; 19:15-23
    Covetous & materialistic. Lk.12:13-21
    Doing their own will. Lk.12:41-48
    Have greater knowledge. Are expected
      to use it. Lk.12:41-48
    Lack of compassion. Mt.18:21-35

Misuse the gifts & possessions given
  by God. Lk.16:1-7; 19:15-23;
  1 Cor.12:1-3
Not watching or expecting Jesus' return. Mt.24:48-51; Lk.12:35-48
Rejecting God's message. Mt.21:33-46;
  Mk.12:1-12; Lk.20:9-19

ACCUSATION, FREE FROM
Meaning. Col.1:22

ACCUSERS, FALSE (See
    SLANDERERS - SLANDEROUS)

ACHAIA
Mentioned. 2 Cor.1:1; 11:10

ACHAICUS
A believer in the early church. 1 Cor.
  16:15-18

ACKNOWLEDGE
Duty.
    To a. the commandments of the Word.
      1 Cor.14:37; 2 Cor.1:13
    To a. the mystery of God. Col.2:2
    To a. the servants of Christ.
      1 Cor.16:18
    To a. the truth. 2 Tim.2:25

ACTS, BOOK OF
Opening and close of. Discussed. Acts
  28:25-29

ADAM
And Christ. Discussed. Ro.5:12-21;
  1 Cor.15:20-23
And Eve. Function of each in God's
  creation. 1 Tim.2:12-14
And history. Focal point of history.
  Ro.5:12-21; 1 Cor.15:20-23
And men.
    Caused sin and death. Ro.5:12-14;
      5:12; 1 Cor.15:20-23
    Passes earthly nature to man. Ro.5:12-14;
      5:12; 1 Cor.15:20-23
    Type or symbol. A representative man
      for all men. Ro.5:12-14; 5:12;
      1 Cor.15:20-23
Choice of.
    Sinned willfully. 1 Tim.2:14
    Vs. the choice people have today.
      Ro.5:12-14
Discussed. Ro.5:12-21
Fact.
    Bore greater sin than Eve. 1 Tim.2:14
    Sinned willfully. Was not deceived.
      1 Tim.2:14
Illustrates the orderly function within the
  family. 1 Tim.2:13
Seed of. Christ. Misunderstood by Jews.
  Jn.1:23
Type of. Christ. Discussed. Ro.5:12-14

ADMINISTER - ADMINISTRATION
Choosing - Appointing.
    Church leaders. Acts 6:1-7
    Deacons. Acts 6:1-7
    Missionaries. Acts 13:1-3
Discussed. Tit.1:5; 1 Pt.5:1-5
How to a.
    The church. 1 Pt.5:1-4
    The overseership. 1 Pt.5:1-4
Problem of. In the early church. Acts
  6:1-7

ADMONISH - ADMONITION (See **INSTINCT**)
Duty.
Believers are to **a.** one another.
Ro.15:14
Fathers are to **a.** children. Eph.6:4
Leaders are to **a.** 1 Th.5:12
To **a.** false teachers. Tit.3:10
To **a.** those who do not work.
2 Th.3:10-15, esp. 15
Source. Scriptures. 1 Cor.10:11

ADOPTED - ADOPTION
Described. Relationship between father &
son. 2 Cor.6:17-18
How one is **a.** - Conditions.
By faith & baptism into Christ.
Gal.3:26-27
By God through redemption & separa-
tion. Lk.8:21
By God's predestination. Eph.1:5-6
By receiving Christ. Jn.1:12
By separation from the world.
2 Cor.6:17-18
By the Holy Spirit. Ro.8:15
By the work of Christ. Jn.8:34-36
Through God's love. 1 Jn.3:1-2
Through redemption. Gal.4:5
Meaning. Gal.4:5-6
To become a child of God. 1 Jn.3:1-2
Of the believer. Discussed. Jn.1:12-13;
Ro.8:15; 2 Cor.6:17-18; Gal.4:4-7; 4:5-6;
1 Jn.3:2
Proof of **a.**
An inner cry toward God. Gal.4:6
Being different from the world.
1 Jn.3:1; 3:10-17
Chastening. Heb.12:5-13
Purifying oneself. 1 Jn.3:2-3
Separation from the world.
2 Cor.6:17-18
Results of **a.**
Access to the Father. Ro.8:16-17;
Eph.2:18
Called sons of God. 1 Jn.3:1
Conformity to Christ's image.
1 Jn.3:2
Exchanges slavery for sonship.
Gal.4:7
God's Spirit bears witness. Gal.4:6
God's Spirit indwells. Gal.4:6
Greatly privileged. Ro.9:4
Inheritance. Ro.8:16-17; Gal.4:7
Righteousness. 1 Jn.3:2-3; 3:10-17
To be glorified with Christ. Ro.8:16-17
To be made just like Christ. 1 Jn.3:1-2
Stages of **a.**
Future: To be conformed to Christ.
1 Jn.3:2
Present: Accepted as children. Gal.
4:6; 1 Jn.3:2
Verses. List of. Lk.8:21

ADORN (See **DRESS MODESTLY**)

ADULTERY - ADULTERESS
Caused by - Is committed.
By having someone else's spouse.
1 Cor.5:1
By looking and desiring. Mt.5:27-30
By marrying a divorced person.
Mt.5:31-32; Mk.10:1-12; Lk.16:17-18
In a party-like atmosphere. Jn.8:3-6
Partying & failing to separate from the
world. Rev.2:20-21

Commandment forbidding. Discussed.
Mt.5:27; Ro.13:9
Described. As remarriage. Mk.10:10-12
Discussed. Mt.5:28; Ro.2:21-24; 13:9;
1 Th.4:1-8
Duty of the **a.**
Not to be deceived. 1 Cor.6:9-11
To pluck out, cut off. Mt.5:27-30
To repent. 2 Cor.12:21
To seek cleansing. 1 Cor.6:11
To seek forgiveness. Jn.8:1-11
Duty of the church.
To converse with. Jn.4:1-42
To discipline. 1 Cor.5:1-13
To forgive. Jn.8:1-11
Toward saved **a.** 1 Cor.5:5, 7, 9-13
Toward unsaved **a.** 1 Cor.5:9-10, 12-13
Kinds of **a.**
Mental **a.** Desiring and lusting.
Mt.5:27-30
Physical **a.** A work of the sinful na-
ture. Gal.5:19-21
Spiritual **a.** Apostasy toward God.
Mt.12:39; Jas.4:4
Meaning. Mt.5:28; 19:9; Mk.7:21; 1 Cor.
6:9; Gal.5:19-21
Misconceptions.
A. is excusable & acceptable.
Mt.5:27-30
Penalty. Death by stoning. Mt.1:19
Results.
Being sent to hell. Rev.21:8
Breaks the union of marriage.
Mt.5:32; 19:1-12
Cheats a brother. To be avenged by
God. 1 Th.4:6-8
Destroys the human body. Five ways.
Ro.13:9
Excludes a person from God's king-
dom. 1 Cor.6:9-11
Four results. 1 Th.4:1-8
In judgment. God will judge.
Heb.13:4
Seriousness of.
Discussed. 1 Cor.6:15-18
Grounds for divorce. Mt.5:31-32; 19:9
Man's body is not designed for.
1 Cor.6:15-20
Sin of.
Acts of: four sins. Mt.5:28
Culprits. Hands and eyes. Mt.5:28
Trait of false teachers. 2 Pt.2:14
Spiritual **a.** (See **ADULTERY,
SPIRITUAL**)

ADULTERY, SPIRITUAL (See
IDOLATRY)
Discussed. Jas.4:4
Meaning Mt.12:39; Jas.4:4
Idolatry. Mt.12:39
Worldliness. Mt.12:39; Jas.4:4
Verses. List of. Jas.4:4

ADVERSARY (See **SATAN**)
Is Satan. 1 Pt.5:8

ADVERSITY
Ministry to. Discussed. Heb.13:3

ADVOCATE (See **JESUS CHRIST**, De-
ity; **Mediator**)
Discussed. 1 Jn.2:1-2
Ministry of. Jesus Christ. Lk.22:32

AENEAS
A man healed of paralysis. Acts 9:32-35

AFFECTION - AFFECTIONS (See
HEARTLESS)

AFFECTION, WITHOUT (See **LOVE,
WITHOUT MEANING**)

AFFLICTIONS (See **DISTRESS;
PERSECUTION; SUFFERINGS;
TRIALS & TRIBULATION**)

AGE
Aged men. Behavior of. Tit.2:2
Aged women. Behavior of. Tit.2:3
Different **a.** Discussed. Tit.2:1-8
New **a.** Ushered in by Christ. Mt.9:14-17
Promised to obedient children. Eph.6:1-3

AGE OF ACCOUNTABILITY
Little children are kept by God. Lk.18:16

AGNOSTIC
Described. Mt.6:14-15
Duty. To be open to the truth. Jn.4:25

AGREEMENT
Meaning. 2 Cor.6:14-16

AGRIPPA, KING HEROD
Almost persuaded. Acts 26:24-32
Discussed. Acts 25:1-26:32
Put Paul on trial. Acts 25:13-27; 26:1-18

ALCOHOL (See **DRUNKENNESS**)
Results. Drinking, partying. Mt.14:6-8;
24:38

ALERT
Meaning. 1 Pt.5:8-9

ALEXANDER
A believer with shipwrecked faith.
1 Tim.1:19-20
A Jew caught up in a riot against Paul.
Acts 19:33-34
A member of the high priest's family.
Acts 4:5-10
A son of the man who carried Jesus'
cross. Mk.15:21

ALEXANDER THE METALWORKER
Discussed. 2 Tim.4:14-15

ALEXANDRIA
A shipping center. Acts 27:6
Alexandria Jews join in Stephen's perse-
cution. Acts 6:9
Apollos' home. Acts 18:24

ALIENATED - ALIENATION (See
MAN, State of - Present; **SEPARATED-
SEPARATION**)

ALIENS
Described as.
An unbeliever. Eph.2:19
Believers. 1 Pt.1:1; 2:11
The Gentiles. Eph.2:19
Discussed. 1 Pt.1:1; 2:11
Meaning. 1 Pt.1:17; 2:11

ALL IN ALL
God is. 1 Cor.15:28
Jesus fills. Eph.1:23

ALLEGIANCE (See **COMMITMENT;
DEDICATION**)

MASTER SUBJECT INDEX

ALMIGHTY
Christ is the Almighty. Rev.1:8
God is the Almighty. 2 Cor.6:18

ALMS--ACTS OF RIGHTEOUSNESS
Meaning. Mt.6:1

ALPHA - OMEGA
Name given to Christ. Rev.1:8; 21:6;
22:12-13

ALTAR
Of believers. Christ's sacrifice is the believer's a. Heb.13:10-11

ALTAR, BRAZEN (See **ALTAR OF
BURNT OFFERING**)

ALTAR OF BURNT OFFERING
In heaven. Place of the martyrs in heaven.
Rev.6:9

AMBASSADOR
Chosen. By Christ to go forth. Jn.15:16
Meaning. Lk.6:13; 2 Cor.5:20

AMBITION - AMBITIOUS (See **SELF-
SEEKING**)
Discussed. Mt.18:1-4; 20:20-28;
Mk.9:33-37; 10:35-44; Lk.14:7-14
Duty.
Not to be a. in pushing ministers for-
ward. 1 Cor.3:3-4; 14:1-5, 12
Not to be envious over gifts.
1 Cor.3:3-4; 14:1-5, 12
Not to glory over self or others.
1 Cor.1:10-16, 26-31; 3:1-4; 3:5-9
Not to love the preeminence, the desire
to be first. 3 Jn.9-11
Not to seek position for self-glory.
Mt.20:20-28
To be as a. for God as unbelievers are
for material things. Lk.16:1-13
To follow after maturity. Ph.3:12-16
To rebuke evil a. 3 Jn.10
To seek to become as a child.
Mt.20:20-28
To seek to win the prize God has
called us. Ph.3:7-16
Evil a. Causes.
An air of superiority. Mt.18:1-4
Arguing & conflict. Mk.9:33-34;
10:41
Compromise. Lk.4:5-8
Embarrassment. Lk.14:7-14
Injustice. Lk.16:1-13
Loving the preeminence. 3 Jn.9
Pride. 1 Tim.3:6
Self-seeking. Lk.9:46-47; 14:7-14;
22:24-30; Jn.11:47-48; 12:10-11;
12:42-43
The fear of losing followers. Jn.12:10-11;
12:42-43
The fear of losing position. Jn.11:47-48;
12:42-43
Evil a. Results in.
Being rebuked. 3 Jn.9-11
God's resistance. Jas.4:4-6
Judgment. Acts 5:1-11; 8:18-25
Examples of.
An a. guest. Lk.14:7-14
Diotrephes: Loving the preeminence.
3 Jn.9-11
James & John: Seeking position.
Mt.20:20-28
Loving the preeminence. 3 Jn.9-11

Motives of. True vs. false. Mt.20:20-21;
Mk.10:36-37
Price of. Sacrifice & pain. Mk.10:38-39
Problem with. Mk.9:33-37; 10:35-45
World's view vs. the Lord's view.
Mk.10:42-43

AMBITIOUS GUEST
Parable of. Importance of humility.
Lk.14:7-14

AMEN
God's promises are assured--Amen.
2 Cor.1:20
Meaning. Mt.6:13
Title. Of Christ. Rev.3:14
Used to close.
Epistles. 1 Cor.16:24
Prayer. 1 Cor.14:16; Eph.3:21

AMPHIPOLIS
Paul passed through on his second missionary journey. Acts 17:1

AMPLIAS
A believer from Rome. Ro.16:8

ANANIAS
A believer in Damascus who witnessed to
Paul. Acts 9:10-18
A believer in Jerusalem who backslid.
Acts 5:1-11
A Jewish high priest who tried Paul.
Acts 23:1-5
Discussed. Acts 5:1-11

ANATHEMA--ACCURSED
Meaning. Gal.1:8-9
The terrifying need for salvation. Ro.9:1-3,
esp. 3; 1 Cor.16:22
Who is a.
Any who call Jesus a. Gal.1:8
Any who preach a false gospel.
Gal.1:8-9

ANCHOR
Illustrates. The a. of the believer's hope.
Heb.6:18-20
The a. of a ship. Acts 27:40

ANDREW, THE APOSTLE
A fisherman. Mt.4:18-19
Asked about the end time. Mk.13:1-4
Call of. Mk.1:16-18
Brought a little boy to Jesus. Jn.6:1-15
Discovered Jesus. Acknowledged Him as
the Messiah, the Christ. Jn.1:35-42
Discussed. Mk.3:18; Jn.6:8-9
Experienced Pentecost. Acts 1:12-15, cp.
2:1-4
One of the first disciples called by Jesus.
Mt.4:18-22
One of the twelve apostles. Mt.10:1-4
Witnessed to his brother, Peter. Jn.1:35-42

ANGELS
Appearances.
In the New Testament. Lk.24:4-8
To Cornelius. Acts 10:3-8
To John. Rev.1:1
To Joseph. Mt.1:18-25
To Mary Magdalene at Christ's resur-
rection. Jn.20:11; 12-13
To Paul. Acts 27:23-24
To Philip. Acts 8:26

To shepherds. Spectacular appearance.
Lk.2:13-14
To the apostles. Acts 1:10-11
To the women at Christ's resurrection.
Mt.28:1-10; Lk.24:4-8
Discussed. Heb.1:4-14
Error concerning.
Men exalt a. over Christ. Heb.1:4-14
Men seek a. as intermediaries & me-
diators to reach God. Heb.1:4-14
Men seek experiences with a.
Heb.1:4-14
Fact.
Aroused to understand and to look into
salvation. 1 Pt.1:12
Stand in stark amazement at the glories
of salvation. Eph.3:10-12, esp. 10;
1 Pt.1:12
Fall of. Some sinned and fell from their
perfect state. 2 Pt.2:4
Fallen a. (See **ANGELS, FALLEN;
SATAN**)
Function toward believers.
To carry out the answers of prayers for
God. Rev.8:1-5
To comfort & assure. Acts 27:23-25
To deliver. Mt.24:30-31
To instruct & direct. Acts 5:17-20; 8:26
To minister. Heb.1:7, 14
Function toward Christ.
To announce His birth. Lk.2:8-14
To announce His conception.
Mt.1:20-21
To ascend & descend upon. Jn.1:50-51
To be subservient to. Heb.1:4-14;
1 Pt.3:22
To guard & protect. Lk.4:10-11
To proclaim His ascension & return.
Acts 1:9-11
To return with Him. Mt.13:40-42;
13:49-50
To strengthen Him in Gethsemane.
Lk.22:43
To witness His resurrection. 1 Tim.
3:16
To worship. Heb.1:4-7
Function toward God.
Avenging agents of God. Rev.15:1;
15:5-8
To be worshippers of God. Rev.4:1-11;
10:1-7
To bind Satan. Rev.12:7-9; 20:1-3
To guard the new Jerusalem. Rev.
21:9-23
To minister to God. Heb.1:4-7
To serve as messengers of God. Acts
27:23-26; Rev.10:1-7
To surround the throne of God.
Rev.7:11-12
Function toward unbelievers.
To avenge God's glory. Rev.15:1;
15:5-8
To execute death. Act 12:20-23
To execute God's judgment.
Mt.13:40-42; Rev.8:1-5; 8:6-7
To harvest unbelievers in the end time.
Mt.13:40-43; 13:49-50; Rev.14:15;
14:17-20
Guardian. Children have guardian. an-
gels. Mt.18:10
In the end time.
To assure Satan's defeat. Rev.20:1-3
To guard the new Jerusalem.
Rev.21:9-23
To seal & protect from judgment.
Rev.7:2-4

6

How **a**. rises to power.
 How he gains control of the world.
  Rev.6:1-2; 6:1-8; 13:1-10; 13:13-17
 The political ruler. 2 Th.2:4-9;
  Rev.13:1-10, cp. 6:1-8
 The religious ruler or prophet. 2 Th.
  2:4; Rev.13:11-18
Methods used by **a**.
 Blasphemy. Rev.13:1; 13:5-6
 Denying Christ's incarnation.
  1 Jn.2:22; 4:1-6; 2 Jn.7
 Forming a confederation of power.
  Rev.13:1-8; 17:7-14
 Persecuting believers. Rev.13:7;
  13:21-23
 Slaying leadership. Rev.11:3-10
 War & conquest. Rev.6:1-2, 3-4;
  13:1-8; 16:13-14; 17:7-14; 17:15-18;
  18:1-24
 Working Satanic miracles. Rev.13:2-3;
  16:13-14
Names - Titles - Identity.
 A deceiver. 2 Jn.7
 A political ruler. Rev.13:1-10
 A religious ruler. Rev.13:11-18;
  16:13; 19:20; 20:10
 Beast, The. Rev.11:7; 13:1-10
 Death & Hell. Rev.6:7-8
 Is a man, a real person, not some force
  or spirit of evil. 1 Jn.2:18
 Many **a**. - now. 1 Jn.2:18-23; 4:1-6;
  2 Jn.7
 Who he is. Rev.13:1
Nature - Character.
 Discussed. 2 Th.2:4; Rev.13:1-5
 Embodiment of Satan. 2 Th.2:8
 Incarnation of evil. Rev.17:8
 "Was...is not...comes up out" of the
  abyss. Rev.17:8
Number of - mark of: 666. Rev.13:17-18;
 14:9; 15:2; 19:20
Origin.
 Of Satan. 2 Th.2:8; Rev.13:1-5
 Out of the abyss. Rev.17:7-13
Power of.
 Chart of nations that will support him.
  Rev.13:2
 Discussed. Rev.13:2; 17:7-14; 17:9-10
 Kings & empires or nations that sup-
  port. Rev.13:2; 17:7-14; 17:9-10
 Political **p**. Nations he rules over.
  Rev.13:1
 Rise to **p**. Rev.13:2-3
 Way he secures **p**. Rev.13:4-8
Prophesied.
 By Daniel. Mt.24:15; Mk.13:1-27;
  13:14
 Chart on prophecies of Revelation &
  Daniel. Rev.13:1; 13:2
 Past & future fulfillment. Mt.24:15;
  Mk.13:14
Warning against.
 Discussed. (See **ANTICHRIST**, Dis-
  cussed) 1 Jn.2:18-12; 4:1-6; 2 Jn.7-13
 Should hear. Rev.13:9
 Should understand. Rev.13:18
When **a**. comes. (See **ANTICHRIST**,
 Appearance)
 In the last time. 1 Jn.2:18
Who escapes from the **a**.
 Believers. Rev.3:10
 Those in the book of life. Rev.13:8-10
 Those sealed by God in their fore-
  heads. Rev.7:1-8; 9:3-6

Those who obey God's command &
 remain faithful to Jesus. Rev.13:10;
 14:12
Those who remain loyal & steadfast to
 Christ. Rev.13:8-10; 14:12
Those who reject the mark of the beast
 or **a**. Rev.14:9-12; 15:2-4
Work.
 To carry on Satan's work. 2 Th.2:9;
  Rev.13:1-5
 To gain power. (See **ANTICHRIST**,
  Power of)
 To set up imperial or state worship.
  2 Th.2:4; Rev.13:11-18

ANTIOCH (See **PISIDIAN OF
ANTIOCH**)
 Church at **A**.
  Became the center of world-wide mis-
   sions. Acts 13:1
  Great church. Reasons. Twofold. Acts
   13:1
  Leadership of. Five leaders. Acts 13:1
  Where believers were first called
   Christians. Acts 11:26
 City of. Discussed. Acts 11:19-30
 Discussed. Acts 11:19-30
 False teachers arose in **A**. Acts 15:1-5
 First great Gentile church. Acts 11:19-30
 Home of one of the first deacons--
  Nicolas. Acts 6:1-7
 Launched the first great missionary thrust
  into the world. Acts 14:26-28
 Paul & Barnabas were ministers of **A**.
  Acts 11:22-26
 Paul was commissioned by **A**. Acts 13:1-3;
  15:35-41
 Sent out the very first missionaries. Acts
  13:1-3

ANTIPATRIS
 Paul spent the night in **A**. as a prisoner.
  Acts 23:31

ANXIETY - ANXIOUS (See **CARES
THE OF WORLD**)
 Caused by.
  A son's absence. Lk.2:48
  Distraction. Lk.10:40
  Facing abuse & persecution.
   Lk.12:11-12
  Fearing judgment. Lk.21:26
  Fearing natural disasters. Lk.21:25
  Lack of necessities. Lk.12:22-34
  Worldliness. Mt.13:22; Lk.21:34
  Worrying about things and life.
   Mt.6:25-34
  Worrying over appearance. Mt.6:27;
   Lk.12:25
  Worrying over household duties. Lk.
   10:40-41
  Worrying over the cares of the world.
   Lk.8:11-15; 21:34
  Worrying over witnessing. Mk.13:9-11
 Discussed. Mt.6:25-34; Lk.12:22-34;
  Ph.4:6-7
 Duty.
  Not to be **a**. over necessities. Lk.
   12:22-34
  To be free from cares, **a**. 1 Cor.7:32
  To cast all your **a**. on God. 1 Pt.5:5-7
 How to conquer.
  Being redeemed. Lk.21:28
  Considering God's provision.
   Mt.6:28-34
  Lifting up one's head. Lk.21:28

Living one day at a time. Mt.6:34
Looking at nature. Mt.6:26-30;
 Lk.12:27
Looking for Jesus' return. Lk.21:27-28
Praying in everything. Ph.4:6-7
Seeking God first. Mt.6:33; Lk.12:31
Sitting at Jesus' feet. Lk.10:38-42
Results. Criticism, murmuring, complain-
 ing. Lk.10:40

APATHY
 Discussed. Heb.3:7-19

APELLES
 A believer from Rome. Ro.16:10

APOLLONIA
 Paul passed through **A**. on his way to
  Thessalonica. Acts 17:1

APOLLOS
 Discussed. Acts 18:23-28; Tit.3:13

APOLLYON
 Meaning. Greek name for the king of evil
  spirits. Rev.9:11

APOSTASY (See **BACKSLIDING;
DENIAL**)
 Caused by--Sources of. Mt.26:69
 Danger - Fate - Judgment of.
  Discussed. Heb.10:26-31
  Impossible to repent of. Heb.6:4-8
  Judgment. 2 Pt.2:1
  Sinning unto death. 1 Jn.5:16
  The blackest darkness. 2 Pt.2:17; 2:10-22
  To be exposed. 2 Tim.3:9
  To be judged according to their works.
   2 Cor.11:13-15
 Deliverance found in.
  Continuing in the Scriptures. 2 Tim.
   3:14-17
  Exhorting one another daily. Heb.
   3:13-19
  Feeding the church of God. Acts
   20:28-31
  Going on to maturity. Heb.6:1-3;
   2 Pt.1:10; Jude 20-25
  Keeping one's self. Jude 21
  Laboring to enter God's rest.
   Heb.4:11-13
  Preaching the Word. 2 Tim.4:2
  Putting on God's armor. Eph.6:10-18
  Reclaiming the lost. Jude 22-23
  Remembering God's judgment. Jude 5-7
  Speaking the truth in love. Eph.4:14-15
  Testing the spirit of teachers. 1 Jn.4:1-6
 Described as.
  A great **a**. 2 Tim.4:3-4
  A time existing now. Mt.13:20-21;
   1 Jn. 4:2-3
   In the church. 2 Tim.3:13; 2 Pt.2:1-3;
    2:10-22
   Men creeping into the church.
    2 Tim. 3:6-9; Jude 4
  A time in the future. The last times.
   2 Tim.3:1-9; 2 Pt.3:3; Jude 18
  A time past.
   At the flood. 2 Pt.2:5
   When Sodom was destroyed. 2 Pt.2:6
   When the angels sinned. 2 Pt.2:4
  Going out into the world. 1 Jn.4:1, cp.
   2:18-19
  Terrible times in the last days. 2 Tim. 3:1
  Sin unto death. 1 Jn.5:16
  Becoming worse and worse. 2 Tim. 3:13

Secured by.
A godly sorrowing. 2 Cor.7:10
Consistency. 2 Cor.6:3
Self-examination. 2 Cor.13:5-6
Spiritual discernment. Ph.1:9-10
Study & diligent work. 2 Tim.2:15
What is **a**. One's ministry. 2 Cor.6:3-4
Who gives **a**.
Believers. Discerning believers.
Ph.1:9-10
Christ. Ph.1:9-10
Who gives **a**.
Christ. 2 Cor.10:18
God. Acts 2:22
Personal **a**. 2 Cor.6:3-4; 7:10-11;
13:5-8

AQUILA AND PRISCILLA
A believer. Discussed. Acts 18:2
Discipled Apollos. Acts 18:24-28
Discussed. Acts 18:2; Ro.16:3-4
Had a church in their home. Ro.16:3-4
Made Ephesus their permanent home.
Acts 18:18-19
Opened their home to Apollos. Acts
18:24-28
Opened their home to Paul. Acts 18:1-3
Paul sent greetings to Aquila when a
prisoner. 2 Tim.4:19
Traveled with Paul. Acts 18:18
Were disciples of Paul. Acts 18:1-2, 18
Were forced to move from Rome to
Corinth. Acts 18:1-2, 18
Worked as tentmakers with Paul. Acts
18:1-2

ARABIA
Citizens of. Present at Pentecost. Acts
2:11
Where Paul got alone with God.
Gal.1:17

ARCHANGEL
Struggled with Satan. Jude 9
Will proclaim the Lord's return. 1 Th.
4:16

ARCHELAUS (See **HEROD, FAMILY
OF**)
Discussed. Mt.2:22

ARCHIPPUS
A believer known by Paul who had a
church in his home. Phile.1:1-2
Discussed. Col.4:17

AREOPAGITE
Dionysius, the **A**., was saved. Acts 17:34

AREOPAGUS
Paul preached from. Acts 17:16-33

ARGUE - ARGUMENTS (See
**CONTENTION; DIVISION;
QUARRELS**)
Described. As vain, empty. Ro.1:21
Discussed. 1 Tim.4:7; 6:20-21;
2 Tim.2:14; 2:16-18; 2:23; 2:24-26
Duty.
Must not **a**. 2 Tim.2:24-26
To cast down. 2 Cor.10:5
To do nothing through strife or **a**.
Ph.2:3-4
To put off the clothing of **a**. Eph.4:31;
Col.3:13
To turn away from. Tit.3:9

Fact.
God scatters the proud in the **i**. of their
heart. Lk.1:51
People imagine empty things against
God. Acts 4:25
Meaning. 2 Cor.10:5
Source - Caused by.
Genuine differences. Acts 15:36-41
Lust. Jas.4:1-2
Self-seeking. Mt.20:20-28
Sin. Mk.6:17-19

ARIMATHEA, JOSEPH OF
Buries Jesus. The conquest of fear.
Jn.19:38-42

ARISTARCHUS
Companion of Paul. Phile.1:24
Discussed. Acts 20:4; Col.4:10

ARISTOBULUS
Household of. Were believers. Ro.16:10

ARK IN HEAVEN
Type-Symbol of. God's new covenant.
Rev.11:19

ARK OF NOAH
Symbol of spiritual cleansing. 1 Pt.3:20-22

ARMAGEDDON, BATTLE OF
Discussed. Rev.11:18; 14:17-20; 16:12-16;
19:17-21

ARMOR OF GOD (See **SPIRITUAL
STRUGGLE--WARFARE**)
Discussed. Eph.6:10-20

ARMOR, SPIRITUAL
Discussed. Eph.6:10-20; 1 Th.5:8
Of light. To put on the **a**. of light. Ro.13:12
Of righteousness. 2 Cor.6:7

ARROGANCE (See **PRIDE**)
Caused by.
Ambition. Lk.9:46-50
Being "lifted up" given responsibility
too soon. 1 Tim.3:6
Boasting in one's knowledge. 1 Cor.8:2
Comparing & judging ministers. 1 Cor.
4:6
Discussed. Lk.7:39
Evil heart. Mk.7:20-22
Feeling oneself is better than others.
Ro.2:19; 12:16
Loving the preeminence. 3 Jn.9-11
Religion of works. Col.2:20-23; 2:23
Roots & heritage. Mt.23:29-33
Seeking attention & recognition. Mt.6:2
Self-centeredness. Ro.3:27
Self-righteousness. Lk.18:11-12
Self-sufficiency. Lk.10:21; 18:9
Selfishness & self-glorying. Ph.2:3-4
Spiritual superiority. "But for the
grace of God, there go I." Mt.8:4
Wealth. Creates the "big I." Mt.19:23;
Mk.10:24
Works. Ro.4:1-3
Worldliness - the world. 1 Jn.2:15-16
Described.
As believing one is good enough to be
acceptable to God. Lk.3:8; 7:39; 18:9
As puffed up air bags. 1 Cor.4:6
As saying, "But for the grace of God,
there go I." Mk.1:44
As the pride of life. 1 Jn.2:15-16

Discussed. Lk.14:7-14; Ro.1:22-23;
3:27; 3:28
Fact. No man is better than another man--
not spiritually. Gal.6:3
Illustrated. Two men of **a**. Jas.2:18
Judgment of. Lk.6:24-26
Abased. Mt.23:12
Death. Lk.12:16-20
Excluded from heaven. Mt.19:23-26
Meaning. Mk.7:22; Rom.1:30; 1 Cor.
13:4-7; 2 Cor.12:19-21; 2 Tim.3:2-4
Overcome by.
Acknowledging one's sinfulness.
Lk.18:10-14
Faith. Ro.3:27-31
Humility. Ph.2:3-4; Col.3:12
Not loving the world. 1 Jn.2:15-16
Serving & giving quietly. Mt.6:3-4
Serving others. Mt.20:26-28
Submitting to others. 1 Pt.5:5-7
Results of **a**.
Boasting. Jas.3:3-5; 4:16
Causes one to act superior, self-sufficient,
& super-spiritual. 1 Cor.4:7; 4:8
Causes one to seek the approval &
honor of men. Jn.5:44
Causes one to seek position. Lk.14:7-11;
19:14-27
Causes one to seek recognition.
Lk.14:12-14; 19:14-27
Causes one to turn from God to idols.
Ro.1:22-23
Conceit. Ro.12:16; 1 Cor.8:2
Elevating oneself over others. Ro.
2:19; 11:18; 12:16
God's resistance. Jas.4:5-6
Idolatry. Ro.1:22-23
Strife. Ph.2:3-4
To be condemned with the devil.
1 Tim.3:6
Verses. List of. Jn.5:44; 8:33
Sin of **a**.
Discussed. The pride of life. 1 Jn.2:15-17
The false minister. What he take **a**. in.
1 Tim.6:4
The sin of the Corinthian church.
1 Cor.4:6; 4:7; 4:8; 5:1; 5:2; 5:6
The sin of the religionists. Ro.3:27-31
Source. Man's claim to be too wise to
believe in God. Ro.1:22-23
Verses. List of. Lk.10:21; 14:11
Vs. humility. Mt.18:1-4; Acts 4:23-24
Vs. the cross of Christ. 1 Cor.1:17-25
Warning against. (See **PRIDE**, Judgment of)
Religious **a**. Mt.23:1-12
To be scattered, lost. Lk.1:51-53

ARTEMAS
Discussed. Tit.3:12

ARTEMIS
A great goddess in Ephesus. Acts 19:24,
27-28, 34-35
Goddess of Ephesians. Acts 19:24, 27-28,
34-35
Paul preached against. Acts 19:23-41

ARTHRITIS
Healed by Jesus. Man more important
than religion. Lk.13:11-13

ASCENSION (See **JESUS CHRIST**, Ascension)

ASCETICISM
Discussed. 1 Cor.8:4-8

ASTROLOGY (See **SORCERY; SUPERSTITION**)
Discussed. Acts 16:16-17
Error of. Causes men to seek fate in the stars & magic. Jn.5:2-4
Vs. Christ. Discussed. Col.2:8-10

ASTRONOMICAL SIGNS, HAPPENINGS
Predicted. In the end time. Mt.24:29-31; Lk.21:11

ASYNCRITUS
Believer from Rome. Ro.16:14

ATHEIST - ATHEISM
Duty. To be open to the truth. Jn.4:25
Fact. Are to face the judgment of God. Ro.2:11-15
Meaning.
  Walking after the course of the world. Eph.2:1-3
  Without God in the world. Eph.2:11-12
Problem with. Becomes immoral. Eph.2:1-3

ATHENS
Discussed. Acts 17:16-21
Paul visited.
  On his second mission. Acts 17:16-21
  Stayed in Athens all alone. 1 Th.3:1

ATHLETES - ATHLETICS
Illustrates. The Christian life. 1 Cor. 9:24-27
Traits. Discussed. 2 Tim.2:5

ATONEMENT (See **JESUS CHRIST**, Death, Sacrifice of; **JUSTIFICATION; PROPITIATION; RECONCILIATION; REDEMPTION**)
Discussed. Lk.18:13; Heb.2:17-18; 1 Jn.2:1-2; 2:2
Meaning. Ro.3:25
Source.
  Christ. Died as our **a**. Ro.5:6-7
  The sacrifice & death of Christ. 1 Jn.4:9-11

ATONEMENT, DAY OF
Discussed. Heb.9:1-10

ATONING SACRIFICE
Discussed. 1 Jn.2:1-2;2:2
Source. The sacrifice & death of Christ. 1 Jn.4:9-11

ATTALIA
Discussed. Acts 14:25

ATTITUDE (See **MIND**)
Duty.
  To be armed with the same **m**. as Christ in facing the trials of life. 1 Pt.4:1-6
  To prepare you **m** for action. 1 Pt.1:13
Essential.
  Is the major weapon for warfare. 1 Pt.4:1
Kinds of. Discussed. Mk.5:22-24; 5:25-34; 5:35-43
Of Christ. Meaning. 1 Pt.4:1-6

ATTRIBUTES (See **GOD**, Deity; **JESUS CHRIST**, Deity)

AUTHOR

Title of Jesus Christ.
  Author & finisher of our faith. Heb.12:2
  Author of salvation. Heb.5:9
Title of God. Author of peace. 1 Cor.14:33

AUTHORITY (See **POWER**)
Dangers of.
  Seeking with evil motives. Mk.10:35-45
  Seeking with selfish motives. Lk.22:24-30
Difference between **a**. and power. Lk.9:1
Discussed. Lk.22:24-30; Ro.13:1-7; Tit.3:1-2; 1 Pt.2:13-17
Duty. To respect **a**. 1 Pt.2:16-17
Exercised by.
  Citizens. 1 Pt.2:13-17
  Rulers. Lk.22:25-26; 1 Pt.2:13-14
  The pastor. 2 Cor.10:8; 13:1-6; Tit.2:15
Instituted. 1 Pt.2:13-14
Of Christ. (See **JESUS CHRIST**, Authority)
  A. of His teaching. Mt.7:28-29; Mk.1:22
  Discussed. Lk.20:1-8
  Over the church. Eph.1:22-23; 2:19-22
Of man. Over nature. Heb.2:5-8
Of the church. Instituted. Mt.16:13-20, esp. 18
Of the family.
  Instituted. Eph.5:31-32
  The child. Eph.6:1-4
  The husband. Eph.5:25-33
  The parent. Eph.6:4
  The wife. Eph.5:22-24
Of the Scribes. Mt.7:29
Purpose.
  To equip and give assurance. Mt.10:1
  To govern & administer. (See **AUTHORITY**, Exercised by)
  To remit & retain sins. Jn.20:23
Rejection of. By false teachers. 2 Pt. 2:10; Jude 8
Source. Of God. Given to the disciples. Mt.10:1; Lk.9:1

AVAILABLE - AVAILABILITY
Essential. Must be **a**. to people.
  Discussed. Mt.15:30-31
  Steps. Mt.15:30-31

AVENGE - AVENGING
Of the elect. God will avenge His elect. Lk.18:6-8

AWE (See **FEAR**)
What to **a**. God
Meaning. Acts2:43

B

BABES - BABIES (See **CHILDREN, LITTLE**)
Symbol of believers.
  Carnal believers. 1 Cor.3:1
  Immature believers. Heb.5:13
  New believers just converted. 1 Pt.2:2-3
Symbol of seekers after God. Ro.2:20

BABYLON
Captivity. God preserved Jews through the Babylon captivity. Mt.1:11
Destroyed. Under the seventh bowl judgment. Rev.16:17-21
In the end time.
  Judgment. Of both the political & religious **B**. Rev.17:1-6; 17:7-18; 18:1-24
  Political.
    Capital of antichrist. Rev.18:1-24
    Destruction of. Rev.18:1-24
  Religious **B**. Destroyed. Rev.17:1-6
  Traits of. Will be embodied in the antichrist. Rev.13:2
  Will be destroyed by God. Rev.14:8
Symbol. Of Rome. 1 Pt.5:13

BACKBITERS - BACKBITING (See **COMPLAINING; GRUMBLING; SLANDERING**)

BACKSLIDING - BACKSLIDERS (See **APOSTASY; DENIAL**)
Caused by.
  Carnal commitment. Lk.22:31-38
  Complacency, lethargy, failing to be steadfast. 2 Pt.1:9
  Failing to become rooted & grounded. Lk.8:11-15
  Fear. Lk.22:54-62
  Forsaking Jesus. Mt.26:55-56
  Looking back. Lk.9:61-62
  Love of money. 1 Tim.6:10
  Lukewarmness. Rev.3:16-17
  Overconfidence. Mt.26:31-35; 26:33-35
  Overemphasizing ritual. Ro.4:11
  Things of the world. Mt.13:7, 22
  Trials & temptation. Lk.8:11-15
  Turning away from Christ to Satan. 1 Tim.5:15
  Two things. 2 Tim.4:3-4
  Why a believer backslides. Mt.13:5-7, 20-22; 18:12; Mk.14:10-11
Described as.
  A failing faith. Lk.22:31-32
  A shipwrecked faith. 1 Tim.1:19
  Being immature. Heb.5:11-6:2
  Compromising & being permissive. Rev.2:18-29
  Denying Christ. Mt.26:31-34, 54-62; Mk.14:27-31; Lk.22:31-34; 22:54-62; Jn.13:36-38; 18:15-18; 18:25-27
  Drifting away. Heb.2:1-4
  Falling away. Heb.5:11-6:8
  Falling away from Christ. Mt.26:31-35; 26:69-75; Mk.14:27-31
  Hardening one's heart - depravity. Heb.3:7-19
  Loving the world. 2 Tim.4:10; 1 Jn.2:15-16
  Missing God's rest. Heb.4:1-13
  Neglecting. Danger of. Heb.12:14-17
  Satan sifting as wheat. Lk.22:31-32
  Withdrawing from the church. Heb. 10:25
Discussed. Ro.6:1-2; 7:14-25; Gal.1:6-9; Heb.10:26-39; 1 Jn.5:16; Rev.2:4; 2:5-6
  Message to backsliders. Gal.2:11-21
Duty.
  Advice for drifters. Heb.10:32-39
  Not to turn back. Gal.4:8-11
  To restore the sinning brother. Gal. 6:1-5
  To seek the **b**. believer. Jas.5:19-20

Examples.
    Disciples. Stumbling & falling away.
        Mt.26:31-35, 56; Mk.14:50-52
    Four examples. Ro.9:5
    Judas. Picture of a ruined life. Mt.
        26:14-16
    Lot's wife. Turning back. Lk.17:31-33
    Peter. Denying Christ. Lk.22:31-34;
        22:54-62
    Peter & Barnabas. Gal.2:11-21
    Verses. List of. Lk.9:61-62
    Views of. Discussed. Ro.6:1-2
    Warning - Precautions against.
        A person can b. so far that he is turned
            over to Satan. 1 Tim.1:20
        Discussed. Heb.10:26-39
        Judgment of the b. will be greater.
            Jn.5:13-14
        What b. is. Great sin of. Heb.10:28-29

BALAAM
    Discussed. Rev.2:14-15
    Example of.
        A false teacher. Jude 3
        Leading others to sin. 2 Pt.2:15-16

BAND (See DETACHMENT)

BANQUET OF GOD, GREAT
    Discussed. Lk.14:15-24; Rev.19:17-21
    Parable of. Jesus' invitation--man's ex-
        cuses. Lk.14:15-24

BANQUETINGS (See CAROUSING)

BAPTISM - BAPTIZED
    Discussed. Mt.3:11; 3:14; 3:15; Mk.1:9-11;
        Jn.1:24-26; Acts 2:38; Ro.6:3-5
        What it is & does. Lk.3:21-22
    Duty.
        To be in a spirit of prayer while being
            b. Lk.3:21
        To obey God. No man is above being
            b. Lk.3:21
    Error. Thinking b. as a ritual saves.
        Ro.2:25-27; 2:28-29; 6:3-5
    Essential. Mt.3:11; 3:14; 3:15; Mk.1:9-11;
        Acts 2:38; Ro.6:3-5
    Kinds of.
        B. of repentance. Meaning. Lk.3:3
        B. with the Holy Spirit & fire.
            Mt.3:11; 3:14; Lk.3:16
        B. of water & of the Spirit. Jn.1:24-26
        Spiritual b. Ro.6:3-5
        Water b. Ro.6:3-5
    Meaning.
        Discussed. Mt.3:11; 3:14; Mk.1:9-11;
            Acts 2:38; Ro.6:3-5
        Illustrated by Noah and the flood.
            1 Pt.3:18-22
        In the Holy Spirit & fire. Mt.3:11;
            3:14; Lk.3:16
        Obedience & approval. Lk.3:21-22
        With water & the Spirit. Jn.1:24-26
    Of Jesus Christ. (See **JESUS CHRIST**,
        Baptism)
    Of John the Baptist. Mt.3:11
        B. only in water, not in the Spirit.
            Mk.1:7-8
        Reason to be b. Jn.1:24-26
    Results. Secures God's approval &
        blessings. Threefold. Lk.3:22
    Views of. Discussed. Mk.16:16
    Why a person must be b. Mt.3:11; 3:14;
        3:15

BARABBAS
    Criminal chosen over Christ. Mk.15:6-10;
        Jn.18:38-40
    Prisoner freed instead of Christ.
        Mt.27:15-25

BARAK
    Faith of. Discussed. Heb.11:32

BAR-JESUS
    False prophet & sorcerer. Discussed.
        Acts 13:7-11

BARNABAS OR JOSES
    Accompanied Paul to Jerusalem to defend
        salvation by grace alone. Gal.2:3-5
    Backslid, drifted away. Gal.2:11-13
    Before the Jerusalem Council. Acts 15:2,
        12
    Call of. Was one of the first two mission-
        aries. Acts 13:1-3
    Defended Paul. Acts 9:23-30
    Discussed. Acts 4:36-37
    Leader of the Antioch church. Acts
        11:19-30; 13:1-3
    Served with Paul. Acts 11:25-26; 12:25;
        13:2-15:40
    Sold land to give to the church. Acts
        4:36-37
    Sought Paul's help in Antioch. Acts
        11:25-26
    Split from Paul. Acts 15:36-40

BARREN (See INEFFECTIVE)

**BARRIERS (See DISCRIMINATION;
DIVISION; PREJUDICE)**
    Between people. Acts 10:1-33
    Described. Physical, ideological, spiri-
        tual. Mt.8:5-13
    Receiving & rejecting men. Mt.8:5-13

BARSABAS
    A believer nominated to replace Judas.
        Acts 1:23
    A believer sent forth by the great Jerusa-
        lem Council to accompany Paul &
        Barnabas. Acts 15:22

**BARTHOLOMEW - NATHANAEL,
THE APOSTLE**
    Discussed. Mk.3:18

**BARTIMAEUS, BLIND (See BEGGAR;
BLIND)**
    Steps to getting help from God.
        Mk.10:46-52

BASIC PRINCIPLES
    B.p. to be destroyed by fire in the end of
        the world. 2 Pt.3:10-13
    Elementary notions of God. Gal.4:1-3;
        4:9-11
    Elementary notions of the world. Col.
        2:8; 2:20-23
    Of the world. Meaning. Col.2:8

BASKET
    Described. Mt.15:37

BATHSHEBA
    Saved by God. Mt.1:6

BE CAREFUL
    Meaning. Mk.8:15; Lk.21:34-35

BEAM (See PLANK)

BEAR - BEARING (See PROTECTS)

BEARING WITH ONE ANOTHER
    Duty.
        To b. with one's fellow workers.
            Eph.6:9
        To b. one another in love. Eph.4:2;
            Col.3:13
        To love by b. with all things. 1 Cor.
            13:7
        To put on b. Col.3:13
    Meaning. Eph.4:1-2

**BEAST OF REVELATION, FIRST (See
ANTICHRIST)**

BEAST OF REVELATION, SECOND
**(See PROPHET OF REVELATION,
FALSE)**

BEATINGS
    By His stripes, the stripes of Christ, we
        are healed. 1 Pt.2:24
    Discussed. Mt.27:26-38; Jn.19:1; 2 Cor.
        6:4-5
    Meaning. Lk.18:32-33
    Of Christ. Discussed. Mt.27:26-38
    Of cords. Meaning. Jn.2:15
    Of Old Testament believers. Heb.11:36
    Of Paul. 2 Cor.6:4-5; 11:24-25
    Paul is beaten. 2 Cor.11:23
    Predicted that believers will suffer b.
        Mt.10:17

BEATITUDES
    Identifies the disciples. Mt.5:1-12
    Meaning. Mk.8:15; Lk.21:34-35
    Of what.
        How one builds the church. 1 Cor.3:10
        Of being a stumbling block. 1 Cor.8:9
        Of Christ's Word. Mk.13:23
        Of covetousness. Lk.12:15
        Of deception. Mt.24:4; Mk.13:5;
            Lk.21:8
        Of despising others. Mt.18:10
        Of division. Gal.5:15
        Of false doctrine & speculations.
            1 Tim.1:4; Tit.1:14
        Of God's judgment. Ro.11:21
        Of ill feelings toward those who of-
            fend one. Lk.17:3-4
        Of oneself & one's ministry. Acts
            20:28; Col.4:17
        Of outward show. Mt.6:1
        Of persecutors. Mk.13:9
        Of pride. 1 Cor.10:12
        Of the light one has. Lk.11:35
        Of the Word of God. Heb.2:1; 2
            Pt.1:19
        Of unbelief. Heb.4:12
        Of watching & praying. Mk.13:33
        Of what & how one hears. Mk.4:24
        Of worldliness. Lk.21:34
    Seven b. of Revelation. Rev.1:3
    Verses. List of. 1 Cor.3:10

BEELZEBUB
    Christ is charged with being possessed
        with **B.**, the devil. Mt.12:24
    Discussed. Prince of the demons.
        Mk.3:22

To do all things for edification.
1 Cor. 10:23-28; 10:29-11:1

To do good to all. Gal.6:6-10

To encourage one another daily.
Eight reasons. Heb.3:13-19

To fellowship. Acts 2:42; 1 Jn.1:3

To greet every saint; to show no
partiality. Ph.4:21-22

To guard against offending others.
Mt.18:5-10; 18:15-17; 18:15-20

To help the needy. Lk.10:29-37

To hold affection for one another.
Gal.4:12-20

To labor for the church. Col.1:29

To live at peace with all. Ro.12:18;
1 Pt.3:8-9

To love all believers. Jn.13:33-35;
1 Pt.4:8; 2 Jn.5-7

To mark those who walk as examples. Ph.3:17-21

To meet needs. Ro.12:13

To meet the needs of new converts.
Acts 9:10-18

To rejoice in the Lord. Ph.4:4

To restore the man who slips.
Gal.6:1-5

To strive for unity. Ph.1:27

To teach the things of salvation &
to teach diligently. 2 Pt.1:12-15

To use one's gifts. Ro.12:6-8;
Eph.4:7-16; 1 Pt.4:10-11

To welcome one another. Mt.18:5

To worship. Acts 2:42; Heb.10:25

Toward leaders. 1 Th.5:12-13

Toward other believers. Mt.6:12;
Ro.12:9-13

Toward the church. 1 Th.2:14-15

Duty in relation to Christ.

Following Christ is not enough.
Mt.26:14-16

How the **b.** is to behave in light of
Christ's return. 1 Th.5:4-11;
1 Th.5:12-18

Not above the Master, but treated
the same as the Master. Lk.6:40

One thing needed. To sit at Jesus'
feet. Lk.10:38-42

To be attached to Christ. Jn.15:1-8

To be changed into the image of
Christ from glory to glory--day by
day. 2 Cor.3:18

To be conformed to Christ. Lk.6:40

To be enriched by Christ, in all
speech & knowledge. 1 Cor.1:4-5

To be enslaved to Christ. Ro.1:1-7;
1:6-7

To be mature witnesses for the Lord
Jesus Christ. Ph.1:12-20

To be prepared for Jesus' return.
Lk.12:35-48

To be sober, alert, & watchful for
the Lord's return. 1 Th.5:4-11

To be steadfast & immovable in the
work of the Lord. 1 Cor.15:58

To be strong in Christ. 2 Tim.2:1-7

To be zealous of good works for
Christ. Eph.2:10; Tit.2:14;
Jas.2:14-26

To bear the cup & baptism of
Christ. Mt.20:22-23

To commit our lives, all we are &
have, to Christ. 2 Tim.1:12

To do greater works than Christ.
Jn.14:12

To do some things since Jesus Christ
is coming again. 1 Pt.2:11-14;
2:15-18

To fear the Lord. Lk.8:25

To fellowship with Christ.
Mt.28:19-20; Jn.14:16-21, esp. 18,
21; 1 Cor.1:9; 1 Jn.1:3; Rev.3:20

To fix one's attention upon Christ.
Heb.3:1

To follow & pattern one's life after
Christ. 1 Cor.11:1

To glorify God & Christ. Jn.11:4;
17:9-11

To grow in Christ. 1 Jn.2:12-13

To help the needy. Lk.10:29-37

To let the love of Christ constrain
us. 2 Cor.5:14

To let the mind of Christ control us.
Ph.2:5-11, cp. 3-4

To live only for Christ who died for
us. 2 Cor.5:14-15

To obey Christ. Jn.14:23; 15:10-14;
2 Th.1:7-9

To "put on" Christ, to be clothed
with Him. Gal.3:26-27

To remember the resurrected Lord.
2 Tim.2:8-13

To seek the things of Christ & of
heaven. Col.3:1-4

To serve the Lord with fervor.
Ro.6:19-20; 12:11

To set one's mind upon Christ
without distraction. 1 Cor.7:35

To suffer for Christ even as Christ
suffered for us. 1 Pt.2:21

To walk & talk about the Lord all
day long. Col.3:17

To walk after Christ. Eph.4:20-24

To walk as Christ walked. 1 Jn.2:6

To walk or live in the Lord. Acts
9:31

To walk just like Christ. Col.1:10

To walk worthy of the Lord. Col.1:10

To watch & be ready for the Lord's
return. Mt.24:42-51

Who it is that Jesus works through.
Acts 3:1-5

Duty in relation to God.

How the believer lives for God.
Gal.2:19-21

Not to abuse or presume upon the
grace of God. Eph.5:5-6

To be a man of God. Marks of.
1 Tim.6:11-16

To be established by God. Ro.16:25-27

To be like God. Mt.5:45; 5:48

To bear God's nature. Gal.5:22-26

To bear the glory & glow of God.
1 Pt.4:14

To believe God. Mk.11:22; Heb.11:6

To do the will & work of God. Jn.
4:31-35

To follow & imitate God. Eph.5:1-7

To glorify God & Christ. Jn.11:4;
17:9-11

To know & learn of the Father. Jn.14:6

To know God. 1 Jn.2:3-6

To long to know the Father. Jn.14:6

To love God & to seek God above
all else. Mt.22:36-38

To obey God's commands. 1 Jn. 2:3-6

To partake of & follow after God's
holiness. Heb.12:10, 14

To walk pleasing to God. 1 Th.4:1-8

Toward God. Several exhortations.
Ro.12:1-3; 1 Th.5:16-22

Duty in relation to ministers & teachers.

To be open to exhortation.
Heb.13:22-25

To beware lest one fall into error.
2 Pt.3:17

To do good to one's teacher.
Gal.6:6-10

To guard against false teaching.
2 Jn.7-13

To guard against impostors.
2 Tim.3:13

To guard oneself. Against four
things. Ph.3:1-3

To ministers (See **MINISTERS;
STEWARDSHIP**)

To highly esteem. 1 Th.5:12-13

To pray for ministers. 1 Th.5:25

To submit to ministers. 1 Pt.5:5-7

To receive true messengers always.
Gal.4:18-20

To shun controversial teachings.
Tit.3:9

To stand against false teachers.
Jude 3

To subject to ministers. 1 Pt.5:5-7

Duty in relation to money. (See
STEWARDSHIP)

Duty in relation to Satan & temptation.
(See **SATAN**, How to Combat;
TEMPTATION)

To be vigilant & to resist the devil.
1 Pt.5:8-9

To bruise Satan under one's feet.
Ro.16:20

Duty in relation to oneself.

Four laws governing. Lk.17:1-16

Fourfold duty. Heb.10:22-25;
13:13-16; Jude 17-25

How to live in light of the new
heavens & earth. 2 Pt.3:11-14

Must not try to serve two masters.
Cannot. Lk.16:13

Not to be anxious, but to pray about
everything. Ph.4:6-8

Not to be conceited. Ro.12:16

Not to be lacking in zeal. Ro.12:11

Not to continue in sin. Ro.6:1-10;
6:11-13; 1 Jn.3:6-7; 3:9

Not to harden one's heart. Heb.3:7-11

Not to think one can sin & sin &
still be forgiven. Eph.5:5-6

Not to think too highly of oneself.
Ro.12:6-8

Not to use one's liberty as a license
to sin. Ro.6:14-23

Not to worry about necessities. Lk.
12:22-34

Rules for discipleship. Lk.6:39-45

Seven marks of believers. Heb.
13:1-8

To abstain from fleshly lusts, sinful
desires. 1 Pt.2:11-12

To accept others. Lk.9:49-50

To add certain things. 2 Pt.1:5-7

To arise & stand up. Mk.3:3

To awaken out of sleep. Ro.13:11-14

To be a peacemaker. Mt.5:9

To be clean-bodied. Eph.5:3

To be clean-mouthed. Eph.5:4

To be completely changed. Gal.
1:10-16

To be diligent in working out one's
own salvation. 2 Pt.1:5-15

To be fearless. 1 Jn.4:18

To be humble & meek. Mt.5:5;
Ph.2:3-4; 1 Pt.5:5-6

To be hungering & thirsting after righteousness. Mt.5:6
To be loving. 1 Th.4:9
To be loyal. Mt.5:10-12; 10:32-33
To be merciful. Mt.5:7
To be mourning. Mt.5:4
To be obedient to God & Christ. Jn.14:21, 23-24; 15:10, 14
To be on fire spiritually & zealous of good works. Ro.12:11; Tit. 2:14
To be poor in spirit. Mt.5:3
To be pure. Mt.5:8; 1 Th.4:1-8
To bear fruit. Mk.4:20; Jn.15:1-8
To beware of some things. Mk. 12:38-40
To boast in the cross. Gal.6:14-17
To build oneself up in the faith. Four warnings. Jude 20-21
To cling to the good. Ro.12:9-10
To combat the sinful nature. Gal.5:16-21
To conquer trials. Ro.12:12
To constantly pray. Ro.12:12
To control one's conversation. Col.4:6
To control one's mind & thoughts. Ro.8:5-7; 2 Cor.10:3-5; Ph.4:8-9
To count one's self dead to sin. Ro.6:1-10
To dedicate one's body as a living sacrifice. Ro.12:1-2
To deny oneself. Mk.8:34
To die to oneself. (See **SELF-DENIAL**)
To discern spiritual things. 1 Cor.2:15-16
To do all in the name of the Lord. Col.3:17
To do the expedient, not just the lawful. 1 Cor.6:12-20
To enjoy life. 1 Pt.3:10-12
To examine oneself. 2 Cor.13:5
To fear certain things. 2 Cor.11:1-15
To flee youthful lusts, the desires of youth. 2 Tim.2:22-26
To follow peace & holiness. Heb.12:14
To forget the past. Ph.3:13
To get up, face circumstances, & conquer. Ph.4:11-14
To give all one is & has--all beyond necessities. Acts 4:32-37
To give generously. Ro.12:13
To give undivided attention to one's task. Jn.21:20-23
To grow in grace & in the knowledge of Christ. 2 Pt.1:18
To guard against immaturity & falling away. Heb.5:11-6:2
To guard against unrighteous character. 1 Cor.6:9-11
To hate evil. Ro.12:9-10
To hold fast. 2 Tim.1:13-18
To keep oneself from idols. 1 Jn.5:21
To keep oneself pure. 1 Tim.5:22
To labor for reward. Mt.10:1-16; Heb.11:1-40; 12:1-4
To labor one hundred percent. Mt.13:8, 23; Lk.19:15-23
To let the gospel abide within. 1 Jn.2:24-27
To live a consistent life. Gal.5:25
To live a life of heavenly behavior & conduct. Ph.3:20-21
To live a morally pure life. 1 Th.4:1-8
To live a quiet life. 1 Th.4:11

To live above reproach. Ro.12:17
To live as a citizen of heaven. Ph. 1:27
To live by the golden rule. Mt.7:12
To live free of sin. 1 Jn.5:16-21
To live in prayer--to pray about everything & know the constant peace of God. Ph.4:6-7
To live worthy of the gospel. Ph.1:27
To look for a new heavens & earth. 2 Pt.3:12-15
To love life for the sake of the gospel. Mk.8:35
To match one's profession. 1 Jn. 2:3-6
To mind one's own business. 1 Th. 4:11
To mortify, put to death, five things. Col.3:5-7
To obey. Not an option. Jn.14:15; Ph.2:12
To obey the truth. Gal.5:7-12
To pass one's time in reverence. 1 Pt.1:17-21
To pray. (See **PRAYER**) Col.4:2-4
To press on. Ph.3:1-21
To purify oneself. 1 Jn.3:3
To put on Christian virtues. Col. 3:12-17
To rejoice in hope. Ro.12:12
To sin no more. After being helped & healed. Jn.5:13-14
To strip off six things. Col.3:8-11
To strive for the faith of the gospel. Ph.1:27
To struggle for deliverance. Ro. 8:23-27
To use one's time wisely. Ro. 13:11-14
To walk as a child of light. Eph. 5:8-14
To walk carefully & strictly. Eph. 5:15-21
To walk humbly. Ro.12:3-5; 12:9-10
To walk in the truth. 2 Jn.4
To walk worthy of one's calling. Eph.4:1-6
To watch. Fear certain things. Lk. 6:39-45
To watch & not be sleepy. 1 Th. 5:2-11
To watch & pray for the end time. Lk.21:34-36
To watch & work for judgment is coming. Mt.25:14-30
To work before the night comes. Jn.11:7-10
To work out one's own salvation. Ph.2:12-13; 2 Pt.1:5-15
Toward oneself. Ro.12:3-8
Traits. Essentials. Mt.4:18-20; 4:21-22
Wise & foolish. Prepared & unprepared. Mt.25:1-13
Duty in relation to the Holy Spirit.
(See **HOLY SPIRIT**, Duty toward)
Not to sin against the Spirit. (See **HOLY SPIRIT**, Sins Against)
To be continually filled with the Holy Spirit. Eph.5:18-21
To be led by the Spirit.
Discussed. Jn.16:13; Gal.5:18
Meaning. Ro.8:14
Through restraint. Acts 16:6-7
To bear the fruit of the Spirit. Gal.5:22-26; Eph.5:9

To follow the Holy Spirit. Jn.21:18-19
To follow the teaching of the Holy Spirit. Jn.14:27
To know the power of the Spirit. Ro.8:1-17
To let the Holy Spirit change us into the image of Christ day by day. 2 Cor.3:18
To pray in the Spirit. Jude 20
To walk in the Spirit. Gal.5:16; 5:25
Duty in relation to the world.
How to live toward the world. Jas.3:14-18
How to walk before unbelievers. 1 Pt.2:11-12
Not to live in envy & strife. Jas.3:14-18
Not to partake of other people's sins. 1 Tim.5:22
Not to repay evil for evil. Ro.12:17
Not to take vengeance. Reasons. Ro.12:18
Not to walk as other men walk. Eph.4:17-19
Response to the world's end. 2 Pt.3:15-18
Responsible for the keys to the kingdom. Mt.16:19
To be a good citizen. Six duties. Tit.3:1-2
To be content with what one has. Not to covet the things of the world. Heb.13:5
To be mature witnesses for the Lord Jesus Christ. Ph.1:12-20
To be responsible. The world's fate depends upon. Mk.6:30
To be unashamed & to exalt Christ. Ph.1:20-26
To be wise or shrewd as snakes; harmless as doves. Mt.10:16
To bear witness to Christ. Jn.21:24-25
To bind & loose. Mt.16:19
To bless persecutors. Ro.12:14
To endure abuse for the gospel. 2 Tim.1:6-12
To identify with & show interest in men. Ro.12:16
To live a peaceful life in the sight of all men. Ro.12:17
To live at peace with all. Ro.12:18; Jas.3:14-18; 1 Pt.3:8-9
To live bearing the fruit of the Spirit. Gal.5:22-23
To love one's enemies. Mt.5:43-48
To love one's neighbor. 1 Jn.2:7-11
To meet the needs of the world. Ro.12:13
To overcome the world. 1 Jn.5:4-5
To possess & live in agape love. 1 Cor.13:1-13
To use one's gifts. Ro.12:6-8
To walk wisely before the world. Col.4:5
To win the respect of the world by living quietly & working diligently. 1 Th.4:11-12
To witness & preach. Mt.16:19; Col.4:2-4
Toward fellow citizens. Ro.13:8-10
Toward the state. Ro.13:1-7
Toward unbelievers. Ro.12:14-21

Example.
 A great Christian man. Philemon.
  Phile.1:1-7
 A haughty outspoken leader. 3 Jn.9-
  11
 A man greatly changed. Onesiums.
  Phile.1:8-21
 A spiritual leader. 3 Jn.1-8
 Reasons for following good examples.
  Ph.3:17-21
Experience of.
 Avenged by God. Lk.18:6-8
 God quickens & makes the believer
  alive. Eph.2:1-2, 4-5
 Spiritual experiences. Described.
  2 Cor.5:21
 The gift of God's grace - salvation.
  Eph.2:8-9
 The work of God's mercy. Eph.2:4-7
Facts.
 Hairs. Are numbered. Mt.10:29-31
 Fall away because of Christ. Reasons.
  Mt.26:31-32
False. (See **DISCIPLE**, False)
Glory of.
 Are transformed daily into the glory of
  God. 2 Cor.3:17-18
 Chart of **b**. glory & Christ's glory.
  Jn.17:22
 Possesses the glory of God Himself.
  Jn.17:22
Growth of. (See **GROWTH,
 SPIRITUAL**)
 Are transformed daily into the glory of
  God. 2 Cor.3:17-18
 Parable of Growing Seed. Mk.4:26-29
Hall of Fame. Many wrote on the life of
 Christ. (See **HALL OF FAME**)
Heirs. (See **INHERITANCE**)
Hope of. (See **HOPE**)
In the end time. (See **END TIME**)
Indwelling presence of Christ. (See
 INDWELLING PRESENCE)
Life - Walk - Behavior. (See **WALK,
 SPIRITUAL**)
 Discussed. Eph.2:1-22; 4:1-6:9;
  Col.2:1-7; 2:6-7; 1 Th.4:9-12;
  Tit.2:11-15; Jude 1-2
 The Believer's Life.
  A child of God vs. a child of Satan.
   1 Jn.3:10-17
  A model life. 1 Th.4:1-12
  Before conversion. Life without
   Christ. Eph.2:1-3
  Beliefs that govern. Col.1:1-2
  Feel scattered abroad. Mt.1:2
  How the **b**. lives for God. Gal.2:19-21
  How to enjoy and love life.
   1 Pt.3:10-12
  How to live under the shadow of
   history's climax. 1 Pt.4:7
  Imperatives for. Jude 17-25
  Is free and spiritual. Gal.5:13-6:18
  Is in a world of religion & religion-
   ists. Jn.16:1-6
  Is "in Egypt" but not "of Egypt"
   (the world). Mt.2:13-18
  Is in this present age. Tit.2:11-15
  Is not to be a stumbling block.
   Ro.14:1-23
  Is to be Christ, that is, wrapped up
   in Christ. Ph.1:20-24; 3:7-16
  Is to be focused upon the great
   things of salvation. 2 Pt.1:5-15
  Is to be mature & strong. Ro.14:1-23;
   15:1-13; Col.1:29; 2:2; Acts 9:10-18

Is to know that following Christ is
 not enough. Mt.26:14-16
Must be strengthened to bear the
 cross. Mt.17:1-13
Objective of. Should long for the
 Father. Jn.14:6
Pillars of. Two great pillars.
 Col.1:3-8
The lot of the **b**. in life. 1 Cor.7:17-24
The "pressing on" of the believer.
 Ph.3:1-21
Three great traits. Ro.15:14
Verse. List of. Ro.8:2-4
The Believer's Walk & Behavior.
 A walk that pleases God. 1 Th.4:1-8
 In light of Jesus' return. Tit.2:11-15
 In light of the end times. 2 Th.2:13-17
 Led step by step. Mt.2:19-23
 Sermon on the Mount was given to
  govern the believer's behavior.
  Mt.5:1-2
 Supreme conduct. Jn.12:3
 The believer & his mission.
  Mt.5:13; 5:14-16
 The faithful vs. the unfaithful.
  Mt.24:42-51; 25:14-30
Marks - Characteristics.
 A strong & true minister. 1 Th.2:1-12
 A strong conversion. 1 Th.1:5-10
 A strong encouragement. 1 Th.3:7-10
 A strong faith. 1 Th.3:1-10
 A strong love. 1 Th.3:11-13
 A strong people. 1 Th.2:13-20
 Come from all races & nations.
  Rev.5:9-10
 Discerns spiritual things. 1 Cor.2:15-16
 Discussed. Ph.1:3-30; 2:12-18
 Eight significant marks. Ph.1:3-11
 Of a child of God. 1 Jn.3:10-17
 Of a great Christian believer. Ph.1:20-26
 Of a mature witness. Ph.1:12-20
 Of God's people. Ph.1:3-30
 Of mature **b**. Ph.1:3-11
 Proof that one really believes in God.
  1 Jn.5:1-21
 Proof that one really knows God.
  1 Jn.2:3-29
 Proof that one really loves God.
  1 Jn.3:1-4:21
 Some distinctives of. Ph.1:1-2
Mature **b**. Discussed. Acts 9:10-18;
 Ro.14:1-23; 15:1-13; 1 Cor.2:15-16;
 Col.1:29; 2:2; 1 Jn.2:12-13
Misconceptions of.
 One can become righteous on his own.
  1 Jn.1:10-2:2
 One can fellowship with God and walk
  in sin. 1 Jn.1:6-7
 One is not totally sinful and depraved.
  1 Jn.1:8-9
Mission. (See **COMMISSION--
 MISSION**)
Motive. (See **BELIEVER**, Duty)
 To magnify Christ. Ph.1:20
Names--Titles.
 A Kingdom & priests. Rev.1:6
 Ambassador for Christ. 2 Cor.5:20
 Believers. Acts 4:32
 Believers are named; unbelievers are
  not. Lk.16:19-21
 Beloved brothers. 1 Th.1:4
 Body of Christ. Ro.12:3-8
 Brotherhood of believers, The.
  1 Pt.2:16-17
 Brothers in Christ. Lk.8:19-21
 Brothers of Christ. Heb.2:12

Builder of the church. 1 Cor.3:10-17
Building stones of the church.
 Mt.16:18
Children of Abraham. Ro.4:11-12
Children of God. Ro.9:6-13; 1 Jn.3:1;
 3:10
Children of Light. 1 Th.5:4-5
Children of the day. 1 Th.5:4-5
Chosen, The. Ro.8:33; Col.3:12
Chosen of God. 1 Pt.1:1-2
Chosen people. 1 Pt.2:9
Christians. Acts 11:26
Circumcision in the spirit, The. Ph.3:1-3
Dear children. Eph.5:1
Dearly loved. Col.3:12
Disciples. Acts 9:25
Friends. Jn.15:14
God's building. 2 Tim.2:19-21
God's flock. Acts 20:28; 1 Pt.5:2
God's simple & humble people.
 1 Cor.1:26-31
God's very own possession. 1 Pt.2:9
Great house. 2 Tim.2:20
Heavenly citizens. Rev.14:1-5
Heirs of God. Ro.8:16-17; Eph.1:11-13
Holy brothers. Heb.3:1
Holy nation. 1 Pt.2:9
Holy priesthood. 1 Pt.2:5
Holy, The. Col.3:12
Light of the earth. Mt.5:14-16
Light of the world. Mt.5:14-16
Little children. 1 Jn.2:1
Living stones. 1 Pt.2:5
Member of Christ's body. 1 Cor.6:15-18;
 6:18
New creature. 2 Cor.5:17
New race of people. 1 Pt.2:9
People who belong to God. 1 Pt.2:9
Peculiar possession of Christ. Tit.2:14
People of God. 1 Pt.2:9
Pilgrims. 1 Pt.2:11
Predestined race of people. Ro.9:6-13
Priests. Rev.1:6
Royal priesthood. 1 Pt.2:9
Saints. Ro.8:27; Acts 9:32
Salt of the earth. Mt.5:13; Lk.14:34-35
Seed of Abraham. Ro.4:13-16; 4:17-25
Servants & only servants. Lk.17:7-10
Servants of the Most High God. Acts
 16:17
Several titles. Mt.21:43
Sheep. Mk.6:34
Six points. Ro.9:25-33
Soldier. 2 Tim.2:3-4
Sons of God. Gal.3:26-27; 4:4-7
Spiritual house. Eph.2:19-22; 1 Pt.2:5
Spiritual people. 1 Pt.2:9
Steward. Mt.16:19
Strangers and aliens. 1 Pt.1:1
Temple of the Holy Spirit. 1 Cor.
 6:19-20
The chosen. Ro.9:25-33
The saved. Lk.13:22-30
The true children of God. Ro.2:28-29;
 9:6-13
The true Israel. Ro.9:6-13
True disciples. Mt.5:1-16
Vessels of honor. 2 Tim.2:21
Witnesses. Acts 1:8
Who believers are. 1 Jn.2:12-14
Nature.
 A changed heart. Col.3:15-17
 A citizen of heaven. Ph.3:20-21
 A new creation. 2 Cor.5:17
 A new person. Col.2:10
 Clothed with Christ. Gal.3:26-27

Compassionate & merciful. Mt.5:7;
   Lk.10:30-37; 1 Pt.3:8
Discussed. Jn.17:11
Godly. 2 Pt.2:9, cp. 2 Cor.7:10;
   Tit.2:12; Heb.12:28; 2 Pt.1:5-7; 3:11
Holy & without blame. Eph.1:4;
   5:27; Col.1:22; 3:12; Heb.3:1;
   1 Pt.1:15-16; 2:5; 2 Pt.3:11
How the **b**. differs from unbelievers.
   2 Cor.6:11-7:1
Humble & meek. Mt.5:5; Ph.2:3-4;
   1 Pt.5:5-6
Identified with Christ. Ro.6:1-10;
   Gal.2:15-16; 2:16; 2:19-21
"In Egypt" but not "of Egypt" (the
   world). Mt.2:13-18
Indwelling presence. Mutual indwell-
   ing. Ro.8:9-10
Indwelt by God's Spirit - corporately.
   Eph.2:21-22
Light. Mt.5:14-16; 1 Th.5:4-11
Light not darkness. Eph.5:8
Loving. 1 Th.4:9
Made children, sons & daughters of
   God. Mk.3:34-35
Not a "lifeless rock" but a "living
   stone."Mt.7:24-25
Not above sin. Mt.26:31-35
Purity. Mt.5:8; Jas.1:27; 1 Pt.1:22;
   2 Pt.3:14
Righteous in Christ. 2 Cor.5:21
Salt. Mt.5:13
Struggle for deliverance. Ro.8:23-27
The temple of God. 2 Cor.6:11-7:1
Zealous of good works. Tit.2:14
Need.
   To be stirred constantly. 2 Pt.1:12-15
   To experience seasons of refreshing.
      Acts 3:19
New **b**.
   Follow up of. Acts 9:10-18
   Must be protected & developed. Acts
      19:9-10
   Must be taught. Acts 11:22-26; 19:9
   Must be teachable. Mt.11:25;
      Lk.10:21
   Must desire the Word of God.
      1 Pt.2:2-3
   Needs of. Acts 9:10-18
Of the early church.
   Discussed. Ro.16:1-16
   Gave all they were & had--all beyond
      necessities. Acts 2:44-45; 4:32-37
   Life of. Discussed. Acts 4:32-37
Position.
   A glorious position in Christ.
      Discussed. Old man "was crucified"
         in Christ. Ro.6:2-5
      Has been baptized, immersed in
         Christ's death. Ro.6:2-5
      Has been crucified with Christ.
         Ro.6:2-5; 6:6-7; Gal.2:19-21;
         5:24Col.3:1-4
      Has been placed "in" Christ.
         Ro.6:3-5; 8:1; 2 Cor.5:17;
         Eph.2:4-7; Col.3:1-4
      Has been raised & exalted with
         Christ. Eph.2:4-7
      Has been resurrected with Christ.
         Col.2:9-10; 2:20; 3:1-4
      Is complete in Christ alone. Col.
         2:9-10
      Is hid with Christ. Col.3:1-4
      Is not above the Master, but treated
         the same as the Master. Lk.6:40

Is possessed and owned by Christ.
   Gal.5:24
Lives with Christ now & forever.
   Ro.6:1-10; 6:2-5
Sits in heavenly places with Christ.
   Eph.2:6
A glorious position in God.
   Called God's Son. Lk.15:30
   Is a son of God. Gal.3:26-27; 4:4-7
   Is dead to sin & alive to God. Ro.
      6:1-10
   Is known by God. Gal.4:9
   Is the temple of God. 2 Cor.6:11-7:1
A high & exalted position.
   A citizen of heaven. Ph.3:20-21
   A new world order. 2 Cor.5:17-6:2
   A spiritual man. 1 Cor.1:15-16
   Discussed 1 Cor.6:2-3
   Greater than Old Testament believ-
      ers. Great privileges. Mt.13:16-17
   Possesses all things. 1 Cor.3:21-23
   What the believer becomes. 1 Pt.
      2:5-6; 2:9
A position of deliverance, salvation, &
   power.
   Freed from condemnation. Ro.8:1-17
   Freed from sin. Ro.6:1-23
   Freed from the law. (See **LAW**)
      Ro.7:1-25
   Lives by the Spirit. Ro.8:1-17
   Discussed. Mt.11:11; Ro.6:1-10
Privileges of. (See **BELIEVER**, Position;
   REWARDS)
   Discussed. Lk.10:21-24
   Fourfold. Ro.1:6-7
   Known by God. Lk.16:19-21
   Trusted by Christ. Lk.8:23
   Truth revealed to. Lk.10:21
Purpose. (See **PERSON**)
   Discussed. Ph.1:20-26
   To be committed to Christ & His mis-
      sion. 2 Tim.3:10-11
   To exalt Christ. Ph.1:20
   To live is Christ, to be totally focused
      upon Christ. Ph.1:21
   To obey God and share in Christ's
      blood. 1 Pt.1:2
   To declare the praises of God.
      1 Pt.2:9
Questioning. (See **QUESTION -
   QUESTIONING**)
Relation - Relationships.
   Believers are given to Christ by God.
      Jn.17:9-11
   Believers are possessed by both God
      & Christ. Jn.17:9-11
   Believers know Christ by His Word or
      voice & Spirit. Jn.20:14-16
   Relationship to Christ.
      As a branch. Jn.15:1-8
      Known by Christ. Intimate knowl-
         edge. Jn.10:14-16
      Very special. Jn.15:9-11
   Relationship to God as Father. Mt.6:9
   Relationship to other believers.
      Jn.15:9-10
   Relationship to religionists. Persecu-
      tion: a bleak picture. Jn.16:1-6
   Relationship to the world. Persecution:
      a bleak picture. Jn.15:18-27
Resources.
   Discussed. 1 Cor.1:4-9
   God's presence & care. (See **CARE**)
      Mt.28:19-20; Jn.16:13; Acts 2:25;
      Heb.13:5

Grace. 1 Cor.1:4-5; 2 Cor.9:8; 2 Cor.12:9
Holy Spirit. (See **HOLY SPIRIT**)
How to face & conquer circumstances
   & problems. Ph.4:11-14
New nature. Jn.14:26; 1 Cor.2:12;
   2 Cor.5:17; Eph.4:24; Col.3:10;
   1 Pt.1:23; 2 Pt.1:4
Power & strength. Eph.1:19-23; 3:20;
   Ph.4:11-14; Col.1:11; 2 Tim.1:7
Spiritual gifts. (See **GIFTS,
   SPIRITUAL**)
Wisdom. Jn.8:32; 1 Cor.1:30; Jas.1:5
Response to Christ. Threefold response.
   Jn.6:66-71
Rewards of. See (**REWARD**)
Security of. (See **ASSURANCE;
   SECURITY**)
Some early Christian believers. Ro.16:1-16;
   1 Cor.16:10-12; 16:15-19; Col.4:7-18;
   2 Tim.4:9-22; Tit.3:12-15; Phile.1:8-21;
   Heb.11:1-40
Some final words to. 1 Th.5:25-28
Spiritual experiences. (See **SPIRITUAL**)
   Described. 2 Cor.5:21
Spiritual struggle. (See **SPIRITUAL
   STRUGGLE - WARFARE**)
Traits of.
   A hypocritical **b**. Jn.12:4-8
   A supreme **b**. Jn.12:3
   B. as sheep. Mk.6:34; Jn.10:27-29
   Discussed. Jn.12:4-8
Types of **b**. (See **BELIEVER**, De-
   scribed) Mt.4:18-22
   Discussed. Jn.12:1-11; 15:1-8;
      1 Cor.2:14-3:4; 1 Jn.2:12-13
   False **b**. (See **PROFESSION,
      FALSE**)
   Natural **b**., carnal **b**., spiritual **b**.
      1 Cor.2:14-3:4
   Secret **b**. Stirred to step forth by the
      cross of Christ. Lk.23:50-56
   Silent **b**. Jn.12:42-43
Unity of. (See **UNITY**)
Value of.
   A great treasure. Mt.13:44, 45-46
   Of more value than sparrows.
      Mt.10:29-31
Warning. (See **WARNINGS**)
   About being offended by Christ.
      Mt.26:31-32
   About causing others to sin. Mt.18:5-10;
      18:15-17; 18:15-20
   About the end time. Mk.13:28-37
   Against being lukewarm. Rev.3:14-22
   Against compromise. Rev.2:18-29
   Against false profession. Rev.3:14-22
   Against idolatry. Rev.2:18-29
   Against losing one's first love. Rev.2:1-7
   Against permissiveness. Rev.2:18-29
   Against Satan's influence. Rev.2:9;
      3:9-10
   Against spiritual deadness. Rev.3:1-6
   Against worldliness. Rev.2:12-17
   Beware of some things. Mk.12:38-40
   Severe warnings of judgment. Eight
      severe judgments in Scripture. 1
      Jn.5:16
   Sin will cause God to reject. 1 Cor.
      6:9-11
   The judgment of the "sin that leads to
      death." 1 Jn.5:16
Who the **b**. is. Lk.13:22-30; 1 Jn.2:12-14

BELOVED (See **DEARLY LOVED**)
Who is **b**.
Believers. Acts 15:25; Ro.16:12; Col.4:7
Christ. Eph.1:6
Church. Ro.1:7; 1 Th.1:4
Israel. Ro.9:25; 11:28
New Jerusalem. Rev.20:9

BELOVED SON
Two precious thoughts. Mt.12:17-18

BENEDICTION
Of Anna: the child Jesus is praised.
Lk.2:36-38
Of Christ. Mt.28:18-20; Acts 1:8
Of Christ upon children. Mk.10:16
Of Elizabeth: a very unusual testimony.
Lk.1:39-45
Of John. Rev.22:20-21
Of Jude. Jude 24-25
Of Mary: God's glorious mercy & deliverance. Lk.1:46-56
Of Paul. Ro.16:20; 1 Cor.16:23-24;
2 Cor.13:14; Gal.6:18; Eph.6:23-24;
Ph.4:23; Col.4:18; 1 Th.4:28; 2 Th.3:18;
2 Tim.4:22; Tit.3:15; Phile.25; Heb.13:25
Of Peter. 1 Pt.5:14; 2 Pt.3:18
Of Simon: Jesus' life & fate foretold.
Lk.2:25-35
Of Zechariah: God's Savior & His forerunner. Lk.1:67-80
Other benedictions. Eph.3:20; 1 Tim.
1:17; Heb.13:20; 1 Pt.5:10

BENEDICTUS
Song of Zechariah. Lk.1:67-80

BENEVOLENCE (See **GIVE - GIVING; MINISTRY; SERVICE; STEWARDSHIP**)

BEREA
Discussed. Acts 17:10-15

BEREAVEMENT (See **GRIEF; SORROW**)

BERNICE
Sister of Herod the king who heard Paul preach. Acts 25:13-27; 26:1-18

BESET, EASILY (See **ENTANGLES, EASILY**

BETHANY
Discussed. Mt.21:17

BETHLEHEM
City of Jesus' birth. Prophesied. Lk.2:3

BETHPHAGE
Discussed. Lk.19:29

BETHSAIDA
Discussed. Mt.11:20-22; Jn.1:44

BETRAYAL (See **APOSTASY; BACKSLIDING; DENIAL**)
Discussed. Jn.13:18-30
Of Christ. By Judas. Picture of a ruined life. Mt.26:14-16
Traits of. Jn.12:4-8

BETROTHED (See **MARRIAGE**)
Engagement before marriage. Lk.1:27
Steps in marriage. Mt.1:18

BEWARE--WATCH OUT (See **HEED, TAKE; SEE TO IT; WATCH**)
Duty.
To **b**. of being led astray. 2 Pt.3:17
To **b**. of covetousness. Lk.12:15
To **b**. of divisive & conniving religionists. Ph.3:2
To **b**. of false teachers. Mt.7:15
To **b**. of five things. Mk.12:38-40, cp. Lk.20:45-47
To **b**. of men, for they will persecute believers. Mt.10:17
To **b**. of the false teaching of religionists. Mt.16:5-11, cp. Mk.8:15; Lk.12:1
To **b**. of unbelief. Acts 13:40-41
Meaning. Mt.7:15; Col.2:8

BIBLE (See **SCRIPTURE; WORD OF GOD**)
Discussed. 2 Tim.3:16
Books and contents of. 2 Pt.1:19-21
Inspired. 2 Tim.3:16
Purpose of. 2 Tim.3:16

BIGOTRY (See **DISCRIMINATION; PARTIALITY; PREJUDICE**)
Caused by.
False convictions & beliefs. Lk.6:7-11;
Acts 26:9-11; 1 Tim.1:13
Racial prejudice Jn.4:9; Acts 10:28
Rejection & ignorance of Christ.
Jn.1:10-11; Tim.1:13
Self-righteousness. Mk.9:38; Lk.19:7;
Ph.3:4-6 Spiritual blindness.
Jn.9:39-41
Results.
Jealousy. Mt.13:53-58, esp. 55-57;
Mk.8:38
Name-calling. Jn.8:48
Persecution. Acts 26:9-11
Rejection of Christ. Lk.9:51-53

BIRDS Are fed & cared for by God.
Mt.8:20; Lk.12:24
Symbolized. Unbelievers lodging in Christianity. Mt.13:31-32
Used in Jewish sacrifice. Lk.2:24
Worshipped by some heathen. Ro.1:23

BIRTH, NEW (See **BORN AGAIN; NEW CREATION; NEW LIFE**)

BISHOP (See **ELDERS; MINISTERS; OVERSEERS**)

BITTER - BITTERNESS
Caused by.
Envy, strife, pride, lying, & denying the truth. Jas.3:14
Failing to be kind & forgiving & tender. Eph.4:31
Not loving & holding the wife's failure against her. Col.3:18-19
Duty.
Not to be **b**. against one's spouse. Col.3:19
Not to even let a root of **b**. spring up. Heb.12:15
To put away all **b**. against others & forgive. Eph.4:31
Meaning. Eph.4:31; Heb.12:15-17

BLAMELESS (See **ABOVE REPROACH; WITHOUT FAULT**)
How to be **b**.
By being diligent & seeking to be **b**. at the return of Christ. 2 Pt.3:14
By God keeping us until the end & making us **b**. in the day of Christ. 1 Cor.1:4, 8
By not murmuring & arguing. Ph.2:14-15
By obeying the charges of the Word. 1 Tim.5:7
By praying for God to sanctify us. 1 Th.5:23
Who is to be blameless.
Believers. 1 Cor.1:8; Ph.2:14-15;
1 Tim.5:7; 2 Pt.3:14
Bishops, elders, ministers. 1 Tim.3:2;
Tit.1:6-7
Deacons. 1 Tim.3:10

BLASPHEMY (See **ABUSIVE; CURSING; SLANDER; SWEARING**)
Against the Holy Spirit. Mt.12:31-32;
Mk.3:29-30; Lk.12:4-12
Caused by.
Backsliding - a shipwrecked faith. 1 Tim.1:19-20
Claiming deity. 2 Th.2:4
Covetousness & worldliness. Jas.2:6-7
False religion. Rev.2:9
Natural & physical difficulties & circumstances. Rev.16:9-11, 21
Not doing to others as we should. 1 Tim.6:1
Not living responsibly & righteously before the world. 1 Tim.6:1; Tit.2:1-5, esp. 5
Persecution. Acts 26:11
Professing Christ, but living a hypocritical life. Ro.2:24, cp. 17-29
Rejection & hatred of Christ. Jn.8:48-59;
Acts 18:5-6
The antichrist. Rev.13:1, 6
The dragon, Satan. Rev.13:4-6
Charged against. Christ. Mt.9:3; Mk.2:6-7;
Jn.10:36
Duty.
Not to speak evil of any person, not a single person. Tit.3:2
To have such a good conscience that those who **s**. will be put to shame. 1 Pt.3:16, cp. 15
To know that people watch to find accusations. Lk.6:7
To live a righteous life, not giving the world any reason for **s**. 1 Pt.2:12
To prepare for the end time: a terrible period of world-wide **s**. 2 Tim.3:1-5, esp. 3
To put away all evil or **s**. speaking. Eph.4:31
To put off **b**. Col.3:8
To rejoice & endure **s**. for the sake of Christ. Mt.5:11-12
Is forgiven. Mk.3:28
Meaning. Mt.9:3; Mk.7:22; Ro.1:30;
1 Tim.3:11-12
Sin of.
Religion can be guilty of **b**. Rev.2:8-11
Will be a trait of the last days. 2 Tim.3:1-2; Rev.6:9-11, 21
Will be committed by the antichrist. Rev.13:4-8

The promise to believers when slandered. To be blessed & greatly rewarded. Mt.5:11-12

Who is often **b**.

Believers. 1 Pt.2:12; 3:16; Acts 2:1-13, esp. 13; 24:5-6; Rev.2:9

Christ. (See **JESUS CHRIST**, Accused - Accusation against)

Ministers & church leaders. Lk.7:33; Acts 6:13; 3 Jn.9-10

Who it is that **b**.

A whole generation of unbelievers who stand against true righteousness. Mt.11:16-19

Corrupt political & religious officials. Lk.22:66-71; 23:1-5

Religious leaders. Acts 6:9-15; 24:1-9

Some church leaders & members who oppose the minister. 3 Jn.9-10

Some religionists. Mt.9:34

The average citizen who mocks spiritual things. Acts 2:1-13, esp. 13

BLAZING LAMPS, SEVEN
Meaning. Rev.4:5-6

BLEMISH, WITHOUT
Meaning. Col.1:22

BLESS - BLESSINGS (See **BELIEVER**, Position; **INHERITANCE; REWARD; SALVATION**, Results)

Duty. To remember & not to forget one's **b**. Jn.5:13-14

Four significant **b**. Ro.1:6-7

Material vs. spiritual **b**. Eph.1:3

Misconceptions. Wealth is a sign of God's **b**. Mt.19:25; Lk.16:14-15

Of God.

Are spiritual **b**. not material. Eph.1:3

Discussed. Sevenfold **b**. Eph.1:3-14

Spiritual. Discussed. Eph.1:13-14

Spiritual. Promised to the world in the end time at Israel's conversion. Ro.11:13-15

What the **b**. are. (See **BELIEVER**, Position; **INHERITANCE; REWARDS; SALVATION**, Results)

All human necessities met. Mt.6:25-34, esp. 33

All needs provided for. Mt.5:1-12

Justification. Gal.3:6-14, esp. 14

Seven great blessings. Eph.1:3-14

The Holy Spirit. Gal.3:13-14

BLESSED
Meaning. Mt.5:3; Rev.20:6

BLESSED OF THE LORD
Meaning. Mk.11:10

BLESSED, THE
Discussed. Ro.4:6-8

Christ is to be **b**.

As the King of Israel. Jn.12:13

As the One over all. Ro.9:5

God is to be **b**. (See **PRAISE; THANKSGIVING**)

To be **b**. as the God & Father of our Lord Jesus Christ. 2 Cor.11:31; Eph.1:3; 1 Pt.1:3

To be **b**. as the only Potentate, the King of kings, & Lord of lords. 1 Tim.6:15

To be **b**. for the gospel. 1 Tim.1:11

To be **b**. forever. Ro.9:5

To be **b**. instead of idols. Ro.1:25

Who are the **b**.

Eight persons. Mt.5:1-12

Mary the mother of Jesus. Lk.1:28

The person who confesses Jesus Christ to be the Son of God. Mt.16:13-17

The person who endures temptation & trials. Jas.1:12

The person who has part in the first resurrection. Rev.20:6

The person who hears & keeps the words of Revelation. Rev.1:3; 22:7

The person who is not offended by Christ. Mt.11:6; Lk.7:23

The person who shall eat in the kingdom of God. Lk.14:15

The person who watches & keeps himself for the Lord's return. Lk.12:37-38; Rev.16:15

They who are called to the marriage supper of the Lamb. Rev.19:9

They who believe Christ. Jn.20:29

They who die in the Lord. Rev.14:13

They who do the Lord's commandments. Rev.22:24

They who hear the Word of God & keep it. Lk.11:28; Jas.1:25

They who serve & minister to the needy. Mt.25:31-40, esp. 34; Lk.14:12-14

They whose iniquities are forgiven. Ro.4:7

BLIND - BLINDNESS (See **HEAL - HEALING; SPIRITUAL BLINDNESS**)

Conflicts between the gospel accounts. Lk.18:35

Steps to getting help from God. Mk.10:46-52; Lk.18:35-43

BLOOD (See **JESUS CHRIST**, Blood of)

BOAST - BOASTING - BOASTERS (See **BOASTFUL; PRIDE; SELF-IMPORTANCE**)

Answer to - Eliminated by.

Faith. Ro.3:27

God. 1 Cor.1:26-31

Law & Scripture. Ro.3:19-20

Caused by.

Boasting about one's flesh. Gal.6:12-13

Churches **b**. in civil leaders who join their fellowship. 1 Cor.5:6

Glorying in men. 1 Cor.3:21-23

Living by a law of works. Ro.3:27; 4:1-3

Pride. Elevating oneself over others. Ro.11:18

Religionists. Ro.2:17-20

Self-centeredness. Ro.3:27

Self-sufficiency. Lk.10:21; 12:19; Jas.3:5

Tongue, the. Jas.3:5

Works of righteousness. Ro.3:19-20; 4:1-3

Discussed. Ro.3:27; Jas.4:16

Duty. Not to boast in oneself, but in Christ. Ro.15:17-19

Fact.

Is disallowed by God's grace & salvation. Eph.2:8-9

Is excluded by the law of faith. Ro.3:27

Is sin. Jas.4:16

The lost are filled with hearts that **b**. Ro.1:18, 30

Will be a trait of the last days. 1 Tim.3:1-2

Meaning. Ro.1:30; 1 Cor.13:4-7

Of ministers. Is sometimes necessary to answer criticism. 2 Cor.11:16-33

True **b**. Discussed. Gal.6:14-17

Warning against. **B**. in conversion. Mt.8:4; Mk.1:44

Who **b**.

Churches. 1 Cor.5:6

False teachers who want to make a good impression outwardly. Gal.6:12-13

Religionists. Ro.2:17-20

The rich & self-sufficient. Lk.12:19

The wise, strong, & noble. 1 Cor.1:26-30

Those who **b**. in gifts & abilities. 2 Cor.10:17-18

BOASTFUL; PRIDE; SELF-IMPORTANCE

Answer to - Eliminated by.

Faith. Ro.3:27

God. 1 Cor.1:26-31

Law & Scripture. Ro.3:19-20

Caused by.

Boasting about one's flesh. Gal.6:12-13

Churches **b**. in civil leaders who join their fellowship. 1 Cor.5:6

Glorying in men. 1 Cor.3:21-23

Living by a law of works. Ro.3:27; 4:1-3

Pride. Elevating oneself over others. Ro.11:18

Religionists. Ro.2:17-20

Self-centeredness. Ro.3:27

Self-sufficiency. Lk.10:21; 12:19; Jas.3:5

Tongue, the. Jas.3:5

Works of righteousness. Ro.3:19-20; 4:1-3

Discussed. Ro.3:27; Jas.4:16

Duty. Not to boast in oneself, but in Christ. Ro.15:17-19

Fact.

Is disallowed by God's grace & salvation. Eph.2:8-9

Is excluded by the law of faith. Ro.3:27

Is sin. Jas.4:16

The lost are filled with hearts that **b**. Ro.1:18, 30

Will be a trait of the last days. 1 Tim.3:1-2

Meaning. Ro.1:30; 1 Cor.13:4-7; 2 Tim.3:2-4

Of ministers. Is sometimes necessary to answer criticism. 2 Cor.11:16-33

True **b**. Discussed. Gal.6:14-17

Warning against. **B**. in conversion. Mt.8:4; Mk.1:44

Who **b**.

Churches. 1 Cor.5:6

False teachers who want to make a good impression outwardly. Gal.6:12-13

Religionists. Ro.2:17-20

The rich & self-sufficient. Lk.12:19

The wise, strong, & noble. 1 Cor.1:26-30

Those who **b**. in gifts & abilities. 2 Cor.10:17-18

BODY, HEAVENLY (See **RESURRECTION**)

Fact. To undergo a radical transformation. 1 Jn.3:2

Discussed.
  A temporary body at death until the resurrection? 2 Cor.5:1-10
  Hope for a heavenly **b**. 2 Cor.5:1-10
Resurrected. To be made just like Christ's **b**. Ph.3:11; 3:21

BODY, HUMAN

Care of. By God. 1 Cor.6:12-20
Described.
  As a tabernacle, a tent. 2 Cor.5:1-4; 2 Pt.1:13
  As a temple. Jn.2:18-22; 1 Cor.6:18-19
  As an earthly house. 2 Cor.5:1
  As an earthly vessel. 2 Cor.4:7
  As picturing the church. 1 Cor.12:12-31; Col.3:15
  As the members of Christ. 1 Cor.6:15
Discussed. Ro.12:1; 2 Cor.5:1-4
Duty.
  Discussed. 1 Cor.6:12-20
  Not to be anxious about the **b**. even if deformed. Lk.12:25
  Not to conform one's **b**. to the world. Ro.12:2
  Not to give one's **b**. over to immorality. 1 Cor.6:13
  Not to let sin control one's **b**. or bodily members. Ro.6:12
  Not to neglect the body nor abuse it through religious rules & over-discipline. Col.2:20-23
  Not to worry about the **b**. Mt.6:25
  Not to yield one's bodily members to sin. Ro.6:13
  To be holy in **b**. & spirit. 1 Cor.7:34
  To be strenuously disciplined. 1 Cor.9:24-27
  To bear in our **b**. the dying of the Lord Jesus. 2 Cor.4:10; Gal.6:17
  To care for the **b**. Acts 9:19; 1 Tim.5:23
  To exercise. 1 Tim.4:8
  To glorify God in our **b**. 1 Cor.6:20
  To have one's **b**. washed with pure water. Heb.10:22
  To keep one's **b**. clean & pure. Eph.5:1-7
  To know that one's **b**. becomes the temple of the Holy Spirit after one receives Christ. 1 Cor.6:19-20
  To know that one's **b**. is dead to sin through Christ. Ro.6:11; 8:10, cp. Ro.6:1-10; 6:11-13; 6:14-23
  To love one's wife as one's own **b**. Eph.5:28
  To magnify Christ in the **b**. Ph.1:20
  To present one's **b**. as a living sacrifice to God. Ro.12:1; Ph.1:20
  To put off the body of the sins of the flesh--by Christ. Col.2:11
  To put to death the deeds of the **b**. Ro.8:13
  To submit one's body to one's own spouse. 1 Cor.7:3-5
  To take care of the **b**. 1 Tim.3:2-3
Facts.
  A person has power over his own **b**. 1 Cor.7:4
  Is a natural **b**. & a spiritual **b**. 1 Cor.15:44
  Is defiled by the tongue. Jas.3:6

Is to be radically changed at the coming resurrection. (See **RESURRECTION**) 1 Cor.15:35-49; 15:50-58
  Surety of - Assurance of. Jn.5:28-29; Ro.8:11
The **b**. means more than things. Mt.6:25
The **b**. of believers will be conformed to the image of Christ. Ro.8:29-30
The **b**. without the spirit is dead. Jas.2:26
The flesh withers. 1 Pt.1:24-25
Will be made blameless by God. 1 Th.5:23
Will be made into a glorious **b**. just like the body of Christ. Ph.3:21
Will be redeemed & made perfect. Ro.8:23
Will face judgment based upon what one has done in his **b**. 2 Cor.5:10
Indulgence of. (See **INDULGENCE**)
Nature.
  Dies because of sin. Ro.5:12; Heb.9:27
  Is corruptible, perishing. 1 Cor.15:50; 2 Cor.4:16; 2 Cor.5:1-4; 1 Pt.1:23
  Is designed to be a temple for God's presence. 1 Cor.3:16; 6:18-19
Purpose of. Discussed. 1 Cor.6:12-20
Sins against.
  Defilement of. Things that defile. Mk.7:14-23
  Homosexuality. Ro.1:24-27
  Immoral looks, dress. (See **DRESS**) Mt.5:27-30
  Immorality. 1 Cor.6:18
  Indulgence. 1 Cor.6:12-13
  Listed. Ro.1:29-32
  Making one's belly one's god. Ph.3:17-19, esp. 19

BODY OF CHRIST, THE (See CHURCH, Nature)

Discussed. Eph.3:6; 4:4-6
Source. God creating a new body of people. Eph.4:4-6

BOLD - BOLDNESS (See CONFIDENCE)

Duty.
  To boldly enter God's presence. Heb.10:19-21
  To boldly magnify Christ in one's body. Ph.1:20
  To boldly preach & teach. Acts 9:27, 29; 14:3; 18:26; 19:8
  To come boldly before God. Heb.4:15-16
Results. Stirs one to step forward for Christ. Lk.23:50-56
Source - Comes by.
  Being faithful in one's duty & service. 1 Tim.3:13
  Being in Christ Jesus our Lord. Eph.3:11-12
  Being with Jesus. Acts 4:13-14
  Believing God's love. 1 Jn.4:16-17
  Knowing that the Lord will provide for one. Heb.13:6
  Living without covetousness & being content with what one has. Knowing that the Lord will provide. Heb.13:6
  Prayer. Acts 4:29; Eph.6:19; Ph.1:19-20
  The blood of Jesus. Heb.10:19
  The Holy Spirit, from His infilling. Acts 4:31

BONDAGE, SPIRITUAL (See ENSLAVEMENT, SPIRITUAL)

Deliverance from.
  By Christ. Lk.4:18-19; Jn.8:36
  By obeying the doctrine, the Word of God. Ro.6:17-23, esp. 17
  By the truth. Jn.8:32
List of. Several things. Lk.9:47
What enslaves - Things that hold men in **b**.
  Corruption & lust. Ro.8:21; 2 Pt.1:4; 2:19
  Death. Ro.5:12; 6:23; Heb.9:27
  Elementary knowledge of the world. Gal.4:3; 4:9-10
  False teachers. Gal.2:4
  Fear. Ro.8:15
  Fear of death. Heb.2:14-15
  Law. Ro.8:3
  Rituals. Gal.5:1
  Sin. Jn.8:34; Ro.6:14-23; 6:16; 6:19-20; 7:23
  The devil. 2 Tim.2:26
  Worldliness. Lk.15:14-16

BOOK OF DESTINY

Discussed. Rev.5:1-4; 5:5-14

BOOK OF LIFE

Described. Rev.13:8
Determines one's destiny. Rev.13:8-10; 17:8; 20:11-15
Discussed. Rev.20:12
Duty. To rejoice that one's name is written in the Book of Life. Lk.10:20
Meaning. Rev.3:4-6
Name is written in heaven. Heb.12:23

BOOK OF RECORDS

A book used to judge unbelievers. Rev.20:12

BORN AGAIN (See NEW BIRTH; NEW CREATION; NEW MAN; SALVATION)

Discussed. Jn.3:1-15; 1 Pt.1:23; 1 Jn.5:1-5
Proof of.
  Doing right - obedience. 1 Jn.2:28-29
  Three evidences. 1 Jn.5:1-5
Results.
  A living hope. 1 Pt.1:3-5
  A new creature. 2 Cor.5:17
  A new life. Ro.6:4-11
  A new man. Eph.4:24; Col.3:10
  An inheritance that can never perish. 1 Pt.1:3-5
  Delivers from sin's enslavement. 1 Jn.3:4-9; 5:19
  Empowers one to overcome. 1 Jn.4:4-6
  Keeps oneself from sin. 1 Jn.5:17-18
  Overcomes false spirits. 1 Jn.4:4-6, cp. 1:1-6
  Overcomes the world. 1 Jn.5:4-5
  Stirs one to be righteous. 1 Jn.2:29
  Stirs one to keep himself from sin. 1 Jn.3:9; 5:17-18
  Stirs one to love others. 1 Jn.4:7-11, esp. 7-8
Source - How one is born again.
  By believing. 1 Jn.5:1
  By confession. 1 Jn.4:14-16
  By God. Jn.1:12-13; Jas.1:18; 1 Jn.3:9; 5:1
  By love. 1 Jn.4:7-8
  By the Holy Spirit and water. Jn.3:5
  By the imperishable Seed. 1 Pt.1:23-25
  By the Word of God. Jas.1:18; 1 Pt.1:23

BORROW - BORROWING (See **LENDING**)
Attitude toward lending. Mt.5:42
Money. (See **MONEY**, Borrowing)
Discussed. Ro.13:8

BOTTLES
Type - Symbol of. New vs. old **b**. New life & joy. The purpose of Jesus. Lk.5:36-39, esp. 37-38

BOTTOMLESS PIT (See **ABYSS**)
Described.
As a great smoking furnace. Rev.9:2
As a prison. Rev.20:7
Ruler over. Discussed. Rev.9:1; 9:11
The beast, that is, the antichrist shall come from. Rev.11:7; 17:8
The destiny of Satan. Satan shall be cast into the **b**. pit for one thousand years. Rev.20:1-3

BOWELS (See **AFFECTION**)

BOWL JUDGMENTS
Discussed. Rev.16:1-21
Preparation for. Rev.15:1-8

BOXER
Illustrates. The Christian life. 1 Cor.9:26

BRAG - BRAGGING
Meaning. Ro.1:30

BRAWLER (See **PEACEABLE, TO BE; QUARRELSOME**)

BRAWLING
Meaning. Eph.4:31

BRAZEN ALTAR (See **ALTAR OF BURNT OFFERING**)

BREAD
Fact.
A necessity of life. Mt.4:2-4; 6:11
Does several things for man's body. Jn.6:33
Man cannot live by **b**., the physical alone. Must live by the Word of God. Mt.4:3
How to secure.
By being faithful to God & receiving His care. 2 Cor.9:8-11, cp. 9:1-7, esp, 6,10
By prayer & trusting God. Mt.6:11
By seeking God first. Mt.6:33, cp. 25-34
By trusting Christ to provide. Jn.6:1-15
By working & earning. Eph.4:28; 2 Th.3:8; 3:12
Meaning. Mt.6:11
Of the Lord's supper. Discussed. Mk.14:22
Spiritual **b**. (See **BREAD OF LIFE; SATISFACTION, SPIRITUAL**)
Symbolizes.
Fellowship with other believers. Acts 2:46; 1 Cor.10:17
The death, the broken body of Christ. 1 Cor.11:24

BREAD OF LIFE
Christ is the Bread of Life. Jn.6:1-71
Discussed. Jn.6:1-71
How one secures & partakes. Jn.6:41-51
Results of partaking. Jn.6:30-36; 6:41-51
Who can partake. Jn.6:59-71

BREAD OF THE PRESENCE, THE (See **CONSECRATED BREAD**)

BREAKING THE LAW (See **LAW**, Breaking)

BREASTPLATE (See **ARMOR, SPIRITUAL**)

BRIBE - BRIBERY
Seeking a **b**.
Felix sought a **b**. from Paul. Acts 24:26
Illustrated. Acts 24:22
Judas accepts a **b**. to betray Christ. Mk.14:10-11
Payoff for favors. Acts 24:26
Simon, a sorcerer, sought to buy the power of the Holy Spirit. Acts 8:18-19
The leaders pay the soldiers to lie about Christ's resurrection. Mt.28:12-15

BRIDEGROOM
Parable of. Mt.9:14-16
Symbolizes. The mission of Jesus Christ. Mt.9:15; Lk.5:35; Jn.3:29-30

BRIGHT MORNING STAR
Name given to Christ. Rev.2:28

BRIGHTNESS (See **SPLENDOR**)

BRIMSTONE, FIRE AND
A place of punishment.
For Satan. 20:10
For the antichrist & false prophet. Rev.19:20; 20:10
For the ungodly. Rev.21:8
Fell upon Sodom in utter destruction. Lk.17:29
The nature of hell & the lake of fire. Rev.19:20; 20:10; 21:8

BROAD ROAD, THE
Those who follow. Mt.7:13

BROTHER - BROTHERHOOD (See **DIVISION; EMPLOYEES; EMPLOYERS; MASTERS; SLAVES; UNITY** and Related Subjects)
Among various ages. 1 Tim.5:1-2; 1 Jn.2:12-14
Basis of.
A blood relationship. Acts 17:26
Christ as our Master. Mt.23:8
Hearing & doing the Word of God. Lk.8:21
God as Creator. Has created all men as one blood. Acts 17:24-27
God as our Father. Mt.23:9
God meshes together. Lk.8:21
Love. Mk.12:31; Ro.13:10; Gal.5:14; Jas.2:8; 1 Jn.4:19-21
Ministering to needy **b**. Jas.2:14-17
Not of flesh or blood or will. Lk.8:20
Principles governing. Fivefold. Lk.6:27-31, cp. Ro.14:1-13; 1 Cor.6:12-20; 8:1-13
Sevenfold basis. The reasons why believers are **b**. Eph.4:4-6
Destruction of **b**. caused by. (See **SIN**)
Bigotry. (See **BIGOTRY**)
Division. (See **DIVISION**)
Judging & criticizing others. Mt.7:1-6; Ro.2:1; 14:3-4

Lack of peace. Ro.12:18
Prejudice. (See **PREJUDICE**)
Satan. Jn.8:41-47, esp. 41, 44
Sin & evil works. 1 Jn.3:11-12
Stumbling blocks. Ro.14:13-15; 1 Cor.8:9; 8:13; 1 Jn.2:10
Discussed. Lk.8:19-21; Jn.15:12-17; Gal.4:12-20; Heb.13:1; 1 Jn.2:7-11; 3:10-17; 4:7-21
Duties - Essential.
Must have patience & endurance to maintain brotherhood. Ro.15:5-6
Not to be a stumbling block. Ro.14:1-23; 1 Cor.8:11-13
Not to cause others to sin. Mt.18:5-10
Not to forsake when persecuted. 2 Tim.1:15-18
Not to judge one another. Ro.14:10-17
Not to speak evil of one another. Jas.4:11
To accept without partiality or favoritism. Ro.15:7-12
To admonish one another to obey the Word of God. 2 Th.3:14-15
To be a **b**. to others. Jn.17:11; 17:20-23
To be giving. Mt.19:16-22, esp. 21-22
To bear the weaknesses of the weak. Ro.15:1-3
To care for one's neighbor. Gal.5:13-15
To correct offending **b**. Mt.18:15-20
To follow Christ. Mk.1:19
To have a forgiving spirit. Mt.18:22
To labor together with God. 1 Cor.3:5-9
To limit one's liberty. 1 Cor.10:14-11:1
To live at peace if possible. Ro.12:18
To live in harmony. 1 Pet.3:8
To live sociably. Heb.13:1-8
To love, care, & support. Ph.1:3
To love one another. 1 Jn.4:7-21
To love one's neighbor as oneself. Mt.22:39; Mk.11:31
To love sincerely without hypocrisy. Ro.12:9-10
To please one's neighbor for his good. Ro.15:1-2
To practice the golden rule. Mt.7:11
To pray for one another. Heb.13:18-19
To seek harmony & to associate with the lowly. Ro.12:16
To strive to keep the unity & peace. Eph.4:3; Ph.1:27
To welcome one another & be tender & gracious. Ro.15:14; 16:1-2
To withdraw from disorderly **b**. 2 Th.3:6
To work for a strong fellowship. Six things. Ro.15:1-13
Toward fellow citizens. Ro.13:8-10
Toward other believers. Ro.12:9-13
Toward the state. Ro.13:1-7
Toward unbelievers. Ro.12:14-21
Example. Demonstrating & showing **b**. vs. not demonstrating. Lk.10:29-37
Failure in.
Causes one to withdraw. Heb.10:25
Some things often put before **b**. Lk.10:29-37
What withdrawing causes. Jn.20:24-25
Meaning. (See **LOVE**) Mt.25:40
One heart & one soul. Acts 4:32
What true **b**. is. Mt.12:46-50; Mk.3:31-35; Lk.8:19-21
Nature of.
A binding force. Jn.17:11
A spiritual, not a blood relationship. Mk.3:33

To catch men; to fish for souls.
Mt.4:18-20; Lk.5:10
To disciple others. Steps to. Lk.6:1-11
To know Christ first. Mt.4:18-20
To take hold of the eternal life. 1
Tim.6:12
To obtain glory. 2 Th.2:14; 2 Pt.1:3
To secure a prize. Ph.3:12-16
To serve God, not religion. Lk.3:2
Twofold. Ro.8:28
Source.
Christ. A command, not an option.
Acts 26:19-21
God. Ro.8:30
God, not man. Gal.2:6; 2:7-10
God's election. Col.3:12
What God's c. is. Eph.1:18
Of God & Christ, not of religion. Lk.3:2
To what. (See CALL, Purpose)
To God Himself. God's great invita-
tion. Mt.22:1-14; Lk.14:15-24
To one's work & profession. 1 Cor.7:20
To repentance. Mt.9:12-13
To the ministry. Discussed. Ro.1:1
Universal c.
Jesus came to give His life for the
whole world. Jn.6:33; Ro.10:13
To all who will. Lk.13:29-30; 14:21-23
Warning. The Holy Spirit does not always
strive with man. Mt.12:14-16; 20:5

CALVARY - GOLGOTHA
Meaning. Lk.23:33
Place where Christ was crucified.
Mt.27:33; Lk.23:33

CAMEL
Cp. to a rich man. Going through the eye
of a needle. Mt.19:24; Mk.10:25

CANA
Discussed. Jn.2:1
Home of Nathanael. Jn.21:2

CANAAN
Type. Of heaven.
An eternal inheritance. Acts 7:2-8;
Heb.13:14
Of the new heavens and earth. Ro.4:13;
Gal.3:16; Heb.11:8-10, 13-14, 16

CANAANITES
Enemies of the Jews. Mt.15:22;
Mk.7:25-26

CANDLE (See LAMP)

CANDLESTICKS (See LAMPSTANDS)

CAPERNAUM
Discussed. Mt.4:12; 4:12-13; 11:23
Headquarters of Jesus. Mt.4:12; Lk.4:31
Is to be judged. Mt.11:23-24
Jesus' ministry in C. Mt.8:14-17; 9:1-8;
Mk.1:21-28; 9:33-50; Lk.4:31-44;
Jn.4:46-54; 6:22-71

CAPITAL PUNISHMENT
Jews were not allowed the right to capital
p. Jn.19:7

CAPTIVE - CAPTIVATED (See
OPPRESSED)
Meaning. Col.2:8
What c.
Satan. 2 Tim.2:26
Sin. 2 Tim.3:1-9

CARE - CARING (See ANXIETY;
WORRY)
Duty to c.
For children. Lk.2:41-52
For great crowds. Jesus' purpose.
Mt.8:14-17
For life. Mk.4:35-41
For ministers. Ph.4:10
For one another. 1 Cor.12:25;
Heb.12:14-17
For one's needs. Mt.6:25-34; 15:29-30;
Mk.8:1-9
For sinful friends. Mt.9:10-11
For the church. 2 Cor.11:28
For the disabled. Mt.9:1-8
For the flock of God. Jn.10:11-18
For the home & the individual.
Mt.8:14-17; Mk.1:29-31
For the less fortunate & the weak. Lk.7:2
For the rejected, hopeless, & helpless.
Mt.9:18-34; Mk.7:24-30
For the spiritual. Mt.6:25-34
For the whole world. Mk.1:32-34
To be touched over suffering. Mt.18:31
To care for God's flock. 1 Pt.5:1-4
To cast all our anxiety on God.
1 Pt.5:6-7
To show c. for all men, even one's
enemies. Lk.10:25-37
To show genuine interest in men's ex-
periences. Ro.12:15
Examples of c.
A Canaanite woman for her daughter.
Mt.15:21-28
A centurion soldier for his servant.
Mt.8:5-13; Lk.7:1-10
A father for his dying daughter.
Mk.5:21-24, 35-43
A father for his son who had a dumb
spirit. Mk.9:14-29
A rejected woman for her daughter.
Mk.7:24-30
Friends of a paralyzed man. Mt.9:1-8
Sisters for their brother. Jn.11:1-46
Some friends for a blind friend.
Mk.8:22-26
Supreme example. Mt.18:11-14
Meaning. 1 Pt.5:6-7
Necessity for c. Mk.8:22-26
Of God.
Discussed. Mt.10:29-31
For man. Verses. List of. Ro.8:34
God's eyes look over the believer.
1 Pt.3:12
Looks after every detail of life for the
believer. Mt.10:29-31
Protects. Acts 28:13-15
Provides the necessities of life for His
people. Mt.6:25-34; Lk.12:22-34
Of Jesus Christ. Identified with man.
Every conceivable experience. Lk.2:40
Steps to c. Threefold. Mk.7:24-30

CAREFUL
Meaning. Mk.8:15; Lk.21:34-35
Of what.
How one builds the church. 1 Cor.3:10
Of being a stumbling block. 1 Cor.8:9
Of Christ's Word. Mk.13:23
Of covetousness. Lk.12:15
Of deception. Mt.24:4; Mk.13:5; Lk.21:8
Of despising others. Mt.18:10
Of division. Gal.5:15
Of false doctrine & speculations.
1 Tim.1:4; Tit.1:14
Of God's judgment. Ro.11:21

Of ill feelings toward those who of-
fend one. Lk.17:3-4
Of oneself & one's ministry. Acts
20:28; Col.4:17
Of outward show. Mt.6:1
Of persecutors. Mk.13:9
Of pride. 1 Cor.10:12
Of the light one has. Lk.11:35
Of the Word of God. Heb.2:1; 2
Pt.1:19
Of unbelief. Heb.4:12
Of watching & praying. Mk.13:33
Of what & how one hears. Mk.4:24
Of worldliness. Lk.21:34
Verses. List of. 1 Cor.3:10

CARES OF THE WORLD (See
ANXIETY; NEEDS--NECESSITIES)
Duty. Not to be anxious over. Lk.12:22-34
Results. Chokes the life out of a person.
Lk.8:11-15

CARNAL - CARNALITY (See SINFUL
NATURE)
Caused by.
Corrupt motives. Jn.6:26-27
Failure to see the cross. Lk.22:33-37
Living after the sinful nature. Ro.8:12-13
Twofold. Jn.13:36-38
Commitment of the c. Mt.26:51-52
Deliverance from.
By Christ.
By condemning sin in the f. Ro.8:3
By His conquest of the f. Jn.1:14
By His death. Eph.2:14-18, esp. 15-
16; Col.1:22; Heb.2:14-16; 9:13-
14; 10:19-20; 1 Pt.3:18
By His giving His f. for the life of
the world. Jn.6:51
By His power over all f. Jn.17:2
By His reconciliation. Eph.2:11-18;
Col.1:22
By His resurrection. Acts 2:30-31;
Ro.1:3-4*
By His suffering in the f. for us.
1 Pt.4:1
By condemning sin in the f. Ro.8:3
By confessing that Christ has come to
earth in the f. 1 Jn.4:2-3; 2 Jn.7
By God.
By His being manifested, revealed
in the flesh. 1 Tim.3:16
By His power over all f. Jn.17:2
By partaking of the f., of the life of
Christ. Jn.6:54-56
By the Holy Spirit. By walking in
Him. Gal.5:16
Deliverance from c. - How to conquer.
Abstaining from fleshly lusts.
1 Pt.2:11-12
Being spiritual minded. 2 Cor.10:5
By prayer. Prayer for a c. church.
2 Cor.13:7-10
By taking certain precautions against
c. Can become weighted down.
Heb.6:9-20; 12:1
By the power of the Spirit. Ro.8:1-17;
8:12-13
Discussed. 2 Cor.10:3-5
Doing no evil. 2 Cor.13:7
Fighting & warring against c.
2 Cor.10:3-5
Praying and fasting. Mk.9:28-29
Purging out c. 1 Cor.5:7
Watching and standing fast. 1 Cor.16:13

Discussed. Ro.7:14-17; 7:18-20;
1 Cor.2:14-3:1-4, 14; Gal.5:16-21;
1 Pt.2:11Heb.5:11-6:3
Being corrupted under a man's ministry. Rev.3:14-22
Better to be cold than lukewarm.
Rev.3:15
Illustrated.
Barnabas' compromise. Gal.2:11-13
Peter's weakness. Lk.22:31-34;
Gal.2:11-13
Meaning. Jn.1:14; Ro.7:5; 8:5-8;
Eph.2:3; 1 Pt.2:11
Spiritual immaturity. 1 Cor.3:1-4;
Heb.5:11-6:3
The carnal mind of man. Ro.8:5-8
The natural, fleshly nature of man.
Ro.7:14-17
The struggle within fighting against
what one should do. Ro.7:14-25;
Gal.5:16-18;1 Th.4:3-5; Jas.4:2; 4:4
Mind of.
Discussed. Ro.8:5-8
Fate of. Ro.8:5-8
Focus of. Ro.8:5-8
Meaning. Ro.8:5-8
Vs. the spiritual **m**. Lk.12:13-21
Nature. Works - Shortcomings of.
Cannot inherit the kingdom of God.
1 Cor.15:50
Cannot make a person perfect. Gal.3:3
Cannot please God. Ro.8:8
Causes man to die. Ro.8:13
Does not justify a person before God.
Ro.3:20; Gal.2:16
Dreams filthy dreams that defiles a
person. Jude 8
Is as grass, withers ever so quickly.
1 Pt.1:24
Is not a part of spiritual beings. Lk.24:39
Is so corrupted that it even spots the
garments worn by a person. Jude 23
Money, silver & gold can consume the
c. Jas.5:3, cp. Mt.6:19-20
No good thing dwells within the **c**.
Ro.7:18
Profits nothing. Jn.6:63
Reaps corruption. Gal.6:8
Serves the law of sin & death.
Ro.7:25; 8:1-4
Stirs a fleshly, carnal commitment.
Jn.13:36-38
Stirs lust. 1 Pt.2:11
Struggles against prayer. Mt.26:41;
Mk.14:38
The carnal vs. the spiritual view of the
c. Lk.22:33-37
The lust of the **c**. is not of God.
1 Jn.2:15-16
Wars against the soul & spirit.
Mt.26:41; Mk.14:38; 1 Pt.2:11
Withers & falls away. 1 Pt.1:24-25
Works of the **c**.
Seventeen works. Gal.5:19-21
Twenty-three works. Ro.1:29-32
Results. (See **CARNAL**, Traits of)
A divided church. 1 Cor.1:10-16, cp.
1 Cor.1:10-4:21
A struggling soul. Ro.7:14-25
Death. Ro.6:23; 8:5-8; 8:12-13
Deforms & stymies growth. One remains
only a babe in Christ. 1 Cor.3:1-2
Dullness of hearing. Heb.5:11
Falling & failing. Lk.22:33-37;
Heb.6:9-20
Grieving the Lord. Mk.9:19-22

Has to be treated as a babe in Christ.
Can receive only the milk of the
Word, not the meat of the Word.
1 Cor.3:1-2; Heb.5:11-6:3
Hurting & cutting a minister. 2 Cor.2:3-4
Self-deception. 1 Cor.3:18-23
Works shall be burned up in the judgment. 1 Cor.3:13-15
Sin of.
A life spent in lusts, cravings. Eph.2:3
Discussed. Lust of the flesh. 1 Jn.2:15-17
Lists of fleshly sins. Ro.1:24-32; 3:9-20;
1 Cor.6:9-11;10:6-10; Gal.5:19-21;
Eph.4:25-32; Col.3:8-9; 1 Tim.1:9-10;
2 Tim.3:1-5; 1 Pt.2:1; 4:3
Vs. the Spirit. Discussed. Ro.8:1-17
Traits of.
A struggling soul. Ro.7:14-25
Allowing the leaven of sin in one's
life. 1 Cor.5:6-8
Being complacent toward sin.
1 Cor.5:1-2; 5:6-13; Rev.3:1-6
Being contentious & divisive.
1 Cor.1:11; 3:3-4
Being enemies of the cross. Ph.3:18-19
Being weak. Ro.15:1-3
Boasting about one's flesh. Gal.6:12-13
Compromising. Gal.2:11-14
Engaging in legal disputes. 1 Cor.6:1-8
Exalting some ministers over others.
1 Cor.3:3-4; 3:5-9; 3:21-23
Faithlessness. Mk.9:19-22
False security. Ro.13:11-14
False teachers. 2 Pt.2:10; Jude 19
Having double standards. Gal.2:11-14
Immaturity. Mt.17:14-21; Mk.9:14-29;
1 Cor.3:1-2
Immorality. 1 Cor.5:1-13
Indulgence. 1 Cor.6:12-20
Judging others. Mt.7:1-5; Ro.2:1;
1 Cor.4:1-5; 4:6-13
Living unrighteously. 1 Cor.6:9-11
Looking progressive, but being dead.
Rev.3:1
Losing one's first love. Rev.2:4
Misusing one's spiritual gifts.
1 Cor.12:1-14:40
Powerlessness. Lk.9:37-45
Prayerlessness. Mk.9:28-29
Rebelling against God. Ro.8:5-8
Unbelief. Mt.17:19-21
Worldly wisdom. 1 Cor.3:18-20; Jas.3:15
Verses. List of. Mk.8:32-33; Jn.6:26-27
Vs. the spiritual man. Ro.8:1-17;
1 Cor.2:14-3:4

CAROUSING
Meaning. 1 Pt.4:3
Sin of. 2 Pt.2:13

CARPENTER (See BUILDING)

CARPUS
Paul had forgotten & left some personal
items at the home of C. 2 Tim.4:13

CAST DOWN (See STRUCK DOWN)

CAST OUT--THROWN OUT
An act of judgment - Who & what is to
be cast out.
Evil spirits & devils. Mt.8:16; 9:33;
10:1; 10:8; 12:28; Mk.1:34; 1:39;
3:15; 6:13; 16:9; 16:17; Lk.13:32
Fallen angels. Rev.12:9
Fear. 1 Jn.4:18

Satan. the prince of this world.
Jn.12:31; Rev.12:9
The beam of wrong in one's eye.
Mt.7:5; Lk.6:42
Those who abuse the temple, the house
of God. Mt.21:12; Mk.11:15;
Lk.19:45
Those who do not come to Christ.
Jn.6:37
Those who have lost the salt of life.
Mt.5:13; Lk.14:35
The reason for judgment. Mt.5:13
Who will not be cast out. Those who
come to Christ. Jn.6:37

CASTAWAY - THROWN OUTSIDE
(See FORFEIT HIS VERY SELF;
DISQUALIFIED; SENT)
Who is **c**.
The undisciplined, those who lack
self-control will be **c**. 1 Cor.9:27
The worthless will be **c**. Mt.25:14-30,
esp. 30

CAUSE
A man needs a **c**. Mt.9:9-13
Dying for a **c**. Not rare. Mt.10:23

CAUSING OTHERS TO SIN
Discussed. Lk.11:44; 17:1-2
Duty.
Not to be **c**. by persecution & ridicule.
Mt.13:21; Mk.4:17; Jn.16:1-4
Not to do anything that will **c**. a
brother. Ro.14:21
Not to **c**. in anything. 1 Cor.10:32;
2 Cor.6:3
Not to **c**. in questionable activities.
Ro.14:1-23; 1 Cor.8:1-13
Not to **c**. 1 Cor.8:9-11; 10:23-28;
10:29-11:1
To be without **c**. until the day of
Christ. Ph.1:10
To cut out of one's life all that **c**.
Mt.5:29-30; 18:7-9; Mk.9:43-48
To mark those who cause division & **c**.
Ro.16:17-18
Fact.
Christ died for our **c**. Ro.4:25
Many will be **c**. because of Christ in
the end time. Mt.24:9-10
The gift of Christ justifies us from
many **c**. Ro.5:16
We all **c**. in many things, especially in
word & tongue. Jas.3:2
How. Six ways. Mk.9:42
Judgment of those who **c**. Shall be cast
into a furnace of fire. Mt.13:37-42
Meaning. Mt.5:29; 17:27; Mk.14:27;
2 Cor.6:3; Ph.1:9-10
Steps to correcting. Mt.18:15-20
Verses. List of. Mk.9:42
Warning against **c**. others. Mt.18:5-10;
Lk.17:1-2
If one **c**. in one point, he is guilty of all
the law. Jas.2:10
Ways one causes others to sin. Mt.18:15
What **c**. men about Christ.
Four things **c**. Jn.6:59-71
His claims. Jn.6:61
His cross, blood. Jn.6:61; 1 Cor.1:23;
Gal.5:11
His Lordship. Jn.6:62
His Person & claims. 1 Pt.2:7-8
His works. Mt.11:1-6, esp. 6;
Mt.13:53-58

CELIBACY
In the end time. Some will devote themselves totally to God - 144,000. Rev.14:1, 4
When a person should practice **c**. Mt.19:12; 1 Cor.7:1; 7:2; 7:7

CEMETERIES
Discussed. Mk.5:3

CENCHREA
Discussed. Acts 18:18

CENSOR - CENSORING (See **JUDGING OTHERS**)
Discussed. Jn.8:3-6
Of church leaders against ministers. 1 Cor.1:10-16; 3 Jn.9-10
Of the self-righteous against the sinner. Jn.8:1-11
Who can **c**. Jn.8:7-9
Who is to be **c**. (See **JUDGMENT**, Who is to be judged)
    All who reject the gospel of Christ. Lk.10:10-16
    False teachers & deceivers who do not confess that Christ has come in the flesh. 2 Jn.7-11, esp. 10
    False teachers who are apostate. Jude 3-16

CENTURION
C. & Christ.
    At the cross.
        Confessed Christ to be the Son of God. Mt.27:54
        Proclaimed Christ to be righteous. Lk.23:47
    Requested Christ to heal his servant. Example of great faith. Mt.8:5-13; Lk.7:1-10
C. & Paul.
    Escorted Paul as a prisoner. Acts 23:17, 23; 27:1-44
    Protected Paul. Acts 22:22-29
    Rescued Paul from a mob. Acts 21:32, 35
    Was led to Christ by Paul. Cornelius. Acts 10:1-48
Discussed. Acts 23:23

CEPHAS (See **PETER, SIMON**)
Peter's name before Christ changed it. Jn.1:42

CEREMONY - CEREMONIAL LAW (See **SCRIBAL LAW; RELIGION; RITUAL**)
Broken - Violated.
    By Jesus. Mk.3:4
    By the disciples of Christ. Mk.2:23-24
Emptiness of. Discussed. Mk.7:1-13
Facts about.
    Does not save. Ro.2:25-27
    Is less important than man & his needs. Mk.2:23-24
    Is stressed before men. Lk.14:3
    Is superseded by need. Lk.6:1-11
    Was rejected & denounced by Christ. Mt.15:1-20; Mk.7:1-23, cp. Lk.11:37-54
Laws of.
    Cleanliness, purity. Washing one's hands. Lk.11:37-38; 11:39-41
    Discussed. Lk.6:2; 6:7
    Eating with unwashed hands. Mk.7:1-13
    Governing the Sabbath. Against working on the Sabbath. Mk.2:23-24
    Over six hundred **l**. Mk.12:28
    Walking over graves. Lk.11:44

CERINTHINISM
Discussed. Col. Introd.

CERTAINTIES (See **ASSURANCE**, Needed in; **SECURITY**)

CHAFF
Meaning. Mt.3:12

CHAMBERING (See **DRUNKENNESS; IMMORALITY; RIOTOUS LIVING; SEXUAL IMMORALITY**)

CHANCE, SECOND
Not given after death.
    To fallen angels. 2 Pt.2:4
    To people in hell. Lk.16:30-31
    To those before the flood. 2 Pt.2:5-6
Not given during life.
    To those who neglect. Heb.12:15-17
    To those who withdraw. Heb.10:26-31

CHARACTER
Of believers. (See **BELIEVER**, Duty, In relation to oneself; Nature)
    Growth of. Developed through trials. Ro.5:3-5; Jas.1:2-4
    Meaning. Ro.5:3-5; Jas.1:2-4
    Weakness of. Mk.6:14-29
Of unbelievers. (See **UNBELIEVERS**, Nature; Who unbelievers are)

CHARGE (See **COMMAND**)

CHARITY - CHARITABLENESS (See **GIVE - GIVING; MINISTRY; SERVICE; STEWARDSHIP**)

CHASTISEMENT - CHASTISED (See **CHURCH DISCIPLINE; DISCIPLINE**)
Chastised - By God. Kinds of. 1 Cor. 11:27-30
Response to. Obedience. Lk.1:59-63
Why a believer is **c**.
    Because God loves him. Heb.12:5-6; Rev.3:19
    For partaking of the Lord's Supper unworthily. 1 Cor.11:27-30
    For unbelief. Not believing the promise of God. Lk.1:20-22
    To bear fruit & more fruit. Jn.15:2
    To prevent sin. 2 Cor.12:7-10; Heb.12:4-13

CHASTITY (See **MORALITY; PURITY**)

CHEAT - CHEATING
Duty.
    Not to **c**. employers. Eph.6:5-8; Col.3:22-25
    Not to **c**. laborers. Jas.5:4, cp. Eph.6:5-9
    Not to covet, take more than what one needs. Lk.3:13, cp. 1 Tim.6:10
    Not to defraud & steal from people. Mk.10:19
    Not to extort & steal from people. 1 Cor.5:10
    Not to overcharge people. Lk.3:13
    To pay a just & fair wage. Col.4:1
    To work so that one will not have to bum off others & cheat. Eph.4:24; 2 Th.3:11-12
Results.
    Shall be judged for cheating. Col.3:25

Shall be rewarded for not cheating. Col.3:24
Shall face judgment & receive exactly what one has done. Eph.6:8; Col.3:24-25
Shall not inherit the kingdom of God. 1 Cor.6:9-10

CHEEK
Striking--slapping. Attitude toward being slapped. Mt.5:39; Lk.6:27-31

CHEER - CHEERFULNESS (See **JOY; REJOICING**)
Duty.
    To accept the presence of Christ with **c**. Mt.14:27; Mk.6:50
    To believe God with **c**. Acts 27:25
    To face trials & temptations, trouble & circumstances with **c**. Acts 27:21-25
    To give with **c**. 2 Cor.9:8
    To rejoice, be cheerful in the Lord. Ph.3:1; 4:4
    To show mercy with **c**. Ro.12:8
    To testify & proclaim the gospel with **c**. Acts 24:10
Source of.
    Christ.
        His presence in the midst of life's storms. Mt.14:27; Mk.6:50
        His victory over the world. Jn.16:33
        His Word & assurance. Acts 23:11; 27:22-25

CHERUBIM
Discussed. Rev.4:6-9
Overlooked the mercy seat of the ark of the covenant. Heb.9:4-5

CHIEF PRIESTS (See **HIGH PRIESTS**)

CHILDBEARING
Brings joy. Jn.16:21
The duties of young women who are believers. 1 Tim.5:14
The promise to the faithful & godly. 1 Tim.2:15

CHILDISH - CHILDISHNESS
Message to. Discussed. Mt.11:16-19
Of this generation. Lk.7:32
Of unbelievers. Lk.7:32

CHILDREN - CHILDLIKENESS, LITTLE
Abuse of.
    Misled & manipulated by a mother. Mk.6:24-25
    Offending - leading astray. Mt.18:5-10
    Slaughtered by Herod. Mt.2:12-18
Acceptance of.
    Discussed. Mt.19:13-15
    What it takes to receive **c**. Mk.9:36-37
Age of accountability. Kept by God. Lk.18:16
Attitudes toward.
    Not important & indulged. Mt.19:13
    Why parents pamper & indulge **c**. Eph.6:4
Created by God. Lk.18:16
Discussed. Mt.19:13-15; Mk.10:13-16; Eph.6:1-4; Col.3:20
Duties of.
    To be faithful to God. Lk.2:49-50
    To be faithful to parents. Lk.2:51

To care for parents. Jn.19:25-27;
1 Tim.5:3-8
To come to Christ. Mk.10:13-16
To honor parents. Eph.6:1-3, cp.
Heb.12:9
To obey parents. Eph.6:1-4
To praise Christ. Proclaim His Messi-
ahship. Mt.21:15-16; 10:13-15
To receive the promise of salvation.
Acts 2:38-40
To respect older adults. 1 Pt.5:5-6
To study & learn the Scriptures.
2 Tim.2:15
To study - learn - share. Lk.2:46-47
To walk in Christ no matter where
they are. 2 Jn.4
Duties toward - Treatment of.
Not to be led astray. Mt.18:5-10
Not to be prevented from coming to
Christ. Mk.10:13
Not to be treated as a nuisance.
Mk.10:13-16
To be protected. Jesus' protection of.
Mk.10:13
To be taught the Scriptures.
2 Tim.1:5; 3:10; 3:16-17
To be warned about the end time.
Mk.13:1-37
To bring c. to Christ. Lk.18:15
Benefits of. Mt.19:13
For dedication. Mt.19:13-15
Why parents do not bring c.
Mt.19:13
To rear c. in the nurture & admonition
of the Lord. Eph.6:4
To receive c. Mt.18:1-4; 18:5;
19:13-15; Lk.9:46-48
Example.
Caring for others. Mt.18:5
Jesus and c.
Discussed. Mt.18:1-4; 19:13-15;
Lk.9:46-48; 18:15-17
Jesus' treatment of. Mt.18:2; Lk.9:47
Received by Jesus. Mt.18:1-4
Nature. Discussed. Mt.18:1-4; Lk.18:16
Needs of. Discussed. Mk.9:36-37
Problems - Weaknesses of.
Immaturity. Example. Salome's de-
pendency upon her evil mother.
Mk.6:24-25
Truth about. Mk.10:13-16
Reactions toward.
Causing c. to sin--lead astray.
Mt.18:5-10
Saved - Salvation of. A benefit of godly
parents. Ro.11:16
Sins of. (See SIN)
Disobedient to parents. 2 Tim.3:2-4
Symbol of believers.
Carnal believers. 1 Cor.3:1
Immature believers. Heb.5:13
New believers just converted.
1 Pt.2:2-3
Teachable babes who see the truth.
Mt.11:25
Truth revealed to. Lk.10:21
Symbol of seekers after God. Ro.2:20
Symbolize - Illustrate - Picture.
Believers.
As children of God. Ro.8:16-17
As children of light. Eph.5:8
As disciples. Mk.10:24
Coming to Christ. Mk.10:13-16
Followers of wisdom. Mt.11:19
God's Kingdom. Mk.10:14-15

Greatness. Mt.18:1-4; Mk.9:36-37;
Lk.9:46-48
Heaven. Mt.18:1-4; 19:13-15;
Lk.18:15-17
New Christians. Mt.18:5-6
Requirements to enter heaven.
Mk.10:15-16
Spiritual growth. 1 Pt.2:2-3
Spiritual immaturity. 1 Cor.13:11;
14:20
Unbelievers. As children of the devil.
1 Jn.3:10
Worshipping God. Mt.21:15-16
Traits.
Contrary, playful, mindless.
Mt.11:16-19
Discussed. Mk.10:14
Easily deceived & misled. Eph.4:14
Humility. Mt.18:1-4
Immaturity. 1 Cor.13:11
Playful. Mt.11:16-19
Several commendable traits. Acts
23:16-22
What provokes a child. Four things. Eph.6:4

CHILDREN OF GOD--SONS OF GOD
(See BELIEVERS, Names - Titles)
Who they are.
Adopted c. of God. Ro.8:15; 8:16-17;
Gal.4:5-6
Not a race, nation, institution, heritage.
Ro.9:6-13
Persons who receive Christ. Jn.1:12-13

CHOSE - CHOSEN
By whom.
Christ. Jn.13:18; Jn.15:16; 2 Tim.2:4
God. Lk.23:35; Eph.1:4; 2 Th.2:13;
Jas.2:5; 1 Pt.2:9
The church under God's direction.
Acts 6:5; 15:22, 25, 40; 2 Cor.8:18-19
Discussed. 2 Th.2:13
Fact. Many are called, but few are c.
Mt.20:16; 22:14
Meaning. Eph.1:5-6; 2 Th.2:13;
1 Pt.1:18-20
Purpose.
To be holy & blameless. Eph.1:4
To be saved through sanctification &
belief of the truth. 2 Th.2:13
To bear the name of Christ. Acts 9:15-16
To go; bear fruit; receive things.
Jn.15:16
To live differently than the world.
Jn.15:18-19
Who the c. are.
Believers. Ro.16:13; 1 Cor.1:27-28;
Eph.1:4;2 Th.2:13; 2 Tim.2:3-4;
1 Pt.2:9; Rev.17:14
Christ, c. of God. Mt.12:18; Lk.23:35
Church officers. Acts 6:5
Messengers of the church. Acts 15:22, 25
Ministers. Acts 1:23-26; 9:15-16;
15:40; 22:14
Six points. Ro.9:25-33
The elect. Mk.13:20
The people of God. Acts 13:17
The poor who love God. Jas.2:5
The twelve disciples. Lk.6:13
Those who love God. Jas.2:5
Witnesses. Acts 10:41-42

CHRISTIAN - CHRISTIANS (See
BELIEVER; SPIRITUAL
STRUGGLE)
Name given to believers. In Antioch.
Acts 11:26

CHRISTIAN LIBERTY (See LIBERTY,
CHRISTIAN)

CHRISTIAN RACE
Discussed. 1 Cor.9:24-27; Heb.12:1-4
Duty.
Not to run with the world. 1 Pt.4:4
To be careful lest one's life be run in
vain. Gal.2:2
To be careful lest someone hinder
one's race. Gal.5:7
To diligently control & discipline
one's body. 1 Cor.9:24-27
To hold forth the Word of life lest one
run in vain. Ph.2:16
To run well. Gal.5:7
To run with patience the race set be-
fore us. Heb.12:1
Fact.
One is not saved by running, of his
own effort & discipline. Jn.1:12;
Ro.9:16
There are three different races of life.
Heb.12:18-24
Inspiration of. The cloud of witnesses
who see everything we do. Heb.12:1

CHRISTIANITY (See CHURCH;
KINGDOM OF GOD)
Accused of.
Being a bloody religion; the worship
of a "grotesque god." Jn.6:61
Being revolutionary. Acts 17:6-7;
19:27-29
Beliefs of.
A look at the beliefs of primitive C.
Ro.1:1-7
Basic beliefs. Col.1:1-2
Elementary teachings. Six t. Heb.6:1-2
Great statements of. Lk.24:36-49
Growth of.
Growth & greatness of.
Mt.13:31-32; Lk.13:19
How C. grows. Mk.4:26-29; 4:30-32
Described as.
A family relationship. Mk.3:31-35
The Way. Acts 18:26; 19:23
Discussed.
Apostate C. To be destroyed.
Mt.13:30; 13:40-42; 13:49-50;
Rev.17:15-18; 18:1-24
Message of. Ro.1:1-7; 1 Cor.15:1-4
Modern day C. Mt.13:1-58
What C. is. Lk.24:36-39
Duty toward.
To bear fruit. Jn.15:1-8
To get past elementary teachings of.
Six teachings. Heb.6:1-2
Nature.
Good and bad within. Mt.13:24-30;
13:31-32; 13:33;13:36-43; 13:47-50
Is a new life & movement brought by
Christ. Lk.5:36-39
Of mercy, not sacrifice. Mt.12:7
Persecution of. (See PERSECUTION)
Attacked, but not overcome. Acts
28:30-31

Satan's influence. Rev.2:8-17; 3:7-13
Sin. Sin will cause God to reject.
1 Cor.6:9-11
Worship. (See WORSHIP)
An early worship service. 1 Tim.4:13
Attendance. Heb.10:25
Neglect of - forsaking. Heb.3:12; 10:25

CHURCH DISCIPLINE
Attitude toward - Spirit of.
Bearing one another's burden. Gal.6:2
Correcting oneself. 1 Cor.4:14-21, esp.21
Discussed. Mt.18:15-20; 2 Cor.1:23-2:4
Edifying - building up the offending
brother. 2 Cor.10:8
Forgiving - showing love to the of-
fending brother. 2 Cor.2:5-11
Gentleness - guarding oneself. Gal.6:1
Purging out - putting out the offending
brother. 1 Cor.5:6-13
Receiving - loving the offending
brother. 2 Cor.7:2-6
Showing a fatherly spirit. 1 Cor.4:14-16
Watching over as a father. Heb.13:17
Authority to discipline.
Church has authority to discipline.
2 Cor.2:5-11
Minister has authority to discipline.
2 Cor.1:23
Described. As being delivered to Satan.
1 Tim.1:19-20
Discussed. Mt.18:15-20; 1 Cor.5:1-5;
5:6-13; 2 Cor.2:5-11
Question of discipline. Mt.13:27-30
Duty.
Not to welcome those who teach false
doctrine. 2 Jn.10-11
To correct offending brothers. Lk.17:3-4
To deal with divisive leaders. 3 Jn.9-10
To discipline & clean sin out of the c.
fellowship. 1 Cor.5:1-5; 5:6-13
To exercise discipline when needed.
2 Cor.13:1-6
To give a chance for repentance first.
2 Cor.10:6
To rebuke teachers who teach false
doctrine. 1 Tim.1:3, cp. 4-11; Tit.1:13-14
To restore a sinning brother. Gal.6:1-5
To withdraw from those who walk
disorderly. 2 Th.3:6-15
How to d.
How to rebuke. 1 Tim.5:1
Steps to discipline. Mt.18:15-20;
2 Cor.2:5-11
Purpose of d.
Discussed. 2 Cor.2:7-8; 2:9
To demonstrate love. 2 Cor.2:7-8
To edify. 2 Cor.10:8
To infuse life to others. 2 Cor.4:12
To keep the teaching & doctrine of the
church pure & sound. 1 Tim.1:3-11;
Tit.1:13-14; 2 Jn.7-11
To lead to forgiveness. 2 Cor.2:5-11
To prevent despair. 2 Cor.2:7-8
To reconcile the offender with the
minister. 2 Cor.7:2-6
To save the offender. 1 Cor.5:1-5
To shame & correct the disorderly.
2 Th.3:14-15
Reasons why some must be d.
They abuse the Lord's Supper. 1 Cor.
11:27-30
They are overtaken in faults. Gal.6:1-5
They do not repent of public sin.
1 Cor.5:1-13

They judge ministers. 1 Cor.1:10-16,
cp. 4:1-5; 4:14-21
They live lives of indulgence and ex-
cess. 1 Cor.6:12-20; 11:18-22, 30
They practice unrighteous deeds.
1 Cor.6:9-11
They teach false doctrine. Tit.1:10-16
Verses. List of. Lk.17:3-4; 1 Cor.5:2;
5:12-13
Who is d.
Divisive leaders. 3 Jn.10
False teachers. 1 Tim.1:3-11; Tit.1:10-16
Five persons. Are driven out by Christ.
Mk.11:15-17
Idle workers. 2 Th.3:6-18
Ministers. 1 Tim.5:19-20
Offending brothers. Mt.18:15-20
The immoral. 1 Cor.5:1-13
Those who abuse the Lord's Supper.
1 Cor.11:27-30
Those who are gripped by indulgence
& excess. 1 Cor.6:12-20; 11:18-22, 30
Those who are overtaken in a fault.
Gal.6:1-5
Those who do not repent of public sin.
1 Cor.5:1-13
Those who judge & criticize ministers.
1 Cor.1:10-16, cp. 4:1-5; 4:14-21
Those who practice unrighteous deeds.
1 Cor.6:9-11

CHUZZA
Herod's steward. His wife Joanna was a
believer who supported Jews. Lk.8:3

CIRCUMCISION
Advantages of. Discussed. Ro.3:1-2
Compared with baptism. Discussed. Ro.4:11
Described as.
Believers c. Ph.3:3
The c., the people who are the real Is-
rael of God. Gal.6:15-16; cp. 12-14
True c. Ph.3:3
Discussed. Acts 7:2-8; 15:1-3; 15:1;
Ro.2:25-27; 4:11; 4:9-12; Gal.5:2-4; 5:5-6;
6:11-18; Ph.3:3; Col.2:11
Of Timothy. Was c. for the sake of ex-
pediency. Acts 16:1-3
Physical c.
A sign of a covenant relationship.
Ro.4:9-12
A sign only, a sign of an inward work,
of righteousness. Ro.2:25-29; 4:9-12
A symbol only. Ro.4:11
Abolished by Christ. Eph.2:11-18, cp.
Gal.5:1-6; 6:15
Performed on the eighth day. Lk.1:59
The time when a child was named.
Lk.1:59-63
Thinking c. or a ritual saves. Ro.2:25-27;
2:28-29
Works nothing. Gal.5:1-6; 6:12-13; 6:15
Spiritual c.
Discussed. Col.2:12-13
Is an operation of God Himself.
Col.2:12-13, cp. Ro.2:28-29
Is of the heart, not by the written code.
Ro.2:28-29
Is performed by God Himself in the
heart of the real Jew (believers).
Ro.2:28-29
Is the true c. Ph.3:2-3; Col.2:11-12
Is worshipping God in the spirit. Ph.3:3

CIRCUMCISION, THE (See JEWS,
THE JUDAIZERS)

CITIZENSHIP (See GOVERNMENT)
Discussed. Mt. 17:24-27; 22:15-22;
Mk.12:13-17; Lk.20:19-26; Ro.13:1-7;
1 Pt.2:13-17
Basis of. True citizenship. Mk.12:15
The believer & his fellow citizens.
Ro.13:8-10
The believer & unbelievers. Ro.12:14-21
The civic duties of believers. Tit.3:1-2
Vs. God. Mk.12:13-17
Duty.
Discussed. The believer & the state
Ro.13:1-7
Good c. Mt.17:24-27
Of believers toward fellow c. Ro.13:8-10
Sixfold. Tit.3:1-2
To leave judgment up to God. 1 Tim. 5:24-25
To obey God rather than men. Acts 5:29
To pay taxes. Mt.17:24-27; 22:15-22;
Mk.12:13-17
To pray for authorities. 1 Tim.2:2
To remember, respect & honor leaders.
Heb.13:7
To submit to the state. 1 Pt.2:13-17
Fact
Believers are strangers and aliens on
earth. 1 Pet.2:11
False concepts of.
Sins common to. Mt.22:16-17
Two false concepts. Mk.12:13; Lk.20:22
Vs. true concepts. Mt.22:15-22
Of the believer.
Has two c. God and Caesar. Mt.22:15-
22; Mk.12:13-17; Lk.20:19-26
Holds c. in a heavenly kingdom.
Mt.17:25
Is a stranger & pilgrim on earth. 1 Pt.2:11
Often misunderstood. Mt.22:15-22;
Mk.12:13-17
Rebellion - Resistance. Discussed. Ro.13:1-2
Views of. The views of the Pharisees and
Herodians. Mt.22:15-16
Vs. God. Lk.20:19-26
Why Christ paid taxes. Six reasons.
Mt.17:27

CITIZENSHIP, HEAVENLY (See
HEAVEN)
Duty. To rejoice because names are
written in heaven. Lk.10:20
Facts.
Are fellowcitizens with all who are
saints, all who are set apart unto
God. Eph.2:19
Believers actually possess c. in
heaven. Ph.3:20
Not everyone will become a citizen of
heaven. Rev.21:27
The names of believers are actually
written down in heaven. Lk.10:20
Reward of.
Will be seated upon thrones, given
positions of authority. Lk.22:30
Will be where Christ is. Jn.14:1-3; 14:3
Will receive a changed body made just
like Christ's body. Ph.3:20-21
Will receive a mansion in heaven.
Jn.14:1-3; 14:3
Will receive an incorruptible inheri-
tance. 1 Pt.1:3-4

CITY - CITIES (See Name of Individual City)
Discussed.
Antioch. Acts 11:19-30
Antioch of Pisidia. Acts 13:14
Athens. Acts 17:16-21
Attalia. Acts 14:25
Babylon. Rev.14:8; 17:1-18:24
Berea. Acts 17:10-15
Cenchrea. Acts 18:18
Colosse. Col. Introd.
Coos. Acts 21:1-3
Corinth. Acts 18:1-17; 1 Cor. Introd.
Cyprus. Acts 13:4
Derbe. Acts 14:21
Ephesus. Acts 18:23-28; Eph. Introd.; Rev.2:1
Galatia, Area of. Gal. Introd.
Iconium. Acts 14:1
Laodicea. Rev.3:14
Lystra. Acts 14:8
Melita. Acts 28:1
Miletus. Acts 20:13-27
Pamphylia. Acts 13:13
Patara. Acts 21:1-3
Perga. Acts 13:13
Pergamos. Rev.2:12
Philadelphia. Rev.3:7
Philippi. Acts 16:12-40; Ph. Introd.
Puteoli. Acts 28:13
Rhodes. Acts 21:1-3
Rome. Ro. Introd.; cp. Acts 16:12-40;
28:13-15; 28:13; 28:16-31; Gal.4:4
Salamis. Acts 13:5
Sardis. Rev.3:1-6
Sidon. Acts 27:3
Smyrna. Rev.2:8
Thessalonica. Acts 17:1-9; 1 Th. Introd.; 2 Th. Introd.
Thyatira. Rev.2:18
Tyre. Acts 21:1-3

CITY, HOLY
Identified. As the new Jerusalem, the heavenly capital, the capital of the new heavens & earth. Rev.21:2

CIVIL AUTHORITIES (See **RULERS**)
Duty toward. (See **CITIZENSHIP**, Duty)
Sins of. Common to civil leaders. Acts 4:5-10

CIVILIZATION (See **CITIZENSHIP**; **SOCIETY**; **WORLD**)

CLAMOR (See **BRAWLING**)

CLAUDIA
Visited Paul in prison & knew Timothy. 2 Tim.4:21

CLAUDIUS LYSIAS
A chief captain of Rome who protected Paul against the rioters. Acts 23:26, cp. 12-35

CLEAN - CLEANLINESS - CLEANSING (See **PURIFY**)
Discussed. Jn.13:6-11
Duty. To **c**. oneself from all filthiness of the body & spirit. 2 Cor.7:1
Essential. For worship. Heb.10:22-25
Heart determines. Mt.23:25-26
How to be cleansed.
By Christ's death. Eph.1:7; 5:26-27
By the Word. Jn.17:17; Eph.5:26-27
Inward **c**. essential. Mt.23:25-28

CLEAVE - CLEAVING--UNITED (See **UNITED**)
In marriage. Mt.19:1-12; 19:5
Meaning. Mt.19:5

CLEOPAS
A disciple to whom Christ appeared after His resurrection. Lk.24:18

CLEOPHAS
Husband of Mary. Jn.19:25

CLIQUES (See **DIVISION**)
Problem with. Discussed. 1 Cor.1:13-16
Results. Division. 1 Cor.1:10-16

CLOAK
Duty. To give one's **c**. when someone asks for it. Lk.6:27-31
Illustrated. A seamstress who made coats for friends. Acts 9:36-39
Of Jesus.
Gambled for. Jn.19:24
Without seams. Jn.19:23

CLOSE-MINDEDNESS (See **HARD - HARDNESS OF HEART; STUBBORN**)
Sin common to false citizenship. Mt.22:16-17

CLOTH & WINE BOTTLES
New & old **c**. Mt.9:14-17

CLOTHE - CLOTHING, SPIRITUAL
Duty. To put on & clothe oneself with Christ. Ro.13:14

CLOTHE
Meaning. 1 Pt.5:5

CLOTHING (See **DRESS**)
Attitude about.
Right vs. wrong. Mt.6:25-34
Duty.
To dress modestly. 1 Tim.2:9
To dress to please God, not to attract attention. 1 Pt.3:1-5
To trust God, not to worry about fashion. Lk.12:22-34
Illustrated.
A seamstress is raised from the dead. Acts 9:36-43
Clothes made by Dorcas for friends. Acts 9:36-39
New **c**. sewn on old **c**. Mk.2:21
Purpose for. Three purposes. Mt.6:28-30
Religious **c**. Problem with. Mt.23:5
Warning.
Against dressing to attract attention. Mk.12:38
Against extravagant styles. Mk.12:38
Against judging people by their clothing. Lk.16:19, cp. 20-31
Against those who dress as sheep (harmless), but inwardly are wolves. Mt.7:15

CLOUD
Descriptive of - symbolic of.
Jesus ascended in. Acts 1:6-11
Jesus returns in. Mt.24:30
Jesus transfigured in. Lk.9:34; 9:35
Meaning. Lk.9:35
Symbol of. Shekinah glory. Mk.9:7

COARSE JOKING
Sin of. Discussed. Eph.5:4

COAT (See **GARMENT**)
Illustrated. A seamstress who made coats for friends. Acts 9:36-39

COEXISTENCE (See **JESUS CHRIST**, Deity)
Of Christ with God. Meaning. Jn.1:1-2; 5:17-30

COHORT
Meaning. A regiment of Roman soldiers. Jn.18:3

COIN
Parable. Of Lost Coin. Lost Sinner in the house. Lk.15:8-10

COLD OR HOT
Describes.
Being spiritually cold or hot. Rev.3:15
Spiritual coldness. Mt.24:12

COLOSSE
Discussed. Col. Introd.

COLT - DONKEY
Discussed. Mk.11:1-7; Lk.19:30; Jn.12:14-15
Jesus used a **c**. in the Triumphal Entry. Mt.21:2-5

COME
To Christ.
To **c**. & become fishers of men. Mk.1:17
To **c**. & inherit the kingdom of God. Mt.25:34
To **c**. & take up the cross & follow Him. Mk.10:21; Lk.9:23
To **c**. for rest. Mt.11:28-29
To **c**. for salvation. Rev.22:17
To God's great banquet. Lk.14:16-24, esp. 17
To the Marriage Supper of the Lamb. Mt.22:1-10, esp. 4

COMFORT - COMFORTED (See **ENCOURAGEMENT**)
Duty.
To be stirred out of self-pity. 2 Cor.1:6-7
To **c**. believers just as a father does his children. 1 Th.2:11
To **c**. believers with the hope of Christ's return. 1 Th.4:18
To **c**. ourselves with the presence of other believers. 1 Th.5:11
To **c**. the hearts of all believers. Eph.6:22; Col.4:8
To **c**. those in trouble. 2 Cor.1:3-4
To forgive & **c**. those gripped by sin. 2 Cor.2:7
To struggle for the hearts of believers to be **c**. Col.2:2
To use worship services to **c**. believers. 1 Cor.14:29-31, esp. 31
Example. Barnabas' very name means consolation, comfort. Acts 4:36
Meaning. 2 Cor.1:3
Present **c**. & eternal **c**. Mt.5:4
Source.
Christ. Mt.9:18-34, esp. 22,25,30,33; Ph.2:1
Fellow believers. Jn.11:19; Col.4:11
God. 2 Cor.1:3-11; 2 Cor.7:6; 2 Th.2:17; Heb.6:18
Love. Phile.7
The faith of believers. 1 Th.3:7
The Holy Spirit. Jn.14:16, 26; 15:26; 16:7; Acts 9:31
The promise to believers.
Their mourning shall cease & they shall be **c**. Mt.5:8
Their suffering upon earth shall end; they shall be **c**. Lk.16:25

COMFORTER, THE (See **HOLY SPIRIT**)

COMMANDMENT - COMMAND
Christ's c.
  Is a new c. Love. Jn.13:34-35
  Is onefold. Love. Jn.13:34-35; 15:12-17
Duty.
  To confess that one has transgressed the c. Lk.15:29, cp. 11-32
  To do God's greatest c.: to believe on the name of God's Son, the Lord Jesus Christ, & to love one another. 1 Jn.3:23
  To obey God's c. Mt.19:17; 1 Cor.7:19; 1 Jn.2:3-6; 2 Jn.5-6
    Is demanded by the death of Christ. Jn.13:31-35
    Proves that one loves God. 1 Jn.5:2-3
  To obey the c. of God. 1 Jn.3:22
  To repent at the c. of God. Acts 17:30
  To stir up one's mind to remember the c. 2 Pt.3:1-2
  To teach the whole world all that Christ has commanded. Mt.28:19-20; Acts 10:42; 13:46-47
  To walk in the c. of truth & love. 2 Jn.4, 6
God's c.
  Are explained by Christ. Mt.5:17-48
  Are holy, just, & good. Ro.7:12
  Are not a burden nor unbearable. 1 Jn.5:3
  Are the c.'s of Christ. Mt.5:17-20
  Are the writings of Paul. 1 Cor.14:37
  Calls & sets people apart for service. 1 Tim.1:1; Tit.1:3
  God's supreme c. To believe on Christ and to love one another. 1 Jn.3:23
  God's unbelievable c. - that His Son, Jesus Christ, die. Jn.10:17-18; 14:31
  Is life everlasting. Jn.12:49-50
Greatest c.
  Discussed. To love God & one's neighbor. Mt.22:34-40; Mk.12:28-34; Lk.10:25-37; 1 Tim.1:5; 1 Jn.4:21; 2 Jn.5-6
  To believe on God's Son, Jesus Christ & to love one another. 1 Jn.3:23
Meaning. 1 Tim.6:17-19
New c. Jn.13:34-35; 1 Jn.2:7-8
Obeying the c.
  Assures acceptance & greatness in the kingdom of heaven. Mt.5:19-20
  Assures answers to prayer. 1 Jn.3:22-24
  Assures God's presence. 1 Jn.3:23-24
  Assures heaven. Rev.14:12-13
  Assures life. Mt.19:17, cp. 16-22
  Assures that one shall enter the eternal city of God & live forever. Rev.22:14
  Assures the very special presence of God & Christ. Jn.14:21
  Guarantees that one is a friend of Christ. Jn.15:14
  Is essential to abide in Christ & God. Jn.15:10, 14-17
  Keeping the c. vs. only professing the c. 1 Jn.2:3-6
  Proves one knows God. 1 Jn.2:3-6
  Proves one's love. Jn.14:15, 21, 24; 15:10, 14

Subjects of the c. (See Subject Desired)
  Adultery. Mt.5:27; 5:27-30
  Anger. Mt.5:21-26
  Divorce. Mt.5:31
  Injury. Mt.5:38-42
  Lighter vs. weightier. Mt.23:23-24
  Love. Mt.5:43
  Murder. Mt.5:21
  Resistance. Mt.5:38-42
  Retaliation. Mt.5:38-42
  Revenge. Mt.5:38-42
  Swearing--Cursing. Mt.5:33-37
  Vengeance Mt.5:38-42
Ten c.
  Are fulfilled by love. Mt.22:34-40; Mk.12:28-34; Lk.10:25-37; Ro.13:8-10
  Real meaning of. Mt.5:21-48
  The c. referred to in the New Testament
    Eighth c. Not to steal. Mt.19:18; Mk.10:19; Lk.18:20; Ro.13:9
    Fifth c. To honor one's father & mother. Mt.15:4; 19:18; Mk.10:19; Lk.8:20; Eph.6:1-3
    Ninth c. Not to bear false witness. Mt. 19:18; Mk.10:19; Lk.18:20; Ro.13:9
    Seventh c. Not to commit adultery. Mt.5:27-32; 19:18; Mk.10:19; Lk.18:20
    Sixth c. Not to kill Mt.19:18; Mk.10:19; Lk.18:20; Ro.13:9
    Tenth c. Not to covet. Ro.7:7; 13:9
    Third c. Not to curse or swear. Mt.5:33-37
Warning.
  Against breaking the c. & misleading people. Mt.5:19-20
  Against claiming to keep God's c. & not doing it (hypocrisy). 1 Jn.2:4
  Against putting traditions before the c. Mt.15:3; Mk.7:9
  Against teaching the c. of men as doctrine. Mt.15:9; Mk.7:7
  Against turning away from the c. 2 Pt.2:21

COMMISSION (See **WITNESSING**)
Described.
  As being sent. Jn.20:21
  As being sent forth as an ambassador. 2 Cor.5:20
  As being sent from the side or heart of God. Jn.1:6
  As preaching. Mk.16:15; 2 Tim.4:1-6
  As proclaiming the resurrection. Jn.20:17-18
  As sharing one's testimony. Mk.5:18-20
Discussed.
  Great charter of the church. Jn.20:19-23
  How to go forth. Lk.10:1-16
  Sent out as ambassadors. 2 Cor.5:25
  Sent out as apostles, as special messengers. Mt.10:2; Ro.1:1; Eph.1:1
  Sent out. Equipped & going out. Mk.6:7-13
  Symbolizes five things. Lk.10:1-16; 10:1
Duty.
  To bear witness to one's own home & to reach out to the whole world. Acts 1:8
  To go forth as Christ went forth. Jn.20:21, cp. Mt.20:28; Lk.19:10
  To go to one's own home & friends first. Mk.2:15
  To preach the gospel to the whole world. Mk.16:15
  To teach & make disciples. Mt.28:19-20; 2 Tim.2:2

Given by.
  Christ. Jn.20:21
  God. Jn.1:6; Eph.1:1
Given to.
  A new convert. Mk.5:18-20
  Believers. Acts 1:8; 2 Tim.2:2
  Disciples. Mt.10:5-15; 28:16-20
  Disciples & preachers. Lk.9:1-9
  Preachers. 2 Tim.4:1-6
Great c. Mk.16:14-20; Jn.20:19-23
  Discussed. Equipping; the task; the method. Acts 1:8
  Fivefold mission. Lk.5:27-39
  Hindrances; reason; promise; confirmation. Mk.16:14-20
  Messiah's final c. to His disciples. Mt.28:16-20
  Threefold mission. Lk.6:17-19
  Zeal for. By Paul. For Israel, his own people. Ro.9:1-3
Meaning. Jn.1:6, cp. Mt.10:2; Ro.1:1; 2 Cor.5:25; Eph.1:1; 2 Pt.1:1
Purpose.
  Discussed. Mk.6:7-13
  Fourfold. Mk.3:13-15
  To be with Christ. Mk.3:14-15
  To be witnesses. Acts 1:8
  To seek & save the lost. Jn.20:21, cp. Lk.19:10
  To warn every man, & teach every man, & present every man perfect. Col.1:28
Urgency of. Jn.9:4
Verses. List of. Mk.1:17-18; 3:14-15

COMMIT - COMMITMENT (See **DEDICATION--DEVOTION**)
Call to c.
  Argument for. Mt.16:21-28
  To be c. to the word of reconciliation, to reconciling people to God. 2 Cor.5:19-20
  To be totally c. to God's Word & to preaching it. 1 Cor.9:16-17; Tit.1:3
  To c. our souls to God in doing good works. 2 Pt.4:19
  To give all one is & has to Christ. 2 Tim.1:12
  To give up all for Christ. Mt.13:44
  To go beyond common sense. Mt. 26:8-9
  To keep that which God has c. to one's trust. 1 Tim.6:20
  To the Lordship of Christ. Acts 4:32
  To the mission of Christ. Acts 4:32
  To total c. Demanded by Jesus' death. Mt.16:21-28
    Anything less is sin. Acts 5:1-4
Degrees of. Mt.13:8, 23
Essential.
  Love is the one basic essential. Jn.21:15; 21:15-17
  Needed desperately for reaching the world. Mk.4:30-32
Kinds of.
  Carnal vs. spiritual. Lk.22:33-37
  Faithful c. 1 Tim.1:11-12
  Half-hearted. Lk.9:57-62
  Reluctant c. Lk.5:4-6; 9:57-62
  Selfish c vs. genuine c. Mt.8:18-22
  Unashamed c. 2 Tim.1:12
Law of. Mt.13:12; 13:13-15
Meaning. Jn.2:23-24
Motive. Determines one's c. Lk.22:33-37
Of the early church. Gave all beyond necessities. Acts 4:34-37

Partial c. Is sin. Acts 5:1-11
Pictures of. Fourfold picture. Mt.26:47-56
Reward. Receives, understands more & more. Mt.13:11-12
What it is that God c. to men.
The gospel. Gal.2:7; 1 Tim.1:11-12
The Word of God & preaching.
1 Cor.9:16-17; Tit.1:3
The word of reconciliation.
2 Cor.5:19-20

COMMON SENSE
To be set aside sometimes for sacrifice. Mt.26:8

COMMUNE - COMMUNION (See DE-VOTION; DRAW NEAR; PRAYER)
Essential to conquer temptation. Mt.4:1
How one can c. with God.
Through abiding in Christ. Jn.15:1-8
Through obedience. Jn.14:16
Through receiving the message that one can fellowship with the Father & His Son. 1 Jn.1:3
Through seeking the things above, the things of Christ. Col.3:1-3
Through separation & commitment to Christ. 2 Cor.6:14-18, cp. Ro.12:1-2; 1 Jn.2:15-16
Meaning. 2 Cor.6:14-16

COMMUNICATION, FILTHY (See LANGUAGE, FILTHY; TONGUE)

COMPASSION
Commanded. Jude 22-23
Duty. To have c. on the prisoner who is a believer. Heb.10:34
To have c. upon the needy. 1 Jn.3:17
To have mercy, not sacrifice. Mt.9:12-13; 12:7
To reach some who waver, doubt. Jude 22-23
To show c. for all men, even for one's enemies. Lk.10:25-37; 1 Pt.3:8
To show c. upon the different. Lk.10:25-37
To show c. upon the neglected and injured. Lk.10:25-37
Essential - Necessary.
Because of the world's condition. Mt.9:36
For ministry. Mt.14:15; 15:32
Involves six things. Mk.8:1-9
To keep the unity among believers. Ph.2:1; 1 Pt.3:8-9
Example.
The Good Samaritan. Lk.10:25-37
The prodigal son. Lk.15:20
Upon prisoners. Heb.10:34
Meaning. Mt.9:36; Lk.7:13; 2 Cor.1:3
Of Christ.
For a mother with a dead son. Lk.7:12-13
For Jerusalem. Mt.23:37-39
For physical needs. Mt.15:29-39, esp. 32
For the desperate. Mt.20:34
For the diseased, the crippled, & the needy. Lk.13:14-16
For the helpless. Mk.9:22
For the ignorant. Heb.5:2
For the most unclean. Mk.1:41; Lk.5:13
For the multitude. Mt.14:14
For the needy. Mk.1:32-34

For the needy who are faithful in wor-ship. Lk.13:14-16
For the scattered and shepherdless. Mt.9:35-38; Mk.6:34
For the tempted. Heb.2:17-18; 4:14-16
For the weary. Mt.11:28-30
For those possessed by evil spirits. Mk.5:1-19, esp. 19; Mk.9:14-29, esp. 22
For those who have gone astray. Heb.5:2
Groans over man's desperate plight. Jn.11:33-36; 11:38-40
Led Christ to teach. Mt.5:1
Reaches out to man. Jn.5:5-9
Verses. List of. Lk.7:12-13
Of God.
For the repentant son. Lk.15:20-24
For the sorrowful & grief-stricken. Lk.7:11-17
Of Paul. For Israel, his own people. Ro.9:1-3
Stirred by.
Four things. Lk.7:12-13
Seeing the world as it really is. Mt.9:36
Verses. List of. Lk.10:29-37; Jn.11:33-36

COMPLACENT - COMPLACENCY
(See SLOTHFUL)
Caused by. Mt.26:40-41
Described.
As arrogance. Ro.11:18; 11:19-21
As drowsiness and sleep. Mt.25:1-13
As softness, being at ease. Mt.11:8
Discussed. Mt.20:3-4; Ro.13:11-14
Duty. To awaken out of sleep. Ro.13:11-12
Law of. Mt.13:12; 13:13-15
Results.
To be judged. Mt.25:24-30
Upon the church. Kills, deadens. Rev.3:1
Warning against. Heb.6:12

COMPLAIN - COMPLAINING
Against Christ & His claims. Jn.6:41-43
Caused by.
Anxiety, worry. Lk.10:40
Hate. 1 Jn.3:15
Characteristic - Trait of. False teachers. Jude 16
Meaning. Ph.2:14
Warning against.
Condemns one. Jas.5:9
Discussed. 1 Cor.10:6-10

COMPLETE (See FULLNESS)

COMPLETE HEALING
Meaning. Acts 3:16

COMPROMISE
Discussed. Jn.18:28-19:15
Errors of. Threefold. Lk.23:13-25
Illustrated. By Pilate. Mt.27:11-25; Mk.15:1-15; Lk.23:13-25; Jn.18:28-19:15
Judgment of. Warning. Lk.6:24-26
Paul and c. Refused to c. Gal.2:1-10
Peter's c. and sin. Gal.2:11-13
Purpose. To quiet dissension. Acts 21:17-26
Results. Upon a church. Rev.2:18-29
Temptation to. Discussed. Mt.4:8; 4:8-10; Lk.4:5-8

CONCEIT - CONCEITED (See PRIDE)
Deliverance from. Discussed. Ph.2:3; 2:4
Discussed. Ro.12:16
Duty.
Believers must not be h. Ro.11:20
Not to be c. Ro.12:16
Not to look upon one's own things. Ph.2:4
Not to think that one is better than an-other person--not spiritually. Gal.6:3
Not to mind high things. Ro.12:16
The rich must not be h. 1 Tim.6:17
To cast down imaginations & every high thing. 2 Cor.10:5
Fact. In the last days men will be h. 2 Tim.3:4, cp. 1-5
Meaning. 2 Tim.3:2-4
Results.
Destroys unity. Ph.2:3
Elevates oneself over others. Ro.11:18

CONCERN (See CARE - CARING; MINISTERING)
Spiritual c. vs. social c. Jn.2:3-5

CONCUPISCENCE, EVIL (See DE-SIRES, EVIL)
Duty.
To resist lustful passion. 1 Th.4:3-5
Meaning. Col.3:5-7
Source. Sin & lust. Ro.7:7-8, cp. Jas.1:14-15

CONDEMN - CONDEMNATION (See JUDGMENT)
Caused by.
Abusing one's leadership. 1 Tim.3:6; Jas.3:1
Abusing the Lord's Supper. 1 Cor.11:27-34, esp. 34
Acting like vipers, biting & poisonous. Lk.3:7
Adam's sin. Ro.5:12-21
Being a false teacher. 2 Pt.2:1-9, esp. 6; Jude 4-5
Being a heretic who has turned away. Tit.3:10-11
Complaining, grumbling, & judging others. Jas.5:9
Disobedience to the law. 2 Cor.3:9
Failing to get right with God. Ro.1:18-3:20
Judging & criticizing others. Ro.2:1
Living an ungodly life. 2 Pt.2:6, cp. 4-6
Swearing, cursing. Jas.5:12
Unbelief. Not trusting Christ. Jn.3:18-21
Violating one's conscience & being a stumbling block. Ro.14:21-23, cp. 1-23
Words, evil & idle words. Mt.12:34-37; Tit.2:8
Deliverance from. Discussed. Jn.3:16-21; Ro.8:1-17
Discussed. Jn.3:18-21
Who can condemn.
Only Christ can c., not man. Ro.8:34
Only God can charge man. Ro.8:31-33
Who escapes c. Jn.3:21

CONFESS - CONFESSING - CONFES-SION (See DENY - DENIAL)
C. of Christ.
Brings salvation. 1 Jn.4:15
Causes Christ to c. believers. Mt.10:32-33

CONSIDERATE; KIND - KINDNESS
Christ is **c.** & lowly. Mt.11:29
Discussed. Tit.3:2
Duty.
  Must correct others in spirit of **c.**
    2 Tim.2:24-26
  To do good works in a **c.** spirit. Jas.3:13
  To dress in a **c.** & quiet spirit.
    1 Pt.3:4, cp. 2-4
  To receive the Word with **c.** Jas.1:21
Meaning. Mt.5:5; Gal.5:22-23; Eph.4:1-2;
  1 Tim.6:11; Ph.4:5
Reward. Three rewards. Mt.5:5
Source. Is a fruit of the Spirit. Gal.5:22-23

CONSISTENCY (See COMMITMENT; CROSS, DAILY; DEDICATION; HEART)
Duty. Areas where believers must be **c.**
  2 Cor.6:3-10

CONSOLATION (See COMFORT; ENCOURAGEMENT)
Duty. To wait for the great day of **c.** Lk.2:25

CONSTANCY (See ENDURANCE; PERSEVERANCE; STEADFASTNESS)

CONSTRUCTION (See BUILDING)
Essential. Must count the cost before
  building. Lk.14:28-32

CONSTRUCTION WORKERS
Tower fell on. Thought to be great sinners being punished. Lk.13:1-5

CONTEMPT (See DESPISE)
Caused by. Threefold. Mt.13:53-58

CONTENT - CONTENTMENT (See JOY)
Discussed.
  Secret to **c.** 1 Tim.6:6-10
Duty.
  To be **c.** in whatever state one is in &
    with what one has. Ph.4:11
  To be **c.** with one's wages. Lk.3:14
  To be **c.** with what one has. Heb.13:5
Meaning. 1 Tim.6:6-8
Source of.
  Godliness, not wealth. 1 Tim.6:6-10
  God's presence. Heb.13:5

CONTENTION - CONTENTIOUS (See ARGUE - ARGUMENTS; CRITICISM; DISAGREEMENT; DIVISION; QUARRELS; SELF-SEEKING)
Caused by.
  Arguing over ministers, which one is
    better. 1 Cor.1:11-16, esp. 11
  Biting & devouring one another.
    Gal.5:15
  Differences of conviction. Acts 15:36-41
Discussed. Acts 15:36-41
Honest **c.** Study of. Acts 15:36-41
Results - Signs of being **c.**
  A great sense of unworthiness. Lk.5:8
  A pricking, convicting, bothersome
    conscience & heart. Acts 9:5
  Obedience. Doing what Christ demands. Acts 9:5-6, cp. 1-11
  Reaction, a defensive attitude.
    Jn.20:24-25, cp. 26-29
  Trembling, but rejecting & becoming
    harder. Acts 24:24-25

CONTEND - CONTENDS
Duty.
  To contend against sin even to the
    point of blood. Heb.12:4
  To **c.** for the faith of the gospel.
    Ph.1:27
  To **c.** for the incorruptible crown.
    1 Cor.9:25
  To **c.** in prayer for ministers & for
    other believers. Ro.15:30
  To **c.** to enter the narrow gate of life.
    Lk.13:24, cp. Mt.7:13-14
Of the Holy Spirit. Does not always **c.**
  with man. Mt.12:14-16
Source of energy to **c.** The working of
  God within one's heart. Col.1:29

CONTINUE - CONTINUING
Condition for salvation. Belief & **c.** Jn.8:31
Duty.
  Not to avenge oneself, but to live in
    peace. Ro.12:18-21
  To **c.** in the teaching of Christ. 2 Jn.9
  To **c.** in the walk and life of Christ.
    1 Jn.2:6; 3:23-24
  To **c.** in Christ. Jn.15:1-8
  To let the Word **c.** or dwell in us.
    Jn.5:38
Meaning. "In" Christ. Acts 2:42; Ro.8:1
Proof that one **c.** in God & Christ.
  A person's obedience. Jn.15:10
  Faithfulness. 1 Jn.2:17
  How one knows God **c.** within.
    1 Jn.3:24
  Love. 1 Jn.4:12-16
  One has God & Christ **c.** within. 2 Jn.9
  Righteousness. 1 Jn.2:29
  The new birth. One is born again.
    1 Jn.2:28-29
Results of **c.**
  Answered prayer. Jn.15:7
  Comfort & help. Jn.14:15-26
  Confident. 1 Jn.2:28-29
  Deliverance from judgment. Jn.15:6
  Discipline and correction. Jn.15:2-3
  Fruit. Jn.15:5-8
  Keeps one from sin. 1 Jn.3:6
  Power. 1 Jn.2:24; 2:27
  Salvation. Jn.8:31
  Unashamedness. 1 Jn.2:28
Reward for **c.** 1 Cor.3:13-15
Source of **c.**
  A Christ-like walk. 1 Jn.2:6
  Christ. Jn.15:1-8
  Christ's love. Jn.15:9-11
  Continuing in the Word & doctrine of
    Christ. Jn.8:31; 2 Jn.9
  Holy Spirit. Jn.14:16-17; 1 Jn.2:27; 3:24
  Loving one another. 1 Jn.4:12-16
  Obedience and discipline. 1 Jn.2:5-6;
    2:17; 3:24
  The gospel. 1 Jn.2:27
  The truth. 2 Jn.2
Things that are to **c.**
  Christ's priesthood. Heb.7:3
  Faith, hope, and love. 1 Cor.13:13
  God Himself. 2 Tim.2:13
  The believer himself. 1 Cor.3:13-15;
    1 Jn.2:5-6, 17, 24, 28
  The believer's anointing. 1 Jn.2:27
  The believer's works. 1 Cor.3:13-15
  The gospel. 1 Jn.2:24
  The obedient. 1 Jn.2:17
Verses. List of. Jn.8:31; 15:4 (See DEVOTED; ENDURANCE; PERSEVERANCE)

CONTRARY (See ARGUE; CONTENTION; CRITICISM; DIVISION)
Duty. To put off being **c.** & grieving the
  Holy Spirit. Eph.4:30
Message to the **c.** Discussed. Mt.11:16-19
Sin of being **c.** Grieving the Holy Spirit.
  Eph.4:30

CONTRITE - CONTRITION (See HUMILITY; REPENTANCE; SORROW, GODLY)
Essential.
  For confession. Mk.3:11-12; Lk.5:8-9
  For forgiveness. Mt.26:75, cp. 69-75
  For mercy & salvation. Lk.18:13, cp. 9-14
  For restoration. Lk.15:20-21; 22:61-62
  Verses. List of. Lk.5:8-9; 5:12

CONTROVERSY
Duty. To turn away from. Tit.3:9

CONVERSATION (See CRITICISM; DIVISION; JUDGING OTHERS; TONGUE; WORDS)
Duty.
  To be clean-mouthed, not filthy
    mouthed. Eph.5:4
  To put away worthless **c.** Eph.4:29
  To waste no time in needless **c.** Lk.10:4

CONVERT - CONVERSION - CONVERTED (See RENEW - RENEWAL; TRANSFORMED; TURN)
Discussed.
  A strong **c.** 1 Th.1:5-10
  Dramatic **c.** Does not last & lacks
    depth. Mt.13:5-6, 20-21; Lk.8:11-15
  Experience of **c.** 2 Cor.4:6
  Various types of **c.** Lk.8:4-15
Duty - Essential.
  Must be willing to be changed. Mk.3:16-19
  To be **c.** & become as little children.
    Mt.18:3
  To be **c.** before preaching the gospel.
    2 Cor.4:6
  To strengthen fellow believers once **c.**
    Lk.22:32
How a person is **c.**
  By a stirred heart. What happens.
    Jn.8:31
  By believers bearing witness. Jas.5:19-20
  By repentance. Acts 3:19
  By turning to God. 1 Th.1:9-10
  Steps to. Discussed. Lk.19:1-10
Illustrated.
  Centurion's confession at the cross.
    Mk.15:39
  Ethiopian eunuch. Acts 8:37-38
  Onesimus' change of life. Phile.1:10-16
  Matthew **c.** was dramatic. Mt.9:9; 9:9-13
  Paul's **c.** was to show God's mercy for
    great sinners. 1 Tim.1:15-16
  Zacchaeus new life. Lk.19:1-10
Many sought to know the Lord. Acts 13:42-45
Marks of. Gal.1:13-16; 1 Th.1:5-10
Meaning. Mt.18:3; Acts 3:19
  A complete change. Gal.1:13-16
  A convulsive experience. Mk.1:25-26
  A repentance. Lk.19:8-10
  A returning after failing. Lk.22:31-34
  A shining of God in one's heart. 2 Cor.4:6
  A washing, a sanctification, a justifying. 1 Cor.6:11
  An awakening from sleep or death.
    Eph.5:14
  Becoming as a little child. Mt.18:1-4

Results.
Given light. Eph.5:14
Hides a multitude of sins. Jas.5:19-20
One's sins are blotted out. Acts 3:19;
Proves the deity of Christ. Lk.20:6
The refreshing presence of the Lord.
Acts 3:19
To Judaism. Discussed. Mt.23:15
Warning.
Can be ignored and forgotten. 2 Pt.1:9
Can be snatched away by the devil.
Lk.8:5, 12
Can blind one's eyes to the need for c.
Mt.13:15; Mk.4:12; Jn.12:40; Acts
28:27

CONVERTS (See **BELIEVERS**)
New c. Needs of. Acts 9:10-18
Various types. Lk.8:4-15

CONVICTION (See **CONFESSION;
CONSCIENCE; REPENTANCE**)
Discussed. Lk.15:17-19
Essential.
Must be c. that Jesus is the Lord. Acts
9:4-5
Must face one's sin to be saved.
Lk.15:17-19; Jn.4:15-18
Must humble oneself despite questions
& doubts. Jn.20:24-29
Three essentials. Acts 4:23-31
Example.
Of Felix. Trembled, but rejected. Acts
24:24-25
Of Paul. Acts 9:5, cp. 1-9
Of Peter. Lk.5:8, cp. 1-11
Meaning. Acts 2:37
Results - Signs of being c.
A great sense of unworthiness. Lk.5:8
A pricking, convicting, bothersome
conscience & heart. Acts 9:5
Obedience. Doing what Christ de-
mands. Acts 9:5-6, cp. 1-11
Reaction, a defensive attitude.
Jn.20:24-25, cp. 26-29
Trembling, but rejecting & becoming
harder. Acts 24:24-25
Source of.
Natural catastrophes. Acts 16:25-31
One's conscience & thoughts. Jn.8:9;
Ro.2:15
The gospel. Acts 2:37-38; 24:25
The Holy Spirit.
Meaning. Jn.16:8-11
Vs. natural man. Mt.16:17
The law. Jas.2:9
Work of. The Holy Spirit. Jn.16:8-11

COOPERATION
Essential.
To bring people to Christ. Mk.2:3
To defend the gospel. Ph.1:27
To maintain unity within the church.
Ph.4:2-3
To pray for & carry on the work of
God. Mt.18:19
To witness. Mk.6:7

CORBAN
Discussed. Mk.7:11

CORINTH
Church of. Life in C., the immoral cesspool of the ancient world. 1 Cor.7:1-40
City of. A cesspool of immorality.
1 Cor.7:1-40

Discussed. Acts 18:1-17
Ministered to by Apollos. Acts 19:1
The bridge of Greece. Acts 18:1-17
Visited by Paul on his second mission.
Acts 18:1-17

CORNELIUS, THE CENTURION
Discussed. Acts 10:1-48

CORNERSTONE, THE--CAPSTONE
Christ is. Discussed. Mt.21:42; 21:44
Title of Christ. 1 Pt.2:6

CORRECT
Duty.
To r. the works of darkness. Eph.5:1-14
To use the Word of God to r.
2 Tim.3:16; 4:2
Meaning. 2 Tim.4:2
What reproves a person.
Believers r. the works of darkness.
Lk.3:19; Eph.5:11-13
Christ. Lk.9:41; 9:55-56; Jn.6:27-29;
7:7; Rev.2:16
God. Heb.12:5-7
God's Word. 2 Tim.3:16
Light. Jn.3:19-20; Eph.5:13
Preaching. Lk.3:18-19; 2 Tim.4:2
The Holy Spirit. Jn.16:8-11

**CORRUPT - CORRUPTION - PERISH-
ABLE** (See **DECAY, PERISH**)
Caused by.
Adam's sinful nature. Ro.5:12-14
Gratifying, sowing to one's flesh. Gal.6:7-8
Lust. 2 Pt.1:4
Sin; being carnal minded. Ro.8:5-8;
·8:12-13
Ultimate cause. Mt.8:17
Characteristic - Trait.
Of evil men. Lk.6:43-44
Of false teachers. 2 Pt.2:12, cp. 10-12;
2:19; Jude 10, cp. 8-11
Deliverance - Escape.
By a radical change of the body.
1 Cor.15:35-58
By being clothed with life. 2 Cor.5:1-4
By Christ.
Christ did not see c. Acts 2:25-36
Conquered by Christ's resurrection.
Acts 13:32-37
By participating of God's nature.
2 Pt.1:4
Of creation itself. Ro.8:19-22
Discussed. 2 Cor.4:16
Meaning. Mt.6:19-20; Acts 2:27; 13:32-37;
2 Pt.1:4
Decaying, aging, deteriorating. Mt.6:19
Flesh and blood which wastes away.
1 Cor.15:50-58
Mortal--mortality. Flesh withering,
falling away, dissolving. 2 Cor.5:1-4
Physical death. 1 Cor.15:42-49
The natural world and body.
1 Cor.15:35-49; Jude 10, cp. 8-10
The world and its desires or lusts will
pass away. 1 Jn.2:17
Problems.
Burdens man with mortality.
2 Cor.5:1-4
Causes pain & infirmities. Ro.8:18;
8:19-22
Causes the world and its desires or
lusts to pass away. 1 Jn.2:17
Enslaves all of creation to the bondage
of c. Ro.8:19-22

Seed of.
The physical vs. the spiritual world &
dimension. Jn.8:23
Within the world. Jn.12:31; 2 Pt.1:4
Verses. List of. Jn.1:14

COS
City of. Discussed. Acts 21:1-3

COUNSEL, GOD'S (See **PURPOSE**, Of
God; **SET PURPOSE**)
Determined the death of Christ. Acts
2:23; 4:25-28
Duty.
To declare the whole c. of God. Acts
20:27
To hear the c. of God. Rev.3:18
Is immutable, unchangeable. Heb.6:17-18
Is rejected by some. Lk.7:30

COUNSELOR (See **HOLY SPIRIT**)

COUNTERFEIT (See **HYPOCRISY;
PROFESSION, FALSE**)

COURAGE (See **BOLDNESS**)
Duty. Not to fear adversaries. Ph.1:28
Example.
A new convert. Mk.3:3
Christ before Pilate. Jn.19:10-11
Joseph of Arimathea. Mk.15:46;
15:47
Failure in c. (See **DENY - DENIAL**)
Jn.12:42-43
In standing with Christ. Mt.26:56, cp.
47-56
In standing with Paul. 2 Tim.4:16-18
Results. Conquers fear - stirs one to stand
up for Christ. Lk.23:50-56
Source.
God. Acts 4:29; 5:29
Having been with Jesus. Acts 4:13-14
Prayer. Acts 4:29

COUNT
Facts.
Faith is c. (counted, credited) to a person
as righteousness. Ro.4:22-25; Jas.2:23
God c. (credits) righteousness without
works. Ro.4:6
God was in Christ, reconciling the
world & not c. (counting, crediting)
their trespasses against them. 2
Cor.5:19
Man is blessed when God does not c.
(credit) sin against him. Ro.4:8
Righteousness is c. (counted, credited)
to a man when he believes on Christ.
Ro.4:11
Sin is not c. (credited) when there is no
law. Ro.5:13
Meaning. Mt.18:24; Ro.4:6-8; 4:9; 4:22;
6:11; 2 Cor.5:18-19

COURTEOUS (See **HUMBLE - HUMIL-
ITY**)

COVENANT (See **COVENANT, NEW;
COVENANT, OLD**)
Covenants with Israel. Listed. Ro.9:4
Established. By Christ. Brings salvation.
Lk.1:68-75
Meaning. Ro.9:4
New covenant. Established by the blood
of Christ. Mk.14:23

COVENANT, NEW (See **COVENANT, OLD**)
Are two **c**.
  C. of grace - from above. Gal.4:21-31
  C. of law - from Mt. Sinai. Gal.4:21-31
Described as.
  A better **c**. Heb.8:6-13
  A better hope. Heb.7:18-19
  Children of promise. Gal.4:22-23, 26-28
  Children of the free. Gal.4:22-23, 26-28
  Everlasting. Heb.13:20
  Forgiveness. Mt.26:26-30
  Heavenly Jerusalem. Gal.4:26
  Heavenly things. Heb.9:23
  Promise of eternal inheritance.
    Gal.3:15-18; Heb.9:15
Discussed. Heb.8:6-13; 9:15-22; 9:23-28;
  12:18-24
  Abrahamic **c**. Gal.3:6-7; 3:15-18
Given.
  By promise, not by law. Gal.3:18
  To Abraham and his seed. Gal.3:16-18
Instituted. (See **COVENANT, NEW**,
  Source)
  By the death of Christ. Mt.26:26-30
Meaning. 2 Cor.3:6; Gal.3:15; Heb.8:6;
  12:18-24; 12:22-24
Minister of the new **c**. Discussed.
  Heb.8:6-13; 9:15-22; 9:23-28
Nature.
  Is a better **c**. Heb.8:6-13
  Is a better hope. Heb.7:19
  Is better than the old **c**. Heb.8:6; 8:6-13;
    12:18-24
  Is heavenly things. Heb.9:23
  Is righteousness. 2 Cor.3:6-11
  Is the promise of eternal inheritance. Heb.9:15
  Is the Spirit giving life. 2 Cor.3:6-11
New **c**. vs. the old **c**. Heb.7:11-24; 8:6-13;
  9:15-28; 9:15-22; 12:18-24
  Six contrasts. 2 Cor.3:6-18
Power of.
  Appoints Christ a priest forever. Heb.
    10:26-31
  Discussed. Heb.8:6; 8:10-12; 12:22-24
  Is an inward, spiritual power.
    Heb.8:10-12; 10:15-18
Source.
  God's promise. Lk.1:68-79, esp. 72-75
  Mediated by Jesus Christ. Heb.8:6; 9:15-28
  The death & blood of Christ. Heb.9:11-14
  To be remembered in the Lord's Sup-
    per. 1 Cor.11:25
  Ushered in by Christ. Heb.7:11-28;
    8:6-13; 9:11-18; 12:18-24
Spiritual vs. legal **c**. Gal.3:15-29; 4:21-31

COVENANT, OLD (See **COVENANT, NEW**)
Are two **c**.
  C. of grace - from above. Gal.4:21-31
  C. of law - from Mt. Sinai. Gal.4:21-31
Described as.
  A type of Hagar. Gal.4:22-25
  Enslaved children. Gal.4:22-25
  Jerusalem which now is. Gal.4:25
  Mount Sinai. Gal.4:25
  Producing bondage. Gal.4:21-25
  The law. Gal.3:15-29
Nature.
  Is condemnation. 2 Cor.3:6-11
  Is death. 2 Cor.3:6-11
  Is legal. Vs. the spiritual. Gal.3:15-18;
    4:21-31
Old vs. new **c**. Gal.3:15-29; 4:21-31; Heb.
  7:11-24; 8:6-13; 9:15-28; 10:11-14; 12:18-24

Powerlessness - Weaknesses of.
  Cannot annul the promise of God to
    Abraham, the Abrahamic covenant.
    Gal.3:17; 3:18
  Discussed. Heb.8:6; 8:7-9; 9:15-22;
    9:23-28; 10:1-5; 10:11-14; 12:18-21
  Gentiles were strangers from. Eph.2:11-
    12
Purpose of.
  To lead to Christ. Gal.3:15-29
  To picture heavenly things. Heb.9:1-28

COVENANT BREAKERS
Discussed. 2 Tim.3:2-4
Meaning. Ro.1:31

COVET - COVETOUSNESS (See
GREED - GREEDY; LOVER OF MONEY)
Discussed. Rom.13:9
Verses. List of. Rom.13:29

COWARDICE (See **FEAR**)

CRAFTINESS (See **DECEPTION**)
Characteristics - Traits of.
  Enemies of Christ. Mt.26:4; Mk.14:1
Is known.
  By Christ. Lk.20:23

CRAVE
Discussed. 1 Pet.2:11
Duty. To **c**. the pure spiritual milk of the
  Word. 1 Pt.2:2-3
Meaning. 1 Pet.2:11; 4:3
Work of. Wars against the soul. 1
  Pt.2:11

CREATION
Deliverance of.
  All **c**. shall be delivered from strug-
    gling & suffering. Ro.8:18-27
  Has been reconciled to God by Christ.
    Col.1:20
Discussed. Col.1:16-17
Misconceptions of **c**. Col.2:8; 2:20-23
Nature of.
  Corruptible & perishing. Ro.8:19-22;
    Heb.1:11-12
  Interrelated & interconnected with
    man. Ro.8:19-22; 10:12
  Suffers & struggles for deliverance.
    Ro.8:19-22
  Sustained - held together by Christ.
    Col.1:16-17; Heb.1:3
Of man.
  Created in the image of God.
    Lk.20:25; Jn.4:23
  Discussed. Jn.4:23
  Every child created by God. Lk.18:16
  Every man owes his existence to God.
    Lk.13:6-9; 20:9
  The purpose & plan for man. Heb.2:6-8
Of the new heavens and earth. Ro.8:19-22;
  2 Pt.3:3-14; Rev.21:1
Purposes of **c**. Jn.4:23-24; Ro.8:17;
  1 Cor.6:13-14; 6:20; Col.1:16; 1:18;
  Heb.2:5-6; 2:9-13
Responsibility for **c**. Man is responsible.
  To bear fruit. Lk.13:6-9
  To subdue **c**. Lk.20:9
Reveals & proves.
  God exists. His power & Deity. Acts
    17:24-25; Ro.1:19
  Much more than God exists. Several
    other things. Ro.1:19

Source of **c**.
  By Christ. Jn.1:1-5; 1:3; Col.1:16-17;
    Rev.3:14
  By God.
    By power. Enormous power. Acts
      4:24
    By the living God. Acts 14:15
    By the Lord of heaven & earth.
      Acts 17:24
    By the Lord who dwells every-
      where. Acts 7:48-50
    By the Word of God. Heb.11:3;
      2 Pt.3:5
    Created all things for Himself.
      Heb.2:9-13
    How we know that God created the
      worlds. Heb.11:3
    Rejected by man. Ro.1:20
    Vs. humanism & evolution.
      Heb.11:3
      Chart contrasting the views of
        the believer & the unbeliever.
        Heb.11:3
State - Condition of. (See **CORRUP-
TION; WORLD**, State of)
  Corruptible, struggling, suffering.
    Ro.8:19-22
  Cursed by God. Discussed. Ro.8:19-22
Verses. List of. 1 Cor.6:13-14
Views of. World's view of creation.
  1 Cor.2:6; Heb.11:3

**CREATURES OF REVELATION,
FOUR LIVING**
Discussed. Rev.4:6-9
Worship Christ continually. For three
  things. Rev.5:8-10

CREDIT - CREDITED
Facts.
  Faith is **c**. (counted, credited) to a per-
    son as righteousness. Ro.4:22-25;
    Jas.2:23
  God **c**. (counts, credits) righteousness
    without works. Ro.4:6
  God was in Christ, reconciling the
    world & not **c**. (counting) their tres-
    passes against them. 2 Cor.5:19
  Man is blessed when God does not **c**.
    (count, credit) sin against him.
    Ro.4:8
  Righteousness is **c**. (counted) to a man
    when he believes on Christ. Ro.4:11
  Sin is not **c**. (counted) when there is no
    law. Ro.5:13
Meaning. Mt.18:24; Ro.4:6-8; 4:9; 4:22;
  6:11; 2 Cor.5:18-19

CREEDS
Fact. Were written by Paul for churches.
  Acts 14:22

CRESCENS
Sent by Paul to minister. 2 Tim.4:10

CRETE
Church of. Tit.1:5; 1:10-12
Island & people of. Tit.1:5; 1:10-12
Paul visited. Acts 27:4-12

CRISPUS
Converted ruler of a synagogue. Acts
  18:8
Discussed. 1 Cor.1:14

CRITICISM - CRITICIZER - CRITI-CIZING (See **ARGUMENTS; CONTENTION; DIVISION; JUDGING OTHERS**)
Characteristic - Trait of.
Divisive people who judge others. Mt.7:1-6; Ro.2:1
False teachers. Jude 16
Prideful, self-centered persons. Ph.2:3-4
The gifted. Jas.4:11-12
Those who judge & compare minis-ters. 1 Cor.1:10-16; 4:1-5; 4:6-13
Described as.
Opposed to love. Gal.5:13-15
The snare of the devil: showing satanic enslavement. 2 Tim.2:24-26
Discussed. Mt.7:1-6; Jas.4:11-12
C. the sacrifice of believers. Jn.12:4-8
Man's c. spirit. Jn.8:3-6
Duty.
Not to c. a fallen brother. Gal.6:1-5
Not to c. or judge. Reasons. Ro.14:3-4
Not to judge & c. Mt.7:1; Ro.2:1
To do all things without complaining & arguing. Ph.2:14
To follow the instructions governing c. Tit.3:2
To mind one's own business. 1 Th. 4:11
To put off all forms of c. Eph.4:31-32
Nature.
Bites & devours. Gal.5:13-15
Blinds a person to his own faults. Mt.7:1-6; Lk.6:41-42
Is being enslaved by Satan. 2 Tim. 2:24-26
Of ministers. (See **MINISTERS**, Duty toward)
Not to c., judge, or compare ministers. 1 Cor.4:1-5; 4:6-13
Reasons why people c.
Are offended by the breaking of tradi-tion. Mt.15:2
Are prejudiced against certain people. Mt.9:11; Mk.2:16; Lk.15:2; 19:7
Are sinners. Have a spirit of judging others. Jn.8:3-6
Are tempted by the devil. 2 Tim.2:24-26
Differ in religious practices. Mt.12:2; Mk.7:2
Oppose a person who differs. Condi-tions of tolerance. Mk.9:38-41
Oppose believers & their sacrifice. Jn.12:4-8
Oppose the claims & works of Christ. Mk.2:7; Jn.6:41
Six reasons. Mt.7:1
Suffer anxiety & worry. Lk.10:40
Warning against.
Are guilty of serious sin. Mt.7:1-6
Are inexcusable. Ro.2:1
Are unworthy of the gospel. Mt.7:1-6; 7:6
Condemns one. Jas.5:9
Is forbidden. Col.2:16-17
Makes a person a hypocrite. Mt.7:5
Sets oneself up as God with the right to judge. Usurps God's authority. Mt.7:1; Ro.14:3-4
Shall be unforgiven. Lk.6:36-37
Watch hypocrisy & c. Four points. Lk.6:41-42
Will be judged. Mt.7:2
Why one should not c. Mt.7:1

CROOKED
Caused by. Sinful nature. Ro.3:10-12

CROSS, DAILY - SELF-DENIAL (See **COMMITMENT; DEDICATION; HEART; JESUS CHRIST**, Cross of; Death of; **SURRENDER**)
Carnal vs. spiritual view of the c. Lk.22:33-37
Discussion. Mt.10:38; Mk.8:34-38; Lk.9:23; 14:25-35
Duty - Essential.
Must abstain from fleshly lust. 1 Pt.2:11-12
Must be crucified with Christ. Ro.6:3-5; 6:6-7
Must count all as loss for Christ. Ph.3:7-11
Must live a crucified life. 1 Pt.4:1; 4:7-11
To bear the c. Mt.16:21-28; Mk.8:34-38; Lk.9:23; 14:25-35
To present one's body as a living sac-rifice to God. Ro.12:1-2
To put sin to death. Col.3:5-11
To put to death the deeds of the body. Ro.8:13
To sacrifice oneself for Christ. Jn.12:23-26
To take up the c. Lk.9:23-27
Meaning. Mk.8:34
Arming self with the Christ's mind. 1 Pt.4:1
Bearing the cross. Mt.10:38; Mk.8:34-38; Lk.9:23; 14:25-35
Crucifying the sinful nature. Gal.5:24
Dying daily. Mt.16:21-28; 2 Cor.4:10
Dying to self. Mt.10:34-39; 2 Cor.4:12
Living the crucified life. 1 Pt.4:1; 4:7-11
Presenting one's body as a living sac-rifice. Ro.12:1-2
Putting off the old man. Eph.4:22
Putting to death one's body members. Col.3:5
Suffering in the body. 1 Pt.4:1
Taking up the cross. Lk.9:23
Misunderstood. By Peter & the disciples. Jn.13:36-38
Necessary to.
Abstain from sinful desires. 1 Pet. 2:11-12
Live a crucified life. 1 Pet 1:23
Pictures conversion. Mk.15:21
Power of. Illust. Mt.27:54
Reactions to.
Discussed. Lk.23:35-36
Man accepts or is repulsed by. Mt.16:22; Lk.2:35
Man rebels against. Mt.16:22
Verses. List of. Jn.12:23-26

CROWDS
Excitement of. Not always wise. Mk.6:45
Fed by Christ. Lk.9:10-17
Feeding of.
Attitudes toward human need & re-sources. Mk.6:35-44
Spiritual food, compassion, evangel-ism. Mk.8:1-9
Followed Christ. By the thousands. Lk.8:4
Followed Jesus. Came from all over. Mk.3:7-8
Thousands followed Christ. Lk.8:4
Why the c. followed Christ. Five reasons. Mt.20:29

CROWN - CROWNS (See **REWARDS**, Crowns)
Described.
As a c. of glory. 1 Pt.5:4
As a c. of incorruption. 1 Cor.9:25
As a c. of life. Jas.1:12; Rev.2:10
As a c. of righteousness. 2 Tim.4:8
As a c. of soul winning. 1 Th.2:19-20
Meaning. 1 Th.2:19-20
To be the reward of.
Believers. 1 Cor.9:25; 2 Tim.2:5
Ministers. Ph.4:1
Soul winners. 1 Th.2:19-20

CROWN OF LIFE
Discussed. Rev.2:10
Meaning. Jas.1:12

CROWN OF RIGHTEOUSNESS
Discussed. 2 Tim.4:8

CRUCIFIXION (See **JESUS CHRIST**, Cross; Death)
Described. Mt.27:26
Was a lingering death. Jn.19:34

CRUSHED
Meaning. Mk.3:5; 8:12; Ro. 2:9; 2 Cor. 4:7-9; 6:4-5; 1 Th.3:7-10

CRY - CRYING (See **SEEKING GOD**)
For deliverance for a child. Mt.15:21-28; 17:15
For mercy. Lk.17:12-14
To Jesus. Essential for healing. Mt. 20:30; Mk.10:47; Lk.17:12-14

CUMMIN
Described. Mt.23:23

CUP, THE
Meaning.
Symbol of Christ's suffering. Jn.18:11
Symbol of three things. Mk.14:36
Of Christ's death & suffering, Gethse-mane. Mt.26:39; 26:42-44
Of hypocrisy. Mt.23:25-26
Of the Lord's Supper. Meaning. Mk. 14:23

CURIOUS - CURIOSITY
Need.
To come to Christ. Mk.1:33
To seek Christ out of c. Mk.2:1-2
What stirs c.
Christ & His person - just who He is.
Stirred the c. of some Greeks. Jn.12:20-21
Stirred the c. of Zaccheus. Lk.19:1:10
Christ & His works.
Stirred the c. of Herod. Lk.9:9
Stirred the c. of the religionist. Jn.2:18
Miracles, unusual happenings. Raising Lazarus from the dead stirred peo-ple's c. Jn.12:9
New ideas & philosophies. Stirred the religionists & philosophers at Ath-ens. Acts 17:21
Suffering & tragedies. Indifferent c. Lk.10:32
The cross, death & resurrection of Christ. Stirred the c. of Peter. Mt.27:46-49; Lk.9:43-45; 24:9-11; Jn.13:36-38

Saved – Secure

Protection
Provision
Peace

Rev. 2:1   Christ abides in the midst of the seven candlesticks.

DAVID

Call. By God. Discussed. Acts 13:22-23
Choosing of. Jn.4:22
Eating consecrated in the tabernacle.
Mt.12:3-4
Example of.
Justification by faith. Ro.4:6-8
Man is more important than rules &
regulations. Mk.2:25-27
Need has precedence over tradition.
Mt.12:3-4
Putting need before religious rules.
Lk.6:1-5
Faith of. Discussed. Heb.11:32
Key of **D.** Meaning. Held by Jesus Christ.
Rev.3:7
Kingdom of. Given to Christ. Mk.11:10;
Lk.1:31-33; 1:32-33; 3:24-31
Predicted - prophesied.
Man's opposition to God. Acts 4:25-28
The death of Jesus. Acts 4:25-28
The Messiah was to be Lord.
Mk.12:35-37; Lk.20:42-44
The resurrection of Jesus. Acts 2:25-31
Seed of. Messiah.
Messiah seen as the Seed of David by
the Jews. Jn.1:23
Promises & fulfillment. Jn.1:45; 1:49

DAY

Uses of the term day to refer:
To a **d.** of judgment. Acts 17:31;
1 Cor.3:13
To believers as children of the **d.**
1 Th.5:5, 8
To Noah's **d.** Mt.24:37
To the **d.** of eternal salvation.
Ro.13:11-12
To the **d.** of evil. Eph.5:16
To the **d.** of Jesus Christ. Ph.1:6
To the **d.** of redemption. Eph.4:30;
2 Pt.1:19
To the **d.** of salvation. 2 Cor.6:2
To the **d.** of the Lord. (See **DAY OF THE LORD**)
To the **d.** of the Lord's return.
Heb.10:25
To the **d.** of wrath. Ro.2:5
To the last days, the present time &
history. Heb.1:2; 2 Pt.3:3
To the Lord's **D.**, the **d.** of worship.
Rev.1:10
To the Son of Man's **d.** Jn.17:24
To the twelve hours of a **d.** Jn.11:9

DAY GOD VISITS US

Meaning. 1 Pt.2:12

DAY OF THE LORD

Discussed. Acts 2:19-20; 1 Th.4:13-5:3;
5:1-3; 5:4-5; 2 Th.2:1-3; 2 Pt.3:10

DAY OF VISITATION (See **DAY GOD VISITS US**)

DAYS, THE LAST (See **TIME, THE LAST**)

Discussed. 2 Pt.3:3

DEBAUCHERY

Characteristic - Trait of. False teachers.
Jude 4
Meaning. Mk.7:22; 2 Cor.12:19-
21;Gal.5:19-21; Eph.4:17-19;1 Pt.4:3,
cp. Ro.13:13

DEACONS

Discussed. Ph.1:1; 1 Tim.3:8-13
Qualifications. 1 Tim.3:8-13
The first **d.** appointed by the early
church. Acts 6:1-6
The first martyr of the early church was a
d. Acts 6:5-15; 7:1-60
Wife of. Discussed. 1 Tim.3:11-12

DEAR (See **VALUED HIGHLY**)

DEARLY LOVED

Meaning. 2 Jn.1

DEATH - DYING

Attitude toward.
Confronting & facing **d.** & reviewing
one's life. 2 Tim.4:6-8
Desire to depart & be with Christ.
Ph.1:21
Fear of **d.** Jn.6:17-19
Is gain to the believer. Ph.1:21
To be an attitude of hope, not despair.
Jn.20:14-16
Caused by - Penalty of.
Adam. Discussed. Ro.5:12-21;
1 Cor.15:21
Backsliding. Jas.5:19-20
Human nature. Jn.8:23
Penalty. Discussed Jn.8:21-22
Satan & his power. Heb.2:14-15
Sin. Ro.5:21; 6:21, 23; 7:5; 8:2;
1 Cor.15:54-56; Heb.2:14-16;
Jas.1:15; 2 Pt.1:4
Is **d.** too severe a punishment for
sin? Ro.5:12
Unbelief. Jn.8:21-22; 8:24
Dead raised.
Dorcas. Conquering death. Acts 9:36-43
Jairus' daughter. The approach that
lays hold of Jesus. Mt.9:18-19, 23-
26; Mk.5:21-24, 35-43
Lazarus. Power over death. Jn.11:38-46
Widow's son. Great compassion &
power. Lk.7:11-17
Deliverance from **d.** 1 Cor.15:5-58
By being faithful & overcoming in
life. Rev.2:11
By Christ's death. Jn.3:14-15; 3:16-17;
Ro.6:8-10;Heb.2:14-16; 1 Jn.3:14
Counteracted by Christ. Ro.5:12-21
By Christ's great power. Jn.11:1-16;
11:41-46; 1 Cor.15:24-26; Col.2:13;
2 Pt.1:3
By confronting **d.** & terrible trials.
Mt.26:36-46
By conversion. Jas.5:20
By faith. Heb.11:13-16
By hearing Christ's words & believing
in God. Jn.5:24
By keeping the words of Christ.
Jn.8:51-52
By loving one another with a pure
heart fervently. 1 Pt.1:24-25
By the coming again of Christ.
Jn.5:28-29; 1 Cor.15:51-58;
1 Th.4:13-18
By the Holy Spirit. Ro.8:1-17
By the love of God. Ro.8:37-39
Power over **d.** Jn.11:38-46
Proof of deliverance. Love. 1 Jn.3:14-17
Through Jesus' return. Jn.14:1-3
Through the divine nature. 2 Pt.1:4

Described.
As a day of accounting. Mt.18:32-34
As a personal presentation to the Lord.
Jn.14:3
As a spirit. Ro.8:2
As dead men's bones. Mt.23:27-28
As departing this life. Ph.1:23
As dissolving this earthly house or
tabernacle. 2 Cor.5:1
As sleep. Lk.8:50; Jn.11:13;
1 Th.4:14-15
As spiritual **d.** Ro.6:23
Verses. List of. Ro.5:12
Discussed. Eph.2:1; Heb.2:14-16; 9:27;
1 Jn.3:14
Death of the saved vs. the unsaved.
Lk.16:19-31
Pain of death for the unbeliever is ter-
rible. Heb.2:14-16
Sin that leads to **d.** 1 Jn.5:16
Why some are taken & others are not.
Acts 12:5-17
Fact.
Comes to the rich. The rich are not ex-
empt. Lk.12:20
Death & hell will be cast into the lake
of fire. Rev.20:13-14
Death for a cause is not rare. Mt.10:23
Death is universal. Ro.5:12; 6:23;
Heb.9:27
There is a difference between Christ's
d. & man's **d.** Mt.26:36-45
There is a need to think about **d.** Rea-
sons. Mt.20:18
Touches Christ. Lk.7:12-13
Kinds of.
By crucifixion. Mt.27:26-44
By drowning. A form of capital pun-
ishment. Mk.9:42
By stoning. Acts 14:19-20
Eternal - second death. Jn.11:25;
Jas.5:20; Rev.2:11; 20:11-15; 21:8
Physical **d.** Jn.11:25; Heb.9:27
Verses. List of. Ro.5:12-14
Spiritual death. Eph.2:1; 2:4-5;
1 Jn.3:14
Caused by.
Sin. Ro.6:23; Jas.1:15
The carnal mind. Ro.8:5-8
Dead while living. Mt.8:22; Lk.15:32;
Jn.5:24-25; 6:52-53; Eph.2:1; 5:14;
Col.2:13; 1 Tim.5:6; Rev.3:1
Described. Ro.6:23
Verses. List of. Ro.1:32
Meaning. Corruption - perishing.
Jn.3:16; Eph.2:1; 2 Pt.1:4; 2:19
Of believers.
A picture of the believer's **d.**
2 Tim.4:6
Emphasis is to be the Father, not
heaven. Jn.14:6
What happens to the believer at death:
a disembodied spirit or given a tempo-
rary body? 2 Cor.5:1-10; 1 Th.4:13-5:3
Where believer goes. Acts 7:59
Will be blessed. Reasons. Rev.14:13
Will be crowned with life. 2 Tim.4:8
Will be delivered from **d.** Quicker than
the blink of an eye (11/100 of a sec-
ond). 2 Tim.4:18
Will be great gain. Ph.1:21
Will be no more **d.** in heaven. Rev. 21:4
Will be present with the Lord. 1 Th.4:14-15
Will meet Jesus at **d.** With Him im-
mediately. Jn.11:25-27; 14:3; 16:4-6
Will never taste **d.** Mt.16:28; 2 Tim.4:18

Preparation for.
How to prepare. Jn.16:4-6
Tasting **d.** vs. seeing God's kingdom.
Mk.9:1
Purpose of **d.** Seven purposes. Jn.11:1-16
Results.
What follows **d.** Lk.16:19-31
With Christ immediately. Lk.23:40-43;
Jn.11:25-27; 14:3; 16:4-6; 2 Tim.4:18
Stages of. Heb.9:27
To self. (See **CROSS--SELF-DENIAL**)
Verses. List of. Jn.6:17-19
View of. Man's view. Col.2:13
Vs. Christ. Col.2:13

DEATH, SECOND (See HELL, LAKE OF FIRE)
Destination of unbelievers. Rev.20:14
Discussed. Jn.11:25; Rev.2:11; 20:8;
20:11-15
Meaning. Rev.20:6; 20:14

DEATH, SPIRITUAL
Caused by.
Sin. Ro.6:23; Jas.1:5
The carnal mind. Ro.8:5-8
Dead while living. Mt.8:22; Lk.15:32;
Jn.5:24-25; 6:52-53; Eph.2:1; 5:14;
Col.2:13; 1 Tim.5:6; Rev.3:1
Described. Ro.6:23
As dead men's bones. Mt.23:27-28
Verses. List of. Ro.1:32

DEBATE (See QUARRELING; STRIFE)

DEBAUCHERY
Meaning. 1 Pt.4:3,

DEBT, SPIRITUAL - SPIRITUAL DEBTOR
Duty.
Not to try to put God in **d.** to oneself
by working for righteousness.
Ro.4:4-5
To pray for God to forgive our **d.**
Mt.6:12
To preach. Obligated & indebted to **p.**
Ro.1:14-15
To seek salvation & righteousness by
faith. Ro.4:4-5; Gal.5:3-5

DEBAUCHERY
Meaning. Ro.13:13

DEBTS (See MONEY)
Discussed. Ro.13:8
Duty.
To owe no man anything. Ro.13:8
To pay all **d.** Ro.13:7
Meaning. Mt.6:12

DECAY
Caused by.
Adam's sinful nature. Ro.5:12-14
Gratifying, sowing to one's flesh.
Gal.6:7-8
Lust. 2 Pt.1:4
Natural heritage - bearing corruptible
seed. 1 Pt.1:23
Sin; being carnal minded. Ro.8:5-8;
8:12-13
Ultimate cause. Mt.8:17
Characteristic - Trait.
Of evil men. Lk.6:43-44
Of false teachers. 2 Pt.2:12, cp. 10-12;
2:19; Jude 10, cp. 8-11

Deliverance - Escape.
By a radical change of the body.
1 Cor.15:35-58
By being born again. 1 Pt.1:23
By being clothed with life. 2 Cor.5:1-4
By being redeemed. 1 Pt.1:18-20
By Christ.
Christ did not see **c.** Acts 2:25-36
Conquered by Christ's resurrection.
Acts 13:32-37
By partaking of God's nature. 2 Pt.1:4
Not by corruptible things. 1 Pt.1:18-20
Of creation itself. Ro.8:19-22
Discussed. 2 Cor.4:16
Meaning. Mt.6:19-20; Acts 2:27; 13:32-
37; 2 Pt.1:4
Decaying, aging, deteriorating.
Mt.6:19
Flesh and blood which wastes away.
1 Cor.15:50-58
Mortal--mortality. Flesh withering,
falling away, dissolving. 2 Cor.5:1-4
Physical death. 1 Cor.15:42-49
The natural world and body.
1 Cor.15:35-49; Jude 10, cp. 8-10
The world passing away. 1 Jn.2:17
Problems.
Burdens man with mortality.
2 Cor.5:1-4
Causes pain & infirmities. Ro.8:18;
8:19-22
Causes the world to pass away.
1 Jn.2:17
Enslaves all of creation to the bondage
of **c.** Ro.8:19-22
Seed of.
The physical vs. the spiritual world &
dimension. Jn.8:23
Within the world. Jn.12:31; 2 Pt.1:4
Verses. List of. Jn.1:14
Vs. incorruption. 1 Pt.1:23

DECEIT - DECEIVE - DECEPTION (See LYING)
Basic errors.
Is a sin common to false citizenship.
Mt.22:16-17
Thinking that Jesus was a deceiver in
claiming that He would arise from
the dead. Mt.27:62-66
Thinking that the claims of Christ were
deceitful. Jn.7:12
Thinks a person can camouflage.
Lk.13:14
Thinks one can be born again without
doing right. 1 Jn.2:24-29; 3:4-9
Thinks one can become righteous on
his own. 1 Jn.1:6-7
Thinks one does not necessarily sin.
1 Jn.1:10-2:2
Thinks one is not totally sinful and de-
praved. 1 Jn.1:8-9
Described as.
Claiming that one is the Christ, the de-
liverer of mankind. Mt.24:5, 11;
Mk.13:6
Empty words. Eph.5:6
Good words & flattering speeches.
Ro.16:18
Mishandling the Word of God. 1 Cor.
2:1-5; 2 Cor.4:2; 1 Th.2:3-5, cp. 6-13
Self-deception. Mk.14:1-2
Turning to false gospels. Gal.1:6-9;
1 Jn.4:1-3
Discussed. Ro.3:13-14; 2 Cor.11:1-15;
Col.2:4; Tit.3:3

Duty.
Must not be deceived.
About bad company. Bad company
corrupts one's morals. 1 Cor.
15:33
About religion. Must bridle one's
tongue. Jas.1:26
About sin & judgment. Sin excludes
a person from God's kingdom.
1 Cor.6:9-10
About the results of sin. A person
reaps what he sows. Gal.6:7-8
Must not **d.** oneself. 1 Cor.3:18; Jas.1:22
Must not preach a **d.** message.
1 Cor.2:1-5; 2 Cor.4:1-5, esp. 1-2;
1 Th.2:1-5, esp. 3-5
Must watch, take heed that no man **d.**
us. Mt.24:4; Mk.13:5
Not to be carried away by the false
doctrine of **d.** Eph.4:14
To guard against **d.** Lk.21:8; 1 Cor.
3:18-23; Eph.5:6; 2 Th.2:3; 1 Jn.3:7
To renounce. 2 Cor.4:1-2
To stop the mouth of **d.**, of false
teachers. Tit.1:10-11
Example of.
Ananias & his wife. Acts 5:1-11
Eve. 2 Cor.11:3; 1 Tim.2:14
Herod. Mt.2:7-18
Judas. Mt.26:16; 26:20-25
Religionists. Mt.22:15-18
Meaning.
What it means not to **d.** Mk.7:22;
Jn.1:47; Ro.1:29; 2 Cor.4:2; Col.2:4;
Tit.1:10; 1 Pt.2:1
Message of **d.**
Denies that Jesus Christ has come in the
flesh. 2 Jn.7, cp. Gal.1:6-9; 1 Jn.4:1-6
False philosophy. Col.2:8-10
Results.
Betrays Christ. Mt.26:48-50
Brings the wrath of God upon a per-
son. Eph.5:6
Makes a person worthy of death.
Ro.1:29-32, esp. 29, 32
Source of.
The heart. Mk.7:14-23, esp. 22-23
The tongue. Ro.3:13
Warning against.
Are many **d.**, many false teachers.
Tit.1:10
Being **d.** by a false gospel & false
teachers. 2 Cor.11:3-4, 13-15; 13:1-6,
cp. Gal.1:6-9
Deceiving oneself. To guard against.
1 Cor.3:18; 2 Cor.11:3-4; 13:5-6;
Jas.1:22
Fourfold warning. 2 Jn.7-13
Receiving a deceiver in one's home or
church. 2 Jn.10-11
The strong **d.** in the last days.
Mt.24:4-5; 2 Th.2:10-12, cp. 9;
2 Jn.7; Rev.13:13-17
Who & what deceives.
False teachers & prophets. Mt.24:11;
Gal.3:1; 2 Th.2:3; 2 Pt.2:13;
1 Jn.2:18-23; 4:1-6
Oneself, one's self-centeredness.
1 Cor.3:18; Gal.6:3; Jas.1:22
Riches, the **d.** of riches. Mt.13:22;
Mk.4:19
Satan.
Blinds the minds of people lest they
believe the gospel. 2 Cor.4:3-4
Is disguised as an angel of light.
2 Cor.11:13-14; Rev.12:9

Satan's messengers. Are disguised as ministers. 2 Cor.11:13-15
Seducing spirits. 1 Tim.4:1
Sin, the **d.** of sin. Ro.7:11; Heb.3:13
The antichrist. 2 Th.2:9; 2:10; 2 Jn.7; Rev.13:13-17
The old man. Eph.4:22
Who is **d.**
  Discussed. 2 Th.2:11
  Unbelievers. Tit.3:3

DECISION
Discussed. Mt.7:13-14
  A man who knows better, but rejects. Acts 24:22-27
  Last minute **d.** Mt.20:6-7
  Of life. Twofold. Mt.7:13-14
  Reasons for indecision & silence. Lk.20:7-8
  Steps involved in. Mk.10:46-52
Duty - Essential.
  Must be a personal **d.** Between Christ & oneself. Jn.11:29
  Must be made. Choice is essential. Lk.2:34
  Must be made now. Now is the accepted time. 2 Cor.6:1-2
  Must choose between two lives. Mt.7:13-14
  Must choose Christ over money & the world. Mk.10:17-22, esp. 21
  Must choose to believe & to follow Christ. Jn.6:67
  Must confess publicly. Jn.1:49
  Must count the cost before making a **d.** Lk.14:28-32
  Must follow Christ.
    Attacked by Satan. Mk.1:12
    Cost of. Mk.1:9
  Must grasp the moment of **d.** Mt.8:21-22
  Must hear the Word of Christ. Lk.9:35
Facts.
  Can wait too late. Lk.13:25
  Christ will not force a **d.** Mt.9:1
  Man hedges in making a **d.** Lk.9:57-62
  Neutrality impossible. Mt.12:30; 12:33; Lk.9:57-62; 11:23; 14:18-20; 16:13
  One decision is required. "He has done everything well." Mk.7:31-37
  The call to Christ is more clear & positive today than the call to Adam. Ro.5:12-14
  The Holy Spirit does not always contend with man. Mt.12:14-16; 20:5; Lk.4:28-30; Jn.7:33-34; 11:54
Rejected.
  By Israel. Mk.12:12
  Deliberate, willful **r.** Mt.13:10-17; 13:13-15; 21:27
  Discussed. Lk.9:57-62; 14:15-24
  Excuses given. Lk.9:57-62; 14:18-20
Responses to Christ.
  Choosing Christ rather than the world. Heb.11:23-26
  King Agrippa. Almost persuaded. Acts 26:24-32
  Three responses. Jn.6:66-71
  Tragic **d.** Mk.11:33
  Two choices men make. Mk.11:27-33
Results.
  Determines a person's destiny. Lk.11:23
  Discussed. Mk.1:12
  Of a wrong **d.**
    Leads to despair & sometimes suicide. Mt.27:1-5, cp. Acts 1:16-19
    Leads to rejection by God. Heb.12:15-17
Verses. List of. Lk.9:61-62

DECLARE
Meaning. 1 Pt.2:9

DEDICATE - DEDICATION (See COMMITMENT; CROSS - SELF-DENIAL; HEART; MINISTRY; SERVICE; SURRENDER)
Degrees of.
  Discussed. Mt.13:8, 23; Mk.4:20; Lk.19:15-23; 19:15; Jn.6:66-71
  Many are less **d.** than worldly men are in their pursuits. Lk.16:8
Described as.
  Half-hearted. Lk.9:57-58
  Spiritual vs. carnal. Lk.22:31-34
Discussed. Mt.13:1-9; Lk.9:23; Ro.12:1-3; Heb.10:38
  Knowing the difference between spiritual & carnal **d.** Lk.22:31-38
Duty.
  Discussed. Lk.16:8
  In the midst of an immoral, cesspool society. Ro.1:8
  To attend upon the Lord without distraction. 1 Cor.7:35
  To be a vessel of honor, sanctified & fit for the Master's use. 2 Tim.2:21, cp. 20-26
  To be an instrument in the Lord's hands. Acts 14:3
  To be as **d.** as the worldly are to their pursuits. Lk.16:8
  To be enslaved to Christ. Ro.1:1-7
  To be enslaved to the gospel. Ro.1:8-15
  To be obedient to the faith & to one's work. Acts 6:6
  To be steadfast, unmoveable, always serving. 1 Cor.15:58
  To **d.** oneself to three things. Mt.6:9
  To forsake all for Christ. Lk.5:11
  To give all one is & has. Mt.19:21-22; 19:23-26; 19:27-30; Lk.14:28-33; Acts 4:32
  To give oneself to Christ before giving money or anything else. 2 Cor.8:5, cp. 1-5
  To God or things. Cannot serve two masters. Lk.16:13
  To labor to the point of exhaustion. Mk.4:35-36
  To remain single if God calls one a celibate life. 1 Cor.7:25-40
  To serve God and not sin. Ro.6:16
  To serve God with the same fervor as you served sin. Ro.6:19-20
  To set one's heart upon Christ. 1 Pt.3:15
  To surrender to the Lordship of Christ. Acts 4:32
  To surrender to the mission of Christ. Acts 4:32
  To withstand temptation. Lk.22:33-34
  To work until Christ returns. Lk.19:13
Example.
  A man who was not a quitter. Ph.2:25-30
  Of martyrdom. Heb.11:35-40
  Of ministers. To give themselves to prayer & preaching of the Word. Acts 6:4
Marks of.
  A great believer. Ph.1:20-26
  A great church. Ph.1:27-30
  A mature witness. Ph.1:12-30
  Sacrificing & doing all one can. Mk.14:8

Meaning.
  Consecration. 2 Cor.6:11-7:1
  Denying oneself. Lk.9:23
  Presenting one's body as a living sacrifice. Ro.12:1-2
  Sacrificial giving. Mt.26:6-13; Mk.10:17-22
  Separation. 2 Cor.6:11-7:1
  Surrender. Mt.6:9; Jn.18:1-11; 21:18-25
Of Jesus Christ. **D.** to do God's will at any cost. Mk.14:33-34; 14:41-42
Proof. Feeding God's people. Jn.21:15-17
Results. God knows & richly blesses. Lk.2:25-27
Stirred by.
  The cross. Jn.12:23-26
  The desire for righteousness & perfection, to arise from the dead. Ph.3:7-10
  The desire to be blameless at the coming of Christ. 1 Th.5:23
  The gospel abiding within one's heart. 1 Jn.2:24
Verses. List of. Lk.17:7-10
Why a person should be **d.**
  A person belongs to Christ in life & death. Ro.14:7-9
  D. determines one's reward. Lk.16:10-12; 19:11-27
  D. is God's great call. Jn.21:18-23
  God warns against being lukewarm. Cold vs. hot. Rev.3:14-22
  Is demanded by Christ's death. Mt.16:21-28
  Must give an account to God. Lk.19:15-23
  One has been purchased by the Lord. Ro.14:7-9
  Reasons for remaining loyal. Discussed. Acts 5:26-42
  The world is often more **d.** than believers. Lk.16:8

DEDICATION, FEAST OF (See FEASTS, RELIGIOUS)
Discussed. Jn.10:22

DEEDS
Vs. faith. Discussed. Jas.2:14-26

DEFILE - DEFILEMENT--UNCLEAN (See FILTHINESS; SIN; UNCLEANNESS)
Cause of **d.**
  An unbelieving & impure mind & conscience. Tit.1:15
  Bitterness against others. Heb.12:15
  Filthy dreams. Jude 8
  The cause is not breaking religious rules & rituals. Mt.15:1-2, 10-20; Mk.7:1-9, 14-23; Jn.18:28
  The heart. Mk.7:14-23
  The tongue. **D.** the whole body. Jas.3:6
  Violating one's conscience, doing something one knows is wrong. 1 Cor.8:7
Discussed.
  Things that **d.** Thirteen things. Mk.7:14-23
  What **d.** a man. Seven things. Mt.15:1-20
Duty.
  To cleanse self from all **d.** 2 Cor.7:1
  To follow peace & holiness. Heb.12:14-15

Fact. The law was given for those who **d.** themselves. 1 Tim.1:9-10

Meaning. Mt.15:17-20

Results.
Will be destroyed by God--if **d.** the body. 1 Cor.3:17
Will be excluded from the new heavens & earth & the holy city. Rev.21:27, cp. 1-5
Will mislead & become a stumbling block to others. 1 Cor.8:7-13

DEGRADATION, SPIRITUAL
Caused by. Selfishness; godless independence. Lk.15:14-16

DEITY (See GOD; JESUS CHRIST; HOLY SPIRIT)

DELIVERANCE (See SALVATION)
Discussed. Jn.14:1-3

Fact.
All of creation shall be **d.** from the bondage of corruption. Ro.8:18-27
Christ was **d.** up to death for us all. Ro.8:32
Death & hell shall **d.** up the dead in them & every person shall face eternal judgment. Rev.20:13

From what.
All evil works. 2 Tim.4:18
Being wild & mean. Mk.5:1-20
Death. 2 Cor.1:10; Heb.2:14-15
Enslavement & helplessness. Mk.1:23-28
Evil spirits. Lk.9:42
Filthy behavior. 2 Pt.2:7-9
Sin. Jn.8:34-36; Ro.3:23-24; Eph.1:7; 1 Pt.2:24
Temptation. 1 Cor.10;13; 2 Pt.2:9
The law & its guilt & condemnation. Ro.7:6
The most severe trials & circumstances. Ro.8:35-37; 2 Tim.3:10-11
The power of darkness. Col.1:12-13
The present evil world. Gal.1:4
The wrath to come. 1 Th.1:10

How one can be delivered.
By Christ. Lk.9:42; Jn.6:15-21; Ro.11:26; Gal.1:4; 1 Th.1:10
By facing up to one's sin. Jn.4:16-18; 8:1-11; 16:8-11
By God. Lk.18:6-7; 2 Cor.1:10; Col. 1:12-13; 2 Tim.4:18; 2 Pt.2:7, cp. 4-6
By listening to the preaching of **d.** Lk.4:18
By prayer. Mt.6:13; Lk.18:6-7; Ro.15:30-32; Ph.1:19; 2 Th.3:1-2

Misconception. Dramatic experience with God will deliver. Jn.14:8

Verses. List of. Mk.6:50-51

DELIVERER
Difference between a **D.** & a Liberator. Lk.22:19-20

Who is the **D.** (See **DELIVERANCE; SALVATION**)

DELUGE (See FLOOD, THE)

DEMAS
Discussed. Col.4:14
Forsook Christ for the world. 2 Tim.4:9
Laborer with Paul. Phile.1:24

DEMETRIUS
A godly church leader. 3 Jn.12
A silversmith at Ephesus. Acts 19:24-31

DEMONS (See EVIL SPIRITS)

DENARII
Discussed. Jn.6:7
Money. One **d.** was the average pay for a day's work. Mk.14:3

DENY - DENIAL OF CHRIST (See CONFESS - CONFESSION)
By whom.
Believers. Fear the world, ridicule, & abuse. Jn.18:15-18; 2 Tim.2:12
Disciples.
Denial foretold. Stumbling, falling away. Mt.26:31-35; Mk.14:27
Reasons. Mk.14:50
False prophets. 1 Jn.4:1-3
False teachers. Tit.1:16; 2 Pt.2:1; Jude 4
Judas
Double-dealing; deception; hypocrisy. Mk.14:43-45
Why a disciple failed & ended up doomed. Mk.14:10-11
Peter. Jn.18:12-27
A lesson in failure. Mk.14:66-72
A look at Peter's **d.** of Christ. Mt.26:69-75
The great tragedy of **d.** Lk.22:54-62
The antichrist. 1 Jn.2:22
The world & the Jews. Jn.18:19-24; Acts 3:13-14
Whosoever--anyone. Mt.10:33; Mk.8:38

Caused by.
Being overconfident. Mt.26:33-35; Mk.14:31
Carnal commitment. Lk.22:33-34
Discussed. Mt.26:69; Mk.14:10-11; 14:66-72
Following at a distance; sitting down among the crowd. Lk.22:54-55
Hypocrisy, false works. Tit.1:16
Two causes. Jn.13:36-38

Discussed. Mt.10:32-33; 1 Jn.2:18-23; 2 Jn.7-13

Duty.
Not to **d.** Christ. Rev.2:13; 3:8
To confess Christ, not deny Him. Mt.10:32; Lk.12:8; Ro.10:9-10; 1 Jn.2:23; 4:15
To **d.** oneself & take up the cross, & follow Christ. Mt.16:24; Mk.8:34; Lk.9:23
To **d.** ungodliness & worldly lusts, not Christ. Tit.2:11-15

Kinds of. Three **k.** Mt.26:69-75; Lk.22:54-62

Meaning. Mt.16:24

Repentance of. Example of Peter. Mk.14:72

Results.
Christ will be ashamed of the person in the day of judgment. Mk.8:38
Determines a person's destiny. Ro.9:5
Shall not have the Father. 1 Jn.2:23
Will be **d.** before the angels of God. Lk.12:9
Will be **d.** before the Father of heaven. Mt.10:33
Will be **d.** the right to reign with Christ. 2 Tim.2:12

Warning against.
D. is illogical & inconsistent. Mt.12:22-30; 12:27-28
Fear denying Christ. Lk.12:4-12
The attacks of Satan. Lk.22:31-38
The great tragedy of **d.** Lk.22:54-62

What it is that people **d.**
Christ & His words. Mk.8:38
Christ Himself. Mt.10:33; Lk.12:9; Tit.1:16
God. Tit.1:16
That Jesus is the Christ, the Savior of the world. 1 Jn.2:22-23, cp. 1 Jn.4:1-3
The doctrine & teachings of the Word of God. 2 Pt.2:1
The faith. 1 Tim.5:8
The faith of Christ. Rev.2:13
The Father & the Son. 1 Jn.2:22-23
The Holy One & the Just, Christ Himself. Acts 3:14
The Lord's death. 2 Pt.2:1
The name of Christ. Rev.3:8
The only God & our Lord Jesus Christ. Jude 4
The power of godliness. 2 Tim.3:5
The resurrection of the dead. Lk.20:27

DENYING SELF (See CROSS, DAILY-- SELF DENIAL)

DEPART
Meaning. Mt.7:23; 2 Tim.4:6

DEPOSIT
Meaning. 2 Cor.1:21-22; 5:5; Eph.1:13-14

DEPRAVED - DEPRAVITY (See MAN, Depravity)
Caused by.
A love of darkness. Jn.3:19
An evil heart. Mt.15:1-20; Mk.7:14-23
Illegitimate birth. Jn.8:41-47
Sinful & evil behavior. Ro.3:9-20
Denied. By man. 1 Jn.1:8
Discussed. Jn.8:41-47; Ro.3:9-20; Eph.2:17-19; Tit.3:3

Duty.
Not to partake of the Lord's Supper with **d.** in one's heart. 1 Cor.5:7-8
Not to use Christian liberty as a cloak, an excuse to hold **d** against someone. 1 Pt.2:16
To be as children in **d.**, having nothing to with **d.** 1 Cor.14:20
To lay aside all **d.** 1 Pt.2:1
To put away **d.**, all **d.** Eph.4:31; Col.3:8

Fact.
Discussed. 1 Jn.1:8
Should not cause man to despair, but lead to his salvation. Ro.3:9-20
Shown by cursing. Mt.5:37
The mind & conscience of all unbelievers are defiled. Tit.1:15-16

Meaning. Ro.1:29; Eph.4:31; Col.3:8-11; 1 Pt.2:1

Of the heart. What defiles the heart. Mt. 15:17-20

Result.
A hard & unrepentant heart. Ro.2:5
Cannot keep from sinning. 2 Pt.2:14
Judgment of. Death. Ro.1:29-32, esp. 32

Trait - Characteristic of.
False leaders & teachers within the church. 3 Jn.10
The ungodly & unrighteous. Ro.1:18, 29-32
Unbelievers. Tit.3:3

To labor so that Christ may be formed in our lives. Gal.4:19

To meditate in God's Word. Let it abide within. Jn.5:38

To offer our bodies as a living sacrifice. Ro.12:1

To sit at Christ's feet. Lk.10:38-42

To take time alone with God & to rest. Lk.9:10

Fact. Are changed into the image of Christ daily. 2 Cor.3:18

Need - Essential.

Concentrating on Christ's death. Mt.20:17

Failure. Reasons. Mt.6:6

Not to stay on the mountain top. Mt.17:14

Paul sought to be alone before facing Jerusalem. Acts 20:13

Sacrificial love & faith. Mt.26:6-13

To be with Jesus. Mt.10:1

To guard against inconsistency. Mt.6:6

To pray night & day. 1 Th.3:10; 1 Tim.5:5

To pray to God always. Acts 10:2

To serve God with fasting & prayer night & day. Lk.2:37

Glory of **d**. Purpose is to minister. Mt.17:14

Of Jesus. (See **JESUS CHRIST**, Prayer Life of)

Arose early in the morning. Mk.1:35

Prepared Himself spiritually. Mk.11:11

Spent the nights of His last week alone with God. Lk.21:37

Purpose of.

To glorify God in our bodies & spirits. 1 Cor.6:19-20

To know the Father. How. Jn.14:6

To minister. Mt.17:14

Results. Boldness and power. Acts 4:13-14

Source - Why God should have our **d**.

Because of Christ's glory in the believer. 2 Cor.3:18

Because of the great price paid for our salvation by Christ's death. 1 Cor.6:19-20; 2 Cor.5:15

Because of the mercies of God. Ro.12:1

Verses. List of. Lk.9:10; 10:41-42

DIANA (See **ARTEMIS**)

DIDYMUS

The Apostle. Discussed. Mk.3:18

DIETARY LAWS (See **LAW**)

DIFFICULTIES

Handled by faith. Mt.17:20

DILIGENCE - DILIGENTLY (See **ENDURANCE; EFFORT; PERSEVERANCE; STEADFASTNESS; ZEAL**)

D. is a special charge given to the minister. 2 Tim.4:1-5

Duty.

Not to lag behind in **d**. Ro.12:11

To abound in all **d**. 2 Cor.8:7

To act & act now. Lk.9:59-60; 17:7-10

To add seven things to one's faith. 2 Pt.1:5-7

To be **d**. & not lazy. Heb.6:11-12

To be **d**. in looking after one another. Heb.12:15

To be **d**. in seeking souls. Ro.9:3; 10:1; 1 Cor.9:22

To keep your spiritual fervor. Ro.12:11

To **d**. follow every good work. 1 Tim.5:10

To **d**. search the Word of God. 1 Pt.1:10

To **d**. seek God. Heb.11:6

To **d**. serve day & night. Lk.17:7-10

To **d**. speak & teach the things of the Lord. Acts 18:25

To **d**. work for the Lord. 1 Cor.15:58

To labor diligently until Jesus returns. Lk.19:13

To labor even if tired. Lk.9:11

To make one's call & election sure. 2 Pt.1:10

To make sure one is found in peace & is blameless before God. 2 Pt.3:14

To rule with **d**., to be **d**. in using one's gifts. Ro.12:8

Meaning. 2 Pt.3:14

DIONYSIUS

A judge in Athens. Led to Christ by Paul. Acts 17:34

DIOTREPHES

Divisive church leader. 3 Jn.9-11

DIRECT

Meaning. 2 Th.3:3-5

DISAGREEMENT

Caused by.

Arguing over ministers, which one is better. 1 Cor.1:11-16, esp. 11

Biting & devouring one another. Gal.5:15

Differences of conviction. Acts 15:36-41

Discussed. Acts 15:36-41; Tit.3:2

Duty. To turn away from. Tit.3:9

Honest **d**. Study of. Acts 15:36-41

Meaning. Ro.2:8; 1 Cor.1:11

Results - Signs of **d**.

A great sense of unworthiness. Lk.5:8

A pricking, convicting, bothersome conscience & heart. Acts 9:5

Obedience. Doing what Christ demands. Acts 9:5-6, cp. 1-11

Reaction, a defensive attitude. Jn.20:24-25, cp. 26-29

Trembling, but rejecting & becoming harder. Acts 24:24-25

Verses. List of. Ro.2:8

DISAPPOINTMENT (See **DISSATISFACTION; DISCOURAGEMENT; SIN**, Results)

DISCERN - DISCERNMENT (See **DISTINGUISHING**)

Duty.

To **d**. both good & evil. Heb.5:14

To test the spirits in teachers. 1 Jn.4:1-6

Source of **d**.

A spiritual gift. 1 Cor.12:10

The Holy Spirit. 1 Cor.2:12-14

The Word of God. Heb.4:12

DISCIPLE - DISCIPLES (See **APOSTLES; BELIEVERS; DISCIPLESHIP; LABORERS; MINISTERS**)

Ambition of. Seek positions of power. Mt.18:1; Mk.9:33-37

Behavior.

Four essential laws. Lk.17:1-10

Rules for. Mt.5:1-7:29

Call. (See **CALL**)

Called, appointed, changed. Mk.3:13-19

Commitment & commissioning **c**. Mt.10:1-4

Jesus chooses His men. Who & why. Lk.6:12-19

Kind of person called. Mk.1:16-20

Of Matthew. Mt.9:9-13

Of the twelve. Mt.4:18-22; 10:1-4

Steps to **c**. Lk.5:1-11; 6:12-19

Three different calls. Mt.10:1-4

To be "with Jesus." Mt.10:1

Who Christ called. Mk.1:16-20

Character - Traits.

Discussed. Mt.5:13-16

Genuine vs. counterfeit **d**. Lk.6:46-49

Heroic **d**. Acts 18:18-22

Hypocritical; counterfeit **d**. Jn.6:61-62; 12:4-8

Indisputable **d**. Acts 18:1-17

Kind of men they were. Mt.4:18-22; 5:13; Mk.1:16-20

Light of the world. Mt.5:14

Salt of the earth. Mt.5:13

Supreme **d**. Jn.12:3

Deserted Christ. (See **APOSTASY; DENIAL**)

Disbelief of.

Disbelieved the predictions of Jesus' death. Lk.9:44-45

Disbelieved the resurrection of Christ. Lk.24:9-11

Discussed. Mt.5:1-2

Duty.

To be conformed to Christ. Lk.6:40

To be responsible. World's fate determined by. Mk.6:30

To be with Jesus. Mt.10:1

To fear hypocrisy. Lk.12:1-3

To go forth. Equipping; six instructions. Mk.6:7-13

Essential.

Compassion & reproduction. Mt.5:1-2

Discussed. Mt.8:19-20; 8:20; 8:21

Must be as a little child. Mt.18:1-4

Personal attachment. Mt.4:18-20

Failure of.

Hiding after the death of Jesus. Jn.20:19-23

Power lost. Lk.9:37-40

Spiritualized Jesus' death & resurrection. Mt.17:22; 18:1

Worldly ambition. Seek worldly greatness & position. Mt.18:1; Mk.9:33-37

False. (See **APOSTASY; DENIAL; PROFESSION ONLY**)

Lays no foundation. Lk.6:49

Impact of Jesus upon.

Attracted to Jesus. Mt.8:21-22

Three responses to Christ. Jn.6:66-71

Young **d**. & theologians. Mk.2:18-22

Message. (See **GOSPEL; MESSAGE; MINISTERS**)

Preeminence of Christ. Mk.1:7-8

Repentance. Mk.6:12

Method.

Number needs to be limited. Mt.10:2

Sent forth two by two. Mt.10:3-4

Mission - Commission. (See **COMMISSION; MISSION**)

Discussed. Mt.5:13-16; 28:19-20

Of Jesus. Numbered many more than just the twelve. Lk.10:1

Position - Privileges. (See **BELIEVER**, Position; Privileges)
  Are sons of God. Lk.15:30; Ro.8:16-17; Gal.4:4-7
  Not above the Master, but treated the same as the Master. Lk.6:40
Power of. (See **POWER**)
Resources. (See **RESOURCES**)
Secret **d**.
  Chief rulers. Jn.12:42
  Joseph of Arimathea. Stirred to step forth by the cross. Lk.23:50-56
  Nicodemus. Jn.3:1-2
Training of.
  Intensive training on the death of Christ. Mt.16:13-20; 16:21-28; 17:1-13; 17:22; 17:24-27; 20:17; 20:20-28
  On the death of Christ. Mt.26:1-2
  Sermon on the Mount given for preparation. Mt.5:1-2

DISCIPLESHIP (See **CROSS--SELF DENIAL; DEDICATION; DISCIPLE; SACRIFICE**)
Call of. Step to **d**. Lk.5:1-11
Cost - Demands of. Mt.8:18-22; 10:34-42
  Discussed. Mk.8:34-38
  Everything. Mk.2:14
  Great cost. Lk.9:57-62
  Must give all that one **is & has**. Mt.19:21-22; 19:23-26; 19:27-30; Lk.14:25-35; 18:18-23
Discussed. 2 Tim.2:2
  New converts. Acts 13:5-6
  Reason people follow Christ. Lk.7:11
  Terms of. Lk.9:23-27
Duty. (See **BELIEVER**, Duty)
  To be conformed to Christ. Lk.6:40
  To be responsible. World's fate is determined by. Mk.6:30
  To disciple young people. Ph.1:1
  To fear hypocrisy. Lk.12:1-3
  To go forth. Equipping; six instructions. Mk.6:7-13
  To make disciples. Acts 13:5-6; 14:21; 16:1-3; Ph.1:1; 1 Tim.1:1-2
Eagerness of Jesus to make disciples. Jn.1:38-39
Essential.
  Compassion & reproduction. Mt.5:1-2
  Four laws. Lk.17:1-10
  Love. Jn.13:34-35
  Love & obedience. Jn.14:15
  Must bear fruit. Jn.15:8
  Must bear one's cross & deny oneself. Mt.16:24; Lk.9:23; 9:57-62
  Must continue in the Word of Christ. Jn.8:31
  Must forsake all that one has. Lk.14:33
  Personal attachment. Mt.4:18-20
  To be with Jesus. Mt.10:1
  To put Christ before all, even one's family. Lk.14:26
Examples of. Lk.9:57-62
  Barnabas discipled. John Mark. Acts 13:5; 15:37
  Paul discipled.
    Aquila & Priscilla. Acts 18:2-3
    John Mark. Acts 13:5
    Several men. Acts 20:4
    Silas. Acts 15:40
    Timothy. Acts 16:1-4

Failure of.
  Being a secret disciple. Lk.23:50-56
  Being an average disciple. Mt.8:21-22
  Failing to count the cost. Lk.9:57-62
  Having a divided allegiance. Lk.9:59-60
  Lack of commitment. Three examples. Lk.9:57-62
  Looking back. Lk.9:61-62
  Putting family before Christ. Lk.9:59-62; 12:49-53; 14:18-20; 14:26
  Putting wealth before Christ. Lk. 18:18-30
  Reluctant to respond to the call of Christ. Lk.5:1-11; 9:57-62
  Seeking worldly greatness & position. Mt.18:1; Mk.9:33-37
False **d**. (See **APOSTASY; DENIAL; PROFESSION, FALSE**)
Meaning. Lk.9:23
Method.
  Method used by Christ. Mk.6:7
  Number needs to be limited. Mt.10:2
  Two by two. Mt.10:3-4
Rules for. Mt.5:1-7:29
Steps to.
  Discussed. Lk.5:1-11
  Illustrated by Andrew. Jn.1:35-37
True vs. false. Two foundations. Lk.6:46-49
Verses. List of. Lk.9:61-62

DISCIPLINE, CHURCH (See **CHURCH DISCIPLINE**)
Described. Handed over to Satan. 1 Tim.1:19-20

DISCIPLINE, GODLY (See **CHASTISEMENT**)

DISCIPLINE, PERSONAL (See **CROSS, DAILY; MIND; SELF-CONTROL**)
Duty.
  To control the mind, cast down arguments or imaginations. 2 Cor.10:4
  To **d**. like an Olympian athlete. 2 Tim.2:5
  To die daily. (See **CROSS**)
  To lay aside every weight. Heb.12:1
  To maintain military **d**. 2 Tim.2:3-4
  To work like a hard-working farmer. 2 Tim.2:3-6
Essential.
  For believers. Great **d**. required. 1 Cor.9:24-27
  For ministers. Great **d**. required. 1 Cor.9:24-27
Without **d**. Meaning. 2 Tim.3:2-4

DISCORD (See **DIVISION; STRIFE**)
Meaning. Gal.5:19-21

DISCOURAGEMENT (See **DISSATISFACTION; HOPELESSNESS; SIN**, Results; **SORROW**)
Caused by. Devastation of hope & life. Lk.24:13-14
Meaning. 2 Cor.4:1
Verses. List of. Ro.5:6-7
Victory over. Paul conquered. Acts 15:41

DISCREET (See **SELF-CONTROLLED**)

DISCRIMINATION (See **BARRIERS; BIGOTRY; DIVISION; PARTIALITY; PREJUDICE**)
Broken down.
  By Christ. Eph.2:13-18
  Jews barricaded the Gentiles from God. Eph.2:11-12

Described. Physical, ideological & spiritual. Mt.8:5-13
Discussed. Ro.12:16; Jas.2:1-13
Example.
  The Syrophencian woman. Mk.7:25
  The woman with a hemorrhage. Mt.9:20
Fact. No **d**. with God. Acts 10:34; Ro.2:11; Eph.6:9; Col.1:26-27; 3:25; 1 Pt.1:17
Jews vs. the Gentiles. One race vs. another. Mk.7:24-30; Eph.2:11-12
Overcome by.
  Compassion. Lk.10:33-37
  Cornelius & Peter. Acts 10:1-48; 11:1-18
  Faith. 2 Pt.1:1
  Jesus. Lk.17:15-19
  Witnessing. Jn.4:1-42

DISEASE (See **HEALING; SICKNESS; SUFFERING**)
Caused by. Ultimate cause. Mt.8:17
Jesus bore our **d**. Mt.8:17
Vs. demon possession. Mk.3:15

DISHONESTY (See **CHEATING; HYPOCRISY; STEALING**)

DISHONOR (See **SHAME**)
Discussed. Jn.4:43-45
Of Christ.
  By His hometown. Jn.4:44
  By some who were close to Him. Jn.4:44

DISOBEDIENCE (See **BACKSLIDING; OBEDIENCE; SIN; TRANSGRESSION; UNBELIEF**)
Caused by.
  Neglecting the great salvation in Christ. Heb.2:2-3
  Stumbling at the Word of God. 1 Pt.2:7-8
  The nature of sin, the depraved nature of man. Ro.5:19, cp. 12-21
  The worldly who deceive. Eph.5:6
Discussed. Ro.2:6-10; Tit.3:3
Influence of. Mt.5:19
Judgment of.
  Shall be called least in the kingdom of heaven. Mt.5:19
  Shall not escape judgment. Heb.2:2-3
  Shall suffer the vengeance of God. 2 Th.1:8
  Shall suffer the wrath of God. Eph.5:6
Meaning. Heb.2:2
To parents. Meaning. Ro.1:30; 2 Tim. 3:2-4
Who is **d**. Mt.5:19

DISORDER
Meaning. 2 Cor.12:19-21

DISPENSATION (See **PUT INTO EFFECT**)
Old vs. New **d**. Lk.16:16; 16:17-18

DISPUTE - DISPUTING (See **ARGUE-ARGUING; CONTENTION; STRIFE**)
Essential. To **d**. in preaching. Acts 17:16

DISQUALIFIED
Meaning. Lk.9:25; 1 Cor.9:27
Who is **d**.
  Sinful angels were. 2 Pt.2:4
  The undisciplined, those who lack self-control will be **d**. 1 Cor.9:27
  The worthless will be **d**. Mt.25:14-30, esp. 30

DISSATISFACTION (See **DISCOUR-AGEMENT; HOPELESSNESS; SIN,** Results)
Caused by.
Sin. Jn.4:15
Worldliness, indulgence, spiritual hunger. Lk.15:14-16
Discussed. Jn.4:15

DISSENSIONS (See **ARGUE; CON-TENTION; DIVISION; STRIFE**)
Against government. Discussed. Ro.13:1-7
Against the Lordship of Christ. Mt. 12:14-16
Answer to **d**.
Being gentle to all men. 2 Tim.2:24
Heeding the Word of Christ. Lk.22:24-27
Humility. Esteeming others better than oneself. Ph.2:3-4
Serving others. Lk.22:24-27
Withdrawing from controversy. 1 Tim.6:4-5
Withdrawing from false teachers. 1 Tim.6:3-5
Characteristic - Trait. Of false teachers. Jude 8, 11
Meaning. Ro.13:13; Gal.5:19-21; Jas. 3:14-16
Result.
Confusion & evil works. Jas.3:16
Shall not inherit the kingdom of God. Gal.5:19-21
Source - What causes **s**.
Carnality. 1 Cor.3:3
Controversial questions. 1 Tim.6:4
False teachers. 1 Tim.6:4, cp. 3-5
Judging ministers. 1 Cor.3:3-4
Selfish ambition. Lk.22:24
The flesh. Gal.5:19-20
The heart. Jas.3:14
Unprofitable talk. 2 Tim.2:14

DISSIPATION
Meaning. Lk.21:34-35

DISTRESS - DISTRESSED (See **AF-FLICTIONS; CRUSHED; SUFFER-ING**)
Caused by.
Being without hope. 1 Th.4:13
Death. To be conquered. Jn.20:14-16
Death of a loved one. Jn.11:28-37; Acts 9:39
Nature of. Often self-centered. Jn.16:5
Meaning. Mk.3:5; 8:12; Lk.16:24; Ro. 2:9; 1 Th.3:7-10

DISTRESS; PERSECUTION; SUFFER-INGS; TRIALS & TRIBULATION
Ct. glory. An eternal glory. 2 Cor.4:17-18
Meaning. 2 Cor.6:4-5; 1 Th.3:7-10

DISTRUST (See **UNBELIEF**)
How one **d**. God. Acts 5:1-4
Nature of. Prefers not to be disturbed. Jn.11:38-40
Results.
Prayerlessness. Jas.4:3
Temptations and trials. Jas.4:3

DIVINE (See **GOD**)

DIVINATION (See **ASTROLOGY; SOOTHSAYER; SORCERY; SUPER-STITION**)

DIVISION--DISSENSION
Answer to.
Being a wise builder. 1 Cor.3:10-17
Being covered by Jesus Christ. 2 Cor.5:18-19; 5:21
Believers are to help heal. Ph.4:3
Discussed.
Four answers. 2 Tim.2:14-26
Steps to correction. Mt.18:15-20
God's wisdom. 1 Cor.2:6-13
Humility. 1 Cor.1:26-31
Knowing one's true father. 1 Cor.4:14-21
Laboring together with God. 1 Cor.3:5-9
Letting God judge. 1 Cor.4:1-5
Marking those who cause **d**. Ro.16:17-20
Not judging ministers. 1 Cor.4:6-13
Prayer. Primary answer is prayer. Mt.18:19
Renouncing self-deception. 1 Cor.3:18-23
Replacing **d**. with the Word. 1 Pt.2:1-3
Sound preaching. 1 Cor.2:1-5
The cross. 1 Cor.1:17-25
Understanding the spiritual stages of man. 1 Cor.2:14-3:4
Caused by.
A divisive man. 2 Cor.2:5
Bad feelings. Proves four things. Mt.6:15
Barriers. Mt.8:5-13
Being arrogant. 1 Cor.4:18-21
Carnal wisdom. 1 Cor.1:17-25; 2:6-13; 3:18-23
Carnality. (See **JUDGING**)1 Cor.3:3
Christ sending a sword to the earth. Mt.10:34-37
Cliques. 1 Cor.1:10-16
Criticism over finances. 2 Cor.11:7-12
Discussed. Ph.2:3-4; 4:2-3
Divided opinion. Acts 15:36-40
Divisive church leaders. 3 Jn.9-11
False teaching. 1 Jn.2:18-19; 2 Jn.10-11
Favoring one minister or preacher over another. 1 Cor.1:12; 3:5-9; 4:1-5; 4:6-13
Five causes. Acts 6:1
Following wrong instructors. 1 Cor.4:15
Judging ministers. 1 Cor.1:10-16; 4:1-5; 4:6-13
Judging others. 1 Cor.4:1-5
Complaining & arguing. Ph.2:14
Opposing one who differs. Mk.9:38
Pride. 1 Cor.3:18-23
Self-glorying. 1 Cor.1:29; 3:21
Super-spirituality. 1 Cor.1:12; 2:6-13
The devil. 2 Tim.2:24-26
Troublemakers. 1 Cor.3:17
Described as.
Earthly, sensual, devilish. Jas.3:14-16
Judging others. Ro.2:1
Discussed. 1 Cor.1:10-16; Tit.3:2; 3:9; 3:10-11
Duty. (See **BROTHERHOOD; LOVE; UNITY**)
Discussed. Ro.16:17-20
To live in peace if possible. Ro.12:18
To mark divisive people. Ro.16:17-20
Examples.
Jews vs. Gentiles. Mk.7:24-30; Eph.2:11-12
Two ladies. Ph.4:2-3
Of families. Caused by Christ. Mt.10:34-37

Of the world. Contrasted with unity. Jn.17:11
Results in.
A divided church. Lk.11:17; 1 Cor.1:10-16; 11:18
A split & in being ruined. Mt.12:25-26
Cliques. 1 Cor.1:10-16
Destruction. Mk.3:22-30
Discussed. 3 Jn.9-11
Divided allegiance. Mt.12:25-26
Judgment. Are to be judged. Ro.2:1-16
Opposing the prayer of Christ. Jn.17:11, 21-23
Three things. 1 Cor.1:13-14
Vs. peacemakers. Mt.5:9

DIVORCE
Allowance for. Mt.5:32; 19:7-8
Caused by.
Adultery. Mt.5:31-32
Hardness of heart. Mk.10:2-6
Marrying a divorced person. Lk.16:18
Discussed.
Christian & unbelieving spouse. 1 Cor.7:12-16
Christian couple & **d**. 1 Cor.7:10-11
The real meaning of divorce. Mt.5:31-32
The sanctity of marriage. Mt.19:1-12
Old vs. New Testament law. Mk.10:5
Problem of. Positions of. Mk.10:1-12
Remarriage is adultery. Lk.16:18
Schools of thought. Conservative vs. liberal. Mk.10:1-12

DOCETISM
Discussed. Col. Introd.

DOCTRINE (See **TEACHING**)
Duty. To preach sound doctrine. 2 Tim.4:2
Elementary **d**. ABC's of **d**. Heb.6:1-2
Fact. Is not enough by itself. Rev.2:1-7
Of church.
Are to guard. 2 Jn.7-11
Discussed. 2 Jn.7-13
Rejected. In the last days people will reject sound **d**. 2 Tim.4:3-4
Source. To be the Word of God. 2 Tim.3:14-17
The message of sound **d**. Tit.2:1-3:11
Theological basis of. The grace of God. Tit.2:11-15

DOCTRINE, FALSE (See **TEACHERS, FALSE; TEACHING, FALSE**)

DOERS (See **OBEDIENCE**)

DOG
Discussed. Mk.7:27
Symbol of.
False teachers. Ph.3:2
Gentiles. Mt.15:26; Mk.7:27
Unbelievers. Mt.7:6; Rev.22:15

DOMINION
Of Christ.
Is due praise & **d**, forever & ever. 1 Pt.4:11; Jude 25; Rev.1:5-6
Is the Creator of all **d**., principalities & powers--of all things. Col.1:16-17
Is to be an eternal **d**. Lk.1:31-33
Over all heavenly angels & beings & rule & authority. 1 Pt.3:22; Eph.1:19-21
Over all things. Jn.3:35

Over death & the fear of death.
Jn.5:28-30; Ro.6:8-10; Heb.2:14-15;
Rev.1:18
Over judgment. Jn.5:22-23, 27
Over man's destiny. Jn.5:24-25
Over nature. Mt.8:23-27; Mk.1:27
Over physical disease. Mk.1:23-27
Over the church. Eph.1:22-23
Of God. Is due glory & **d**. forever & ever.
1 Pt.5:11
Of man.
Has **d**. over animals. Jas.3:7
Is held responsible for the world.
Lk.13:6-9; 20:9
Is interrelated with creation & the
world. Ro.8:19-22
Lost his **d**. over the world, but is to
have it returned in the future.
Heb.2:6-8
Of Satan.
Has power over death. Heb.2:14-16
Is the father of unbelievers. Jn.8:44,
cp. 42-44
Is the prince of the power of the air. Eph.2:2
Is the prince of the world. Jn.12:31; 14:30
Rules over men. Acts 26:18; 1 Jn.3:10
Rules over principalities, powers, rul-
ers, & spiritual wickedness. Eph.6:12
Rules over the world. Mt.4:8-10;
Lk.4:6; Jn.12:31; 14:30; 2 Cor.4:4

DOOR (See **GATE**)
Symbolic use of.
The **d**. of Christ. He is the **d**. of the
sheep. Ro.5:2; Eph.2:18; Heb.10:19-22
The **d**. of faith. Acts 14:27
The **d**. of opportunity. 1 Cor.16:9;
2 Cor.2:12; Col.4:3; Rev.3:8
The **d**. of Revelation. Three **d**. de-
scribed. Rev.4:1-2
The **d**. of salvation. Mt.25:10
The **d**. of the heart. To open & invite
Jesus to enter. Lk.24:28-32; Rev.3:20
The **d**. of the Lord's return. Mt.24:33
The **d**. of heaven.
Discussed. Rev.21:12-13
Shall never be shut. Rev.21:25
The **d**. of hell cannot prevail against or
stop the gospel. Mt.6:18
The **d**. of life. A broad & a narrow **d**.
Mt.7:13-14
The narrow **d**. Make every effort to enter.
Lk.13:24

DORCAS
Discussed. Acts 9:36-43

DOUBLE-MINDED (See **DECISION;
FICKLENESS; INSTABILITY; NEU-
TRALITY**)
Described. Mental assent. Ro.10:16-17
Duty.
Cannot fellowship with the Lord & the
world. 1 Cor.10:21
Cannot serve two masters. Lk.16:13
Not to waver in faith, tossed to & fro.
Jas.1:5-8
To decide. Not to be double-minded.
Lk.9:57-62; 11:23; 14:18-20; 16:13;
Jas.1:5-8
To purify the heart from **d**. Jas.4:8
Fact.
Is unstable. Jas.1:6-8
Shows a need to purify the heart. Jas.4:8
Results. Makes one unworthy to be a
leader. Lk.23:2-7

DOUBLE TONGUED (See **SINCERE**)
Meaning. 1 Tim.3:8

DOUBT - DOUBTING (See **UNBELIEF**)
Deliverance from **d**.
By doing the will of God. Jn.7:16-17
By guarding against being carried
away with doubts & strange teach-
ings. Heb.13:9, cp. Col.2:8
By guarding against empty discussion.
1 Tim.1:5-6; Tit.1:10
By guarding against perverse & wrong
teachings. Acts 20:28-31
By not listening to false teaching &
speculations & questions. 1 Tim.1:3-4
By searching the Scripture. Jn.5:39;
Acts 17:11-12; 2 Tim.3:16; Heb.4:12
By turning away from all fables, all
fictional & false teaching. 1 Tim.1:4;
4:7; 2 Tim.4:4; Tit..1:14; 2 Pt.1:16
Duty. Must believe and not **d**. Jas.1:5-8
Results of **d**.
Chastisement & punishment. Lk.1:19-20,
cp. 5-22
Insecurity & instability. Jas.1:5-8
What is questioned & doubted.
The claims of Christ to be the Messiah,
the Savior of the world, the Son of
God. Lk.7:19-23; Jn.7:3-5; 7:25-31;
7:40-44; 8:12-59; 10:22-39
The power of Christ to raise the dead.
Jn.11:39
The power of God to deliver one from
terrible trouble & circumstances.
Mk.4:40; Acts 12:14-15
The power of God's healing power to-
day. Mt.14:31; 17:17
The preaching of the cross. 1 Cor. 1:17-
25
The resurrection of Christ. Jn.20:24-29
The resurrection of the human body.
1 Cor.15:12
The return of Christ & the end of the
world. 2 Pt.3:3-4
The Word of God. Lk.24:25

DOVE
Described. Mt.10:16
Discussed. Jn.1:32-33
Symbol of.
Being harmless & peaceful. Mt.10:16
The Holy Spirit. Jn.1:32-34

DRAGNET
Described. Mt.13:47
Parable of. Separating the bad from the
good. Mt.13:47-50

DRAGON OF REVELATION, THE (See
SATAN)
Discussed. Rev.12:1-5; 12:6-17; 13:4; 13:11

DRAW - DRAWN - DRAW NEAR (See
**DEVOTION - DEVOTIONS; COM-
MITMENT**)
Source.
God Himself. God **d**. man for salva-
tion. Jn.6:44-46; 6:65
Hope. The hope for perfection.
Heb.7:19
To Christ. God **d**. people to Christ by the
cross. Jn.6:44-46; 6:65
To God. Duty.
To draw near God. Heb.10:22
To draw near God & repent. Jas.4:8

DREAMS
Characteristic - Trait of. False teachers.
Jude 8
Kinds of. Two kinds. Jude 8
Sin of. Jude 8
Used by God.
To give direction. Mt.1:19-20; 2:11-13, 19
To reveal truth. Acts 10:9-17
To warn people. Mt.27:19

DRESS (See **CLOTHING**)
Can cause problems.
Anxiety & pressure. Mt.6:28-34
Being attracted & being in submission
to someone other than one's own
spouse. 1 Tim.2:9-10; 1 Pt.3:1; 3:5
Being extravagant & wasteful in dress
& life. Lk.7:25; 16:19
Being identified with the world & the
heathen. Mt.6:32
Being immodest & insensitive.
1 Tim.2:9-10
Ignoring God and people. Lk.16:19-31
Ignoring inner beauty. 1 Pt.3:1-6
Rebelling & being unfaithful.
1 Tim.2:9-15; 1 Pt.3:1-6
Discussed. 1 Tim.2:9-15; 1 Pt.3:1-6; 3:3;
3:4-6
Duty - Proper **d**.
Must be based upon faith & love.
1 Tim.2:15
Not to dishonor or embarrass one's
spouse. 1 Cor.11:2-16
Not to dress to attract attention.
Mk.12:38; Lk.20:46; 1 Tim.2:9-10
Not to judge people by their **d**., nor
give preference to people because of
their clothing. Jas.2:1-4
To attract one's own spouse. 1 Pt.3:1; 3:4-6
To be modest. 1 Cor.11:2-16; 1 Tim.2:9-10
To be modest & sensitive. 1 Tim.2:9-10
To dress as a godly person. 1 Tim.2:9-10,
cp. Mt.3:4
To seek God first. Mt.6:31-34
To show pure behavior. 1 Pt.3:2
Watch one's dressing - demeanor.
1 Tim.2:9-10
How to **d**. 1 Pt.3:1-6
Results of proper dress.
Discussed. 1 Tim.2:9-15
Makes one a daughter of faith. 1 Pt.3:4-6
Saves one in childbearing. 1 Tim.2:15
Wins an unbelieving spouse. 1 Pt.3:1-2
Warning against.
Being overly dressed - living extrava-
gantly. 1 Tim.2:9
D. to draw attention. Mk.12:38;
Lk.20:45-47
D. in extravagant styles. Mk.12:38;
Lk.7:25
Exposure of the body. Drinking &
dancing parties. Mk.6:24-25
Worrying, thinking too much about **d**.
Mt.6:28-34

DRESS MODESTLY
Meaning. 1 Tim.2:9-10

DRINK - DRINKING
Symbol of.
D. Christ, the living water. Jn.4:13-14
Partaking of Christ's blood & becom-
ing related to Him. Jn.6:52-58
The Holy Spirit & the abundant life He
gives to believers. Jn.7:37-39

DROWN - DROWNING
Form of capital punishment. Mt.18:6; Mk.9:42
Symbol of. **D**. in lusts. 1 Tim.6:9

DRUGS (See **DRUNKENNESS**)
Sin of. 1 Pt.4:3

DRUNKENNESS
Discussed. Eph.5:18
Duty.
Leaders are to abstain from **d**. 1 Tim.3:2-3
Not to be filled with wine, but with the Spirit of God. Eph.5:18
To separate from those who drink. 1 Cor.5:11; Gal.5:19-21
Fact.
Is a characteristic & trait of the world, not of believers. 1 Pt.4:1-5
Is a work of the flesh, a work that struggles & war against the spirit. Gal.5:19-21
Judgment of. God shall judge. 1 Cor.5:13, cp. 11
Shall give an a count to Christ who is ready to judge. 1 Pt.4:3-5
Shall not inherit the kingdom of God. 1 Cor.6:9-10
Meaning. Ro.13:13; 1 Cor.5:11; 6:10; Gal.5:19-21; 1 Pt.4:3
Results. In a partying & lustful spirit. Mt.14:6-8; 24:38; Mk.6:21-22
In being unprepared for the coming of Christ. Mt.24:37-39; Lk.21:34-35
In dulling one's ability to watch for the coming of Christ. 1 Th.5:5-7
In immorality. Ro.13:13; 1 Pt.4:3-4
Six results. Lk.21:34-35

DULL - DULLNESS, SPIRITUAL (See **SLOW**)
Caused by.
Closing one's heart to the truth. Acts 28:27
Failure to be rooted in the Word of God. Heb.5:11-14
Failure to hear the Word of Christ. Jn.8:43
Failure to recognize & discern that Christ is the Savior of the world. Lk.12:56
Failure to seek after God. Ro.3:11
Sin, the love of sin. 2 Tim.3:1-7, esp. 7
Spiritual insensitivity. Lk.9:44-45
Unbelief. Not believing all of the Word of God. Lk.24:25
Describes. Depraved nature. Ro.3:10-12
Verses. List of. Lk.9:44-45

DUTY (See the Subject Desired, Duty of)
Misuse of. Placed before compassion. Lk.10:29-37

DWELL - DWELLING (See **INDWELLING PRESENCE; LIVE; LIVES**)

DYING TO SELF (See **CROSS - SELF-DENIAL**)

E

EAGLES (See **VULTURES**)
Meaning. Lk.17:37
Symbol of judgment. Mt.24:25-28

EAR (See **HEAR - HEARING**)
Fact.
Deaf **e**. can be healed by the power of Christ. Mk.7:32-35
What one speaks to the ears in secret shall be revealed. Lk.12:2-3
The **e**. of believers.
Hears the things of God. 1 Cor.2:9-10
Is blessed, gloriously blessed. Mt.13:16-17
Is to hear the Holy Spirit's message to the church. Rev.2:7, 11, 17, 29; 3:6, 13, 22; 13:9
Is to proclaim what it hears from Christ. Mt.10:27
The **e**. of unbelievers.
Is incapable of hearing (grasping) the things God has prepared for those who love Him. 1 Cor.2:9
Is spiritually deaf. Acts 7:51
Is spiritually dull. Mt.13:15
Itch for teaching that will allow them to live like they want. 2 Tim.4:3-4

EARNEST (See **DEPOSIT**)

EARTH (See **CREATION; END TIME**)
Destruction of. Discussed. 2 Pt.3:10; 3:12
Fact.
Has been corrupted by sin. Ro.8:18-22
Not approved by Christ. Mt.10:34-37
The believer is to inherit the **e**. & the world. Ro.4:13
The destroyers of the **e**. shall be destroyed. Rev.11:18
The meek shall inherit the **e**. Mt.5:5
Fate of.
Natural catastrophes in the end time. Rev.8:6-12; 16:1-21
To be remade, perfected. Surety of. Lk.21:33; 2 Pt.3:10; 3:13
To be shaken, created anew. Heb.12:26-27
Heart of. Meaning. Mt.12:40

EARTH & HEAVENS, NEW
Discussed. Ro.8:18-22; Heb.1:10-12; 12:26-29; 2 Pt.3:1-10; Rev.21:1-8; 22:1-5

EARTHLY NATURE
Meaning. Col.3:5-7

EARTHQUAKE
At Jesus' death. Mt.27:51
At Jesus' resurrection. Mt.28:2
At Philippi. Acts 16:25-26
In the end time.
A catastrophic **e**. will destroy most major cities. Rev.16:18-21
Predicted in the last days. Mt.24:7; Lk.21:11

EASY
Meaning. Mt.11:29-30

EAT - EATING (See **FOOD**)
Described. As partying, drinking, carousing. Mt.24:38
Duty.
Eating too much is a habit of many who walk after the flesh. Ph.3:19
Must not be a stumbling block in **e**. Ro.14:13-21
Not to worry about food. Mt.6:25-34
To give thanks for food. Acts 27:35; 1 Tim.4:4-5
To work for what one **e**., not to bum off others. 2 Th.3:10-12

Warning.
Eating too much makes a person's belly his god. Ph.3:18-19
Eating was the trait of the world that was destroyed in Noah's day. Mt.24:38
The glutton will be emptied & made to hunger. Lk.6:25

EDIFY - EDIFICATION (See **BUILD EACH OTHER UP**)
Duty.
To do all things for **e**. 2 Cor.12:19
To do things that **e**. & not just the things that are lawful. 1 Cor.10:23
To **e**. one another. 1 Th.5:11
To follow after the things that **e**. others. Ro.14:19
To seek to **e**. one's neighbor. Ro.15:2; 1 Th.5:11
To speak only that which **e**. others. Eph.4:29
To use one's spiritual gifts to **e**. the church. 1 Cor.14:3-12; Eph.4:11-12
Hindrances to **e**.
False teaching. 1 Tim.1:3-4
Misusing one's gifts. 1 Cor.14:1-19, esp. 4, 17
How a person **e**. others.
By commending them to the Word of God's grace. Acts 20:32
By exercising one's authority to discipline when needed. 2 Cor.10:8; 13:10
By love. 1 Cor.8:1
By using spiritual gifts for their intended purpose. 1 Cor.14:3-12; Eph.4:11-12
Result. A church grows. Acts 9:31

EDUCATION (See **TEACHERS; TEACHING**)

EFFEMINATE - HOMOSEXUALITY
Meaning. 1 Cor.6:9

EFFORT
Meaning. 2 Pt.3:14

EGNATIAN WAY
The great Roman road. Acts 17:1-9

EGYPT
Jesus led to **E**. for 6 years Mt.2:13-18
Jews often fled to **E**. Mt.2:13
Type. Of the world. Mt.2:13-18

EIMI
I AM. The most basic Name of deity. Meaning. Jn.1:1-2

ELDER SON (See **OLDER SON**)

ELDERLY (See **FAMILY; OLDER MEN AND WOMEN**)
Aged men. Behavior of. Tit.2:2; 1 Tim.5:1
Aged women. Behavior of. Tit.2:3; 1 Tim.5:2
E. fathers. The needed testimony. 1 Jn.2:12-14
E. parents. To be cared for by children. Mk.7:11; 1 Tim.5:4-8

ELDERS (See **BISHOPS; MINISTERS; OLDER MEN AND WOMEN**)
Authority of. Believers to submit to the authority of **e**. 1 Pt.5:5
Discussed. Ph.1:1; 1 Tim.3:1-7; 5:17-20; Tit.1:5-9
Duty of **e**. 1 Pt.5:1-4
Discussed. Tit.1:5-9
To consider & handle problems within the church. Acts 15:6, cp. 15:1-35
To do a good job, do their work well. 1 Tim.5:17
To minister to those in need. Acts 11:29-30
To pray for & minister to the sick. Jas.5:14-15
Duty toward **e**.
Discussed. 1 Tim.5:17-20
To ordain **e**., set them apart. Tit.1:5, cp. Acts 14:23
Example of. Peter. 1 Pt.5:1

ELDERS OF REVELATION, TWENTY-FOUR
Discussed. Rev.4:4
Function. Rev.4:10-11
Worship & praise Christ. For three things. Rev.5:8-10

ELECT - ELECTION (See **CHOSEN ONES; PREDESTINATION**)
Blessings of.
An eternal inheritance. 1 Pt.1:2-4
Grace & peace. 1 Pt.1:2
No charge will ever be made by God against His **e**. Ro.8:33
The **e**. shall be gathered & taken home to be with Christ. Mt.24:31; Mk.13:27
The **e**. will be avenged of all the injustices done against them. Lk.18:7-8
The **e**. will receive salvation with eternal glory. 2 Tim.2:10
Discussed. Ro.9:7-13; 9:14-24; 2 Th.2:13
Duty.
To be diligent to make our calling & **e**. sure. 2 Pt.1:10
To put on several Christian virtues. Col.3:12-13
To stand against deception--no matter how strong. Mt.24:24; Mk.13:22
Fact. God puts up with evil men in order to share His glory with believers. Ro.9:22-24
Proof of. Jacob & Esau. Ro.9:7-13; 9:10-15
Purpose. To separate from the world & to be set apart to God. Col.3:12-14
Source - Basis of **e**.
Faith & acknowledgment of the truth. Tit.1:1, cp. 2 Th.2:13
God's foreknowledge. 1 Pt.1:2
God's grace. Ro.11:5-6
God's purpose. Ro.9:11
The faith & godliness of forefathers. Ro.11:28-29, cp. 25-32
The gospel. 1 Th.1:4-10
Who is **e**.
Angels. 1 Tim.5:21
Believers. Mt.24:22; Mk.13:20; 1 Pt.1:2
Christ. 1 Pt.2:6
Christian women. 2 Jn.1, 13
Church. 1 Pt.5:13
Six points. Ro.9:25-33

ELEMENTARY ELEMENTS - ELEMENTS OF THE WORLD (See **BASIC PRINCIPLES**)

ELEMENTARY TEACHINGS
Duty. To get past the elementary **t**. & to move on & mature. Heb.5:11-6:3

ELEMENTARY TRUTHS
Duty. To move beyond the elementary truths of God's Word & grow. Heb.5:11-6:3

ELEMENTS (See **BASIC PRINCIPLES**)
E. to be destroyed by fire in the end of the world. 2 Pt.3:10-13
Of the world. Meaning. Col.2:8

ELIJAH
Appeared at the transfiguration of Christ. Reason. Mt.17:3; Mk.9:2-4; Lk.9:30-31
Misunderstanding about. Was expected to personally return to earth. Jn.1:20-22
Prophecy. Foresaw the remnant of Israel. Ro.11:2-4
Spirit of Elijah will be present in the last days. Rev.11:5-6

ELIZABETH, MOTHER OF JOHN THE BAPTIST
A picture of godly parents. Lk.1:5-25
A supernatural proclamation. An unusual testimony. Lk.1:39-45

ELYMAS
The title of a sorcerer. Acts 13:8-11

EMBARRASSED
Christ can be put to an open shame. Heb.6:6
Discussed. Things that **e**. one. Lk.9:26
The needs of **e**. men met. Mt.9:1-8

EMBEZZLEMENT
Of the Lord's "possessions" (life, talents, money). Lk.16:1-13
Warning. Discussed. Mt.21:33-41

EMMANUEL
A name of deity. Mt.1:23

EMMAUS
City of. Discussed. Lk.24:13
Two disciples on the road to **E**. joined by Jesus. Lk.24:13-35

EMOTIONS
Sins of. Discussed. Col.3:8-11
Stirring of. Not always wise. Mk.6:45

EMPATHY (See **SYMPATHY**)

EMPLOYEE (See **WAGES**)
Discussed. Eph.6:5-9; Col.3:22-4:1; 1 Tim.6:1-2; 1 Pt.2:18-20
A major world problem. Eph.6:5-9
Discipline of idle workers. 2 Th.3:6-18
Disorderly work. 2 Th.3:6-11
Not to be menpleasers. Eph.6:6
Submit to masters or employers. 1 Pt.2:18-20
The believer & his work. Col.3:22-4:1
Work & employment. 2 Th.3:6-18
Work under God's authority. Eph.6:5-9

Duty.
To be content with one's wages. Lk.3:14
To submit to one's employer. 1 Pt.2:18-20
To work & do what one is hired to do--without complaint. Mt.20:1-16
To work with one's own hands & to not bum off people. 1 Th.4:11-12
Toward a Christian supervisor. 1 Tim.6:1-2
Why God demands that we work. 1 Th.4:11-12
Example of. Paul. Acts 18:3
Fact. Is worth a just wage. Mt.10:10
Problems of. Can a believer serve Christ in any job? 1 Cor.7:20-23
Warning to **e**. Discussed. Mt.21:33-41

EMPLOYER (See **WAGES**)
Discussed. Eph.6:5-9; Col.4:1; Jas.5:4-6
Duty. To pay a just wage. Mt.10:10

EMPLOYMENT (See **LABOR; SERVICE**)
Discussed. Work & **e**. 2 Th.3:6-18
Duty. To follow God's will in one's **e**. Col.1:1
Evil **e**. Disturbed by the gospel. Acts 19:21-41
Example of.
Jesus worked. He was a carpenter by trade. Mk.6:3
Paul worked. He was a tent maker. Acts 18:1, 3
Failure in. Can know four things. Mt.6:33

EMPTY - EMPTINESS (See **FULLNESS, SPIRITUAL**)
Answer to.
Not to walk as other men walk, in the **e**. of their mind. Eph.4:17
Seeking Jesus. Lk.5:27-29; 5:30-32
Caused by.
False teaching. 2 Pt.2:18; Jude 12
Sin. Jn.4:15
Worldliness, indulgence, selfishness, spiritual hunger. Lk.15:14-16
Characteristic - Trait of.
False teachers. Jude 12
The unregenerate, the unsaved & lost. Eph.4:17
Those who only reform their lives & refuse to be transformed by Christ. Mt.12:43-45
Fact. The **e**. are loved by Christ & by genuine believers. 2 Jn.1-2

EMULATIONS (See **JEALOUSY**)

ENCOURAGE - ENCOURAGEMENT
A strong **e**. 1 Th.3:7-10
Discussed. Ph.2:1
Duty.
Must **e**. Eight reasons. Heb.3:13-19
To be stirred out of self-pity. 2 Cor.1:6-7
To bear the burdens of believers. Ro.15:1; Gal.6:2
To **e**. believers just as a father does his children. 1 Th.2:11
To **e**. believers with the hope of Christ's return. 1 Th.4:18
To **e**. ourselves with the presence of other believers. 1 Th.5:11

Expectations of believers.
A new heavens & a new earth.
2 Pt.3:11-14
Discussed. 2 Pt.3:11-14; 3:15-18
Fact.
Every knee shall bow & worship
Christ. Ph.2:9-11; Rev.20:11-15
Surety of the end times, the end of the
world will take place. Mt.24:3, 14;
1 Th.4:16; 2 Th.1:7-10; 2 Pt.3:3-10
False prophet of. (See **PROPHET OF
REVELATION, FALSE**)
Great Tribulation. (See **DISTRESS,
GREAT**)
Believers to be delivered from.
Rev.3:10
Judgments of. (See **END TIME**, Events
of; **JUDGMENTS**, Of Revelation)
Great mourning & fear will sweep the
earth. Mt.24:29-31
Political Babylon will be destroyed.
Rev.18:1-24
Religious Babylon, that is, false re-
ligion, will
be destroyed. Rev.17:1-6; 17:7-18
The bodies of the dead will be eaten
by vultures. Mt.24:28
The door to heaven will be shut.
Mt.25:1-13, esp. 10-12
The evil will be condemned to eternal
death. Mt.24:48-51
The ungodly will be punished with ev-
erlasting destruction. 2 Th.1:7-10
The wicked will be cast into outer
darkness. Mt.25:30
The wicked will be cut off from God
& cast into everlasting fire. Mt.25:41-
46
There will be great separation of peo-
ple & judgment. Mt.24:40-41
Millennium (See **MILLENNIUM**)
One hundred forty four thousand Jews.
Discussed. Rev.7:4-8; 14:1-5
Satan (See **SATAN**)
Seventieth week of Daniel. Mk.13:1-27
Signs of - Events.
A wicked & evil people. 2 Tim.3:1-17
Abomination that causes Desolation.
(See **ANTICHRIST**)
Antichrist. (See **ANTICHRIST**)
Apostasy. Lk.18:8
Astronomical events. Mk.13:24-25;
Lk.21:25-26
Clearly seen. Parable of the Fig Tree.
Lk.21:29-33
Day of the Lord. Acts 2:22-24
Discussed. Mt.24:1-14; Mk.13:1-37
Eighteen signs. 2 Tim.3:2-4
False teachers intensify. Lk.21:8
Godlessness. 2 Tim.3:2-4
Great distress or tribulation.
Mk.13:14-23; 13:24-27
Lawlessness. Mt.24:12; 2 Th.2:4-12
Listed. Acts 2:22-24; 3:21
Mockers & scoffers. Jude 17-19;
2 Pt.3:3-7
Persecution. The tragic sign.
Lk.21:12-19
Powerless religion. A form of godli-
ness, but denying the power.
2 Tim.3:5
Rejecting sound doctrine. 2 Tim.4:3-4
Restoration of all things. Acts 3:21
Return of Christ. Mk.13:24-27
Surety of. Absolute & certain.
Lk.21:33

Terrible times. 2 Tim.3:1
The book of destiny. Mk.13:1-37
To happen in one generation.
Mk.13:30; Lk.21:32
Worldliness. As Noah's day. Carous-
ing. Mt.24:37-39
World's end. Mt.24:15-28
Warning to believers. (See **END TIME**,
Duty) Mk.13:28-37
Against being deceived about the end
time. Lk.21:5-8
Against calamities & disasters & trials
of. Lk.21:34-35
To watch & pray for. Lk.21:34-36
World religion in. (See **STATE, WOR-
SHIP OF**)

ENDURE ENDURANCE (See **PERSE-
VERANCE; STEADFASTNESS**)
Call to. 2 Cor.6:3-10
Duty.
Discussed. 2 Cor.6:3-10
Not to be slothful. Heb.6:12-15
To continue in the love of Christ.
Jn.15:9-10
To e. all things. 2 Tim.2:10
To e. chastening. Heb.12:7
To e., combating temptation & trials.
Jas.5:7-11
To e. grief even if one suffers wrong-
fully. 1 Pt.2:19
To e. hardness just like a soldier.
2 Tim.2:3-4
To e. in prayer. Lk.11:5-10
To e., keeping one's eyes fixed upon
the return of Christ. Jas.5:7-11
To e. persecutions, even if severe.
Heb.10:32-33; 2 Tim.3:10-12
To e. trials & temptations. Jas.1:12
To e. trials. Ro.5:3-5; 12:12; 1 Pt.1:6-9
To patiently race for Christ. Heb.12:1-4
To resist sin to the point of blood.
Heb.12:4
Essential. For salvation. Mt.24:43-44
Example of.
Christ. The Supreme example.
Heb.12:1-29
Great heroic believers. Heb.11:32-40
Moses. Heb.11:27
Meaning. Ro.12:12; 2 Cor.6:4; 2 Th.1:4
Outline of. Jas.1:3-8
Result.
Assures a crown of life. Jas.1:12
Assures salvation. Mt.10:22;
Mk.13:13
Brings happiness. Jas.5:11
Fulfills God's will. Heb.10:35-36
Gives one a strong witness.
2 Tim.2:10
Obtains the promise. Heb.6:12-15;
10:35-36
Stirs great character. Ro.5:3-5
Things that are to e.
The Word of God. 1 Pt.1:23
Verses. List of. Jn.8:31

ENEMIES (See **BROTHERHOOD;
FORGIVENESS, HUMAN**)
Attitude toward. (See **PERSECUTION**)
Discussed Mt.5:43; 5:44; 5:44-48; 5:48;
Lk.6:20-23; 6:27-31
Duty toward.
Discussed. Ro.12:14-21
Love. Mt.5:43; 5:44; 5:44-48; 5:48;
Lk.6:27, 35
How to treat. Reasons. Ro.12:19-21

ENEMIES OF GOD
Judgment & end of.
Shall be condemned & shall perish.
Jn.3:16-21, esp. 16, 18
Shall be condemned to eternal death
by God. Ro.1:28-32, esp. 32
Shall be put under the feet of Christ.
1 Cor.15:25; Heb.10:13
Meaning. Col.1:21-22
Who & what are the e. of God.
All who have not approached God
through Christ, who have not been
reconciled to God by Christ. Ro.5:10,
cp. 8-11; Col.1:21-22
All who oppose Christ. Mt.22:44, cp.
41-46; Ro.5:10, cp. 8-11
Death. 1 Cor.15:26; 15:54-57
Satan. Mt.13:39, cp. 37-43; Lk.22:31;
1 Pt.5:8
Spiritual wickedness. Eph.6:12
The world & worldliness. Jas.4:4;
1 Jn.2:15-16
Those who do evil. Mt.13:25-28, 39;
Col.1:21
Those who hate God. Ro.1:28-31, esp. 39
Those who walk & live as enemies of
the cross. Ph.3:18-19

ENGAGED (See **BETROTHED; ES-
POUSED**)

ENSLAVEMENT, SPIRITUAL
By what. Sin. Lk.15:14-16; Jn.8:33-40;
Col.2:20-22
Denied. Two reasons. Jn.8:33
Deliverance from. (See **JESUS CHRIST**,
Death, Purposes of; **SALVATION**)
Fear. Ro.8:15
Result. Despair, misery, hopelessness.
Ro.6:14-15
Verses. List of. Jn.8:34-36

ENTANGLE - ENTANGLEMENT - TRAP
Meaning. Mt.22:15

ENTANGLES, EASILY
Meaning. Heb.12:1

ENTICE - ENTICEMENT (See **DECEP-
TION; SEDUCE - SEDUCTION**)
Discussed. Col.2:4
Meaning. Jas.1:14-16; 4:1; 4:2
What it is that e.
Enticing words. Col.2:4, cp. 1 Tim.1:4-7;
4:1-2; 4:6-7; 6:3-5; 2 Tim.2:14-18,
23-26; 3:7; 4:3-4; Tit.1:9-14; 3:9-11
Lust. Jn.8:44; Jas.1:14
Man's wisdom. 1 Cor.2:4

ENTICING WORDS (See **FINE-SOUND-
ING ARGUMENTS**)

ENVY (See **JEALOUSY; SELF-
SEEKING**)
Affects one's attitude & one's behavior
toward others. Mt.20:15
Answer to - Deliverance from.
Conversion. Turning one's life over to
Christ. Tit.3:3-7
Crucifying the flesh with its affections
& lusts. Gal.5:24-26
Love. 1 Cor.13:4, cp. 1-4
The fruit of the Spirit. Gal.5:22-23,
cp. 19-21
Trusting & governing one's life by the
wisdom from above. Jas.3:13-18
Discussed. Tit.3:3

Duty.
Not to e. one another. Gal.5:26
Not to make a false profession: having a heart full of e., yet professing the truth. Jas.3:14
Not to walk in e. Ro.13:13
To lay aside all e. 1 Pt.2:1
Evil of
Causes carnality & division. 1 Cor.3:3; 2 Cor.12:20
Causes confusion & every evil work. Jas.3:16, cp. 14-16
Excludes one from God's kingdom. Gal.5:19-21, esp. 21
Is a work of the flesh. Gal.5:19-21
Stirs controversy & opposition against the gospel & believers. Acts 13:45; 17:5
Was the very reason the religionists plotted against Jesus. Mk.15:10; 27:18
Meaning. Mk.7:22; Ro.1:29; 13:13; 1 Cor.13:4-7; Gal.5:19-21; 1 Pt.2:1
Trait of.
False teachers. 1 Tim.6:3-5, esp. 4
Some ministers. Ph.1:15
The carnal, those who live flesh-centered lives. 1 Cor.3:3
Those who reject & rebel against God. Ro.1:28-32, esp. 29

EPAPHRAS
Discussed. Col.4:12-13
Imprisoned for his faith. Phile.1:23

EPAPHRODITUS
A man who was not a quitter. Ph.2:25-30
Delivered a gift to Paul when Paul was a prisoner. Ph.4:18
Discussed. Ph.2:25-30

EPHESUS
Church.
Discussed. Eph. Introd.; Rev.2:1
Message to. By Christ. Rev.2:1-7
One of the seven churches of Revelation. Rev.2:1-7
Paul left Timothy to minister in E. 1 Tim.1:3
Paul sends the minister Tychicus to E. Eph.6:21
Paul's exhortation to the c. leaders. Acts 20:23-38; Eph. Introd.
Represents the orthodox, but unloving church. Rev.2:1-7
City. Discussed. Acts 18:23-28
Visited by Paul on his second mission. Acts 18:18-22
Visited by Paul on his third mission. Acts 18:23-28

EPICUREANS
Discussed. Acts 17:18

EPILEPSY
Caused shame. Mk.9:14-18

EPIMENIDES
Greek poet quoted by Paul. Tit.1:12

EQUALITY OF MAN (See **ONENESS; UNITY**)
Basis of.
Creation. All men are of one blood. Acts 17:26
Death & judgment. Heb.9:27; 2 Cor.5:10
God's love. Jn.3:16

Human nature & death. Ro.5:12, cp. Ro.3:10-18; 3:23
The sacrifice of Christ. Tit.3:4-7; 1 Pt.3:18; 1 Jn.2:1-2
What is equal in God's eyes.
All men. Acts 10:28
All races. Ro.10:12
Male & female. Gal.3:28
Position, education, profession, titles, relationships. Mt.23:8
Slaves (employees) & free men (employers). Gal.3:28
The poor & the rich. Jas.2:1-5

EQUIP - EQUIPPED
Discussed. Mt.5:48; Heb.7:1-24
Duty.
To be e. by God & Christ. Heb.13:20-21
To be e. even as God is e. Mt.5:48
To be e. in every good work. Heb.13:20-21
To be the believer's great aim. Ph.3:12-13
To go on to perfection. Heb.6:1
To live in the Word of God. 2 Tim.3:16-17, cp. 2 Tim.2:15; 1 Pt.2:2-3
To e. holiness. 2 Cor.7:1
To e. one's faith. 1 Th.3:10
To praise God in perfection. Mt.21:15-16
To rely upon the strength of Christ for being e. 2 Cor.12:9
To seek & pursue perfection 2 Cor.13:9; Ph.3:12-16
Essential. To live in God's presence. Ph.3:7-11; 3:7-16
Fact.
Believers do not achieve perfection on earth. Ph.3:12-16
Love is the way to e. 1 Cor.13:8-12
Man is not e. & cannot secure being e. Gal.2:15-16
The person who sets his life apart unto God is perfected forever through Christ. Heb.10:14
Meaning. Jn.17:23; 1 Cor.2:6; Jas.1:3-41 Pt.5:10
Need for being e.
By man. Discussed. Heb.7:1-24; 9:9
Met by Christ. Heb.2:9-10; 5:9; 7:1-24; 7:11-247:25-28; 9:11-14; 11:39-40
His strength. 2 Cor.12:9
Source - How one is e.
A spiritual union with God & Christ alone. Jn.17:23
Controlling one's tongue & words. Jas.3:2
Discussed. Heb.7:11-24, esp. 11-12, 18-19
Following after perfection. Ph.3:12, cp. 7-16
Giving all one is & has to Christ & the poor. Mt.19:21, cp. 16-30
God. Heb.13:20-21; 1 Pt.5:10
Help from faithful ministers. Eph.4:11-16; Col.1:28; 4:12; 1 Th.3:10
Hope. Heb.7:19
Living in Christ's presence. An absolute essential. Ph.3:7-11; 3:7-16
Love. Col.3:14; cp. 1 Jn.4:17-18
Not by sacrifice or law. Heb.10:1-4
Overcoming & conquering trials & temptations. Jas.1:2-4
Prayer. 1 Th.3:10

Presenting one's body as a living sacrifice to God. Ro.12:1-2
Scripture. 2 Tim.3:16-17
The blood of Christ. Heb.10:1-18; 12:22-24; 13:20-21
The Holy Spirit. Gal.3:3, cp. 1-5
The perfect life of Christ. Secured by suffering as a Man upon earth. Heb.2:10
The perfect sacrifice & death of Christ. Heb.10:1-4, esp. 1-4, 14
Warning & teaching every person. Col.1:28
Work & faith. Jas.2:22

ERASTUS
Became a minister who served with Paul. Acts 19:22
Ministered in Corinth. 2 Tim.4:20
Was the city treasurer for Corinth. Ro.16:23

ERROR (See **SIN; TRANSGRESSION**)

ESAU
Character. Sensual, profane. Heb.12:16-17
Example of. Neglecting his inheritance. Heb.12:16-17
Son of Isaac. Rejected by God as the heir of the promises. Ro.9:7-13

ESCAPE, NO
What a person must escape from.
False teachers. 2 Pt.2:18
Temptation. 1 Cor.10:13
The corruption that is in the world. 2 Pt.1:4
The judgment of God. Ro.2:3
The terrible judgments of the end time. Lk.21:36, cp. 5-36
The world & its pollutions. 2 Pt.2:20
Who will not escape.
False religionists. Mt.23:33, cp. 13-39
Those who judge & criticize others. Ro.2:1-3, esp. 3
Those who neglect salvation. Heb.2:3
Those who refuse to hear Christ. Heb.12:25
Those who rest in a false & worldly security. 1 Th.5:3
Those who turn away from Christ & become entangled again with the world. 2 Pt.2:20

ESCAPISM
Of this generation. Discussed. Lk.7:33-34
Peace does not come from e. Jn.14:27
Results in.
Hard hearts. Lk.7:33-34
Rejection of Jesus Christ. Lk.7:33-34
Shirking of duty. Lk.23:1-7; 7:33-34

ESPOUSED
Discussed. Engagement before marriage. Lk.1:27
Steps in marriage. Mt.1:18

ESTABLISH - ESTABLISHED (See **ASSURANCE; GROWTH, SPIRITUAL; SECURITY; STRENGTHEN; STRONG, MAKE**)
Duty.
Must be e. & kept from evil. 2 Th.3:3
Must be e. in every good word & work. 2 Th.2:16-17

Must be **e.** in heart. Jas.5:8
Must be **e.** in holiness. 1 Th.3:12-13
Must be **e.** in order to bear up under suffering & death. 1 Pt.5:10
Must be **e.** in the faith. Ro.1:4-12; Col.2:6-7; 1 Th.3:1-2
Must be **e.** time & again in the truth. 2 Pt.1:12
Must be **e.** with believers. 2 Cor.1:21
Must have one's heart **e.** with grace & not with rituals, ceremonies, & religious rules. Heb.13:9
Source.
　Christ. 1 Th.3:12-13; 2 Th.3:3
　God. Through the gospel & the preaching of Jesus Christ. Ro.16:25; 1 Pt.5:10
　God & Christ together. 2 Th.2:16-17
　Ministers & preachers. Ro.1:18
　Oneself. One's own determination & commitment to be **e.** Jas.5:8

ESTEEM
Fails. Several ways. Mt.6:5

ETERNAL - ETERNITY
New heaven & earth. Discussed. Rev.21:1-8
Vs. the temporal. 2 Cor.4:17-18

ETERNAL LIFE
Assurance of.
　Discussed. Jude 24-25
　God preserves the believer for eternal life. 2 Tim.4:18; 1 Jn.5:13-15
Discussed. Mk.10:17; 10:18; 2 Cor.5:1-10; 1 Jn.2:25
　As eternal rest & rewards. Rev.14:13
　Cost of. Lk.18:18-30
　Problem of. Mk.10:17-22
　Reality. Mt.22:29
Duty.
　To make eternal life one's great aim in life. Ph.3:12-16
　To preach. Tit.1:2-3
Fact.
　Believers are preserved eternally. 2 Tim.4:18
　Believers are to be transferred into. Jn.11:25-27; 2 Tim.4:18
　Believers groan for. 2 Cor.5:1-10
How to secure.
　By being clothed from heaven. 2 Cor.5:2-4
　By believing in Christ. Jn.3:15; 3:16; 5:24; 11:25; 20:31
　By believing in God who sent Christ. Jn.5:24
　By coming to Christ, partaking of the living bread. Jn.6:35, 51, 58
　By eating & partaking of the bread of life - of Christ. Jn.6:51, 58
　By giving everything--all one is & has. Feared, neglected by men. Mt.19:21-22; 19:23-26; 19:27-30;Mk.10:21-22; Lk.10:25-37;Ph.3:12-16
　By hating one's life in this world. Jn.12:25
　By hearing Christ's voice and following Him. Jn.10:27
　By hearing God's commands. Jn.12:50
　By knowing God and Christ. Jn.17:3
　By living a fruitful & holy life. Ro.6:21-22

By making eternal life one's first & supreme aim in life. Ph.3:11, cp. 3:7-11
By obeying God. 1 Jn.2:17
By obeying God's commandment. Jn.12:50
By seeing the Son and believing. Jn.6:40
By self-denial. Mt.19:28; 19:29
By serving Christ. Jn.12:25-26
Discussed. Mk.10:17-22; Lk.10:25-37
Four steps. Mt.19:16-22
Verses. List of. Ro.2:7; 6:21-22
Meaning. Ro.2:6-10
　Being delivered from death. Jn.8:51
　Being present with the Lord & absent from the body. 2 Cor.5:8
　Having a well of water springing up within one's heart. Jn.4:14
　Having mortality swallowed up of life. 2 Cor.5:4
　Knowing Christ & being in Him. 1 Jn.5:20
　Knowing the only true God & Christ. Jn.17:2-3
　Living forever. 1 Jn.2:17
　Living - never ceasing to live. Jn.11:25-26
　Never being snatched out of Christ's hand. Jn.10:28
　Never dying. Never experiencing death anymore. Lk.20:36-38; Jn.11:26
　Never hungering and never thirsting again. Jn.6:35
　Not being dissolved. 2 Cor.5:1-4
　Possessing eternal rest & rewards. Rev.14:13
Misconception.
　Eternal **l.** can be secured by good works. Mk.10:17; 10:18
　Eternal **l.** is only a human idea & allegory. Mk.12:25
　Man's idea of. Discussed. Mt.19:17
Nature. (See **ETERNAL LIFE**, Meaning)
　Differs from this life. Lk.20:36; 20:37-38
　Discussed. Mk.12:25
　Is a perfect life. Mt.19:28
　Is of the spiritual world & dimension. Mt.22:29
Results.
　In an eternal inheritance. Heb.9:15, cp. 1 Pt.1:3-4
　In being resurrected to life. Jn.5:28-30; 6:40; 11:23-27
　In being transported into the presence of God immediately at death. Never losing consciousness. Jn.11:25-27; 2 Tim.4:18
　In eternal comfort. 2 Th.2:16
　In eternal glory. 1 Pt.5:10
　In eternal salvation. Heb.5:9
　In knowing the only true God and Christ. Jn.17:2-3
　In never being condemned but being saved. Jn.3:17-21; 5:24
　In never being snatched out of Christ's hand. Jn.10:28
　In never dying. Jn.11:25-27
　In never perishing. Jn.3:15-16; 10:28
　In the glory of God and Christ. Jn.17:1-4
　In three great things. Jn.6:54

Results of rejecting.
　Will be found naked. 2 Cor.5:3
　Will be punished with everlasting destruction. 2 Th.1:7-8
　Will rise to be condemned. Jn.5:29
　Will face the wrath of God. Jn.3:36
　Will lose one's life. Mt.16:25; Mk.8:35; Lk.9:24
　Will never see life. Jn.3:36
Seeking. How to seek. Mk.10:17; 10:18
Source.
　God.
　　Is given by God in Christ. 1 Jn.5:11-12
　　Promised by God. 1 Jn.2:25
　Jesus Christ. Ro.5:19-21
　　Promised by Christ. Jn.3:16-17; 4:14; 5:24-29; 6:35, 40, 51, 58; 10:28; 11:25-27; 12:25, 50; 17:3; 20:31
　　The death of Christ. Jn.3:14-15
　　The eternal redemption provided by Christ. Heb.9:12-14
　The gospel. Promised by the gospel. 1 Jn.2:24-25
Verses. List of. Jn.8:51; 11:25-27; 17:2-3
Vs. existence. Mt.19:16
Vs. temporal. 2 Cor.4:17-18

ETHICS
God's case against the moralist. Ro.2:1-16

EUBULUS
Visited Paul in prison & knew Timothy. 2 Tim.4:21

EUNICE
Grandmother of Timothy. 2 Tim.1:5

EUNUCH
Discussed. Mt.19:12; 1 Cor.7:25-40

EUODIA
Discussed. Ph.4:2-3

EUPHRATES RIVER
In the end time. Dried up. Rev.16:12-16
Place where four fallen angels are bound. Reason. Rev.9:14-15

EUROPE
Cradle of society changed to **E.** Acts 16:6-11

EVALUATION
Needed. Time for **e.** is essential. Lk.9:10

EVANGELISM - EVANGELIZE (See **COMMISSION; MISSIONS; WITNESSING**)
And Jesus. **E.** was the ministry of Jesus. Lk.4:17-19; 19:10, cp. Mt.28:19-20
Basis of. Discussed. Ro.10:14-15
Dangers to.
　Fear of being shamed. Ro.1:16; 2 Tim.1:8, cp. 6-7
　Sensationalism. Jesus tempted to use sensationalism. Lk.4:9-12
　Unbelief & hardness. Mk.16:14
Discussed. Acts 1:8
　Equipping; task; method. Acts 1:8
　How to **e.** Lk.10:1-16
　Picture of. Acts 13:4-13
　Response to. Four **r.** Acts 13:42-52
　Vs. pastoring. Acts 14:21-28

Duty.
Great call to world **e.** Acts 16:6-11
To be faithful in **e.** that one may be
free from the blood
of all men. Acts 20:26-27
To be ready to preach the gospel.
Ro.1:14-16
To have a world-wide vision.
Ro.15:22-33
To preach, warn, & teach every man.
Col.1:28
To reach our homes & friends for
Christ. Gal.1:18-20; 1:21
To reach out & go world-wide. Acts
28:30-31; 1 Tim.3:16
To use trials for **e.** Acts 28:4-9
Essentials for **e.** Four **e.** Acts 9:31
Method.
Discussed. Acts 13:14-16; 13:46-47;
14:1
House **e.** Lk.9:4; 10:5-6
Meaning. Lk.8:1
Pattern of **e.** Acts 14:1-7
Paul's personal method. Acts 20:17-27
Paul's plan for world-wide **e.** Acts
19:21-23
Strategy for.
In large cities. Steps. Acts 28:16-31
Of Paul in Rome. Acts 28:16-31
To be centered in homes. Lk.9:4;
10:5-6
Of the world.
Peter gains a world-wide vision. Acts
11:1-18
The first launch of **e.** to the Gentiles.
Acts 10:1-48
The strategy of Paul to reach the
world. Acts 19:21-41
Predicted. The whole world will be **e.**
Mk.13:10; Rev.14:6-7
Resources to e.
God's power. 2 Tim.1:7-8
The Holy Spirit. Jn.16:7-11; Acts 1:8
The name of Christ. Mk.16:17-18
Who is to e.
Believers. Mt.28:19-20; Mk.16:15;
Jn.20:21, cp. Lk.19:10; Acts 1:8; 1
Pt.3:15
Minister. (See **MINISTERS**, Duty, In
relation to preaching)
The church. To be the church's first
duty. Mt.28:19-20; Acts 1:8;
Rev.3:8
The laymen of the church. Acts 8:1-4
Why e.
Discussed. Acts 13:4-13
The fields are ripe for harvest. Jn.4:35
The gospel is the power of God unto
salvation. Ro.1:16
The harvest is great. Lk.10:2
Zeal for. (See **ZEAL**)
By Paul. For Israel, his own people.
Ro.9:1-3
By the Pharisees. Were strong in **e.** for
their religion. Mt.23:15

EVANGELIST
Duty toward. To welcome and support.
3 Jn.3-4, 5-8
Example of an e.
Philip. Acts 21:8
Timothy. 2 Tim.4:5
Gift of. Meaning. Eph.4:11

EVE, THE FIRST WOMAN
And Adam. Function of both in creation.
1 Tim.2:12-14
Error - Mistake of. Was deceived.
2 Cor.11:3
Fact. Was deceived, but not Adam.
1 Tim.2:14

ETERNAL FIRE (See **FIRE, ETERNAL**)
Meaning. Mt.25:41

EVERLASTING LIFE (See **ETERNAL
LIFE**)

EVERYTHING THAT HINDERS
Meaning. Heb.12:1

EVIL (See **LOST; SIN**)
Concept of. Threefold. Mk.7:23
Deliverance from. (See **EVIL**, Duty)
By Christ, His redemption. Tit.2:14
By God. God delivers from.
2 Tim.4:16-18
By God, His mercy & promise not to
remember our sins & **e.** any more.
Heb.8:12
By the death of Christ. Gal.1:4
Duty.
Not to rejoice in **e.** 1 Cor.13:6
To avoid every kind of **e.** 1 Th.5:22
To cast **e.** out of one's life. Discussed.
Mt.12:43-45
To depart from **e.** 2 Tim.2:19
To expel **e.** & wicked persons from the
church. 1 Cor.5:13
To guard against an **e.** heart of unbe-
lief. Heb.3:12
To guard against **e.** boasting. Jas.4:16
To guard against **e.** thoughts. Jas.2:4
To have our hearts sprinkled from an
e. conscience. Heb.10:22
To rebuke those who do **e.** 2 Pt.2:16
To redeem the time because the days
are **e.** Eph.5:16
To shun; to abhor **e.** Ro.12:9-10
To turn away from **e.** and to do good.
1 Pt.3:11
Facts about - Traits.
Abounds & causes love to become
cold. Mt.24:12
Enslaves & binds a person. Acts 8:23;
Ro.6:19
Is at work in the world now. 2 Th.2:7
Is hated by Christ. Heb.1:9
Is not of love. 1 Cor.13:4-7, esp. 6
The tongue is a world of **e.** Jas.3:6
Will be a trait of the end time.
Mt.24:12
Final triumph over evil. Great announce-
ment of. Rev.10:1-11
In the church (See **KINGDOM OF
HEAVEN**)
In the Kingdom of Heaven (See **KING-
DOM OF HEAVEN**)
In the world. Questioned. Why is **e.** in the
church & in the world? Mt.13:27
Judgment of those who do e.
Shall be put away from Christ.
Mt.7:21-23
Shall be put out of Christ's kingdom &
cast into a furnace of fire. Mt.13:41-42
Meaning. Mt.7:23; 24:12
Law of. Ro.7:21-23
Means both evil & the evil one or Sa-
tan. 2 Th.3:3-5

Problem of.
Discussed. Mk.7:14-23
From within, not without. Mk.7:14-23
Man makes three mistakes in dealing
with **e.** Mk.7:23
Restraint of. By God. 2 Th.2:6-8
Results. Causes swearing. Mt.5:37
Source.
A depraved nature. Ro.3:10-12
The heart. Mt.12:35; Mk.7:23
The heart within man. Mt.23:28
What can be e. & wicked.
A man. Mt.12:35
A whole generation of people.
Mt.12:39, 45
Appearance. 1 Th.5:22
Boasting & rejoicing. Jas.4:16
Days. Eph.5:16
Deeds. 2 Jn.9-11
Persons. 1 Cor.5:13
Satan, the wicked one or the **e.** one.
Eph.6:16
The conscience. Heb.10:22
The heart. Heb.3:12
The present **e.** age. Gal.1:4
Things. Ro.12:9
Thoughts. Jas.2:4

EVIL ASSOCIATIONS (See **SEPARA-
TION**)
Danger of.
Can cause a person to deny Christ.
Lk.22:54-62; Jn.18:18-25
Corrupts good morals. 1 Cor.15:33
Duty.
Not to associate with people who do
evil. 1 Cor.5:11
Not to be unequally yoked together
with unbelievers. 2 Cor.6:14
Not to have fellowship with the un-
fruitful works of darkness. Eph.5:11
To come out from & to be separate
from evil **a.** 1 Cor.6:17-18
To save oneself from this evil genera-
tion. Acts 2:40

EVIL DESIRE (See **DESIRE**, Bad & Evil;
LUST)

EVIL DOERS
Duty.
Not to suffer reproach because of evil
doing. 1 Pt.4:14-15
To save oneself from this evil genera-
tion. Acts 2:40
Facts.
Believers are sometimes falsely ac-
cused of evil doings. 2 Tim.2:9;
1 Pt.2:13; 3:16
Can characterize a whole generation.
Lk.9:41
Rulers are appointed to control evil
doers. 1 Pt.2:14, cp. Ro.13:1-4

EVIL EYE (See **ENVY**)
Affects one's attitude & one's behavior
toward others. Mt.20:15

EVIL FOR EVIL
Duty. Not to repay evil for evil.
Ro.12:17

EVIL HEART

Fact. Is the source of evil. Mt.12:35; Mk.7:21

Traits - Characteristics of.
Covetousness. 2 Pt.2:14
Full of extortion & excess. Mt.23:25
Produces all kinds of evil things. Mk.7:21
Unbelief. Heb.3:12

EVIL SPEAKING (See **SPEAKING, EVIL; TONGUE; WORDS**)

EVIL SPIRITS

Acknowledged Jesus' deity. But were rejected by Jesus. Reasons. Mk.1:23-26; 3:11-12; Lk.4:33-37; 4:41; Acts 16:16-17

Delivered from. (See **JESUS CHRIST**, Work of, Destroying Satan & Evil Spirits)
A boy possessed by a spirit that robbed his speech. Spiritual immaturity & powerlessness. Mk.9:14-29
A daughter.
Caring for the rejected. Mk.7:24-30
How to receive things from God. Mt.15:21-28
A demon-possessed girl. The power of money vs. the power of Jesus' name. Acts 16:16-24
A dumb man. The quiet approach for sanity. Mt.9:32-33
An only child. Rebuke of this present generation. Lk.9:37-45
By Christ's death & power. Mt.8:28-34; Mk.3:7-12, esp. 11; Col.2:15
Many possessed persons. Jesus' power. Mt.4:24; Lk.4:41
Many seeking & fearing Christ. Mk.3:7-12, esp. 11
The most enslaved. Mk.1:23-28; 1:34; 3:11-12; 5:1-20
The most unclean. Lk.4:33-37
The most wild & mean. Mk.5:1-20
Two possessed men. Saving men. Mt.8:28-34

Discussed. Mt.8:28-34; 9:32-34; 17:15-16; Mk.5:1-20; Lk.9:39; Eph.6:12
Deliverance from the forces of evil. Mt.8:28-34
Evil **s.** conquered. By the cross. Mt.8:28-34
The character & work of evil **s.** Lk.8:26-39
The dark world of the occult. Acts 16:16-17
The denial of evil **s.** Mt.8:28-34

Duty.
To put on the armor of God for protection against evil **s.** Eph.6:10-20
To test the spirits of teachers. 1 Jn.4:1-6
To wrestle against. Mt.8:28-34

In the end time.
Described.
As locusts. Afflict men. Rev.8:13-9:11
As military horseman & horses. Kill men. Rev.9:12-21
Will kill one third of the ungodly & evil. Rev.9:16-19

King of evil **s.** (See **SATAN**)
Discussed. Rev.8:11

Nature.
Are devils. Mt.4:24; 8:16; 8:28; 8:33
Are evil. Lk.7:21; 8:2; Acts 19:11-12
Are forces of evil. Mt.8:28-34; 17:15; Eph.6:12
Are spiritual beings, not physical beings. Lk.24:39; Eph.6:12
Discussed. Mk.5:6-7; Lk.8:26-33
Is different from mental illness & insanity. Mt.4:24

Power over.
By believers. Must put on the armor of God. Eph.6:10-18, esp. 11-12
By Christ.
Acknowledged by religionists. Mk.3:22-23
Impact upon. Mk.3:11-12
Many in a mass meeting. Mk.1:34, cp. 1:33
Many when confronting Christ. Mk.3:7-12
Proves the deity of Christ. Lk.11:14-28
By disciples. Mk.6:7
By ministers. Given power over. Lk.10:17-18
To free men. Lk.8:26-39

Relation to God & Christ. Four facts about. Mk.5:6-7

View of.
Man's view. Col.2:15
The denial of evil **s.** Mt.8:28-34; Eph.6:12

Vs. Christ. Col.2:15

Work of.
Discussed. Lk.8:26-33
Effects of work. Described. Sixfold. Mk.5:2-5
Seek to inhabit men. Lk.11:24-26
To bear false witness to Jesus. Acts 16:16-17
To deceive into false teaching. 1 Tim.4:1-2
To deceive through fortune-telling. Acts 16:16-17
To enslave, control, possess, & ruin man. Mk.1:23-24; 5:1-20; Acts 19:13-16
To enslave through the occult. Acts 16:16-17
To heighten & aggravate existing conditions. Mk.9:17-18
To hurt God by enticing people to the things & gods of this world. 1 Cor. 10:20
To possess people. Mk.1:23-28; 3:11-12; 5:1-20; 9:14-29; Jn.13:27-30

EVIL THINGS, INVENTORS OF
Meaning. Ro.1:30

EVIL THOUGHTS (See **THOUGHTS**)

EVIL WORKS OR EVIL DEEDS
Fact.
The Lord delivers believers from every evil work. 2 Tim.4:18
The works of the world are evil. Jn.7:7

Results.
Disturbs the soul. 2 Pt.2:8
Shall not inherit the kingdom of God. Gal.5:19-21, esp. 21
Shall suffer the judgment of the Lord. Jude 14-15
What are evil works.
Envy & strife. Jas.3:16
Murder. 1 Jn.2:12
Murder & lying. Jn.8:41, 44-47
Receiving & associating with false teachers. 2 Jn.9-11
The works of the flesh. Gal.5:19-21

EXALT - EXALTATION (See **BOASTING; JESUS CHRIST**, Exaltation of; **PRIDE; SELF-EXALTATION; SELF-SEEKING; SELFISHNESS**)

Duty. To **e.** Christ & not self. Jn.3:29-30
Fact.
Man has been **e.** over animals. Mt.6:26; 12:12; Jas.3:7
Of Christ. (See **JESUS CHRIST**, Exaltation)
Of God. (See **GOD**, Nature)
Results in.
Joy. Jas.1:9
The reward of eternal rule & reign. (See **REWARDS**) Lk.19:17; 1 Cor.6:2; Rev.3:21; 5:10; 22:5
Selfish & evil exaltation.
Comes from - Caused by.
Lust for power. Jas.1:14-15; 4:1-3; Rev.13:2-3; 13:4-8
Lust for recognition. Acts 12:21-23; 2 Th.2:4. Cp. Mt.23:5-10
Satan. Mt.4:8-9
Self-seeking. Mt.10:35-37
Who is to be **e.**
The person of low degree, who walks in lowliness of mind. Lk.1:52; Jas.1:9
The person who cries out for the mercy of God. Lk.18:10-14, esp. 13-14
The person who humbles himself & serves others. Mt.23:11-12; Lk.14:11, cp. 7-10; 1 Pt.5:5
The person who humbles himself under the mighty hand of God. 1 Pt.5:6
The person who responds to the gospel, who is led to Christ. 2 Cor.11:7

EXAMINE - EXAMINATION (See **TEST - TESTING**)

Duty.
To **e.** one's own life before **e.** & judging others. Mt.7:5, cp. 1-6
To **e.** ourselves, make sure we are worthy to partake of the Lord's Supper. 1 Cor.11:28, cp. 17-34
To **e.** ourselves to see if we are truly in the faith. 2 Cor.13:5
To **e.** the spirits to see if they are truly of God. 1 Jn.4:1-3

EXAMPLE (See **TESTIMONY**)
Meaning. 1 Pt.2:21; Tit.2:7-8

EXCESS (See **INDULGENCE**)

EXCITEMENT
Of crowds. Not always wise. Mk.6:45
Problem with. Stirred by worldly desires. Mk.6:45

EXCOMMUNICATION (See **CHURCH DISCIPLINE**)
Right use of **e.** (See **CHURCH DISCIPLINE**)
To discipline & clean sin out of the church's fellowship. 1 Cor.5:1-5; 5:6-13
To **e.** false teachers. 2 Jn.7-11
Wrong use of **e.**
Wrong to use **e.** against true believers. Jn.16:1-3
Wrong to use **e.** against true ministers of the gospel. 3 Jn.9-10
Wrong to use **e.** to threaten people. Jn.9:22, cp. 1-41
The spirit needed in **e.** (See **CHURCH DISCIPLINE**)

EXCUSES
E. for not following Christ.
Discussed. Mt.8:18-22; 22:1-14; Lk.9:57-62; 14:15-24
Is not condoned. No matter the **e.**, a person is still guilty. Acts 3:17-18
Will be severely judged & condemned. Mt.25:24-30; 25:44-46
Fact. Sin & unbelief are absolutely inexcusable. Ro.1:20, cp. Ro.1:18-32
For not accepting God's great invitation. Mt.22:1-14; Lk.14:16-24

EXHAUSTION (See **BURDENED; PRESSURE; TIRED; YOKE**)
Need for rest. Dangers of too much rest. Mk.6:30-34

EXHORT - EXHORTATION (See **EDIFY; ENCOURAGED - ENCOURAGEMENT; PREACHING; URGE**)
Duty. To receive the word of **e.** Heb. 13:22
How **e.** is to be given.
By prophesying, proclaiming the message of God. 1 Cor.14:3
Not wrongfully, in deceit; but in truth, **e.** people in the Word of God. 1 Th.2:3-13, esp. 3-6, 11-13
With all longsuffering & doctrine. 2 Tim.4:2
Meaning. 1 Tim.2:1
The message of **e.**
Employment.
To be quiet & to work diligently. 2 Th.3:12
To honor & obey employees. 1 Tim.6:1-2; Tit.2:9-10
Prayer. To pray for all men. 1 Tim.2:1
Salvation. To be saved from this crooked generation. Acts 2:40
The Christian walk. To walk so as to please God. 1 Th.4:1
The faith.
To continue in the faith. Acts 14:22
To earnestly contend for the faith. Jude 3
The promises & deliverance of God. Acts 27:22-25
The true grace of God. 1 Pt.5:12
Witnessing & ministering. 1 Th.5:14
When **e.** is to be given.
Constantly, always. 1 Tim.4:13
On a daily basis. Heb.3:13; 10:25
When churches experience a revival. Acts 11:23, cp. 19-30
When churches need help. Acts 18:27

When people request a word of **e.** Acts 13:15
When preaching. Lk.3:18, cp. 1-18
When traveling about from church to church. Acts 20:1-2
Who is to be **e.**
All believers. Acts 14:22
All men, everyone. Tit.2:15, cp. 1-15
Believers who are being chastened by the Word. Heb.12:5
Elders & ministers. 1 Pt.5:1
Those who oppose the minister. Tit.1:9
Young men. Tit.2:6

EXISTENCE - EXISTING
Of man. **E.** forever with or without God. Mt.19:16

EXORCISTS (See **EVIL SPIRITS**)
Jewish **e.**
In Jesus' day. Mt.12:27-28; Mk.3:22-23; Lk.11:19
In Paul's day. Acts 19:13-20

EXPECTATION (See **HOPE**)

EXPEDIENCY
Reasons for. Lk.20:7-8

EXPOSURE - EXPOSED
Of all things. Discussed. Lk.8:17; 1 Cor.4:5
Of sin. Known by God. Jn.1:47-48; 2:24-25; 5:42; 13:19-20;Ro.2:2-5; 2:16
Verses. List of. Lk.8:17; 12:1-3

EXTORTION (See **SWINDLERS**)
Duty.
Must face the fact & repent if we are guilty of **e.** Mt.23:25
Not to take more than what is due one. Lk.3:13-14

EXTRAVAGANCE (See **INDULGENCE; RICHES; SELFISHNESS; WEALTH**)

EYE - EYES
Described as. Healthy vs. diseased. Man has either healthy or diseased eyes. Lk.11:33-36
Evil. Meaning. Mk.7:22
Fact.
Is the culprit in immorality. Mt.5:28; 5:29
Is the gate to the Mind. Mt.6:21-23
The **e.** has never seen the glory prepared for those who love God. 1 Cor.2:9
Sins of.
Closing one's **e.** to the truth. Mt.18:13-16
Having **e.** full of adultery. 2 Pt.2:14
Lust of. Mt.5:27-29; 1 Jn.2:15-17
Refusing to open one's **e.** to the truth. Mk.8:17-18
Retaliating, demanding an eye for an eye. Mt.5:38
Seeing the faults of others & judging them. Mt.7:3-5
Seriousness of. Mk.9:47-48
Working only to catch the **e.** of the supervisor, only when he is looking. Eph.6:6

F

FABLES (See **MYTHS**)
Duty.
Not to pay attention to **f.**, false & speculative teaching. 1 Tim.1:4; Tit.1:14
Fact.
F. turn people away from the truth. 2 Tim.4:3-4
People will turn aside to **f.** in the end time. 2 Tim.4:3-4, esp. 4
Salvation, the power & coming of Christ, is not a **f.** 2 Pt.1:16
The true minister does not follow nor proclaim cunningly devised **f.** 2 Pt.1:16
Results.
Arouse questions & doubt instead of edifying. 1 Tim.1:4
Destroy godliness. 1 Tim.4:7
Turn people away from the truth. 2 Tim.4:3-4

FACTION - FACTIONS
Discussed. 2 Pt.2:1
How to deal with **f.** Tit.2:10-11
Duty. To reject a heretic. Tit.3:10
Fact.
Christianity was called a **f.** Acts 24:5, 14
Is destructive. 2 Pt.2:1
Meaning. Gal.5:19-21, esp. 20

FAILED THE TEST
Described. 2 Tim.3:1-9, esp.8
Meaning. 2 Cor.13:1-6

FAILURE
Caused by.
Building upon the wrong foundation. Mt.7:27, cp. 24-27; 1 Cor.3:11-15, esp. 15
Failing to count the cost. Lk.14:25-33
Four things. Mk.14:66
Lack of prayer & fasting. Mt.17:16, cp. 14-21
Unbelief. Heb.4:5-6

FAINT - FAINTING (See **LOSE HEART**)
Duty.
Not to **f.** in laboring & standing fast for the Lord. Rev.2:2-3
Not to **f.** in prayer. Lk.18:1
Not to **f.** in the ministry. 2 Cor.4:1; 4:16
Not to **f.** under the chastening of the Lord. Heb.12:5
Meaning. Mt.9:36
Reward of those who do not **f.**
Shall not be hurt by the second death. Rev.2:3, 11
Shall reap life everlasting. Gal.6:1

FAINT NOT (See **HEART, DO NOT LOSE**)

FAIR HAVENS
Port of Crete where Paul's ship docked. Acts 27:8

FAITH

Attitude. Wrong **a.** vs. right **a.** Mk.5:35-43
Described as.
  A household. Gal.6:10
  A law & a principle. Ro.3:27
  A mustard seed. Mt.17:20; Lk.17:5-6
  Discussed. Heb.11:1-6
  Great. Mt.8:8-10
  Logical. Ro.4:4-5
  Precious. 2 Pt.1:1
  The Shield of Faith. Eph.6:16
Discussed. Mt.9:18-34; Mk.11:22-23
  Dead vs. living **f.** Jas.2:14-26
  Growth in. 2 Th.1:3
  Of a great believer.
    A heroic **f.** Heb.11:32-34
    An enduring **f.** Heb.11:35-40
  Of Abraham. An obedient, hopeful **f.**
    Heb.11:8-10
  Of Barak. Heb.11:32
  Of David. Heb.11:32
  Of Gideon. Heb.11:32
  Of Isaac. A repentant **f.** Heb.11:20
  Of Israel.
    A conquering **f.** Heb.11:30
    A delivering **f.** Heb.11:29
  Of Jacob. A worshipping **f.** Heb.11:21
  Of Jephthae. A heroic **f.** despite op-
    position. Heb.11:32
  Of Joseph. An undying **f.** Heb.11:22
  Of Moses. A self-denying **f.**
    Heb.11:24-28
  Of Moses' parents. A loving & fear-
    less **f.** Heb.11:23
  Of Noah. A fearful & reverent **f.**
    Heb.11:7
  Of Rahab. A saving **f.** Heb.11:31
  Of Samson. A man of heroic **f.**
    Heb.11:32
  Of Samuel. A heroic **f.** in the midst of
    an unbelieving generation.
    Heb.11:32
  Of Sarah. An impossible **f.** Heb.11:11-12
  Of the Patriarchs. A pilgrim's **f.**
    Heb.11:13-16
  Of the Prophets. Men of heroic **f.**
    Heb.11:32
  The righteous will live by **f.** Ro.1:17;
    Gal.3:11; Heb.10:38
  The way for the world to get right with
    God. Ro.3:21-5:21
  What a person must believe. Mk.1:15
  What it takes to enter God's Kingdom.
    Mt.21:28-32
Duty.
  Not to deny the **f.** Rev.2:13
  Not to keep on laying the foundation
    of **f.** time & again. Heb.6:1
  Not to profess the **f.** of Christ & then
    show partiality & prejudice. Jas.2:1
  Not to waver in **f.** Jas.1:5-8
  To add certain qualities to one's faith.
    2 Pt.1:5-7
  To add seven things to our **f.** 2 Pt.1:5-7
  To be an example. in **f.** 1 Tim.4:12
  To be established in the **f.** Col.2:7
  To be nourished in the words of **f.**
    1 Tim.4:6
  To be patient, endure in **f.** 2 Th.1:4
  To be steadfast in **f.** Col.2:5
  To be strong in **f.** 1 Th.3:1-10
  To believe "nothing is impossible."
    Lk.1:36-37
  To believe the miraculous. Lk.1:34-35
  To build up oneself by building upon
    one's **f.** Jude 20

To comfort believers concerning their
  f. 1 Th.3:2
To contend for the **f.** against false
  teachers. Jude 3
To continue in the **f.** Acts 14:22;
  Col.1:21-23, esp. 23; 1 Tim.2:15
To die in **f.** Heb.11:13
To examine oneself to make sure one
  is truly in the **f.** 2 Cor.13:5
To follow after **f.** 1 Tim.6:11-12;
  2 Tim.2:22
To follow the **f.** of spiritual leaders.
  Heb.13:7
To have a **f.** that grows & grows.
  2 Th.1:3
To have **f.** in Christ. Concerns three
  things. Acts 24:24-25
To have **f.** in God. Mk.11:22
To hold **f.** in a pure conscience. 1 Tim.3:9
To hold fast sound words in **f.** & love.
  2 Tim.1:13
To hold fast the profession of our **f.**
  Heb.10:23-24
To hold on to one's **f.** 1 Tim.1:18-19
To keep above all the law of judgment,
  mercy, & **f.** Mt.23:23
To keep the **f.** of Jesus. Rev.14:12
To labor in **f.** & love & patience of
  hope. 1 Th.1:3
To live by the **f.** of Christ. Gal.2:20
To make sure one is in the **f.** 2 Cor.13:5
To make sure that one's **f.** stands in the
  power of God, not in the wisdom of
  men. 1 Cor.2:4-5
To perfect what is lacking in **f.** 1 Th.3:10
To persevere in **f.** Jn.4:48-49
To preach the word of **f.** Ro.10:8-10;
  Gal.1:23
To pray for Christ to increase one's **f.**
  Lk.17:5
To pray in **f.** Jas.1:6
To pray that one's **f.** does not fail.
  Lk.22:32
To proclaim repentance toward God &
  f. toward Christ. Acts 20:21; 24:24-25
To rebuke men to be sound in the **f.**
  Tit.1:13
To resist Satan by being steadfast in
  the **f.** 1 Pt.5:9
To sacrifice oneself in order to build
  up the **f.** of others. Ph.2:17
To stand fast in the **f.** 1 Cor.16:13
To strive for the **f.** of the gospel. Ph.1:27
To take hold of the shield of faith in
  combating the devil. Eph.6:11, 16
To teach in **f.** & truth. 1 Tim.2:7
To teach sound doctrine that men may
  be sound in the **f.** Tit.2:1-2
To trust God to take care of needs &
  necessities. Lk.10:4
To walk by **f.** & not sight. 2 Cor.5:7
Essential - Importance of **f.**
  Discussed. Mk.1:15
  For answered prayer. Mk.2:3-4
  For forgiveness. Mk.2:3-4; Acts 10:43
  For power. Acts 3:16
  For receiving answers to prayer.
    Mt.9:22
  For receiving the Holy Spirit. Gal.3:2, 5
  For removing mountains, that is,
    problems. Mk.11:22-23
  For salvation. Verses. Acts 10:43
  Must be accompanied with repentance.
    Mk.1:15
  Must be in Christ. Meaning. Mt.8:8-10

Must be stirred & initiated by God.
  Acts 3:16
Must have genuine **f.** Lk.17:5-6
Must have two essential beliefs.
  Heb.11:6
Must know that **f.** is one of the two
  great pillars of life. Col.1:3-8
Must know that whatever is not of **f.** is
  sin. Ro.14:23
Must not doubt at all. Mt.21:20-21
Must stand by **f.** 2 Cor.1:24, cp.
  Ro.11:20
Evidence of - Proofs of.
  Discussed. Jn.4:43-45; 1 Jn.2:3-29
  Obedience. Heb.5:9
  Two proofs. Jn.4:43-45
Example of.
  Abraham. Justification by **f.** Ro.4:1-25;
    Gal.3:6-7
  Barnabas. A man full of **f.** Acts 11:27
  Centurion. Great **f.** in a soldier.
    Lk.7:1-10
  Friends.
    Their **f.** brings about forgiveness.
      Lk.5:18-20
    Their **f.** saves a friend. Mt.9:2;
      Mk.8:22-26
    Their **f.** saves another. Mt.9:18-34
  Paul. A life of consistent **f.**
    2 Tim.3:10; 4:7
  Philemon. Phile.4-5
  Picture of sacrificial love & **f.**
    Mt.26:6-13
  Stephen. A man full of **f.** Acts 6:5, 8
Fact.
  All believers have the *same kind of*
    faith, a **f.** like everyone else.
    2 Pt.1:1; Tit.1:4
  Christ knows the **f.** & works of a
    church. Rev.2:13; 2:19
  It is impossible to please God without
    f. Heb.11:6
  It is of critical importance, but not as
    important as love. 1 Cor.13:2, 13
  The door of **f.** is now opened to the
    Gentiles. Acts 14:27
  There is only one **f.** Eph.4:4-6
  Unbelief cannot void **f.** Ro.3:3
Founder of the **f.** The Lord Jesus Christ.
  Heb.12:2
Gift of. Discussed. The spiritual gift of **f.**
  Ro.12:3-6; 1 Cor.12:8-10
Great **f.**
  Described. Mt.15:28
  Found in a ruler. Mt.9:18
  Found in a soldier. Lk.7:1-10
  Found in two blind men. Mt.9:27-28
  Jesus acknowledged great **f.** Two
    times. Mt.8:10; 15:28
  Meaning. Mt.9:2
  Misunderstood. Not amount of **f.**, but
    "having" genuine **f.** Lk.17:5-6
Growth in **f.**
  A growing **f.** 2 Th.1:3
  Martha's growth in **f.** Jn.11:17-27
Lack of. (See **UNBELIEF**)
Law of. Discussed. Ro.3:27
Meaning. Mk.16:16; Lk.7:6-8;
  1 Tim.6:11
  Commitment. Jn.2:24
  Discussed. Mk.11:22-23
  Obedience. Mt.21:20-21; Lk.17:14;
    Jn.3:36; 4:50; 4:51-53; 5:5-9; 9:6-7;
    Acts 2:38; 5:32; Heb.5:9
  The substance of things hoped for.
    Heb.11:1

Object of. Discussed. Mt.9:18-34;
  Mk.11:22-23
Power of. (See **FAITH**, Work of)
Purpose. To edify & unify all believers in
  the **f.** until they are conformed to Christ.
  Eph.3:11-13
Results. (See **FAITH**, Work of)
  Are given the hope of righteousness.
    Gal.5:5
  Are given the presence of Christ
    within one's heart. Eph.3:17
  Assures a good testimony & boldness.
    Ro.1:8; Eph.1:15; Col.1:4; 1 Th.1:8;
    1 Tim.3:13
  Become children of God. Gal.3:26
  Edifies people in godliness. 1 Tim.1:4
  Gives access into God's presence &
    grace. Ro.5:2; Eph.3:12
  Gives assurance of cleansing. Heb.
    10:22
  Gives an understanding of creation, of
    its source. Heb.11:3
  Heals a person. Acts 3:16; 14:9-10;
    Jas.5:15
  Makes a person whole. Mt.9:22;
    Mk.5:34; 10:52; Lk.8:48; 17:19
  Raises one up with Christ. Col.2:12
  Reconciles a person if he continues in
    the **f.** Col.1:21-23
  Salvation. Lk.7:50; 18:42; Eph.2:8-10
  Shall receive the inheritance of the
    promise. Gal.3:22; Heb.6:12
  Stirs & develops more & more endur-
    ance. Jas.1:3
  Stirs joy. Ph.1:25-26
  Strengthens churches more & more.
    Acts 16:5
  Will lead to the glory & honor of
    Christ. 1 Pt.1:7
  Will receive the end of our **f.**, even our
    salvation. 1 Pt.1:9
Reward. (See **FAITH**, Work of)
Source of **f.**
  Belief in God. Belief in the God who
    raised Jesus from the dead. Ro.4:23-25
  Established by Christ.
    A new & living **f.** Heb.10:19-21
    By His crucifixion. Gal.2:20
    By His grace. 1 Tim.1:14
    By His resurrection. 1 Cor.15:14, 17
    By sanctification. Acts 26:18
    Discussed. Mt.4:3-11
    The author and finisher of. Heb.12:2
    The power of Jesus. Lk.7:6-8; 7:9-10
    The supreme author of. Heb.10:19-
      11:40
    Through His blood. Ro.3:2
    Through the power of His name.
      Acts 3:16
  God & God alone. Ro.4:17
    By purifying the heart. Acts 15:9
    God works by **f.** not by signs.
      Mt.4:3-11; 12:38-40
    Is the gift of God. Initiated by God.
      Acts 3:16
    Is the gift of righteousness, even the
      gift of our Savior Jesus Christ.
      2 Pt.1:1
    Through the resurrection of Christ.
      1 Pt.1:21
    Word of God. Ro.4:18-21; 10:16-17
  Love. Gal.5:6
  Ministers. Eph.4:11-13, esp. 13
  The Holy Spirit. Gal.5:22-23
Stages - Kinds of.
  Beginning **f.** Jn.8:31

Complaining, limited **f.** Jn.11:21-22
Confirmed **f.** Jn.4:53
Dead **f.** Jas.2:14-26
Declared **f.** Jn.11:25-27
Discussed. Jn.4:46-54; Ro.10:16-17
Does not believe. Jas.1:5-8
Faltering **f.** Mt.14:28-31
Fundamental **f.** Jn.11:23-24
Great **f.** (See **FAITH**, Great) Mt.8:10;
  Lk.7:1-10
Growing **f.** 2 Th.1:3
Intercessory **f.** Saves a friend.
  Mk.8:22-26
Little **f.** Mt.6:30; 8:26; 14:31; 16:8;
  Lk.12:28
No **f.** Mk.4:40
Persevering **f.** Mk.2:3-5
Persistent **f.** Jesus answers persistent
  faith. Mt.9:1-8; Lk.5:18-20; 8:41-42;
  8:49-56
Pessimistic; questioning; unswerving **f.**
  Jn.6:1-15
Prevailing **f.** Mk.5:21-43
Reluctant **f.** Lk.5:4-11
Resting, unlimited **f.** Jn.6:10-13;
  11:21-22; 11:40
Silent **f.** Jn.12:42-43
The most holy **f.** Jude 20
Three kinds of **f.** Jn.11:17-27
True vs. false **f.** Jas.2:14-26
Unlimited, resting **f.** Jn.11:21-22;
  11:40
Weak **f.** Mt.6:30; 8:26; 14:31; 16:8;
  Jn.6:7; 6:8-9
Strength of.
  God & God alone. Mk.11:22-23
  God's Word & God's Word alone.
    Ro.4:18-21
Verses. List of. Acts 10:43
Vs. fear. Faith eliminates fear. Mk.5:36;
  Lk.8:25
Vs. feelings. Heb.10:38
Vs. seeking proof & signs. Mt.4:3-11;
  12:38-40
Vs. the law. Discussed. Ro.4:13-16;
  Gal.3:6-14
Vs. works or deeds.
  Discussed. Mk.16:16; Jn.6:28-29;
    Ro.4:11; Gal.2:15-16; 3:1-5; 3:6-14;
    Jas.2:14-26
  F. apart from works. Jn.4:50
  Illust. in Abraham. Ro.4:1-3
Warning.
  A person can be damned for casting
    off his **f.** 1 Tim.5:12
  A person can be reprobate concerning
    the **f.** 2 Tim.3:8
  A person can deny the **f.** & be worse
    than an infidel. 1 Tim.5:8
  A person can miss the righteousness of
    God. Ro.9:32
  All men do not have **f.** 2 Th.3:2
  F. can be shipwrecked. 1 Tim.1:19-20
  F. without works & fruit cannot save a
    person. Jas.2:14-26
  False teachers can overthrow the **f.** of
    some. 2 Tim.2:18
  Hearing the preached Word does not
    profit a person without **f.** Heb.4:2
  Money can turn a person away from
    the **f.** 1 Tim.6:10
  Some seek to turn believers away from
    the **f.** Acts 13:8
  Some shall depart from the **f.** 1 Tim. 4:1

There is the danger that the earth will
  have no **f.** when Christ returns.
  Lk.18:8
Worldly & empty talk & false knowl-
  edge & speculations can turn a per-
  son away from the **f.** 1 Tim.6:20-21
Work of - What **f.** does--Results.
  Answers prayer. Mk.11:22-23
  Assures salvation. Lk.7:50; Eph.2:8-10
  Causes God to count one righteous.
    Heb.11:4
  Discussed. Ro.3:27-31; 4:1-25; 4:13-16
  Establishes & upholds the law. Ro.3:31
  Gives a person both righteousness &
    salvation. 2 Pt.1:1
  Imparts great power. Mt.17:14-21;
    21:22; Lk.17:5-6; Heb.11:4-5
  Justifies a person. Gal.2:15-16; 2:16;
    2:19-21; 3:1-5; 3:6-14; 3:15-18
    Faith alone justifies. Ro.4:1-25
    Proven by logic. Ro.4:1-25, 1-8
  Lays hold of Jesus' power. Mk.5:21-43;
    Lk.8:40-54
  Makes a person a child of Abraham.
    Gal.3:6-9
  Makes a person whole. Lk.17:19
  Makes all things possible. Mk.9:23
  Overcomes the world. 1 Jn.5:4-5
  Provides a life of **f.** (hope). Gal.3:11
  Puts an end to boasting. Ro.3:27-31
  Quenches the fiery darts of the
    wicked. Eph.6:16
  Removes mountains. Mt.17:20;
    Mk.11:22-23
  Saves a person. Lk.18:42
  Secures the righteousness of God.
    Ro.1:17; 4:4-5; Ph.3:9
  Stirs arduous labor. 1 Th.1:3
  Threefold work. Ro.4:16; Gal.3:23-29

FAITH, THE CHRISTIAN
  Duty.
    Not to deny the **f.** of Christ. Rev.2:13
    To be established in the **f.** Col.2:7
    To be obedient to the **f.** among all na-
      tions of people. Ro.1:5
    To continue in the **f.** Acts 14:22; Col.1:23
    To earnestly contend for the **f.** Jude 3
    To establish the church in the **f.** Acts 16:5
    To examine to see if one is truly in the
      f. 2 Cor.13:5
    To fearlessly proclaim the **f.** to rulers.
      Acts 24:24-25
    To hold fast the profession of our **f.**
      Heb.10:23
    To hold the **f.** in a pure conscience.
      1 Tim.3:9
    To keep the **f.** 2 Tim.4:7
    To keep the **f.** of Jesus. Rev.14:12
    To preach the **f.** Gal.1:23
    To rebuke & make sure believers are
      sound in the **f.** Tit.1:13
    To stand fast in the **f.** 1 Cor.16:13
    To strive for the **f.** of the gospel. Ph.1:27
  Facts.
    False teachers are rejected by the **f.**
      2 Tim.3:8
    Some Jewish priest were obedient to
      the **f.** Acts 6:7
    The **f.** is the **f.** of God's elect people,
      the saints. Tit.1:1; Rev.13:10
    There is a household of **f.**, a body of
      true believers who follow Christ &
      do good to all men. Gal.6:10
    There is *only one f.* Eph.4:4-6
    True believers hold to the same **f.** Tit.1:4

Foundation of the **f**. The Lord Jesus Christ. Heb.12:2
Meaning. Acts 14:22
Purpose of. To edify & unify all believers in the **f**. until they are conformed to Christ. Eph.3:11-13
Warning.
  Any person who does not provide for his family denies the **f**. & is worse than an infidel. 1 Tim.5:8
  Empty speculations & false knowledge has turned some away from the **f**. 1 Tim.6:20-21
  Money has caused some to turn away from the **f**. 1 Tim.6:10
  Some seek to turn believers away from the **f**. 2 Tim.3:8
  Some shall depart from the **f**. in the end times. 1 Tim.4:1
  The **f**. of some has been overturned by false teachers. 2 Tim.2:17-28

FAITHFUL - FAITHFULNESS
Duty.
  Children of deacons must be **f**. Tit.1:6
  Employees must be **f**. in serving their employers. 1 Tim.6:2
  Of all believers.
    To be a **f**. layman. Col.4:9
    To be **f**. despite imprisonment. Acts 28:30-31
    To be **f**. despite persecution. Rev.2:9; 2:13
    To be **f**. despite the lack of blessing from God. Lk.1:8-9
    To be **f**. in all things. 1 Tim.3:11-12
    To be **f**. in helping & ministering to fellow believers & to strangers. 3 Jn.5
    To be **f**. in small matters as well as large matters. Lk.16:10
    To be **f**. in the service of the Lord, **f**. until He returns. Mt.24:45-47
    To be **f**. to Christ despite great trial. Acts 9:23-30
    To be **f**. to the church. Acts 9:26-28
    To be **f**. until Jesus returns. Lk.12:41-48; 19:15-23
    To be **f**. unto death. Rev.2:10; 2:13
    To be steadfast & unmoveable. 1 Cor.15:58
    To hold fast to the **f**. word. Tit.1:9
    To labor to the point of exhaustion. Mk.4:35-41
    To train **f**. men so that they in turn can share the gospel. 2 Tim.2:2
    To watch & work. Because judgment is coming. Mt.25:14-30
  Of ministers.
    Are called to be **f**. 1 Cor.7:25
    God calls ministers because He counts them **f**. 1 Tim.1:12
    To be a **f**. minister for the church. Col.1:7; 4:7; 1 Pt.5:12
    To be found **f**. 1 Cor.4:2; 4:17; Eph.6:21
  Wives of deacons must be **f**. 1 Tim.3:11
Essential. For power. Mk.1:39
Example. Paul's **f**. in evangelism. Acts 28:17
Fact. The gospel is a **f**. message. 1 Tim.1:15; 4:9; 2 Tim.2:11; Tit.3:4-8, esp. 8
Meaning. Col.1:2; 1 Tim.6:11

Need for **f**. In the midst of an immoral, cesspool society. Ro.1:8
Of all believers.
Of Christ. (See **JESUS CHRIST**, Obedience; Sinless)
  Is the **f**. High Priest. Heb.2:17
  Is the **f**. witness. Rev.1:5; 3:14
  To the believer. In three areas. 2 Th.3:3-5
  Was **f**. to God who had appointed Him. Heb.3:2
Of God.
  Is a **f**. Creator who will look after the souls of believers. 1 Pt.4:19
  Is **f**. even if one does not believe. 2 Tim.2:11-13
  Is **f**. in forgiving sins when they are confessed. 1 Jn.1:9
  Is **f**. to complete the work He began in one's heart. Ph.1:6
  Is **f**. to confirm the believer until the end & make him blameless. 1 Cor.1:8-9
  Is **f**. to create a new world, both heavens & earth. Rev.21:5, cp. 1-5; 22:6; cp. 2 Pt.3:10-13
  Is **f**. to deliver the believer from temptation. 1 Cor.10:13
  Is **f**. to His promise. Heb.10:23; 11:11
  Is **f**. to keep one from evil. 2 Th.3:1-5
  Is **f**. to keep one from falling. Jude 24-25
  Is **f**. to preserve the believer. Jn.10:28-29; 1 Th.5:23-24; 1 Pt.1:5
Results.
  Determines the reward for believers. Mt.25:20-23; 25:24-30; Lk.19:15-23
  Secures more & more. Lk.8:18
  Will be given the crown of life. Rev.2:10
  Will be made ruler over all that God has. Lk.12:42-45
  Will be made ruler over many things. Mt.25:19-23
Stirred by. The hope for heaven. 2 Cor.5:1-4
Title of. Believers.
  Are called "**f**. brothers in Christ." Col.1:2
  Are called "the **f**. in Christ Jesus. Eph.1:1
Verses. List of. Lk.17:7-10; 19:15-23
Vs. unfaithfulness. Mt.25:14-30
Who the **f**. are. Eph.1:1-2

FAITHFUL BROTHERS - HOLY BROTHERS
Discussed. Acts 9:32; 1 Cor.1:2; 1 Pt.1:15-16
Meaning. 1 Cor.1:2; Ph.1:1; Col.1:2

FAITHLESS - FAITHLESSNESS (See DOUBT; UNBELIEF; UNFAITHFULNESS)
Discussed. Mt.17:14-21; 17:17-18
Jesus' death reveals weak faith. Jn.13:36-38
Meaning. Lk.9:41; Ro.1:31; Gal.5:22-23; 2 Tim3:2-4
Sin of.
  Not believing all that the Scripture says. Lk.24:25
  Not trusting the presence & care of Christ. Lk.8:22-25
  This present generation. Mt.17:17; Lk.9:41

FALL OF MAN (See MAN, Fall of)

FALLING AWAY - FALL, SPIRITUAL (See APOSTASY; BACKSLIDING; DENIAL; REBELLION)
Discussed. Lk.11:44; 17:1-2; Heb.5:11-6:3; 2 Pt.1:10
Duty.
  Not to **f**. by persecution & ridicule. Mt.13:21; Mk.4:17; Jn.16:1-4
  Not to do anything that will make a brother **f**. Ro.14:21
  Not to **f**. in anything. 1 Cor.10:32; 2 Cor.6:3
  Not to **f**. in questionable activities. Ro.14:1-23; 1 Cor.8:1-13
  Not to cause others to **f**. 1 Cor.8:9-11; 10:23-28; 10:29-11:1
  To be without **f**. until the day of Christ. Ph.1:10
  To cut out of one's life all that **f**. Mt.5:29-30; 18:7-9; Mk.9:43-48
  To mark those who cause division & **f**. Ro.16:17-18
Fact.
  Christ died for our **f**. Ro.4:25
  Many will be **f**. because of Christ in the end time. Mt.24:9-10
  The gift of Christ justifies us from many **f**. Ro.5:16
  We all **f**. in many things, especially in word & tongue. Jas.3:2
How. Six ways. Mk.9:42
Judgment of those who **f**. Shall be cast into a furnace of fire. Mt.13:37-42
Meaning. Mt.5:29; 17:27; Mk.14:27; 2 Cor.6:3; Heb.6:6; Ph.1:9-10
Precautions against. Six precautions. Heb.6:9-20
Steps to correcting. Mt.18:15-20
Verses. List of. Mk.9:42
Warning against **f**. others. Mt.18:5-10; Lk.17:1-2
  If one **f**. in one point, he is guilty of all the law. Jas.2:10
Ways one causes others to sin. Mt.18:15
What **f**. men about Christ.
  Four things **f**. Jn.6:59-71
  His claims. Jn.6:61
  His cross, blood. Jn.6:61; 1 Cor.1:23; Gal.5:11
  His Lordship. Jn.6:62
  His Person & claims. 1 Pt.2:7-8
  His works. Mt.11:1-6, esp. 6; Mt.13:53-58

FALSE ACCUSERS (See SLANDEROUS)

FALSE MINISTERS (See TEACHERS, FALSE)

FALSE PROFESSION (See HYPOCRISY; PROFESSION, FALSE)

FALSE PROPHETS (See TEACHERS, FALSE)

FALSE TEACHERS (See TEACHERS, FALSE)

FALSEHOOD (See DECEPTION; HYPOCRISY; LYING)

FAME - FAMOUS (See **HONOR;
PRIDE; RECOGNITION**)
Duty. Not to seek after. Mt.6:1-5
Facts about. Fourfold. Mt.14:5
Rejected. By Christ. Mt.4:5-10
Seeking. Discussed. Mt.18:1-4

FAMILY - FAMILIES (See **FATHERS;
MOTHERS; PARENTS**)
Basis of.
A spiritual union, a cleaving wrought
by Christ. Mt.19:5-6; 19:5
Discussed. Mt.19:1-12; 19:5; Lk.8:19-21
Love & submission. Eph.5:22, 25, 33;
Col.3:18-19
Marriage. Mt.19:5-6; Eph.5:31
Mutual respect. Recognizing the order
of creation. 1 Cor.11:7-10; Tit.2:4-5
Responsible children. Honoring &
obeying their parents. Eph.6:1-4;
Col.3:20
Responsible parents. Being gentle &
nurturing children in
the Lord. Eph.6:4; Col.3:21
The right order with the husband as the
head. 1 Cor.11:3; Eph.5:23; Tit.2:4-5
Children. (See **CHILDREN**)
Dangers - Failures facing the **f.**
A child becoming self-righteous.
Lk.15:25-32
A child going astray. Lk.15:11-16, cp.
17-24
A lost **f.** member. Discussed. Lk.15:8-10
Adultery. (See **ADULTERY**)
Division over Christ. Mt.10:34-37;
Mk.13:12-13; Lk.12:49-53
Divorce. (See **DIVORCE**)
Doubting & questioning Christ & His
claims. Mt.12:46-50; Jn.7:2-5
Indulging & pampering a child.
Eph.6:4
Opposing & persecuting **f.** members.
A believing member of the family.
Mt.10:21; 10:34-37; 10:35-37;
12:46-50
Overcontrolling or undercontrolling a
child. Eph.6:4
Putting family before Christ. Lk.9:59-62;
12:49-53; 14:18-20; 14:26
Discussed.
The believing & unbelieving spouse.
1 Cor.7:12-16
The believing wife & husband are to
walk in a spirit of submission & love.
Eph.5:22-23
The Christian & the family. Col.3:18-21
Duty.
Function of husband & wife. 1 Tim.
2:12-14; 1 Pt.3:1-6; 3:7
Leaders must manage their **f.** well.
1 Tim.3:4-5; 3:11-12
Not to be affected by a **f.** member's
sin. Mt.18:25
Not to put the **f.** before Christ.
Lk.12:49-53
Not to use the **f.** as an excuse for re-
jecting Christ. Lk.14:18-20
To achieve its potential. Cannot with-
out Christ. Mt.10:35-37
To be godly.
Essential for service. Mt.4:18-20
Picture of. Lk.1:5-25
To be reached first. Mt.10:5-6
To be the center of the church's minis-
try. Lk.9:4

To be the strongest of relationships.
Mt.10:35-37
To care for all members, even elderly
parents. Mk.7:11; 1 Tim.5:4-8
To esteem highly. Example of. Christ.
Mt.12:46-47
To go & reach first. Mt.9:4-7
To guard against false teachers.
2 Jn.10-11
To open one's home to believers. Acts
18:2
To put Christ first. Lk.14:18-20
To witness to one's **f.** Lk.8:38-39;
Jn.4:53-54
Fathers. (See **FATHERS**)
Husbands. (See **HUSBAND**)
Ministry of. To be the center of the
church's ministry. Lk.9:4; 1 Cor.16:19
Mothers. (See **MOTHER**)
Nature. Is a miniature of the church.
1 Tim.3:4-5, cp. Eph.5:22-33
Needs of. (See **NEEDS**, Met - Provided for)
Jesus cares & meets. Mt.8:14-17
Of apostles. Greatly influenced them.
Mt.10:2
Of Jesus. (See **JESUS CHRIST**, Family)
Order of. (See **FAMILY**, Basis - Foun-
dation of)
As established by God. Eph.5:22-24;
1 Cor.11:2-16
Orderly arrangement necessary.
1 Tim.2:12-14
Place of man & woman. 1 Cor.11:2-16
Parents. (See **PARENTS**)
Protected. By law on divorce. Mt.5:32
Wives. (See **WIFE - WIVES**)

FAMILY OF GOD
Basis of.
A father-child relationship. Mt.7:11
A true spiritual kinship, not a blood or
social relationship. Mk.3:33-35
Discussed. Mt.12:48-50
Not of man's heritage, flesh, or will.
Lk.8:20
Described. As the church & household of
God. Eph.2:19
How one becomes a member of God's **f.**
By being adopted as a child of God.
Ro.8:15-17
By being born of God. 1 Jn.3:9-10
By doing the will of the Father, the
Father of the Lord Jesus Christ.
Mt.12:50
By faith in Christ Jesus. Gal.3:26, cp.
Jn.1:12
By receiving Christ. Jn.1:12
By separating oneself from the world.
2 Cor.6:17-18
By the redemption of Christ. Gal.4:4-5
The blessings of being a member of
God's **f.**
Becomes a child of the living God.
Ro.9:26
Becomes an heir of God, an equal heir
with Christ. Ro.8:16-17; Gal.3:29;
4:7; Tit.1:7; 1 Pt.1:3-4. Cp. Heb.1:14;
6:17; 11:7
Is given open access into the very
presence & care of God Himself.
Gal.4:6-7
Is made a member of God's very own
household, a household of all races
& nations of people. Eph.2:19

Is made one with other believers &
made a brother to Christ. Heb.2:11,
cp. Ro.8:29
Is reconciled with all other believers--
no matter the race
or nation. Eph.2:19, cp. 2:11-18
Shall be delivered from the bondage of
corruption. Ro.8:21, cp.
1 Cor.15:42-44; 15:50-58
Shall be raised from the dead & never
die anymore. Lk.20:35-38

FAMINE
Fact. To be severe in the last days.
Rev.6:5-6
Predicted in last days. Will be intensified.
Lk.21:11

FAN INTO FLAME
Meaning. 2 Tim.1:6

FARMER (See **SOWER, PARABLE OF
THE SOWER OR FARMER**)
Illustrates.
Patience needed to combat temptation
& trials & to wait for the Lord's re-
turn. Jas.5:7-9
Traits. Discussed. 2 Tim.2:6

FASHION - FASHIONED (See **CON-
FORM - CONFORMED**)
Fact.
Believers are not to **f.** themselves after
their former lusts. 1 Pt.1:14
Jesus Christ left heaven & became **f.**
as a man. Ph.2:7-8
The **f.** of the rich man fades away.
Jas.1:11
The **f.** of the world passes away.
1 Cor.7:31
Meaning. Ph.3:20-21

FAST - FASTING
Dangers. Fourfold. Mt.6:16
Duty - Essential.
Discussed. Mt.6:16-18; 6:16
For preparation & temptation. Mt.4:1
To sometimes separate oneself from
one's spouse & **f.** 1 Cor.7:5
Examples of **f.**
God-fearing men. Acts 10:1-2, 30
Jesus.
Criticized because He fasted so lit-
tle. Lk.5:33-34
Fasted 40 days & nights. Mt.4:1-2
Questioned about **f.** Mk.2:18-22
Ministers. 2 Cor.6:4-5
Paul. Acts 9:9; 2 Cor.11:27
The church. Acts 14:23
The dedicated woman. Lk.2:37
Jesus' disciples questioned about.
Mt.9:14-17
Motive. Right vs. wrong **f.** Mt.6:16-18
When to **f.**
Discussed. Mt.6:16-18
Two times. Mk.2:18-22
Vs. when not to **f.** Mt.9:15
When a person is ordained to the min-
istry. Acts 13:1-3
When courage is needed. Mk.14:66-72

FATE (See **DEATH; DESTINY; JUDG-
MENT**)
Man's words determine his **f.** Mt.12:31-37

FATHER, GOD AS (See **GOD, NAMES - TITLES OF**)

FATHER - FATHERS
Duty.
　Discussed. Eph.5:25-33
　Not to provoke his children. Eph.6:4; Col.3:20-21
　Not to seek to replace God in the eyes of children. Mt.10:34-37; 23:9
　To chasten & discipline his children. Heb.12:5-7, esp. 7
　To exhort, comfort, & charge his children. 1 Th.2:11
　To forgive & receive a repentant child. Lk.15:20-24
　To love his wife. Eph.5:25-33; Col.3:19
　To provide for his children. Mt.7:9-10
　To put the call of God before one's **f**. Mt.4:21-22
　To rear his children to be obedient. Eph.6:1-4; Col.3:18-21
　To seek Christ in behalf of a sick child. Mk.5:21-24, 35-43; Lk.8:41-42, 49-56
Duty toward one's **f**.
　Not to rebuke a **f**. 1 Tim.5:1
　To honor & take care of one's **f**. when he is aged. Mt.15:3-6; 1 Tim.5:4-8
　To leave one's **f**. & mother when one marries. Mt.19:5
　To obey. Eph.6:1; Col.3:20
　To put the call of Christ before one's **f**. Mt.4:21-22
　To serve & work with one's father. Mt.4:21; Ph.2:22
Mistakes of. Threefold. Mt.7:11

FATHERLESS (See **ORPHANS**)

FAULT-FINDERS (See **CRITICISM**)
Against Christ.
　His claim to be the Messiah, the Savior of the world. Jn.6:41-51, esp. 41
　His power to forgive sins. Mk.2:5-12
Against God & His coming judgment. Ro.2:4-5; 9:19-21
Caused by.
　A desire for prominence, recognition & position. 3 Jn.9-10
　Greed. Jn.12:3-6
　Judging people by man-made rituals & rules & religious tradition. Mt.12:1-2; 15:1-2; Mk.7:1-3
　Self-righteousness. Mt.9:10-13; Mk.2:16-17; Lk.5:27-32, esp. 29-31; 15:1-2; 19:7
　Unbelief in Christ. Mk.2:5-7; Jn.6:41-42
Described. Mt.11:16-19
　By Jesus Christ. (See **HEAL - HEALING; JESUS CHRIST**, Power Of)
　He **f**. & chastens the irresponsible & sinning believer. Heb.12:5
　He **f**. disease. Lk.4:39
　He **f**. His disciples for being worldly & carnal. Mk.8:27-33, esp. 33; Lk.9:55-56, cp. 51-56
　He **f**. nature & delivers men. Mt.8:26; Mk.4:39; Lk.8:24
　He **f**. sickness & evil spirits. Mt.17:14-21; Lk.4:38-39
　He **f**. the devil & evil spirits & sets people free. Mt.17:18; Mk.1:25; 9:25; Lk.4:35; 9:42
　He **f**. those He loves. Rev.3:19

Duty.
　Not to despise the rebuke of the Lord. Heb.12:5-7
　Not to **f**. an elder, but appeal to him as a father. 1 Tim.5:1
　To be without **f**. in the midst of a crooked & perverse nation. Ph.2:15
　To call upon the name of the Lord in rebuking Satan. Jude 9
　To **f**. & convict people. Tit.2:15
　To **f**. a faithless & perverse generation. Lk.9:41
　To **f**. a judgmental spirit. Lk.9:55-56
　To **f**. false teachers. Tit.1:13-14
　To **f**. hypocritical living. Mt.3:7-10; Gal.2:11-13
　To **f**. sinning brothers. Lk.17:3-4
　To **f**. those who resist the Holy Spirit. Acts 7:51
　To **f**. those who sin before all. 1 Tim.5:20
　To use the Word of God to **f**. people. 2 Tim.3:16; 4:2
　To willingly receive the **f**. of the Lord. Heb.12:5-7
Meaning. 1 Tim.5:1; 2 Tim.4:2

FAVOR - FAVORED (See **BLESSED, THE; BLESSINGS; GRACE; PROMISES**)

FAVORITISM (See **DISCRIMINATION; PARTIALITY; PREJUDICE**)
And God.
　Does not show **f**. Lk.13:29-30; Acts 2:17-21; 10:23-33; 10:34-35; Ro.2:11-15; 3:29-30
　Judgment will be without **f**. Ro.2:11-15
Discussed. Jas.2:1-13
Duty. Of the minister. Not to show **f**. 1 Tim.5:21
Feeling as though one is a **f**. of God. Mk.10:36-37
Meaning. Jas.3:17-18
Temptation of.
　Discussed. Jas.2:1-13
　Feeling that "but for the grace of God, there go I." Mt.8:4

FEAR
Caused by - What men fear.
　Civil & religious authority. Jn.7:13; 12:42; 20:19; Gal.2:12
　Coming judgment. Heb.10:26-27; 11:7; 1 Jn.4:17-18
　Coming of Christ. Lk.21:25-26
　Darkness. Being in the dark; spiritual blindness. Jn.6:17-19
　Death. Heb.2:15
　Evil associations & worldliness. Lk.22:54-62
　Jesus' power. Lk.7:16
　List of ten things. Lk.9:26
　Men.
　　F. men seeking to harm. Jn.9:22; 20:19
　　F. the displeasure & opposition of one's peers. Gal.2:12
　　F. the loss of position & livelihood. Jn.12:42; 19:38
　　F. to stand up for Christ. Mt.26:56; Lk.23:50-56
　　F. to witness. 2 Tim.1:7-8
　　F. what men can do. **F**. men more than fear God. Reason. Jn.19:13-15
　Persecution. Jn.20:19; 2 Tim.1:6-12; 1 Pt.4:12-13
　Signs of the end time. Lk.21:25-26
　Unexplainable events. Mt.27:54; 28:4

Deliverance from Overcome by.
　Christ's power. Mt.8:23-27
　Christ's presence. Mk.10:32; Jn.6:19-21
　Discussed. Jn.6:16-21; 1 Jn.4:18
　Faith & love. 1 4:16-18
　God's power, love, & self-discipline. 2 Tim.1:7
　Love. 1 Jn.4:18
　The acts of God. Acts 2:43; 5:5, 11; 19:17
　The death of Christ. Heb.2:14-15
　The Holy Spirit & spiritual adoption. Ro.8:15
　The promise of God. Mt.6:33-34; Lk.12:31-32
Discussed. Ro.8:15; 2 Tim.1:6-12; 1 Jn.4:18
Duty.
　Must cry for help. Mk.6:47-49
　Must fear. Reason. Heb.4:1
　Must fear God. Ro.3:18; 1 Pt.1:17-21; 1:17; 2:16-17
　Must not fear. Mt.10:30-31; 2 Tim.1:7
　Not to **f**. persecution. Rev.2:10
　To live pure lives with **f**. 1 Pt.3:2
　To move upon earth in **f**. of God's coming judgment. Heb.11:7
　To perfect holiness in the **f**. of the Lord. 2 Cor.7:1
　To preach the Word without **f**. Ph.1:14
　To save people for Christ with **f**. Jude 23
　To submit ourselves one to another in the **f**. of God. Eph.5:21
　To walk in the **f**. of the Lord. Acts 9:31
　To work & serve with **f**. & trembling. Eph.6:5; 1 Pt.2:18
　To work out one's salvation with fear & trembling. Ph.2:12
In the end time. Discussed. Lk.21:25-26; Rev.6:15-16
Kinds. Godly **f**. vs. bad **f**. Mt.8:26
Meaning. Mt.10:28; Lk.7:16-17; 1 Pt.1:17-21
Results - Causes one to.
　Act as dead, asleep, & unnoticed. Mt.28:4
　Be ashamed, embarrassed. 2 Tim.1:7-8
　Be silent - failing to witness. Jn.9:22; 2 Tim.1:7-8
　Compromise. Jn.19:12-16
　Deny Christ. Mk.14:66; Lk.22:54-62
　Desert Christ. Mk.14:50; 14:51-52
　Disbelieve. Three fears. Jn.11:47-48
　Fail in heart. Lk.21:26
　Fail to stand up for Christ. Lk.23:50-54
　Glorify God. Lk.7:16
　Pretend, deny, curse. Mk.14:66-72
　Reverence the Lord. Lk.8:25
Vs. faith. Mk.5:36; Lk.8:25
What to fear.
　Being rejected by God. Ro.11:20
　Civil authorities. Ro.13:7
　Covetousness & selfishness. Lk.12:13-21
　Discussed. Acts 9:31; 2 Cor.11:1-15
　False teaching. 2 Cor.11:1-15
　God. Mt.10:28; Lk.7:16-17; Heb. 12:28-29; 1 Pt.1:17-21; 1:17; Rev.14:7
　Godly conviction. 2 Cor.7:10-11
　God's awesome presence & power. Heb.12:21, cp. 18-21
　Judgment. Mt.10:28; Lk.12:20-21
　Meaning. Acts 2:43
　Missing the promises of God. Heb.4:1
　Not persecution. Mt.10:28
　Not to **f**. men. Reasons. Mt.10:28; Lk.12:4-12

MASTER SUBJECT INDEX

The awesome responsibility to preach
the gospel. 1 Cor.2:1-5, esp. 3
The holy presence of Christ.
Rev.1:17-18
The power of Christ. Mk.4:37-41, esp.
41; 5:33, cp. 25-33; Lk.5:26; 8:37
Things to **f**. & not to **f**. Lk.12:1-12;
12:13-21
Unbelief. Ro.11:20

FEARLESSNESS (See **COURAGE**)
Duty.
To preach the Word without fear. Ph.1:14
To witness without fear. 2 Tim.1:7
Source.
God's care & provision. Mt.10:30-31
Love. 1 Jn.4:18
The death of Christ. Heb.2:14-15
The Holy Spirit. Ro.8:15
The promise of God. Acts 27:25, cp.
2 Pt.1:4

FEASTS, RELIGIOUS
Discussed. Three major **f**. of the Jews.
How fulfilled in Christ. Acts 2:1
Of Dedication. Jn.10:22
Of Pentecost. Acts 2:1
Of Tabernacles. Jn.7:37
Of the First Fruits or the **F**. of Harvest.
Acts 2:1
Of unleavened bread. Mt.26:17; Lk.22:1

FEED - FEEDING, SPIRITUAL (See
SHEPHERD)

FEEDING OF THE FIVE THOUSAND
Discussed. Jn.6:1-15
Essentials for ministry. Mt.14:15-21
Miracle of. By Christ. How to minister.
Lk.9:10-17

FEELING - FEELINGS
Discussed. Eph.4:17-19; Heb.10:38
Vs. faith. Heb.10:38

FELIX
Discussed. Acts 24:1-27

FELLOWSHIP (See **ABIDE - ABIDING;
BROTHERHOOD; UNITY**)
Based upon - Source of.
Abiding in Christ. Jn.15:1-8
Discussed. Lk.8:21
Forgiving others. Eph.4:31-32
God & Christ. 1 Jn.1:3
Opening one's heart. Rev.3:20
Receiving the Word & continuing in
its teaching. Acts 2:42
The gospel of the Lord Jesus Christ.
Ph.1:5
The Holy Spirit. Ph.2:1
Treating others as we should. 1 Pt.3:8
Walking in the light. 1 Jn.1:7
Danger - Problems - Errors - Mistakes.
Destroyed by false teachers. Jude 12
F. with the world. 2 Cor.6:14-16
Revelling in **f**. and not witnessing.
Jn.20:17-18
Withdrawing. What causes. Jn.20:24-25;
Heb.10:25
Discussed. Jn.6:56; Acts 2:42
Marks of a strong church **f**. Ro.15:1-13
F. was the very purpose for Jesus
coming. 1 Jn.1:3-4

Duty.
Not to **f**. with devils & false worship.
1 Cor.10:20
Not to **f**. with unbelievers. 2 Cor.6:14-18
Not to have **f**. with the works of dark-
ness. Eph.5:11
To **f**. & be sociable. Jn.2:1-2
To know the **f**. of Christ's sufferings.
Ph.3:10
Meaning - Nature. 2 Cor.6:14-16
A spiritual bond of friends. Jn.15:14-15
Is spiritual. Acts 4:32; 1 Jn.1:3; 1:7
One heart & one soul. Acts 4:32
Results.
Eternal **f**. with God in the new heavens
& earth. Rev.21:3-4
Forgiveness of sins. 1 Jn.1:7
Joy. 1 Jn.1:3-4
The **f**. of Christ. Is desired by Christ.
Lk.19:5-6
Unity. Ph.2:1
What believers share. (See **INDWELL-
ING PRESENCE**)
Everything: worship, prayer, food,
money, & possessions. Acts 2:41-47
Ministry. 2 Cor.8:4
The **f**. of Christ. Mt.18:20; Lk.24:15,
32; Acts 4:13; 1 Cor.1:9; Ph.3:10;
1 Jn.1:3; Rev.3:20
The **f**. of Christ's sufferings. Ph.3:10
The **f**. of God in the new heavens &
earth. Rev.21:3-4
The **f**. of God the Father. Heb.7:19;
10:22; Jas.4:8; 1 Jn.1:3
The **f**. of God's Son. 1 Cor.1:9
The **f**. of ministering & giving.
2 Cor.8:4
The **f**. of other believers. Acts 2:41-47;
1 Jn.1:3, 7
The **f**. of the gospel. Ph.1:5
The **f**. of the Holy Spirit. Jn.14:16-17;
Ro.8:14-15, 26; Ph.2:1
The **f**. of the mystery of Christ.
Eph.3:9
The **f**. of the mystery of the church.
Eph.3:9
The gospel. Ph.1:5
True **f**. Mk.3:33-35

FERVENT - FERVENCY (See **FERVOR;
ZEAL**)
Duty.
To arise and stand forth. Mk.3:3
To be **f**. in loving one another.
1 Pt.4:8
To be **f**. in prayer. Jas.5:16
Example. Apollos. Acts 18:25

FERVOR
Duty.
To arise and stand forth. Mk.3:3
To have **f**. in loving one another.
1 Pt.4:8
To have **f**. in prayer. Jas.5:16
To keep your spiritual **f**.. Ro.12:11
Example. Apollos. Acts 18:25
Meaning. Ro.12:11

FESTUS
Discussed. Acts 25:1-26:32

FICKLENESS (See **DOUBLE-MINDED;
INSTABILITY; WAVERING**)
Caused by.
False doctrine & teaching. Eph.4:14;
Heb.13:9
False teachers. Acts 14:8-19, esp. 19;
Eph.4:14
Fearing religious or civil authorities.
Gal.2:12
Lack of faith. Jas.1:6
Lacking the heart to continue on. Acts
13:13
Listening to & accepting another gos-
pel. Gal.1:6-9
Trait - Characteristic of.
Many converts. Mt.13:5-7, 20-22;
Mk.4:16-19
This age & period of history. Lk.7:29-35
Unbelievers. Acts 14:8-19

FIDELITY (See **DEDICATION**)

FIERCE (See **BRUTAL**)

FIERY LAKE; FIRE
Discussed. Rev.20:14
Who will be in the fiery lake.
Sinners: a list of the doomed.
Rev.21:8
The beast & the false prophet.
Rev.19:20
Satan will be thrown into. Rev.20:10
Unbelievers. Rev.20:15

FIG TREE
Cursed by Christ.
A fruitless life. Mk.11:12-14
Why Jesus destroyed. Mt.21:17-22
Discussed. Jn.1:48
Parable of. Must bear fruit or perish.
Lk.13:6-9
Symbolized.
A fruitless, barren life. Mt.21:19
Israel. Mt.21:19; Mk.11:20-21
Judgment in all of life. Mk.11:12-14
The Lord's return. Mt.24:32-35

FILTHY - FILTHINESS (See **DEFILE -
DEFILEMENT; OBSCENITY; UN-
CLEANNESS**)
Duty.
Not to have any part of anything that is
f. Eph.5:3-4
To lay aside all **f**. Jas.1:21
Results. Keeps one out of the kingdom of
God. Eph.5:5
Trait - Characteristic of.
False teachers. 2 Pt.2:10
Religionists, hypocrites. Mt.23:27
Unbelievers, the old man. Ro.6:19

FILTHY LUCRE (See **LOVER OF
MONEY**)

FINANCES (See **MATERIALISM;
MONEY; RICHES; STEWARDSHIP**)
Policies of. Paul's **f**. policy criticized.
2 Cor.11:7-12

FINANCIAL SUPPORT (See **GIVE -
GIVING; STEWARDSHIP; TITHE**)

FINE-SOUNDING ARGUMENTS
Meaning. Col.2:4

FLOG - FLOGGING
Discussed. Mt.27:26-38; Jn.19:1;
2 Cor.6:4-5
Meaning. Lk.18:32-33
Of Christ. Discussed. Mt.27:26-38
Of cords. Meaning. Jn.2:15
Of Old Testament believers. Heb.11:36
Of Paul. 2 Cor.6:4-5; 11:24-25
Predicted that believers will suffer **b.**
Mt.10:17

FLOOD, THE
Facts.
Covered the earth. 2 Pt.3:5-6
Guarantees that the whole world will
be judged in the future. 2 Pt.2:4-9
Was a judgment upon a sensual & un-
believing world. Mt.24:37-39
Was escaped by Noah through believ-
ing the Word of God. Heb.11:7
Was preceded by a great demonstra-
tion of God's longsuffering.
1 Pt.3:20
Symbol - Type of.
Baptism. 1 Pt.3:20-22
Coming judgment. 2 Pt.3:5-18
The return of Christ. Mt.24:37-39

FOLLY
Discussed. 2 Tim.3:3
Fact. The preaching of the cross is **f.** to
the unbeliever. 1 Cor.1:18
Meaning. Mk.7:22

FOLLOW - FOLLOWING JESUS
Discussed. Lk.9:23
Duty.
To **f.** Jesus, seeking salvation & truth.
Jn.1:35-37
To **f.** immediately after healing & sal-
vation. Lk.18:43
To **f.** the steps of Jesus in suffering.
1 Pt.2:21; Rev.14:4
Meaning. Mt.16:24; Mk.8:34; Jn.1:43;
1 Pt.2:21
Results.
Proves that one belongs to Christ.
Jn.10:27
Shall receive the light of life. Jn.8:12
Will be with Jesus where He is--in
heaven. Jn.12:26

FOLLOW THROUGH - FOLLOW-UP
Duty. To strengthen the church. Acts
14:21-28
Essential for God's leadership. Mt.2:12
Of a new church. By the mother **c.** Acts
11:22-24

FOOD (See EATING; GLUTTONY;
NEED - NECESSITIES)
Attitude about. Right vs. wrong attitude.
Mt.6:25; 6:31-32
Duty. Not to worry about **f.** God pro-
vides. Mt.6:25-34; Lk.12:22-34
What defiles a man. Mt.15:17-20

FOOD, SPIRITUAL (See FULLNESS,
SPIRITUAL; HUNGER, SPIRITUAL;
SATISFACTION, SPIRITUAL)

FOOLISH - FOOLISHNESS (See
FOLLY)
Discussed. 2 Tim.3:3
Fact. The preaching of the cross is **f.** to
the unbeliever. 1 Cor.1:18

FOOLISH, THE VS. THE WISE
BUILDER
Discussed. Mt.7:24-27

FORBEAR - FORBEARANCE (See
BEARING WITH ONE ANOTHER;
ENDURANCE; PERSEVERANCE;
STEADFASTNESS)
Duty.
To be **f.** with one's fellow workers.
Eph.6:9
To love by **f.** with all things. 1 Cor.13:7
To put on **f.** Col.3:13
Meaning. Eph.4:1-2

FORBEARANCE OF GOD
Duty. Not to despise the **f.** of God.
Ro.2:4
Is the source of salvation, the very reason
we are saved. Ro.3:25

FOREIGNER
Described.
As an unbeliever. Eph.2:19
As Gentiles. Eph.2:19

FOREKNOWLEDGE OF GOD (See
CHOSEN; ELECTION; PREDESTI-
NATION)
Fact.
Election is based upon. 1 Pt.1:2
God foretold the death of Christ. Acts
2:23; 3:18
God knows all future events.
Mt.24:36; Acts 15:18
Guarantees a remnant of believers.
Ro.11:2
Predestination is based upon. Ro.8:29
Meaning. Acts 2:23; Ro.8:29; 1 Pt.1:2
Verses. List of. Acts 2:23

FOREORDAINED - FOREORDINA-
TION (See CHOSE - CHOSEN;
ELECTION; PREDESTINATION)

FORERUNNER
Christ is the **f.** of the believer. Heb.6:18-20
John the Baptist was the **f.** of Christ.
Mt.3:1-3

FORFEITED HIS VERY SELF
Meaning. Lk.9:25; 1 Cor.9:27
Who is **f.**
Sinful angels were. 2 Pt.2:4
The undisciplined, those who lack
self-control will be **f.** 1 Cor.9:27
The worthless will be **f.** Mt.25:14-30,
esp. 30

FORGETFULNESS, SPIRITUAL
Discussed. 2 Pt.1:8-11
Duty.
Must not forget to be hospitable.
Heb.13:2
Must not forget to do good & to give.
Heb.13:16
Must not forget the Word of God.
Jas.1:22-25, esp. 25

FORGETTING THE PAST
Discussed. Ph.3:12-16

FORGIVENESS, HUMAN
Attitudes toward. Mt.6:14-15
Discussed. Mt.6:12; 6:14-15; 26:28;
Ro.4:6-8

Duty - Essential.
To be kind, tenderhearted, & forgiving
of one another. Eph.4:24
To forbear one another & to forgive
one another. Col.3:13
To forgive all offenses. Mk.11:25
To forgive an unlimited number of
times. Mt.18:21-35, esp. 21-22;
Lk.17:3-4
To put on a forgiving spirit. Col.3:12-14,
esp. 13
Importance of.
Assures that one's prayers will be an-
swered (being forgiven). Mt.6:14-
15; Mk.11:25
Assures the **f.** of God. Mk.11:25;
Lk.6:37
Cleanses one's conscience. 1 Jn.3:20-21
God does not **f.** if we do not **f.**
Mt.6:14-15; Mk.11:25-26; Lk.6:37;
1 Pt.3:9
Is the basic principle of prayer.
Mt.6:14-15
Is the most important thing in life.
Mt.6:14
Relationships are impossible without **f.**
Mt.18:22
Motive. Why we should **f.** others. Be-
cause God has forgiven us. Eph.4:32
Spirit of. Mt.18:21-35; Acts 7:60
Verses. List of. Ro.4:6-8
Who is to be **f.**
A divisive person. 2 Cor.2:5-11
All believers. Eph.4:32; Phile.1:8-21
Those who fail us & forsake us.
2 Tim.4:16
Those who offend. Mt.6:14-15;
Eph.4:32
Those who persecute us. Lk.23:34;
Acts 7:60

FORGIVENESS, SPIRITUAL (See RE-
MISSION)
Attitudes toward. Mt.6:14-15
Condition - Prerequisites for **f.**
Discussed. Mt.6:14-15
Repentance. Lk.3:3
F. of others. Essential. Time after time.
Mt.6:14; 18:21-35, esp. 21-22;
Mk.11:25-26; Lk.6:37; 17:3-4
Described. Mt.18:22
Discussed. Mt.6:12; 6:14-15; 26:28; Acts
2:38; 10:43; Eph.1:7; Col.1:14;
1 Jn.1:9
Believers given authority to remit &
retain sins. Jn.20:23
God's **f.** unlimited. Lk.17:3-4
Man's dark sinfulness & God's great **f.**
Jn.8:1-11
Steps to **f.** Lk.5:17-26
Duty.
Must be cleansed of sin before serving
Christ. Jn.13:6-11
Not to think one can sin & sin & still
be **f.** Eph.5:5-6
To be cleansed & washed of sins.
Heb.10:22
To pray for **f.** Mt.6:12; Lk.11:4
To preach repentance & **f.** of sins.
Lk.24:47-48; Acts 26:18, cp. 12-18
How one receives.
By believing in Christ. Acts 10:43
By coming & believing. Mk.2:3-4
By confessing our sins. 1 Jn.1:9
By forgiving others. Mt.6:14-15;
Mk.11:25-26; Lk.11:25-26; 1 Pt.3:9

By God's grace & love. Lk.7:42;
Ro.4:7-8; Eph.2:1-10; 4:32;
Col.2:13; Tit.3:3-7
By repentance. Acts 2:38; 8:22
Through Christ. Mt.9:2; Mk.2:8-11;
3:28; Acts 5:31; 13:38; Eph.1:7;
1 Jn.1:9; 2:1-2
Through Christ's blood. Mt.26:26-28;
Ro.3:25; Col.1:14; 2:13; Heb.9:13-
15; 9:22
Through prayer. Lk.11:2-4; Jas.5:14-15
Through redemption. Eph.1:7;
Col.1:14; Heb.9:12-15
Importance of.
F. is the basic principle of prayer.
Mt.6:14-15
F. is symbolized in the Lord's Supper.
Mt.26:26-30
F. is the most important thing in life.
Mt.6:14
Meaning. Mt.26:28; Acts 2:38; Eph.1:7
Misconceptions - Errors - Mistakes.
Thinking that man can become sinless
& righteous on his own. 1 Jn.1:10-2:2
Thinking that man can fellowship with
God & walk in sin. 1 Jn.1:6-7
Thinking that man is not totally sinful
& depraved. 1 Jn.1:8-9
Thinking that one can sin & sin & still
be f. Eph.5:5-6
Power to forgive.
Anyone can be f.--no matter how great
the sin. Mk.3:28
The most helpless. Mk.2:1-12;
Lk.5:17-26
The most unclean. Mk.1:41-42
The power is possessed by Christ.
Mt.9:6; Mk.2:10; Lk.5:24; 7:47-48;
Acts 5:31; 13:38-39
Verses. List of. Ro.4:6-8
Why God does not f. Mt.6:14-15

FORM - FORMALISM (See CERE-MONY; RELIGION; RELIGIONISTS; RITUAL)
Discussed.
A trait of the last days. 2 Tim.3:1-5,
esp. 5
God's case against f. Ro.2:17-29
The mistakes of f. Ro.2:17-20
Duty.
To turn away from a religion of f. to
Christ. Ph.3:4-16
To turn away from those who have
only a religion of f. 2 Tim.3:5
Example of. Paul. Ph.3:4-6
Warning against.
A woe is pronounced. Mt.23:23
All f. perishes. Col.2:20-22
One loses one's reward. Col.2:18-23,
esp. 20-22
Stressing f. before people. Lk.14:3
The ministry is performed in vain.
Gal.4:10-11

FORNICATION (See MARITAL UN-FAITHFULNESS; SEXUAL IMMOR-ALITY; SEXUAL SIN)

FORSAKING
F. all. (See SELF-DENIAL)

FORTUNATUS
Christian believer in the early church.
1 Cor.16:15-18

FORTUNE-TELLING
Discussed. Acts 16:16-17

FORUM OF APPIUS
Believers encouraged Paul at Appius Fo-
rum. Acts28:15

FOUNDATION, SPIRITUAL
Of God's building or church. Discussed.
1 Cor.3:9; Eph.1:19-22;2 Tim.2:19-21
Of life.
Must be based upon Christ. 1 Cor.3:11
Must be built upon the f. of the apos-
tles & prophets of Jesus Christ.
Eph.2:20
Must count the cost before laying the
f. Lk.14:28-29
Must lay up a good f. against the judg-
ment to come. 1 Tim.6:19, cp. 17-19
Must mature & move on beyond the f.
of repentance. Heb.6:1
Two f. True discipleship & false dis-
cipleship. Lk.6:46-49, cp. Mt.7:24-27
Reward for laying a spiritual f.
Assurance & security. 2 Tim.2:19
Eternal life. 1 Tim.6:19
The basis of the spiritual f.
Christ, the chief & head cornerstone.
Mt.21:42; Acts 4:11; Eph.2:20;
1 Pt.2:6
Christ, the foundation upon which man
must build his life. 1 Cor.3:11;
Eph.2:19-22, esp. 20

FOUNTAIN OF LIFE (See THIRST, SPIRITUAL; WATER, LIVING)
Promised to those who thirst. Rev.21:6
Source of. The Lamb of God, Jesus
Christ. Rev.7:17

FRANKINCENSE
Given as a gift to Christ when He was a
baby. Mt.2:11

FREEDOM
Believers.
Are called to f. Gal.5:13
Are free & spiritual. Gal.5:13-6:18
Are freed from condemnation. Ro.8:1-17
Are freed from sin. Ro.6:1-23; 6:20-23
Are freed from the law. Ro.7:1-25
Are set free by Christ. Jn.8:34-36;
Gal.5:1-6
Are set free from five things. Jn.8:32;
2 Cor.3:17-18
Are set free, not enslaved. Gal.4:21-31
Discussed. Ro.6:14-15; 14:1-23
Shall be freed from struggling & suf-
fering. Ro.8:1-39
Creation. Shall be set free from bondage.
Ro.8:18-27; 2 Pt.3:8-14; Rev.21:1-5
Described as.
The law of the spirit of life. Ro.8:2
The perfect law that gives f. Jas.1:25
Discussed. Ro.14:1-23; 1 Cor.6:12; 8:1-13;
10:14-11:1; Gal.5:1-6; 5:13-15
Duty.
How to live in f. 1 Pt.2:16-17
Not to be a stumbling block. Ro.14:1-23;
1 Cor.8:1-13
Not to follow false teachers who abuse
Christian f. Gal.2:4-5
Not to use f. as an excuse to disobey
the laws of the state. 1 Pt.2:16-17
Not to use f. to indulge the flesh. Gal.
5:13-15

To be controlled by love. Gal.5:13-15
To continue in the law of f. Jas.1:25
To do the expedient, not just the law-
ful. 1 Cor.6:12-20
To serve righteousness. Ro.6:17-23
To stand firm in the liberty of Christ.
Three points. Gal.5:1-6
True f. keeps the law. Jas.1:25
Gift of God. To use f. to care for the
world. Mk.12:1
Is conditional. Must continue in the truth,
the Word of Christ. Jn.8:31-32
Limits of. What is allowed vs. not al-
lowed. Ro.14:1-23; 1 Cor.8:1-13;
10:14-11:1
Questions concerning.
Liberty & personal rights. 1 Cor.8:1-
11:1
Limits of f. Christian believers & their
freedom. 1 Cor.10:14-11:1
Principles of f. 1 Cor.6:12
Questionable pleasures & socials.
1 Cor.8:1-13
Questionable social activities. Dis-
cussed. Ro.14:1-12
Results. (See LIBERTY, Believers) Jas.1:25
Source.
Christ. Col.2:20
The gospel. Ro.6:17-18
The Holy Spirit. Ro.8:2; 2 Cor.3:17
The Lord. 2 Cor.3:17
Truth. Liberated from five things. Jn.8:32
Tests of l. Questions to ask. 1 Cor.10:23-28
Vs. license. Ro.6:1; 1 Pt.2:16-17
Discussed. Acts 15:1-35
Is a very real danger. Gal.5:13-15
Is abused. 2 Pt.2:10
Unbelievers reject both approaches to
the gospel. Lk.7:33-34
Why a person is not free to sin.
Gal.5:13
Why belief does not lead to the freedom
to sin. Gal.5:13

FREEDOM, CHRISTIAN
Vs. license. 1 Pet.2:16-17

FREEDOM, SPIRITUAL (See FREE-DOM, CHRISTIAN)

FREE WILL
Call to exercise one's free will.
To evaluate one's faith & behavior.
Jas.2:5-6, cp. 1-8
To examine all things & hold to that
which is good. 1 Th.5:21
To hearken to Christ. Mk.7:14-15
To hold fast our confidence & hope in
Christ until the end. Heb.3:6
To hold fast our profession without
wavering. Heb.4:14; 10:23
To redeem the time, every opportunity.
Eph.5:16; Col.4:5
God trusts man. Gave him free will.
Mt.21:33
Of man.
Chooses sin. Result is condemnation.
Ro.1:24
God will not coerce man, will not vio-
late his free w. Ro.1:24
Man is allowed to walk as he wills.
Acts 14:14-18

FRIENDLESS
Caused by. Loss of worldly possessions.
Lk.15:14-16

FRIENDS - FRIENDSHIP (See **BROTH-ERHOOD**)

FRIGHT
In the end time. Discussed. Rev.6:12-17

FRUGAL - FRUGALITY
Duty. To be industrious, **f.**, & saving. Mt.4:21-22; 14:20-21; Mk.6:43

FRUIT BEARING (See **BELIEVER**, Life - Walk; **DEDICATION**)
Conditions for fruit bearing.
Abiding in Christ the Vine. Jn.15:1-8
Accepting the death of Christ. Jn.12:24
Being chosen by Christ. Jn.15:16
Being pruned by God. Jn.15:2
Hearing & understanding the Word of God. Mt.13:23; Mk.4:20
Prayer. Jas.5:18, cp. 14-20
The gospel. Col.1:4-6, esp. 6
Degrees of. Mt.13:8, 23
Discussed. Mt.13:8, 23; Jn.15:1-8
Duty.
To be **f.** in all good works. Col.1:10
To be filled with the **f.** of righteousness. Ph.1:11
To bear **f.** Mt.13:26
To bear seven things. 2 Pt.1:5-8
To bear the **f.** of holiness. Ro.6:22
To bear the **f.** of patience & endurance waiting for the Lord's return. Jas.5:7-8
To bear the **f.** of righteousness. Jas.3:18
To bear the **f.** of the Spirit. Gal.5:22-23; Eph.5:9
To bear the **f.** of witnessing & of converts. Jn.4:36; Ro.1:13; Jn.15:1-8; Ph.4:17; Col.1:6
To bring forth **f.** unto God. Ro.7:4
To give **f.** to God. Lk.13:6-9; 20:10-12
To offer the **f.** of praise to God continually. Heb.13:15
To repent & bear **f.** Mt.3:8; Lk.3:8
Essential.
Judgment is based upon. Lk.13:6-9
Must bear **f.** or perish. Lk.13:6-9; 20:10-12
No **f.** apart from the vine. Jn.15:4
Two times **f.** is expected. Mt.21:19
Meaning. What **f.** is. Three things. Jn.15:1-8
Purpose.
Of believers. Are chosen to bear **f.** Jn.15:16
Of the world. The relationship of Jesus to the people of the world. Jn.15:1-8
The very reason Jesus came. To seek fruitful men. Mk.11:12
Results.
Are assured of some **f.** if one sows seed. Mk.4:1-20; 4:3-9; 4:30-32
Discussed. Jn.4:36-38; 15:1-8
Eternal life. Jn.4:36; Ro.6:22
Reveals one's nature. Mt.12:33; Lk.6:43-45
Steps to producing a crop. Threefold. Mk.4:20
Warning. (See **UNFRUITFULNESS**)
False teachers are like trees whose fruit withers. Jude 12
The unfruitful shall be cut down & burned. Mt.3:10; 4:19; Lk.3:9; Jn.15:6
Worldliness & money keep a person from bearing **f.** Lk.8:14

FRUIT, GOOD
Basis. Good **f.** will be the basis of judgment. Mt.25:31-46
Described as. Dead **f.** Heb.6:1
Discussed.
Of the church. Rev.2:19
Right vs. wrong motives for good **f.** Mt.6:1; 6:1-4
What it takes to enter the kingdom of God. Good **f.** Mt.21:28-32
Duty.
To be a pattern, an example of good **f.** Tit.2:7
To be rich in good **f.** 1 Tim.6:18
To cease from working for salvation. Heb.4:10
To do good to all men. Gal.6:10
To do good to one's enemies. Mt.5:44
To do good works. Jn.3:21; 1 Pt.3:11
To do good works quietly & in secret. Mt.6:3-4
To do good works that stir people to glorify God. 1 Pt.2:12
To do greater works than Jesus. Jn.14:12
To do the works of God, to believe on Christ. Jn.6:29; 1 Jn.3:23
To give good **f.** precedence over religious law. Mt.12:5
To give to all who ask or take. Mt.5:40; 5:41; 5:42
To have a faith that does good works. Jas.2:14; 2:17-18, 20, 26
To keep on doing good works. Tit.3:8
To know that a man is not justified by **w.** Gal.3:1-4:7
To let our good works be seen by men. Mt.5:16
To love one's enemies & do good. Lk.6:35
To move on from the foundation of repentance from dead **f.** Heb.6:1
To purge one's conscience from dead **f.** Heb.9:14
To repent from dead **f.** Heb.6:1
To stir others to love & do good works. Heb.10:24
To work tirelessly for the Lord. 1 Cor.15:58
Essential.
To follow Christ in doing good works. Mk.1:16
To have a faith that does good works. Jas.2:14; 2:17-18, 20, 26
Meaning. Mt.16:25-28; Jas.2:14-26; 3:17-18
Nature of **f.**
Is a law, a principle. Ro.3:27
The **f.** of the world are evil. Jn.7:7
Purpose.
Are redeemed to be a special people, zealous of good **f.** Tit.2:13-14
The very reason we are saved is to do good works. Eph.2:10
To lead men to believe. Jn.2:9-11; 2:23
To lead men to glorify God. Mt.5:16
To silence critics by one's good works. 1 Pt.2:15
Results.
Are good, beneficial, & fruitful to men. Tit.3:8
Good **f.** follow believers to heaven. Rev.14:13

Secures the acceptance & approval of God. Acts 10:34-35; Heb.13:16
Secures the esteem of other believers. 1 Th.5:13
Secures the praise of rulers & leaders. Ro.13:3
F. lead some to believe. Jn.2:23-25
F. make faith perfect. Jas.2:22
F. plus faith justify a man. Jn.2:24
F. prove that one follows God. Jn.3:21
F. prove the believer's faith. Mt.25:34-40
Will be given power to rule. Rev.2:26-27
Vs. faith.
Discussed. Jn.6:28-29; Ro.4:1-8; 4:9-12; Gal.2:1-21; 2:15-16; 2:16; 2:17-18; 3:1-5; Eph.2:8-9; Jas.2:14-26
Faith apart from **f.** Jn.4:50
Illust. in Abraham. Ro.4:1-3
Obedience & love tied together. Jn.14:23
Vs. love. Mk.12:31
Vs. salvation.
Discussed. Acts 15:1-35; 2 Tim.1:9
The issue of works vs. faith was answered in the Great Jerusalem Council. Acts 15:1-35
Vs. self-denial. Lk.6:32-34
Weakness of. (See **PERFECT - PER-FECTION**)
Believing one is saved because of **f.** 2 Tim.1:9
Discussed. Col.2:20-23; 2:23
Emptiness of **f.** Mk.7:1-13
Man cannot do enough good **f.** to become perfect. Gal.2:15-16
F. are opposed to the believer's rest. Heb.3:7-19; 4:1-13
F. are unacceptable for salvation. Mt.5:20
F. cannot justify a person before God. Ro.3:20; Gal.2:15-16; 2:16; 3:1-4:7
F. cannot make a person acceptable to God. Ro.4:1-8
F. cannot make one acceptable to Christ. Mt.7:22-23
F. cannot make one righteous. Ro.4:1-8, esp. 4-7; 9:30-32; Gal.2:15-16; 3:19-22, esp. 21-22
F. cannot save a person. Gal.3:1-5; Eph.2:8-9; 2 Tim.1:9; Tit.3:4-5
F. cannot void the boastings of men. Ro.3:27
F. give man reason to glory, but not before God. Ro.4:2
F. lead to pride & false humility. Col.2:23
F. put a man under the curse. Gal.3:10-12

FULL, THE (The Glutton)
Judgment of. Are warned. Lk.6:24-26

FULLNESS
Meaning. Col.2:9-10; Jas. 1:1-3

FULLNESS OF TIME (See **TIME HAS COME, THE**)
Discussed. Gal.4:4; Eph.1:10
Fulfilled by Christ. Discussed. Lk.3:1-6; 3:1-2
World prepared by a forerunner. Three ways. Jn.1:23

FULLNESS, SPIRITUAL (See **HUN-GER, SPIRITUAL; SATISFACTION**)
Duty.
To be filled with the fullness of God. Eph.3:19
To be filled with the Spirit. Lk.4:1; Eph.5:18
To be full of faith & of the Holy Spirit & power. Acts 6:5, 8; 11:24
To be full of good works. Acts 9:36
To be full of goodness. Ro.15:14
To be full of light. Mt.6:22; Lk.11:36
To be full of mercy & good fruits. Jas.3:17
To examine & guard oneself in order to receive a full reward. 2 Jn.8
To fully preach & teach the gospel of Christ. Ro.15:19; 2 Tim.4:17
To grow to the full stature of Christ. Eph.4:13
To have a heart full of glory. 1 Pt.1:8
Source - Provision of.
All the fullness of God Himself. Eph.3:19
Discussed. Jn.6:30-36
God. Acts 2:28
Grace upon grace. Jn.1:16
Jesus Christ. Jn.1:16-17; 10:9; Col.1:19; 2:9; 1 Pt.1:8
Joy. Jn.15:11
The fullness of Christ. Jn.1:16
The fullness of the Holy Spirit. Eph.5:18
The knowledge of God's will. Col.1:9
The Word of God. 1 Jn.1:4
Verses. List of. Jn.6:34-35; 6:55; 10:9

FUNERALS
Atmosphere needed. Mt.9:23-26

FUTURE (See **END TIME; JESUS CHRIST**, Return of; **JUDGMENT; PROPHECY; WORLD**, Future of)
Attitudes toward. Three **a**. Mt.6:34
Is revealed by Christ. Jn.13:19
The Holy Spirit. Jn.16:13
Is unknown to man.
The Lord's return is not known. Mt.24:27; 24:36; Lk.12:40; 1 Th.5:2; Rev.16:15
The time when a man is to die is not known. Lk.12:16-21

G

GABRIEL
Angel. Discussed. Lk.1:19
Work of. Sent to an unknown person with God's message. Lk.1:26

GADARANES
A place east of the Sea of Galilee. Mk.5:1
Jesus healed two demon possessed men in **G**. Mt.8:28-34; Mk.5:1-20; Lk.8:26-40

GAIUS
A believer in Corinth.
Discussed. Acts 20:4-6
Opened his home to Paul & the church. Ro.16:23
A beloved leader in the church. 3 Jn.1-8
Discussed. 1 Cor.1:14
The recipient of 3 John. 3 Jn.1

GALATIA
Discussed. Gal. Introd.
Mission to. Message preached. Acts 13:14-41
Paul instructed the churches of Galatia on stewardship. 1 Cor.16:1
Peter wrote to the churches in **G**. 1 Pt.1:1
Visited by Paul.
On his first mission. Acts 13:13
On his second mission. Acts 15:41-16:5
On his third mission. Acts 18:23

GALILEANS
Slaughtered by Herod. Thought to be great sinners. Lk.13:1-5
Speech & accent was distinct. Mk.14:17; Lk.22:59
Were receptive to Jesus & His ministry. Jn.4:45

GALILEE
Discussed. Mt.4:12; Jn.4:43; Acts 18:12-17
Population: 200 cities with a population of over fifteen thousand each. Mk.3:7-10

GALILEE, SEA OF
Discussed. Mk.1:16

GALL
Mixed with vinegar. An intoxicating drink. Offered to Christ on the cross. Mt.27:26-38
Symbol of. Bitterness of sin. Acts 8:23

GAMALIEL
Discussed. Acts 5:34

GARMENT (See **CLOTHING; DRESS**)
Attitude about.
Right vs. wrong. Mt.6:25-34
Duty.
To dress modestly. 1 Tim.2:9
To dress to please God, not to attract attention. 1 Pt.3:1-5
To trust God, not to worry about fashion. Lk.12:22-34
Illustrated.
A seamstress is raised from the dead. Acts 9:36-43
Clothes made by Dorcas for friends. Acts 9:36-39
New **c**. sewn on old **c**. Mk.2:21
Of Jesus. Gambled for. Jn.19:23-24
Parable of. New vs. old. To bring a new life & joy. Lk.5:36-39
Purpose for. Three purposes. Mt.6:28-30
Religious **c**. Problem with. Mt.23:5
Warning.
Against dressing to attract attention. Mk.12:38
Against extravagant styles. Mk.12:38
Against judging people by their clothing. Lk.16:19, cp. 20-31
Against those who dress as sheep (harmless), but inwardly are wolves. Mt.7:15

GATE (See **DOOR**)
Symbolic use of.
The **g**. of Christ. He is the **g**. of the sheep. Jn.10:7-10, cp. Jn.14:6; Ro.5:2; Eph.2:18; Heb.10:19-22
The **g**. of faith. Acts 14:27

The **g**. of opportunity. 1 Cor.16:9; 2 Cor.2:12; Col.4:3; Rev.3:8
The **g**. of Revelation. Three **g**. described. Rev.4:1-2
The **g**. of salvation. Mt.25:10
The **g**. of the heart. To open & invite Jesus to enter. Lk.24:28-32; Rev.3:20
The **g**. of the Lord's return. Mt.24:33
The **g**. of heaven.
Discussed. Rev.21:12-13
Shall never be shut. Rev.21:25
The **g**. of hell cannot prevail against or stop the gospel. Mt.6:18
The **g**. of life. A broad & a narrow **g**. Mt.7:13-14

GEHENNA (See **HELL**)

GENEALOGY
Error of. Discussed. 1 Tim.1:4
Honoring, relying upon. Mt.23:29-33
Of Jesus Christ. Mt.1:1-17; 1:1; Lk.3:23-38

GENERATION
Described.
As childish, playful, mindless. Mt.11:16-19
As evil. Reasons. Lk.11:31
By Jesus. Threefold. Lk.7:29-35
Discussed.
Jesus' great invitation to this **g**. Mt.11:28-30
The answer to an evil **g**. Mt.12:38-45
The message to a childish **g**. Mt.11:16-27
Rebuke of. Lk.9:37-45
Welfare of. Determined by a people's concern for righteousness. Lk.10:2

GENNESARET, LAKE OF
Discussed. Mt.14:34; Mk.1:16

GENTILES
After Christ.
Barriers broken down between the **G**. & the Jews.
By Peter & Cornelius. Acts 10:1-48
By Philip in Samaria. Acts 8:5-8, 14-17, 25
G. were made fellow-heirs of the gospel. Eph.3:6
God turned from the Jews to the **G**. Ro.10:18-21
God's great invitation was extended to the **G**. Mt.9:10; 22:1-14; 22:7
The door to the **G**. was opened by God. Scripture proves. Acts 15:13-21
The door to the **G**. was opened by Paul & Barnabas. Acts 14:21-28
The door to the **G**. was opened by Peter. Acts 10:1-48; 10:48
The first great gentile church was established. Acts 11:19-30
The **G**. received the gospel. Through Israel's fall. Ro.11:11-16
The **G**. received the Holy Spirit. Acts 10:44-48
The **G**. were turned to by God. Mt.21:43; 22:1-14
The **G**. were turned to by Paul. To receive the gospel instead of the Jews. Acts 13:46-48; 28:25-29

Age of - Times of.
  Full number of the G. Meaning.
    Ro.11:25-26
  Shall end & Israel shall be restored.
    Lk.21:24
Before Christ.
  Did not follow after righteousness. Ro.9:30
  Did not have the law of God. Ro.2:14
  Did not know God. 1 Th.4:5
  Many G. turned to Judaism. Acts 13:42-45
  Many lived lives of unrighteousness &
    ungodliness. Ro.1:18-32; 1 Pt.4:3-5
  Rejected & denied the only living &
    true God. Ro.1:18-32
  Were religious, but worshipped idols,
    not God. 1 Cor.12:2
  Were under sin. Ro.3:9; Eph.2:1
  Were without Christ & God & did not
    have any hope. Eph.2:11-12
  What G. life was like before Christ.
    Eph.2:11-12
Parable describing. Wild olive branch.
  Ro.11:17-24
Prophecy of G. salvation.
  At Jesus' birth. Lk.2:28-32
  Conversion of. Mt.8:11; Ro.15:7-12;
    9:25-33; 10:18-21
  In the end time. Multitudes will be
    saved. Rev.7:9-17
  To be a part of the Abrahamic covenant -
    to be blessed through Abraham. Gal.3:8
  To be evangelized. Foreshadowed by
    Christ. Mk.7:24
  To come from the four corners of the
    world. Lk.13:29-30
  Trusting Christ. Mt.12:21
Sins of. Executed Jesus. Mt.17:22
Vs. the Jews.
  Accepted. Jews cut off. Ro.11:17
  Described as "dogs." Mk.7:27
  Discussed. Acts 10:1-33; 10:11-16;
    10:28-29
  Prejudice between. Lk.7:4; Acts
    10:1-33; 10:11-16; 10:28-19
  Relationship between the Jew & G.
    Ro.11:17-24
  Warning to both the Jew & G.
    Ro.11:17-24

GENTILES, COURT OF THE
  A court of the temple. Discussed.
    Mt.21:12-16

**GENTLE - GENTLENESS (See CON-
SIDERATE; KIND - KINDNESS)**
  Christ is g. & lowly. Mt.11:29
  Duty.
    Must be strengthened with God's
      power to be g. Col.1:11
    Must correct others in spirit of g.
      2 Tim.2:24-26
    To be longsuffering in living for
      Christ. 2 Tim.3:10-12
    To be longsuffering in ministering:
      preaching, teaching, etc. 2 Tim.4:2
    To be longsuffering in persecution.
      2 Tim.3:10-12
    To be longsuffering in trials. 2 Cor.6:6-7
    To do good works in a g. spirit. Jas.3:13
    To dress in a g. & quiet spirit.
      1 Pt.3:4, cp. 2-4
    To put on g. Col.3:12
    To receive the Word with g. Jas.1:21
    To show forth all g. as a pattern for
      other believers. 1 Tim.1:16
    To walk in longsuffering. Eph.4:1-2

Duty - Essential.
  Of the elderly.
    To be characterized by g. Tit.2:2
    To be sound in faith, love, & g. Tit.2:2
  Of the minister. To be g. 1 Tim.3:3;
    2 Tim.2:24
  To add g. to one's faith. 2 Pt.1:5-7
  To be g. in combating all temptations
    & trials. Ro.5:3-5; Jas.5:7-11
  To be g. in continuing to do good
    works. Ro.2:6-7
  To be g. in keeping one's eyes fixed
    upon the return of Christ. 2 Th.3:5;
    Jas.5:7-8; 5:7-11
  To be g. in persecution & trials.
    2 Th.1:4; 1 Pt.2:20
  To be g. in standing against false
    teachers. Rev.2:2
  To be g. in the hope of the Lord Jesus
    Christ. 1 Th.1:3
  To be g. in waiting for one's eternal
    salvation. Ro.8:23-25
  To be g. toward all men. 1 Th.5:14
  To follow after love & g. 1 Tim.6:11
  To minister in g. 2 Cor.6:4; 12:12;
    2 Tim.3:10-11
  To pray for strength to be g. Col.1:9-11,
    esp. 11
  To run with g. the race set before one.
    Heb.12:1
  To wait upon God. Jn.11:6
Example of.
  Abraham. The g. needed to endure.
    Heb.6:13-15
  The prophets & Job. Perseverance
    needed to combat temptation & tri-
    als. Jas.5:10-11
  The farmer. Perseverance needed to
    wait for the Lord's return. Jas.5:7-8
  Meaning. Col.1:11; 2 Th.1:4; 1
    Tim.3:2-3; 2 Tim.3:10-11; Jas.1:3-4;
    2 Pt.1:5-7
Meaning. Mt.5:5; 2 Cor.6:6-7; Gal.5:22-23;
  Eph.4:1-2; 1 Tim.6:11; 2 Tim.3:10-11;
  4:2; Ph.4:5
Of God.
  God endures with much g. the vessels
    of wrath. Ro.9:22
  The g. of the Lord means salvation.
    2 Pt.3:15
  Why God is g. to men. Ro.2:4; 2
    Pt.3:9; 3:15-16
Proves.
  That one has truly been called of God.
    1 Tim.1:16
  That one walks worthy of God. Eph. 4:1-2
Reasons. God knows the exact time, the
  best time to act. Jn.11:6
Result.
  Determines one's reward. Ro.2:7
  Glory, honor & immortality. Ro.2:6-7
  Inherits the promises. Heb.6:12; 10:36
  Joy. Col.1:11
  Keeps & saves one's soul. Lk.21:19
Reward. Three rewards. Mt.5:5
Source.
  An honest & good heart. Lk.8:15
  God. Ro.15:5; 2 Th.3:5
  God's power. Col.1:11
  Hope. Ro.8:25
  Is a fruit of the Spirit. Gal.5:22-23
  The Holy Spirit. Gal.5:22-23
  The trials & testing of one's faith.
    Ro.5:3-5; 12:12; Jas.1:2-4
  The Word of God, the Scriptures.
    Ro.15:4

GETHSEMANE
  Jesus & G.
    Confronting death & terrible trial.
      Mt.26:36-46; Mk.14:32-42; Lk.
      22:39-46
    Often went to the garden of G. to pray.
      Lk.22:39; Jn.18:1-2. Cp. Mt.26:30, 36
    Sweating blood; an angel strengthens.
      Lk.22:43-44
  Meaning. Mt.26:36

GIDEON
  Faith of. Discussed. Heb.11:32

GIFTED, THE
  How the g. enter heaven. Mt.19:16-22

**GIFTS OF GOD & CHRIST (See RE-
WARD; SALVATION)**
  G. of Christ.
    A crown of life. Rev.2:10
    Eternal, everlasting life. Jn.4:14; 6:27;
      10:28; 17:2
    Food from the tree of life. Rev.2:7
    Manna to eat & a new name. Rev.2:17
    Peace. Jn.14:27, cp. 16:33
    Power over all the evil. Lk.10:19
    Power over the nations. Rev.2:26
    Rest. Mt.11:28, cp Heb.4:1-11
    Reward or punishment based upon
      one's works. Rev.22:12, cp. 2 Cor.5:10
    Strength. Ph.4:13; Col.1:10; 2 Cor.
      12:8-9
    The grace of God. 1 Cor.1:4
    The keys to the kingdom of heaven.
      Mt.16:19
    The water of life. Rev.21:6
    The words & wisdom to stand against
      one's enemies. Lk.21:15
  G. of God.
    All things. Ro.8:32; 1 Tim.6:17;
      Eph.3:20
    Answer to prayer. Jn.15:16; 16:23
    Eternal life in Jesus Christ. Verses.
      Ro.5:15-18
    Good things. Mt.7:11; Jas.1:17
    Grace. Jas.4:6; 1 Cor.1:3; 2 Cor.9:8
    His Son, the Lord Jesus Christ. Jn.
      3:16
    Peace. 1 Cor.1:3; Ph.4:6-7, 9
    Repentance that leads to life. Acts
      11:18
    Security & assurance of eternal life.
      Jn.10:29
    The Holy Spirit & His strength.
      Lk.11:13; Jn.14:16; Eph.3:16
    The necessities of life. Mt.6:33, cp.
      25-34
    The provision to meet all needs.
      Ph.4:19, cp. 11-13
    Wisdom & knowledge. Eph.1:17;
      Jas.1:5

GIFTS, SPIRITUAL
  Described as.
    A measure of faith. Ro.12:3
    A trust - to hold on to. 2 Tim.1:14
  Discussed - Listed. Mt.25:14-15;
    Eph.4:7-16
    Apostle. 1 Cor.12:28; Eph.4:11
    Distinguishing, discerning of spirits.
      1 Cor.12:8-10
    Evangelist. Eph.4:11
    Encouragement. Ro.12:6-8
    Faith. 1 Cor.12:8-10
    Giving. Ro.12:6-8

Government (administration).
1 Cor.12:27-30
Healing. 1 Cor.12:8-10; 12:28
Helps. 1 Cor.12:27-30; 12:28-30
Interpreting tongues. 1 Cor.12:8-10;
12:30
Knowledge. 1 Cor.1:5-7; 12:8-10
Leadership (administration). Ro.12:6-8
Love. 1 Cor.13:1-13, cp. 12:31; 14:1
Mercy. Ro.12:6-8
Ministry. Ro.12:6-8
Miracles. 1 Cor.12:8-10; 12:28
Pastor. Eph.4:11
Prophecy - Prophet. Ro.12:6-8;
1 Cor.12:8-10; Eph.4:11
Special lists of.
Eight **g**. 1 Cor.12:28
Nine **g**. 1 Cor.12:8-10
Professional or office-bearing gifts
in the church. Eph.4:11
Seven **g**. Ro.12:-8
Teacher. Eph.4:11; 1 Cor.12:28-30
Teaching. Acts 13:1; Ro.12:6-8;
1 Cor.12:28;Eph.4:11; 1 Tim.2:7;
2 Tim.1:11-12; Jas.3:1
Tongues. 1 Cor.12:8-1; 12:28
Tongues contrasted with prophecy.
1 Cor.14:1-25
Utterance. 1 Cor.1:5-7
Wisdom. 1 Cor.12:8-10
Word of knowledge. 1 Cor.12:8-10
Duty. (See **GIFTS, SPIRITUAL**, Pur-
pose)
To control. 1 Cor.14:29-33
To covet the best **g**. 1 Cor.12:31; 14:1
To focus upon the central thing: Love
not gifts. 1 Cor.13:1-13
To guard against misuse. Strong **g**. can
become one's weakness. Mt.26:15
To hold on to. 2 Tim.1:14
To stir up the **g**. of God. 2 Tim.1:6
To use & minister to one another.
1 Pt.4:10-11
To use, being set aflame for Christ.
Ro.12:6-8
To work & use one's gifts. Mt.25:14-30
History of - Overview of. Discussed.
1 Cor.12:1-14:40
Illustrated. By the body. Ro.12:3-5;
1 Cor.12:12-31
Nature - Value.
Are different, yet mutually dependent.
Ro.12:3-8; 1 Cor.12:27-30
Cost God an unbelievable price.
Eph.4:7-16
Problems - Dangers surrounding.
Controversy. 1 Cor.12:4-11
Dangers surrounding. Less gifted vs.
more gifted. 1 Cor.12:12-31
Ignorance about **g**. 1 Cor.12:1-3
Potential abuses of the **g**. 1 Cor.14:36-38
There are counterfeit gifts. (See
TEACHERS, FALSE) Acts
19:13-14; 1 Cor.11:13-15
Thinking that gifts are of men & can
be bought. Acts 8:18-24
Purpose.
Discussed. 1 Cor.12:1-14:40
Threefold purpose. Eph.4:12-16
To care for the church. 1 Cor.12:24-26
To establish believers in Christ.
Ro.1:11
To predict & encourage others in their
call & duty. 1 Tim.1:18
Questions concerning. 1 Cor.12:1-14:40

Source - The Giver of spiritual **g**.
Christ. Eph.4:7
Cost the greatest possible price. Eph.4:8-10
God. Ro.12:3; 1 Cor.12:18; 12:28; Jas.1:17
God gives varying degrees of faith for
the gifts. Ro.12:6
Unity of. Discussed. 1 Cor.12:4-7

GIVE - GIVING - GIFTS (See **CROSS,
DAILY - SELF-DENIAL; HELP -
HELPING; STEWARDSHIP;
WORKS**)
Attitudes toward. Human need & **g**.
Mk.6:35-44
Described.
As a grace. 2 Cor.8:6-7
As the great Christian ethic. Mt.5:42
Discussed. Mt.5:40; 5:41; 5:42;
2 Cor.8:1-15; 9:1-7; 9:8-15
The challenge to give. 2 Cor.8:1-15
The widow's offering. Mk.12:41-44
Duty.
To be sacrificial, to **g**. "out of need."
Lk.21:3; 2 Cor.8:1-5
To give according to one's ability.
Lk.11:41; Acts 11:29; 2 Cor.8:12
To give all one is & has. Mt.19:21-22;
19:23-26; 19:27-30;Lk.9:23; 12:33;
Acts 4:34-37;Ro.12:13; 2 Cor.8:12;
9:6-7; 1 Tim.6:17-19
To give quietly & without show. Mt.6:1-4
To give readily & generously; to meet
needs unselfishly. Lk.6:38;
10:34-35; Acts 11:29;
To give through the offerings of the
church upon the first day of the
week. 1 Cor.16:2
To give to all who ask or take.
Mt.5:40; 5:41; 5:42
To give to help meet the needs of the
needy. Lk.6:27-31; Acts 20:35
To give to spread the gospel.
Ro.10:14-15; Ph.4:16
To give what one has. Verses. List of.
Jn.6:10-13
To give when asked. Lk.6:27-31
To give without charge. Mt.10:8
To seek heavenly treasures by **g**.
Lk.12:31-34
To work so that one will have to **g**. &
meet the needs of others. Lk.12:31-34;
Eph.4:28
Example of.
Jesus Christ. 2 Cor.8:9
Strong example. Macedonian
churches. 2 Cor.8:1-5
Facts - Principles.
Giving determines how much one gets
in life. Mk.4:24-25
God judges one's giving by how much
one has left. Mk.12:43
One is judged by the amount kept
back, not given. Lk.21:3
The more one gives, the more one re-
ceives. Mk.4:24-25; Lk.6:38
How to give. Two descriptive ways.
Mt.6:3
Meaning. Mt.6:1; 19:21-22; 19:23;
19:25; Lk.9:23
Motive.
Discussed. Mt.6:1-4; 2 Cor.9:8-15
Wrong motive. Mt.6:2
The spiritual gift of giving. Discussed.
Ro.12:6-8
Verses. List of. Mk.10:21-22;
Lk.9:16-17; 11:42

GLASS, SEA OF
In front of God's throne. Discussed.
Rev.4:5-6; 21:18, 21

GLORY - GLORIFIED (See **GLORY OF
CHRIST; GLORY OF GOD**)
Ct. afflictions. 2 Cor.4:17-18
Described.
An eternal weight of **g**. 2 Cor.4:17-18
Shekinah **g**. Mt.17:5-8; Lk.2:8-12;
Jn.1:14
Discussed. Ro.3:23
Fact.
Is seen in the face of Christ. 2 Cor.4:6
Is the supreme purpose of all things.
1 Pt.4:10-11
Is the supreme purpose of Jesus' life &
death. Jn.12:27-30; 17:4
Was experienced by Moses.
2 Cor.3:7, 13
Meaning. Ro.2:7
Source. - How to secure **g**.
By dying to self & committing oneself
to service. Jn.12:23-26
By prayer & receiving Jesus' presence.
Lk.9:29
Verses. List of. Ro.2:7; 5:2
Vs. earthly **g**. Discussed. 2 Cor.4:17-18

GLORY, CROWN OF
Meaning. 1 Pt.5:4

GLORY, ETERNAL (See **GLORY OF
BELIEVERS**, Promise of glory)
Of the believers. Discussed. Ro.8:30
Verses. List of. Ro.2:7; 5:2

GLORY OF BELIEVERS
Are transformed into the **g**. of the Lord
daily. 2 Cor.3:17-18
Chart of the **g**. of Christ & of the be-
liever. Jn.17:22
Discussed. Jn.17:22; 2 Th.2:14
Duty. (See **GLORY OF CHRIST**, Duty;
GLORY OF GOD, Duty)
To **g**. in infirmities & weaknesses.
2 Cor.11:30; 12:8-10
To **g**. in the cross of Christ. Gal.6:14
To **g**. in the faithfulness of believers.
2 Th.1:4
To **g**. in trials Ro.5:3
To let the Word of God be glorified in
us. 2 Th.3:1
Promise of **g**.
Are called to God's kingdom & **g**.
1 Th.2:12
Are changed from **g**. to **g**. by looking
into the face of Christ. 2 Cor.3:18
Are to receive the **g**. of our Lord Jesus
Christ. 2 Th.2:14
Is assured of **g**. Predestined by God.
Ro.8:30
Is called to eternal **g**. 1 Pt.5:10
Is called to **g**. & virtue. 2 Pt.1:3
Is given the hope of **g**. in the very
presence of Christ. Col.1:27
Is made a partaker of the **g**. that shall
be revealed. 1 Pt.5:1
Will appear with Christ in **g**. Col.3:4
Will be brought to **g**. by Christ.
Heb.2:10
Will be glorified when Christ returns
to earth. 2 Th.1:10
Will be glorified with Christ.
Ro.8:16-17; 8:30

Will be shown & experience the riches of God's **g**. Eph.1:18
Will be transformed into the image of the glorious body of Christ. Ph.3:21
Will behold the **g**. of Christ. Jn.17:24
Will experience a glorious day of deliverance & redemption from corruption. Ro.8:21, 23
Will experience a glow of **g**. when one is persecuted. 1 Pt.4:14
Will experience **g**. daily. 2 Cor.3:18
Will experience joy unspeakable & full of **g**. 1 Pt.1:8
Will experience the **g**. of salvation & eternity. 1 Pt.1:10-11
Will have our bodies raised from the dead in **g**. 1 Cor.15:42-44, esp. 43
Will receive the salvation which is in Christ Jesus with eternal **g**. 2 Tim. 2:10
Will stir suffering to produce an eternal weight of **g**. within us. 2 Cor. 4:17

GLORY OF CHRIST (See **MAJESTY**, Of Christ)
Described. Mt.17:2; Mk.9:2-4; Jn.1:14; 12:23-26; 17:1
Christ is called the Lord of **g**. Jas.2:1
Discussed. Jn.13:31-32
Duty.
To glorify Christ by receiving eternal life. Jn.17:1-4
To look for the glorious appearance of Christ. Tit.2:12-13
Fact.
Christ existed in *pre-existent* **g**. Jn.17:5-8
Is seen only as through a glass. 2 Cor.3:18
Jesus demonstrated His glory when upon earth. Jn.2:11
Was witnessed by the early disciples. Jn.1:14
Is accomplished.
By believers spending eternity with Christ. Jn.17:24
By Christ living in believers & giving them the hope of **g**. Col.1:27
By the commitment & life of believers. Jn.17:9-10
By the death of Christ. Lk.24:25-26; Jn.12:23-26; 13:31-32; 17:1
By the exaltation of Christ. Jude 24-25
By the resurrection of Christ. Acts 3:13-15; 1 Pt.1:21
By the return of Christ. Mt.16:27; 24:30; Mk.8:38; 13:26; Lk.21:27; 2 Th.1:10; 1 Pt.4:12-13
By the testimony of believers. Acts 21:20; Gal.1:24; 2 Th.1:11-12
By the word & power of God. Jn.12:28; 13:31-32
By the work of the Holy Spirit. Jn.16:13-14
By the works of Christ. Jn.11:4
Is in the believer. 2 Cor.3:17-18
Meaning. 2 Cor.4:6
Was determined by God. Heb.5:5
Will be witnessed when He returns. 2 Th.1:10

GLORY OF GOD
Described.
God is called the Father of glory. Eph.1:17
God is called the God of glory. Acts 7:2

Discussed. Mt.6:9; Jn.13:31-32; Ro.3:23
Duty toward the **g**. of God.
To be strong in faith, giving **g**. to God for His promises. Ro.4:20-21
To boast in God alone. Eph.2:8-9
To do all to the **g**. of God 1 Cor.10:31
To fear & glorify God no matter who we are. Rev.15:4
To fear God & give **g**. to Him. Rev. 14:7
To focus one's eyes on heaven's **g**. 2 Cor.4:17-18
To glorify God after being blessed & healed. Mt.9:8; 15:31; Mk.2:12; Lk.5:26; 13:14-16; 17:15-19; 18:43; 23:47
To glorify God for His mercy. Ro.15:9
To glorify God for keeping & preserving us until His heavenly kingdom. Ro.16:25-27; 2 Tim.4:18; Heb.13:20-21; 1 Pt.5:10-11
To glorify God for sending Christ to redeem us. Gal.1:4-5; Eph.1:5-6
To glorify God for the suffering that comes our way. 1 Pt.4:16
To glorify God in our bodies & spirits. 1 Cor.6:19-20
To glorify God with other believers. Ro.15:6
To honor & glorify God. Mt.6:9-10
To hope for the **g**. of God. Ro.5:1-2
To praise God for His glory as the Creator & Savior of all things. Ro.11:36; 1 Tim.1:17
Fact.
Failure to glorify God is the great sin of unbelievers. Ro.1:20-21
God's **g**. is so great & brilliant that it will outshine the sun in the new heavens & earth. Rev.21:23
God's **g**. raised Christ from the dead. Ro.6:4
Is the supreme purpose of all things. 1 Pt.4:10-11
Is the supreme purpose of Jesus' life & death. Jn.12:27-30; 17:4
Sustains the minister. 2 Cor.4:15; 4:17-18
How God is glorified - Is accomplished. Mt.6:9-10; Jn.13:31-32; 1 Pt.4:10-11
By believers bearing much fruit. Jn.15:8
By believers being filled with the fruits of righteousness. Ph.1:11
By Christ answering the prayers of believers. Jn.14:13
By Christ receiving & saving us. Ro.15:7
By His inheritance in believers. Eph.1:18
By His meeting & supplying all our needs. Ph.4:19-20
By the birth of Christ. Lk.2:14
By the coming judgment that will force all men to bow & confess Christ (God's Son) to be Lord. Ph.2:10-11
By the creation of man. 1 Cor.11:7
By the death of Christ. Jn.12:27-32; 13:31-32; 17:1-4
By the death of faithful believers. Jn.21:18-19
By the faithful life & ministry of believers. Mt.5:16; Acts 4:21; 11:18; 13:48; 21:20; Gal.1:24
By the **g**. of God seen in the face of Christ. 2 Cor.4:6
By the good works of believers. 1 Pt.2:12
By the life & works of Christ. Jn.17:4; Eph.3:21; Heb.1:3

By the praises of believers. 2 Cor.4:15
By the promises given in Christ. 2 Cor.1:20
By the sickness of believers. Jn.11:4, 40
By the subjection of believers to the gospel. 2 Cor.9:13

GLORY OF MAN
Fact.
Fades away as quickly as the grass & flowers. 1 Pt.1:24
Is seen in the great creation & dominion of man upon earth. Heb.2:6-8
Man is short of God's glory. Ro.3:23
Will be excluded from the **g**. of God. 2 Th.1:9

GLORY, SHEKINAH (See **SHEKINAH GLORY**)

GLORYING IN MAN (See **BOASTING; MAN; MOVE TO BOAST; PRIDE; SELF-SUFFICIENCY**)

GLUTTONY
Fact. Some make their stomachs their god. Ph.3:18-19
Judgment of.
Are warned. Lk.6:24-26
Will face destruction. Ph.3:18-19

GNASHED - GNASHING
Meaning. Mt.8:12; Lk.13:28; Acts 7:54

GNOSTICS - GNOSTICISM
Belief of. In the church today. Eph.5:5-6
Discussed. Col.1:15; 1 Tim.4:3
Teaching of.
How to approach God. Col.1:15
Mediators. Col.1:15
Of the body as evil. Col.1:15

GOATS
Type. Of unbeliever. Mt.25:33

GOD (See **TRINITY**)
Access to. (See **ACCESS**)
And Christ.
Is a mutual indwelling between God & Christ. Jn.5:17-30; 8:15-16; 14:10
Is an intimate knowledge between God & Christ. Jn.5:17-30; 10:14-16
Is One with Christ. Jn.5:17-30; 8:15-16; 10:14-16; 14:10
Verses. List of. Jn.5:19; 8:54-59
Is pleased with Christ. Mt.3:17; Jn.12:27-30
Is God's beloved Son. Verses. List of. Jn.5:20
Is the dearest thing to God's heart. Jn.3:16; 3:35-36; 5:20
Revealed all His works through Christ. Jn.5:20
Revealed Himself in Christ. Jn.8:19; 12:45; 14:7; 14:9; 16:15Col.2:9; 1 Tim.3:16; Heb.1:3
Armor of. Eph.6:13-20
Blessings of. (See **BLESSINGS**)
Care of. (See **CARE - CARING**)
Chastisement of. (See **CHASTISEMENT**)
Commands of. (See **COMMAND**)
Duty. To obey. 1 Jn.2:3-6
Keeping of proves that one knows God. 1 Jn.2:3-6
Creator. (See **CREATION**)

What God is like - Attributes.
Cannot be overthrown, stopped, defeated. Acts 5:33-40
Cannot lie. Three reasons. Tit.1:2-3
Comforting. 2 Cor.1:3
Discussed. Acts 17:24-25
Eternal. Jn.1:1-2; 1 Jn.1:1-4; Rev.1:8
Faithful. 1 Cor.1:9; 10:13; Heb.6:18; 1 Pt.4:19
Faithful & just. 1 Jn.1:9
Faithful. Will preserve the believer. 1 Th.5:23-24
Frightening vs. loving. Heb.12:18-24
Glorious. (See GLORY, Of God)
God is One. Gal.3:20
Good. Jas.1:17-18
Good & severe. Mk.11:12-14
Gracious. (See GRACE)
Holy. (See HOLY - HOLINESS, Of God)
Immutable. (See GOD, Nature, Unchangeable)
Impartial. Ro.3:29-30; 1 Pt.1:17
Invisible. Jn.1:18; 5:37-38; 8:19
Never seen by man. Jn.8:19; 1 Cor.3:18-23
Verses. List of. Jn.5:37-38; 1 Tim.6:16
Is God righteous? Ro.9:14
Just. (See JUSTICE, Of God)
Just & true. Rev.15:3
Kind & loving. Tit.3:4-5
Life. Acts 17:24-25
Light. 1 Jn.1:5
Longsuffering. (See GOD, Longsuffering; LONGSUFFERING)
Love. (See GOD, Love; LOVE, Of God)
Merciful. (See GOD, Mercy; MERCY, Of God). 2 Cor.1:3; Tit.3:4-5
Not unjust because He chooses to reward some persons. Mt.20:11-14
Omnipotent. (See GOD, Power; POWER, Of God)
Omnipresent - Present everywhere. (See GOD, Presence of)
Omniscient - All-knowing. (See GOD, Knowledge of)
One God. Universal Fatherhood. Mk. 12:29-31; Ro.3:29-30; 1 Cor.8:4; Eph.4:6; 1 Tim.2:3-7; 1 Jn.5:7
Perfect--no imperfection whatsoever. 1 Tim.2:3-7
Providence. (See GOD, Providence of)
Righteous. (See GOD, Righteousness; RIGHTEOUSNESS, Of God)
Self-sufficient. Acts 17:24-25
Sovereign. (See GOD, Providence of)
Guides history, even of each person. Acts 17:26
Spirit. Jn.4:23-24; 4:24; Acts 17:24; 2 Cor.3:17
Triune. The Trinity. (See TRINITY)
True. Jn.3:33; 2 Cor.1:18
Unchangeable. Ro.11:29; Tit.1:2; Heb.1:2; 6:17-18; Jas.1:17
Unsearchable. Ro.11:33-36; 1 Cor.2:16
Omniscient. (See GOD, Knowledge - Omniscience; KNOWLEDGE, Of God)
Patience of.
Discussed. Mt.22:1-14; 22:4; 2 Pt.3:9; 3:15-16

Is not willing for any to perish. 2 Pt.3:8-10
Means salvation for man. 2 Pt.3:11-15
Why God is longsuffering toward man. 2 Pt.3:9
Power of. (See JESUS CHRIST, Power)
All things are possible to God. Mt.19:26; Lk.1:36-37; 1:58
Answers prayer--far beyond what is asked or thought. Lk.1:34-35; Eph.3:20-21
Is a keeping power. Ro.16:25; Ph.1:6; Jude 24-25
Is enormous. Created the universe. Acts 4:24
Is for the believer. Eph.1:3-23; 3:1-21
Is seen in two events. Mt.1:11-16
Is the mighty hand of God. 1 Pt.5:6-7
Raised & exalted Christ. 1 Cor.6:14; 2 Cor.13:4;Eph.1:19-23
Sent the Messiah, born of a virgin. Lk.1:49-50
Uses power in a loving & caring way. Ro.1:16
Will resurrect believers. 1 Cor.6:14; 2 Cor.13:4
Presence of.
Effect. Mt.9:15
Invisible. (See GOD, Nature, What God is like, Invisible) Jn.1:18; 5:37-38; 8:19
Not distant & far off. Jn.14:9
Omnipresent. Not limited. Acts 7:42-53
Spirit. Jn.4:23-24
Profession of. (See CONFESSION; PROFESSION, FALSE)
Proof of. (See GOD, Existence)
Providence - Sovereignty.
A picture of God's providence & man's deception. Acts 23:12-35
Chose Paul before his birth. Gal.1:15
His right is as the potter over the clay. Ro.9:19-21
His right is to do as He wills. Ro.9:19-21
His right is to elect as He wills. Ro.9:10-13
His right is to show mercy & justice as He wills. Ro.9:14-33
Is immutable. Heb.6:17; Jas.1:17
Overrules events to fulfill His will. Acts 4:25-28
Overrules events to fulfill Scripture. Christ's birth. Lk.2:1-6
Overrules the affairs of men. Mt.2:7-8
Overrules the world. Heb.2:5-13
Overrules unbelief & uses it for good. Verses. List of. Jn.11:55-57
Reversed the order of things on earth. Lk.1:51-53
The futility of struggling against. Acts 5:38-39
Works all things after the counsel of His will. Eph.1:11
Purpose of.
Discussed. Ro.8:29; 9:6-13; 9:14-33; 2 Tim.1:8-10
His plan for the ages. Jn.4:22
His purpose is eternal. 2 Tim.1:8-10
Reaction toward. (See GOD, Misconceptions)
Denied.
By false teachers. Tit.1:16; 2 Pt. 2:1; Jude 4
By works. Tit.1:16
Doubted. By worldly wisdom. 1 Cor.2:6
Mocked. God will not be mocked. Gal.6:7-9

Opposed.
As an enemy by all men. Ro.5:10
By three kinds of men. Acts 4:25-28
Rejected. Evidence is denied. Lk.7:30; Ro.1:19; 1:20; 1 Th.4:8
Some hate God. Ro.1:30
Revealed - revelation of.
Is Jesus Christ. Jn.8:19; 12:45; 14:6-7; 14:9; 16:15;Col.2:9; 1 Tim.3:16; Heb.1:1-3;2:9-13
Is not revealed by man, but by Christ. Jn.1:18; 3:13; 3:31; 1 Cor.3:18-20
Is revealed through nature & creation. Acts 14:14-18; 17:24-25; Ro.1:20
Righteousness of.
Discussed. Ro.3:21-26; 10:1-11
Is Jesus Christ. Ro.3:21-22; 10:4; 1 Cor.1:30;2 Cor.5:21; Ph.3:9
Is revealed in the gospel. Ro.1:16-17
Revelation of. Ro.3:21-26
Salvation of. (See SALVATION) 2 Pt.1:1-21
Sins against. (See SIN; UNBELIEF; Related Subjects)
Source of.
Creation. (See CREATION)
Life. Jn.5:26
Of all that concerns His people. 2 Cor.1:1-2
Peace. (See PEACE)Ph.4:6-7; 4:9
Salvation. (See SALVATION)
Testimony.
Discussed. 1 Jn.5:6-15
Throne of.
Discussed. Rev.4:1-11. Cp. Rev.20:11
Heaven is God's throne. Mt.5:34
Trinity. (See TRINITY)
View of. (See GOD, Misconceptions of; Reaction toward)
Vs. Satan. (See SATAN, Purpose; Work of)
Will of.
Cannot be overthrown, stopped or defeated. Acts 5:33-40
Christ came to do the will of God. Jn.6:38; 6:39; 6:40
Discussed. Mt.6:10; Col.1:9
For believers. That believers might be assured & secured. Never lost. Jn.6:39; 6:40
For Christ. That Christ might have many followers & brothers. Jn.6:39; Ro.8:29
For man. (See GOD, Purpose of; MAN, Purpose of) 1 Jn.5:13-15
Overrules events to fulfill His will. Acts 4:25-28
Submission to. Lk.1:26-38
The mystery of God's will. Eph.1:9-10
The right to do as He wills. Ro.9:19-21
To save men. Jn.4:31-35
Wisdom of. (See WISDOM, Of God)
Threefold witness within man. Ro.2:11-15
Works of. (See WORKS OF GOD. Also see Subjects Desired)
Discussed. Jn.9:4
Incarnation, The. 2 Cor.5:18-19; Gal.4:4-7;1 Tim.3:16
Steps to getting help from God. Lk.18:35-43
To assure salvation. (See ASSURANCE; SALVATION)
Has assured it by an oath. Heb.6:16-20
To be "in Christ" reconciling the world. 2 Cor.5:18-19

To be the Savior, Provider, & Justifier.
Ro.8:31-33

To draw man to Christ. Jn.6:37-39; 6:44-46

To govern & control history. Lk.1:46-56

To guarantee the believer's home in
heaven. 2 Cor.5:5

To indwell believers. 2 Cor.4:7; Eph.3:19

To justify man. Ro.8:31-33

To make the believer a temple for
God's Holy Spirit. To indwell the
believer. 2 Cor.6:16

To reveal Himself in Christ. Jn.5:20

To reverse the order of five things.
Lk.1:51-53

To save men. (See **SALVATION**).
Jn.4:31-35

To supply all the needs of believers.
Ph.4:19

To testify about His Son, the Lord Jesus Christ. 1 Jn.5:7; 5:9-12

What God does for the believer. Jude
24-25

Wrath of. (See **WRATH OF GOD**)

GOD, DAY OF
Discussed. 2 Pt.3:12

GODS, FALSE (See **IDOLS - IDOLATRY**)
Fact.
Are not gods--only notions, ideas, &
imaginations of men. Acts 17:29;
19:24-26; Ro.1:22-23; 1:24-25;
1 Cor.8:4-8; Gal.4:8; 4:9-11;
Col.2:20-23; 2 Pt.1:16
Idols are dumb & lifeless. 1 Cor.12:2
Man worships one of two things. Acts
14:14-18
Names - Titles.
Beelzebub.
Ancient god of the Philistines. Dis-
cussed. Mk.3:22
Christ was charged with being pos-
sessed by Beelzebub. Mt.3:22-23
Diana.
Ancient goddess of the Greeks.
Discussed. Eph. Introd.
Worshippers of Diana attacked
Paul. Acts 19:21-41, esp. 27-34
Hermes (Mercurius). Ancient god of
the Romans. Discussed. Acts 14:8-13
Zeus (Jupiter). Ancient god of the
Romans. Discussed. Acts 14:8-13
Source. Created by man's imaginations,
ideas. Jn.8:54-59

GOD, SUPPER OF
Discussed. Rev.19:17-18
The great invitation of God & man's ex-
cuses. Lk.14:15-24

GOD-FEARERS
Prospects for the gospel. Acts 17:17

GODLESS - GODLESSNESS (See **SIN;
UNGODLY**)
Caused by.
Being lost & alienated from God. Eph.2:12
Choosing sin over God. Ro.1:18-32
Self-centeredness. Ro.3:10-12
Violating & rejecting the law of God.
1 Tim.1:9
Duty. To deny ungodliness. Tit.2:12-13
Meaning. 2 Tim.3:2-4; Heb12:15-17
Result. Cannot save oneself. Ro.5:6-7
Sign of the end time. But deny the power.
2 Tim.3:2-4; 3:5

GODLY - GODLINESS (See **HOLY -
HOLINESS**)
Duty.
To lead a quiet & peaceable life in all
g. 1 Tim.2:1-2
To exercise oneself to **g**. 1 Tim.4:7
To follow after **g**. 1 Tim.6:11
To live **g**. in this present world, look-
ing for the glorious appearing of
Christ. Tit.2:12-13
To live like one should in all holy be-
havior & **g**., looking for the day of
God. 2 Pt.3:10-12
To teach & subject oneself to the doc-
trine which stresses **g**. 1 Tim.6:3
Fact.
Every **g**. tree brings forth godly fruit.
Mt.7:17-20
G. can be perverted, used as gain.
1 Tim.6:5
Meaning. 1 Tim.6:11; Tit.2:12-13;
2 Pt.1:3; 1:5-7; 3:11
Mystery of. 1 Tim.3:16
Results. Contentment. 1 Tim.6:6-8
Source. The power of God. 2 Pt.1:3
Vs. ungodly man. Mt.14:1-14

GOG AND MAGOG
Discussed. Rev.20:7-10

**GOLDEN CANDLESTICKS OF REVE-
LATION** (See **GOLDEN LAMP-
STANDS OF REVELATION**)

**GOLDEN LAMPSTANDS OF REVE-
LATION**
Identified. The seven churches of the
Revelation. Rev.1:12; 1:20

GOLDEN RULE
Discussed. Mt.7:12; Lk.6:31

GOLGOTHA
Hill on which Christ was crucified.
Mt.27:26-38
Meaning. Mk.15:22

GOMORRHA
Discussed. Mt.10:15
Example of. The judgment of God. Jude 5-
7

GOOD - GOODNESS (See **GOOD
WORKS**)
Discussed. The great struggle to do **g**.
Ro.7:14-25
Duty.
To do **g**. Ro.12:9-10; 1 Pt.3:11
To do **g**. to those who hate us. Lk.6:27
To follow that which is **g**.. 1 Th.5:15
To love enemies & do **g**.. Lk.6:35
To minister for the **g**. of others.
Ro.13:4; 15:2
To minister to one's enemies.
Ro.12:20
Example.
Barnabas. Acts 11:24
Joseph. Lk.23:50
Mary. Mt.26:6-13, esp. 10; Mk.14:3-9,
esp. 6
Meaning. Mt.7:11; Ro.15:14; Gal.5:22-23;
Eph.5:9; 1 Pt.2:12; 2 Pt.1:5-7
Misconception of. (See **SELF-
RIGHTEOUSNESS**)
Of Christ. Went about doing good &
helping all who had need. Acts 10:38

Of God.
Discussed. Jas.1:17-18
God's **g**. is despised by some. Ro.2:4
God's **g**. leads men to repentance.
Ro.2:4
Is showered upon both **g**. & evil men
upon earth. Mt.5:45; Acts 14:17
There is none **g**. but one, that is, God.
Mt.19:17
Result - Reward. Glory, honor, & peace
will be given to the person who does **g**.
Ro.2:10

GOOD NEWS OF GOD
Preached by Jesus Christ. Mk.1:14-15

GOOD SAMARITAN
Parable of. Supreme questions of life.
Lk.10:25-37

GOOD WORKS (See **DEEDS; WORKS**)

GOODMAN OF THE HOUSE (See
OWNER OF THE HOUSE)

GOSPEL (See **MESSAGE; PREACH-
ING; SALVATION**)
Beginning of. Discussed. Mk.1:1-8; 1:1-2
Described as.
A mystery. Eph.6:19, cp. Eph.3:1-6
A treasure. Mt.13:44
An additive only. Some only add the
gospel to other things in life.
Mt.13:7, 22
Revolutionary. Acts 17:6-7
The Word of the Lord. 1 Pt.1:25
Discussed. 1 Cor.15:1-11
Eight points. Col.1:5-6
How men receive the **g**. Mt.13:1-9
The message that turned the world
upside down. Acts 17:1-9
The preaching of Paul. Acts 13:14-41;
17:1-9; 17:22-34;26:19-23
Duty.
Not to be ashamed of the **g**. 2 Tim.1:8
Not to preach in word only. 1 Th.1:5
Not to preach to please people.
1 Th.2:5
To be enslaved to the **g**. Ro.1:8-15
To be open to the **g**. Jn.4:24
To be separated, given over totally to
the **g**. Ro.1:1
To be unashamed of the **g**. Ro.1:16-17
To believe the **g**. Acts 15:7; Eph.1:13-14
To defend the **g**. Gal.2:1-10; Ph.1:7,
17, 27
To endure abuse for the **g**. 2 Tim.1:6-12
To fully preach the **g**. Ro.15:19
To guard & protect the **g**. Lk.10:5-6
To honor the **g**. by our behavior & life.
Ph.1:27
To let the **g**. remain in you. 1 Jn.2:24-27
To lose one's life for the sake of the **g**.
Mk.8:35
To plant the **g**. in a world that is barren
& lost. Mk.4:30-321 Cor.1:17;
2 Cor.10:14; 11:7
To preach a pure **g**. 1 Th.2:3-6;
Gal.1:8-11
To preach the **g**. Lk.9:6; 20:1; Acts
8:2; 8:25; 14:7;
To preach the **g**. as a witness for &
against man. Mt.24:14
To preach the **g**. as it should be
preached. 1 Th.1:5

To preach the **g.** boldly. Eph.6:19;
1 Th.2:2

To preach the **g.** despite weaknesses,
sickness, & suffering. Gal.4:13

To preach the **g.** to all nations.
Mk.13:10; 16:15

To preach the **g.** to the poor. Mt.11:5;
Lk.7:22

To preach the **g.** with compulsion.
1 Cor.9:16-23

To preach the **g.** with the presence of
the Holy Spirit. 1 Pt.1:12

To sacrifice one's house & family for
the sake of the **g.**--if need be.
Mk.10:29

To spread the **g.** by peaceful means.
Mt.5:9

To submit to the **g.** 2 Cor.9:13

To take the **g.** to the world. Ro.10:14-15

Fact.
A critical, judgmental person is unde-
serving of the **g.** Mt.7:16

Has been taken from the Jews & given
to the Gentiles. Acts 28:25-29

Is not a fable, a cleverly invented
story. 2 Pt.1:16

Is sent to the Gentiles. Acts 28:25-29

Is universal, for all men. God has no
favorites. Mt.24:14; Acts 28:19-20;
Mk.13:10; 16:15; Lk.24:47; Acts
1:8; Ro.10:13; 10:12-21; 10:14-15;
Col.1:26-27; Rev.14:16

Ministers & believers are called & entrusted with the **g.** Acts 16:10;
1 Th.2:4; 1 Tim.1:11

Reached the whole world. Acts 28:30-31

Some are ashamed of the **g.** Ro.1:16

The feet of those who go forth &
preach the **g.** are counted beautiful.
Ro.10:13-15, esp. 15

Was carried to Judaea & Samaria.
By laymen scattered all over the
world. Acts 8:1-9:31
By Peter. Acts 9:32-35; 9:36-43

Was carried to the Gentiles. The door
was swung wide open. Acts 10:1-48;
11:1-18

Will be used as the instrument of
judgment. Ro.2:16

False. Teaching of. Is a story, a creation
of man's mind. 1 Pt.3:12

In the end time. Will be preached to the
whole world. Rev.14:6-7

Meaning. 1 Cor.15:1-11

Message of.
Angels desire to look into. 1 Pt.1:12

Certainty of. The truth of the Word.
Lk.1:1-4

Concerns the Lord Jesus Christ. Lk.1:1

Discussed. Acts 2:14-24; 2:25-36;
3:12-16;9:20; 13:14-21; Tit.1:2-3

Fact of. Five facts. 1 Cor.15:1-11

Great facts of. Col.1:6-8

Greatness of. Gal.1:8-9

Importance of. 1 Cor.15:1-2

Is a gospel of peace. Eph.6:15

Is a gospel of rest. Heb.4:1-13

Is Christ, not the ideas of man or religion. Mk.1:1-2; Acts 1:8

Is heaven & hope. Col.1:3-5

Is life & immortality. 2 Tim.1:10

Is revolutionary. Misinterpreted.
Causes believers to do foolish things.
1 Cor.7:17-24

Is the gospel of hope. Col.1:23

Is the gospel of salvation. Eph.1:13

Is the kingdom of God. Mt.24:24;
Mk.1:14-15

Is the kingdom of the Lord. Mt.3:2; 4:23

Is the old, old message. 1 Jn.2:24

Is the resurrection of Christ. 2 Tim.2:8

Is the Word of the Lord. 1 Pt.1:25

Outline of. Ro.1:2

Reveals the righteousness of God.
Ro.1:16-17

The message that turned the world
upside down. Acts 17:1-9

The message to preach to a heathen
people. Acts 17:22-34

The message to preach to the world.
Acts 10:34-43

The points of the gospel. Mt.3:1-12;
4:17; Acts 4:5-10

There is only one gospel. Gal.1:6-9

Was preached by Jesus Christ. Mk.1:14-15

Was proclaimed by John. Mt.3:1-12

Of Luke.
Is an historical, orderly, & accurate
account. Lk.1:1-4

Is based upon many written accounts.
Lk.1:1

Power of. Has transforming power.
Mt.13:33; Lk.13:21; Ro.1:16-17

Preached.
First sermon. Message of the gospel.
Acts 2:14-24; 2:25-36

Second sermon. Message of the gospel. Acts 3:12-16

To a heathen people. Acts 17:22-34

To a superstitious people. Acts 14:8-20

To all in the end time. Rev.14:6-7

To the world. Col.1:6-8; 1:20-23

Purpose. Jn.20:30-31

Response to.
Attacked. But never overcome. Acts
28:30-31

Four responses. Acts 13:42-52

Hardened to.
Danger of. Jn.4:25
Reasons. Mt.13:4, 19

Rejected by the Jews. Acts 28:25-29

Resisted. Jn.6:44

Some refuse to hear. Lk.6:27-31

Two encouragements. Mt.13:47-48

Results.
A new birth, a new life. 1 Cor.4:15

Established & made strong. Ro.16:25

Faith, love, & hope. Col.1:5-6

Hope. Col.1:5

Penetrated Herod's household. Lk.23:8

Receive the promises of God. Eph.3:6

Salvation. Ro.1:16-17

Sealed with the Holy Spirit. Eph.1:13-14

Spiritual rest. Heb.4:1-13

The glory of our Lord Jesus Christ.
2 Th.2:13-14

Source - Comes from.
Eyewitnesses. Lk.1:2

God. Lk.1:3; Ro.1:1-3; Gal.1:10; 1:11-12

Jesus Christ. Mk.1:14-15; Ro.1:1-4;
2 Cor.2:12; 4:4; Tit.2:11-15

John the Baptist. Mk.1:1-4

Ministers of the Word. Lk.1:2;
Ro.1:1-3; 1 Th.3:2; 1 Pt.1:12

The grace of Christ. Gal.1:6

The grace of God. Acts 20:24

The power of God. Ro.1:16

The prophets. Ro.1:1-4, esp.2

The revelation of Jesus Christ.
Gal.1:11-12

The Scriptures of the Old Testament.
Ro.1:1-2; Gal.3:8

Tragic facts.
A man who knows better but rejects.
Acts 24:22-27

About the **g.** Discussed. Gal.1:6-9

Jews are blinded to the **g.** 2 Cor.3:14-15

Some are moved away for the **g.**
Col.1:23

Some believers do not walk according
to the **g.** & cause serious problems.
Gal.2:14

Some do not obey the **g.** & are
doomed. 2 Th.1:8-9

Some ministers hinder the **g.** by their
greed & worldliness. 1 Cor.9:11-12

Some pervert the **g.** Gal.1:6-9

The **g.** is hidden to the lost. 2 Cor.4:3-4

There are false gospels. Acts 17:1-9

Universal. Ro.10:13; 10:12-21; 10:14-15

Value of. Discussed. Mt.13:44; 13:45-46

Verses. List of. Ro.10:11

Writing of. Include only a few of Jesus'
miracles. Jn.20:30-31

GOSPEL, FALSE (See **TEACHING,
FALSE**)
Duty. To fear a false gospel. 2 Cor.11:4

Teaching of. Is a fable, a creation of
man's mind. 2 Pt.1:16. Cp. Acts 17:29;
19:24-26; Ro.1:22-23; 1:24-25; 1 Cor.
8:4-8; Gal.4:8; 4:9-11; Col.2:20-23

GOSSIP - GOSSIPERS (See **BUSY-
BODY; SLANDER; TONGUE**)
Discussed. Jas.4:11-12

Meaning. Ro.1:29; 2 Cor.12:19-21;
Tit.2:3

Prevented. By watching one's behavior
around the opposite sex. Jn.4:27

GOVERNMENT (See **CITIZENSHIP**)
And God.
The question of civil & religious
authority. Mk.12:13-17

Which is supreme: government or
God? Lk.20:19-26

Concepts of. Two false concepts.
Mk.12:13; Lk.20:22

Destruction of. In the end time.
Rev.14:8; 18:1-24; 19:17-21

Discussed. Lk.20:24-25; 1 Pt.2:13-17

Disciples argued over the positions in
Christ's **g.** Lk.22:24-30

G. & the believer. Ro.13:1-7

Purpose of. Ro.13:1-7

When **g.** is to be obeyed & when it is
not. Ro.13:1-7

Duty.
To honor civil authorities. 1 Pt.2:16-17

To obey & be subject to **g.** Reasons.
Ro.13:1-7; 1 Pt.2:13-17; Tit.3:1

To pray for. 1 Tim.2:1-3

To submit to **g.** Reasons. 1 Pet.2:13-17

Fact.
Is ordained of God to execute just
laws. Mk.12:16-17; Ro.13:1-7

Is under the power & control of God.
Jn.19:10-11; Ro.13:1-4

Paul's witness reached into the very
halls of **g.** Ph.1:13; 4:22

In the end time. (See **ANTICHRIST;
END TIME**)
A confederation of states. Rev.13:1-2;
13:8-10; 16:12-16;17:2; 17:7-18;
19:17-21

Discussed. Rev.13:1-10; 13:11-18

Godless g. Will be destroyed by God.
Rev.14:8; 18:1-24; 19:17-21
The g. of the antichrist.
Will be against God. 2 Th.2:1-12
Will seduce other governments to
follow its evil. Rev.14:8
Worship of. In the end time. Imperial
worship. Rev.13:4-8; 13:13-17; 17:1
Leaders.
Example of a believer. Ro.16:23
Opposed Christ. Lk.13:31-33
Sins of. Mk.12:14
To respect. 1 Pt.2:16-17
Were ignorant of God's ways.
1 Cor.2:7-8
Official. Came to Jesus for help. Jn.4:46-47
Rebellion - Resistance to g.
Discussed. Ro.13:1-7; 1 Pt.2:13-14
When rebellion is permitted. Ro.13:1-7;
1 Pt.2:13-14
Work of. Things involved in g. Rev.11:15

GRACE
Danger - Sin against.
Abusing & presuming upon the g. of
God. Eph.5:5-6
Falling from g. Discussed. Heb.
12:15-17; Gal.5:3-4
Feeling one is a favorite of God.
Mt.8:4
Frustrating the g. of God. Gal.2:21
Is often twisted & perverted by false
teachers. Jude 4
Pride. But for the g. of God, there go I.
Mt.8:4
Thinking one can sin & be forgiven
time & again. Eph.5:5-6
Using g. as an excuse to sin. Ro.6:1-2;
6:14-15; Eph.5:5-6
Discussed. Ro.5:2; 6:14-15; 1
Cor.1:4;Eph.2:8-10; 2 Tim.2:1;Tit.2:11-15
Dispensation of. Eph.3:1-13
Duty.
To always speak with g. Col.4:6
To be strong in the g. that is in Christ.
2 Tim.2:1
To call upon God for g. in time of
need. Heb.4:15-16
To come boldly to the throne of g.
Heb.4:16
To establish our hearts with g.
Heb.13:9
To grow in the g. & knowledge of our
Lord Jesus Christ. 2 Pt.3:18
To hope for the g. of redemption when
Christ returns. 1 Pt.1:13
To let only good proceed out of our
mouth so that it will minister g. to the
hearers. Eph.4:29
To possess & have g. in serving God.
Heb.12:28
To receive abundance of g. Ro.5:17
To sing & praise God with g. in our
hearts. Col.3:16
Fact.
About believers.
Are under g. not under the law.
Ro.6:14
G. is the distinctive of believers.
Ph.1:2
Have received g. Jn.1:16
Stand before God in g. Ro.5:1-2
G. led Jesus Christ to give up unbe-
lievable riches for man. 2 Cor.8:9
G. twisted & perverted by false teach-
ers. Jude 4

Meaning. Jn.1:14; 1:16-17; Ro.4:16;
5:2;1 Cor.1:3; 1:4; 1 Th.1:1;Tit.2:11-15;
2 Pt.1:2; 2 Jn.3;Rev.1:4
The condescension of Christ. 2 Cor.8:9
Misconceptions about. Grace gives the
right to sin. Ro.6:1
Of God.
Amazes spiritual beings. Eph.3:10-12
Gift of. Eph.2:8-10
God's glorious g. Mt.20:1-16
Mystery of. Eph.3:1-13
The work of God's g. Eph.2:8-10
Vs. works. Tit.3:4-7
Purpose of g. To share the riches of
God's glory with believers.
Ro.9:22-24; Eph.2:4-7
Results - Work of.
Assures us of the promises of God.
Ro.4:16
Builds us up through the Word of God.
Acts 20:32
Calls us to reveal Christ & to preach
Him. Gal.1:15-16
Causes a person to reign in life.
Ro.5:17
Causes God to accept us in Christ.
Eph.1:6
Enriches us in all speech & knowl-
edge. 1 Cor.1:4-5
Gives us a righteousness that leads to
eternal life. Ro.5:21
Gives us everlasting consolation &
hope. 2 Th.2:16
Gives us great power & makes us great
witnesses. Acts 4:33
Gives us special gifts for ministry.
Ro.12:3, 6
Gives us the knowledge of the riches
of God. Eph.2:7
Justifies us. Ro.3:24
Makes us an heir of God. Tit.1:7
Makes us heirs of life with our spouse.
1 Pt.3:7
Makes us sufficient for all things.
2 Cor.9:8
Redeems us & forgives our sins.
Eph.1:7
Saves us. Acts 15:11; Ro.3:24; 11:6;
Eph.2:5; 2:8-9; Tit.2:11; 3:7
Stirs belief. Acts 18:27
Stirs faith & love within us. 1 Tim.
1:14
Stirs us to use our gifts & to minister
to others. 1 Pt.3:10
Strengthens us through all infirmities
& weaknesses. 2 Cor.12:9-10
Teaches us how to live. Tit.2:12-13
Teaches us to look for Christ's return.
Tit.2:12-13
Source.
Discussed. Jn.1:16-17
God. Jas.4:6; 1 Pt.5:5, 10; Rev.1:4
Has the right to show g. & justice as
He wills. Ro.9:14-33
Jesus Christ. Jn.1:17; Acts 15:11;
Ro.1:5, 7; 5:15
Type - Symbol of. Sarah & Isaac.
Gal.4:21-31
Under g. Meaning. Ro.6:14-15
Vs. the law.
Believer is under g. not law. Meaning.
Ro.6:14-15
Contrasted with the law. Heb.12:18-24
God is not a hovering judge. Ro.6:14-15
Two problems with salvation by g.
alone. Ro.6:1

GRANDFATHER
Duty. Discussed. Tit.2:1-2

GRANDMOTHER
A g. of great faith. 2 Tim.1:5
Duty. Discussed. Tit.2:3-5

GRATITUDE (See THANKFUL -
THANKSGIVING)
Discussed.
Five facts. Lk.17:11-19
G. shown for the minister of God.
Acts 28:10, cp. 1-10
Lesson on need & g. Lk.17:11-19

GRAVE (Adjective; See HELL; WOR-
THY OF RESPECT)

GRAVE - GRAVEYARDS
Discussed. Mk.5:3
Fact.
All that are in the g. shall arise to
judgment. Jn.5:28-29
Christ raised Lazarus from the g.
Jn.11:38-46, cp. 17
The g. will not triumph over those who
trust Christ & His power.
1 Cor.15:55, cp. 50-58
The power of Christ over the g. is
boldly proclaimed. Jn.12:17, cp.
1 Cor.15:12-58

GREAT COMMISSION (See COMMIS-
SION, GREAT)

GREAT - GREATER - GREATNESS
Attitudes toward g. By the world & by
the Lord. Lk.22:24-30
Christ is declared to be g. (See JESUS
CHRIST, Supremacy - Superior)
Great Author of faith. Heb.10:19-21
Great Creator & sustainer of the uni-
verse. Col.1:16-17; Heb.1:3
Great Door to God. Jn.10:7-8; 14:6
Great Example of endurance.
Heb.12:1-29
Great God & Savior. Tit.2:12-13
Great God who entered history.
Jn.1:1-3
Great High Priest, God's Son.
Heb.4:14-8:5
Great King & Lord. Rev.19:16
Great Mediator. 1 Tim.2:3-7
Great Minister. Heb.8:1-10:18; 8:1-5;
10:1-18
Great Power. Rev.11:16-17
Great Revelation, God's Son.
Heb.1:1-4:13
Great Ruler. Lk.1:32-33
Great Sacrifice. Heb.10:1-18
Great Shepherd of the sheep.
Heb.13:20-21
Great Son of God. Jn.3:16; 5:20
Greater than all principality & power.
Col.2:9-10
Greater than Jonah. Mt.12:41
Greater than religion. Mt.12:1-8
Greater than Solomon. Mt.12:42
Greater than the angels. Heb.1:4-14
Greater than the law. Mt.5:17;
Mk.1:41-42; Ro.8:3
Greater than the prophets. Heb.1:1-3
The great, Ideal, & Perfect Man, the
very Son of Man Himself. Mt.5:17;
8:20; 26:1-2; Mk.2:28; Lk.9:58;
Col.2:12; 2:20

MASTER SUBJECT INDEX

Conditions for.
  Discussed. Mt.18:1-4
  How one achieves. Jn.13:4
Demonstrated by. Jesus. Royal service.
  Jn.13:1-17
Discussed.
  The conditions for g. Mt.18:1-4
  The dispute over g. Lk.22:24-30
  The price & meaning of g. Mt.20:20-28
  The problem of ambition. Mk.9:33-37;
  10:35-45
  The way of g.: humility. Lk.9:46-50
Duty.
  Not to neglect so g. a salvation. Heb.2:3
  To count the reproach of Christ g.
  riches than the possessions of the
  world. Heb.11:26
  To have & develop g. faith. Mt.8:10;
  Lk.7:9
  To have a g. zeal for believers in
  prayer & ministry. Col.4:12-13
  To know that God is g. than our heart
  & knows all things. 1 Jn.3:20
  To know that greater is God who is in
  us than he (the devil) who is in the
  world. 1 Jn.4:4
  To know that the servant is not g. than
  his master. Jn.13:16; 15:20
  To know that we shall receive the g.
  condemnation, for we know the
  truth. Jas.3:1
  To know the g. power of God in our
  lives. Eph.1:19-23
  To love, for the greatest thing is love.
  1 Cor.13:13
  To tell the g. things the Lord has done
  for us. Mk.5:19; Lk.8:39
  To witness with g. power. Acts 4:33,
  cp. Acts 1:8; 2 Tim.1:7-8
Great things to avoid & escape.
  The g. darkness of an evil eye. Mt.6:23
  The g. day of God's wrath. Rev.6:12-17,
  esp. 17
  The g. gulf between heaven & hell.
  Mt.16:26, cp. 19-31
  The g. tribulation. Mt.24:21-22
  The g. trouble & flame of fire caused
  by the tongue. Jas.3:4-6
  The g. white throne judgment of God.
  Rev.20:11-15
  The greed & lust for g. possessions.
  Mt.19:16-22, esp. 22
Great things to pursue.
  The g. Christian race. Heb.12:1
  The g. commandment, love. Mt.22:36-40
  The g. fall of a house (life) built upon
  the sand. Mt.7:27, cp. 24-27
  The g. harvest. Lk.10:2
  The g. mystery of godliness. 1 Tim. 3:16
  The g. power of the Holy Spirit for
  witnessing. Acts 4:33, cp. Acts 1:8
  The g. salvation of Christ. Heb.2:3
  The greatness of a child. Mt.18:1-6;
  Mk.9:33-37; Lk.9:46-50
  The greatness of love. 1 Cor.13:13,
  cp. 1-13
  The pearl of g. price. Mt.13:46
Price of g.
  Keeping & teaching the command-
  ments of God. Mt.5:19
  Receiving Christ & walking as a little
  child upon earth. Mt.18:1-6;
  Mk.9:35-37; Lk.9:46-50
  Serving & ministering to others--
  diligently. Mt.20:26; 23:11;
  Mk.10:43; Lk.22:24-30

GREAT BANQUET
  Discussed. Rev.19:17-18

GREAT SUPPER (See **GREAT BAN-QUET**)
  Discussed. Rev.19:17-18
  Parable of. Great invitation to man &
  man's excuses. Lk.14:15-24

GREECE, ANCIENT
  Traits of. Will be embodied in the antichrist. Rev.13:2

GREED (See **COVET - COVETOUS-NESS**)
  A picture of. Acts 27:4-12
  Discussed. Mt.26:15
  Four significant facts. Mk.14:10-11
  Example of.
  A people choose possessions over
  Christ. Mk.5:14-18
  Fortune-telling. Acts 16:16-17
  Judas. Mt.26:15
  Seeking payoff, bribery for favors
  done. Acts 24:26
  Meaning. Mk.7:22; Ro. 1:29
  Power of.
  Is the root of evil. 1 Tim.6:10
  What it causes. Acts 16:16-24
  Results.
  Brings judgment. Jas.5:3
  Causes sorrow. 1 Tim.6:10
  Sin of. Enslaved by c. 2 Pt.2:14
  Trait of false teachers. 2 Pt.2:14
  Verses. List of. Mk.14:11

GREEKS
  Fact.
  A great number of Greeks accepted
  Christ.
  In Corinth. Acts 18:4
  In Iconium. Acts 14:1
  In Thessalonica. Acts 17:1-4
  Some Greeks seek & approach Jesus.
  Four misunderstandings. Jn.12:20-36
  The Greeks sought after wisdom, not
  after Christ. 1 Cor.1:22
  The Greeks were considered unclean
  by the Jews. Acts 21:28
  Paul & the Greeks.
  Paul felt that he was in debt to preach
  the gospel to the Greeks. Ro.1:14-16
  Paul preached the gospel to the Greeks
  throughout all Asia. Acts 19:10
  Paul preached the message of repen-
  tance to the Greeks. Acts 20:21

GREETINGS
  Meaning. Mt.28:9
  Warning. Against using titles for atten-
  tion. Mk.12:38

GRIEF - GRIEVE - GRIEVED (See
DISTRESSED; SORROW)
  Caused by.
  Being without hope. 1 Th.4:13
  Death. To be conquered. Jn.20:14-16
  Death of a loved one. Jn.11:28-37;
  Acts 9:39
  Duty. Not to g. the Holy Spirit. Eph.4:30
  Nature of. Often self-centered. Jn.16:5

GRIPING (See **COMPLAINING;
TONGUE**)
  Warning against. 1 Cor.10:6-10

GROWTH, SPIRITUAL - MATURITY
  Assured. (See **ASSURANCE**)
  No need for discouragement. Mk.4:28
  Discussed. Acts 9:10-18
  Great prayer for. Eph.3:14-21
  Marks of. Ph.1:3-11
  Maturity is revealed by the tongue.
  Jas.3:1-12
  Parable of the Seed. Four facts.
  Mk.4:26-29
  The danger of immaturity. Heb.5:11-6:3
  Duty.
  Must do the will & work of God.
  Jn.4:31-35
  Must not let suffering or disability
  hinder spiritual g. Mt.12:9-10
  To follow Christ who is perfect. Heb.
  2:10-13; 5:9; 7:19; 10:14;12:23; 13:21
  To grow in Christ. 1 Jn.2:12-14
  To press on. Ph.3:1-21
  To put off the old man & put on the
  new man. Eph.4:22-24, cp. 4:25-32;
  Col.3:8-10
  To put on seven things. Ro.13:14
  To seek perfection. Ph.3:7-16;
  Heb.6:1-2
  Essential.
  Discussed. Eph.3:14-21; Heb.5:14
  Must abide in Christ. Jn.15:5
  Must add seven things to one's faith.
  2 Pt.1:5-11
  Must be constantly purged by God.
  Jn.15:2
  Must feast on God's Word. Acts
  20:32; 1 Pt.2:2-3
  Must go on to maturity. Heb.6:1
  Must grow before serving. Lk.5:14
  Must grow in grace & in the knowl-
  edge of Christ. 2 Pt.3:18
  Must meditate upon the truth & the
  Word. 1 Tim.4:15
  Must not be children in understanding.
  1 Cor.14:20
  Must pray in the Holy Spirit & keep
  oneself in the love of God. Jude 20-21
  Must put away childish things.
  1 Cor.13:11
  Must speak the truth in love. Eph.4:15
  Need for. To grow strong in spirit.
  Lk.1:80
  Source - How one g.
  By the working of God. 2 Cor.9:10;
  1 Th.3:12
  Feasting on God day by day. Jn.6:54
  How one grows.
  By edification. Eph.4:12-16
  By faith, not by the flesh. Gal.3:3
  Is transformed daily into the glory of
  God. 2 Cor.3:17-18
  Steps to satisfaction. Jn.6:30-36
  States - Levels of.
  Discussed. 1 Jn.2:12-14
  Twofold. Col.1:2

GRUMBLING (See **COMPLAINING;
TONGUE**)
  Against Christ & His claims. Jn.6:41-43
  Caused by.
  Anxiety, worry. Lk.10:40
  Hate. 1 Jn.3:15
  Characteristic - Trait of. False teachers.
  Jude 16
  Meaning. Ph.2:14
  Warning against. 1 Cor.10:6-10

GUARD (See **BEWARE; WATCH**)
Discussed. Mt.24:42
Duty.
To **g**. Rev.3:2
To **g**. & be sober. 1 Th.5:6; 1 Pt.4:7
To **g**. & keep one's clothing lest one
be found naked. Rev.16:15
To **g**. & stand fast in the faith. 1
Cor.16:13
To **g**. against false teachers. Acts
20:28-31, esp. 31
To **g**. because history's climax is at
hand. 1 Pt.4:7-11
To **g**. for the Lord's return. Mt.24:42-51;
25:13; Mk.13:35; Lk.12:35-40;
21:36; Acts 20:31
To **g**. in all things. 2 Tim.4:5
To **g**. in prayer. Eph.6:18; 1 Pt.4:7
To **g**. & pray for the end time.
Lk.21:34-36
To **g**. & pray in great trials.
Lk.21:34-36, esp. 36
To **g**. & pray not to enter into
temptation. Mt.26:41; Mk.13:33;
14:38; Lk.22:45-46; Col.4:2
Essential. To **g**. self & the church. Areas
to **g**. Acts 20:28
Meaning. Mt.24:42; 1 Cor.16:13-14
Need to. Rules for discipleship. Fourfold.
Lk.6:39-45
Warning.
Danger in failing to **g**. Mt.26:40-41
Must **g**. or one will fall short of God's
grace. Heb.12:15-17

GUESTS
Courtesies to. Lk.7:44

GUIDANCE
Assurance of **g**. In God's purpose & will.
Mt.4:12
By whom. The Holy Spirit. Jn.16:12-13
Promise. Discussed. Jn.16:12-13

GUILE - GUILELESSNESS (See **DECEIT;
DECEPTION; NOTHING FALSE**)

GUILT (See **REPENTANCE**)
Caused by. Unbelief. Jn.20:24-25
Deliverance from.
By God's love. 1 Jn.3:20-21
By the conviction of the Holy Spirit.
Jn.16:8-11
Described. Mt.6:14-15; 14:1-14
Discussed. 1 Jn.3:18-19; 3:20-21
Example of.
A multitude. Acts 2:37
Esau. Heb.12:16-17
Herod's sinful life. Mk.6:14-29
Strict religionists. Jn.8:9
The ruler Felix. Acts 24:25
Godly vs. worldly sorrow. 2 Cor.7:10

H

HADES (See **HELL**)
Meaning. Lk.16:23

HAGAR
Type - Symbol of.
The flesh, the sinful nature. Ro.9:7-13
The law. Gal.4:21-31

HAIL - REJOICE (See **GREETINGS**)

HAIR
Discussed.
How men & women are to wear their
hair. 1 Cor.11:13-15
Women are not to fix their hair to at-
tract attention. 1 Pt.3:3
Women are to fix their hair in a mod-
est way. 1 Tim.2:9-10
Is used to symbolize & picture.
Commitment & sacrifice to God.
Mt.3:4; Mk.1:6
Humility & devotion to Christ.
Jn.12:3
Man's inability to do certain things.
Mt.5:36

**HALF-HEARTED - HALF-
HEARTEDNESS** (See **DOUBLE-
MINDED; INDECISION; NEUTRAL-
ITY**)

HALL OF FAME, BELIEVER'S
Believers of the early church. Ro.16:1-16;
1 Cor.16:10-12; 16:15-19; Col.4:7-18;
2 Tim.4:9-22; Tit.3:12-15; Phile.1:8-21;
Heb.11:1-40

HALLELUJAH
Meaning. Rev.19:1-6

HALLOWED
Meaning. Mt.6:9

HANDICAP
Duty. Must care for the **h**. Mk.8:22-26

HANDS
Duty. To guard against using in immor-
ality. Mt.5:27-30
How **h**. lay hold of Jesus. Mk.14:46
Sins of.
How. Seriousness of. Mk.9:43-44
Is the culprit in immorality. Mt.5:27-30
Washing. Part of Jewish ceremonial law.
Purity, cleanliness. Lk.11:37-38

HANDS, LAYING ON OF
Discussed. Acts 6:6
In ordination.
In bestowing the Holy Spirit. Acts
8:15-17
In blessing people. Mt.19:13-15
In healing. Mt.9:29
Of deacons. Acts 6:1-6
Of ministers. Acts 13:1-4; 1 Tim.4:14

HAPPY - HAPPINESS (See **FULLNESS,
SPIRITUAL; JOY**)
How to secure **h**.
By doing what one knows to do & not
condemning oneself. Ro.14:22, cp.
14:1-23
By enduring all trials & afflictions.
Jas.5:10-11
By following the example of Christ in
humility & in serving others.
Jn.13:17, cp. 1-20
By suffering for righteousness' sake.
1 Pt.3:14
By suffering for the name of Christ.
1 Pt.4:14
Of the world. Judgment of. Warning to.
Lk.6:24-26

**HARD - HARDENED - HARDNESS OF
HEART** (See **HEART**)
Caused by.
Disbelieving the resurrection.
Mk.16:14
Forgetting. Being attached to the earth.
Mk.6:52
God.
He hardens whom He wills. Ro.
9:18, cp. 15-18
He refuses to overlook the rejection
of men. Jn.12:39-41
Ignoring the Lord's will. Lk.22:49-50
Resisting the Holy Spirit. Acts 7:51
Sin. Heb.3:13
Unbelief in Christ. Jn.12:37-41
Danger of.
Continually rejecting Christ. Jn.4:25
Forgetting the works & power of
Christ. Mk.6:52; 8:17
Discussed.
Are not to **h**. our hearts. Heb.3:7-19; 4:7
H. in & out of marriage. Mt.19:8
Reasons why a person becomes **h**.
Mt.13:4, 19
Warning against. Mk.8:16-20;
Heb.3:7-19
Example of.
Disciples. Mk.6:52; 8:17
Herod. Lk.23:8-12
Religionist. Mk.3:5
Kinds of.
Corrupt **h**. Mk.7:14-23
Four kinds. Mk.4:13-20
Hard **h**. Mk.3:5; 6:52; 8:17
Israel's close-mindedness. Ro.10:18-21
Judas hardened his heart time & again.
Mt.26:15
To guard against. Ro.9:15-18
Result.
Blinds to the truth. Mk.6:52
Brings judgment upon oneself. Jude 15
Closes one's mind to the truth.
Lk.8:9-10
Corrupts the heart. Mk.7:14-23
Grieves the heart of Christ. Mk.3:5
Reacts against God. Lk.15:11-13
Rejects Christ. Lk.4:28-30; 7:33-34;
Jn.5:40-41
Rejects the Word of God. Lk.8:11-15
Stores up wrath against oneself in the
day of judgment. Ro.2:5
Trait of.
False teachers. 2 Pt.2:10
Unbelievers, the unregenerate of the
world. Tit.3:3
Verses. List of. Lk.15:11-13

HARDLY
Meaning. Mt.19:23

HARDPRESSED
Deliverance from. Jn.14:1-3
Meaning. 2 Cor.4:7-9

HARDSHIPS
Meaning. 2 Cor.6:4-5

HARLOT (See **ADULTERY; IMMOR-
ALITY**)

HARMLESS (See **PURE**)

HARVEST

H. of judgment. Mt.13:30, cp. 37-43
H. of souls.
Discussed. Mt.9:37-38
Ripe for reaping. Jn.4:35
H. of stewardship. 2 Cor.9:6
H. of the godly. Rev.4:14-16, esp. 15-16
H. of the ungodly. Rev.14:17-20

HASTEN

Meaning. 2 Pt.3:12

HATE - HATRED

Ct. with love thy neighbor. Mt.5:43-44
Discussed. Mt.5:43-48; 2 Tim.3:3
Duty.
Not to **h.** but love. 1 Jn.3:15; 4:19-21
Not to **h.** one's brother. 1 Jn.2:9; 2:11
Not to **h.** one's enemies, but to love
them. Mt.5:43-44
Not to **h.** one's wife. Eph.5:29
To **h.** evil, not to do evil. Jn.3:19-20
To **h.** one's life in this world. Jn.12:25
To **h.** worldliness. Rev.2:6
To remember that the world **h.** Christ;
therefore, it will **h.** us. Jn.15:18;
1 Jn.3:13
Examples.
Herodias. Mk.6:18-19
Misdirected religionists. Acts 23:12
Fact.
Christ **h.** the deeds of worldliness.
Rev.2:6
Christ loves righteousness & **h.** sin.
Heb.1:9
H. is a work of the flesh. Gal.5:19-21,
esp. 19
Meaning.
Discussed. Mt.5:21-26; Gal.5:19-21
Is murder. 1 Jn.3:15, cp. 3:11-12
Results - Effects.
Bars one from eternal life. 1 Jn.3:15
Blinds & erases purpose. 1 Jn.2:9-11
Blinds & puts one in darkness.
1 Jn.2:9-11
Marks one as a child of Satan.
1 Jn.3:10
Proves one does not know God.
1 Jn.2:9-11; 4:19-21
Proves one does not love God.
1 Jn.4:19-21
Who is hated.
Believers.
Stated. Mt.10:22; 24:9; Mk.3:13;
Lk.21:17
Why believers are **h.** Jn.15:18-21;
17:14
Christ.
Is **h.** without just cause. Jn.15:24-25
Some reject Him as the Savior of
the world. Jn.19:6
Some reject His reign over them &
the world. Lk.19:14
Some reject His testimony that the
world is evil. Jn.7:7
God. Jn.15:24; Ro.1:30
One's enemies. Mt.5:43-48, cp. 21-26
Those who do good. 2 Tim.3:1-5, esp. 3

HAUGHTY - HAUGHTINESS (See AR-ROGANCE; BOASTING; PRIDE; SELF-SUFFICIENCY)

HEADY (See RASH)

HEAL - HEALING

And forgiveness. **H.** is less important
than forgiveness. Mk.2:1-12
By Jesus Christ.
All diseases & sicknesses. Jesus'
power. Mt.4:24; 8:16-17; 9:35;
11:5;15:29-31; Lk.4:40
Arthritis, curvature of the spine. Man
is more important than religion.
Lk.13:11-13
Blind & dumb (mute) man. Proves the
Messiah's power. Mt.12:22-24
Blind Bartimaeus. Steps for getting
help. Mk.10:46-52; Lk.18:35-43
Blind man. Necessity for caring.
Mk.8:22-26; Jn.9:1-7
Blind men. The unceasing cry for
sight. Mt.9:27-31; 20:20-34
Canaanite woman's daughter. How to
receive the things of God. Mt.15:21-28
Centurion's servant. Receiving & re-
jecting men. Mt.8:5-13; Lk.7:1-10
Deaf & could hardly speak (mute).
Doing all things well. Mk.7:31-37
Demon possessed.
A boy whose speech was robbed by
a spirit. Spiritual immaturity &
powerlessness. Mk.9:14-29
A daughter. Caring for the rejected.
Mk.7:24-30
A daughter of a Canaanite woman.
How to receive things from God.
Mt.15:21-28
A demon-possessed girl. Power of
money vs. the power of Jesus'
name. Acts 16:16-24
A dumb man. The quiet approach
for sanity. Mt.9:32-33
A man. Hope for the most wild &
mean. Mk.5:1-20
A son. A rebuke to the present gen-
eration. Lk.9:37-45
Delivering the most enslaved.
Mk.1:23-28; 1:34; 3:11-12; 5:1-20
Delivering the most unclean.
Lk.4:33-37
Many possessed persons.
Jesus' power. Mt.4:24; Lk.4:41
Seeking & fearing Christ.
Mk.3:7-12
Many possessed with evil spirits.
Mk.1:23-28; 1:34; 3:11-12; 5:1-20
Two possessed men. Saving men.
Mt.8:28-34
Unclean spirits. Meeting the needs
of people. Acts 5:16
Dropsy. The religionists & their error.
Lk.14:1-6
Dumb (mute) man. The quiet approach
for sanity. Mt.9:32-34; 12:22;
Lk.11:14
Hemorrhaging woman. The secret
hope for health. Mt.9:20-22;
Mk.5:24-34;Lk.8:43-48
Impotent man. Power to meet the
world's desperate need. Jn.5:1-16
Lame man. Lessons for witnessing.
Acts 3:1-11
Leper.
Proves deity. Mt.8:1-4
Ten lepers. Lesson on need &
gratitude. Lk.17:11-19
The most unclean. Mk.1:23-28;
1:40-45
The most untouchable. Lk.5:12-16

Man with a withered hand. Under-
standing true religion. Mk.3:1-2;
3:1-6; Lk.6:6-11
Many among the crowds. Seeking &
fearing Christ. Mk.3:7-12
Many sick. Meeting the needs of peo-
ple. Acts 5:16; 19:12
Neglected. Reason. Lack of power &
faith. Lk.9:11
Nobleman's son. The stages of faith.
Jn.4:46-54
Forgiveness of sins. Mk.2:1-12
Paralytic. Aeneas. Making men whole.
Acts 9:32-35
Paralyzed man. Forgiving sin. Mt.9:1-8;
Lk.5:18-26
People in the streets. Caring for the
whole world. Mk.1:32-34
Peter's mother-in-law. Caring for the
home & for individuals. Mt.8:14-15;
Mk.1:29-31;Lk.4:38-39
Raised the dead.
Dorcas. Conquering death. Acts
9:36-43
Jairus' daughter. A desperate, be-
lieving approach. Mk.5:21-24,
35-43; Lk.8:40-42,49-56
Lazarus. Power over death.
Jn.11:41-46
Ruler's daughter. Hopeless cry for
life. Mt.9:18-19, 23-26
Shriveled hand. Man is greater than
religion. Mt.12:9-13
Widow's son. Compassion &
power. Lk.7:11-17
Discussed. Acts 9:32-35
Duty.
To minister to those who are sick.
Mt.25:36, cp. 31-40; Lk.10:34
To pray for healing when seriously
sick. Jas.5:14-15
Errors of. Mentioned. Mt.9:35
Gift & power of **h.**
Discussed. 1 Cor.12:8-10
Involves the infusion of great power
into the sick & diseased. Lk.8:46
Is a God-given power. Mt.4:24;
Mk.3:15; 16:17-18; Acts 19:11-12
Why the gift of **h.** is given. Mt.10:1
Kinds.
Spiritual **h.** The very special mission
of Christ was to **h.** man spiritually.
Lk.4:18
Spiritual, physical, mental. The whole
man. Mt.4:24
Meaning.
Being **h.** Lk.17:15-19; Acts 4:9
Of both soul & body. Mt.14:36; Acts
3:16
Through & through. Soul & body.
Mt.14:36
Method. Anointing with oil. Mk.6:8-13;
Jas.5:14-15
Request for **h.** Mt.9:20; 14:36
Source of wholeness.
Christ. The name of the risen Lord.
Acts 4:9-10
Faith. Mk.10:51-52
Steps to.
Being made whole. Mt.14:34-36
Discussed. Mk.6:53-56
Why God does not always heal. Mt.8:1-4

HEAR - HEARING
Duty.
Not to deliberately close one's ears. Mt.13:13-15
To be obedient of the Word not a hearer only. Ro.2:11-15; Jas.1:22
To be quick to **h**. & slow to speak. Jas.1:19
To desire to **h**. the Word of God. Acts 13:7, 44
To **h**. God's Son. Mt.17:5; Mk.9:7
To **h**. the Word. Eph.1:13-15; Col.1:5; 1 Th.2:13; 2 Tim.1:13; 1 Jn.2:7
To **h**. the Word & keep it & bear fruit. Lk.8:15
To **h**. the Word of Christ. Lk.9:35; Ro.10:16-17
To **h**. what the Spirit says to the churches of Revelation. Rev.2:11
To heed what we **h**. Mk.4:24; Lk.8:18
To proclaim what we **h**. about the Lord. Acts 4:20; 1 Jn.1:3-5
Fact.
Many **h**. but do not understand. Acts 28:26, cp. 25-27; Jn.8:42-43
Many have turned their ears away from the truth & followed fables. 2 Tim.4:4, cp. 1-4
People cannot **h**. without a preacher. Ro.10:13-15
Proof that a person **h**.
He follows Christ. Jn.10:3
He keeps the Word of God & bears fruit. Lk.8:15
Results of hearing the Word.
Will be blessed. Rev.1:3
Will receive everlasting life. Jn.12:47-50
Results of not hearing & not understanding the Word.
A person forgets who he is & what he needs. Jas.1:23-24
Destruction. Mt.7:24-27; Acts 3:23
Satan snatches away what a person does **h**. Mt.13:19
Shall be judged by the very words of Christ. Jn.12:47-48

HEART
Discussed.
Condition of. Hard, shallow, thorny, soft. Mk.4:1-20
Defilement of. Things that defile, make unclean. Mt.15:17-20; Mk.7:14-23
Known, exposed by God. Acts 1:24; 15:8; Ro.2:2-5; 8:27
The inside vs. the outside of man. Purity, cleanliness. Lk.11:39-41
Duty - Essential.
Must be broken for salvation. Mk.3:11-12
Must be cleansed. Lk.11:39-41
Must be opened by Christ. Acts 16:14
Must bear fruit. Mt.13:8, 23
Not to deceive one's **h**. Jas.1:26
To be meek & lowly in **h**. Mt.11:29
To be open in looking at God's call to separation. 2 Cor.6:11-13
To be open to the truth. Jn.4:25
To draw near God with a true **h**. Heb.10:22
To establish the **h**. with grace. Heb.13:9
To give one's **h**. to God. Lk.11:39-41
To have a clean **h**. 1 Jn.3:18-24
To have a pure **h**. Mt.5:8

To have a renewed **h**. Heb.8:10-12
To let Christ dwell in one's **h**. Eph.3:17
To let the peace of God & the Word of Christ rule in one's **h**. Col.3:15
To live for Christ out of a pure **h**. 2 Tim.2:22
To love out of a pure **h**. 1 Tim.1:5; 1 Pt.1:22
To open the door of one's **h**. to Christ. Rev.3:18-20
To open the eyes of the **h**. to know God. Eph.1:17-18
To possess the law of God in one's **h**. Heb.10:15-18
To receive the Word of God within one's **h**. Four ways. Mk.4:1-20
To sanctify the Lord in one's **h**. 1 Pt.3:15
To stand steadfast in **h**. 1 Cor.7:37
To work the will of God from the **h**. Eph.6:6
Hard - Hardened. (See **HARD - HARD-NESS OF HEART**)
Kinds of.
Blind **h**. Eph.4:18
Clean **h**. 1 Jn.3:18-24
Corrupt **h**. Mt.15:15-20
Covetous **h**. 2 Pt.2:14
Darkened. Cannot see. Ro.1:21
Enlightened **h**. 2 Cor.4:6
Glad & single **h**. Acts 2:46
Hard **h**. Mt.13:4, 19; Heb.3:7-11
Honest & good **h**. Lk.8:15
Indifferent. Lk.8:11-15
Perverse. Lk.9:41
Pure **h**. Mt.5:8; 1 Tim.1:5; 2 Tim.2:22; 1 Pt.1:22
Seven descriptions. Acts 16:14
Sincere **h**. Meaning. Heb.10:22
Sinful, unbelieving **h**.. Heb.3:12
Thorny. Worldly. Mt.13:7, 22
Troubled **h**. Deliverance from. Five-fold. Jn.14:1-3
Uncircumcised **h**. Acts 7:51
Meaning. Mt.22:37; Mk.7:21; 12:29-31
Set on.
Earthly or heavenly treasure. Mt.6:21-23
Exposed by words. Mt.12:34-35
Money or God. Lk.16:14-15
The new life in Christ. Col.3:15-17
Treasure. A person's treasure is where the **h**. is. Mt.6:21-23
Source. Of evil. Mk.7:23; Lk.11:39-41
What the heart does.
Commits adultery. Mt.5:28
Commits covetousness. 2 Pt.2:14
Defiles a person, makes him unclean. Mt.15:10-20; Mk.7:14-23
Determines speech. Lk.6:45
Determines the outside of a person. Mt.23:25-26
Develops a blindness to the truth. 2 Cor.3:15; Eph.4:18
Develops a hardness against Christ. Mk.3:5; 6:52; Ro.1:21
Does evil. Mt.9:4; Lk.6:45
Does good things & evil things. Mt.12:35
Experiences conviction. Acts 2:37
Experiences rejoicing. Acts 2:26
Experiences sorrow. Jn.16:6; Ro.9:2
Experiences the love of God. Ro.5:5
Gives assurance. 1 Jn.3:9
Gives purpose, initiative, drive. 2 Cor.9:7

Grows in the understanding of Christ. Mt.13:15; Jn.12:40; Acts 28:27
Lies. Acts 5:3
Loves God. Mt.22:37
Questions. Ro.10:6-7, cp. 8-10
Sanctifies. 1 Pt.3:15
Stirs belief. Lk.8:15; Ro.10:10; Acts 8:37
Stirs doubt. Mk.11:23
Stirs obedience. Ro.6:17
Suffers trouble & lack of peace. Jn.14:1; 14:27

HEART, DO NOT LOSE
Meaning. 2 Cor.4:1, 4:16

HEARTLESS
Discussed. Ro.1:31
Evil **h**. Meaning. Col.3:5-7

HEART OF THE EARTH
Meaning. Mt.12:40

HEATHEN - HEATHENISM - HEA-THENISTIC
Message to.
Discussed. Acts 14:8-20
Preached to. Acts 17:22-34
Modern man is **h**. Discussed. Acts 28:4-9
Seeking God. A **h**. who truly seeks God is heard by God. Acts 10:1-6; 10:1-8
The judgment of the **h**. Discussed. Ro.2:11-15
What happens to the **h**. who never hears of Christ. Ro.2:11-15

HEAVEN (See **HEAVEN & EARTH, NEW; KINGDOM OF HEAVEN**)
Believers.
Are citizens of **h**. Ph.3:20-21
Are not to make **h**. their object, but God. Jn.14:6
Are preserved for **h**. 2 Tim.4:18
Are to be rewarded with **h**. Mt.5:11-12
Are to be transported into **h**. immediately. Never lose consciousness. Jn.11:25-27; 2 Tim.4:18
Are to undergo an eternal transformation. 1 Cor.15:47-49, cp. 42-57; 1 Jn.3:1-3
Have a house, a building in **h**. 2 Cor. 5:1-4
Position in **h**. Mt.11:11
Characteristics Nature.
Is eternal & incorruptible. 2 Cor.5:1-4
Life in. (See **INHERITANCE; RE-WARDS**)
Differs from this life. Lk.12:41-48; 16:10-12; 19:15-19;20:36; 20:37-38; Jn.11:25-27
Experiences eternal rest. Rev.14:13
Experiences no corruption. 1 Cor.15:42-49; 15:50-57
Experiences no curse. Rev.22:3; Ro.8:18-22
Experiences no death. Lk.20:36-38; Rev.21:4
Experiences no sorrow, crying, or tears. Rev.7:17
Experiences no thieves or stealing. Mt.6:20
Foretaste of. Described. Mt.17:2; 17:3; 17:4; 17:5-8; 17:5
Has a great reward. Mt.5:12; Lk.6:23
Has all relationships perfected. Mk.12:25
Has love perfected. Mk.12:25

Has no defilement or wicked person. Rev.21:27; 22:15
Has no night. Rev.22:5
Inherits a mansion. Jn.14:2-3
Involves a changed body.
1 Cor.15:42-49; 15:50-57
Involves praise, singing & rejoicing. Rev.5:9-12; 7:11-12; 11:17;
14:2-3; 19:5-6
Involves reigning with Christ forever & ever. Rev.22:5
Involves serving & working for
Christ. Rev.7:15; 22:3
Is glorious. Mk.9:2-13; Ro.8:17-18
Is like the spirit of a child. Lk.18:17
Undergoes an eternal transformation.
1 Cor.15:47-49, cp. 42-57; Rev.21:4
Will experience standing before
Christ & seeing Him face to face.
Rev.22:4
Will receive an inheritance that is incorruptible & undefiled. 1 Pt.1:3-4
Three **h**. Mt.6:9
Citizens of.
A countless multitude from every nation & every tribe. Rev.7:9-17; 19:6
Angels. Heb.12:22
Believers. Ph.3:20-21
Christ. Jn.14:2-3; Acts 7:55; 2
Cor.5:1; Heb.9:24; 1 Pt.3:22
God. Mt.18:10; 24:36; Lk.11:2; Acts
7:49, 55; 17:24; Heb.12:22
Heavenly beings. Rev.5:11
Holy Spirit. Jn.1:32; 1 Pt.1:12
Special witnesses for God. Rev.7:1-8;
14:1-5
Ct. hell.
Picture of a man in heaven & hell.
Lk.16:19-31
Unsaved shall see believers in heaven.
Lk.13:28; 16:23
Described as.
A house, building, mansion. 2 Cor. 5:1-4
God's house. Jn.14:1-3
The continuing city. Heb.13:14
The **h**. city. Heb.11:10
The **h**. country. Heb.11:13-16
The **h**. Jerusalem. Heb.12:22
The new **h**. & earth. 2 Pt.3:13
The pattern of earthly things. Heb.8:1-5;
9:23-28
The pattern receiving a better sacrifice.
Heb.9:23-28
The promised land. Acts 7:2-8
The third heaven. 2 Cor.12:2
The true priesthood. Heb.8:1-5
The true worship. Heb.8:1-5
Discussed.
Difference between **h**. & this world.
Lk.20:27-38; 2 Cor.4:17-18
Earthly worship is a shadow of **h**.
things. Heb.8:1-5
Minister of. Supreme minister is Jesus
Christ. Heb.8:1-5; 8:1-9:28
Mysteries of **h**. Mt.13:1-58
The least in **h**. Mt.11:11
The pattern of earthly things. Heb.8:1-5;
9:23-24
The pattern that receives a better sacrifice. Heb.9:23-28
The tabernacle of the sanctuary. Worship of. Heb.9:1-14
Witnesses of **h**. to Christ. 1 Jn.5:6-8

Duty.
Not to swear by **h**. Mt.5:34; Jas.5:12
To be perfect even as our Father in **h**.
is perfect. Mt.5:48
To earnestly desire **h**. 2 Cor.5:1-8;
Ph.1:22-23
To give all we are & have in order to
secure **h**. Lk.12:33
To hope for **h**. Col.1:5
To lay up treasure in **h**. Mt.6:20
To look for the coming of the new **h**.
& earth. 2 Pt.3:10-12, esp. 12. Cp.
Heb.11:10
To pray for God's will to be done even
as it is in **h**. Mt.6:10; Lk.11:2
To rejoice because our names are
written in **h**. Lk.10:20
To seek **h**. Heb.13:13-16
Abraham sought. Heb.11:10
Patriarchs sought. Heb.11:13-16
To wait with anticipation for Christ's
return from **h**. Ph.3:20; 1 Th.1:10;
4:16; 2 Th.1:7
Fact.
Beings in **h**. stand in stark amazement
at God's grace to believers.
Eph.3:10-12
Cannot be penetrated by man. Lk.10:22;
Jn.3:13; 3:31; 8:14; 8:15-16; 8:19;
8:23; 8:42-43; 1 Cor.2:6-13; 3:18-20
Hope is laid up in **h**. Col.1:5
Is a world of righteousness. 2 Pt.3:13
Is another world, a spiritual dimension
of being. Mt.9:35; 19:16; 22:29
Is the real world, the spiritual world &
dimension. Jn.11:25-27
To be a new **h**. & earth. 2 Pt.3:10; 3:13
To be shaken & created into a new **h**.
Heb.12:26-27
How to enter.
By bearing the image of Christ.
1 Cor.15:47-49
By becoming as a child. Lk.18:17
By being diligent to make one's call
sure. 2 Pt.1:10-11
By being poor in spirit. Mt.5:3
By looking for **h**. 2 Pt.3:12-14
By obedience, keeping God's commandments. Rev.22:14
By putting one's treasure in **h**. Lk.12:33
Discussed. Eph.2:6
How a rich man enters **h**. Mt.19:16-22
Is difficult for a rich man to enter **h**.
Mt.19:24
Must be counted worthy to enter **h**.
Lk.20:35
Must have one's name written in the
book of life. Lk.10:20
Requires more righteousness than a
religionist has. Mt.5:20
What it takes to enter **h**. Mt.21:28-32
Meaning.
A new **h**. & earth - recreated.
2 Pt.3:12-14
Another dimension of being, the
spiritual world & dimension.
Mt.9:35
Heavenly kingdom of God. 2 Tim.4:18
Symbolized by. The promised land.
Heb.11:10; 11:13-16
The third heaven. 2 Cor.12:2
Three heavens. Mt.6:9
Misconceptions - Errors. Idealize, materialize, humanize **h**. Mk.12:25

Search for.
By Abraham. Heb.11:8-10
By believers. Heb.12:22-24
By man. 2 Cor.5:1-4; 2 Pt.3:12-14
By the patriarchs. Heb.11:13-16
Man's futile search for Messiah - utopia - heaven. Jn.8:21-24
Vision of.
A countless multitude of Gentiles is
seen in **h**. Rev.7:9-17
Jewish converts are seen in **h**.:144,000
converts. Rev.7:1-8
Redeemed Jews are seen in **h**. Rev.14:1-5

HEAVEN & EARTH, NEW
Assurance of. Rev.21:4-6
Capital of. New Jerusalem. Rev.21:2;
21:9-23; 21:24-22:5
Discussed. Ro.8:18-22; Heb.1:10-12;
12:26-29; 2 Pt.3:1-10; Rev.21:1-8;
21:24-22:5

HEAVEN, KINGDOM OF (See **KINGDOM OF HEAVEN**)

HEAVENLY BEINGS
Observe God's grace to man & stand in
stark amazement. Eph.3:10-12

HEAVENLY BODIES (See **END TIME**,
Events of; Signs of)
Fate of. Will pass away. Lk.21:33
In the end time. Greatly affected.
Mt.13:24-25; Lk.21:25-26; Rev.6:2-14

HEAVENLY BODY, MAN'S (See **RESURRECTION**)
Discussed. 1 Jn.3:2

HEAVY - HEAVINESS (See **SUFFER
GRIEF**)
Deliverance from the **h**. of sin & sorrow.
By coming to Christ. Mt.11:28-29
Duty.
To let the **h**. of soul drive one to God.
Jas.4:9-10
To suffer **h**. in behalf of others who
suffer. Ph.2:26
To suffer **h**. of soul for the lost. Ro.9:2
Fact.
Many are burdened down with **h**.
Mt.11:28
Sin causes **h**. Jas.4:9
Temptation causes **h**. 1 Pt.1:6

HEBREWS
Meaning. Acts 6:1

HEED, TAKE (See **BE CAREFUL; BEWARE; CAREFUL; WATCH**)
Of what.
Of being a stumbling block. 1 Cor.8:9
Of Christ's Word. Mk.13:23
Of covetousness. Lk.12:15
Of deception. Mt.24:4; Mk.13:5;
Lk.21:8
Of despising others. Mt.18:10
Of division. Gal.5:15
Of false doctrine & speculations.
1 Tim.1:4; Tit.1:14
Of God's judgment. Ro.11:21
Of ill feelings toward those who offend one. Lk.17:3-4
Of oneself & one's ministry. Acts
20:28; Col.4:17
Of outward show. Mt.6:1

Of persecutors. Mk.13:9
Of pride. 1 Cor.10:12
Of the light one has. Lk.11:35
Of the Word of God. Heb.2:1; 2 Pt.1:19
Of unbelief. Heb.4:12
Of watching & praying. Mk.13:33
Of what & how one hears. Mk.4:24
Of worldliness. Lk.21:34

HEIRS (See **INHERITANCE, EARTHLY; INHERITANCE, SPIRITUAL**)

HELL - HADES - SHEOL
A temporary place. Lake of fire is the permanent place. Rev.9:2
And Jesus.
Bore h. for man. Mt.27:52
Jesus descended into h. Mt.26:52-53; Eph.4:8-10, esp. 9;1 Pt.3:19-20
Deliverance. Now available. Acts 1:8
Discussed. Mt.5:22
Prisons, cell blocks, compartments, & sections of h. 1 Pt.3:18-22; 19:20
Two compartments to h. Lk.16:23
Man within. (See **HELL, What h. will be like**)
Begged for another chance. Lk.16:30
Discussed. Lk.16:23-31
Is able to see believers in heaven. Lk.13:27-30
The body & soul of some will be destroyed in h. Mt.10:28; Lk.12:5
The body of some will be cast into h. Mt.5:29-30
Meaning. 1 Tim.3:8; Tit.2:2; Acts2:27
Prepared for. The devil & his angels. Mt.25:41
What h. will be like. (See **SALVATION**)
A furnace of fire. Mt.13:30, 42
A lake of fire. Rev.20:14
An abyss. Rev.9:2
Anguish, torment. Lk.16:23-31
Damnation. Mt.23:33
Darkness. Mt.8:12
Eternal destruction. 2 Th.1:9
Eternal fire. Mt.25:41; 25:46; Mk.9:43-44
Eternal punishment. Mt.25:46
Excluded from the presence of the Lord. 2 Th.1:9
Gnashing of teeth. Mt.8:12; 13:42
Unquenchable fire. Lk.3:17
Weeping. Mt.8:12; 13:42
What h. is not. Mt.25:41-45
Who is to be in h.
Angels who sinned. 2 Pt.2:4; Jude 6
Discussed. Rev.21:8
Goats. People who do not minister or help others in life. Mt.25:41
Satan. Rev.20:10
Sinners. Offenders. Mt.18:8
The beast (antichrist) & false prophet of Revelation. Rev.19:20
The extravagant, indulgent, hoarding, & non-sacrificial person who does not give all he is & has. Mt.19:21-22; 19:23-26; 19:27-30; Lk.12:13-21; 16:19-21
The unfruitful. Mt.3:10; 7:19
The unrighteous. Mt.25:41-46
The wealthy & the materialist. Reason. Lk.16:19-21
The "whosoever" of judgment. Rev.20:15
The worshipers of the antichrist. Rev.14:9-12
Those who do not know God. 2 Th.1:8
Those who do not obey the gospel. 2 Th.1:8
Weeds. All who offend & do iniquity. Mt.13:41-42, 50

HELLENISTS
Meaning. Acts 6:1

HELP - HELPING (See **GIVE - GIVING; WORKS**)
Duty.
Discussed. Mt.5:40; 5:41; 5:42
To help all who need help, no matter who they are. Lk.10:34
To help those who labor in the gospel. Ph.4:3
To submit to those who h. in the gospel. 1 Cor.16:15-16
Of Christ. Helps us in time of need. Ro.8:27; Heb.4:14-16
Of God. Ro.8:28-39; Heb.13:5-6
Of the Holy Spirit. Helps our infirmities. Jn.14:16-17; Ro.8:26

HELPLESS - HELPLESSNESS
Meaning. Mt.9:36
Needs met. (See **HEAL - HEALING**)
By Jesus. Lk.4:40
Of man.
Cannot always do good; cannot keep from sinning. Ro.7:14-21
Cannot come to Christ except the Father draw him. Jn.6:44
Cannot save himself. Ro.5:6-7

HEMORRHAGING WOMAN
Healed by Jesus. Reward of true faith. Lk.8:43-48

HERALD, A
Meaning. Who a p. is. 1 Tim.2:3-7; 2 Tim.1:11-12

HEREDITY
What is passed on from generation to generation.
A corruptible body. 1 Cor.15:42, 50, 53; 2 Pt.1:4
An earthly nature. 1 Cor.15:47-49
Death. Ro.5:12, cp. 1 Cor.15:21-22
Flesh & blood. 1 Cor.15:50; Heb.2:14
Flesh, a natural body. Jn.3:6; 1 Cor. 15:44, 46
Sin. Ro.3:23. Cp. Ro.3:9-18; Eph.2:1
The soul. 1 Cor.15:45

HERESY (See **FACTIONS; TEACHERS, FALSE**)
Discussed. 2 Pt.2:1
How to deal with h. Tit.2:10-11
Duty. To reject a heretic. Tit.3:10
Fact.
Christianity was called a h. Acts 24:5, 14
Is destructive. 2 Pt.2:1

HERITAGE
Honor of. By religionists. Error of. Lk.11:47-51
Of Israel. Ro.9:5
Weakness of.
Does not make one acceptable to God. Jn.8:33
Family cannot save. Mt.3:7-10
Inadequate to save. Mt.1:7-8; 3:7-10
Not saved by h. Ro.9:7

HERMAS
Believer in Rome. Ro.16:14

HERMES
Believer in Rome. Ro.16:14
False god. Discussed. Acts 14:12

HERMOGENES
Forsook Paul. 2 Tim.1:15

HEROD, FAMILY OF
Archelaus. Discussed. Mt.2:22
Herod Agrippa I (AD 41-44). Discussed. Acts 12:1-25
Herod Agrippa II (AD 53-70). Discussed. Acts 25:1-26:32
Herod Antipas (BC 4 - AD 39)
Discussed. Mt.14:1-14; Mk.6:14-29; Lk.3:1-6
Disturbed by the disciples' teaching. Lk.9:7-9
Murdered John the Baptist. The immoral vs. the righteous. Mt.14:1-14; Mk.6:14-29
Reaction to Jesus.
Guilty conscience. Mk.6:16-23
Plotted to kill Jesus. Lk.13:31-33
Trial of Jesus. Shirked concern for the truth. Lk.23:8-12
Herod the Great, Ruler of Judea (BC 37 - AD 4)
Discussed. Mt.2:3-4
Reacts to Jesus' birth. Mt.2:1-11
Slaughters the children. Mt.2:13-18
Philip, Tetrarch of Ituraea & Trachonitis. Discussed. Lk.3:1

HERODIANS
Discussed. Mt.22:16; Mk.12:13
Joined forces with the Pharisees. Mk.3:6
Plotted Jesus' death. Mk.3:6

HERODIAS
Discussed. Mt.14:6-11
Wife of Herod. Plotted John's death. Vengeful. Mk.6:24-25

HERODION
Believer in Rome. Ro.16:11

HIDDEN TREASURE
Parable of. Mt.13:44

HIDE - HID
Duty.
Not to hide our talents. Mt.25:24-30
To dress & adorn the hidden man of the heart. 1 Pt.3:4
To renounce the hidden things of darkness. 2 Cor.4:2
Fact.
A light on a hill cannot be hid. Mt.5:14
All the treasures of wisdom & knowledge are hid in Christ. Col.2:3
Everything hid shall be revealed. Mt.10:26; Mk.4:22; Lk.8:17; 12:2
Hidden things will be revealed. 1 Cor.4:5
The believer's life is hidden with Christ in God. Col.3:3
The gospel is hidden to the lost--Satan blinds their minds. 2 Cor.4:3-4
Truth is hidden from the wise & revealed to babes. Mt.11:25
Works cannot be hidden. 1 Tim.5:25

HIERAPOLIS, CITY OF
A church was established in H. Col.4:13

HIGH IN LIFE, THE (See **CONCEITED; RICH, THE**)

HIGH PRIEST - CHIEF PRIESTS (See **RELIGIONISTS**)
A political office in Jesus' day. Mt.26:3
And Jesus. Stood against Jesus. Mt.26:3-5
Discussed. Mt.26:3; Jn.7:32; 11:49;
Heb.3:1; 5:1-4; 7:4-24; 8:1-10:18

HIGH PRIESTHOOD (See **JESUS CHRIST**, Priesthood of)

HIGHEST
Meaning. Mt.21:9; Mk.11:10

HIGH-MINDED (See **CONCEITED**)
Duty.
Believers must not be **h**. Ro.11:20
Not to mind high things. Ro.12:16
The rich must not be **h**. 1 Tim.6:17
To cast down imaginations & every high thing. 2 Cor.10:5
Fact. In the last days men will be **h**. 2 Tim.3:4, cp. 1-5
Meaning. 2 Tim.3:2-4

HILLEL SCHOOL
Liberal school of thought. Mt.19:1-12; Mk.10:1-12; 19:1-12

HISTORY (See **END TIMES**)
Book of destiny. Rev.5:1-4; 5:1
Center of civilization changed. Acts 16:9
Christ & history.
Adam & Christ, two representatives of mankind. Ro.5:12-21
Christ made an invasion into **h**. Divided the ages & time. Lk.7:28
Christ ushered in a new age. Mt.9:14-17
Christ was the pivotal point of **h**. Ro.5:12-21; 1 Cor.15:20-23
H. was changed by the death of Christ. Jn.21:24
Supreme fact of **h**. - the incarnation of Jesus Christ. Jn.1:10
The eternal God enters **h**. 1 Jn.1:1-5
Daniel's seventieth week. Mt.24:15
End of. (See **END TIMES**)
Discussed. Rev.6:1-7:17
Living under the shadow of history's climax. 1 Pt.4:7-11
Future of.
Climax has already come. 1 Cor.10:1-13
God's glorious plan for **h**. Eph.1:9-10
God & **h**.
God's plan for the ages. Jn.4:22; Heb.2:5-13
H. is guided by God. Acts 17:26
Salvation came through the Jews. Jn.4:22
The eternal God enters **h**. 1 Jn.1:1-5
The throne of God is the focal point of **h**. God controls **h**. Rev.4:1-11; 5:1
Hope of. Final triumph over evil. Great announcement of. Rev.10:1-11
Overview of - Perspective of.
From God's perspective. Mt.21:33-46; Eph.2:11-18
God's plan for **h**. Acts 13:14-41
Parable of the Wicked Tenants. Lk.20:9-18
Pivotal points of.
Abraham. Ro.4:11-12
Adam. Ro.5:12-21; 1 Cor.15:20-22
Believers. Ro.8:29
Christ. Coming of. Lk.3:1-6; 7:28; 11:23
Death of Jesus Christ. Mk.15:16-41

Discussed. Mt.5:17-18; 1 Cor.15:20-22
Launched by. John the Baptist. Lk.3:1-6
Symbolized. Mt.1:1-17
World measures years & calendar by Christ. Mt.8:18-22

HISTORY, SPIRITUAL & BIBLICAL HISTORY
Is inspired. 2 Tim.3:16
Periods of. Mt.1:17

HOLD FAST (See **ENDURANCE; HOLD ON; PERSEVERANCE; STEAD-FASTNESS**)
Duty.
To hold fast our hope to the end. Heb.3:6
To hold fast our profession without wavering. Heb.4:14; 10:23
To hold fast sound words. 2 Tim.1:13
To hold fast that which is good. 1 Th.5:21; Rev.3:11
To hold fast the faithful Word that has been taught. Tit.1:9
To hold fast until Christ returns. Rev.2:25
To hold fast what we have received & heard. Rev.3:3

HOLD ON
Duty.
To hold on. Rev.2:24-25
To hold fast our hope to the end. Heb.3:6
To hold fast our profession without wavering. Heb.4:14; 10:23
To hold fast sound words. 2 Tim.1:13
To hold fast that which is good. 1 Th.5:21; Rev.3:11
To hold fast the faithful Word that has been taught. Tit.1:9
To hold fast until Christ returns. Rev.2:25
To hold fast what we have received & heard. Rev.3:3

HOLOCAUST
Of antichrist. Millions slaughtered. Rev.6:9-11; 7:9; 7:13-14; 11:1; 11:2; 11:3-13; 17:6

HOLY - HOLINESS
Discussed. Ph.1:1; Heb.12:14; 1 Pt.1:15-16
Duty.
Of aged women. To live in **h**. Tit.2:3
Of believers.
The great duty of believers. Heb.12:14
To be holy. Verses. List of. Jn.20:12-13
To bear the fruit of **h**. Ro.6:21-22
To build up ourselves on our most **h**. faith. Jude 20
To enter into the holiest (God's presence) by the blood of Christ. Heb.10:19-22
To follow after peace & **h**. Heb. 12:14
To hold fast our profession without wavering. Heb.4:14; 10:23
To hold fast that which is good. 1 Th.5:21
To hold fast the confidence of our hope. Heb.3:6
To hold fast what we have. Rev. 2:25; 3:3; 3:11

To live a life of **h**. behavior & godliness. 2 Pt.3:10-12, esp. 11
To live a life of purity. 1 Th.4:1-8
To partake of God's holiness. Heb.12:10
To perfect **h**. in the fear of God. 2 Cor.7:1
To pray, lifting up **h**. hands to God. 1 Tim.2:8
To put on the new man which is created in righteousness & true **h**. Eph.4:24
To seek & pursue holiness. 1 Pt.1:13-16; 1:15-17
To serve God in **h**. & righteousness all the days of our lives. Lk.1:75
To yield our body members as servants of righteousness & **h**. Ro.6:19
Of married women. To continue in faith, love, & **h**. 1 Tim.2:15
Of ministers. Must be **h**. Tit.1:8
Of single women. To strive to be **h**. in both body & spirit. 1 Cor.7:34
Fact. Man has no **h**. within himself to minister or serve God. Acts 3:12
Meaning. 1 Cor.1:2; 2 Cor.1:12; Eph.1:4; Ph.1:1; Col.1:22; 1 Pt.1:15-16;
Of God.
Declared by Mary. Is pure being & pure in being; perfect being & perfect in being. Lk.1:49-50
Discussed. 1 Pt.1:15-16
Fact.
God is **h**. & true; therefore He will judge the earth. Rev.6:10
God is praised day & night for His holiness. Rev.4:6-9
God is to be feared & worshipped because He is **h**. Rev.15:4
H. is the very name of God. Jn.17:11
The presence of God makes the very ground where a person stands **h**. Acts 7:33
Of Jesus Christ. (See **JESUS CHRIST**, Sinless)
Described. Glimpsed in the transfiguration. Lk.9:29; 9:32-33
Discussed. Rev.3:7
Fact.
Is the High Priest for us, the High Priest who is holy. Heb.7:26-27
Is the Holy One. 1 Jn.2:20; Rev.3:7
Is the Holy One of God. Mk.1:24
Is the Holy One who could not suffer corruption. Acts 2:27; 13:35
Was the holy child Jesus who was anointed by God. Acts 4:27, 30
Was raised from the dead by the Spirit of holiness. Ro.1:4
Purpose.
Believers are being built up as an **h**. priesthood. 1 Pt.2:5
God has called us to be holy & without blame before Him. Eph.1:4; 5:27; Col.1:22
Results.
Assures us.
That we shall see the Lord. Heb.12:14
That we will be presented unblameable before God. Col.1:22; 1 Th.3:12-13
Frees us from sin. Ro.6:1-21
Makes us partakers of God's holiness. Heb.12:10

Source of - Comes through.
    Hope. 1 Jn.3:3, cp. 3:1-3
    Not man, but Christ. Acts 3:12-13
    Obedience. 1 Pt.1:14
    The blood of Christ. Heb.10:19-20
    The blood of the cross & reconcilia-
      tion. Col.1:20-22
    The call of God. Eph.1:4; 2 Tim.1:9
    The chastening of God. Heb.12:10
    The work of Christ within the heart.
      1 Th.3:12-13
Stages of. Progressive stages of holiness.
    Ph.1:1
Symbolized. By white clothing.
    Jn.20:12-13
Verses. List of. Ro.6:21-22
What is holy.
    Days of worship & celebration. Col.2:16
    Faith. Jude 20
    New Jerusalem, the capital of the new
      heavens & earth. Rev.21:10
    Prophets of the Old Testament.
      2 Pt.3:2; Rev.22:6
    Scripture. Ro.1:2; 2 Tim.3:15
    The call of God to believers.
      2 Tim.1:9
    The commandments of God. Ro.7:12;
      2 Pt.2:21
    The inner sanctuary of the tabernacle.
      Heb.9:3, 8
    The kiss & brotherly affection be-
      tween believers. Ro.16:16; 1
      Cor.16:20;
      2 Cor.13:12; 1 Th.5:26; 1 Pt.5:14
    The temple or church of God.
      1 Cor.3:17; Eph.2:21
    The things of the ministry & worship.
      1 Cor.9:13
    The very ground where the presence of
      God is manifested. Acts 7:33; 2 Pt.1:18
    The call of God to believers. 2 Tim.1:9
Who is holy.
    Angels. Acts 10:22; Rev.14:10
    Apostles & prophets. Rev.18:20
    Believers. Col.3:12; 1 Th.5:27;
      Heb.3:1; Rev.22:11
    Believers who have a part in the first
      resurrection. Rev.20:6
    The children of believers. 1 Cor.7:14
    The new man. Eph.4:24
    The single woman who strives to be
      holy in both body & spirit. 1 Cor.7:34
    Women of history who trusted God.
      1 Pt.3:5
    Writers of Scripture. 2 Pt.1:21

HOLY PLACE - HOLY OF HOLIES
(See **MOST HOLY PLACE**)
    Christ entered once. Heb.9:11-14
    Curtain of.
      Torn at Christ's death: symbolizes
        open access to God. Mt.27:50-51
    Discussed. Heb.9:1-10; 9:15-22; 9:23-28
    Entrance into. Not by the blood of animals,
      but by Christ. Heb.9:11-14; 10:19
    Purpose for. Heb.9:1-14

HOLY SPIRIT
    Baptism of.
      Discussed. 1 Cor.12:12-13
      Historical occasions of the Holy
        Spirit's baptism. Acts 2:1-13; 10:44
      How to receive. Acts 1:4-5
      Possible because Christ has come.
        Verses. List of. Mk.1:7-8
      Vs. infilling of. Acts 2:1-4

Came upon - Received by.
    A small prayer band. Acts 4:31
    Christ.
      Discussed. Jn.1:32-33; 3:34;
        5:32;Acts 10:38-39
      Indwelt Christ fully. Mt.3:16; 12:18
    Disciples. Jn.20:22; Acts 13:52
      At Pentecost. Acts 2:1-13
    Disciples of John. Acts 19:6
    Gentiles. Acts 10:44-48; 11:15
    Jews. Acts 2:1
    Mary. Mt.1:18; Lk.1:34-35
    Paul. Acts 9:17
    Samaritans. Acts 8:14-17
    Those who obey God. Acts 5:32
Deity of.
    Discussed. Jn.15:26-27; 16:16
    Is called God. Acts 5:3-4
    Is eternal. Heb.9:14
    Is sovereign over man (omnipotent).
      1 Cor.12:11
    Knows the things of God (omniscient).
      1 Cor.2:10-11
Discussed. Jn.14:15-26; 16:7-15; Acts
    2:1-13;Ro.8:1-17
    All the verses in the Book of Acts.
      Acts Introd.
    Essential for salvation. Acts 19:1-9
    Given by Christ. Breathed on the dis-
      ciples. Jn.20:22
    Jesus Christ was completely dependent
      upon. Acts 1:1-2
    The law of the Spirit of Life. Ro.8:2-4
    Why His presence is better than hav-
      ing Christ with us. Jn.16:7
Duty toward.
    Must depend upon. Acts 1:1-2
    Must follow. Jn.21:18-19
    Must receive. Is conditional. Jn.14:16
    Not to grieve. Eph.4:30
    Not to put out the Spirit's fire. 1 Th.5:19
    Not to sin against the Holy Spirit. (See
      HOLY SPIRIT, Sins Against)
    To be continually filled with the Spirit.
      Eph.5:18-21
    To be full of the Holy Spirit. Acts 6:3,
      5; 9:17; Eph.5:18-21
    To be led & guided by the Holy Spirit.
      Jn.16:13; Ro.8:14; Gal.5:18
    To be sensitive to the leadership of the
      Spirit. Acts 16:6-11
    To bear the fruit of the Spirit.
      Gal.5:22-26; Eph.5:9
    To follow the teaching of the Holy
      Spirit. Jn.14:26
    To let the Holy Spirit change us into
      the image of Christ day by day.
      2 Cor.3:18
    To obey the Spirit. Acts 16:6-11
    To pray in the Holy Spirit. Jude 20
    To receive the unction, the anointing
      of the Spirit. 1 Jn.2:20-21; 2:27
    To walk in the Spirit. Gal.5:16; 5:25
Fruit of.
    Discussed. Gal.5:22-26
    Is goodness, righteousness & truth.
      Eph.5:9
Gifts of. (See **GIFTS, SPIRITUAL**)
How to receive.
    By being born again. Jn.3:5
    By faith, not by works nor by law.
      Gal.3:2
    By obeying God. Acts 5:32
    By repentance. Acts 2:38
    By the baptism of the Spirit. Acts 1:4-
      5; 1 Cor.12:12-13

Indwelling presence - Indwells the be-
    liever.
    Indwells the church in a special way.
      1 Cor.3:16-17
    Is the sustaining power of the believer.
      2 Cor.4:7-9
    Lives with the believer. Jn.14:17
    Proves.
      That Christ abides within a person.
        1 Jn.3:24; 4:12-13
      That God is within a person.
        1 Jn.3:24; 4:12-13
      That one is truly saved. 1 Jn.3:24;
        4:12-13
    Requires separation. 2 Cor.6:16-18
    The believer is the temple of the Holy
      Spirit. 1 Cor.6:19-20
    Verses. List of. Jn.14:17; 1 Cor.6:19-20
Infilling. (See **HOLY SPIRIT**, Work of)
    Discussed. Jn.14:21-22; Acts 2:1-4;
      2:2; Eph.5:18-21
    Follows obedience & the discipline of
      God. Lk.1:67
    Is due to obedience. Lk.1:41
    Is necessary to answer accusers & per-
      secutors. Acts 4:5-10
    Meaning of. The Holy Spirit being
      poured out. Acts 2:17-21
    Response to. By the public. Acts 2:14-16
    Upon Simeon. Lk.2:25
    Verses. List of. Jn.14:21
Names - Titles.
    Abiding Presence of the Trinity.
      Jn.14:23-25
    Christ in the believer. Jn.14:20
    The Comforter. Jn.14:16; 14:26;
      15:26-27; 16:7
    The Counselor
    The Eternal Spirit. Heb.9:14
    The Law of the Spirit of life. Ro.8:2-4
    The Living Water. Jn.7:37-39
    The Promise of the Father. Acts 1:4
    The Seal, Earnest, or Guarantee.
      2 Cor.1:21-22; 5:5; Eph.1:13-14
    The Seven Spirits. Rev.1:4; 3:1
    The Spirit of Adoption. Ro.8:15
    The Spirit of Christ. Ro.8:9
    The Spirit of glory & of God. 1 Pt.4:14
    The Spirit of God's Son. Gal.4:6
    The Spirit of holiness. Ro.1:4
    The Spirit of Life. Ro.8:2
    The Spirit of prophecy. Rev.19:10
    The Spirit of the Father. Mt.10:20
    The Spirit of Truth. Jn.15:26-27;
      16:13; 1 Jn.5:6
    The unction or anointing of God.
      1 Jn.2:20-21; 2:27
    Who He is. Jn.14:15-26
Power of.
    Discussed. Ro.8:1-17
    Works within the believer. Eph.3:20
Prophecies concerning - Foretold.
    By Jesus. Acts 1:5, 8
    Given to believers by God. Acts 5:32;
      15:8
    Poured out in the last days. Acts 2:17-21
Sins against.
    Blasphemy. Unpardonable sin.
      Mt.12:31-32; Mk.3:29-30;Lk.12:4-12
    Insulting the Spirit's conviction &
      work within the heart. Heb.10:28-29
    Discussed. 1 Th.5:19
    Grieving. Eph.4:30
    Lying to the Holy Spirit. Acts 5:1-4
    Quenching or putting out the Spirit's
      fire. 1 Th.5:19

Rejected.
  A person turns away. Mt.12:14-16
  Does not always contend with man.
    Mt.12:14-16; 20:5; Lk.4:28-30;
    Jn.7:33-34; 11:54
Source of the Holy Spirit.
  Christ. Jn.7:37-39; Tit.3:6
  God.
    Given in answer to prayer.
      Lk.11:11-13
    Gives the Holy Spirit to all who ask
      Him. Lk.11:11-13
Work of.
  Discussed. Jn.16:7-15; Ro.8:1-17
  In relation to Jesus Christ.
    Anointed Christ. Acts 10:38-39
    Bears witness to Christ. 1 Jn.5:6-8
    Came upon Christ as a dove.
      Jn.1:32
    Came upon Christ without measure.
      Jn.1:32-33; 3:34; 5:32
    Conceived Christ in the womb of
      Mary. Mt.1:20
    Convicts men that Jesus Christ is
      the Son of God. Mt.16:17
    Gave Christ the power to offer Him-
      self without spot to God. Heb.9:14
    Glorifies Christ. Jn.16:14-15
    Identified Christ as the Messiah for
      John. Jn.1:30-34
    Justified Christ. 1 Tim.3:16
    Led Christ. Lk.4:1
    Proves Christ is the Son of God.
      Ro.1:4
    Raised up Christ from the dead.
      Ro.1:4
  In relation to Scripture.
    Gave Scripture by speaking through
      holy men of God. 1 Pt.1:21, cp.
      Acts 1:16; 28:25-27
    Uses the Word of God as a sword.
      To convict. Heb.4:12
      To defend against the attacks of
        evil. Eph.6:17, cp. 10-18
  In relation to the believer.
    To convict justify, save, assure, &
      deliver the believer.
      Assures the believer. 1 Jn.3:24;
        4:12-18
      Baptizes the believer.
        1 Cor.12:12-13
      Bears witness to the believer.
        Witnesses to four things.
        Heb.8:10-12; 10:15-18
      Convicts of sin, righteousness &
        judgment. Jn.16:8-11
      Enters, matures, & enables the
        believer. Gal.3:2-5
      Frees from sin & death. Ro.8:2
      Gives access into God's pres-
        ence. Eph.2:18
      Gives evidence of salvation.
        Acts 19:1-7
      Indwells & assures the believer.
        Gal.4:4-7
      Justifies. Ro.4:25
      Places a witness within.
        1 Jn.5:6-12
      Quickens. Jn.6:63
      Regenerates. Jn.3:5-6, cp. 3-6;
        Tit.3:5
      Restrains sin. 2 Th.2:6-8
      Reveals God's wisdom.
        1 Cor.2:10-13
      Reveals new truth. Jn.3:5-6

Reveals the things of God.
  1 Cor.2:10-13
Saves. Ro.5:10
Seals & guarantees the believer.
  Ro.5:5; 2 Cor.1:21-22;
  Eph.1:13-14
Witnesses to Christ. Jn.5:32;
  15:26-27
Works in both the believer & un-
  believer. Jn.16:7-15; Acts 1:4-5
To grow & mature the believer.
  Brings about unity & peace be-
    tween believers. Eph.4:3
  Comforts & helps. Jn.14:16
  Enters, matures, & enables the
    believer. Gal.3:2-3
  Equips the believer to understand
    the Word. 1 Cor.2:10-13
  Give abundant life. Jn.7:38-39
  Gives rivers of living water.
    Jn.7:37-39
  Helps the believer to struggle
    against the sinful nature.
    Gal.5:16-18
  Infills. Jn.14:21-22
  Intercedes for the believer. Ro.8:34
  Leads believers. Gal.5:18
  Pours out His love into our
    hearts. Ro.5:5
  Renews day by day. 2 Cor.3:18;
    Tit.3:5
  Reveals God's wisdom.
    1 Cor.2:10-13
  Reveals new truth. Jn.3:5-6
  Reveals the things of God.
    1 Cor.2:10-13
  Sanctifies believers. 1 Pt.1:2
  Strengthens believers to wait for
    the hope of salvation. Gal.5:5;
    Eph.3:16
  Teaches & helps the believer to
    remember. Jn.14:26
  Teaches the believer the things
    God has prepared for him.
    1 Cor.2:10-13
  Works in the life of the believer.
    Acts 1:8; Ro.8:1-17
To live, stand fast, serve & witness.
  Anoints, equips the believer for
    learning. 1 Jn.2:20-21; 2:27
  Bears fruit. Gal.5:22-23
  Delivers through trials. Ph.1:19
  Empowers for witnessing. Acts
    1:8
  Enables the believer to hold fast.
    2 Tim.1:13
  Equips the believer.
    With a special unction. 1 Jn.2:20
    With power. Lk.24:44-49
  Foretells one's trials. Acts 20:22
  Gives gifts. 1 Cor.12:4-11
  Gives power for witnessing.
    Acts 1:8
  Gives power to believers. Acts
    1:8; Ro.8:1-17
  Gives special experiences with
    Jesus Christ. Jn.14:21-22; 14:21
  Gives the believer inspiration
    when needed. Lk.12:4-12
  Gives victory over the world.
    Jn.15:26-27
  Guides & leads by restraint.
    Acts 16:6-7
  Guides & leads the believer.
    Jn.16:12-13; Acts 16:6-11;
    Gal.5:18

Indwells the believer. Ro.8:9;
  1 Jn.4:12-13
Protects against false teaching.
  1 Jn.2:20-23; 2:27
Speaks through the believer
  when needed. Lk.12:4-12
Stirs confidence & courage.
  2 Cor.5:6-8
In relation to the church.
  Appoints leaders within the church.
    Acts 20:28
  Appoints ministers & missionaries
    of the church. Acts 13:1-4
  Baptizes us all into one body, into
    the church. 1 Cor.12:13
  Comforts the church. Acts 9:31
  Indwells the church. 1 Cor.3:16;
    Eph.2:22; 3:16
  Sends forth & directs the ministers
    & missionaries of the church.
    Acts 8:29; 13:4
  Stirs fellowship within the church.
    Ph.2:1
In relation to the world
  Causes a person to be born again.
    Jn.3:5-6
  Convicts & quickens the gospel to
    the hearts of men. Jn.6:44-46;
    16:8-11
  Restrains evil. 1 Th.2:6-8

HOMAGE
  Demonstrated by obedience. Mt.21:6-7

HOME (See **FAMILY; MARRIAGE**)
  Duty.
    To care for the **h**. & the individual.
      Mk.1:29-31
    To invite the presence of Jesus into the
      h. Mk.1:29-31
    To live for God first of all at home.
      1 Tim.5:4
    To take care of one's **h**. & family. Tit.2:5
    To witness to one's own **h**. & family.
      Mk.5:19; Lk.8:38-39
  Essential. Jesus' presence. Mk.1:29-31
  Hope of. Jesus Christ. Mk.1:30; 1:31
  To be the center of the church's ministry.
    Lk.9:4

HOMELESS
  Christ had no home. Lk.9:58
  Paul had no home. 1 Cor.4:11

HOMOSEXUAL - HOMOSEXUALITY
  Discussed. Ro.1:26-27

HONEST - HONESTY (See **GOOD**)
  Duty - Essential.
    Ministers (churches) to use their
      money for **h**. things. 2 Cor.8:20-21
    Must choose men of **h**. to serve as
      deacons. Acts 6:3
    Not to corrupt, cheat, or wrong any
      man. 2 Cor.7:2
    Not to do evil, but that which is **h**.
      2 Cor.13:7
    Not to seek bribes. Acts 8:18-24;
      24:23-26, esp. 26
    To always do what is right & **h**. in the
      sight of everyone. Ro.12:17
    To do what is **h**. in the eyes of both the
      Lord & men. 2 Cor.8:21
    To focus one's thoughts upon things
      that are **h**. Ph.4:8

To have a good conscience, living **h.** in all things. Heb.13:18

To have an **h.** & good heart in hearing the Word of God. Lk.8:15

To live an **h.** life before the world. 1 Pt.2:12

To live as a citizen in all godliness & **h.** 1 Tim.2:2

To owe nothing to anyone except love. Ro.13:8

To renounce the hidden things of dishonesty. 2 Cor.4:2

To walk honestly, not unrighteously. Ro.13:13

To work that one may walk **h.** before the world. 1 Th.4:12

Example of.
Nathanael. Did not deceive, bait or mislead. Jn.1:47
Zacchaeus. Repays what he had stolen. Lk.19:8, cp. 1-10

Results.
A good, clear conscience. Heb.13:18
A good testimony before the world. 1 Pt.2:12
An **h.** heart keeps the Word & brings forth fruit. Lk.8:15
Peace. Ph.4:8-9

HONOR - HONORED (See GLORY - GLORIFIED; RESPECT)

Discussed. Jn.4:44

Duty.
Husbands are to give **h.** to the wife. 1 Pt.3:7
Not to **h.** Christ only with one's lips. Mt.15:8; Mk.7:6
To count one's employer worthy of all **h.** 1 Tim.6:1
To count one's minister as worthy of double **h.** 1 Tim.5:17
To give **h.** to whom **h.** is due. Ro.13:7
To give preference to others in **h.** Ro.12:10
To **h.** God. 1 Tim.1:17
To **h.** Jesus Christ. Lk.11:19; Jn.4:44
To **h.** one's father & mother. Mt.15:4; 19:19; Lk.18:20; Eph.6:2
To **h.** the elderly & widows who are true widows. 1 Tim.5:1-3
To **h.** the Son & the Father. Jn.5:23
To possess one's body in **h.**, especially sexual **h.** 1 Th.4:4
To proclaim **h.** & glory to God forever & ever. 1 Tim.1:17; 1 Tim.6:16
To seek for glory, **h.**, & immortality. Ro.2:7
To stand fast in temptation so that one's faith will be proven honorable when Christ returns. 1 Pt.1:6-7

Fact.
A prophet is without **h.** in his own country. Mt.13:57; Mk.6:4; Jn.4:44
Christ did not seek the **h.** of men. Jn.5:41
God **h.** any man who **h.** His Son. Jn.12:23-26
If a person does not **h.** the Son, he does not **h.** the Father. Jn.5:23
Marriage is honorable & the bed undefiled. Heb.13:4
Ministers of Christ are to be faithful whether **h.** or dishonored. 2 Cor.6:4-10, esp. 8
Some persons are vessels of **h.** & some of dishonor. 2 Tim.2:10-21
Some refuse to **h.** Christ. Jn.4:44

Meaning. Ro.2:7

Of Christ.
Discussed. Jn.4:44
H. by God. Jn.8:54-59; 2 Pt.1:17
Has more **h.** then man because He is the Builder & Creator. Heb.3:3-4
Is worthy of **h.** Rev.4:11; 5:12-13; 7:12; 19:1, 7
Should be **h.** Jn.4:44; 5:22-23
Verses. List of. Jn.3:29-30

Of self.
Discounted, ignored, distasteful. Jn.8:54-59
Results in rejecting Christ. Jn.5:44
Seeking **h.** for self. Verses. List of. Jn.5:44

Of the believer.
To be rewarded in eternity. Ro.2:6-10
Will be **h.** by God. Jn.12:26

Seeking. (See AMBITION)
Loving to receive **h.** is wrong. Mt.23:5
Worldly **h.** Discussed. Lk.11:43; 14:7-14; 20:45-47
Verses. List of. Ro.2:7
Warning. Against seeking **h.** for oneself. Mk.12:39

HOPE (See INHERITANCE, SPIRITUAL; REWARD)

Acts - Word of. Stirs endurance in labor. 1 Th.1:3

Basis of.
Believer's life. Col.1:5-8
Faith & love. Col.1:5-8

Described as.
A living hope. 1 Pt.1:3-5
A refuge & anchor of the soul. Heb.6:18-20
Better. Heb.7:19
Blessed. Tit.2:13
Good. 2 Th.2:16
Secure & steadfast. Heb.6:19

Discussed. Ro.5:2; 8:24-25; 1 Pt.1:3-5
Verses. List of. Ro.8:24-25

Duty.
Not to be moved away from the **h.** of the gospel. Col.1:23
To answer every man who asks about one's **h.** 1 Pt.3:15
To be diligent in being assured of God's **h.**--to the end. Heb.6:11
To flee to God & lay hold upon the **h.** set before us. Heb.6:18-19
To **h.** for the comfort & growth of other believers. 2 Cor.1:7; 10:15
To **h.** in believers, that they will be acceptable & approved when Christ returns. 1 Th.2:19
To **h.** in Christ for both this life & the next life. 1 Cor.15:19; Col.1:27; 1 Th.1:3; 1 Tim.1:1
To **h.** to the end of life. 1 Pt.1:13
To hold fast the rejoicing of **h.** to the end. Heb.3:6
To labor, plow & reap in **h.** 1 Cor.9:10
To live in faith, **h.**, & love. 1 Cor.13:13
To look for the blessed **h.** & glorious appearing of Christ. Tit.2:12-13
To persevere in **h.** seeking God's help. Jn.4:46-47
To put on the **h.** of salvation. 1 Th.5:8
To rejoice in **h.** Ro.12:12

Fact.
Unbelievers are without God & have no **h.** Eph.2:12
Unbelievers have no true **h.** beyond death. 1 Th.4:13

For what.
A redeemed body. Ro.8:23-27
Deliverance, life, & spiritual rest. Acts 2:25-31
Eternal life. Tit.1:2-3; 3:7; 1 Pt.1:3
Eternal transformation. 1 Jn.3:2
Glory. Col.1:27
God's calling. List of what a call is. Eph.1:18
Heaven. 2 Cor.5:1-4; Col.1:4-8
Righteousness. Gal.5:5-6
The glory of God. Ro.5:2
The resurrection. Jn.6:37-40, 44; Acts 23:6; 24:15; 26:6-8, cp. Ph.3:10-11
To be like Christ. 1 Jn.3:2
To receive eternal rest & reward. Rev.14:13
To stand unashamed before Christ. Ph.1:20

H. for man.
H. for depraved man. Ro.3:9-20
Only **h.** for survival is the Kingdom of God. Acts 1:3

Meaning. Ro.5:2; 8:24-25; 1 Cor.13:4-7

Results of **h.** (See HOPE, Believer's hope)
Anchors the soul. Heb.6:19
Eases fear when persecuted. Lk.12:4-12
Erases shame. Ro.5:5
Greatly blessed. Lk.2:36
Lets the believer draw near God. Heb.7:19
Purifies the believer. 1 Jn.3:3
Salvation. Ro.8:24

Source of **h.** - Comes through.
Christ. 1 Tim.1:1; 1 Th.1:3; 1 Tim.1:1
Christ & God. 2 Th.2:16
Experience through trials. Ro.5:3-5
God. Ro.15:13; 1 Pt.1:21
God's promises. Acts 26:6-7; Tit.1:2-3
Scriptures. Ro.15:4
The call of God. Eph.4:1, 4
The gospel or the Word of God. Col.1:5-8
The resurrection of Christ. 1 Pt.1:3
Threefold. 1 Pt.1:3
Verses. List of. Lk.12:14; Ro.5:2; 8:24-25

HOPELESS - HOPELESSNESS (See DISCOURAGEMENT; DISSATISFACTION; SIN, Result)

Answer to.
Christ's power to meet the **h.** Mt.9:18-34
Discussed. Mk.5:25-34

Caused by.
Death. 1 Th.4:13
Seeking God through works & the law. Ro.6:14-15
Six things. Eph.2:11-12

Results. Hardness, emptiness, prejudice. Jn.1:46

State - Condition.
Cannot save oneself. Ro.5:6-7
Discussed. Ro.6:14-15
Verses. List of. Ro.5:6-7

HORSEMEN OF APOCALYPSE, FOUR

Discussed Rev.6:1-8

HOSANNA

Meaning. Mt.21:9; Mk.11:9; Jn.12:12-13

HOSPITABLE
Discussed. Heb.13:2; 1 Pt.4:9
Duty.
  Discussed. Lk.10:8-9
  Of believers.
    Not to forget to entertain strangers.
      Heb.13:2
    To have a strong testimony in **h.**
      3 Jn.3-4, 5-8
    To practice **h.** Ro.12:13
    To use **h.** without complaining.
      1 Pt.4:9
    To welcome evangelists, prophets,
      & traveling ministers. 3 Jn.3-4, 5-8
  Of Christian widows. To have a strong
    testimony of **h.** 1 Tim.5:10
  Of ministers. Must be given to **h.**
    1 Tim.3:2; Tit.1:8
Example. Ro.16:23
  Gaius. Ro.16:23
  Island people. Acts 28:2, 7
  Justus. Acts 18:7
  Lydia. Acts 16:14-15
  Martha. Lk.10:38-42
  Philemon. Phile.1:1-2
  Philip the evangelist. Acts 21:8
  Priscilla & Aquila. Acts 18:2
  The jailer. Acts 16:33-34
  Zaccheus. Lk.19:7
How ministers are to be received.
  Mt.10:40-42; Phile.1:22
Meaning. 1 Tim.3:2-3
Who to receive & welcome into one's
  home.
  Believers. Ro.12:13
  Ministers. Acts 16:14-15; 18:2;
    3 Jn.3-4, 5-8
  Not false teachers. 2 Jn.10-11
  Strangers. Witnessing to them.
    Mt.25:33-35; 1 Tim.5:9-10; Heb.13:2

HOSPITALITY (See HOSPITABLE)

HOUR - HOURS (See TIME)
Of the day. Discussed. Mk.1:32; 6:48
Used symbolically of.
  The **h.** of Christ's death. Mt.26:45;
    Mk.14:35; Jn.2:4; 7:30; 8:20; 12:23-
    27; 17:1
  The **h.** of God's judgments. Rev.14:7
  The **h.** of great tribulation in the end
    time. Rev.3:10
  The **h.** of persecution. Mk.13:11
  The **h.** of salvation in Christ. Jn.4:21-23
  The **h.** of the end time & Christ's re-
    turn. Mt.24:36, 42, 44-50; 25:13;
    Mk.13:32; Lk.12:40-46
  The **h.** of the glorification of Christ.
    Jn.13:1

HOUR, THE
Meaning. Jesus' death. Jn.12:23-24
Urgency of. Lk.10:4
Used symbolizing the **h.** of man's ac-
  claim, not Jesus' acclaim. Jn.7:6-9

HOUSE - HOUSEHOLD
Described as.
  Built upon rock & sand. True vs. false.
    Lk.6:46-49
  Divided **h.** cannot stand. Lk.11:17-18
  Of the rich. Lk.7:36
Discussed. Lk.5:19
Duty. To trust God for shelter & not to
  worry. Lk.12:22-34
Of Jesus' day. Discussed. Mk.2:4

Parable of the household. Devotion,
  study, sharing. Mt.13:51-52
Rooftops. Discussed. Mt.24:17
Used symbolically of.
  A divided **h.** that cannot stand.
    Lk.11:17-18
  A life built upon either rock or sand.
    Lk.6:46-49
  Heaven. Jn.14:1-3
  The family of God, the church.
    Heb.10:21
  The heart of man. Rev.3:20
  The household of a nation of people.
    Mt.10:6; 15:24; Acts 2:36; Heb.8:8-10
  The household of faith. Gal.6:10
  The household of God, the church.
    Eph.2:19; 1 Tim.3:15; Heb.10:21;
    1 Pt.4:17
  The household of the Son. Heb.3:6
  The human body. 2 Cor.5:1

HOUSE OF GOD, THE (See CHURCH; TEMPLE)
Is the church of the living God. 1 Tim.3:15
Is the tabernacle. Mt.12:4; Mk.2:26;
  Lk.6:4; 1 Tim.3:15

HOUSING
Attitude about. Right vs. wrong. Mt.6:26

HUMANISM - HUMANIST (See UNBE-LIEF; WORLDLINESS)
Described. Lk.10:21
Discussed. Lk.10:21; Ro.1:22-23;
  1:24-25; Jas.4:13-17
Error of. Deifying men. Acts 14:8-13
Fact. Preached by some ministers. 1 Tim.6:5
View - Position.
  Of the end time. Rev.13:4-8; 14:8;
    14:9; 17:2; 18:2-7
  Of the state. Lk.20:22
  Reject the demands of Christ.
    Lk.2:34-35
Warning to. Lk.9:23
  Inadequate to meet man's needs.
    Mt.14:15-21
  To be judged. LK.10:21

HUMILIATE - HUMILIATION
Caused by.
  Not counting the cost or planning
    ahead. Lk.14:27-30
  Seeking worldly recognition, honor, &
    position. Lk.14:7-14
  Self-sufficiency. Lk.22:31-34
  Sin. Lk.15:15
Deliverance from - Prevention against.
  Counting the cost & planning.
    Lk.14:27-30
  Humility. Lk.14:7-11
  Repentance & confession of wrong.
    Lk.15:17-21
Of Christ. (See JESUS CHRIST, Con-
  descension)

HUMBLE - HUMILITY (See MEEK-NESS)
Christ is **h.** & lowly. Mt.11:29
Discussed. Lk.14:11; 14:27-30; Tit.3:2;
  Ph.2:3; 2:4; 2:5-8; 1 Pt.3:8; 1 Pt.5:5-7
  An aspect of gentleness. Gal.5:22-23
  Condition for greatness. Mt.18:1-4;
    Mk.9:33-37; Lk.9:46-50
  Importance of. Lk.14:7-14
  Men fear **h.** Reasons. Mt.18:4
  Steps involved. Mt.18:4

Duty.
  Not to push oneself forward. Jn.1:20-22
  Not to think too highly of oneself. Ro.12:3-5
  Of ministers. To walk as a brother, not
    as a superior. 1 Cor.1:1
  Threefold duty. 1 Pt.5:5-7
  To associate with the lowly. Ro.12:16
  To do good works in a **h.** spirit. Jas.3:13
  To dress in a **h.** & quiet spirit.
    1 Pt.3:4, cp. 2-4
  To esteem others better than oneself.
    Ph.2:3-4
  To exalt Christ & not oneself. Jn.3:29-30
  To give preference to others. Ro.12:9-10
  To humble oneself. Jas.4:10
  To prefer one another. Ro.12:9-10
  To put on **h.** Col.3:12
  To receive the Word with **h.** Jas.1:21
  To seek forgiveness in **h.** Lk.5:12
  To seek the help of Christ in **h.** Jn.4:46-47
  To serve the Lord with all **h.** of mind.
    Acts 20:18-19
  To submit to each other. Eph.5:18-21
  To walk in **h.** before other believers.
    Ro.15:14
Essential.
  Because we fail to serve perfectly.
    Lk.1:29-30; 17:7-10
  Discussed. Mt.8:5-9
  For God to use. Lk.1:47-48
  For greatness. Mt.18:4
  For true confession. Mk.3:11-12
  Necessary for greatness. Lk.9:46-50
  To sense "nothingness." Lk.1:47-48;
    7:37-38; 18:13
Example.
  Canaanite woman. Mt.15:26-27
  Centurion. Great **h.** Mt.8:5-9; Lk.7:3
  Christ. Mt.12:19; 18:4
  Jesus washing the feet of the disciples.
    Royal service. Jn.13:1-17
  John the Baptist. Mt.3:14
  Mary, the mother of Jesus. Lk.1:47-48
  Matthew. Mt.10:3-4
  Peter & John. After a spiritual experi-
    ence. Not puffed up. Acts 4:23-24
Meaning. Mt.5:5; Lk.14:11; Gal.5:22-23;
  Eph.4:1-2; 1 Pt.5:5; 1 Tim.6:11
Results.
  Exaltation. Lk.14:11; 22:28-30; 22:30;
    Jas.4:10
  God pours out His grace upon the
    humble. Jas.4:6; 1 Pt.5:5
  Greatness. Mt.18:1-4; Mk.9:33-37;
    Lk.7:46-48
  Justification. Lk.18:9-14
  Unity. Ph.2:1-18
Reward. Three rewards. Mt.5:5
Source. Is a fruit of the Spirit. Gal.5:22-23
Source - Comes by.
  Abasing oneself. Lk.1:47-48; 14:11
  Acknowledging one's sinfulness &
    unworthiness. Lk.7:37-38; 15:17-21;
    18:9-14
  Acknowledging who one is.
    1 Cor.1:26-31
  Coming to Jesus. Mt.11:28-30
  Counting all things loss for Christ.
    Ph.3:4-8
  Following the example of Christ.
    Ph.2:5-8
  Having the right attitude toward
    Christ. Mt.3:14
  How to become humble. Mt.18:4
  Ideal humility. Jesus Christ. Mt.12:19;
    Ph.2:5-8

Sitting at Jesus' feet & hearing His Word. Lk.10:38-42, esp. 39
Vs.
False **h.** Caused by a religion of works. Col.2:18, 23
Puffed up pride. Acts 5:1-4

HUMBLE IN LIFE, THE
Discussed. Jas.1:9-11

HUNGER & THIRST
Caused by.
Failing to receive help & support from churches. 2 Cor.11:27
Famine. Lk.15:14-16
Fasting. Lk.4:1-2
Missing meals - failing to eat. Mt.12:1; Mk.11:12; Acts 10:10
Not having the means to secure food. Ph.4:12
Fact.
The person who hungers & thirsts after righteousness will be filled. Mt.5:6
To be severe in the last days. Rev.6:7-8
Will be no hunger or thirst in the new heavens & earth. Rev.7:16-17

HUNGER, SPIRITUAL (See **FULL-NESS, SPIRITUAL; LIFE; SATIS-FACTION, SPIRITUAL**)
Answer to.
God & His Word, not physical food. Lk.4:3-5
Jesus Christ, the Bread of Life. Jn.6:30-36; 6:41-51; 6:53; 6:52-58
Jesus Christ, the Living Water. Jn.4:10-14; 7:37-39
Met by man's great **h.** Jn.6:22-29
Verses. List of. Jn.6:34-35; 6:55
Caused by. Selfishness & godless independence. Lk.15:14-16; 15:17-19
Duty.
To **h.** for the Word of God. Lk.5:1; 10:38-42, esp. 39; Acts 17:11
To seek an answer & do something about one's **h.** Jn.1:43-44
Meaning. Mt.5:6; Lk.6:20-23
Satisfied by believing, not by works. Jn.6:28-29
Verses. List of. Lk.5:1

HUSBAND (See **FAMILY; FATHERS; MARRIAGE; WIFE**)
Discussed.
The believer & his family. Col.3:18-21
The believing wife & husband. Eph.5:22-33
The questions concerning marriage. 1 Cor.7:1-40
Duty.
Not to deprive one's wife - physically, sexually. 1 Cor.7:4-7
Not to put away one's wife through separation or divorce. 1 Cor.7:11
Of ministers. Must be the **h.** of only one wife. 1 Tim.3:2; Tit.1:6
To one's wife. Eph.5:25-33
To provide for his wife. 1 Tim.5:8
Fact.
Is head of the wife. Eph.5:23
Is sanctified by a believing wife. Cor.7:14
Putting away a spouse & marrying another person is adultery. Lk.16:18
Putting away **h.** or wife is adultery. Mk.10:12

HUSBANDMAN, WICKED (See **TEN-ANTS, WICKED**)

HYMENAEUS
Discussed. 1 Tim.1:19-20
Taught that the resurrection of believers had already passed. 2 Tim.2:16-18

HYPOCRISY - HYPOCRITE - HYPO-CRITICAL (See **PROFESSION, FALSE**)
Answer to.
Correcting one's own life before correcting others. Mt.7:5; Lk.6:42
God's wisdom. His wisdom is pure & without any **h.** Jas.3:17
The one essential. Lk.10:40
Caused by.
Appearing fruitful, but bearing no fruit. Mk.11:12-14
Being religious, but not controlling one's tongue. Jas.1:26
Being spiritually blind. Mt.15:12-20; 23:16-22
Claiming & teaching, but not living. Mt.23:3
Coveting & exploiting people. 2 Pt.2:3
Criticizing & gossiping about those who fall. Mt.7:1-6
Criticizing others. Mt.7:1-5, esp. 5
Deceiving people. Verses. List of. Jn.12:4-8
Desiring recognition. Mt.23:5-7
Doing one thing & teaching another. Lk.13:15-16
Drawing near God with one's lips, but not with one's heart. Mt.15:8
Fasting for recognition. Mt.6:16
Giving for recognition. Mt.6:2
Having double standards. Lk.13:14-16; Gal.2:11-21
Honoring God with one's lips & one's heart. Mt.15:7-8; Mk.7:6
Judging others. Mt.7:5
Leaven, false teaching. Lk.12:1-3
Lusting, yet praying for what one desires. Jas.4:3
Making a false profession. Mk.7:6
Placing form & ritual before people in need. Lk.13:14-16
Praying for recognition. Mt.6:5
Seeking God through form & ritual. Lk.13:14-16
Seeking the world's garbage. Lk.15:16
Self-righteousness. Lk.18:9-14
Stressing ritual, tradition, rules & regulations. Mt.15:1-11
Teaching the commandments of men as doctrine. Mt.15:8-9
Using science & false knowledge to oppose the truth. 1 Tim.6:20
Characteristics - Traits of.
Counterfeit disciples. Jn.6:59-71
Counterfeit ministers. 2 Cor.11:14-15
False apostles & deceitful workers. 1 Cor.11:13
False brothers who try to mislead us. Gal.2:3-4
False prophets. 1 Jn.4:1-3
False religion. Mt.23:1-36
False teachers. Mt.23:3; 23:13-36; 2 Pt.2:1
People in the last days. 1 Tim.4:1-2
Satan's deception. 2 Cor.11:13-15
Self-righteousness. Lk.18:9-14
Discussed. Mt.23:13; Ro.2:17-29
Message to. Lk.18:9-14; Gal.2:11-21

Duty.
Not to fast as **h.** do. Mt.6:16-18
Not to give as **h.** do. Mt.6:2-4
Not to pray as **h.** do. Mt.6:5-6
To fear being a **h.** Lk.12:1-3
To lay aside all **h.** 1 Pt.2:1
Examples of. (See **APOSTASY; DENY - DENIAL**)
Ananias. Acts 5:1-11
Judas. Mt.26:45-49; Jn.12:4-6
Peter. Jn.12:4-6; Gal.2:11-14
Pharisees - religionists. Mt.15:1-9; 22:18; 23:1-33
Meaning. Mt.23:13; 1 Pt.2:1
Mistakes of. Ro.2:17-29
Results - Warning against.
Close the Kingdom of heaven to men. Mt.23:13
Deceives the hearts of the unsuspecting. Ro.16:17-18
Discussed. Mk.11:12-14
Does not discern the signs of the time. Mt.16:3-4
Fills one's heart with robbery & indulgence. Mt.23:25
Fills one's heart with uncleanness. Mt.23:27
Makes one hopeless. Mt.7:26-27
Makes people children of hell. Mt.23:15
Omits the weightier matters of life. Mt.23:23
Shall not escape the damnation of hell. Mt.23:33
Shall receive the judgment of **h.** Mt.24:51
Steals from widows. Mt.23:14
Verses. List of. Lk.12:1-3

HYPOCRISY, WITHOUT (See **SIN-CERE**)

I

I AM
Basic name of deity. Meaning. Jn.6:20

ICONIUM
Discussed. The ancient city. Acts 14:1
Fact.
Believers of Iconium knew & thought well of Timothy. Acts 16:1-2
Had a large number of Greek & Jewish believers. Acts 14:1
Persecuted Paul. Acts 14:2, 19; 2 Tim.3:11

IDENTIFY - IDENTIFYING
Duty. To **i.** with people. Lk.10:8-9
Of Christ with believers. Lk.10:16

IDLE - IDLENESS - CARELESS (See **LAZY**)
A symbol of lostness. Mt.20:3-4
Discussed. Work & employment. 1 Th.4:11-12
Duty.
Not to be **i.**, wandering from house to house as talebearers. 1 Tim.5:13
To accept the call of Christ & go to work. Mt.20:1-7
To work & not be idle. 1 Th.4:11-12
To work before the night comes. Jn.9:4
Meaning. Mt.12:36

IDOLS - IDOLATRY (See **GODS, FALSE; RELIGION**)
Described as.
  Detestable. 1 Pt.4:3
  An empty, darkened mind. Eph. 4:17-19
  Covetousness. Eph.5:5; Col.3:5
  Dumb. 1 Cor.12:2
  Imperial worship of Caesar & the state or government. Rev.13:4-8; 13:13-17; 17:1
  Irrational, foolish. Acts 17:29
  Mental image of God. Mt.13:57
  Several things. Acts 17:24-25
  Worship of angels. Col.2:18
  Worship of antichrist. 2 Th.2:3-4; Rev.13:4-18
  Worship of man. Acts 10:25-26
  Worship of Satan. Jn.8:44, cp. 41-47; Rev.13:4
Discussed. Acts 17:22-34; Ro.1:22-23; 1:24-25; 2:21-24; 1 Cor.10:14-22; 2 Cor.6:14-16; Eph.4:17-19; Rev.2:20-21
  In Athens. Full of idols. Acts 17:16
Duty.
  Not to associate with **i**. 1 Cor.5:9-11; 10:20
  Not to be idolaters as some Jews were. 1 Cor.10:7
  To abstain from pollutions of **i**. Acts 15:20, 29; 21:25
  To flee. 1 Cor.10:14-22
  To keep oneself from idols. 1 Jn.5:21
  To separate from. 2 Cor.6:14-18, esp. 16
  To turn from. Acts 14:15
  To turn to God from **i**. 1 Th.1:9-10
Error of.
  Deifies men. Acts 14:8-13
  Discussed. Acts 17:22-34
  Honors man too much. Acts 10:25-26
  Works the will of the worldly, the rebellious, & the lost of the world. 1 Pt.4:3-5
  Worships something that is nothing in this world, that is not God. 1 Cor.8:4; 10:19
Facts.
  A whole city can be given over to **i**. Acts 17:16
  Covetousness is **i**. Col.3:5
  God's temple & church have nothing to do with **i**. 2 Cor.6:16-18
  I. cannot see nor hear nor walk. Rev.9:20
  I. is a work of the flesh. Gal.5:19-21
Meaning. 1 Cor.5:9-10; 6:9; Eph.4:17-19; 5:5;Gal.5:19-21; 1 Pt.4:3
Nature. Are not gods--only notions, ideas, imaginations of men. Acts 17:29; Ro.1:22-23; 1:24-25; Gal.4:8; 4:9-11; Col.2:20-23;2 Pt.1:16
Results - Effects of.
  Causes God to give man up to **i**. Ro.1:24-32
  Enslaving. Gal.4:8-9
  Judgment. Acts 17:29-31; 1 Pt.4:3-5
  Shall have no part in the new heavens & earth. Rev.22:15
  Shall have their part in the lake of fire. Rev.21:8
  Shall not inherit the Kingdom of God. 1 Cor.6:9; Gal.5:19-20

Source - Origin.
  Demons. 1 Cor.10:19-21
  Man's irrationality. Acts 17:29
  Man's mind & imagination. Creates his own "gods." Acts 17:29; Ro.1:22-23; 1:24-25; Gal.4:8
  Man's own thinking. Acts 17:29
  Pride. Man's claim to be "wise." Ro.1:22-23; 1:24-25
Verses. List of. 1 Cor.5:9-10

IGNORANCE - IGNORANT
About Christ.
  Men are **i**. that Christ is the only approach to God. Jn.4:22
  Verses. List of. Jn.4:22
About God.
  Caused by. Man.
    Blindness of the heart. Eph.4:18
    Depraved nature. Ro.3:10-12
    I. in not knowing God. Jn.7:25-31; 8:19; 1 Cor.2:6-13
    I. in their worship of God. Jn.4:22
    Questioning God's existence. Jn.14:4-5
    Walking in darkness. 1 Jn.2:11
  Verses. List of. Jn.4:22; 7:25-31; 8:19
Duty. To have compassion on the **i**. Heb.5:2
Results.
  A life of lusts. 1 Pt.1:14
  Alienation. Eph.4:18
What people can be **i**. about.
  Christ & His salvation. Jn.8:19; 1 Tim.1:12-15, esp. 13
  God. Jn.8:55
    As Creator. 2 Pt.3:5
    His righteousness. Ro.10:3
  Satan's desires. 2 Cor.2:11
  Spiritual gifts. 1 Cor.12:1
  The end & fate of the world. 2 Pt.3:3-15
  The longsuffering of God. 2 Pt.3:8-15
  The mystery of the Jews. Ro.11:25
  The return of Christ. 1 Th.4:13; 2 Pt.3:8-15
  The Scriptures. Mt.22:29; 1 Cor.10:1
  The suffering & persecution of ministers. 2 Cor.1:8
  Worship. Acts 17:22-23

ILLOGICAL
What is **i**.
  Denial. Mt.12:27-28
  Rejection. Mt.13:13-15

IMAGE OF GOD (See **LIKENESS**)
Believers are.
  Constantly changed into God's **i**. 2 Cor.3:18
  Renewed in God's **i**. Col.3:10
Christ. Is the **i**. of God. Col.1:15
Man.
  God's **i**. is stamped upon man. Lk.20:25; Jn.4:23
  Is created in the **i**. of God. Jn.4:23
Meaning. Heb.1:3

IMAGINATION (See **ARGUMENTS; THINKING**)
Fact.
  God scatters the proud in the **i**. of their heart. Lk.1:51
  People imagine empty things against God. Acts 4:25

IMAGINATIONS, EVIL
Creates false gods. (See **IDOLATRY**, Source of) Jn.8:54-59
Prevented. By guarding oneself around the opposite sex. Jn.4:27

IMMANUEL
Name of deity. Mt.1:23

IMMATURITY, SPIRITUAL
Conquered. Two ways. Mk.9:28-29
Discussed. Heb.5:11-6:3
Problem. Spiritual **i**. & powerlessness. Mk.9:14-29

IMMORAL PERSON
Behavior of - Error.
  Fall from their steadfastness. 2 Pt.3:17
  Hypocrisy. Mt.22:15-18, esp. 18; Acts 8:18-24, esp. 22
  Immoral, unprincipled behavior. 2 Pt.2:7
  Sin & take pleasure in those who sin. Ro.1:32
  Twist the Scriptures. 2 Pt.3:16-17
Described as.
  A sin of omission. Lk.19:15-23
  Being short of God's glory. Mt.18:32-34
Judgment of. (See **JUDGMENT; PUNISHMENT**)
  Are worthy of death. Ro.1:28-32, esp. 29, 32
  Excluded from God's kingdom. Gal.5:19-21
Meaning. Mk.7:22; Ro.1:29
Source of. The heart. Mk.7:20-23, esp. 22
Who is **i**.
  Evil spirits & forces. Eph.6:12
  Hypocritical religionists. Lk.11:37-39
  Immoral persons. 2 Cor.5:1, 13
  Satan. Mt.13:19; Eph.6:16
  The antichrist. 2 Th.2:8-9
  The ungodly & unrighteous. Ro.1:29
  The unsaved, those alienated from God. Col.1:21
  The whole world. 1 Jn.5:19
  This generation. Mt.12:43-45, esp. 45; 16:4
  Those who crucified Christ. Acts 2:23
  Unfaithful men. Mt.25:14-30, esp. 26-27; Lk.19:12-27, esp. 22-23
  Unjust men. Mt.18:23-35, esp. 32-33
  Unreasonable & **i**. men. 2 Th.3:2

IMMORALITY (See **ADULTERY; FORNICATION; LUST; SEXUAL IMMORALITY**)
Caused by.
  Partying & failing to separate from the world. Rev.2:20-21
  Threefold. Mt.5:27-30
Described. As several things. Eph.5:3; 5:4; 5:5
Discussed. Mt.5:27-30; Ro.13:9; 1 Cor.5:1-10
Duty.
  Not to fellowship with immoral persons. 1 Cor.5:11
  Not to look upon a person with lust. Mt.5:27-28
  Not to talk or joke about **i**. Eph.5:3-12
  Not to touch a woman. 1 Cor.7:1
  To avoid **i**. through marriage. 1 Cor.7:2
  To dress modestly. 1 Tim.2:9-10; 1 Pt.3:1-6
  To keep a pure body. Heb.10:22
  To live a pure life. Lk.1:26; 1 Th.4:3-7; Tit.2:5

Example of.
  At a party held by Herod. Suggestive dancing. Mk.6:21-22
  Woman. Repents & is saved. Lk.7:36-50
In the church.
  A case of public incest. 1 Cor.5:1-13
  Moral laxity. 1 Cor.5:1-6:20
Meaning. Mt.5:28
Misconception of. Is acceptable & excusable. Mt.5:27-30
Prevention - cure. Discussed. Mt.5:28; 5:30
Results.
  Causes God to give man over to i. Ro.1:26-27
Sin of. Is a sin against the person's own body. 1 Cor.6:18
Verses. List of. Ro.13:9

IMMORTALITY (See **ETERNAL LIFE; HEAVEN; RESURRECTION, THE**)
Duty. To seek for i. Ro.2:7
Meaning. Ro.2:7
Source - How to secure.
  By believing in Christ. Jn.11:26
  By continuing to do good works. Ro.2:7
  By earnestly desiring to be enclosed in our house in heaven. 2 Cor.5:1-2
  By fearing God who can destroy both body & soul in hell. Mt.10:28
  By Jesus Christ.
    Abolished death & brought i. through the gospel. 2 Tim.1:10
    Is the only Person who has i. 1 Tim.6:14-16, esp. 16
  By keeping the sayings of Christ. Jn.8:51
Surety of.
  Guaranteed by the Spirit. 2 Cor.5:5
  Resurrected believers cannot die any more. Lk.20:36
  The mortal shall put on i. 1 Cor.15:50-58, esp. 53
Verses. List of. Ro.2:7

IMPARTIAL - IMPARTIALITY (See **DISCRIMINATION; FAVORITISM; PARTIALITY; PREJUDICE; WHOSOEVER**)
And God.
  Does not show i. Ro.3:29-30; Gal.2:6
  Judgment is i. Ro.2:11-15
  Shows no favoritism. Acts 10:23-33; 10:34-35
  Treats all men just alike. Ro.3:29-30; 10:12
  Ways all men are related to God. Four ways. Ro.10:12
Discussed. Jas.2:1-13
Duty. Not to act superior or exclusive. 1 Cor.1:2
Duty. Of the minister.
  Not to show i. 1 Tim.5:21
  Not to show i. in choosing workers. Acts 15:36-41
  Not to show p. in sharing salvation. Acts 10:34-43
  Not to show i. to any person, no matter position, power, or importance. 2 Cor.5:16, cp. 12
  Not to show i. within the church. Jas.2:1-3
Fact.
  God is i. in accepting people.
    He accepts all who call upon Him. Ro.10:12
    He accepts all who fear Him & works righteousness. Acts 10:34-35
  God is i. in His blessings. Mt.5:45
  No i. with God. Col.3:11
Temptation to show i. Discussed. Jas.2:1-13

IMPATIENCE (See **ANXIETY**)
What causes i.
  People who do not do what we think they should. Lk.10:38-42, esp. 39-40
  People who embarrass us. Mt.15:21-23
  People who reject Christ. Lk.9:51-55, esp. 54

IMPENITENCE (See **HARD - HARDNESS; REBELLION; REPENTANCE; STUBBORN**)

IMPERFECTION (See **PERFECT - PERFECTION; SIN; UNBELIEF**)
Discussed. Man is imperfect, therefore unacceptable to a perfect God. 1 Tim.2:3-7; Heb.7:1-24; 7:27;9:1-10
Fact.
  All men offend in many things. Jas.3:2
  Man is short of the glory of God. Ro.3:23

IMPERIAL WORSHIP
Of the state & government. Rev.2:12; 13:4-8; 13:13-17; 17:1

IMPERISHABLE
Vs. perishable. 1 Pt.1:4; 1:23

IMPOSSIBLE
What is i.
  I. for God to lie. Heb.6:18
  I. that offenses & sins will not come. Lk.17:1
  I. to please God without faith. Heb.11:6
  I. to renew those who were once enlightened & fall away. Heb.6:4-6
  Nothing is i. to the person who has true faith. Mt.17:20
  Nothing is i. with God. Mt.19:26; Mk.10:27; Lk.1:37; 18:27

IMPURITY (See **ADULTERY; FORNICATION; IMMORALITY; LUST**)
Attitude toward. By the church. Mk.2:15
Deliverance - Cleansing. Discussed. Mk.1:40-45
Duty.
  Not to touch any i. thing, but to live a separated life. 2 Cor.6:17-18
  To guard against doing the things that people consider i. Ro.14:13-15, esp. 14
  To live a moral & clean life. 1 Th.4:6-8
  To put to death i. Col.3:5-7
Meaning. Ro.1:24-25; 2 Cor.12:19-21; Gal.5:19-21; Eph.4:17-19; 5:5

IMPUTE - IMPUTATION (See **CREDIT; COUNT**)
Facts.
  Faith is i. (counted, credited) to a person as righteousness. Ro.4:22-25; Jas.2:23
  God i. (counts, credits) righteousness without works. Ro.4:6
  Man is blessed when God does not i. (count, credit) sin against him. Ro.4:8
  Righteousness is i. (counted, credited) to a man when he believes on Christ. Ro.4:11
  Sin is not i. (counted, credited) when there is no law. Ro.5:13
Meaning. Mt.18:24; Ro.4:6-8; 4:9; 4:22; 6:11

IN CHRIST (See **ABIDE - ABIDING**)
Meaning. Ro.8:1; 2 Cor.5:17

INCARNATION (See **JESUS CHRIST**, Virgin Birth)
Discussed. Mt.1:16; 1:23; Jn.1:14-18; Ro.1:1-4; 2 Cor.5:18-19; 1 Jn.1:1-4; 1 Jn.4:2-3
  Cost of the i. What it cost God to give His Son to the world. Jn.3:16
  Six facts. 1 Tim.3:16
  The pivotal point of history. Mt.5:17-18
  Why the i. was necessary. Lk.3:32-38
Duty - Essential.
  Must believe in the Incarnation. 1 Jn.2:22-23; 4:2-3; 4:9-11; 5:19-20; 2 Jn.7, 10-11
  To guard the doctrine of. Jn.5:23; 1 Jn.5:20
How.
  Jesus Christ became flesh. Jn.1:14; Ro.1:3; 8:3; Ph.2:7; 1 Tim.3:16; Heb.2:14; 1 Jn.4:2; 2 Jn.7
  Jesus Christ came to earth "out of" heaven. Jn.3:13; 3:31; 6:33; 7:17-19; 7:25-31; 8:14; 8:23
  Jesus Christ came to earth through a woman. Lk.1:31, 34-35; Gal.4:4-7
  The eternal God entered history. 1 Jn.1:1-3
  The Incarnation came by the Word of God, not by some grotesque method. Jn.1:10; 6:61
Proof of.
  A persons' salvation. 1 Jn.2:22-23; 4:9-11
  Four proofs. Jn.1:14-18
  God's love. Jn.3:17
Purpose.
  Discussed. Lk.4:16-21; Heb.10:5-10
  To become the perfect High Priest for man in order to save him to the uttermost. Heb.7:24-28
  To come to earth in a body in order to do the will of God as the Ideal Man. Heb.10:5-10
  To deliver men from the fear of death. Heb.2:14-16
  To deliver men from this present evil world. Gal.1:4
  To establish fellowship between God & man. 1 Jn.1:1-3
  To fulfill all righteousness. Mt.3:15; 5:17-18; Ro.8:3
  To give God's Son many brothers. Ro.8:29
  To give life. 1 Jn.4:9-11
  To keep men from perishing by giving them everlasting life. Jn.3:16; 5:24
  To minister & to give His life as a ransom for many. Mt.20:28
  To reconcile man to God. 2 Cor.5:19-21
  To represent man before God and God before man. Lk.3:32-38
  To reveal God to man. Jn.14:6-11
  To reveal God's love toward man by Christ's death. Ro.5:8; 1 Pt.2:24; 1 Pt.3:18
  To seek & save the lost. Lk.19:10
Results. Some deny that God's Son, Jesus Christ, has come in the flesh. 1 Jn.2:18; 2:22-23; 4:2-3;2 Jn.7
Reveals. The power of God. Lk.8:22-23

INCONSISTENCY - INCONSISTENT
Example of. Peter. Gal.2:11-13
How people are i.
  In being unmerciful.
    By encouraging the needy but not
      helping them. Jas.2:15-16
    By putting rules above the needs of
      men & of mercy. Jn.7:23
  In false profession.
    By professing Christ, yet disobey-
      ing Him. Lk.6:46
    In professing Christ, yet denying
      Him by one's works. Tit.1:16
  In judging & criticizing. By judging &
    criticizing others when we are guilty
    of sin ourselves. Mt.7:3; Ro.2:1
  In speech.
    By loving only in word & tongue,
      not in deed & truth. 1 Jn.3:18
    By using one's mouth to bless &
      curse. Jas.3:10
  In teaching & not practicing. By not living
    what one preaches & teaches. Ro.2:21
Results.
  Brings the judgment of God upon one-
    self. Ro.2:1-16
  Causes the way of truth to be spoken
    against, slandered, & abused. 2 Pt.2:2
  Condemns oneself. Ro.2:1
  Dishonors the name of God among the
    lost. Ro.2:23-24

INCONTINENT (See **SELF-CONTROL, WITHOUT**)

INCORRUPTION - INCORRUPTIBLE--IMPERISHABLE (See **CORRUPTION**)
Assurance of. God is able to present be-
  lievers without fault. Jude 24-25
Fact.
  Believers are born again of an i. seed. 1 Pt.1:23
  Corruption cannot inherit i. 1 Cor.15:50
  God is **I**. Ro.1:23
Meaning. 1 Cor.15:42-44; 15:53; 1 Pt.1:3-4;
  1 Pt.1:23
The reward of believers.
  Shall be given an i. crown. 1 Cor.9:25
  Shall be given an i. inheritance. 1 Pt.1:3-4
  Shall be raised & given an i. body.
    1 Cor.15:42-44; 15:50-58

INCORRUPTION, CROWN OF
Meaning. 1 Cor.9:25

INCREASING MEASURE
Meaning. 2 Pt.1:8-11

INDECENT - INDECENCY
Meaning. 1 Cor.13:4-7

INDECISION - INDECISIVENESS (See **DOUBLE MINDED; NEUTRALITY**)
Example of.
  Felix. Acts 24:24-26
  Pilate. Mt.27:11-25; Mk.15:2-5
Fact.
  A choice has to be made. Mt.4:10; 6:24
  Cannot serve two masters. Lk.16:13
Reasons for. Lk.20:7-8
Results.
  Makes a person double minded, un-
    stable. Jas.1:5-8
  Makes a person lukewarm, neither hot
    nor cold. Rev.3:15-16
  Makes a person unfit for God's king-
    dom. Lk.9:61-62
Verses. List of. Mk.15:2-5; 15:6-10

INDEPENDENCE (See **SELF-SUFFICIENCY**)

INDIFFERENCE (See **HARDNESS; UNBELIEF**)
Describes. Sinful nature. Ro.3:10-12
Toward what.
  God. Ro.1:19-32
  Sin & evil. Lk.17:26, 28; Ro.3:9-18
  The evil behavior of the lost. Mt.24:12
  The invitation of Christ. Rev.3:15-16, 20
  The invitation of God. Mt.22:1-6
  The needy. Lk.10:30-37
  The resurrection of the dead.
    1 Cor.15:12
  The return of Christ & the end of the
    world. 2 Pt.3:3-15
  The works of the flesh. Gal.5:19-21

INDIGNATION (See **ANGER; WRATH**)
Of believers.
  Against believers who give large &
    special gifts to Christ. Mt.26:6-13
  Against self-seeking believers. Mt.20:24
Of God.
  Against the followers of antichrist.
    Rev.14:10
  Against the selfish & unrighteous. Ro.2:8
  Against those who willfully sin after
    receiving the truth. Heb.2:26-27
Of religionists.
  Against others for breaking religious
    ceremonies & rituals & rules. Lk.13:14
Of the world. Against believers for wit-
  nessing. Acts 5:17

INDULGE - INDULGENCE
Caused by. Selfishness & godless inde-
  pendence. Lk.15:11-13
Described as.
  Extravagant living. Lk.12:13-21
  Indulgence, drunkenness, & worldli-
    ness. Lk.21:34-35
  Wild partying, indulgent living.
    Lk.15:11-13
  Trying to save one's life in this world.
    Lk.9:24
Example.
  Prodigal son. Lk.15:11-24
  Rich fool. Lk.12:13-21
Judgment of.
  Causes a person to lose his soul.
    Lk.16:19-31
  Why God does not forgive a person
    who indulges time & again.
    Mt.6:14-15
Sin of.
  Discussed. Lk.14:15-24
  Is not love. Ro.3:5-8
Verses. List of. Lk.12:15-19
Vs. giving one's life to Christ. Lk.9:24

INDWELLING PRESENCE (See **UNION WITH CHRIST**)
Discussed. 2 Cor.4:7-18
Is a mystery. Col.1:26-27
Indwelling of Christ in the believer.
  Discussed. The Spirit of Christ. Ro.8:9
  Mutual i. between Christ & the believer.
    Stated. Jn.6:56; 1 Cor.6:15-18; 6:18
    Verses. List of. Jn.6:56
  Stated. Jn.14:18-20; 14:21; 14:23-24;
    Gal.2:19-21; Eph.3:17
  Verses. List of. Jn.14:20

Indwelling of God in the believer.
  Called a "treasure in earthen vessels."
    2 Cor.4:7
  Discussed. 2 Cor.4:7
  Is conditional based upon love.
    1 Jn.4:12-13
  Makes a believer different from an un-
    believer. 2 Cor.6:16
  Mutual i. between God & the believer.
    1 Jn.4:13
  Overcomes false spirits. 1 Jn.4:4-6,
    cp. 1-6
  Stated. Eph.3:19; 1 Jn.4:12-13
  The believer is the temple of God.
    2 Cor.6:16
Indwelling of the Holy Spirit in the be-
  liever.
  I. between God & Christ. Jn.5:17-30;
    8:15-16; 10:14-16; 10:37-39; 14:10;
    17:10
  I. between God, Christ & the believer.
    Jn.14:18-20; 14:23-24
  I. of the Trinity. Jn.14:23-24; Eph.3:19
  Proven by.
    Obedience. 1 Jn.3:24
    The Spirit within. 1 Jn.3:24; 4:12-13
  Verses. List of. Ro.8:9

INEFFECTIVE
Discussed. 2 Pt.1:8-11

INFERIORITY
Caused by. Discussed. Mt.13:53-54

INFIDEL (See **UNBELIEF; UNBE-LIEVER**)

INFIRMITIES (See **WEAKNESSES**)

INFLUENCE
Evil i. (See **STUMBLING BLOCK**)
  A little leaven leavens the whole lump.
    1 Cor.5:6; Gal.5:9
  Doing questionable things. Ro.14:1-23;
    1 Cor.8:1-13
Good i. (See **TESTIMONY**)

INGRATITUDE (See **UNGRATEFUL**)
Trait of men.
  After being blessed. Lk.17:15-19
  Is seen in rejecting God despite all the
    evidence that God exists. Ro.1:21

INHERITANCE, EARTHLY
Dispute over. Jesus was asked to settle a
  dispute over an earthly i. LK.12:13-14
Fact.
  An i. can be stolen. Mt.21:33-46, esp.
    38-39; Mk.12:7-8; Lk.20:14-15
  An i. can be wasted. Lk.15:11-24, esp.
    12-14
Law governing. Lk.12:13-14; 15:12

INHERITANCE, SPIRITUAL (See **RE-WARD**)
Discussed. Mk.25:34-40; Tit.3:6; 1 Pt.1:4
  Christ is God's heir. Heb.1:4-14, esp. 4-9
Nature.
  Glorious. Ro.8:16-17
  Imperishable, undefiled, can never
    fade away. 1 Pt.1:4
  Is eternal. Tit.3:7; Heb.9:15
  Is heavenly, of another dimension, the
    eternal world. 1 Pt.1:4, cp. Mt.21:43
  Is light. Is the possession of saints in
    light. Col.1:12

Of Abraham.
  Promised that he would inherit the world. Ro.4:13; Gal.3:16; 3:18; Heb.11:8
  To inherit righteousness & eternity. Gal.3:18; 3:29
Of Israel & the church. Mt.21:43
Source of - How a person receives the **i**.
  By being sanctified by faith in Christ. Acts 26:18
  By faith & patience. Heb.6:12
  By faith, not by works. Gal.3:18
  By hearing the Word & believing. Eph.1:11-13
  By overcoming the world. Rev.21:7
  By promise, not by law. Gal.3:18
  By the death of Christ. Heb.9:14-15
  By the Lord Jesus Christ. Gal.3:29; Eph.1:11; Col.3:24
  By the Word of God. Acts 20:32; Eph.1:13-14
  By trusting Christ. Eph.1:13-14
Surety of.
  Discussed. 1 Pt.1:3-5
  Is a covenant. Gal.3:15-18
  Is confirmed. Heb.6:16-20
  Is guaranteed by the Holy Spirit. Eph.1:11-13
  Is not by law, but by faith. Ro.4:13-16
What the **i**. is.
  A blessing. 1 Pt.3:9
  A kingdom. Mt.25:34; Jas.2:5
  A treasure within - God Himself. 2 Cor.4:7
  Being made the cherished possession of God. Eph.1:11-13; 1:18
  Crucifixion, the death of the old person. Ro.6:3-5
  Discussed. Ro.8:17; Eph.1:11-13; Col.1:12
  Everlasting life. Mt.19:29; Jn.3:16; 5:24. Cp. Mk.10:17; Lk.10:25; 18:18
  Freedom from sin & death. Ro.6:6-7
  Glory, to be glorified with Christ. Ro.8:16-17
  Life with Christ. Ro.6:8-10
  Listed. Lk.16:10-12; Tit.3:6; 1 Pt.1:4; Rev.14:13
  Newness of life with Christ & God. Ro.6:1-10
  Possessing all things. 1 Cor.3:21-23; Rev.21:7
  Reward. (See **REWARD**)
  Righteousness & justification & eternity. Ro.4:23-25; Gal.3:18; 3:29; Heb.11:7
  Salvation. Heb.1:14
  Sharing equally with Christ--being made an heir of God. Jn.16:14-15; Ro.8:16-17; Gal.3:23-29; 4:4-7; Eph.3:6; Tit.3:7; Heb.2:11-13
  The grace of life. 1 Pt.3:7
  The new birth - the imperishable seed. 1 Pt.1:23
  The promises given to Abraham. Ro.4:13; Gal.3:2; 3:16; 3:18; 3:29; Heb.11:8
  The promises of God. Mt.1:2
  The resurrection to eternal life. Ro.6:3-5; 6:8-10; 8:11; 1 Pt.1:3-4
  The spiritual dimension. Mt.21:43; 1 Pt.1:4
  The world itself. Ro.4:13; Gal.3:16; 3:18
  Verses. List of. Ro.8:17

Who shall not receive the **i**.
  The profane & immoral. Heb.12:16-17
  The unrighteous. 1 Cor.6:9-10; Eph.5:3-5
  Those who live by the flesh. Gal.5:19-21
  Those who trust man, flesh & blood, alone. 1 Cor.15:50
Why God chose to give the **i**., the promises, to the younger men in the Old Testament. Ro.9:13

INIQUITY (See **EVIL; SIN; WICKEDNESS**)
Deliverance from.
  By Christ, His redemption. Tit.2:14
  By God, His mercy & promise not to remember our sins & **i**. any more. Heb.8:12
Duty.
  To depart from **i**. 2 Tim.2:19
Facts about - Traits.
  Abounds & causes love to become cold. Mt.24:12
  Enslaves & binds a person. Acts 8:23; Ro.6:19
  Is at work in the world now. 2 Th.2:7
  Is hated by Christ. Heb.1:9
  The tongue is a world of **i**. Jas.3:6
  Will be a trait of the end time. Mt.24:12
Judgment of those who do **i**.
  Shall be put away from Christ. Mt.7:21-23
  Shall be put out of Christ's kingdom & cast into a furnace of fire. Mt.13:41-42
Source. The heart within man. Mt.23:28

INITIATIVE (See **COMMITMENT; DEDICATION; ZEAL**)
Essential.
  To seize & grasp every opportunity. Mk.1:21; Jn.11:7-10
  To work while it is day before the night comes. Jn.11:7-10

INJURY
Law governing. Discussed. Mt.5:38; 5:39-41; 5:40;5:41; 5:42
Personal **i**. Discussed. Mt.5:39-41; 5:41
Property **i**. Discussed. Mt.5:40

INJUSTICE (See **JUSTICE**)
A charge sometimes made against God.
  In His blessings, reward, & payment. Mt.20:1-16, esp. 10-16
  In salvation & service. Ro.9:11-13; 9:14-33, esp. 14-21
Caused by. Compromising with the world. Lk.23:13-16
Fact.
  All **i**. are to be straightened out. Mt.19:30
  Christ is returning to execute justice. Rev.1:7
  Judgment will be perfect justice, exactly what a person deserves. Lk.19:15-23; Jn.12:39-41; Ro.2:6-10;
Results. Makes one unworthy to rule. Lk.23:13-25

INNER MAN (See **NEW PERSON**)
Duty. To renew day by day. 2 Cor.4:16
Meaning. 2 Cor.4:16

INSANITY
Fact.
  Causes some people to destroy themselves. Mt.17:15
  Is different from demon-possession. Mt.4:24
  Sin is said to be **i**. Lk.15:17-19

INSECURITY
Caused by.
  Building one's life upon sand. Mt.7:26-27
  False teachers. Jude 12
  Trusting oneself--one's own strength. 1 Cor.10:12
  Trusting the world & its security. 1 Th.5:2-3
  Trusting wealth & possessions. Mk.10:23-25; Lk.12:16-21, esp. 19-20; 1 Tim.6:17
  Worldliness. Lk.12:16-21
Characteristic - Trait of. False teachers. Jude 12
Deliverance from.
  Knowing God & Christ personally. Ph.4:19
  Seeking the kingdom of God first. Mt.6:25-34, esp. 33

INSIGHT (See **SPIRITUAL SIGHT; UNDERSTANDING**)

INSOLENT
Caused by. Three things. Mt.13:53-58
Discussed. 2 Tim.3:2-4
Duty.
  Employees (servants) are not to **i**. their employers (masters). 1 Tim.6:1
  Not to **i**. the poor. Jas.2:1-4
  Strong believers are not to **i**. weak believers. Ro.14:3
Example of **i**. Christ.
  I. His claims. Jn.10:20, cp. 1-21
  Mocking & **i**. His preaching. Lk.16:14, cp. 13-18
  Mocking His claim to be the Son of God. Mt.26:67-68
  Mocking His miraculous works & power. Mk.15:29-30
  Questioning His earthly birth. Mt.13:53-58
Meaning. Lk.18:9; Ro.1:30; Heb.12:5-7
Warning against.
  I. the offer of salvation & heaven by God. Mt.22:1-10, esp. 7-8
  I. young believers. Mt.18:10
  Ways **i**. Mt.18:10

INSPIRATION OF THE SCRIPTURE (See **SCRIPTURE**, Inspiration of)

INSTABILITY (See **FICKLENESS; WAVERING**)
Caused by.
  Doubting & wavering. Jas.1:2-8, esp. 6-8
  False teaching. Gal.1:6-7; Eph.4:14; Heb.13:9; 2 Pt.2:18; Jude 12
  Lacking the commitment to follow Christ through difficult situations. Acts 13:13
  Not accepting Christ & His provision. Jn.6:66, cp. 6:59-71
Characteristic - Trait of. False teachers. Jude 12

INSTANT (See **PREPARED**)

INSTINCT
Duty.
  Believers are to **a**. one another. Ro.15:14
  Fathers are to **a**. children. Eph.6:4
  Leaders are to **a**. 1 Th.5:12
  To **a**. false teachers. Tit.3:10
  To **a**. those who do not work. 2 Th.3:10-15, esp. 15
Meaning. Ro.15:14
Source. Scriptures. 1 Cor.10:11

INSTRUCT - INSTRUCTION (See **TEACH - TEACHER**)
Duty.
Not to be hypocritical & self-sufficient in **i**. Ro.2:17-24, esp. 20-24
To **i**. believers, but more importantly, to be a father to believers. 1 Cor.4:14-16
Meaning. 1 Cor.4:14; 4:15
Source of. The Scripture. 2 Tim.3:16

INTEGRITY (See **HONEST - HONESTY**)

INTELLECTUAL PRIDE
Result. Blinds to the truth. Mt.11:25-27

INTELLIGENCE (See **KNOWLEDGE; UNDERSTANDING**)
Weakness of. 2 Tim.3:6-9

INTERCESSION (See **PRAYER**)
Example of **i**.
A Canaanite woman interceded for her daughter. Mt.15:22
A man interceded for his son. Lk.9:37-42, esp. 37-39
Elijah made **i**. against Israel. Ro.11:2
Meaning. 1 Tim.2:1
Of believers.
For all believers. Eph.3:14; 6:18
For God to delay judgment. Lk.13:6-9
For ministers. Eph.6:19
For the healing of a friend. Mk.8:22-26; Jas.5:14-18
For the lost. Ro.10:1
Of Jesus Christ. (See **JESUS CHRIST**, Intercessor; Mediator; Priesthood of)
For believers. Jn.17:9
For man's salvation. Ro.8:34; Heb.7:25
For the lost & rebellious. Lk.23:34
For weak believers. Lk.22:32
Of the Holy Spirit. Helps us to pray. Ro.8:26-27

INTOLERANCE (See **BIGOTRY; DISCRIMINATION**)
Reasons for. Lk.9:49-50

INTOXICATION (See **DRUNKENNESS**)

INTRIGUE
Of Herod. Against the baby Jesus. Mt.2:1-8
Of Judas. Described as on the prowl after Christ. Mt.26:16
Of the religionist. Against Christ. Jn.7:11-13, 19-20, 30, 32, 44

INVITATION (See **CALL; COME; DECISION**)
Extended by Christ.
He invites men to become fishers of men. Mk.1:17
He invites men to open the door of His heart. Lk.24:28-32; Rev.3:20
He invites people to God's great banquet. Mt.22:4; Lk.14:16-24
He offers rest. Mt.11:28-30
He offers salvation. Rev.22:17
He seeks to gather people as a mother hen. Mt.23:37
He takes the initiative. Jn.1:39-40

Extended by God.
God extends an **i**. to Israel & the Gentiles. Ignored. Mt.22:5
God must draw man. Jn.6:44
God sends message after message. Mt.22:1-10
God sets a great feast before people. Mt.22:1-10; Lk.14:16-24
Kinds of. Severalfold. Mt.22:4
Rejected.
Excuses given. Mt.8:18-22; Lk.14:15-24
God's great invitation. Mt.22:1-14
Verses. List of. Mk.1:33

IRRESPONSIBILITY
Behavior of. Lk.10:29-37
Described as.
Escapism. Of duty. (See **ESCAPISM**) Lk.23:6-7
Selfishness. Lk.15:11-16

ISAAC
Faith of. A repentant faith. Heb.11:20
Type. Symbol of.
Grace & righteousness by faith. Gal.4:21-31
The death & resurrection of Christ. Heb.11:17-19

ISAIAH
Chart of the prophecies of the O.T. & their fulfillment in the N.T. Jn.1:45
Isaiah's prophecies concerning Christ. (See **PROPHECY**)
The bearing of our infirmities & sicknesses. Mt.8:17
The death of Christ. Acts 8:28, 32-33
The forerunner of Christ. Mt.3:3; Lk.3:4; Jn.1:23
The hardening of people's hearts & rejection of Christ. Mt.13:14-15; 15:7-8; Mk.7:6; Jn.12:38-41; Acts 28:25
The ministry & salvation of Christ. Mt.4:14; Lk.4:17-19
The special anointing by God & His ministry to the Gentiles. Mt.12:17-18
Isaiah's prophecies concerning other things.
A remnant of Israel is to be saved. Ro.9:27-29
Few would believe the message. Ro.10:16
The conversion of the Gentiles. Ro.10:20-21; 15:8-12

ISHMAEL
Type - Symbol of.
The law. Gal.4:21-31
The sinful nature. Ro.9:7-13

ISRAEL (See **JERUSALEM; JEWS**)
And the gospel of righteousness.
The callous on Israel's heart is a warning to others. Ro.11:17-24
The callous on Israel's heart is not final--there is to be a restoration. Ro.11:11-16
The callous on Israel's heart is not total--there is a remnant. Ro.11:1-10
The gospel is not for Israel alone. Ro.10:12-21
The privileges of Israel & their failure. Ro.9:1-5
The restoration of Israel & its surety. Ro.11:25-36
The true mistake of Israel--missing God's righteousness. Ro.10:1-11

Blessings of.
Discussed. 1 Cor.10:1-5
Privileges of. Ro.9:1-5
Chosen by God.
Four purposes. Lk.1:68
Purpose. Jn.4:22
Discussed. Mt.10:12; 21:33-46; 21:43; 22:1-14; Lk.6:7
Israel & God. Parable of the Wicked Tenants. Mk.12:1-12
Who Israel really is. Rev.3:9-10
Duty toward.
To be reached first. Reasons. Mt.10:5-6
Why Israel was to be evangelized. Mt.10:5-6
Example of.
Is an example of judgment upon believers. Jude 5-7
Is an example to believers. 1 Cor.10:1-13
Fact.
Attacked by Satan.
Down through history. Rev.12:3-4
Tried to destroy the seed of Israel. Rev.12:3-4
God still loves. Rev.11:3-13
Failure - Errors - Mistakes - Sins of.
Discussed. 1 Cor.10:1-13; 1 Th.2:15-16
Hard hearts. Heb.3:7-11
In the wilderness. Jude 5-7
Is an example to believers. 1 Cor.10:1-13
Missed God's righteousness. Ro.10:1-11
Persecuted God's messengers. Mt.23:37
Reasons for failure & fall. Ro.11:17-24
Rejected God's servants. Mk.12:3
Rejected the Messiah & His love. Mt.23:37
Slept & slumbered. False security. Ro.11:6-9
Was gripped by unbelief. Discussed. Heb.3:7-11
Faith of Israel
A conquering faith. Heb.11:30
A delivering faith. Heb.11:29
History.
Blessed by God. Three blessings. Mk.12:1
Discussed. Lk.6:7; Jn.4:22
Future of Israel Foretold by Christ. Mk.12:1-12
God's great invitation to Israel. Mt.22:1-14
God's perspective, dealings with Israel. Mt.21:33-46; 21:43; 22:1-14; Lk.20:9-18
Overall view of Israel Discussed. Lk.20:9-18
Period of Israel. Lasted through John the Baptist. Christ begins a new order. Lk.16:16
Symbolizes the spiritual journey of a person. Mt.1:17
The "binding force" that held the nation together. Mt.12:10
In the end time.
How Israel turns to God. Rev.11:3-13
Satan attacks & tries to destroy Israel Holocaust. Rev.12:1-17; 12:6; 12:7-9; 12:12; 12:13-17
Two witnesses to Israel. Rev.11:3-13
Will be one hundred forty-four thousand witnesses from Israel. Rev.7:4-8; 14:1-5

Judgment of Israel.
    By God. Discussed. Mt.21:17-22;
    21:33-46
        Turned from Israel to Gentiles.
        Ro.10:18-21
    Discussed. Lk.20:15-16
    Fall of. Lk.19:43-44
    Fate of. Sealed. During the end time of
    Revelation. Rev.7:1-8
    God's great invitation. Mt.22:1-14
Laws of. (See CEREMONIAL LAWS)
    Capital punishment was not allowed
    by the Romans. Jn.19:7
Love for.
    By God. Rev.11:3-13
    By Paul. Ro.9:1-3; 11:13-15
Name. "Israel." History of. Ro.9:4
Parables describing.
    Parable of the Marriage Feast.
    Mt.22:1-14
    Parable of the Olive Tree. Ro.11:17-24
    Parable of the Wicked Husbandman.
    Mt.21:33-46; Mk.12:1-12
Purpose.
    Fourfold purpose. Lk.1:68
    Why God chose Israel. Jn.4:22
Rejection of. (See JESUS CHRIST, Re-
sponse to; RELIGIONISTS, Opposed
Christ)
    Christ. Parable of the Wicked Tenants.
    Mt.21:33-46; Mk.12:1-12
    Jesus, the Messiah. Mt.21:33-46;
    Lk.13:31-35
    Sceptre departed from Judea. Five
    proofs. Lk.2:1-24
Religionists of Israel. (See RELIGION-
ISTS)
Remnant.
    144,000 saved during the tribulation of
    the end time. Rev.7:1-8; 14:1-5
    How Israel turns to God. Rev.11:3-13
    Paul a proof of. Ro.11:1
    Proofs that there is a remnant. Ro.11:1-10
Restoration of. (See JEWS, Restoration)
    At the end of the "times of the Gen-
    tiles." Lk.21:24
    Discussed. Ro.11:25-26; 11:25-36
    How Israel turns to God in the end
    time. Rev.11:3-13
    Surety of. Ro.11:11-16; 11:25-26
        Predicted by the prophets. Ro.11:2-4
        Prophecy. Will proclaim Messiah.
        Mt.23:39
        Sixfold surety. Ro.11:25-36
        The forefathers are surety of the
        restoration. Ro.11:16; 11:28
    To be wrought by Christ Himself.
    Ro.11:26-27
State of. Scepter departed from Judea.
Five proofs. Lk.2:1-24
True Israel.
    A new creature. Gal.6:15
    Abraham's true seed. Ro.4:11-12;
    4:16; 4:18-22; Gal.3:27-29
    All who believe. Ro.4:11-12; 4:16;
    4:18-22
    Discussed. Ro.9:6-13
    Persons who are Christ's. Gal.3:27-29
    The Israel of God. Gal.6:15-16
    Those who are of faith. Gal.3:6-9; 5:6; 6:15
Vs. the Gentiles.
    Relationship to. Ro.11:17-24
    Warning to both Israel & the Gentiles.
    Ro.11:17-24
    Who is really following God, the Jew
    or the Gentile. Ro.9:6

ITALY
    Aquila, Paul's co-worker in Corinth, had
    come from Italy. Acts 18:2
    Believers in Italy sent greetings to the
    Hebrew believers. Heb.13:24
    Cornelius & his band of soldiers were
    from Italy. Acts 10:1
    Paul sailed into Italy. Acts 27:1
    The Jews were expelled from Rome by
    Claudius the Emperor. Acts 18:2

J

JACOB
    Chosen by God. Over Esau. Ro.9:7-13
    Faith of. A worshipping faith. Heb.11:21
    History of. Place in God's plan. Acts
    7:8-16; 7:17-41
    Ladder of. Meaning. Jn.1:51

JAILER
    At Philippi. Led to Christ by Paul. Acts
    16:25-40

JAIRUS
    Daughter raised from the dead.
        How to approach Jesus. Mk.5:21-24,
        35-43
        Reward of true faith. Lk.8:40-56
    Ruler of a synagogue. Discussed.
    Mt.9:18-19

JAMBRES
    Religious leader in Egypt who opposed
    Moses. 2 Tim.3:8

JAMES
    Men in the New Testament named James.
    Lk.5:10

JAMES THE APOSTLE, THE SON OF ALPHAEUS
    Discussed. Mk.3:18; Acts 1:13
    Had a believing mother. Mt.27:56; Mk.16:1
    Returned to the upper room. Acts 1:13

JAMES THE APOSTLE, THE SON OF ZEBEDEE
    Brother of John. Discussed. Mk.3:17
    Called Boanerges, son of thunder (anger).
    Mk.3:17
    Called to be a disciple. Mk.1:19-20
    Discussed. Mt.10:2; Mk.3:17
    Fate of. Martyred by Herod. Mt.20:23;
    Mk.10:39; Acts 12:2
    Misunderstood Jesus' mission. Lk.9:52-54
    One of Jesus' inner circle. Mt.17:1
    Returned to the upper room. Acts 1:13
    Self-seeking. Sought a chief position.
    Mk.10:35-45
    Wealthy. Father owned a fishing busi-
    ness. Mk.10:36-37

JAMES, THE BROTHER OF JESUS
    Became a believer. Acts 1:14
    Became pastor of the great Jerusalem
    church. Acts 15:13-22
    Confesses the deity of Jesus. Jn.1:14
    Did not believe in Jesus, not at first.
    Jn.7:3-5
    Discussed. Mt.13:55-56; Jas.1:1
    Identified as an apostle. Gal.1:18-20
    Jesus appeared to James after His resur-
    rection. 1 Cor.15:7

JANNES
    Religious leader in Egypt who opposed
    Moses. 2 Tim.3:8

JASON
    Believer in Thessalonica. Acts 17:1-9
    Relative of Paul. Ro.16:21

JEALOUSY (See ENVY)
    Caused by.
        The flesh. Gal.5:19-21, esp. 20
        The life & blessings of others.
        Lk.15:28
        The pay and labor of others. Mt.20:12
        The position of others. Lk.9:49-50
    Results - Judgment of. Excludes a person
    from the kingdom of God. Gal.5:19-21,
    esp. 21

JEPHTHAE
    Faith of. Discussed. Heb.11:32

JERICHO
    Destruction of. By God under Joshua &
    Israel. Heb.11:30
    Discussed. Mk.10:46; Lk.18:35

JERUSALEM (See ISRAEL)
    Duty toward.
        To love & weep over. Mt.23:37-39;
        Lk.19:41-44
        To preach the gospel to Jerusalem.
        Lk.24:47; Acts 1:8
    Is to be a heavenly Jerusalem or city.
    (See JERUSALEM, NEW)
        Is the inheritance of the believer.
        Gal.4:24-28
    Jesus & Jerusalem.
        Jerusalem rejected Christ. Lk.13:31-35
        Jesus' crucifixion at Jerusalem.
        Mt.27:26-56; Mk.15:16-41; Lk.9:31;
        23:43-49; Jn.19:16-37
        Jesus' great journey to. Lk.9:51-19:28
        Jesus' love for.
            Great lament over Jerusalem.
            Mt.23:37-39
            Wept over. Lk.13:34-35; 19:41-42
        Jesus' ministry in. John covers; other
        Gospels say little. Mk.11:1-13:37
        Jesus' triumphal entry into Jerusalem.
        Mt.21:1-11; Mk.11:1-11; Lk.19:28-40;
        Jn.12:12-19
    Paul & Jerusalem.
        Paul attended the great Jerusalem
        council. Acts 15:1-35
        Paul did not visit Jerusalem again until
        fourteen years later. Gal.2:1
        Paul visited Jerusalem three years after
        his conversion. Gal.1:18
        Paul was arrested in Jerusalem. Acts
        21:30-23:10
        Paul's face was set for Jerusalem.
        Acts 20:13-18
    Prophecy concerning.
        In the end time.
            One tenth of the city will be de-
            stroyed by an earthquake.
            Rev.11:13
            To be trampled & ruled over by the
            Gentiles. Rev.11:1-2
            Will be spiritually apostate.
            Rev.11:1-2; 11:8
        Of judgment & destruction. Mt.24:15-28;
        24:29-31; Lk.19:41-44; 23:28-31

Foreseeing. Pressure, weight of.
Lk.9:28-36
Glory of Christ's death.
   Great glory of His condescension
     was His death. Jn.13:3-5
   Supreme glory was His death.
     Jn.12:23-26; 12:27-30; 14:30-31;
     15:9; 16:11
   Threefold glory. Jn.13:31-32
Meaning.
   Died as the Ideal Man, as the substi-
     tute for man. Mk.8:31
   Died as the Son of Man, as the
     substitute for man. Mt.26:1-2
   Died for us, instead of us, as our
     substitute. Ro.5:6-7
Misunderstood by disciples. Spiritual-
   ized. Lk.18:34
Necessity of. (See **JESUS CHRIST**,
   Death, Destined)
   Dear to the heart of Christ.
     Mt.20:18
   Misunderstood & spiritualized. By
     disciples. Mt.20:20-21; Mk.9:32
   Must. Meaning. Mk.8:31; 9:31; 10:32
   Reasons. Threefold. Mk.10:32
   Set for Jerusalem. Driven toward
     Jerusalem. Death. Mk.10:32;
     Lk.9:51-56; 19:28
   To be in Jerusalem. Reason.
     Lk.13:31-33
Plotted. Mt.20:17-19; 26:3-5; 26:57-68;
   Jn.5:16; 11:47-57
   A picture of the Passover & Jesus'
     d. Picture of deception & lies.
     Mk.14:1-2
   By religionists. Reasons. Mk.14:1-2
   By the Jews. Acts 2:22-24, 36;
     3:13-15
   Culprits involved in death.
     Mt.16:21; 27:1-10
   Groups involved in **d**. Mt.16:21;
     27:26-44
Predicted - Foretold. Mt.9:15; 17:12;
   17:22-2320:17-19; Mk.2:19;
   Lk.9:22; 9:44-45; 12:50; 13:33;
   17:25; 18:31-34; 22:37; Jn.3:14;
   6:51; 7:33-34; 10:11; 10:17-18; 12:7-8;
   12:31-36; 13:31-14:3; 14:30-31;
   17:11, 13; Acts 3:18; 1 Cor.15:3
   A violent death. Mk.2:20
   By Jesus. Mk.8:31-33; 9:11-13;
     9:30-32;10:32-34; 12:6-8;
     14:18-21; 14:41-42
   By Simeon when Jesus was a child.
     Lk.2:34-35
   Demands total commitment.
     Mt.16:21-28
   Discussed. Lk.9:44-45; 18:31-34
   Indoctrinated into the disciples.
     Shook them. Mk.8:31; 8:32-33
   Misunderstood by the disciples.
     Spiritualized. Mk.9:32; Lk.18:34;
     Jn.14:8
   Predictions intensified. Launched a
     new stage. Mt.16:21-28; 17:1-13;
     17:22; 17:24-27; Mk.8:31
   Reason for predictions. Mk.9:31
   Second prediction. Lk.9:44-45
   Teaching the disciples about His
     death. Mk.9:30-32
   What disciples thought. Their inter-
     pretation. Jn.14:8

Prepared for.
   All verses in N.T. given. Mt.17:23
   Anointed for **d**. Sacrificed love &
     faith. Mt.26:6-13
   By the transfiguration. Mt.17:1-13;
     Mk.9:2-13
   Confronting death & terrible trials.
     Gethsemane. Mt.26:36-46
Prophesied.
   All prophecies in John. Jn.20:20
   By the high priest. Jn.11:49-53
   Most verses & their fulfillment.
     Lk.3:23-38; 1 Cor.15:4
   The O.T. prophecies about Jesus &
     their fulfillment. Jn.1:45
   To be sacrificed for the people.
     Jn.11:49-53
Prosecutors of.
   Discussed. Mt.20:19
   Whole world symbolized.
     Mk.10:33
Purchased the church by His death.
   Acts 20:28-31
Purpose. Jn.4:22; Tit.2:11-15
   Died for the ungodly, the sinner, &
     enemies. Ro.5:6-11
   Died for the whole world. Mk.10:33
   Discussed. Mk.9:31; 10:32;
     2 Cor.5:21
   The purposes involving His death.
     To deliver man from perishing.
       Jn.3:14-15
     To deliver man from sin, death,
       the law, and evil spirits.
       Col.2:13-15
     To descend into hell for man &
       to conquer death. Mt.27:52-53
     To die for the spiritually dead.
       2 Cor.5:14-16
     To taste death for every man.
       Heb.2:9-13
   The purposes involving life, both
    abundant & eternal life.
     To bring us to God. 1 Pt.3:18
     To draw men. Mk.10:32
     To freely give us all things. God
       spared not. Ro.8:31-33
     To give eternal life. Jn.3:14-15
   The purposes involving sin.
     To be the sacrifice for man's
       sins. Heb.7:27
     To bear & die for the sins of the
       world. Gal.1:4-5; 1 Pt.2:24;
       3:18
     To bear man's sin, the guilt &
       punishment for man. Ro.8:3;
       1 Cor.15:3
     To bear the curse of the law for
       men. Gal.3:13-14
     To die for every man's sin. Acts
       3:13-15
     To show man the supreme act of
       love. Jn.15:12-13
     To take away sin. 1 Jn.3:5
   The purposes involving the devil.
     To defeat evil spirits & forces of
       the universe. Col.2:15
     To deliver man from sin, death,
       the law, and evil spirits.
       Col.2:13-15
     To destroy the works of the
       devil. Heb.2:14-15; 1 Jn.3:8
     To preach to the spirits in prison.
       1 Pt.3:18-22

The purposes involving the world.
   To deliver us from this evil
     world. Gal.1:4-5
   To reconcile all things to God.
     Col.1:20
Threefold purpose. 2 Cor.5:14-16;
   Tit.2:14
Twofold purpose. Mt.17:23
Why God's Son, the Lord Jesus
   Christ, had to die.
   A perfect ransom was needed.
     Ro.5:6-7; 1 Tim.2:3-7
   A perfect sacrifice was needed.
     Ro.5:6-7; Heb.10:1-18; 10:5-10;
     13:20; 1 Jn.2:2
   A perfect substitute was needed.
     Ro.5:8-9; Gal.3:13-14
   Justification was needed.
     Ro.5:1; 2 Cor.5:14-16
   Propitiation was needed. Ro.5:6-7
   Reconciliation was needed.
     Ro.5:10-11; 2 Cor.5:17-21;
     Eph.2:13-18
   Redemption was needed. Ro.5:6-7
   Salvation was needed. Ro.5:10-11;
     1 Tim.2:3-7
   The Author & Source of eternal
     salvation was needed. Heb.5:5-
     10
   The supreme act of obedience to
     God was needed. Jn.10:11;
     10:17-18; 12:27-30; 14:30-31;
     15:9; 16:11; Eph.5:2
   The supreme love & sacrifice of
     God was necessary. Ro.5:2
   Why man crucified Christ.
     1 Cor.2:6-9
Response to Jesus' death. Mt.27:57-66;
   Lk.23:35-36
   Dejection of the disciples over.
     Lk.24:13-14
   Rebelled against.
     By natural man. Mk.8:32-33
     Considered repulsive by some.
       Mt.16:21-23; Jn.6:61;
       Heb.10:28-29
Results - Effects.
   Destroyed the rule & reign of sin,
     the old man & death. Ro.6:1-10
   Discussed.
     Is the theme of preaching.
       1 Cor.2:2
     What Christ's death does.
       Jn.13:31-14:3
   Fourfold result. Lk.12:49-53
   In relation to God & Himself. A
     threefold glory. Jn.13:31-32
   In relation to man.
     Brings faith and righteousness.
       Justification. 2 Pt.1:1
     Brings freedom from the law.
       Ro.7:4
     Brings joy & deliverance from
       wrath. Ro.5:8-9
     Brings redemption. (See **RE-
       DEEM - REDEMPTION**)
     Established a new covenant.
       Mk.14:23
     How His death should affect His
       disciples. Lk.5:35
     Made propitiation for sins.
       1 Jn.2:1-2
     Several results. Mt.9:15
     Should cause fasting. Mt.9:15
     Transforms a secret disciple.
       Lk.23:50-54

In relation to Satan & evil forces.
(See **JESUS CHRIST**, Work of,
Destroying Satan)
Judged & condemned Satan.
Lk.10:18; Jn.16:11
In relation to the world & history.
Brought the fire of judgment to
the world. Four ways.
Lk.12:49-53
Changed face & fate of history &
men. Jn.21:24
History revolves around **d**.
Mt.17:22-23
Proves.
That He is God, the great I AM.
Jn.8:28
That the world does not know
God's wisdom. 1 Cor.2:6-9
Purchased the church by His death.
Acts 20:28-31
Sacrifice - Sacrificial death. 1 Jn.2:1-2
Called the sacrificial Bread of God.
Jn.6:33
Cost God an unbelievable price.
Jn.3:16
Covers all things in heaven & earth.
Heb.9:12-24
Discussed. Heb.9:11-14; 9:15-22;
9:23-28; 10:1-18; 10:19-21
Seven pictures of Jesus' death.
Jn.12:20-36
Propitiation. (Atoning sacrifice)
1 Jn.2:1-2; 1 Jn.4:9-11
Substitutionary. (See **JESUS
CHRIST**, Death, Substi-
tutionary)
Verses. List of. Jn.11:49-53
Was the perfect sacrifice. Ro.5:7-7;
Heb.9:23-28; 10:1-18; 10:19-21;
1 Jn.2:2
Willingness. To die as God willed.
Jn.18:1-11
Spiritualized. By the disciples. Misun-
derstood. Mt.17:22; 18:1; Mk.9:32
Substitutionary. (See **JESUS
CHRIST**, Death. Sacrifice)
Discussed. Mk.10:45; Jn.1:29; 1 Cor.
5:7; 15:3; 2 Cor.5:14-16; Gal.1:4-5;
3:13-14; Eph.2:8-9; 5:2; Col.1:20;
1:21-22; 1 Th.5:8-10; Heb.2:9-13,
esp. 9; 2:17-18; 9:11-14; 9:15;
9:15-22; 9:23-28; 10:5-10; 1 Pt.
1:18-20; 2:21-24; 3:18; 1 Jn.3:16;
Rev.1:5-6
Gave His life as the sacrifice for
man's sins. Heb.7:27
Need to know that Jesus died for us.
Lk.22:33-37; Jn.1:29-30; 10:11;
10:17-18; 11:49-53; 18:38-40
Sufferings of.
At death. Mt.27:26-38
Bore ultimate degree of pain.
Mt.20:19; Mk.10:33
Described. Fourfold. Lk.18:32-33
Different from man's **d**. Several
ways. Mt.26:37-38
Discussed. Mt.26:37-38
Felt in Gethsemane. Mt.26:37-38
Forms of torture. Physical, mental,
spiritual. Mt.26:37-38; Mk.10:33;
Lk.22:43-44
Picture of the world's treatment of
God's Son. Mt.27:26-44
Purpose of. Sixfold. Mk.10:34
Strengthened to bear the cross.
Mt.17:1-13

Suffered every trial of man. Listed.
Lk.2:40
Suffered separation from God.
Mt.27:46-49
To be completed by the faithful be-
liever. Col.1:24
Tortured, physically beaten, ridi-
culed. Mt.26:67-68
Type of.
As the King of sinners. Jn.19:18
By the Passover Lamb. Lk.22:1;
1 Cor.5:7
By the snake raised up by Moses.
Jn.3:14-15
By the temple being destroyed &
raised up. Jn.2:18-21
By the curtain of the tabernacle &
temple. Heb.10:19-21
The conquest of death. Mt.27:52-53
Those who pierced Christ shall see
Him. Rev.1:7
Time of. 3 P.M. in the afternoon.
Mk.15:25
Triumphant. Mt.27:50
Verses.
All the verses in the N.T. given.
Mt.17:23
List of. Jn.3:16; 12:23-26; Ro.5:6-7;
5:8-9; 8:2
Vicarious. (See **JESUS CHRIST**,
Death, Substitutionary)
Victory over. Mk.16:1-20
Voluntary - Willingness. (See **JESUS
CHRIST**, Death; Sacrifice)
Discussed. 1 Pt.2:21-24
Was a passing experience. Rev.2:8
Way of God's Messiah vs. man's
messiah. Mk.8:31-32
Why He would not defend Himself.
Mk.15:2-5
Deity. (See **JESUS CHRIST**, Claims;
Names - Titles; **MESSIAH - MESSI-
AHSHIP**)
Acknowledged as Lord. Meaning.
Mt.8:5-9
Advocate - worshipped. Lk.24:50-53
Apostle of God.
Entered history. 1 Jn.1:1-5
Seen as the special representative of
God. Mt.15:31
Sent by God. Jn.3:32-34
Verses. List of. Jn.3:32-34; 3:34;
8:26-27; 14:6;15:14-15
Spoke of God Himself. Heb.12:25
Teaching, doctrine was of God.
Jn.7:16-19; 1 Cor.3:11
The Messenger of God. Jn.7:16-19
Verses. List of. Jn.3:32-34; 3:34
The Spokesman for God. Jn.3:32-
34; 8:26-27; 14:6; 14:10; 1
Cor.3:11
Verses. List of. Mk.1:22; Jn.
3:32-34; 3:34; 8:26-27;14:6;
15:14-15
The witness of God. Jn.8:14
The Word of God, the spokesman
for God. Heb.1:1
Approved of God. Proof. Acts 2:22-24
Chosen Servant, The. Mt.12:18
Christ emptied Himself. Ph.2:7; 2:8
Christ has the very nature of God.
All judgment is committed to Him.
Verses. List of. Jn.5:22-23
Embodiment of all wisdom &
knowledge. Col.2:3
Eternal. Jn.1:30-31; Heb.1:10-12

First & last. Rev.2:8
Head of all authority & power.
Col.2:9-10
Holy One. Rev.3:7
Is wrapped in the glory of God.
Mt.16:27; 17:2
Of God. (See **JESUS CHRIST**,
Nature - Origin)
Of God vs. of man. Mk.12:35-37
Omniscient. (See **JESUS CHRIST**,
Knowledge). Jn.1:47; 2:23-25
Righteousness of God. Ro.3:21-22
Sees all & knows all. Eyes like a
flame of fire. Rev.2:18
Unchangeable. Heb.1:10-12
Christ is God.
Called God. Acts 20:28-31
Called God by God the Father.
Heb.1:7-9
Coexistent with God. Jn.1:1-2;
5:17-30
Did the works of God. 1 Tim.3:16
Equal with God. Prayed to.
1 Th.3:11
God incarnated in human flesh. (See
INCARNATION) 2 Cor.5:18-19;
1 Tim.3:16
God indwelt Him. (See **IN-
DWELLING PRESENCE**)
God was in Christ. 2 Cor.5:19-20
God-Man. Jn.1:14
Verses. List of. Jn.10:30-33
Is God, that is, Elohim & Jahweh.
Jas.1:1
Is the Amen, the beginning. Rev.3:14
Is the image of God. Heb.1:3
Is the Lord. Meaning. Acts 2:36;
Ph.2:9-11
Not just a man, but God. Mt.19:17
Of God, out of heaven. Jn.3:31; 3:34
Possesses oneness with the Father.
Jn.5:17-30; 8:15-16; 14:10
Verses. List of. Jn.5:19; 8:54-59
Possesses the fullness of God.
Jn.1:16; Col.1:19; 2:9-10
Possesses the glory of God.
2 Cor.4:6
Self-existent. Jn.1:1-2; 5:26
The revelation of God. Jn.1:50;
14:6; 14:8-11
Verses. List of. Jn.14:6
The Word of God. Jn.1:1-5; 1:14;
1 Jn.1:1; 5:6-8
Christ is the King.
Discussed. Verses & fulfillment of
Davidic prophecies. Lk.3:24-31
King of Israel. Jn.1:43-45
King of kings & Lord of lords.
Rev.19:16
King of the universe. Jn.12:20-22;
19:19
Christ is the Savior & Messiah.
Discussed. Jn.4:42
False concept of. Jn.12:12-13
Messiah. Jn.1:35-42
Messianic heir: Prophet, Priest, &
King. Verses & fulfillment.
Lk.3:23-38
Prophet, Priest, & King. Rev.1:13-16
The One prophesied. Jn.1:43-45
Christ is the Son of God. Mt.1:16;
1:23; 3:16-17
Called the Son of God. Rev.2:18
Claimed to be the Son of God.
Lk.22:70

Declared to be the Son of God.
Ro.1:1-4
Discussed. Jn.1:1-2; 5:25; 2 Cor.1:19
Verses. List of. Mk.3:21; Jn.9:35-38
God's beloved Son. Mt.12:18
God's heir. Heb.1:7-9
God's only Son. Heb.1:7-9
His Person. Mt.12:17-18; Heb.1:1-3
List of references in the N.T. Jn.1:34
The Supreme High Priest, God's
Son. Heb.4:14-7:28
The Supreme revelation, God's Son.
Heb.1:1-4:13
Christ is the Son of Man.
Claimed by Christ. Lk.22:69
Discussed. Mt.8:20; 26:1-2;
Mk.2:28; Lk.9:58
Meaning. Mt.8:20
Verses. List of. Jn.1:51
Citizenship. Origin. Of heaven, God's
kingdom. Mt.17:25-26
Claims. (See **JESUS CHRIST**, Claims)
Creator. Jn.1:1; Col.1:16; Heb.1:2;
Rev.3:14
Davidic heir. (See **PROPHECY**,
Fulfilled by Christ)
Discussed. Acts 13:22-23
Demonstrated. Deity & Sovereignty.
Lk.8:22-25
Denial of deity. 2 Jn.7-13
Discussed. Mt.11:25-27; 22:41-46;
Ph.2:5-11
Eight facts. Heb.1:1-3
Fifteen or more claims to deity.
Jn.10:25
Witnesses to. 1 Jn.1:1-4
False concepts of deity.
Conqueror, Provider, Indulgent
Lord. Jn.12:12-13
Vs. true concept. Jn.12:12-19
Great confession. Who Jesus is.
Mk.8:27-30
Greater than religion. Mt.12:1-8
Has the key of David. Rev.3:7
Holy Spirit. Possessed the Spirit with-
out measure. Jn.1:32-33
Ideal, Perfect Man.
Discussed. Col.2:12; 2:20
Meaning. Mt.8:20; 26:1-2; Mk.2:28;
Lk.9:58
Pattern, The. Mt.5:17
Is the mystery of God. Col.1:26-27
Life. Possesses the energy of life.
Verses. List of. Jn.5:26
Mediator. Lk.13:24; Jn.3:17; 4:22;
10:7-8;14:6; 1 Tim.2:5; Heb.1:3; 4:4-
14; 7:25; 8:6; 9:15; 9:23-28; 12:24;
1 Jn.2:1
Verses. List of. Mk.1:15; Lk.11:31-32;
Jn.3:17;1 Cor.3:11; 10:7-8
Misunderstood.
Four misunderstandings. Jn.12:20-36
Questioned by John the Baptist.
Mt.11:1-6
Reasons truth missed. Mk.12:36-37
Unacceptable confessions.
Mt.16:13-14
Mutual indwelling. In the Father & the
Father in Him. Jn.14:10
Mutual possession. Between the Father
& Christ. Jn.17:10
New Master. Proof. Jn.3:22-36
Predicted - Foretold. Jn.13:33-36;
14:1-3; 14:4-5
Preeminence of. Jn.1:30-31; 3:29-30
Verses. List of. Mk.1:7-8; Jn.3:29-30

Priest. Verses & fulfillment. Lk.3:32-38
Proclaimed.
Before birth. Lk.1:43-44; 1:67-75
In dedication of - as a child in the
temple. Lk.2:28-33
To be Messiah as a child. Lk.2:28-33
Proofs of deity. Mk.12:6-8
By His works & signs. Jn.2:23;
5:36; 10:38; 20:30-31
Discussed. 2 Pt.1:16-21; 1 Jn.1:1-4
Foretold. Jn.8:12-20
Four proofs. Lk.5:22-26
Great proofs of His resurrection.
Lk.11:29-36
Is the Son of God. Men fail to see.
Lk.12:54-57
Lived a sinless life. 1 Jn.2:29
Nine proofs. Jn.5:17-30
Scripture. 2 Pt.1:19-21
Six proofs. Lk.11:14-28
The eyewitness account. 2 Pt.1:16-18
The resurrection. 1 Tim.3:16;
2 Tim.2:8
The signs given to Jesus & the pres-
ent generation. Mk.8:11
Three possibilities. Lk.20:1-8
Three proofs at His baptism.
Mt.3:16-17
Two choices. Jesus was of God or
of man. Mk.11:27-33
Sinless. (See **JESUS CHRIST**, Na-
ture, Sinless) Acts 3:13-15; 1 Pt.1:19
Has the Spirit of holiness. Sinless &
divine. Ro.1:1-4; 5:10-11; 8:3
Is the righteous one. 1 Jn.2:1-2
Lived a sinless & perfect life.
Jn.8:46; 2 Cor.5:21; 1 Tim.3:16;
Heb.1:9; 4:15; 7:26; 9:14;
1 Pt.1:18-20; 2:21-24
Verses. List of. Mk.1:15; Jn.7:16-
19; 2 Cor.5:21
Was perfectly obedient. Is the Ideal
& Perfect Man. Mk.1:15; Jn.6:38;
7:18; 8:47;2 Cor.5:21; Col.1:21-22;
Heb.7:25-28; 7:26
Spirit endowed fully. Mt.12:18
Superior to the angels. Heb.1:4-14
Superior to the prophets. Heb.1:1-3
Vs. false teaching. Col.2:8-23; 2:8-10;
2:11-12; 2:13-15; 2:16-19; 2:20-23
Witnesses to. 1 Jn.5:6-12
Five witnesses. Jn.5:31-39
Works. Mt.12:19-21
Denial. (See **DENY - DENIAL**)
Must not deny Christ. Rev.3:8
To guard against. 1 Jn.4:1-6; 2 Jn.7-13
Descendant. Of Abraham & of David.
Mt.1:1-2
Descent into hell. Mt.27:50; 27:52;
Eph.4:8-10; 1 Pt.3:19-20; 3:19-22
Described.
Eyes are like a flame of fire. Rev.2:18
Feet are like brass. Rev.2:18
Has a sharp two-edged sword in His
mouth. Rev.2:12
Has the key of David. Rev.3:7
Has the seven spirits of God. Rev.3:1
Has the seven stars. Rev.3:1
Holds the churches in His hands. Rev.2:1
Is the Ideal Man, the Ideal Righteous-
ness. Ro.3:31; 5:10-11; 5:10; 8:3
Was dead & is alive. Rev.2:8
Deserted. (See **APOSTASY; BACK-
SLIDING; DENY - DENIAL**)
Destined - Determined. In the fullness of
time, in due time. Ro.5:6-7

Devotion to. (See **COMMITMENT;
DEDICATION**)
Disciples of. (See **APOSTLES; DISCI-
PLES**)
Discussed. Ro.5:1
Dwelling within the believer. (See **JE-
SUS CHRIST**, Indwelling Presence;
INDWELLING PRESENCE)
Early life. (See **JESUS CHRIST**, Child-
hood)
Education. (See **JESUS CHRIST**,
Childhood)
Questioned by religionists. Jn.7:11-15
Endured - Endurance.
E. temptation. Heb.12:4
E. to the point of blood. Heb.12:4
Supreme example of endurance.
Heb.12:1-29
Exalt - Exaltation.
A heavenly, spiritual ministry.
Heb.8:1-5
A perfect appointment. Heb.7:28
All are to bow & worship. Ph.2:9-11
Described. Rev.1:9-20
Discussed. Acts 2:33-36; 2:36; Ph.
2:9-11; Heb.1:1-3; 1:4-14; 1 Pt.3:22;
Rev.1:9-20
Has an awesome appearance. Rev.1:9-
20; 5:5-14
Has entered heaven. 1 Pt.3:22
His message to the churches as the
exalted Lord. Rev.1:9-3:22
How the power of the exaltation af-
fects believers. Mt.26:64; Eph.1:20
Predicted. Jn.14:4-5; 14:6
Proof of.
Seen by John. A vision of the ex-
alted Christ. Rev.1:9-20
Seen by Paul. Acts 9:1-9, esp. 4-6
Seen by Stephen. Acts 7:55-56
Seen in the ascension. Acts 1:9-11
Prophesied by David. Acts 2:33-36
Sits on the right of the throne of God.
Heb.8:1; 12:2
To be a day of godly supremacy. De-
scribed. Lk.13:35
To rule & reign. 1 Tim.3:16
Verses. List of. Ro.8:34
Faithfulness of. To the believer. In three
areas. 2 Th.3:3-5
Fame of. Discussed. Mt.4:23-25
Family.
A humble family. Mt.13:53-58
Answer to doubting families.
Mt.12:46-50
Brothers. Mocked & disbelieved Him.
Jn.7:1-9; 7:3-5
Brothers & sisters listed. Mt.13:53-58;
13:55; Mk.6:3
Cousin to John the Baptist. Jn.1:30-31
Doubted & misunderstood Him.
Mt.12:46-47
Father, Joseph, probably died early.
Mt.13:53-58
Joseph died early. Jn.2:1-2
Mother. Mary. Submission to God's
will. Lk.1:26-38
Parents.
Were faithful in worship. Lk.2:41-42
Were poor. Lk.2:24
Poor. Mt.2:19-23
Tenderness shown to His mother,
Mary. Jn.2:3-5; 19:25-27
Were embarrassed over Jesus & His
claims. Mk.3:31-35; Lk.8:19

Life of.
Carpenter. Knew building. Mt.7:24-27
Daily activities. Mt.4:23-25
Last day on earth. Acts 1:6-11
Last week on earth. Mk.11:1-11
Ministered to by angels. 1 Tim.3:16
Picture of. Devotion--worship--
mission. Jn.8:1-2
Pivotal point of history. Mt.5:17-18
Predicted when Jesus was a child.
Lk.2:28-35
Result of. Causes many to rise & many
to fall. Lk.2:34
Typical day in the life of Jesus.
Lk.21:37-38
Living within the believer. (See **JESUS
CHRIST**, Indwelling Presence; **IN-
DWELLING PRESENCE**)
Love of.
Constrains the minister & believer to
serve Christ. 2 Cor.5:14-16
Discussed. Jn.11:33-35; 13:33-35;
15:9-11; 21:15-17
Does not condemn the believer; He
died for the believer. Ro.8:34-39
Duty.
To continue in His love. Jn.15:9-10
To understand. 1 Jn.3:16
For believers. Is a great love.
Jn.13:33-35; 15:9; 15:12; 21:15-17
For each person individually. Jn.11:5
Great lament for Jerusalem. Rejected.
Mt.23:37-39
His great love. Jn.15:9-11
Nothing separates the believer from
the love of Christ. Ro.8:34-39
Supreme demonstration of. Sacrificial
death. Eph.5:2
Loved. By God.
God's beloved Son. Verses. List of.
Jn.5:20
Reasons. Threefold. Jn.15:9
The dearest thing to God's heart.
Jn.3:16; 3:35-36; 5:20
Marriage of the Lamb.
Discussed. Mt.25:1-13; Rev.19:1-10
Feast of. God's great invitation.
Mt.22:1-14
Mediator.
Claimed by Jesus. Jn.12:44-45; 14:6
Described. In four ways. Jn.14:13-14
Discussed. Jn.1:51; 12:44-46; 14:6;
1 Tim.2:3-7; Heb.4:4-14; 8:6; 9:15;
1 Pt.2:9; Rev.3:7
Fact. A human mediator is no longer
needed. 1 Pt.2:9-10
How Christ became the Mediator. (See
JESUS CHRIST, Death)
By becoming a man & bringing us
into fellowship with God.
1 Jn.1:1-3
By becoming man's advocate.
1 Jn.2:1
By His blood. Eph.2:13;
Heb.10:19-21
By His body becoming the temple
of men. Jn.2:18-21
By His body, His death & His res-
urrection. Jn.2:18-21; 1 Tim.2:3-7
By His death. 1 Tim.2:5; Heb.9:15;
12:24-25;1 Jn.2:1-2
Meaning. Jn.12:44

Work of Christ as Mediator.
Appears in the presence of God for
us. 1 Tim.2:3-7; Heb.1:3; 7:25; 9:24
Becomes the perfect sacrifice for
sins. Heb.7:27; 10:1-18
Intercedes for the believer. Jn.14:13-
14
Makes worship possible. Jn.4:22
Provides a better covenant. Heb.8:6
Provides an eternal inheritance.
Heb.9:15
Provides justification & reconcilia-
tion with God. Ro.5:6-11, esp. 10
Provides salvation. Jn.3:17; 4:22;
10:7-8; 14:6
Verses. List of. Jn.3:17; 10:7-8
Provides the only Door to God.
Jn.10:7-8; 14:6
Provides the way to God. Jn.14:6;
Eph.2:18
Verses. List of. Mk.1:15
Message of. (See **GOSPEL**)
Differed in five ways. Mk.1:22
God is light. 1 Jn.1:5
Repent. Mt.4:17; Mk.1:14-15
The Kingdom of heaven. Mt.9:35;
Mk.1:14-15
Method.
Used the synagogue & established re-
ligion. Mk.1:39
Went everywhere. Mt.9:35
Mind of.
Discussed. Ph.2:5; 1 Pt.4:1
Meaning. 1 Pt.4:1
Minister.
Of the superior covenant. Heb.8:6-13
Of the tabernacle. Heb.8:1-5; 9:1-14
The exalted **m.** Heb.8:1-5
The supreme **m.** Heb.8:1-10:18
Ministry. (See **JESUS CHRIST**, Work of)
A day in the life of Christ. Lk.4:31-44;
21:37-38
A hoax. If He is not the Christ, He is a
deceiver. Mt.16:15-16
Age when launched. Lk.3:23
Baptized people. Jn.3:22-26
Between His baptism & John the Bap-
tist's death. Mk.1:14
Composure. Calm assurance.
Mt.26:62-63
Continues.
Presence & power are still active.
Acts 3:6-8
Seen in the Book of Acts. Acts 1:1-5
Galilee **m.** Synoptic gospels concen-
trate on. Mk.11:1-13:37
Jerusalem **m.** Only John covers in de-
tail. Mk.11:1-13:37
Last day on earth. Acts 1:6-11
Ministered all night. Mk.1:32
Overview of. Acts 1:1-5
Phases of. Judean, Galilean, traveling
m. Mk.10:1-4
Power & tenderness of. Mt.9:18-19,
23-26
Predicted. Lk.4:17-19
Prophesied. Lk.7:22
Same yesterday and today and forever.
Heb.13:8
Side-tracked. Did not allow. Lk.4:43-44
Successful. Mt.4:23-25
To Gentiles. Discussed. Mt.15:29
To purchase the church of God by His
blood. Acts 20:28-31

Misconceptions of.
Death & resurrection. Mt.17:22; 18:1;
20:20-28; 20:21
Four false concepts. Mt.16:13-14;
Jn.7:10-19
Only a good man, a deceiver, unimpor-
tant. Jn.7:11-15
Only a man. Mt.19:17; Mk.6:3;
Jn.8:19
Mission. (See **JESUS CHRIST**, Works of)
Announced & rejected. Lk.4:16-30
Came by water (baptism) and blood
(the cross). 1 Jn.5:6-8; 5:6; 5:8
Discussed. Mt.9:35-38; Lk.4:17-19;
8:1
A great mission. Lk.5:27-39
His mission is good, not divisive &
destructive. Mk.3:22-30
Misunderstood & explained.
Lk.9:51-56
The work of His mission.
Mt.12:18-21
Purpose of the Lord's mission.
One primary purpose: people.
Mt.4:15-16
Three purposes. Mt.4:15-16; 9:35-38
To baptize with the Spirit. Mk.1:7-8
To break into Satan's house.
Mk.3:27
To bring a new life & spiritual
movement. Lk.5:36-39
To bring joy. Lk.5:33-34
To bring peace & judgment to the
world. Lk.12:49-53
To call sinners, not the righteous to
repentance. Lk.5:30-32
To cast evil out of lives. Mk.3:24-26
To destroy Satan. Mk.3:26
To die. (See **JESUS CHRIST**,
Death)
To do the will of God. Jn.4:34;
5:30; 6:38-40
To do the works of God. Jn.5:17;
9:4
To give light to man. Jn.1:4-5; 1:9
To minister & give His life as a ran-
som. Mt.20:28
To open the eyes of man. Jn.9:1-7
To preach. Mt.4:17; 4:23; Mk.1:36-
38; 1:39; Lk.8:1
To reach out & evangelize. Lk.8:1
To save from sins. Mt.1:21
To save life. Lk.9:55-56
To save man. 1 Tim.1:15-16
To save, not to condemn. Lk.13:34
To secure salvation. Lk.9:51
To seek & save the lost. Jn.1:38-39;
1:43-44
To usher in a new age & life &
covenant. Mt.9:14-17
Urgency of. Jn.9:4
Mother. Mary. Chosen. Submission to
God's will. Lk.1:26-38
Multitudes follow. Thousands. Lk.12:1
Mystery of Christ. Discussed. Eph.3:1-13
Name. Power of Jesus' name. Acts 3:6
Names - Titles.
Advocate, or Defender - stirs to worship.
Lk.24:52-53; 1 Jn.2:1-2
Almighty, The. Rev.1:8
Alpha & Omega, the beginning & the
end. Rev.1:8; 21:6; 22:12-13
Amen, The. Rev.3:14
Apostle of God. Jn.3:32-34; 3:34;
Heb.3:1
Author of eternal salvation. Heb.5:9

Author of Life. Acts3:15
Author of our faith. Heb.12:2
Beloved Son. Mt.3:17
Bread of God. Jn.6:32
Bread of Life. Jn.6:33-34; 6:35; 6:47-51
Bread, The true. Jn.6:35
Bridegroom. Mt.9:15; 25:1-13;
  Jn.3:29-30
Bridge builder. Heb.3:1
Bright & morning star. Rev.22:16
Builder of the house. Heb.3:3-4
Chief Cornerstone, Capstone.
  Eph.2:20; 1 Pt.2:5-8
Chief Shepherd. 1 Pt.5:4
Chosen Servant of God. Mt.12:18
Christ Jesus our hope. 1 Tim.1:1
Christ - Messiah. Mt.1:18; 16:13-16,
  20; Mk.1:1; Acts 2:30; 4:26; 9:20, 22
Christ, the Son of the Living God.
  Mt.16:15-16; Mk.8:29; Jn.6:69;
  1 Jn.5:1
Communicator, The great. Jn.14:6
Eternal. Jn.1:1-2
Faithful witness. Rev.1:5-6
First & last. Rev.2:8
Firstborn. Rev.1:5-6
Foundation Rock. True vs. false dis-
  cipleship. Lk.6:46-49
Foundation Stone. 1 Pt.2:5-8
Gate of the Sheep. Jn.10:7-10
God Himself. Mt.22:41-46; Jn.10:30-33;
  Acts 20:28-31
God's Apostle. Jn.3:32-34; 3:34
God's Beloved. Mt.12:18
God's servant. Mt.12:17-21; Acts
  3:12-13
God's Son, Jesus. Acts 3:13, 26
Good Shepherd. Jn.10:11-21
Great shepherd of the sheep. Heb.13:20
Head cornerstone. Mt.21:42; 21:44
Head of the church. Eph.1:22-23;
  Col.1:18
High Priest. Jn.19:23-24; Heb.2:17-18;
  3:1; 6:19-20
Highest. Lk.1:76
Holy Child, Jesus. Acts 4:27, 30
Holy One of God. Mk.1:24; Acts
  2:27; 3:14
Horn of Salvation. Lk.1:69
I AM. Mt.14:27; Mk.14:62; Jn.1:1-2;
  4:26; 6:20
Ideal man, The. Jn.5:27
Image of God. 2 Cor.4:4
Immanuel. God with us. Meaning.
  Mt.1:23
Intercessor. Lk.22:32; Heb.3:1
Jesus. Mt.1:21; Mk.1:1; Lk.1:31;
  2:21; Acts 2:32; 5:30
Jesus Christ. Acts 3:20; 9:34; 10:36
Jesus of Nazareth. Jn.1:45; Acts 2:22;
  10:38
Judge. Acts 10:42
Just, The. Acts 3:14
King. Mk.11:1-7; Lk.19:29-40
King of Israel. Jn.1:49; 12:20-22;
  18:37
King of kings & Lord of lords.
  Rev.17:14; 19:16
King of the Jews. Mk.15:2-5
Lamb of God. Mt.26:17-30; Jn.1:29-34;
  Rev.5:6-7
Liberator
  The great. Jn.14:6
  Vs. Deliverer. Lk.22:19-20
Life, The. Jn.1:4-5; 1:4; 14:6; 1 Jn.1:2

Light.
  Function. Tenfold. Jn.1:9
  Of life. Jn.8:1-9:41
  Of man. Jn.1:9-13
  Of the world. Jn.3:19-21; 8:12;
    12:35-36; 12:46
Lion of Judah. Rev.5:5
Living Stone. 1 Pt.2:5-8
Living water. Jn.7:37-39; cp. 4:10-14
Lord. Lk.1:43-44; Jn.13:13-14; Acts
  2:36
Lord & Christ. Acts 2:36
Lord Jesus. Acts 19:5
Lord Jesus Christ. Acts 16:31; 20:21
Lord of all. Acts 10:36
Master. Mt.8:19; Lk.17:11-14;
  Jn.11:28; 13:13-14
Mediator. 1 Tim.2:5; Heb.8:6; 9:15;
  12:24
Messiah. (See **MESSIAH - MESSI-
  AHSHIP**)
  Meaning. Jn.1:20
    The witness of Andrew. Jn.1:35-42
  Named before birth. Lk.1:31-33
New Master. Jn.3:22-36
One prophesied. Jn.1:45
One who is, was, & is to come.
  Rev.1:4; 1:8
One who died & came to life. Rev.2:8
One with double sword in His mouth.
  Rev.2:12
Overseer. 1 Pt.2:25
Perfecter of our faith. Heb.12:2
Pioneer, The. Heb.2:10
Prince of the kings of the earth.
  Rev.1:5-6
Prophet of the Most High. Lk.1:76
Propitiation, atoning sacrifice for sin,
  The. 1 Jn.2:2; 4:10, 12-13
Resurrection and life. Jn.11:25-27
Revelation of God. Jn.14:6; 1 Jn.1:2
Righteous One, The. 1 Jn.2:1
Rising sun. Lk.1:78
Rock that makes them fall. Ro.9:32-33
Root & offspring of David. Rev.5:5;
  22:16
Ruler. Acts 5:31
Ruler of God's creation. Rev.3:14
Savior. Lk.2:11; Acts 5:31
Savior of the world. 1 Jn.4:14
Seed of Abraham. Gal.3:16, cp. 3:6-9
Shepherd. 1 Pt.2:25
Shepherd of the Sheep. Jn.10:1-6;
  10:11-21
Son of Adam. Lk.3:32-38
Son of David.
  Discussed. Lk.1:31-33; 1:32-33;
    18:38
  Meaning. Mt.1:1; 1:18; 3:11; 11:1-6;
    15:22
  Prophecies & fulfillment. Lk.3:24-31
Son of God. Mt.1:16; 1:23; 3:17; 14:33;
  Mk.1:1; Lk.1:35; Acts 9:20;
  2 Cor.1:19; Heb.4:14; 1 Jn.5:5; 5:9-13;
  Rev.2:18
  List of N.T. references. Jn.1:34;
    5:25
Son of Man. (See **JESUS CHRIST**,
  Deity, Son of Man)
  List of references in John. Jn.5:27
  Meaning. Mt.8:20; 26:1-2; Mk.2:28;
    Lk.9:58
Son of the Most High. Lk.1:32
Spokesman, God's. Jn.3:32-34; 3:34

Stone. Mt.21:44; Mk.12:10-11;
  Lk.20:17-18; Acts 4:10-12
Stumbling stone. Ro.9:32-33
Suffering Servant of God. Lk.22:33-37
Teacher. Jn.3:2
True Vine. Jn.15:1
Truth, The. Jn.14:6; 2 Jn.1-2
Way to God. Jn.14:6
Who men said He was. Mt.16:14
Word of Life, The. Jn.1:1-5; 1:14;
  1 Jn.1:1; 5:7
Nature - Origin. (See **JESUS CHRIST**,
  Deity)
  Discussed. Divine & human nature.
    Ro.1:1-4
  Nature as God.
    All knowing (omniscient). (See **JE-
      SUS CHRIST**, Knowledge of)
    All powerful (omnipotent). (See
      JESUS CHRIST, Power of)
    Equal with God. Jn.5:17-30
    Eternal. Preexistent, coexistent,
      self-existent. Jn.1:1-2; 1:30-31
    Ever present (omnipresent). Mt.18:20
    Full embodiment of God. Jn.14:8-14
    Fullness of God. Col.1:19
    God Himself. Jn.1:1-2; 10:33;
      14:8-14
    Holy - the Son of God. Lk.1:34-35
    Image of God. Heb.1:3
    Immortal, King of kings & Lord of
      lords. 1 Tim.6:13-16
    Immutable. (See **JESUS CHRIST**,
      Nature, Unchangeable)
    Is God. Ph.2:5-12
    Is God's righteousness. Ro.10:4
    Miraculous - of the Holy Spirit.
      Mt.1:18; cp. 1:16; 1:23
    Not a lifeless rock, but a "living
      stone." Mt.7:24-25
    Omnipotent--all powerful. (See **JE-
      SUS CHRIST**, Power)
    Omnipresent - ever present.
      Mt.18:20; 28:20; Heb.13:5
    Omniscience--all intelligent. (See
      JESUS CHRIST, Knowledge -
      Omniscience)
    One with God the Father. Jn.5:17-30;
      5:19; 10:30-33; 14:10
    Preexistent. 1 Jn.1:1-4
      As God. Jn.1:1; 1:30-31
      Dwelt in the glory & fullness of
        God. 2 Cor.8:9
    Righteousness. Is the righteousness
      of God. Ro.3:21-22; 10:4; 1
      Cor.1:30; 2 Cor.5:21; Gal.2:16;
      2:19-23; Ph.3:9
    Son of God. Jn.1:34; 5:25; 10:34-36
    Spirit of holiness. Sinless, divine.
      Ro.1:1-4
    Unchangeable. Heb.7:24-25; 13:8
  Nature as Man.
    Approachable. Mt.18:2; 18:3
    Approved of God. Meaning. Acts
      2:22-24
    Gentle. Mt.11:29
    Innocent. Mt.27:4
    Possessed the energy of life. Jn.1:4;
      5:26; 14:6; 17:3
    Possessed the full measure of the
      Spirit. Jn.3:34; 5:32
    Righteous. 1 Jn.2:29

To cleanse the most defiled.
Mt.8:1-4
To free men from evil spirits.
Lk.8:26-39; 9:1; 9:42-43
To heal. (See **HEALS - HEAL-
ING**) Mk.5:25-34
Power to preach & minister.
Promised to disciples. Mt.28:19-20
To preach. Lk.4:31-32, 43-44
Power to save & give life to man.
Creative power. To meet man's
need for regeneration. Jn.2:1-11
To change lives. Mk.2:18-22
To give life. Jn.5:21
To save men. Mt.8:28-34
To usher in a new age, life,
covenant. Mt.9:14-17
Response to.
Scorned. Mt.9:23-26
Sought & trusted. Steps to being
made whole. Mt.14:34-36
Power over nature & life.
Over God's house, the temple.
Jn.2:12-22
Over nature, a storm. Lk.8:22-25
Conquering fear. Mt.8:23-27;
Jn.6:20
Five wise lessons. Mk.6:45-52
Rest & peace. Mk.4:35-41
The power of His presence.
Mt.14:22-33
Over the physical universe.
Fig tree destroyed. The source of
power. Mt.21:17-22
Storm calmed. The power of Je-
sus' presence. Mt.14:22-33
Praise of. By children. Proclaimed His
Messiahship. Mt.21:15-16
Prayer life.
Discussed. Mk.1:35-39; Lk.11:1
High Priestly prayer. Jn.17:1-28
Model prayer. Mt.6:9-13; Lk.11:2-4
Reasons for prayer. Lk.9:28-36
Teaches how to pray. Lk.11:1-13
When Jesus prayed. Lk.6:12
Who & what He prayed for.
Before the call of the disciples.
Lk.6:12
For future believers. Jn.17:20-26
For Himself. Jn.17:1-8
For Himself. Sought to be re-
strengthened. Lk.4:42
For His disciples. Jn.17:9-19
For strength. Persevered in. Gethse-
mane. Mt.26:36-46; Mk.14:32-42
Got alone with God after preaching.
Mk.6:46
The quickening of the disciples.
Lk.9:18
Withdrew to pray. Lk.5:16
Preexistence. (See **DEITY**, Preexistence)
As God. Jn.1:1; 1:30-31
Dwelt in the glory & fullness of God.
2 Cor.8:9
Presence. (See **INDWELLING PRES-
ENCE**)
Calms fear. Mk.6:49
Instilled sense of God's presence.
Mt.9:15
Power of. Mt.14:22-33
Priesthood. (See **JESUS CHRIST**, Exal-
tation; Intercessor; Mediator)
Ct. man's **p**. Heb.5:1-10; 7:11-24; 8:1-5

Described as.
The eternal High Priest. Heb.7:11-24
The exalted High Priest. Heb.8:1-5
The great High Priest. Heb.4:14-5:10
The great sacrificial work of Christ.
Heb.9:15-22; 9:23-28
The greater. Heb.7:1-24
The High Priest after order of
Melchisedek. Heb.6:18-20; 7:1-24
The mediator of the superior cove-
nant. Heb.9:15-22; 9:23-28
The minister of a superior covenant.
Heb.8:6-13; 9:15-22; 9:23-28
The minister of the tabernacle.
Heb.9:1-14
The perfect High Priest. Heb.7:25-28
The supreme author of faith.
Heb.10:19-21
The supreme example of endurance.
Heb.12:1-29
The supreme High Priest. Heb.4:14-
8:5
The supreme minister. Heb.8:1-9:28
The supreme sacrifice. Heb.10:1-18
Discussed. Heb.2:17-18; 3:1; 4:14-16;
5:1-10
How Christ changed the **p**. Heb.7:1-24
Is a heavenly, spiritual **p**. Heb.8:1-5
Predicted. Heb.5:5-10
Priestly office. Transferred to Christ.
Mt.17:3
Prophecies of. To be High Priest. Verses
& their fulfillment. Lk.3:32-38
Purpose for.
Fourfold Purpose. Heb.2:17-18
Reconciliation. Heb.2:14-18
To bring about a changed Priest-
hood. Heb.7:11-24
To offer up the perfect sacrificial
blood. Heb.10:19-21
To provide a perfect salvation.
Heb.7:25-28
To secure supremacy for man.
Heb.2:9-13
To secure the right to receive tithes.
Heb.7:4-10
To suffer bitterly to become High
Priest. Heb.5:5-10
Verses & their fulfillment. Lk.3:32-38
Qualifications for the heavenly priest-
hood. Met by Christ. Heb.8:1-5
Prophecies concerning. (See **PROPH-
ECY**, Concerning Christ)
Prophecies fulfilled by. (See **PROPH-
ECY**, Fulfilled by Christ)
Prophet - Prophetic office.
Prophet of the Highest. Lk.1:76
Prophet, Priest, & King. Rev.1:13-16
Verses of prophecy & their fulfill-
ment. Lk.3:32-38
Transferred to Christ. Mt.17:3
Purpose. (See Related Subjects)
Christ's purpose in relation to God.
Sent by God. Jn.3:32-34
Supreme **p**. To glorify God.
Jn.12:27-30
To be the Apostle, the Spokesman
for God. Jn.3:32-34
To be the Revelation of God.
Jn.1:1; 14:6; 14:8-14
To declare God. Jn.1:18
To do & to fulfill God's will.
Jn.6:38
To do God's will at any cost.
Mk.14:33-34; 14:41-42
To glorify God. Jn.8:48-50

Christ's purpose in relation to His
death, resurrection, & exaltation.
Set to go to Jerusalem. To die.
Lk.9:51; 19:28
To die and arise. Mk.10:34
To die on the cross. The supreme
act of obedience. Jn.12:27-30
To die. Willingness to die.
Mt.26:53-54
To rule on David's throne. Acts
2:29-36
Christ's purpose in relation to man's
salvation & life.
Misunderstood. Jn.12:27-30
Not to sanction the world & its sin.
Mt.10:34-37
To be a Prince & a Savior. Acts
5:30-32
To bear the infirmities & sicknesses
& sins. Meaning. Mt.8:16-17
To become the Ideal Man & to se-
cure righteousness for man.
Ro.3:31; 8:3
To bring division between family
members. Lk.12:49-53
To bring fire & division to the
earth. Lk.12:49-53
To bring joy & new life. Lk.5:33-34;
Ro.5:10-11
To bring peace. Mk.11:1-7
To bring security. Jn.17:11
To cause division. Mt.10:34-37
To come to earth in a body in order
to carry out the will of God for
man. Heb.10:5-10
To deliver man from condemnation
& death & to give him everlasting
life. Jn.3:16; 5:24
To deliver man from this present
evil world. Gal.1:4
To execute judgment. Jn.5:27
To free the believer from the law.
Ro.7:4
To fulfill all righteousness.
Mt.3:15; 5:17-18; Ro.8:3
To give fellowship with God. 1 Jn.1:3
To give life abundantly. Jn.5:26,
40; 6:37-40; 7:37-39; 10:10
To give light to men in darkness.
Lk.1:76-79
To give repentance & forgiveness.
Acts 5:30-32
To heal the bruised, not to condemn
them. Mt.12:20
To keep man from dying & perish-
ing. Jn.3:16-17; 6:47-51
To make it possible for Him to have
many brothers. Ro.8:39
To make it possible for men to live
righteously. Lk.1:68-75
To minister & to give His life as a
ransom for many. Mt.20:28
To preach. Lk.4:43-44; 8:1; 24:47
To reconcile man to God.
2 Cor.5:19-21
To redeem man. Discussed.
2 Cor.5:21
To restore man to his exalted state.
Heb.2:5-13
To reveal God to man. Jn.14:6-11
To reveal God's love toward man
through His death. Ro.5:8;
1 Pt.2:24; 3:18
To save lives. Lk.9:56
To save, not to judge the world.
Jn.3:17; 12:47

To secure supremacy for man.
Heb.2:5-13

To seek & save the lost. Mt.18:11-14;
Lk.19:7-8; 19:9-10

To send a sword, not peace on
earth. Mt.10:34-37

To serve others - sacrificially.
Jn.13:1-17

To teach. Lk.4:31-32

Twofold. Mt.11:4-6

Christ's purpose in relation to Satan &
his works.

To destroy Satan. (See **JESUS
CHRIST**, Work of, Destroying
Satan) Mt.12:25-26; 12:29;
Lk.9:1; 9:42-43; 10:18; 11:21-22;
Col.2:15; Heb.2:14-15; 1 Jn.3:8

Discussed. Before His birth. Lk.1:67-75

Stated. Verses. Lk.1:1

Questioned. (See **JESUS CHRIST**, Accused; Challenged)

Raises dead. (See **HEAL - HEALING**)

Redeemer. (See **REDEEM - REDEMP-
TION**)

Rejected.

Scornfully neglected. Heb.10:28-29

Trampling Christ under foot.
Heb.10:28-29

Relationship.

To believers.

Knows believers--intimately.
Jn.10:14-16; 15:9-11

Very special. Jn.15:9-11

To God. Intimate knowledge.
Jn.10:14-16

To people of the world. Jn.15:1-8

Discussed. Jn.15:1-8

God's case against all men. Ro.3:9-20

God's case against the indulgent.
1 Cor.6:12-20

God's case against the moralist.
Ro.2:1-16

God's case against the religionist.
Ro.2:17-29

God's case against the ungodly &
unrighteous. Ro.1:18-32

God's case against the unrighteous
character. 1 Cor.6:9-11

Life before conversion. Eph.2:1-3

Natural man vs. the spiritual man.
1 Cor.2:14-3:4

Separated from God. Eph.2:11-12

Response to.

By individuals - Groups.

By a city: callously rejected.
Mk.5:14-17

By authorities. Rejection & opposition. Jn.7:32-36; 12:19

By His brothers. Rejected. Jn.7:1-9

By His family. Embarrassed by
Him. Mk.3:31

By His friends. Thought insane &
mad. Seven reasons. Mk.3:21

By His hometown. Why Jesus was
rejected. Mk.6:1-6

By Israel. Reacting instead of re-
penting. Mk.12:12

By leaders. Holding the wrong view
of the Messiah.   Mt.12:24;
Mk.12:12

By people. Hoped that He was the
Messiah. Mt.12:22-24; Jn.7:20-
31; 12:17-18

By pilgrims. Thought He was demon-
possessed & insane. Jn.7:20-24

By religionists. (See **RELIGION-
ISTS**, Opposed Christ) Mt.12:22-24

Sought to kill. Mk.3:6; 11:18;
14:1-2

By sinners. Felt comfortable with.
Mt.9:10-11

By the demon-possessed & insane:
questioning, unbelief. Jn.7:20-31

By the Jews and the people.
Jn.7:10-19

By the witnesses of Lazarus' resurrection. Witnessed His works.
Jn.12:17

Crowds followed.

Crowded Him. Mk.3:7-10

Thousands. Lk.8:4

Herod's response. A guilty conscience. Mk.6:16-23

Many thousands followed. Innu-
merable. Lk.12:1

Three responses. Jn.6:66-71

Discussed. Four specific responses to
Him. Jn.12:1-11

Mistreating Christ.

Mockery, ridicule, unbelief. Answer
to. Jn.7:6-9

Murmuring against His claims.
Jn.6:41-43

Misunderstanding Christ.

Ashamed of. Lk.9:26

Divided opinions. Jn.7:37-53

Fear. Questioning who He is.
Mk.4:41

Four false concepts. Jn.7:10-19

Mere man - merely a good man.
Jn.7:20-24; 7:25-31

Not to fall away because of C.
Lk.7:23

Offended by Him. Four reasons.
Jn.6:59-71

Unimportant. Counted as. Lk.23:8-12

Rejected - rejection. Mt.8:34; 13:53-58;
Jn.1:10-11; 5:40-47; 6:36, 64-66

Angered, filled with madness
against Christ. Lk.6:11

By all men. Every man guilty. Acts
3:13-15

By the citizens of the world.
Lk.19:14

By His hometown, Nazareth. Tried
to kill Him. Mt.13:53-58;
Lk.4:16-30

By religionists. (See **RELIGION-
ISTS**, Opposed Christ)

Sought to kill Him. Lk.19:47-48;
22:1-2

By the world. Tragic. Reasons.
Jn.1:10-11

Denied. 1 Jn.2:18-23

Five facts. Lk.20:13-15

Lordship rejected. Mt.12:14-16

Nothing to do with. Jn.7:32-36

Reasons.

He is a threat to doing as one
wishes. Jn.7:32

Obstinate unbelief. Mt.12:24;
12:31-32; 13:13-15; Jn.11:47-57

Unbelief & opposition. Jn.11:54

Rejected as King. Jn.12:37-50

Rejected His claim to be equal with
God. Jn.14:9

Scornfully rejected. Heb.10:28-29

Tragic rejection. Lk.13:31-35

Trampling Christ under foot.
Heb.10:28-29

Seeking - receiving Christ

Accepted. Jn.1:12-13; 1:35-51

Believed on. Jn.10:42; 11:45;
12:11

All men sought Him. Mk.1:37, 45

Amazed - astonished - glorified
God. Mk.1:21-22, 27-28; 2:12;
7:36-37; Lk.4:31-32, 36; 5:26;
7:16-17; 9:43; 17:18; 18:43

Begged to stay. Lk.4:42-43

By crowd. Amazed - astonished.
Followed and crowded Him.
Mt.4:25

Glorified God. Mt.7:28-29; 9:8, 33

Questioned who He was.
Mk.1:27-28

Received by one family in particular. Jn.11:1-3

Receiving. (See **SALVATION**)

Results of. Jn.6:52-58

Sought after. For help. Jn.12:17-18

Spread His fame. Mk.1:28, 45;
7:36-37

Why Jesus disturbs people. Mt.2:3

Resurrection.

All verses in N.T. given. Mt.17:23

Appearances to.

Chosen witnesses. Reasons. Acts
10:40-41

Disciples. Mt.28:16-20; Mk.16:14;
Jn.20:19-23; 20:24-29

Great Statements of Christian
faith. Lk.24:36-49

Five appearances. 1 Cor.15:5-10

Five hundred people at one time.
1 Cor.15:6

Last appearance. The ascension.
Lk.24:50-53

Official appearance was to be in
Galilee. Mt.26:32

Peter. Lk.24:34

Some women. Mt.28:9

Ten appearances mentioned. Acts
1:3

Two on the road to Emmaus.
Lk.24:13-35

Denying Christ's resurrection. Consequences. 1 Cor.15:12-19

Described. As a lamp. Lk.11:33-36

Discussed 1 Cor.15:4

Was the subject of early preaching.
Acts 2:25-36; 3:15, 26; 10:40-41

With His death. Does three things.
Mt.20:19

Doctrines of. Listed. Jn.21:24

Essential.

Belief in the resurrection is essential
for salvation. Ro.10:8-10

Necessity of. Christ had to be resurrected to complete salvation.
Lk.13:31-33

To focus upon the Father, not
heaven. Jn.14:6

To remember the resurrection of
Christ. 2 Tim.2:8-13

Events of. (See **JESUS CHRIST**,
Resurrection, Appearances to)

Angels appeared. Mk.16:5-6;
Lk.24:4-8; Jn.20:11-18

Appearance to Mary Magdalene.
Mk.16:9; Jn.20:11-18

Appearance to the disciples.
Jn.20:19-23; 20:24-29

Appearance to two disciples.
Mk.16:12

Body missing. Lk.24:3

State of the world when Christ returns.
People will either be ashamed or confident at His return. 1 Jn.2:28
People will mourn. Mt.24:30
When Christ returns, the world will be as Noah's day. Mt.24:37-39; Lk.17:26-30
When & how Christ is coming.
After two events. 2 Th.2:3
Believers will know & not be caught off guard. Mt.24:37
Can be generally discerned. Mk.13:28-29
Within one generation. Mt.24:32-35; Lk.21:32
Discussed. Mt.24:32-41; Mk.13:24-27; Lk.17:20-37; 1 Cor.15:51-52;1 Th.4:13-5:3; 2 Pt.3:3-14
Four things about Christ's return. Mt.24:25-28
How coming. Four facts. Sudden, unexpected, shattering. Mt.24:37-39
Known only to God. The hour & day. Mt.24:36
Two returns for believers. At death & at Christ's return. Jn.14:1-3
Unknown. Mk.13:30
Why Christ has not returned. Mt.25:5; 2 Pt.3:8-10; 3:15-16
World's attitude toward.
Disbelief in. 2 Pt.3:1-7
First thing to know: scoffers shall come. 2 Pt.3:1-7
Unprepared. Missed first coming; shall miss second coming. Lk.2:7
Results. The righteous judgment of God. 2 Th.1:6-12
Revelation - revealed. (See **REVELATION**)
Christ is revealed as.
God's great love. Jn.3:16-17
The answer to man's great hunger. Jn.6:22-29
The Assurance & Security of believers. Jn.6:37-40
The Authority over life. Jn.5:1-47
The Authority over the Sabbath. Jn.5:1-16
The Bread of Life. Jn.6:1-71
The Coming King. Jn.12:12-50
The Creative Power of the universe. To regenerate man. Jn.2:1-11
The Deliverer from fear. Jn.6:16-21
The Embodiment of God. Jn.14:8-14
The Gate. Jn.10:7, 9
The Glorified Son of Man. Jn.12:12-50
The Great Intercessor. Jn.17:1-26
The Great Minister. Jn.13:1-16:33
The Light of Life. Jn.3:19-21; 8:1-9:45; 12:35-36
The Living Water. Jn.4:1-14
The Mediator. Jn.14:4-7
The New Master. Jn.3:22-36
The Object of Faith. Jn.4:43-54
The only One who can reveal heaven & truth. Jn.3:31
The Only Way to God. Jn.14:4-7
The preeminent Christ. Col.1:12-23
The Provision for human needs. Jn.6:1-15
The Resurrection & Life. Jn.11:1-12:11
The Shepherd of Life. Jn.10:1-42
The Son of God. Jn.2:1-3:21

The Source of Spiritual Satisfaction. Jn.6:30-36
The Suffering Savior. Jn.18:1-19:42
The Supreme One over God's house. Jn.2:12-22
The Supreme Revelation of God. Jn.1:1, 10; 14:6-7
The Word. Jn.1:1-5; 1:14; 1 Jn.1:1; 5:7
Christ revealed.
God.
Discussed. Jn.1:50; Heb.1:1-3; 1 Jn.1:1-3
Has not left man in the dark, groping & grasping. Jn.14:6; 14:6-7
Man's condemnation. Jn.3:18-21
Christ was revealed. To John the Baptist. Sign given by God. Jn.1:32-34
Reactions to.
Four reactions. Jn.12:1-11
Tragedy of. Supreme tragedy. Jn.1:10-11
Witnesses to. Jn.1:1-51
Savior. (See **JESUS CHRIST**, Claims; Deity; **SALVATION; SAVIOR**)
False concept of. Jn.12:12-13
Seed of.
Abraham. Never seen by Jews. Lk.19:9-10; Jn.1:23; 4:22; Ro.4:1-25; Gal.3:7-8, 16, 19, 29, cp. 3:6-29
Adam. Never seen by Jews. Jn.1:23
Seek - seeking. (See **SEEK - SEEKING**)
Sent by God. (See **JESUS CHRIST**, Deity). Jn.3:32-34; 3:34; 4:31-35; 8:42
Shepherd.
Contrasted with false shepherds. Jn.10:16
Discussed. Jn.10:22-42; 1 Pt.2:25
Great claims of. Jn.10:22-42
Is the door of the sheep. Jn.10:7-10
The Shepherd of life. Jn.10:1-42
The Spokesman for God. Jn.14:10
The title of Christ. Four titles. 1 Pt.5:4
Work of. 1 Pt.5:4
Sinless - Perfectly obedient. Jn.6:38; 7:18; 8:45-47; 2 Cor.5:21;Heb.7:25-28; 7:26
Discussed. 1 Pt.2:21-24
Nothing in Him for Satan. Jn.14:30-31
Son of God. (See **JESUS CHRIST**, Claims; Deity)
Son of Man. (See **JESUS CHRIST**, Claims; Deity)
The Ideal Man. Ro.3:31; 5:10-11; 8:3; Col.1:21-22;1 Tim.2:3-7
Verses. List of. Ro.1:1-4
Verses. List of. Jn.7:16-19
Without blemish & spot. 1 Pt.1:19
Sovereignty. (See **JESUS CHRIST**, Deity)
Stone. (See **JESUS CHRIST**, Names - Titles)Lk.20:17-18
Suffering of. (See **JESUS CHRIST**, Death, Sufferings of) Mk.14:33-34
Supremacy - Superior. (See **JESUS CHRIST**, Names - Titles)
Beloved Son of God. Jn.3:16; 5:20
Creator & Sustainer of the universe. Col.1:16-17; Heb.1:3
Eternal God who entered history. 1 Jn.1:1-3
Eternal High Priest. Heb.7:11-24
Exalted Minister. Heb.8:1-5

Great God & Savior. Tit.2:12-13
Great Power. Rev.11:16-17
Great Ruler. Lk.1:32-33
Great Shepherd of the sheep. Heb.13:20-21
Greater than Abraham. Jn.8:53-59
Greater than Jacob. Jn.4:12-14
Greater than John the Baptist. Mt.11:11; Lk.7:28; Jn.5:36
Greater than Jonah. Mt.12:41
Greater than religion. Mt.12:1-8
Greater than Solomon. Mt.12:42
Head of all principality & power. Col.2:9-10
Ideal, Perfect Man - Son of Man.
Discussed. Mt.8:20; 26:1-2; Mk.2:28; Lk.9:58;Col.2:12; 2:20
Meaning. Mt.8:20; 26:1-2; Mk.2:28; Lk.9:58
Pattern, The. Mt.5:17
King of kings & Lord of lords. Rev.19:16
Minister of a superior covenant. Heb.8:6-13
Only Door to God. Jn.10:7-8; 14:6
Only Mediator. (See **JESUS CHRIST**, Mediator) 1 Tim.2:3-7
Superior to Moses. Heb.3:1-6
Superior to the angels. Heb.1:4-14
Superior to the law. (See **LAW**) Mt.5:17; Ro.8:3
Superior to the prophets. Heb.1:1-3
Supreme Author of faith. Heb.10:19-21
Supreme Example of endurance. Heb.12:1-29
Supreme High Priest, God's Son. Heb.4:14-8:5
Supreme Minister. Heb.8:1-10:18
Supreme Revelation, God's Son. Heb.1:1-4:13
Supreme Sacrifice. Heb.10:1-18
Teaching.
Authority of. Meaning. Mt.7:29
By parables. Why He used parables. Mk.4:33-34
Differed from man's teaching in five ways. Mk.1:22
Discussed. Four facts. Lk.21:37
Effect. Astonished & amazed. Mt.7:28-29
Fact.
Authority of. Taught with authority. Meaning. Mk.1:22; Lk.4:31
Launched a new ministry. Mk.1:21-22
Method. Mt.9:35
Was God's teaching. Jn.7:16-17; 1 Cor.3:11
Was the Messenger of God. Jn.3:32-34; 3:34; 7:16-19; 8:26-27
Was the Word, the Spokesman for God. Jn.1:1-2; 8:26-27; 14:10; Heb.1:1
Temple of Jesus' body. Becomes temple of men. Jn.2:18-21
Temptation of. (See **TEMPTATION**)
Conquering--victory over. Lk.4:1-15
Dealing with temptation. Mk.1:12-13
Discussed. Mt.4:1-11
Tomb of. Discussed. Mt.27:65-66
Training of the disciples. (See **DISCIPLES**, Training of)
Transfiguration.
A glimpse of heaven's glory. Mk.9:2-13
Approved for the cross. Mt.17:1-13
Events of. Lk.9:28-36

Trials, Legal.
  Accusers. False witnesses. Mt.26:60-61
  Before Caiaphas. Mt.26:57-68;
    Jn.18:19-24
  Before Herod. Lk.23:8-12
  Before Pilate.
    Indecisive compromise. Jn.18:28-19:15
    Picture of a morally weak man.
      Mk.15:1-15
    Second trial. A compromising man.
      Lk.23:13-25
    Tragedy of an indecisive man.
      Mt.27:11-25
  Before Pilate & Herod. Shirking of
    duty & concern. Lk.23:1-12
  Before the Gentiles. Jn.18:28-19:15
  Before the Sanhedrin, the Jewish
    court.
    A picture of wrong repentance &
      human religion. Condemned to die
      by the Sanhedrin. Mt.26:57-68;
      27:1-10
    Six trials. Lk.22:66
    The claims of Jesus. Lk.22:54;
      22:63-71
    Three charges against Christ. Lk.23:2
    Weak & strong character.
      Mk.14:53-65
  Behavior.
    Composure. Calm assurance.
      Mt.26:62-63
    Strong, controlled, impressive.
      Mt.27:11-14
  Charges against.
    Blasphemy. Mt.26:65-66
    Revolutionary. Mt.26:60-61;
      Mk.14:55-59
    Three charges against. Jn.2:18;
      18:19
  Life threatened time after time.
    Mt.2:12-23
  Physically beaten & ridiculed.
    Mt.26:67-68
Trials - Tribulations. (See **JESUS
CHRIST**, Condescension; Death; Fam-
ily; Finances of; Sufferings; Tempta-
tions of; Related Subjects)
  Great composure under trials. Calm
    assurance. Mt.26:62-63
Triumph - Victory of. (See **JESUS
CHRIST**, Exaltation; Resurrection;
Return)
  In the end time. Assured. Rev.14:1-20;
    19:1-10; 19:11-20:15;21:1-22:5
Triumphal Entry.
  A dramatic warning. Mk.11:1-11
  Christ's claim to be King. Lk.19:28-40
  Demonstrates Jesus' Messiahship.
    Mt.21:1-11; 21:12-16; 21:17-22
  Proclaimed as King & Messiah.
    Jn.12:12-19
Versus.
  Evil spirits. Col.2:15
  False philosophy & astrology. Col.2:8
  False religion. Col.2:11-12
  False teaching. Col.2:8-23
  Rules & ritualism. Col.2:16-17
  Satan. (See **JESUS CHRIST**, Death;
    Purpose, Purpose involving the
    devil)
  Sin. Col.2:13
  Spiritism. Col.2:18-19
  The law. Col.2:14
Virgin Birth. (See **VIRGIN BIRTH**)
  Discussed. Mt.1:16; 1:23; Lk.1:27;
    1:34-35

Vision.
  A world white unto harvest. Mt.9:37-38
  Discussed. (See **JESUS CHRIST**,
    Deity; Nature; Person; & Related
    Subjects)
Who Jesus Christ is. Lk.9:18-22
Why crowds followed Jesus. Five rea-
  sons. (See **JESUS CHRIST**, Re-
  sponse to) Mt.20:29
Will of. Distinct, separate from God.
  Jn.6:38
Witness of God. (See **JESUS CHRIST**,
  Deity)
Witness to.
  By Andrew. The Messiah. Jn.1:35-42
  By Christ. Threefold. Jn.1:50-51
  By John the apostle.
    Five witnesses to. Jn.5:31-39
    The Light of men. Jn.1:9-13
    The Word. Jn.1:1-5
    The Word became flesh. Jn.1:14-18
  By John the Baptist.
    God became flesh. Jn.1:15
    Special witnesses to. Jn.1:6-8
  By Nathanael. The Son of God, the
    King of Israel. Jn.1:46-49
  By Philip. The One prophesied. Jn.1:43-45
Words of Christ. (See **JESUS CHRIST**,
  Deity, Apostle of God)
  Prove His deity. Jn.14:10; 14:11; 15:15
  Rejected. Jn.5:47; 8:37
  To be heard & listened to. Lk.9:35
  Were the Words of God. Jn.7:16-19;
    14:10
Work of - Ministry. (See **JESUS
CHRIST**, Mission)
  Bears witness.
    To His deity. Jn.5:19; 5:20; 5:36;
      10:25; 14:10; 20:30-31
    To His Messiahship. Mt.12:25-26;
      12:29
  Described. Mt.4:23-25
  Discussed. Mt.4:16-17; 9:35-38;
    12:18-21; Lk.1:67-80; 2:25-35; 21:37-
    38; Acts 2:14-24; 10:34-43; Gal.1:4;
    4:4-7; Eph.2:13; 1 Pt.1:18-20
    Proclaimed by John. Five works.
      Lk.3:4
    Why Christ came. 1 Jn.3:8
  Fact.
    Busy, very busy. Mt.4:23
    Concerned with every need. Jn.6:1-71
    Continues. Seen in the Book of
      Acts. Acts 1:1-5
    Knocks on the door of man's heart.
      Rev.3:18-20
    Revealed. By Christ Himself.
      Lk.5:27-39
    Sent forerunners ahead to prepare
      for His coming. Lk.10:1
  His work in caring, helping, & healing
    man.
    Preaching, teaching, & healing.
      Mt.9:35
    To care for the rejected. Mk.7:24-30
    To help man. Heb.2:17-18
    To help those rejected by family.
      Jn.7:3-5
    To meet all the needs of man.
      Lk.11:29
    To open the eyes of man. Jn.9:1-7
    To pray for sinners. Lk.23:34
    To pray for weak believers.
      Lk.22:32
    To reach & preach every place He
      could. Mk.1:35-39

His work in destroying Satan & evil
  spirits.
    To cast out evil spirits. Proves His
      deity. Lk.11:14-28
    To conquer all the evil forces of the
      universe. Six forces. Rev.5:5
    To defeat Satan & evil spirits & evil
      forces of the universe. Col.2:15
    To destroy the power of the devil.
      Heb.2:14-18
    To destroy the devil's works.
      1 Jn.3:8
    To secure the ideal & perfect right-
      eousness for man. Mt.5:17;
      Eph.2:6; Col.2:14;1 Pt.1:2
    To vindicate salvation before the
      spirits in the prison of hell.
      1 Pt.3:19-20; 3:19-22
His work in meeting man's need for
  life, both abundant & eternal.
    To awaken the sleeping, the spiri-
      tually dead. Eph.5:14
    To be the light of world. Jn.1:9
    To break down all barriers.
      Gal.3:28
    To bring peace, joy & security.
      Jn.14:27-31
    To bring salvation & enable men to
      survive. Acts 1:1-2
    To bring satisfaction. Jn.6:30-36
    To deliver men from the fear of
      death. Heb.2:14-16
    To fellowship with believers.
      1 Jn.1:3-4
    To free from five things.
      2 Cor.3:17-18
    To give gifts to men. Eph.4:7-16
    To give liberty. 2 Cor.3:17
    To give life & immortality.
      2 Tim.1:8-10; 1 Jn.4:9; 5:20
    To give light. Lk.1:76-79
    To give special insight. 1 Jn.5:20
    To give the Holy Spirit to believers.
      Tit.3:5; Rev.3:1
    To indwell the believer. Eph.3:17
    To make believers the heirs of God.
      Tit.3:7
    To make man perfect. Heb.10:1-4;
      10:9-10; 10:14
    To make man secure. Jn.10:9
    To quench man's spiritual thirst.
      Jn.4:15
    To remove spiritual blindness from
      man's mind. 2 Cor.3:14-18
    To resurrect & give life. Jn.11:25-26
    To save man to the uttermost.
      1 Tim.1:15; Heb.7:25; Rev.1:5-6
    To secure supremacy for man.
      Heb.2:5-13
    To seek man. Mt.13:44; 13:45
    To serve & teach. Jn.13:1-17
    To set men free from the law.
      Gal.5:1-6
    To stand with & strengthen believ-
      ers. 2 Tim.4:16-18
His work in relation to God.
    To do God's works. Jn.5:19; 5:20
      Verses. List of. Jn.5:20
    To subject Himself to God.
      1 Cor.15:24-28
His work in relation to judgment.
    Judgment committed to. Reasons.
      Jn.5:22
      Verses. List of. Jn.5:22-23
    To judge ministers. 1 Cor.4:1-5
    To judge people. Ro.2:16

To judge the living & the dead.
Acts 10:42
To judge the world. Jn.5:22
To present the kingdom to God,
ending all things. 1 Cor.15:24-28
To reverse the order of three things.
Lk.1:51-53
His work in relation to ministers.
To hold ministers in His hand. (See
MINISTERS) Rev.2:1; 3:1
His work in relation to the church.
In the midst of the churches.
Rev.2:1
Reveals the church. Mt.16:13-20
Reveals union with God. Jn.5:20
To be the foundation of the church.
1 Cor.3:11
To cleanse God's temple.
Mk.11:15-19; Lk.19:45-56;
Jn.2:12-22
Walks in the midst of the churches--
examining. Rev.2:1-3:22
His work in relation to the High
Priesthood, the Mediator & Interces-
sor.
To be the High Priest. Verses of
prophecy & fulfillment. Lk.3:32-38
To be the Mediator, the Messianic
High Priest. Verses of prophecy &
fulfillment. Lk.3:32-38
To be the minister of the heavenly
sanctuary. Heb.9:11-14
To be the minister of the superior
covenant. Heb.8:6-13
To be the sympathetic High Priest.
Heb.4:14-16
To the Prophet of God. Verses of
prophecy & fulfillment. Lk.3:38
To become the High Priest for man.
Heb.2:17-18
To bring perfection to man & his
worship. Heb.9:11-14
To fulfill the qualifications of the
priesthood perfectly. Heb.5:1-10
To live & undergo the experiences
of men. Heb.4:14-16
To mediate a better covenant.
Heb.8:6-13, cp. Jer.31:31-34
To meet the heavenly qualifications
of the High Priest. Heb.8:1-5
To minister in heaven for man.
Heb.8:1-5
His work in securing righteousness &
dying for man.
Not to condemn but to die for man.
Ro.8:34
To abolish death. 2 Tim.1:8-10
To be the ideal & perfect Man &
Sacrifice. 1 Pt.1:2
To be the propitiation, atoning sac-
rifice for our sins. 1 Jn.2:1-2
To be the Savior of the world.
1 Jn.4:14
To become man. Ph.2:7
To become sin for man. 2 Cor.5:21
To become the substitute for man.
2 Cor.5:21
To bring peace, reconciliation, ac-
cess--all by the blood of the cross.
Eph.2:13
To bring redemption. (See **RE-
DEEM - REDEMPTION**)
1 Tim.2:5-7
To condemn sin in the sinful nature.
Ro.8:3
To conquer death. Ro.6:8-10

To deliver from condemnation.
Ro.8:34
To deliver from the law. Gal.4:4-7
To deliver from the law's curse.
Gal.3:13-14
To die & deliver us from this evil
world. Gal.1:4-5
To die, arise, & ascend to the right
hand of God. Ro.8:34
To end securing righteousness by
law. Three ways. Ro.10:4
To experience & suffer every trial
of man. Lk.2:40
To forgive sins. Eph.1:7; Col.1:14;
1 Jn.1:6-2:2; 1 Jn.3:5
To fulfill Scripture. Mt.4:12-17
To fulfill the law. Mt.5:17; Ro.3:31;
8:3; 1 Cor.15:57; Gal.4:4-7;
Col.2:14; Rev.2:5-6
To identify perfectly with man.
Heb.4:15-16
To justify. Tit.3:6-7
To lay down His life for man.
1 Jn.3:16
To live a sinless, perfect & ideal
life. Ro.8:3
To make propitiation for man.
Heb.2:17-18
To open & shut the door to God's
presence. Rev.3:7
To reconcile man. 2 Cor.5:17-21
To redeem men. Gal.4:4-7;
1 Pt.1:18-20
To sacrifice Himself. Eph.5:2
To sacrificially offer Himself for
man. Heb.9:23-28
To satisfy the law. To be a perfect
satisfaction. Mk.1:15
To save the sinner. Mt.9:12-13
To take away sins. 1 Jn.3:5
Worship of.
As king.
By the magi. Mt.2:1-11
Every knee shall bow. Ph.2:9-11
Faithful in worship. Mk.1:21
To be a day of universal worship.
Jn.7:6-9

JEWISH LEADERS (See **RELIGION-
ISTS; PHARISEES; SADDUCEES;
TEACHERS OF THE LAW;
HERODIANS; ELDERS**)

JEWS (See **ISRAEL; JERUSALEM**)
Advantages.
Had the privileges & the blessings of
God. Ro.9:1-5; 1 Cor.10:1-5
Had the Word of God. Ro.3:1-2
Salvation is of the Jews. Jn.4:22; Acts
10:34-35
Birth of.
Father of the Jews. Abraham. Ro.4:1-25
The Jews as a people. Call & life of
Abraham. Acts 7:2-8
Call of. Purpose. Acts 10:1-22
Charges against. Eightfold. Acts 7:42-53
Covenants of. (See **COVENANT**)
Discussed. Jn.5:10
Errors - Mistakes of.
Claimed the heritage of God; claim to
be the children of Abraham. Jn.8:33
Counted some laws weightier, others
lighter. Mt.22:36
Cried for Jesus' blood to be upon
them. Mt.27:25

Discussed. Mt.12:10; Ro.2:17-29
Exalted Moses & the law above God.
Acts 7:30-38
God's case against the Jews. Ro.2:17-29
Misinterpreted God's promises.
Jn.4:22
Opposed - Rejected God's Son, the
Lord Jesus Christ. (See **JESUS
CHRIST**, Opposition)
Despite all kinds of evidence.
Mk.12:6-8
Opposed the Messiah & the Day of
Salvation. Lk.19:44
Persecuted Jesus. Jn.5:16; 7:13-15, 19
Plotted & killed Jesus. Accused of.
Mt.17:22-23
Reasons. Mt.12:1-8; 12:9-13; 12:10
Rejected the gospel. Acts 28:25-29
Sought to kill Jesus. Jn.5:16, 17-18;
7:13, 19; 8:40, 59;10:31-33, 39
Ways opposed. Mt.12:10
Persecuted God's true messengers, the
servants of God's Son Christ. Mt.23:37
Rejected the Messiah. Mt.23:37-39;
23:37
Required a sign. Mt.12:38-45
Worshipped false gods. Acts 7:42-53
Fact.
The gospel was taken from the Jews &
given to the Gentiles. Acts 28:25-29
The Jews were turned away from. By
Paul. He turned to the Gentiles. Acts
28:25-29
Their minds are blinded to the gospel.
2 Cor.3:14-15
Hellenist Jew vs. Hebrew Jew. Acts 6:1
History. Lk.6:7
Descendants of Jacob. Mt.1:2
Fled to Egypt often. Mt.2:13-18
Refugees. Preserved by God. Mt.1:11
The "binding force" of the Jewish na-
tion. Mt.12:10
Tragic. Rejection of God time and
again. Acts 7:2-8
Hope. Is Christ & Christ alone. Mt.1:2
In the end time.
One hundred forty four thousand. Seen
in heaven. Rev.7:4-8; 14:9-12
Redeemed Jews seen in heaven.
Rev.14:1-5
Judgment of.
Because of sins. Mt.23:37-39; 23:38-39
Discussed. Lk.20:15-16
Gospel taken from the Jews & given to
the Gentiles. Acts 28:25-29
Threefold judgment. Mt.23:38-39
Laws of.
Capital punishment. Not allowed by
the Romans. Jn.19:7
Dietary Laws. Acts 10:9-22; 10:11-16
Sabbath. Mt.12:1-9
Love for the Jews.
Messiah's great lament for Jerusalem.
Mt.23:37-39; Lk.13:34-35; 19:41-42
Messiah's patience & care & protec-
tion. Mt.23:37
Of the diaspora. Jas.1:1
Purposes of. Reasons the Jews were cho-
sen by God. Jn.4:22
Religion of.
Rules & regulations. Mt.15:1-20
Stressed outside, external appearance.
Mt.15:1-20
Stressed tradition. Mt.15:1-20; 15:6-9
Remnant.

144,000 saved during the tribulation of the end time. Rev.7:1-8
Conversion of multitudes of Jews in the last days. Rev.11:3-13
Protected in the end time. Rev.11:1-2
Some claim to be Jews but are not. Rev.2:9
Restoration.
  At the end of the "times of the Gentiles." Lk.21:24
  Discussed. Ro.11:25-26; 11:25-36
  Predicted. Will proclaim Messiah. Mt.23:39
  Surety of.
    Forefathers. Ro.11:16; 11:28
    Predicted by the prophets. Ro.1:2-4
    Prophecy. Jews will proclaim Messiah. Mt.23:39
    Sixfold surety. Ro.11:25-36
  To be wrought by Christ Himself. Ro.11:26-27
Seed of. Discussed. Jn.4:22; Ro.4:1-25; Gal.3:7-8, 16,19, 29, cp. 3:6-29
Sins of. 1 Th.2:15-16
Teachers of the Jews. Some teachers in Jesus day. Lk.2:46-47
The true Jew.
  A new creation. Gal.6:15
  Abraham's true seed. Ro.4:11-12; 4:16; 4:18-22;Gal.3:27-29
  All who believe. Ro.4:11-12; 4:16; 4:18-22
  Discussed. Ro.9:6-13
  Persons who are Christ's. Gal.3:27-29
  Persons who are of faith. Gal.3:6-9; 5:6; 6:15
  The Israel of God. Gal.6:15-16
  What a true Jew is. Rev.3:9-10
  Who a true Jew is. Ro.2:28-29; 9:6-13
Vs. the Gentiles.
  Bitter enemies of Canaanites. Mk.7:25-26
  Cut off & Gentiles accepted. Ro.11:17
  Discussed. Acts 10:1-33; 10:11-16; 10:28-29
  Example. Mt.15:23-28
  Prejudice between. Lk.7:4-5; Acts 10:1-33; 10:11-16; 10:28-29
  Racial barriers are broken by Christians. Mk.7:24-30
Wept over. By Christ. Lk.19:41-44
Why Jesus came to earth as a Jew. Jn.4:22
Why Jews did not believe the gospel. Ro.10:18-21

JEZEBEL
Discussed. A prophetess who seduced believers. Rev.2:20-21

JOANNA
Discussed. Supported, Jesus. Lk.8:3
One of the first to proclaim the resurrection of Jesus. Lk.24:10

JOB
Example of.
  Patience needed to combat temptation & trials. Jas.5:11
  Patience needed to wait for the Lord's return. Jas.5:11

JOHN, MEMBER OF THE HIGH PRIEST FAMILY
Mentioned. Acts 4:5-10

JOHN THE APOSTLE
A successful businessman. Mk.1:20
Called to be a disciple. Mk.1:19-20
Death of. Mt.20:23
Discovered the Lord's empty tomb. Noticed strips of linen still in its fold & believed. Jn.20:7-10
Discussed.
  A companion to believers in three things. Rev.1:9
  Fate of. Mk.10:39
  Received the N.T. Book of Revelation from Christ. Rev.1:1-3
Exiled. On the island of Patmos. Rev.1:9
Misunderstood Jesus' mission. Lk.9:52-54
Slipped into the sin of self-seeking. Sought the chief position in Christ's kingdom. Mk.10:35-45
Task of. Completed. Jn.21:24-25
Testimony of. 1 Jn.1:1-4
Witness to Christ.
  Discussed. 1 Jn.5:13-15
  The Word. Jn.1:1-5
  Word became flesh. Jn.1:14-18

JOHN THE BAPTIST
Baptism of. Meaning. Mt.3:11-12; Mk.1:7-8
Death.
  Beheaded. The immoral vs. the righteous. Mk.6:14-29
  Imprisoned & martyred. A godly vs. an ungodly man. Mt.14:1-14
Discussed. Mk.1:1-8; Lk.3:1-6
Forerunner.
  Discussed. Mt.11:10
  Pivotal point of history. Lk.3:1-6
  Why a forerunner was necessary. Jn.1:23
Greatest among men. Mt.11:11; Lk.7:28
In prison. Discussed. Mt.11:2-3
Life of.
  A life of self-denial. Mk.1:6
  A priest, but not a religionist. Jn.1:19
  His birth & naming. An event for all generations. Lk.1:57-66
  Sufferings of. Discussed. Mk.10:39
  Was cousin to Jesus Christ. Jn.1:1:30-31
Message of. Mt.3:1-12; 3:2-6; 3:7-10; 3:11-12; Lk.3:7-20
Messenger of God. Mk.1:1-8; Jn.1:19-27
Ministry.
  Discussed. Mt.11:7-15
  Ended the age of Old Testament prophecy. Mt.11:14
  Needed assurance. Questioned Jesus' Messiahship. Mt.11:1-6; Lk.7:18-28
Mission of. Mk.1:3
Parents of. Picture of godly **p**. Lk.1:5-25
Prophecy predicting.
  The forerunner. Mk.1:2; 1:15
  His person & ministry. Why he was sent into the world. Lk.1:76-80
Proved deity of Christ. Lk.7:21-23; 20:5-6
Response to.
  By sinners & people. Lk.7:29-31
  Impact. Mk.1:3
Vindicated. By Christ. A reminder to fickle people. Mt.11:7-15
Vs. Herod. Mt.14:1-14
Who he was & was not. Mt.11:7-15
Witness to Christ.
  God became flesh. Jn.1:15
  The Lamb of God - Son of God. Jn.1:29-34
  The special witness to Christ. Jn.1:6-8

JOKING
Sin of. Discussed. Eph.5:4

JONAH
Compared with Christ. Mt.12:41
Symbolized - Type of. The resurrection of Christ. Mt.12:38-40; Lk.11:30

JOSEPH, CALLED BARSABBAS
Nominated as a candidate to replace Judas. Acts 1:23

JOSEPH OF ARIMATHEA
Buried Jesus.
  A discussion of courage. Mk.15:42-47
  A secret disciple stirred to step forward. Lk.23:50-56
  Discussed. Mt.27:57-60
  The conquest of fear. Jn.19:38

JOSEPH, SON OF JACOB & RACHAEL
Discussed. Acts 7:8-16
Faith of. An undying faith. Heb.11:22
Symbolized - Type of Christ. Acts 7:8-16

JOSEPH, THE FATHER OF JESUS
Discussed. Mt.1:18-19; 1:20-21

JOSHUA
Symbolized - Type of. One of the two witnesses of Revelation. Rev.11:3-4

JOY
Discussed. Jn.14:28-29; 15:11; 1 Jn.1:4
Duty.
  Not to let the world or persecution destroy one's joy in Christ. Mt.13:20-21
  To be faithful & enter the joy of the Lord. Mt.25:14-30, esp. 21, 23
  To finish the course of one's life with joy. Acts 20:24
  To joy in salvation. Lk.10:20
Essential. To combat temptation. Jas.1:2-4
Experience of. Involves three experiences. Mt.13:44
Meaning. Lk.10:21; Jn.14:28-29; 15:11; Gal.5:22-23
Of Jesus.
  Over souls saved. Lk.10:21
  Over the glorious day of redemption. Heb.12:2
Source of - Stirred by.
  Access to God. Jn.16:23-27
  Being assured of eternal life. 1 Jn.1:2, 4, cp. 1:1-4
  Comes from two things. Lk.6:20-23
  Faith in Christ. 1 Pt.1:8
  Fellowship with God. 1 Jn.1:3-4
  Fellowship with men. 1 Jn.1:3-4
  Future reward. Mt.25:21
  How to have **j.** in trials. Jas.1:2-4
  Jesus Christ.
    His death. Ro.5:10-11
    His presence. Lk.5:33-34
    His promises & Word. Jn.15:11
    His resurrection. Jn.16:20-22
    The life He brings. Mk.2:19
  Jesus' purpose. Jn.15:11
  Knowing eternal life. 1 Jn.1:2, 4, cp. 1:1-4
  Leading a person to Christ. Great **j.** over one lost person saved. Mt.18:14

Salvation. Meeting Christ face to face. Jn.1:45

Salvation of souls. Lk.15:1-7; 15:8-10; 15:22-24

The fact that one's name is written in the Book of Life. Lk.10:20

Verses. List of. Ro.5:10-11

JUDA, THE REVOLUTIONARY
Discussed. Acts 5:36-37

JUDAISM
Converts. Many Gentiles & many women because of a corrupt society. Acts 16:14

Converts to. Many Gentiles. Reasons. Mt.23:15

Why Gentiles turned to Jesus. Acts 13:42-45

JUDAIZERS (See **RELIGIONISTS**)
Discussed. Acts 11:1-3; 11:2; Gal.2:3-5; 2:4; 2:11-13

Teachings of. Gal.1:6-7; 2:3-5; 2:4; 2:11-13

JUDAS ISCARIOT, THE APOSTLE
Betrayed Christ.
 Double-dealing, deception, hypocrisy. Mk.14:43-45
 Picture of a ruined life. Mt.26:14-16; 26:47-56
 Predicted. Jn.13:18-30
 Reasons. Mk.14:10-11
 Terrible sins against Christ. Lk.22:47-53

Discussed. Mk.3:19

Entered by Satan twice. Lk.22:5

Failure and fate.
 Allowed Satan to enter twice. Lk.22:5
 Committed suicide. Despair. Hopelessness. Mt.27:1-5
 Discussed. Acts 1:12-26

Fall of. Discussed. Lk.22:47-48

Given a last chance.
 Called to repent. Mt.26:20-25
 The appeals to a sinner. Mk.14:12-21

Life of. Discussed. Mk.14:10

Repentance of. Wrong repentance & human religion. Mt.26:1-10

Traits of.
 A thief. Stole money. Jn.12:4-8
 Sinful trait. Threefold. Jn.12:4-8

Was treasurer of disciples. Jn.12:4-8

JUDAS THE APOSTLE, SON OF JAMES
Discussed. Mk.3:18

JUDE
Became a believer & wrote the epistle of Jude. Acts 1:14; Jude Introd.

Brother of Christ. Mt.13:55

Did not believe in Christ at first. Jn.7:3-5

JUDEA
A providence ruled over by Roman governors. Lk.3:1

Scepter departed from. Five proofs. Lk.2:1-24

Wilderness of. Discussed. Mt.3:1

JUDGING OTHERS (See **CRITICISM**)
Discussed. Mt.7:1-6; Ro.2:1; Jas.4:11-12

Duty.
 Not to judge fallen brothers. Gal.6:1-5
 Not to j. Reasons. Ro.14:3-4
 Watch j. Lk.6:41-42

Error - Sin of.
 Censoring, condemning. Jn.8:3-6
 Common to the gifted. Jas.4:11-12
 Discussed. Mt.7:1-6
 J. by appearance. Jn.7:24
 Sets oneself up as God. Ro.14:3-4
 Usurps God's right to j. Makes one as God. Jas.4:12

How we judge others.
 Discussed. Mt.13:54-56; 19:30
 Try to separate the bad from the good. Mt.13:47-50

Illust. The unmerciful servant. Mt.18:28-31; 18:28; 18:30

J. Ministers, servants. (See **MINISTERS**, Duty toward)
 Discussed. 1 Cor.4:1-5; 4:6-13
 Not to compare, criticize, & judge ministers. 1 Cor.4:1-5; 4:6-13

Meaning. Mt.7:1

Reasons why people j. others. Six reasons. Mt.7:1

Results.
 Causes cliques & division. 1 Cor.1:10-16
 Causes super-spirituality. 1 Cor.1:10-16

Who has the right to j.
 Discussed. Jn.8:7-9; 1 Cor.4:1-5
 Is to be left up to Christ alone. 1 Cor.4:1-5

Why one should not j. Mt.7:1
 Is forbidden. Col.2:16-17
 Is often inaccurate. Mt.19:30
 Makes one unworthy of the gospel. Mt.7:1-6; 7:6
 To be judged for the very thing one judges another person for. Mt.7:2
 Usurps God's authority. Makes one as god. Mt.7:1

JUDGMENT (See **END TIME**)
Attitudes toward.
 Man scoffs at & is ignorant of. 2 Pt.3:1-7
 Many think God is too good to j. Ro.2:2-5; 3:5-8
 Many think they will escape j. Ro.2:2-5

Basis of - What God uses to j. man.
 A person's failure to minister. Mt.25:41-45
 A threefold witness within man. Ro.2:11-15
 Man's evil deeds. Jn.3:19
 Man's privilege. J. is to be based upon privilege. Mt.11:20-24; Lk.12:47-48
 Man's words. Mt.12:31-37
 Man's works.
  Ministering, serving, helping. Mt.25:31-46
  To be based upon deeds, works. Mt.16:27; Ro.2:6-10; 1 Pt.1:17;Rev.20:12; 22:12
 The Book of Life & the Books of Records. Rev.20:12
 The gospel of Jesus Christ. Ro.2:16
 The law.
  Failing to keep the l. Ro.2:11-15
  Obeying the l. Ro.2:11-15
  Under the law's curse. Gal.3:10-12
 The Word of Christ. Jn.12:47-50

Degrees of.
 Based upon privilege. Lk.10:10-15; 12:47-48
 Reason. Mt.11:20-24
 Rewards and punishment. Lk.12:41-48

Deliverance. Three persons shall escape. Rev.14:12

Described as. (See **JUDGMENT**, How God judges) Mt.22:11-14
 A curse. Gal.3:10-12
 A day of accounting. Mt.18:28; 18:30; 18:32-34
 A day of judgment & perdition. 2 Pt.3:7
 A day of reckoning & accountability. Mt.25:19
 A day of wrath. Ro.2:5
 A great shaking of the earth & heaven. Heb.12:26-27
 A terrible end. 1 Pt.4:17-18
 All things being revealed. Lk.8:17-18
 Being beaten with blows. Lk.12:47-48
 Being burned. Branches that are cast into the fire. Jn.15:6
 Being condemned. Jesus reveals condemnation. Jn.3:18-21
 Being cut into pieces. Lk.12:46
 Being deserted, desolated, & blinded. Mt.23:38-39; Lk.13:34
 Being destroyed. 1 Cor.3:17
 Being destroyed. Meaning. Lk.20:15-16; Acts 3:22-24; 3:23
 Being enslaved to sin. Ro.1:24
 Being killed. Lk.19:27
 Being spit out of Christ's mouth. Rev.3:16-17
 Being thrown away & burned. Jn.15:4-6
 Being thrown out. Mt.5:13
 Chaff that is to be burned. Mt.3:12; Lk.3:17
 Desolation. Lk.13:34
 Final j. Of nations, of sheep & goats. Mt.25:31-46
 Fire & burning sulfur. Lk.17:26-30; Rev.14:10
 Gnashing of teeth. Mt.8:12; Lk.13:28
 God "giving man up." Ro.1:24-32; 1:24
 God's great confrontation with man. Mt.22:11-14
 Hell. Mt.5:22
 J. that fell in Noah's day. Lk.17:26-30
 Judicial blindness. Mt.13:13-15
 Judicial j. Jn.12:39-41; Ro.1:24; 11:7-10
 Perfect justice. Lk.19:15-23
 Punishment and destruction. 2 Th.1:9
 Punishment, terrible punishment. Ro.2:6-10
 Salted with fire. Mk.9:49
 Separation & being cast into eternal fire & punishment. Mt.25:41, 25:46
 Separation, exclusion, shut out. Jn.7:33-34; 8:21-22
 Separation from the righteous. Lk.13:29-30; 16:24
 Severe punishment. Four punishments. Ro.2:6-10
 Spiritual abandonment. Ro.1:24
 Stripping & separation. Mt.25:24-30
 Suffering loss. 1 Cor.3:13-15
 Tares that are gathered & burned. Mt.13:30
 The Day God Visit's us. 1 Pt.2:12
 The great day of God's wrath. Rev.6:12-17; 6:16-17
 The great white throne j. Rev.20:11-15
 The Messianic fire of j. Mt.1:1; 3:11; 11:1-6; 11:2-3; 11:6; 11:4-6
 The wrath of God. Ro.1:18; 2:5; Rev.14:8; 14:10; 14:18-19
 Unquenchable fire. Lk.3:17
 Weeping. Mt.8:12; Lk.13:28
 Wrath of God. Ro.1:18, 25; Eph.2:3; Rev.14:8; 14:10; 14:18-19

Discussed. Ro.2:16; Heb.10:26-39;
  Rev.14:9-12
    Eight serious warnings. 1 Jn.5:16
    Four facts. Ro.2:1-16
    Love requires **j**. Ro.3:5-8
    The Day of the Lord. Rev.14:17-20
    The Parable of the Wicked Tenants.
      Lk.20:9-18
    The picture of heaven and hell. Lk.16:19-31
    The righteousness of God. 2 Th.1:6-12
    Three facts about God's **j**. 1 Pt.1:17
Duty - How to escape **j**.
    Discussed. Ro.2:6-10
    Must be convicted of the judgment to
      come. Jn.16:8-11
    Must be justified by Christ. Ro.3:23;
      3:24
    Must be saved. Ro.1:16-18
    Must believe & prepare for judgment.
      Lk.17:26-30
    Must fear & reverence God. 2 Cor.5:11
    Must guard against being a castaway.
      1 Cor.9:27
    Must have boldness. 1 Jn.4:17
    Must hope for deliverance. A day of
      victory is coming. Mt.12:20
    Must labor for Christ. 2 Cor.5:9-10
    Must leave **j**. up to God. 1 Tim.5:24-25
    Must not neglect salvation. Heb.2:3
    Must not turn away from Christ.
      Heb.12:25
    Must prepare. Discussed. 2 Pt.3:11-14
    Must respond to the conviction of the
      Holy Spirit. Jn.16:8-11
    Must seek the verdict of faithfulness.
      Mk.7:31-37
    Must turn from sin to Christ. Ro.6:23
    Three persons shall escape. Rev.14:12
Example of.
    Angels. Jude 5-7
    Herod Agrippa. Acts 12:18-23
    Israel. Jude 5-7
    Sodom and Gomorrha. Jude 5-7
How God judges. (See **JUDGMENT**,
  Described)
    Abandons man - "gives man over."
      Ro.1:24-32; 11:7-10
    Allows life to perish & corrupt. Jn.3:16;
      2 Th.2:10-12; 1 Pt.1:23; 2 Pt.1:4
    Allows man freedom--to live under
      God's wrath. Eph.2:1-3
    Appoints man to death & **j**. Heb.9:27
    By allowing a judicial judgment.
      Jn.12:39-41; Ro.1:24; 11:7-10;
      2 Th.2:11
    By being exact; business-like.
      Mk.12:2
    By Christ. Lk.12:4-12; 12:49-53;
      Jn.5:22-23;5:27
        Will be more severe under Christ
          than under the law. Heb.2:1-4
        Will bow every knee before Christ.
          Ph.2:9-11
    Four ways. Ro.1:24-32
    In justice.
        Assures justice. Jn.12:39-41;
          Ro.2:6-10
        Straightens things out. Mt.19:30
        The judicial judgment of God.
          Jn.12:39-41; Ro.1:24; 11:7-10;
          2 Th.2:11
    To be impartial, without respect of
      persons. Ro.2:11-15
    To be reciprocal. Jas.2:12-13
In the end time. (See **JUDGMENTS OF
  REVELATION; END TIME**)

Kinds.
    The eternal separation from God. Mt.25:41;
      25:46; Lk.13:29-30;16:24; Jn.7:33-34;
      8:21-22;2 Th.1:9; Rev.20:11-15
    The judicial **j**. of God or the reciprocal
      j. of God. Jn.12:39-41; Ro.1:24;
      11:7-10;2 Th.2:11; Jas.2:12-13
    Spiritual abandonment. God gives man
      up to his sin. Ro.1:24-32; 1:24
Meaning. Mt.19:28
Misconceptions of - reactions against.
    Men scoff at. Think God is too good to
      j. Ro.2:2-5; 3:5-8
    Most men think they will escape. Ro.2:2-5
Of believers.
    Fact.
        Believers are almost cursed. Are
          barely saved. Heb.6:3-8
        J. is already paid in the cross of
          Christ. Jn.12:31-32
        J. stirs believers to labor.
          2 Cor.5:9-10
        Works are to be tested by fire.
          1 Cor.3:13-15
    For what.
        For becoming useless & destructive.
          Mt.5:13
        For defiling God's temple. 1 Cor.3:17
        For false profession. Threefold.
          Mt.7:21; 13:30
        For how one builds the church.
          1 Cor.3:10-17
        For partaking of the Lord's Supper
          unworthily. 1 Cor.11:27-30
        For righteousness sake. 1 Pt.3:13-17
        For works. 1 Cor.3:10-17
    Discussed. 1 Cor.3:10-17; 2 Cor.5:9-10; 5:10
        The Judgment Seat of Christ.
          2 Cor.5:9-10
    Reason. Mt.5:13
    Warnings of **j**. to believers. Eight seri-
      ous warnings. 1 Jn.5:16
Of the church.
    Crown taken away. Rev.3:11
    Death. Rev.2:23
    Discussed. 1 Pt.2:9-10; 4:17-18
    God's personal opposition. Rev.2:16; 3:3
    Great tribulation. Rev.2:22-23
    Removed by Christ. Rev.2:5-6; 2:16
    Spit - thrown out. Rev.3:16
Of the followers of antichrist. Discussed.
  2 Th.2:11; 2:12
Of unbelievers.
    Fate.
        Destroyed. Meaning. Lk.20:15-16;
          Acts 3:22-24; 3:23
        Four terrible things. Rev.14:10-11
        The face of God is against. 1 Pt.3:12
        The lake of fire. Rev.20:14
    Great white throne **j**. Rev.20:11-15
    To be destroyed. Meaning. Acts 3:22-
      24; 3:23
    To be **j**. by words of Christ. Reason.
      Jn.12:47-50
Results. (See **JUDGMENT**, Kinds of)
    A terrible end. 1 Pt.4:17-18
    Cast out. Mt.5:13
    No second chance. Lk.16:30
    Separated from God & the saved.
      Mt.25:41; 25:46; Lk.13:29-30;16:24;
      Jn.7:33-34; 8:21-22;2 Th.1:9;
      Rev.20:11-15
    Severe punishments. (See **JUDG-
      MENT**, Described) Ro.2:6-10
    Sin exposed. (See **EXPOSURE - EX-
      POSED**) Lk.12:1-3

Surety.
    Because a day of accounting must
      come. Lk.20:10-12
    Because God will quickly bring judg-
      ment for His chosen ones. Lk.18:6-8
    Because God will vindicate the truth
      someday. Mt.10:26
    Because injustices must be straight-
      ened out. Mt.19:30
    Because **j**. is inevitable. No escape. Is
      definitely coming. Lk.12:58-59
    Because man is without excuse.
      Ro.1:18-23
    Because of the love & justice of God.
      Mk.11:12-14
    Because reciprocal **j**. must be exe-
      cuted. Jas.2:12-13
    Discussed. Mk.9:49; Ro.2:6-10;
      2 Pt.3:8-14
    Verses. List of. Mk.9:49; Ro.1:18;
      2:6-20; 2:16; 3:5-8
    Verses. List of. Lk.10:10-15; 11:47-51;
      12:41-48
What is to be judged. (See **JUDGMENT**,
  Who is to be judged)
    Babylon, the capital of the antichrist.
      To be burned. Rev.17:16; 18:8
    Man's unprofitable & sinful works.
      1 Cor.3:13-15
    The heavens & earth. To be destroyed
      & remade. Heb.12:26-27
    The works of the earth. To be burned.
      2 Pt.3:10
    The world.
        A day is appointed. Acts 17:31
        By fire. 2 Pt.2:7; 3:10-18
        By water in the days of Noah.
          2 Pt.2:5; 3:1-7
When will God **j**.
    After death, immediately after.
      Heb.9:27, cp. Lk.16:19-31
    At the day of the Lord. 2 Th.2:1-3;
      2 Pt.3:10
    At the Great White Throne **j**.
      Rev.20:11-15
    At the Judgment Seat of Christ.
      Ro.14:10-12; 2 Cor.5:9-10
    At the resurrection, at the Lord's re-
      turn. A separation will occur.
      Mt.25:1-13; Acts 3:19; 2 Th.1:6-12
    Delay means salvation to many more.
      2 Pt.3:15
    Now - presently. The judicial **j**. or re-
      ciprocal **j**. of God. Jn.12:39-41;
      Ro.1:24; 11:7-10;2 Th.2:11;
      Jas.2:12-13
Who escapes **j**. Three persons. Rev.14:12
Who executes **j**.
    Christ.
        All **j**. is committed to Christ.
          Jn.5:22; 5:27
        To **j**. the living & the dead. Acts 10:42
        To reveal all things. 1 Cor.4:4-5
        Verses. List of. Jn.5:22-23; 5:28-30
    The judge. Heb.10:30-31
    The Word of God. 2 Pt.3:5-7
Who is to be **j**. (See **JUDGMENT**, What
  is to be judged)
    All who make excuses. Lk.9:61-62;
      14:24
    All who reject Jesus Christ. Lk.10:10-16
    All who reject the invitation to God's
      Supper. Lk.14:15-24
    False professors. Threefold. Mt.7:21
    Five persons. Mk.11:15-17
    Israel. Discussed. Lk.20:15-16

Some in the kingdom. Who they are. Mt.13:41

The believer. (See **JUDGMENT**, Of Believers)

The covetous & selfish. Lk.12:20-21

The doers of evil. Lk.13:27-28

The first. The first to be last. Mt.19:30

The foolish. Door shut to **f**. Mt.25:10-12

The heathen.
  Basis of. Ro.2:11-15
  Fallen angels. Discussed. 2 Pt.2:4
  False teachers.
    Discussed. Jude 4, 5-7, 11, 14-15
    Ordained by God. Jude 4
    Surety of. Jude 5-7
  Sodom & Gomorrha. Reason. 2 Pt.2:6-7
  What happens to heathen who never hear of Christ. Ro.2:11-15

The indulgent & selfish. Lk.16:19-21

The Jews. Described. Deserted, blinded. Mt.23:38-39

The lost - the unbeliever. 1 Pt.2:9-10; 3:12

The nations. Meaning. Mt.25:31-46; 25:32

The person who builds upon a false foundation. Lk.6:49

The rejected. Lk.10:10-15

The self-righteous. Jn.9:41

The unbeliever. (See **JUDGMENT**, Of Unbelievers)

The unfaithful steward. Lk.12:41-48

The unprepared & evil. Mt.24:51

The unrighteous & sinners. Ro.5:12; 6:23; 1 Cor.6:9-10;Jas.1:15; Rev.21:8

The wealthy & materialist. Lk.16:19-21

The world. In the end time. Mt.24:15-28; 24:25-28

This generation. Lk.11:30-32
  Ninevah to testify against. Mt.12:41

Those who commit the sin that leads to death. 1 Jn.5:16

Those who do not know God or retain God in their knowledge. Ro.1:28-32

Those who do not love the Lord. 1 Cor.16:22

Those who fall away. Heb.6:4-8

Those who live by the flesh. Gal.5:19-21

Those who make false professions. Mt.7:21

Those who pierced Christ. Rev.1:7

Those who show partiality. Jas.2:12-13

Those who sin with the body & the mouth. Eph.5:5

Two men doomed. Mt.21:44

Why God **j**.
  Because love requires **j**. Ro.3:5-8
  Because of the worst holocaust in history. Rev.15:2-3
  Discussed. Ro.1:18-23; 2:6-10; 2:11-15
    The world's need to get right with God. Ro.1:18-3:20
  God has a case against all men. The great indictment of sin against man. Ro.3:9-20
  God has a case against all unrighteousness & ungodliness. Ro.1:18-32
  God has a case against the moralist, the self-righteous. Ro.2:1-16
  God has a case against the religionists. Ro.2:17-29
  God sees all men. He stands against the evil. 1 Pt.3:12

God's great indictment of sin against man. Ro.3:9-20

Man fails to bear fruit. Lk.3:9

Man fails to believe on the Lord Jesus Christ. Jn.3:19; 3:36; 8:24; 2 Th.2:12

Man fails to do the will of God. Mt.7:22-23

Man fails to obey the gospel of the Lord Jesus Christ. 2 Th.1:8

Man is accountable. Mk.12:2

Man is slothful. Mt.25:24-30

Man loves evil. Ro.1:18-32

Man is under the law's curse. Gal.3:10-12

Man refuses to hear Christ. Acts 3:22-24

Winds of. Discussed. Rev.7:1

JUDGMENT OF REVELATION

An overall picture of the very end. Rev.11:14-19

Judgment upon man himself, his cities & society.
  Armageddon. Rev.16:12-16
  Demon-like horsemen. Rev.9:12-21
  Demon-like locusts. Rev.8:13-9:11
  Earth's great harvest will take place. Rev.14:14-16; 14:17-20
  Effects upon unbelievers. Rev.6:15-16
  Evil spirits. Rev.16:12-16
  Justice is executed. Rev.14:9-12
  Of believers. Rev.14:14-16
  Of political Babylon. Rev.18:1-24
  Of religious Babylon, that is, false religion. Rev.17:1-6; 17:7-18
  Of the nations. Rev.19:11-21; 11:18; 14:17-20; 16:12-21
  Of the ungodly & evil. Rev.14:17-20
  One third of the fish & the fishing & shipping industry destroyed. Rev.8:8-9
  Shut out from the city. Rev.14:20
  Society destroyed. Rev.16:17-21; 19:17-21
  The great day of God's wrath upon earth pictured. Rev.16:12-16; 17:1-2; 19:11-21
  The harvest of the wicked is come. Rev.14:14-20
  Ulcerous sores. Rev.16:2

Judgment upon nature.
  An astronomical eclipse. Rev.8:12
  Astronomical happenings. Rev.6:12-14
  Darkness, thick darkness. Rev.16:10-11
  Euphrates dried up. Rev.16:12-16
  Fierce storms. Rev.8:6-7
  Fresh waters polluted. Rev.16:4-7
  Great earthquake. Rev.6:12-14
  Great hailstorm. Rev.16:17-21
  Meteoric mass. Rev.8:10-11
  Natural catastrophes & disasters. Rev.8:6-12; 16:1-21
  One third of the vegetation destroyed. Rev.8:6-7
  One third of the water supply destroyed. Rev.8:10-11
  Scorching heat from the sun. Rev.16:8-9
  Sea polluted. Rev.16:3
  The mystery & judgment of Babylon. Rev.17:1-18:24
  Ungodly cities to be devastated by a great earthquake. Rev.16:17-21
  Volcanic explosion. Rev.8:8-9

Purpose of **j**. Rev.9:20-21

Reason for **j**. Rev.14:9-12

Seven bowls judgments. Preparation. Rev.15:1-16:21

Seven seals judgments.
  Antichrist. Rev.6:1-8
  Events preceding the tribulation. Rev.6:1-7:17
  Famine. Rev.6:5-6
  Hunger & starvation. Rev.6:7-8
  Pestilence. Rev.6:7-8
  Savagery. Rev.6:7-8
  War. Rev.6:3-4; 6:7-8

Seven trumpets judgments.
  Astronomical eclipse. Rev.8:12
  Demonic-like horses & riders. Rev.9:12-21
  Demonic-like locusts. Rev.8:13-9:11
  Fierce storms. Rev.8:6-7
  Meteoric mass. Rev.8:10-11
  Natural catastrophes. Rev.8:6-12
  One third of the fish & the fishing & shipping industry destroyed. Rev.8:8-9
  One third of the vegetation destroyed. Rev.8:6-7
  One third of the water supply destroyed. Rev.8:10-11
  Volcanic explosion. Rev.8:8-9

The wrath of God. Rev.6:16-17; 14:10-11; 15:1; 16:1-21

The wrath of Satan. Rev.12:12

JUDICIAL BLINDNESS

Law of. Discussed. Mt.13:13-15; Jn.12:39-41; Ro.1:24; 11:7-10

JUPITER

False god. Discussed. Acts 14:8-13

JUST - JUSTICE (See **RIGHTEOUSNESS**)

Duty.
  To meet the needs of the poor & oppressed. Lk.11:42; Heb.6:10
  To preach social justice. Lk.3:10-14

Fact.
  All injustices to be corrected. 2 Th.1:6; Rev.6:10; 8:2-4
  J. is essential. 2 Th.1:6
  J. is more important than religion. Lk.11:42
  Love require **j**. Ro.3:5-8

Hope of. Day of victory coming. Mt.12:20

In legal disputes. (See **LEGAL DISPUTES**)

Meaning. Mt.12:18

Misconception - Error of. Thinking God is love & not **j**. Ro.2:2-5; 3:5-8

Of God.
  God has the right to show **j**. as He wills. Ro.9:14-33
  God will avenge His elect. Lk.8:6-8
  Is based upon love. Ro.3:5-8
  Will be executed in the end time. Rev.14:9-12
  Will be impartial & without respect of persons. Ro.2:11-15
  Will be perfect **j**., exactly what a person deserves. Lk.19:15-23; Jn.12:39-41;Ro.2:6-10
  Will judge the living & the dead. Acts 10:42

Prayer for. Rev.8:2-4

Promise of. At the final judgment.
Ro.2:2-5
Surety.
All injustices are to be straightened
out. Mt.19:30
Christ's return. Is returning to execute
j. Rev.1:7
God will not forget. Heb.6:10
Weakness of. Lacks love, compassion, &
mercy. Mt.18:28; 18:30

JUSTIFIED - JUSTIFICATION
Depth of. Discussed. Ro.5:6-11
Discussed. Ro.1:17; 4:1-3; 4:22; 5:1;
2 Cor.5:18-19; 5:21; Gal.3:1-5:12;
1 Tim.3:16; 1 Pt.1:2
The fivefold appeal to be justified by
faith alone. Gal.4:8-5:12
The proof that a man is justified by
faith alone & not by works. Gal.3:1-4:7
Example of.
Abraham. Ro.4:9; 4:17-25; Gal.3:6-14
David. Ro.4:6-8
Meaning. 1 Cor.6:11; Gal.2:15-16
Being counted worthy. Lk.18:14; 20:35
Faith is counted for righteousness.
Ro.4:1-3; 4:22; 5:1
Seen in Abraham. Ro.4:1-25; 4:1-3;
4:9-12
Need for. The world needs to get right
with God. Ro.3:21-5:21
Proves. God's righteousness & justice.
Ro.3:25-26
Results of. (See **SALVATION**)
A continuous experience of God's
love. Ro.5:5
Access into the presence of God.
Ro.5:2
Five results. Ro.5:1-5
Forgiveness of sin. Acts 13:38-39
Frees from the law. Ro.7:4; Gal.5:1-6
Hope for the glory of God. Ro.5:2
Inheritance. Tit.3:7
Justified from all things. Acts 13:38-39
Peace. Ro.5:1
Righteousness. 2 Cor.5:21
Sins forgiven. Ro.4:6-8
Victory & glory through trials &
temptations. Ro.5:3-5
Source - How man is **j**.
By faith in Jesus Christ.
Discussed. Ro.4:1-3; 4:22; 5:1;
Gal.2:15-16; 3:1-5
Proven by logic. Ro.4:1-8
By God & God alone. Ro.3:24; 3:25
By the blood of Christ. Ro.5:9; 5:6-11
By the cross. Jn.12:32
By the death of Christ. Ro.5:6-11
By the grace of God. Ro.5:1; Tit.3:7
By the love of God. Gal.1:6-9
By the resurrection of Christ. Ro.4:25
By the Spirit of God. Ro.8:2-4
By the true God--the only true God.
Ro.3:29-30; 4:5
The wrong way to seek **j**.
By law or works. Ro.3:27-31; 4:1-8;
4:13-16; Gal.3:1-5:12
By professing faith without works.
Jn.2:14-26
By ritual. Ro.4:9-12; Gal.4:1-3; 4:8-11;
5:1-6; 5:7-12
By self-righteousness & religion.
Ro.10:1-3
Verses. List of. Ro.5:1
Who is **j**. A major lesson on who is **j**.
Lk.18:14

JUSTUS
A believer who opened his home to Paul.
Acts 18:7
Discussed. Col.4:11

K

KEEP - KEEPING (See OBEDIENCE; PROTECT)
Duty.
To keep oneself from idols. 1 Jn.5:21
To keep oneself from sin. 1 Jn.5:18
To keep oneself in the love of God. Jude 21
To keep oneself pure. 1 Tim.5:22
To keep oneself unspotted from the
world. Jas.1:27
To keep the commandments of God.
Mt.19:17
To keep the faith. 2 Tim.4:7
To keep the Lord's commandments.
Jn.14:21; 15:10, 14; 1 Jn.5:2
To keep the trust, the gift of God--that
which God has entrusted to oneself.
1 Tim.6:20
To keep the words of the Book of
Revelation. Rev.22:7, 9
To keep this commandment: fight the
good fight of faith & lay hold on
eternal life. 1 Tim.6:11-14
To strive to keep the unity of the
Spirit. Eph.4:1-3, esp. 3
Reward.
Will abide in the love of Christ. Jn.15:10, 14
Will be blessed. Rev.1:3; 22:7
Will be blessed & given rest forever &
ever. Rev.14:13
Will be loved by God & Christ. Jn.14:21
Will enter into life. Mt.19:17

KEPT - KEEPING POWER OF GOD (See ASSURANCE; PREDESTINATION; SECURITY)

KILL - KILLING (See MURDER)
Discussed. Ro.13:9; 2 Tim.3:1-4, esp. 3

KIND - KINDNESS (See CARE - CARING; MINISTERING)
Duty.
To add brotherly **k**. to our faith. 2 Pt.1:7
To be **k**. Ro.12:9-10
To clothe oneself with **k**. Col.3:12
Meaning. 1 Cor.13:4-7; 2 Cor.6:6-
7; Gal.5:22-23; Eph.4:32
Of God. Tit.3:4-5
Leads to man's salvation. Tit.3:4-7,
cp. Eph.4:32
Revealed to man through Christ.
Eph.2:7; Tit.3:4-7

KING
Jesus Christ.
Approached as **K**. Jn.12:20-36
Christ is **K**. Verses & fulfillment of
Davidic prophecies. Lk.3:24-31
Claimed to be **K**. Jn.18:33-37
K. of kings & Lord of lords. Rev.19:16
K. of the universe. Jn.12:20-21; 19:19
Rejected & accepted as **K**. Jn.12:37-50
What gives Christ the right to be **K**.
His person, resurrection, & exalta-
tion. Acts 2:33-36; 13:22-23
Reception of. How a **k**. was received.
Mk.11:1-7

KINGDOM OF CHRIST
Entrance into. Transferred into by God.
Col.1:13, cp. 2 Tim.4:18
Nature of. Exists now, as well as in the
future. Col.1:13

KINGDOM OF DAVID
Promised.
To Christ. Eternally. Lk.1:31-33;
1:32-33; Acts 2:33-36; 13:22-23
Verses & fulfillment. Lk.3:24-31

KINGDOM OF GOD (See ETERNAL LIFE; HEAVEN; KINGDOM OF HEAVEN)
Citizens of.
Are blessed. Lk.14:15
Only those who become as children
are citizens of the **k**. Lk.18:16-17
The least person in the **k**. is greater
than the greatest of prophets.
Lk.7:28
Who is unfit for the **k**. Lk.9:62
Climax - Consummation of. Discussed.
1 Cor.15:24-28
Discussed. Mt.19:23-24; Lk.17:20-37
Duty.
To be the concern of believers.
Ro.14:16-18
To pray for God's **k**. to come. Mt.6:10
To preach the **k**. Lk.9:60
To seek the **k**. first. Mt.6:33;
Lk.12:13-33; 16:16
To struggle & press to get into the **k**.
Lk.16:16; 17:22
To work together with other believers
for the **k**. of God. Col.4:11
Facts about.
Harlots go into the **k**. before religion-
ists. Mt.21:31
Is different for a rich person to enter.
Mt.19:24; Mk.10:23; Lk.18:24
Not controlled by man. Lk.17:22;
17:23-24
Several facts. Lk.13:19; 13:20-21
Growth of. Mk.4:26; 4:30-33
Meaning. Both within & without man.
Lk.17:20-21; 17:22
Message of.
Discussed. Mk.1:14-15
Misunderstood. Lk.18:16-17
Preached by Jesus. Lk.8:1
The subject & focus of Jesus' message
& teaching. Lk.8:1; 17:20-37; Acts
1:3
To be preached. Lk.9:60
Misunderstood - Misconception.
By men. Lk.16:16; 18:16-17
By the disciples. Acts 1:6-7
The true vs. the false concept of the **k**.
Acts 1:6-7
Thought to be an earthly **k**. Vs. the
spiritual **k**. Jn.13:36-38
Thought to be an earthly rule & reign.
Acts 1:6-7
Wrong concept. Lk.19:11
Nature of.
Age of the **k**. vs. the age of promise.
Lk.7:28
Is a new social order. Vs. the old so-
cial order. Lk.16:16
Is internal & external, within & with-
out a person. Lk.17:20-21; 17:22
Is not of this earth, but spiritual.
Mk.15:2-5

Is righteousness, peace, & joy.
Ro.14:16-18
Is universal. Lk.13:20-21
Is ushered in by Christ. Lk.7:28;
16:16
Meaning & stages. Lk.17:20-37
Two periods of history. Lk.16:16
What it is like. Mk.4:30-32; Lk.13:18-21
Parables of. (See **PARABLES**)
Positions in. Disciples argue over.
Lk.22:24-30
Power of.
A delivering power. Col.1:12-14
A transforming power. Lk.13:21
Promised.
To believers. As the reward. Lk.6:20;
9:27
To Christ. Eternally. Lk.1:31-33;
1:32-33
To the poor in spirit. As a reward.
Lk.6:20
Rewards of. (See **REWARDS**)
Signs of. Will be clearly seen in the end
time. Lk.21:29-33
Stages of. Mt.19:23-24
Time of.
Began after John the Baptist.
Lk.16:16
Is come to men. Lk.11:20
Is near. Lk.10:11
Is not controlled by man. Lk.17:22;
17:23-24
Is the coming day of God's k. & Jesus'
return. Lk.17:20-37
Is within a person. Lk.17:21
Will be ushered in.
By a new period & social order.
Lk.16:16
By Christ. Lk.11:20
The true vs. the false concept of the **k.**
Acts 1:6-7
The unsaved shall see the **k.** Lk.13:27-30
Triumph of. Final triumph over the king-
doms of this world. Rev.11:14-19
Who receives, enters, & inherits the **k.**
Not church members & not those who
practice sin. 1 Cor.6:9-11; Gal.5:19-
21; Eph.5:3-5
Not flesh & blood, nor anything of
corruption. 1 Cor.15:50
Not those who look back. Lk.9:62
Those appointed & chosen by Christ.
Lk.22:39
Those called by God. 1 Th.2:12
Those who become as a little child.
Lk.18:16-17
Those who continue in the faith & suf-
fer for the **k.** Acts 14:22
Those who have been delivered from
darkness & redeemed by Christ.
Col.1:12-14
Those who press into the kingdom.
Those born again. Jn.3:3-5
Those who seek the **k.** Lk.12:31-34

KINGDOM OF HEAVEN (See **ETER-
NAL LIFE; HEAVEN; KINGDOM OF
GOD**)
Concept of. Discussed. Mt.18:1
Discussed.
As a fisherman's net. Mt.13:47
As a priceless treasure. Mt.13:44
As leaven or yeast. Cp. evil. Mt.13:33
Mysteries of the **k.** of heaven.
Mt.13:1-58
Parables of the **k.** of heaven. Mt.13:1-52

Fact.
Can have a rich welcome into.
2 Pt.1:8-11
Religionists shut up the **k.** of heaven to
others. Mt.23:13
There is to be judgment within the **k.**
Who is to be judged. Mt.13:41
Growth of. Greatness of. Mt.13:31-32
How one enters.
By becoming as a little child. Mt.18:3
By being poor in spirit. Mt.5:3, 10
By having a righteousness that ex-
ceeds the righteousness of religion-
ists. Mt.5:20
By repentance. Mt.3:2; 4:17; 10:7
Not by professing the Lord, but by
doing the will of God. Mt.7:21
Now & eternally. Mt.5:3
Meaning. Mt.19:23-24
Message of.
Proclaimed by Jesus. Mt.4:17
Proclaimed by John. Mt.3:2-6
Nature.
Comes violently. Mt.11:12
Greatness of believers in. Mt.11:11
Keys to the **k.** of heaven. Mt.16:19
Misunderstood. By the disciples. Mt.18:1
Mixture of good & bad, presently.
Mt.13:1-58; 3:1-9; 13:24-30;13:31-
32; 13:33; 13:47-50
Surpasses the world in two ways. Mt.4:23
What the **k.** of heaven is like.
Mt.13:24, 31, 33, 44, 45, 47, 52;
18:23; 20:1; 22:2; 25:1, 14
Position in. Least in. Greater than John
the Baptist. Mt.11:11
Value of.
Giving up all for Christ. Mt.13:44
The Parable of the Hidden Treasure.
Mt.13:44

KINGDOMS OF WORLD (See **WORLD**)
Triumph over. By God & Christ in the
end time. Rev.11:14-19

KINSHIP (See **BROTHERHOOD; FAM-
ILY**)
Basis. Discussed. Lk.8:19-21

KISS
Of love. Meaning. 1 Pt.5:14

KNOW - KNOWING - KNOWLEDGE
(See **SPIRITUAL SIGHT; UNDER-
STANDING**)
Duty.
To add **k.** to our faith. 2 Pt.1:5
To cast down imaginations & every-
thing that exalts itself against the **k.**
of God. 2 Cor.10:5
To control **k.** with love. Ph.1:9
To grow in grace & in the **k.** of Christ.
2 Pt.3:18
To **k.** how to control one's body. 1
Th.4:4
To **k.** nothing (religiously) but Jesus
Christ & Him crucified. 1 Cor.2:2
To **k.** that knowledge puffs up, but
love builds up. 1 Cor.8:1
To **k.** that one has eternal life. 1 Jn.5:12-13
To **k.** that the conversion of a sinner
saves a soul from death. Jas.5:20
To prove that we are wise persons; to
prove our **k.** & wisdom by good be-
havior. Jas.3:13
How to **k.** God. Jn.7:16-19; 8:31-32

Meaning. Ro.15:14; Col.2:3;Jas.1:5-8;
3:13; 2 Pt.1:2; 1:5-7
Of Christ. (See **JESUS CHRIST,**
Knowledge of)
Believers know Christ by His Word or
voice & Spirit. Jn.20:14-16
Duty toward **k.** Christ.
To do the will of God, then one will
k. Christ. Jn.7:17
To **k.** & believe that Christ is in
God & God in Him. Jn.10:38
To **k.** about Christ before one can
seek Him. Mt.18:1
To **k.** Christ & the power of His
resurrection. Ph.3:10
To **k.** Christ, the fact that God sent
Him. Jn.17:3
To **k.** the love of Christ. Eph.3:19
To receive the special revelation of
God & Christ. Lk.10:22
Given to believers. 1 Jn.5:20
Intimate knowledge between Christ &
believers. Jn.10:14-16; 11:5
Intimate knowledge between Christ &
God. Jn.8:55; 10:14-16
Knows about all men. Lk.12:1-3;
Jn.2:24-25
Knows believers intimately.
Jn.10:14-16; 11:5
Possesses all the treasures of wisdom
& **k.** Col.2:3
Of God. (See **GOD**, Knowledge; **EXPO-
SURE**)
An anointing is necessary. 1 Jn.2:20;
2:27
Discussed. Heb.8:10-12; 10:19-20;
10:21
Depth & riches of God's **k.** are un-
searchable. Ro.11:33-36
Duty toward God.
To grow in the **k.** of God.
Eph.1:15-18; Col.1:10
To **k.** God personally, that He is the
source of eternal life. Jn.17:3
To **k.** the only living & true God.
Identified. Eph.1:17-18
Proof that one **k.** God.
Few people care about knowing
God. 1 Jn.2:3-6
One obeys God's command.
1 Jn.2:3-6
Seven tests. 1 Jn.2:3-29
Results. Of **k.** God. Eph.1:18
Some do not have the **k.** of God.
1 Cor.15:34
Of man.
A person who does not **k.** God will
suffer the vengeance of God.
2 Th.1:8
Does not know God by wisdom.
1 Cor.1:21
Man's **k.** of God is an elementary or
basic **k.** Gal.4:3; 4:9-11
Professes that he **k.** God, but he denies
Him by his works. Tit.1:16
Professes to be wise, but is a fool in
his rejection of God. Ro.1:19-22, cp.
18-32
Some are so steeped in sin that they
never come to a **k.** of God.
2 Tim.3:6
Without an understanding of God &
reality. Ro.3:10-12
Of the new birth. Complete assurance, **k.**
Jn.3:9-11

Of the world.
  Are ignorant of God. 2 Pt.3:5-6
  Described. Is as an elementary or basic
  k. Gal.4:3; 4:9-11
Source of **k.**
  Doing the will of God. Jn.7:17
  Jesus Christ. Col.2:3; 1 Jn.5:20
  Receiving a special revelation from
    God & Christ. Lk.10:22
  Receiving the anointing of God.
    1 Jn.2:20; 2:27
  Studying & learning. Jn.7:15;
    2 Tim.2:15
  The Holy Spirit. 1 Cor.2:12-16
  The Scriptures. Studying the Scrip-
    tures. Acts 17:11; 20:32;
    2 Tim.2:15; 3:16-17
Spiritual **k.**
  Gift of. Meaning. 1 Cor.1:5-7; 12:8-10
  Results.
    Frees one from error. Jn.8:31-32
    Gives one eternal life. Jn.17:3
    Leads to salvation. 2 Tim.3:15
  Secured by.
    Obedience. Jn.7:16-17
    The Scriptures. 2 Tim.3:15
  Vs. love. 1 Cor.8:1-3
  Weakness of. 2 Tim.3:6-9

KNOWLEDGE, ELEMENTARY
Of the world. Discussed. Col.2:8

KNOWLEDGE, MESSAGE OF
Gift of. Discussed. 1 Cor.12:8-10

KORAH
Example. Of false teacher. Jude 11

L

LABOR - LABORERS (See **BELIEV-
ERS; DISCIPLES; MINISTERS;
WORK**)
  Call of. (See **CALL - CALLED**)
  Discussed. Mt.20:1-16; Eph.6:5-9;
    Col.3:22-4:1; 1 Pt.2:18-20
    Need for labor. Mt.9:37-38
    Power of laborers. Lk.10:17-20
    Privileges of laborers. Lk.10:21-24
    Purpose. Eph.4:28
    Subject of labor. For God. Jn.4:31-42
    The mission of laborers. Lk.10:1-16
  Duty.
    Discussed. 2 Th.3:6-18
    To be diligent. To **l.** & care for the
      earth. Lk.20:9
    To care for the world & the church.
      Mt.21:33
    To count **l.** in the Word as worthy of
      double honor. 1 Tim.5:17
    To earn one's own living. 1 Th.4:11-12;
      2 Th.3:6-12
    To follow God's will. Col.1:1
    To hold forth the Word of life lest one
      l. in vain. Ph.2:16
    To know them who **l.** among us.
      Col.1:29; 1 Th.5:12
    To **l.** Demanded by God. Imperative!
      Today! Mt.21:28
    To **l.** & suffer reproach because one
      trusts in the living God. 1 Tim.4:10
    To **l.** for Christ's name's sake.
      Rev.2:3

To **l.** for money to meet the need of
  others. Lk.12:31-34
To **l.** for the food that leads to everlast-
  ing life. Jn.6:27
To **l.** in love. 1 Th.1:3; Heb.6:10
To **l.** in order to support the weak.
  Acts 20:35
To **l.** in prayer. Col.4:12
To **l.** night & day preaching the gos-
  pel. 1 Th.2:9
To **l.** one hundred percent. Lk.19:16-17
To **l.**, striving according to God's
  working within oneself. Col.1:29
To **l.** to be accepted by God. 2 Cor.5:9
To **l.** to enter into God's rest. Heb.4:11
To **l.** working with one's own hands.
  Eph.4:28
To love Christ so much that one strives
  to **l.** more abundantly than all others.
  1 Cor.15:10
To pray for laborers. Mt.9:37-38;
  Lk.10:2
To watch & work for judgment is
  coming. Mt.25:14-30
To keep away from idle **l.**
  2 Th.3:6-11
To work with one's own hands.
  1 Th.4:11-12
Toward employers. 1 Tim.6:1-2;
  Tit.2:9-10
Why God demands that we **l.**
  1 Th.4:11-12
Fact.
  Are laborers together with God.
    1 Cor.3:9
  If a person is able & does not work, he
    should not be given handouts.
    2 Th.3:10
  The harvest is ripe, but laborers are
    few. Mt.9:37; Lk.10:2
  There is work for all to do. Mt.20:1
Failure - Sins of.
  Believer can know four things.
    Mt.6:33
  Caused by the temptation of Satan.
    1 Th.3:5
  Cheating laborers out of their wages.
    Jas.5:1-6
  Complaining about wages. Mt.20:11-16,
    cp. 1-16
  In different professions. Lk.3:10-14
  Laboring for food that perishes. Jn.6:27
  Mistreating **l.** Mt.21:33-46, esp. 35-39
  Not working & bumming off other
    people. 1 Th.4:11; 2 Th.3:6-12
  Why there are not more laborers.
    Mt.9:37-38
Invitation to laborers. To come To Christ
  Mt.11:28-30
Kinds of labor.
  Enforced. Mt.5:41
  Industrious. The kind of man Christ
    calls. Mk.1:16
  Six kinds. Mt.20:3-4
Meaning. 2 Cor.6:5
Reward for faithful **l.**
  Is counted worthy of his hire & re-
    ward. Lk.10:7; 1 Tim.5:18
  Will be the first to partake of the fruits.
    2 Tim.2:6
  Will not be in vain. 1 Cor.15:58

LADY, THE ELECT
Discussed. 2 Jn.1-4

LAKE OF FIRE (See **FIERY LAKE;
FIRE**)

LAMB
Sacrificial. Type of Christ. Mt.26:17-30
Symbol - Type of. Ministers. Lk.10:3

LAMB, MARRIAGE SUPPER OF THE
Discussed. Rev.19:1-10

LAMB OF GOD
Christ is the Lamb of God.
  Discussed. Jn.1:29-30; Rev.5:6-7
  Sacrificed Himself as the Lamb of God
    without blemish & without spot.
    1 Pt.1:19
  Sacrificed Himself for us as the Lamb
    of God. 1 Cor.5:7
  Stands in heaven as the slain Lamb of
    God. Rev.5:6; 6:1
Fact.
  Believers shall stand before the Lamb
    of God when they are in heaven.
    Rev.7:9
  Heaven's great song is the song of the
    Lamb of God. Rev.15:3
  The Lord God Almighty & the Lamb
    of God, Christ Himself, are the very
    temple of heaven. Rev.21:22

LAME, SPIRITUALLY
Meaning. Heb.12:13

LAMP
Described. Mt.25:7
Parable of. Truth & man's duty.
  Mk.4:21-25

LAMPSTAND
Of revelation. Symbol in the church.
  Rev.1:13; 1:20

LANGUAGE, FILTHY
Duty. To strip off. Col.3:8-11

LAODICEA
Church of.
  One of the seven churches of Revela-
    tion. Rev.3:14-22
  Represents the affluent, but lukewarm
    & half-committed church. Rev.3:14-22
City of. Discussed. Rev.3:14
Epistle to. Discussed. Col.4:15-16

LASCIVIOUSNESS (See **DEBAUCH-
ERY; DEFILEMENT; FILTHINESS;
LEWDNESS; SENSUALITY; UN-
CLEANNESS**)

LAST DAYS (See **END TIME**)
Age of. Lk.21:5-38

LAST TIMES (See **END TIME**)
Age of. Lk.21:5-38
Discussed. Jude 17-19

LAST WILL & TESTAMENT (See
**COVENANT; WILL, LAST WILL &
TESTAMENT**)
Discussed. Heb.8:6-13; 9:15-22

LAUGH - LAUGHTER
Of the world. Judgment of. Lk.6:24-26

LAW (See **SCRIBAL LAW; COMMANDMENT**)
Breaking.
  Breaking one l. makes one guilty of breaking all laws. Jas.2:8-11
  Criteria for breaking the l. Mt.12:3-4
  Influencing others to break the l., to sin. Mt.5:19
  Satisfaction, payment must be made once the l. is broken. Mk.1:15
  Voiding the l. Mt.5:19
Ceremonial l. (See **CEREMONIAL LAW; SCRIBAL LAW**)
Defined as.
  The greatest l. Is love. Mt.22:34-40; Mk.12:28-34
  The standard for behavior. 1 Jn.3:4
Deliverance from.
  By Christ. Ro.4:1-3; 4:22; 5:1; 10:1-11; Gal.2:15-16
    His being born under the l. to redeem believers. Gal.4:4-7
    His death. Ro.7:4; Col.2:14
    His fulfilling the law. Mt.5:17; 5:17-48; 5:17-20; Ro.3:31;8:3; 1 Cor.15:57; Gal.4:4-7; Col.2:14; Rev.2:5-6
  By faith & justification. (See **JUSTIFICATION**) Ro.3:27-31; 4:1-3, 13-16, 22; 5:1;10:1-11; Gal.3:1-5:12
Described as.
  A prison for man. Gal.3:23-25
  A teacher or guardian. Gal.3:23-25
  An elementary (child's) knowledge of God. Gal.4:1-3; 4:9-11
  The law of evil. Meaning. Ro.7:21-23
  The law of faith. Discussed. Ro.3:27
  The law of righteousness. Christ ended the law. Three ways. Ro.10:4
  The law of sin. Meaning. Ro.7:21-23; 7:25
  The law of "Spirit & Life." Meaning. Ro.8:2-4
  The law of the "inward man." Ro.7:21-23
  The law of "the mind." Ro.7:21-23
  The law of "works." Discussed. Ro.3:27
  The "oldness of the letter." Ro.7:6
  The strength of sin. 1 Cor.15:54-56
Discussed. Mt.5:17-20
  Dietary law. Acts 10:11-16; 10:9-22
  Thirteen points. Gal.3:10
Duty.
  Must die to the l. Gal.2:19-21
  To be controlled by love. Mt.22:40
  To be obedient, not a hearer of the l. Ro.2:11-15
  To obey. Seriousness of. Mt.5:19
Fulfilled by Christ.
  As a child. Lk.2:21-23
  Two reasons. Lk.2:39
Importance.
  Of the l. of God. Lk.16:16; Jn.1:17; Ro.2:12-15;3:19-20; 5:20-21; 7:12; 7:14;Gal.3:24; 1 Tim.1:9
  Shall not pass away. Lk.16:16
  To the Jewish nation. Lk.6:7
  To the Teachers of the Law & Pharisees. Mt.5:17-18
Jews view of. Fourfold. Mt.5:17
Kinds.
  Ceremonial & ritual l. (See **CEREMONIAL LAW; RITUAL**)
  Civil l. (See **CIVIL LAW**)

Conditioning l. Are eight laws of condition. Jn.12:39-41
Man-made l. Less important than man & his need. Mt.12:9-13
Misconception - Misunderstanding of. One of three great misconceptions of men. Lk.16:17-18
Nature of the l.
  Is established & upheld by faith. Ro.3:31
  Is holy, just, & good. Ro.7:12
  Is spiritual. Ro.4:14
Old vs. new l. Lk.16:16; 16:17-18
Principles. Discussed. Mt.5:17-48
Purpose of the l.
  Discussed. Ro.7:7-13; 1 Tim.1:8-11
  Fivefold. Ro.3:19-20
  To arouse sin. Ro.7:5; 7:8
  To bring us to Christ. Gal.3:23-25
  To govern behavior & unbelief. Jn.12:39-41
  To point out sin & transgression. Ro.4:14-15; 5:19-21; 5:20; 7:5; 1 Jn.3:4
  To reveal man's depravity. Ro.3:9-20
  To reveal sin. Ro.7:7
  To stop boasting & make all the world guilty before God. Ro.3:19-20
  To work or bring wrath. Ro.4:14-15
Relation to believers.
  Believers are delivered from the l. (See **LAW**, Deliverance)
  Believers are freed from the l. Ro.7:1-25
  Is fulfilled in love. Ro.13:8-10
  L. is "dead" to believers. Ro.7:1-6
  To avoid foolish questions about. Tit.3:9
Relation to man. (See **LAW**, Breaking; Duty; Related Subjects)
  Man's view of. Col.2:14
  Not charged when there is no law. Ro.5:13
  Requires two witnesses to support one's testimony. Jn.8:17-18
  Two positions of the l. to man. Ro.7:1-6
Scribal. (See **CEREMONIAL LAW; SCRIBAL LAW**)
Source.
  Brought, mediated by angels. Heb.2:2
  God gave the l. through mediators, both angels & man (Moses). Gal.3:19-20
Vs. Christ. Col.2:14
  Before Christ vs. after Christ. Mt.5:17-18
  To stand fast in the liberty of Christ, not in the l. Gal.5:1-6
Vs. faith.
  Discussed. Ro.4:13-16; Gal.2:15-16; 2:16;2:17-18; 2:19-21; 3:6-14; 3:15-18; 5:1-6
  Given 430 years after the promise given to Abraham. Gal.3:17
  Voids faith; brings wrath; points out sin. Ro.4:14-15
Vs. grace. Heb.12:18-24
  Believer is under grace, not l. Meaning. Ro.6:14-15
  Christ ended the law. Three ways. Ro.10:4
  Discussed. Act 15:1-35
    Hagar & Sarah illustrate l. vs. grace. Gal.4:21-31
Vs. liberty. Acts 10:9-15, 28, 34-35; 11:5-10;15:1-22; 21:17-26
Vs. love & forgiveness. Mt.5:17-20
Vs. salvation. Acts 13:45-46, 50; 14:2, 19; 15:1-11; 17:5-9, 13; 18:19
Vs. the new covenant. 2 Cor.3:6-18
Weakness & powerlessness of.

Are two positions of the l. to man. Ro.7:1-6
Arouses sin. Ro.7:5; 7:8
Breaking of the l. is sin. 1 Jn.3:4
Cannot give the reward nor fulfill the promise of God. Ro.4:13
Causes sin to dominate a person. Ro.6:14-15
Creates & stirs fear. Heb.12:18-21
Creates pressure, tension, discouragement, & defeat. Being "under l." Ro.6:14-15
Demands perfection or else results in judgment. Gal.3:10-12
Demands that every l. be kept. Gal.3:10-12
Discussed.
  Eleven points. Ro.7:7-13
  Fivefold weakness. Gal.3:19-22
Does not produce righteousness. Ro.3:21-22
Does not receive an inheritance. Ro.4:13-16
Does not save. Acts 15:4-5
Enslaves - entangles. Gal.3:10-12; 4:1-3; 4:8-11; 4:24-25
Enslaves one to do all the l. Gal.3:10-12; 5:3
Fails just as idolatry does. Gal.4:9-11
Forces a man to live under the l. Gal.3:10-12
Holds the world in bondage. Gal.4:1-3
Imprisons & teaches. Gal.3:23-25; 4:1-3
Is against man. Ro.3:19-20
Is "alive" & "active" to the unbeliever. Ro.7:1-6
Is contrary to man. Col.2:14
Is excluded & voided by faith. Ro.3:27-31
Is overcome by the Spirit. Ro.8:2-4
Is the strength of sin. 1 Cor.15:50-58
Is the wrong way to seek justification. Ro.4:13-16
Judges man. Gal.3:10-12
Justifies no man. Gal.3:1-4:7
Lacks love, compassion, & mercy. Mt.18:28; 18:30
Leaves a consciousness of sin. Heb.10:1-4
Makes man a sinner. 1 Jn.3:4-9
Makes nothing perfect. Heb.7:11-12; 7:19
Man cannot keep enough l. to become perfect & acceptable to God. Gal.2:15-16
Offers an imperfect system. Heb.10:1-10
Puts man under a curse. Gal.3:10-12
Threefold weakness. Ro.4:14-15
Weightier vs. lighter matters. Mt.22:34-36; 23:23-24

LAW-BREAKING
Caused by.
  Adam's sin. Ro.5:13-14
  Being deceived. 1 Tim.2:14
  Breaking the law. Ro.4:14-15
  Committing sin. 1 Jn.3:4
Counteracted - Delivered from. By Christ.
  He was counted among the transgressors. Lk.22:37
  He died to redeem us from our l. Heb.9:15
Discussed. Ro.4:14-15; Eph.2:1-2

Meaning. Mt.6:14; Eph.2:1-2; Heb.2:2;
1 Jn.3:4
Of the law. Breaking one law makes a
person guilty of breaking all the laws.
Jas.2:8-11

LAW, CIVIL
Discussed. Mt.17:24-27; 22:15-22;
Mk.12:13-17; Lk.20:19-26; Ro.13:1-7;
1 Tim.2:2; Tit.3:1; Heb.13:7;1 Pt.2:13-17

LAWLESSNESS
Meaning. 1 Jn.3:4

LAWLESSNESS, MAN OF
Antichrist, The. (See **ANTICHRIST**)
2 Th.2:3

LAWYER--AN EXPERT OF THE LAW
(See **TEACHERS OF THE LAW**)
Described. Mt.22:35
Jesus accused lawyers of burdening men
down with laws & rules. Lk.11:45-52
Seek to discredit Jesus. Lk.10:25-37
Zenas, a l. who was a committed believer.
Tit.3:13

LAY ASIDE (See **RID YOURSELF**;
THROW OFF)

LAYMEN (See **BELIEVERS**)
Of the early church.
Discussed. Acts 8:1-3; 11:19-30; 13:1-3
Established mission churches. Acts
8:3; 11:19-30; 13:1-14:28
Preached everywhere in the early
church. Acts 8;1-4
Were persecuted & scattered. Acts
8:1-4; 11:19-30
Witness of.
Are to disciple l. to witness.
Mt.28:19-20; Jn.20:21, cp. Lk.19:10;
Acts 1:8; 2 Tim.2:2; 1 Pt.3:15
Great witness in the early church.
Acts 8:1-4

LAZARUS, THE BEGGAR
And the Rich Man. The self-indulgent vs.
the man of faith. Lk.16:19-31

LAZARUS, THE BROTHER OF MARY
& MARTHA
And Jesus. Power over death. Jn.11:38-46
Death of. Purposes of death. Jn.11:1-16
Religionists sought to kill Lazarus.
Jn.12:9-11

LAZY - LAZINESS (See **IDLE - IDLE-
NESS**; **SLOTHFUL**)
Discussed. Ro.13:11-14
Work & employment. 2 Th.3:6-18
Duty.
Not to lack zeal. Ro.12:11
To awaken out of sleep & l. Ro.13:11-12
To be diligent & not l. Heb.6:11-12
To stay awake, always working &
preparing for the Lord's return.
Mt.25:1-13, esp. 5
Example. Reluctant to obey. Lk.5:4-5
Fact. A l. person is useless to Christ.
Mk.1:16
Law of. Mt.13:12; 13:13-15
Meaning. A l. servant. Mt.25:24-30, cp.
14:30; Ro.12:11

Result. Secures little if anything. Lk.8:18
Result - Judgment of. Shall be cast into
outer darkness, hell. Mt.25:26-30, cp.
14-30
Reward. Receive less & less. Mt.13:12;
13:13-15
Verses. List of. Lk.8:18

LEADERS - LEADERSHIP (See **DEA-
CONS**; **MINISTERS**; and Related Sub-
jects)
Call of. To be ambassadors & shepherds.
Lk.6:13
Choosing. Discussed. Acts 1:12-26
Duty.
To obey & submit to--respect & fol-
low. Heb.13:17
To pray for l. Heb.13:18-19
To remember l. & follow them.
Heb.13:7
Essentials. Acts 1:12-15
Gift of. Discussed. Ro.12:6-8
How to lead. Discussed. 1 Pt.5:1-4
Message to. Last words of Paul to l. Acts
20:28-38
Names - Titles within the church. 1
Cor.12:28
Apostle. Eph.4:11
Deacon. 1 Tim.3:8-13
Elder. Ph.1:1; 1 Tim.3:1-7; 5:17-20;
Tit.1:5-9
Evangelist. Eph.4:11
Minister. (See **MINISTER**)
Overseer. Acts 20:28-31
Pastor. Eph.4:11
Prophet. Ro.12:6-8; 1 Cor.12:8-10;
Eph.4:11
Teacher. 1 Cor.12:28-30; Eph.4:11
Problem. Shortage of.
Cannot minister to everyone. Acts 6:1
Causes grumbling & complaining.
Acts 6:1
Reward of believers. For faithfulness.
Lk.12:41-48
Seeking l. Discussed. Acts 11:25
Sins common to l. Acts 4:5-10
Blind l leading the blind. Lk.6:39
Staff of a church.
Lay staff chosen. Acts 6:1-7
Ministerial staff formed. Acts 11:22-26

LEADING ASTRAY
Warning against. Mt.18:5-10

LEARN FROM ME
Meaning. Mt.11:29

LEARNING (See **TEACH - TEACHING**)

LEAVEN--YEAST (See **YEAST**)

LEGACY
Of the lost. Lk.16:22

LEGAL DISPUTES
How to handle. Discussed. 1 Cor.6:1-8

LEGALISM - LEGALIST (See **CERE-
MONIAL LAW**; **PHARISEES**; **RE-
LIGIONIST**; **RITUAL**; **SCRIBES**)
Discussed. Lk.6:7; Gal.2:3-5; 2:4; 2:11-13
In the Jewish religion. Reason for.
Lk.6:7
Message to. Gal.2:11-21
Paul did not preach l. Gal.5:10-12
Questionable social activities.
Ro.14:1-23; 1 Cor.8:1-13
Strict vs. loose behavior. Mt.5:17-18

Error - Problem with - Results.
Eliminates the right to worship at the
cross. Heb.13:10-11
Enslaves one to do the law. Gal.5:2-4
Lacks love, compassion, & mercy.
Mt.18:28; 18:30
Lays heavy burdens upon men.
Mt.23:4
Often becomes a witch hunt. Acts
21:20-26
Places form & ritual before people in
need. Lk.13:14-16
Results - Judgment.
Makes one a false brother. Gal.2:3-5;
2:11-13
Voids one's right to receive the inheri-
tance. Gal.4:30

LEND - LENDING (See **BORROWING**)
Discussed. Mt.5:42; Ro.13:8
Duty. To lend when asked. Mt.5:42;
Lk.6:27-31; 6:35
Example of. Bankruptcy. Mt.18:23-27

LEPER - LEPROSY
Discussed. Mt.8:1-4; Mk.1:40-45;
Lk.5:12; 17:12-14
Healed by Jesus.
One leper. Mt.8:1-4
Ten lepers. Lk.17:17-19
Legal requirements for a healed leper.
Mt.8:1-4; 8:4
Symbolized. The most unclean.
Mk.1:40-45
Type of. Sin. Mt.8:1-4; Mk.1:40-45

LETHARGY (See **SLOTHFUL**)

LETTERS
Of commendation. Discussed. 2 Cor.3:1-5

LEVI
Another name for the apostle Matthew.
Call of. Mk.2:14

LEVI, TRIBE OF - LEVITES
Discussed. Jn.1:19
Work - Function of. Served as priests for
Israel. Heb.7:5

LEVITE MARRIAGE
Discussed. Lk.20:27-33; 20:28

LEWDNESS
Characteristic - Trait of. False teachers.
Jude 4
Meaning. Mk.7:22; 2 Cor.12:19-
21;Gal.5:19-21; Eph.4:17-19;1 Pt.4:3,
cp. Ro.13:13

LIBERAL - LIBERALS
Errors of. Twofold. Mk.12:24
Vs. conservative.
Two schools in Christ's day. Mk.10:2-
4
Unbelievers reject both approaches to
the gospel. Lk.7:33-34

LIBERATOR
Is Christ. Difference between a liberator
& a deliverer. Lk.22:19-20
Jesus the liberator. Jn.8:34-36; 14:6

LIBERTY, CHRISTIAN (See **DELIV-ERANCE; FREEDOM; SEPARA-TION**)

Believers.
Are called to l. Gal.5:13
Are free & spiritual. Gal.5:13-6:18
Are freed from condemnation. Ro.8:1-17
Are freed from sin. Ro.6:1-23; 6:20-23
Are freed from the law. Ro.7:1-25
Are set free by Christ. Jn.8:34-36; Gal.5:1-6
Are set free from five things. Jn.8:32; 2 Cor.3:17-18
Are set free, not enslaved. Gal.4:21-31
Discussed. Ro.6:14-15; 14:1-23
Shall be freed from struggling & suf-fering. Ro.8:1-39
Creation. Shall be set free from bondage. Ro.8:18-27; 2 Pt.3:8-14; Rev.21:1-5
Described as.
The law of the spirit of life. Ro.8:2
Discussed. Ro.14:1-23; 1 Cor.6:12; 8:1-13; 10:14-11:1; Gal.5:1-6; 5:13-15
Duty.
Not to be a stumbling block. Ro.14:1-23; 1 Cor.8:1-13
Not to follow false teachers who abuse Christian l. Gal.2:4-5
Not to use l. as an excuse to disobey the laws of the state. 1 Pt.2:16-17
Not to use l. to indulge the flesh. Gal.5:13-15
To be controlled by love. Gal.5:13-15
To do the expedient, not just the law-ful. 1 Cor.6:12-20
To serve righteousness. Ro.6:17-23
To stand firm in the liberty of Christ. Three points. Gal.5:1-6
True l. keeps the law. Jas.1:25
Is conditional. Must continue in the truth, the Word of Christ. Jn.8:31-32
Limits of. What is allowed vs. not al-lowed. Ro.14:1-23; 1 Cor.8:1-13; 10:14-11:1
Questions concerning.
Liberty & personal rights. 1 Cor.8:1-11:1
Limits of l. Christian believers & their freedom. 1 Cor.10:14-11:1
Principles of l. 1 Cor.6:12
Questionable pleasures & socials. 1 Cor.8:1-13
Questionable social activities. Dis-cussed. Ro.14:1-12
Source.
Christ. Col.2:20
The gospel. Ro.6:17-18
The Holy Spirit. Ro.8:2; 2 Cor.3:17
The Lord. 2 Cor.3:17
Truth. Liberated from five things. Jn.8:32
Tests of l. Questions to ask. 1 Cor.10:23-28
Vs. license. Ro.6:1; 1 Pt.2:16-17
Discussed. Acts 15:1-35
Is a very real danger. Gal.5:13-15
Is abused. 2 Pt.2:10
Unbelievers reject both approaches to the gospel. Lk.7:33-34
Why a person is not free to sin. Gal.5:13
Why belief does not lead to the freedom to sin. Gal.5:13

LICENSE (See **INDULGENCE; SELF-ISHNESS; SIN**)

Believers do not have l. to sin. Ro.6:1; 6:14-23; 1 Cor.6:12-20; 8:1-13; 10:14-11:1

Discussed. Ro.6:1-10; 14:1-3; 1 Cor.6:12-20; 8:1-13; 10:14-11:1
Meaning. Giving l. is not love. Ro.3:5-8
Sin of. Discussed. Rev.2:5-6
Vs. liberty. Gal.5:13; 1 Pt.2:16-17
Unbelievers reject both approaches to the gospel. Lk.7:33-34

LIE - LIARS - LYING (See **DECEP-TION; HYPOCRISY**)

Discussed. Jn.8:44-45; Acts 25:6-7; Ro.13:9; Eph.4:25
Duty. To strip off. Col.3:8-11
Fact.
Men of the end time will be given over to l. through hypocrisy. 1 Tim.4:1-2
No l. is of the truth. 1 Jn.2:21
Some people l. so much that they have the very reputation of being l. Tit.1:12
The law is made for liars. 1 Tim.1:10
The teaching of God's Spirit is not a l. 1 Jn.2:27
Judgment of.
Excluded from the holy city, heaven itself. Rev.21:23-27; 22:14-15
To be put into the lake of fire. Rev.21:8, 27
Kinds of - How one lies.
By claiming to love God, yet hating one's brother. 1 Jn.4:20
By denying God & His Son, the Lord Jesus Christ. 1 Jn.2:22
By denying that Jesus is Christ, that He has come in the flesh. 1 Jn.2:22-23, cp. 1 Jn.4:2-3
By denying that one has not sinned or that man is not a sinner. 1 Jn.1:8, 10
By not believing the Word of God, that God has sent His Son. 1 Jn.5:10
By not keeping God's commandments 1 Jn.2:4
By professing Christ, yet walking in darkness. 1 Jn.1:6
Six kinds. Ro.13:9
Sin of.
Being deceived & believing a lie. 2 Th.2:11
Changing the truth of God into a lie. Ro.1:25
Committed by man & Satan. Jn.8:44-45
Lying to God is sin. Discussed. Acts 5:1-4
Will be committed by the antichrist. 2 Th.2:8-12

LIFE (See **SALVATION**)

Answers to life - How to secure life - Source of life. (See **ETERNAL LIFE**)
Belief. Jn.3:16; 3:36; 5:24; 11:25; 20:31
Building l. Mt.7:24-27
Christ. Mk.2:18-22; Jn.1:4; 5:21; 5:26; 5:40-41; 7:37-39; 11:25-27; 14:6; 17:2-3; Gal.2:20; Col.2:9-10; 3:3; 1 Jn.1:1-2; 1:1; 5:9-12
Came to bring l. Lk.5:36-39; Jn.10:10
Energizes & quickens l. Jn.6:58; Ro.8:11
Is the only gate to l. Jn.10:10
L. is found in Christ. Col.2:9-10
Receiving Him. Jn.6:52-58
Verses. List of. Jn.5:26
The reason He came. To give l. 1 Jn.4:9-11
Verses. List of. Jn.5:26

Counting oneself alive to God. Ro.6:11
Eagerness of Christ to give l. Jn.1:38-39
Faith. Gal.3:1-5
Four ways. Mk.2:20
Fullness & grace of God. Jn.1:16-17
God. Jn.1:4; 5:21; 5:26; 17:2-3; 1 Jn.5:9-12
The power of God. 2 Pt.1:3
Love. Loving Christian brothers. 1 Jn.3:14
Man himself. By doing the will of God. 1 Jn.2:17
Mortifying, putting to death the deeds of the body. Ro.8:13-14
Righteousness. Ro.8:10
Steps to l. Fourfold. 1 Pt.3:10-12
The Holy Spirit & His power. Ro.8:1-17; 8:1-4; 8:11
The Word of God. 1 Pt.1:23, cp. Jn.3:4-8
Assurance of. (See **ASSURANCE**)
Discussed. 1 Jn.5:9-12; 5:13-15
Perfected. In the new heaven & earth. Rev.21:4-6
The Word & promise of Christ. Jn.5:24
Attitude about - Concepts of.
Living one day at a time. Mt.6:34
Men think l. consists in things. Lk.12:15-19
Right vs. wrong l. Mt.6:25-34
Threefold. Mk.8:32-33
What men call life. Mt.10:39
Christ & l.
Christ brings a new l. Lk.5:36-39
Christ is the Way, the Truth, & the Life. Jn.14:6
Christ's authority over l. Jn.5:1-47
Kinds of l. Christ brings. Mk.2:18-22
Life is to exalt Christ. Ph.1:20-21
The life of Jesus is to be manifested in our flesh. 2 Cor.4:11; Gal.2:20
The Light of l. Meaning. Jn.8:12-13
To live *is* Christ. Ph.1:21
Crown of l. A reward to be given to faith-ful believers. Discussed. Rev.2:10
Dangers - Problems - Errors of.
A person can ruin his l. Mt.26:6-13; 26:14-16
L. can be choked by three things. Lk.8:11-15
L. is a mystery to man. Mt.19:11-22; 19:23-26; 19:27-30; Lk.10:25-37
L. is uncertain. Jas.5:7
L. is wasted in worldly & indulgent living. Lk.12:15-19; 15:11-16; 16:19-20
Unbelief. Separates one from l. 1 Jn.5:9-12
What life means to men. Ph.1:21
Defined.
As being "hid" in Christ. Col.3:3
As the energy of Christ Himself. Jn.1:4; 14:6; 17:3; 1 Jn.1:1; 1:1-2
As the energy of God Himself. Jn.1:1, 4; 17:3
Described.
As a race. Heb.12:1-4
As grace for grace. Discussed. Jn.1:16-17
As the narrow road. Mt.7:13-14
As the spirit of l. Ro.8:2-4
As the wise & foolish builder. Mt.7:24-27
As two choices in l. Mt.7:13-14
As two roads. Five descriptions. Mt.7:13-14

Described as.
  Active, not inactive. Mt.22:39
  Loving people, not doing religious
    things. Mt.22:39
  The greatest commandment.
    Mk.12:29-31
  Unfeigned l. Meaning. 2 Cor.6:6-7
Discussed. Mt.5:44; 22:37-40; Mk.
  12:28-34;Lk.10:25-37; 1 Cor.13:1-13;
  Gal.5:13-15; 1 Th.3:11-13;1 Pt.4:8;
  1 Jn.2:7-11; 3:10-24;4:7-21; 2 Jn.6
  A picture of sacrificial l. & faith.
    Mt.26:6-13
  A strong l. 1 Th.3:11-13
  The great command of. 2 Jn.5-6
  The Greek words for l. Four words.
    Mt.5:44
  The new commandment of l. Meaning.
    Jn.13:33-35
  What l. involves. Mt.22:37-38
Duty.
  Discussed. Lk.6:27-38; Jn.15:17;
    Jn.21:15-17
  Essential.
    L. must control questionable pleas-
      ures & social functions. 1 Cor.8:1-3
    Must abide in Christ's l. Jn.14:21;
      15:10
    Must base belief upon l. Jn.20:2, 8
    Must be the great law of the be-
      liever. Gal.5:13-15
    Must be the mark of disciples.
      Jn.13:33-35
    Must demonstrate the acts of l.
      Listed. Gal.5:14; 2 Jn.6
    Must grow more & more in l.
      Ph.1:9-10; 1 Th.4:9-10
    Must labor in l. Heb.6:10
    Must l. & love sacrificially. Jn.12:3
    Must l. with actions and not with
      words only. 1 Jn.3:18-19
    Must l. oneself. Mt.22:39;
      Mk.12:31
    Must l. the ministry. L. is absolutely
      essential. Jn.21:15; 21:15-17
    Must owe nothing to anyone but
      love. Ro.13:8
    Must put on l. Col.3:13
  Meaning. Jn.14:15; 14:23; 15:9;
    15:12;21:15-17
  Must love believers.
    To live in brotherly l. Heb.13:1
    To love another in the truth (in
      Christ & in the Word of God).
      2 Jn.1-2
    To love as brothers. 1 Pt.3:8
    To love as Christ loved. Eph.5:1-2
    To love believers with the l. of
      Christ. Jn.13:33-35; 15:9; 15:12
    To love one another fervently.
      1 Pt.1:22-25; 1 Jn.4:7-21
    To love the brotherhood, the
      church. 1 Pt.2:16-17
    To love those who criticize & mis-
      treat. 2 Jn.5
    To love with kindness. Ro.12:9-10
    To love without hypocrisy.
      Ro.12:9-10
    To provoke believers to l.
      Heb.10:24
  Must love Christ.
    Basic thing God wants. Jn.20:1-2;
      20:7-10
    Before family. Mt.10:35-37
    Meaning. Jn.14:15; 14:23

Must love God.
  Chief duty. To love God first--with
    all of one's heart. Mt.22:37-38;
    Mk.12:29-31
  How do we know that we really l.
    God? Discussed. 1 Jn.3:1-3
  Must respond to His love. 1 Jn.3:1-3
  Proven by our love for one another.
    1 Jn.4:19-21
  Proven by several tests. 1 Jn.3:1-4:21
  To love God. Mk.12:29-31; Lk.10:25-37
Must love one's enemies. Mt.5:44;
  Lk.6:27-31
Must love one's neighbor. 1 Jn.2:7-11
  As oneself. Ro.13:8-10
  The second great commandment.
    Mt.22:39; Mk.12:31; Lk.10:25-37
Example of.
  A mother's great love for her child.
    Mt.15:22
  Peter at the civil trials of Jesus. Mk.14:54
  Philemon's reception of his runaway
    slave. Phile.1:17-21
Importance of - Why one must l. (See
  LOVE, Results)
  Assures boldness in the day of judg-
    ment. 1 Jn.4:17
  Discussed. 1 Cor.13:1-3; 1 Jn.4:7-21
  Embraces all the commands.
    Mt.22:40; Ro.13:8-10
  Fulfills all the law. Ro.13:8-10
  God commands l. 1 Jn.3:23-24
  Involves fifteen of the greatest acts of
    behavior. 1 Cor.13:4-7
  Is not a new command 1 Jn.2:7-8
  Is one of the two great commands of
    God. 1 Jn.3:23-24
  Is one of the two great pillars of life.
    Col.1:3-8
  Is superior to spiritual gifts.
    1 Cor.13:1-13; 13:13
  Is the commandment of Christ.
    Mt.22:34-40
  Is the greatest commandment.
    Mt.22:37-39
  Is the law of life. Gal.5:13-15
  Is the supreme commandment. 1 Jn.2:7-8
  Keeps one from stumbling. 1 Jn.2:7-11
  Perfects one. 1 Jn.2:5; 4:12; 4:18
  Permanence of. 1 Cor.13:8-12
  Preeminence of. 1 Cor.13:8-13
  Proves seven things. 1 Jn.4:7-21
  Reasons for l. Is the new commandment
    of Christ. Jn.13:34-35; 15:12-17
  Stirs diligent labor. 1 Th.1:3
  Supremacy of. 1 Cor.13:13
Kinds of. Jn.21:15-17
  Agape, godly l. Jn.21:15-17;
    1 Cor.13:1-3;2 Pt.1:5-7; 2 Jn.5
  Brotherly l. 1 Th.4:9-10; 2 Th.1:3;
    Heb.13:1;1 Pt.3:8
  Fervent l. 1 Pt.4:8
  Four kinds. Agape, phileo, storge,
    eros. Mt.5:44; 1 Cor.13:1-13;
    1 Th.3:12;2 Jn.5
  Increasing l. 2 Th.1:3
  Philadelphia, brotherly l. 1 Pt.1:22-25
  Phileo, brotherly l. Jn.21:15-17
  Unfeigned l. 2 Cor.6:6-7
L. of Christ. (See **CHRIST**, Love of)
  Constrains a minister to serve.
    2 Cor.5:14-16
  Duty. To understand the l. of Christ.
    Eph.3:19; 1 Jn.3:16
  For believers. Jn.13:33-35; 15:9;
    15:12; 21:15-17

L. of God. (See **GOD**, Love of)
L. of self. Legitimate. Are to love self.
  How. Mt.22:39
Meaning. (See **LOVE**. Kinds of)
  Jn.21:15-17; 1 Cor.13:1-13; Gal.5:22-23;
  Eph.2:4-5; 2 Jn.5
  Of *philadelphia* love. 1 Pt.1:22-25
Misconceptions - Errors of. Thinking
  God is l. & not just. Ro.2:2-5; 3:5-8
Nature.
  Requires justice & judgment. Ro.2:2-5;
    3:5-8
  What l. involves. Mt.22:37-38;
    Mk.12:29-31
Perfected.
  By confession & love. 1 Jn.4:14-19
  By obeying God's Word. 1 Jn.2:5
Proof of. Obedience. Jn.14:15, 21, 23-24;
  15:10
Proves.
  Seven things. 1 Cor.13:8-13
  Six things. 1 Jn.4:7-21
  That God is one's Father. Jn.8:42
  That God's Spirit is within. 1 Jn.4:12-13
  That one is a child of God. 1 Jn.3:10
  That one is born again. 1 Jn.4:7
  That one is either of God or of Satan.
    1 Jn.3:10
  That one really l.'s God. 1 Jn.4:8
  That one really l.'s God & others.
    1 Jn.5:1-3
Results. (See **LOVE**, Importance of)
  Are not to l. the praise of men.
    Jn.12:43
  Assures boldness in the day of judg-
    ment. 1 Jn.4:17
  Covers a multitude of sins. 1 Pt.4:8
  Delivers from fear. Perfect l. 1 Jn.4:18
  In obedience. Jn.14:15; 14:23
  In the new birth. 1 Jn.4:7-8; 4:14-16
  In unity. Ph.2:1
  In witnessing. Jn.13:34-35; 21:15-17
  Is the way one knows God. 1 Jn.4:7-21
  Keeps one from stumbling. 1 Jn.2:7-11
  Obeys God's commands. 1 Jn.5:2-3
  Makes one complete. 1 Jn.2:5; 4:12;
    4:18
  Presents one blameless before God.
    1 Th.3:13
  Proves seven things. 1 Jn.4:7-21
  Proves that one knows God. 1 Jn.2:7-11
  Proves whether one is a child of God
    or of the devil. 1 Jn.3:10
  Purifies the soul. 1 Pt.1:22
  Stirs ministry & service. 2 Cor.5:14-16
Study of l. Mt.22:34-40
  Jesus' anointing at Bethany. Mk.14:3-9
  Verses. List of. Lk.10:25-28
Views of l. In the Old Testament.
  Mt.5:43
Vs. doing religious things. Mk.12:31
  Discussed. 1 Pt.1:22-25; 4:8
What one is not to l.
  Not to l. money. 1 Tim.6:10
  Not to l. the praise of men. Jn.14:42-43
  Not to l. the world nor the things of the
    world. 1 Jn.2:15-16
Work of l. Discussed. 1 Jn.3:10-17

LOVE, SELF
Discussed. 2 Tim.3:2-4

LOVE, WITHOUT MEANING
Meaning. 2 Tim.3:2-4

LOVER OF MONEY
Caused by. Money. One of three misconceptions of men. Lk.16:14-15
Described as.
    Idolatry. Eph.5:5; Col.3:5
    Root of all kinds of evil. 1 Tim.6:10
Discussed. Lk.12:13-21; Ro.13:9; Heb.13:5-6
Duty.
    Ministers are not to be given over to covetousness. 1 Tim.3:3
    Not to let covetousness be mentioned even once among us. Eph.5:3
    Not to use a cloak to hide a covetousness heart. 1 Th.2:5
    To be without covetousness Heb.13:5
    To beware of covetousness Lk.12:15
    To put to death covetousness. Col.3:5
Example.
    Ananias. Acts 5:1-11
    Judas. Mt.26:14-15
    The rich fool. Lk.12:13-21
Legitimate lover of money. To covet gifts. 1 Cor.12:31
Meaning. Mk.7:22; Lk.12:15; Ro.1:29; 1 Cor.5:9-10; 6:10; Eph.5:3; Col.3:5;
    Meaning. 1 Tim.3:2-32 Tim.3:2-4
    Being rich & hoarding. 1 Tim.6:9
    Desiring material things. Heb.13:5
    Love of money. Acts 5:1-11; 1 Tim.6:10
    Preferring property over Christ. Mt.8:28-34
Results in.
    Acute mental anguish. 1 Tim.6:10
    Being barred from the kingdom of God. 1 Cor.6:9-11; Eph.5:5
    Death, spiritual & eternal death. Ro.1:28-32, esp. 32
    Deception, hypocrisy. Verses. List of. Jn.12:4-8
    Disqualification of pastoral call. 1 Tim.3:3
    Enslavement. 1 Tim.6:9
    Failure to use wealth wisely. Lk.12:13-21
    Falling spiritually. 1 Tim.6:9
    Judgment. Lk.12:20-21
    Lying. Acts 5:1-11
    Many hurtful desires. 1 Tim.6:9
    Many temptations. 1 Tim.6:9
    Reaction & rejection of Christ. Reasons. Mt.8:33-34; 8:34-37
    Rejection of the Lord's preaching. Lk.16:13-14
    Wandering. 1 Tim.6:9
Sin of.
    Desiring, lusting for more & more. Mt.26:15
    Enslaved by covetousness 2 Pt.2:14
    Judas. Lk.22:4-6
    The big sin of the world. Lk.12:15-19
    The religious. Lk.16:14-15
Trait.
    Of false teachers. 2 Pt.2:14
    Of men in the last days. 2 Tim.3:1-5, esp. 1-2
    Unregenerate man. Ro.1:28-32, esp. 29
Verses. List of. Lk.12:15-19; 12:15; Ro.13:9; 1 Cor.5:9-10

LOW - LOWLINESS - LOWLINESS OF MIND (See HUMILITY)

LOWLY IN LIFE, THE (See HUMBLE IN LIFE, THE)

LOYAL - LOYALTY (See COMMITMENT; DEDICATION)
Carnal vs. spiritual l. Discussed. Lk.22:33-37
Duty. To be l. in the face of opposition. Rev.2:9; 2:13
Essential. To follow Christ. Mt.8:21-22
Reasons for being l. Discussed. Acts 5:26-42
Stumbling, faltering l. Jn.13:36-38

LUCIUS
Relative of Paul. Served with Paul in Corinth. Ro.16:21

LUCIUS OF CYRENE
Leader of the Antioch church. Acts 13:1

LUCRE, FILTHY (See MONEY, LOVE OF)

LUKE
A doctor who left all to be with Paul. Phile.1:24
Our beloved friend, the doctor. Col.4:14
Discussed. Acts 16:10
Luke based his gospel upon the writings of many. Lk.1:1
Only believer to stay with Paul in his final days. 2 Tim.4:11
Truth of Luke's gospel account. Lk.1:1-4
When Luke joined Paul. Acts 16:10

LUKEWARM - LUKEWARMNESS
Discussed. Mt.22:1-14, esp. 5; Lk.24:12; Rev.3:15

LUST--EVIL DESIRE (See CARNAL; COVET; CRAVE; CRAVINGS; DESIRES; FLESH; PASSIONS; SINFUL DESIRE)

LYDDA
Area evangelized. Acts 9:32-35
Discussed. Acts 9:32

LYDIA
Businesswoman. Discussed. First convert of Europe. Acts 16:12-15

LYSANIUS
Discussed. Lk.3:1-6

LYSIAS
Chief captain who rescued Paul from a Jewish mob. Acts 21:31-23:30; 24:7-8, 22

LYSTRA, THE FRONTIER TOWN
Discussed. Acts 14:8
Visited by Paul on his first mission. Acts 14:8-20

M

MACEDONIA (A district covering northern Greece)
The call to preach in Europe came from M. Acts 16:6-11
The churches of M.
    Received the Word from & had the example of the Thessalonians to follow. 1 Th.1:6-8; 4:9-10
    Supported missions financially. Ro.15:26; 2 Cor.8:1-5; 11:9
    Were ministered to by Paul. Acts 16:6; 17:14; 19:21
    Were ministered to by Silas & Timothy. Acts 18:5
    Were ministered to by Timothy & Erastus. Acts 19:21
    Were poor & suffered great trial. 2 Cor.8:1-2
    Were strong in the Lord, so strong that their testimony was used to stir other churches. 2 Cor.9:1-4

MAGI
Discussed. Mt.2:1
Worshipped Jesus as King. Mt.2:1-11

MAGNIFICAT
Song of Mary. Lk.1:46-56

MAGOG, GOG AND
Discussed. Rev.20:7-10

MAJESTY
Meaning. 2 Pt.1:16-18
Of Christ. (See GLORY OF CHRIST)
    Has been anointed with the oil of gladness above all beings. Heb.1:9
    Has been exalted & given a name above every name. Ph.2:9
    Has been exalted to the right hand of God to be a Prince & a Savior. Acts 5:31
    Has gone into heaven & is on the right hand of God--all angels & authorities & powers being subjected to Him. 1 Pt.3:22
    Is both Lord & Christ--Jesus the One crucified. Acts 2:36
    Is continually praised by all heavenly beings as being worthy to receive power & honor & glory. Rev.5:12
    Sits on the right hand of the power of God--as the Son of Man. Lk.22:69
    Was raised from the dead & sat at the right hand of God in the heavenlies. Eph.1:19-20
    Was received up into heaven & sat on the right hand of God. Mk.16:19
Of God. (See GLORY OF GOD)

MALICE - MALICIOUSNESS - MALIGNITY (See DEPRAVITY; HATE - HATRED; SLANDER)
Behavior of - Error.
    Fall from their steadfastness. 2 Pt.3:17
    Hypocrisy. Mt.22:15-18, esp. 18; Acts 8:18-24, esp. 22
    Immoral, unprincipled behavior. 2 Pt.2:7
    Sin & take pleasure in those who sin. Ro.1:32
    Twist the Scriptures. 2 Pt.3:16-17
Described as.
    A sin of omission. Lk.19:15-23
    Being short of God's glory. Mt.18:32-34
Discussed. Tit.3:3
Duty.
    Not to partake of the Lord's Supper with m. in one's heart. 1 Cor.5:7-8
    Not to use Christian liberty as a cloak, an excuse to hold m against someone. 1 Pt.2:16
    To be as children in m., having nothing to with m. 1 Cor.14:20
    To lay aside all m. 1 Pt.2:1
    To put away m., all m. Eph.4:31; Col.3:8

Judgment of. (See **JUDGMENT; PUN-ISHMENT**)
  Are worthy of death. Ro.1:28-32, esp. 29, 32
  Excluded from God's kingdom. Gal.5:19-21
Meaning. Mk.7:22; Col.3:8-11; 1 Pt.2:1
Results - Judgment of. Death.
Source of. The heart. Mk.7:20-23, esp. 22
Who is **m**.
  Evil spirits & forces. Eph.6:12
  Hypocritical religionists. Lk.11:37-39
  Immoral persons. 1 Cor.5:1, 13
  Satan. Mt.13:19; Eph.6:16
  The antichrist. 2 Th.2:8-9
  The ungodly & unrighteous. Ro.1:29
  The unsaved, those alienated from God. Col.1:21
  The whole world. 1 Jn.5:19
  This generation. Mt.12:43-45, esp. 45; 16;4
  Those who crucified Christ. Acts 2:23
  Unfaithful men. Mt.25:14-30, esp. 26-27; Lk.19:12-27, esp. 22-23
  Unjust men. Mt.18:23-35, esp. 32-33
  Unreasonable & **m**. men. 2 Th.3:2
Trait - Characteristic of.
  False leaders & teachers within the church. 3 Jn.10
  The ungodly & unrighteous. Ro.1:18, 29-32
  Unbelievers. Tit.3:3

MALICIOUS TALKER
Accusations against; **TONGUE**)
Against the Holy Spirit. Mt.12:31-32; Mk.3:29-30; Lk.12:4-12
Caused by.
  Backsliding - a shipwrecked faith. 1 Tim.1:19-20
  Claiming deity. 2 Th.2:4
  Covetousness & worldliness. Jas.2:6-7
  False religion. Rev.2:9
  Natural & physical difficulties & circumstances. Rev.16:9-11, 21
  Not doing to others as we should. 1 Tim.6:1
  Not living responsibly & righteously before the world. 1 Tim.6:1; Tit.2:1-5, esp. 5
  Persecution. Acts 26:11
  Professing Christ, but living a hypocritical life. Ro.2:24, cp. 17-29
  Rejection & hatred of Christ. Jn.8:48-59; Acts 18:5-6
  The antichrist. Rev.13:1, 6
  The dragon, Satan. Rev.13:4-6
Charged against. Christ. Mt.9:3; Mk.2:6-7; Jn.10:36
Discussed. Tit.3:3; Jas.4:11-12
Duty.
  Not to be a **s**. 1 Cor.6:9-11
  Not to fellowship with a railer. 1 Cor.5:11
  Not to partake of the Lord's Supper with **s**. in one's heart. 1 Cor.5:7-8
  Not to rail, even when railed against. 1 Pt.3:9
  Not to speak evil of any person, not a single person. Tit.3:2
  Not to use Christian liberty as a cloak, an excuse to hold **s** against someone. 1 Pt.2:16
  To be as children in **s**., having nothing to with **s**. 1 Cor.14:20
  To bless when **s**. 1 Cor.4:11-13

To have such a good conscience that those who **s**. will be put to shame. 1 Pt.3:16, cp. 15
To know that people watch to find accusations. Lk.6:7
To lay aside all **s**. 1 Pt.2:1
To live a righteous life, not giving the world any reason for **s**. 1 Pt.2:12
To prepare for the end time: a terrible period of world-wide **s**. 2 Tim.3:1-5, esp. 3
To put away all evil or **s**. speaking. Eph.4:31
To put away **s**., all **s**. Eph.4:31; Col.3:8
To put off **s**. Col.3:8
To rejoice & endure **s**. for the sake of Christ. Mt.5:11-12
To suffer being reviled even as Christ did. 1 Pt.2:21-24
Is forgiven. Mk.3:28
Meaning. Mt.9:3; Mk.7:22; Ro.1:29-30; 1 Cor.5:11; 6:10; 2 Cor.12:19-21; Col.3:8-11; Eph.4:31; Col.3:8-11; 1 Tim.3:11-12; 2 Tim.3:2-4; 1 Pt.2:1
Of what.
  Believers. Mt.5:11-12; 1 Pt.2:21-24
  Christ upon the cross. Mt.27:39-44; 1 Pt.2:21-24, esp. 23
Results.
  Judgment of. Death. Ro.1:29-32, esp. 32
  The **s**. shall not inherit the kingdom of God. 1 Cor.6:9-10
Sin of.
  Religion can be guilty of **b**. Rev.2:8-11
  Will be a trait of the last days. 2 Tim.3:1-2; Rev.6:9-11, 21
  Will be committed by the antichrist. Rev.13:4-8
The promise to believers when slandered. To be blessed & greatly rewarded. Mt.5:11-12
Trait - Characteristic of.
  False leaders & teachers within the church. 2 Pet.2:10-12; 3 Jn.10
  The ungodly & unrighteous. Ro.1:18, 29-32
  Unbelievers. Mk.15:29-32; Lk.23:39; Tit.3:3
Who is often **s**.
  Believers. 1 Pt.2:12; 3:16; Acts 2:1-13, esp. 13; 24:5-6; Rev.2:9
  Christ. (See **JESUS CHRIST**, Accused - Accusation against)
  Ministers & church leaders. Lk.7:33; Acts 6:13; 3 Jn.9-10
Who it is that **s**.
  A whole generation of unbelievers who stand against true righteousness. Mt.11:16-19
  Corrupt political & religious officials. Lk.22:66-71; 23:1-5
  Religious leaders. Acts 6:9-15; 24:1-9
  Some church leaders & members who oppose the minister. 3 Jn.9-10
  Some religionists. Mt.9:34
  The average citizen who mocks spiritual things. Acts 2:1-13, esp. 13

MALIGNITY (See MALICE)

MAN (See JUDGMENT; LUST; SIN; Related Subjects)
Achievements of. Discussed. Ro.3:27; 3:28
Attitude. To the world & the soul. Mk.8:36-37

Blessed. (See **BLESSED - BLESSINGS**)
Case against.
  All men. Ro.3:9-20
  The moralist. Ro.2:1-16
  The religionist. Ro.2:17-29
  The Godlessness & wickedness of men. Ro.1:18-23; 1:24-32
Classes of.
  Average person & citizen.
    Ignores Christ. Acts 17:5
    Is a prospect for the gospel. Acts 17:17
  Disorderly, loafers, idle. Acts 17:5
  God-fearers. Prospects for the gospel. Acts 17:17
  Pleasure seekers. Discussed. Acts 17:18
  Religionists. Acts 17:5
  Three classifications. 1 Cor.2:14-3:4
Concepts of God. (See **GOD**, Misconceptions of)
Creation of. (See **CREATION**) Lk.20:25
  By God. Every man owes his existence to God. Lk.13:6-9
  Created superior to the animals. Mt.10:31
  Discussed. Jn.4:23
  Every child created by God. Lk.18:16
  Every person owes his existence to God. Lk.13:6-9; 20:9
  Given the intelligence & knowledge of God. Ro.1:19-22; 2:14-15; Col.3:10
  In the image of God. Lk.20:25
  Made of one blood. Acts 17:21
  Purpose of creation.
    For God's glory & pleasure. Rev.4:11
    To have all the good things of life. 1 Jn.5:13-15
    To have dominion over the earth. Heb.2:5-13
    To worship & serve God. Jn.4:23-24
Decision. (See **DECISION**)
Deliverance of. (See **DELIVERANCE; SALVATION**) Mk.5:1-20
  By a new approach to God. The old approach is changed. Heb.7:19; 12:18-24
  By all barriers being broken down in Christ. Gal.3:28
  By being reconciled to Christ. Col.1:20-23
  By being stirred from dead works to serve God. Heb.9:14
  By being succored by Christ. Heb.2:17-18
  By Christ securing supremacy for **m**. Heb.2:5-13
  By faith & justification. Ro.4:1-25; 5:1
  By God suffering & bearing with **m**. & sin. Acts 13:17-22
  By God's plan for **m**. Heb.2:6-8
  By having **m**.'s body radically changed at the coming resurrection. 1 Cor.15:35-49; 15:50-58
  By hearing the words of Christ & living now. Jn.5:24-25
  By heeding how **m**. draws near God. Eph.2:13-18; Heb.7:19; 10:18-22; 10:22-25
  By **m**.'s eyes being opened spiritually. Stages of. Jn.9:8-41
  By not continuing in sin, not yielding his body members to sin. Ro.6:11-13
  By the blood of Christ. Heb.9:14
  By the gospel of salvation & the cross of Christ. Ro.1:16-32; 1 Cor.1:17-25

From darkness. Jn.9:1-7; 1 Jn.1:6-7
From death & perishing. Jn.3:16;
  Heb.2:14-16
From sin. 1 Jn.1:8-9; 2:1-2
  Is conditional. Jn.8:31-32
From spiritual hunger. Jn.6:30-36;
  6:41-51; 6:52-58
God & m. Col.1:12-14
Not of man's efforts. Eph.2:8-9
What God has done for man. Ro.5:6-11;
  Col.1:12-14
Depravity of **m**. (See **DEPRAVITY;**
  MAN, Nature; Origin; State of)
  A dark carnal nature. Jn.8:1-11; 8:44
  Abandoned by God. Ro.1:24-32
  Born illegitimately. Jn.8:41-47
  Dead because of sin. Eph.2:1; Col.2:13
  Debt of sin is huge. Mt.18:24
  Described. As children of the devil.
    Jn.8:38
  Discussed. Eph.2:1-3
  Enslaved. Commits sin continually.
    Jn.8:34-36; 1 Jn.3:4-9
  Exposed by words. Mt.12:34-35
  Follows the devil. Jn.8:38; 8:41-47;
    1 Jn.3:8
  Has no light in him. Jn.3:19; 8:12;
    Eph.5:8. Cp. Jn.3:19;   Ro.13:12
  Has not obtained mercy. 1 Pt.2:10
  Hungers for material things.
    1 Tim.6:9-10
  Is condemned & perishing.
    1 Cor.1:18; 2 Cor.5:14-15;2 Th.2:12
  Is imperfect; therefore, unacceptable to
    God. 1 Tim.2:3-7
  Is not of God. 1 Pt.2:10
  Is of the devil. Jn.8:38; 8:41-47;
    1 Jn.3:8
  Is the reason **m**. dies. Ro.5:12
  Is under sin. Ro.1:18-3:20
  Is under the influence of evil. Mk.1:23-24
  Is worthy of being hated. Reasons.
    Tit.3:3
  Life without God. Eight traits. Tit.3:3
  Progress of sin within. Mk.7:21
  Proven by nature & the law. Ro.3:9-20
  Reasons. Fourfold. Mt.8:28-31
  Rejects the evidence within him &
    without him. Ro.1:19; 1:20
  Short of perfection. Incomplete.
    Mk.14:27-31; Ro.3:23; Eph.2:1-3;
    1 Tim.2:3-7; Heb.7:1-24; 9:9;10:1-4
  Shown by cursing. Mt.5:33-37
  Sinful.
    From within. Mk.7:18-23
    Utterly sinful. Ro.3:9-20, cp.
      1:18-3:8
  What defiles a **m**. Mt.15:1-20
Described.
  As a humanist. (See **HUMANISM;**
    SELF-SUFFERING) Jas.4:13-17
  As an evil generation. Answer to.
    Mt.12:38-45
  As childish: contrary, playful, mind-
    less. Mt.11:16-18
  As sheep gone astray. 1 Pt.2:25
  As sheep without a shepherd. Mt.9:36;
    Mk.6:34
  As wise & foolish. Mt.25:1-4
Destiny of **m**.
  Foretold by Christ. Jn.7:33-34
  In the hands of Christ. Jn.5:24-25
  Returns to the earth, to dust. Jn.8:23
  To face God two different times.
    Jn.14:3

Duty - Behavior of.
  Determines his own fate. Ro.8:12-13
  Discussed.
    Things of men & things of God.
      Mk.8:34-9:1
    Truth & man's duty. Mk.4:21-25
  Not to be anxious about the body.
    Lk.12:22-34
  Not to rebel & be a non-conformist in
    custom. 1 Cor.11:2-16
  To be open to the truth. Jn.4:25
  To be wise as serpents; harmless as
    doves. Mt.10:16
  To beware of some things. Mk.12:38-40
  To care for the earth in behalf of God.
    Lk.13:6-9; 20:9
  To give fruit to God. Lk.13:6-9;
    20:10-12
  To have a healthy eye, not a diseased
    eye. Lk.11:33-36
  To love God supremely. Mk.12:29-30
  To love himself. Mk.12:31
  To love his neighbor. Mk.12:31
  To oversee the world for God. Mk.12:1
  To rejoice in whatever state he is in.
    Jas.1:9-11
  To walk in light & to believe in light.
    Jn.12:34-36
Duty toward. To honor all men.
  1 Pt.2:16-27
Errors - Mistakes of. (See **SIN**)
  Discussed. Mk.8:32-33
    Gross errors of. Lk.12:49-59
    Six errors. Jn.5:40-47
  Errors in relation to Christ.
    Blinds himself to the Messiah.
      Mt.11:25-27
    Insensitive & inconsiderate toward
      Christ. Mk.15:24
    Is offended by the death of Christ.
      Jn.6:57-66
    Makes no room in his heart for the
      Word of Christ. Jn.8:37
    Makes three errors in looking at the
      cross. 1 Cor.1:22-24
    Misses the truth of Christ. Reasons.
      Mk.12:36-37
    Misunderstands Christ. Tragic failure
      to understand Christ. Jn.8:25-30
    Rejects Christ. Jn.5:40-47
    Rejects the invitation of Christ &
      makes excuses. Lk.14:15-24
    Shrinks Christ to a mere man.
      Mt.13:57
    Thinks Christ came only to bring
      peace. Lk.12:49-53
    Thinks Christ is just a man. Mt.19:17
    Thinks the Messiah has not yet
      come. Lk.12:54-57
  Errors in relation to God.
    Claims to be of God & to know
      God. Jn.8:41-47
    Creates his own gods, mental images of
      God. Mt.13:57; Ro.1:22-23; 1:24-25
    Denies the supernatural. 2 Pt.3:1-7
    Does not love God. Jn.5:42
    Feels God is far away. Mk.12:7
    Opposes God. Acts 4:25-28
    Professes God, but does not know
      God. Jn.8:54-59
    Rejects the evidence of God.
      Ro.1:19; 1:20
    Senses no need for God. Lk.10:21
    Thinks there is no need to "make
      peace with God." Lk.12:58-59

Errors in relation to himself.
  Allows division within & without
    himself. Mt.10:34-36
  Deceives himself. Acts 23:12-15;
    Ro.3:1-8
  Follows the devil. Jn.8:38; 8:44
  Grasps for help in the stars, magic,
    & sorcery. Jn.5:2-4
  Guilty of serious sin. Jn.8:1-11
  Is deceived by religion. Lk.13:10-17
  Is idle & doing nothing. Mt.20:3
  Is inconsistent. Mt.11:16-19; 11:19
  Is self-confident, overly confident
    in himself. Mk.14:31
  Is self-righteous not humble.
    Mt.19:17; Lk.18:9-14
  Lives either a loose or a strict life.
    Mt.11:16-19; 11:19
  Plans, but his plans will come to
    nothing. Acts 5:33-40
  Seeks recognition. How. Failure of.
    Mt.6:5
  Sets the wrong priorities. Mt.6:25
  Thinks man is good & can achieve
    goodness. Mt.19:17
Errors in relation to others.
  Despises others. Lk.18:9
  Is insensitive & inconsiderate.
    Lk.23:8
  Places tradition over people.
    Lk.13:10-17
Errors in relation to the gospel of sal-
  vation.
  Argues against the fact of sin.
    1 Jn.1:8-2:2
  Fails to do the works of Abraham:
    to believe. Jn.8:39-40
  Is hypocritical & unbelieving.
    Jn.12:4-8
  Is unbelieving & fails to under-
    stand. Lk.11:29
  Misses the truth of eternal life.
    Mt.19:17
  Misunderstands two things.
    Jn.11:37
  Objects.
    Several objections. Ro.3:1-8
    To the gospel. Discussed.
      1 Jn.1:6-2:2
  Opposes the righteousness & moral-
    ity of Christianity. Acts 19:21-41
Errors in relation to the world.
  Focuses on the material & physical
    world. Jn.6:30-31
  Hungers for material things.
    1 Tim.6:9-10
  Is wrapped up in this world. Rea-
    sons. Mt.6:31-32
  What man is given by the world.
    Lk.15:4
Fall of.
  Caused by.
    Adam's sin. Ro.5:12-19
    Adam's willful disobedience.
      1 Tim.2:14
    Eve's transgression. 1 Tim.2:14
    Satan's seduction of Eve.
      2 Cor.11:3
  Discussed. Heb.2:5-13
  Results - Consequences. (See **DE-**
    PRAVITY; MAN, Depravity)
    An evil heart. Mt.15:15-20;
      Mk.7:20-23
    Death. Ro.5:12; 1 Cor.15:21-22

Depravity. (See **DEPRAVITY; MAN**, Depravity)
Discussed. Six results. Eph.4:17-19
Enslaved to Satan. 1 Jn.3:8, cp. Jn.8:41-47
Enslaved to sin. Jn.8:34; 1 Jn.3:4-6
Is born with a corruptible nature & body. Ro.5:12-14; 1 Cor.15:45-50, cp. Jn.3:6
Is under sin. Ro.1:18-3:20; Gal.3:22; 1 Jn.5:19
Mind & conscience are defiled. Tit.1:15-16
Must face the eternal judgment of God. Heb.9:27
Spiritual & eternal death. Eph.2:1; Col.2:13
Free will. (See **FREE WILL**)
Hunger - Thirst of. (See **SPIRITUAL HUNGER; SEEK - SEEKING**) Jn.6:30-36
Described. Jn.4:15
For deliverance. Jn.4:15
Searches for a human deliverer & utopia. Jn.6:26-29; 8:21-24
The physical vs. the spiritual. Jn.4:13
Lost. (See **LOST**)
Love for **m**. (See **GOD**, Love of; **JESUS CHRIST**, Death; Love of; **LOVE**, Essential - Duty) Lk.10:29-37
Misconception of. (See **MAN**, Errors - Mistakes of)
Life. What life is. Mk.8:32-33
One can become righteous on his own. 1 Jn.1:10-2:2
One can know God & walk in sin. 1 Jn.1:6-7
One is not totally sinful & depraved. 1 Jn.1:8-9
Thinks man is basically good. Ro.2:2-5; 3:5-8
Three great misconceptions. Lk.12:49-59; 16:14-18
Names - Titles.
A son of man. Heb.2:5-13
Builders. 1 Pt.2:7
Natural **m**.
Cannot save himself. Mt.16:17
Discussed. 1 Cor.2:14
Failure - Weaknesses. Cannot know the things of God. 1 Cor.2:6-13; 2:10-13; 4:14; 4:15
Life without God. Eight traits. Tit.3:3
Nature of. Natural & corruptible. (See **CORRUPTION**) 1 Cor.15:35-49
Nature of **m**. (See **MAN**, Depravity; State of)
Meaning. The outward vs. the inward form. Ro.12:2
Nature in relation to his own behavior & person.
All men have the same nature--like passions. Acts 14:14-18
Can be enslaved. By evil spirits. Mk.1:23-24
Cannot change his stature. Mt.6:27
Esteem. Fails. Several ways. Mt.6:5
Has no light in him. Jn.11:7-10
His human nature cannot solve the sin problem. Ro.7:14-17
His human will cannot solve the sin problem. Ro.7:18-20
Is corruptible. 1 Cor.15:50; 2 Cor.4:16; 5:1-4
Is fickle & forgetful. Mt.11:7-15

Is fierce, wild, mean. Reasons. Mt.8:28-31
Is flesh, soul, spirit. Jn.4:23
Is imperfect; therefore, unacceptable to God. 1 Tim.2:3-7
Is religious. Acts 17:22; 17:23
Is short of perfection. Self-centered. Mk.14:27-31; Eph.2:1-3; 1 Tim. 2:3-7; Heb.7:1-24; 9:9;10:1-4
Is spiritually blind. Mk.8:10-13; 2 Cor.3:14-15; 4:3-4;11:3
Is superstitious. Acts 17:22; 17:23
Is unspiritual, carnal. Ro.7:14-17
Is unstable. Acts 28:4-9
Some are like wolves. Mt.10:16
Nature in relation to God, Christ, & heaven.
All men are sinners, ungodly & enemies of God. Ro.5:6-11
An adversary to God. Mt.16:21-23
Called branches. Attached or unattached to the vine(Christ). Jn.15:1-8
Cannot penetrate the spiritual world & dimension. Jn.8:14; 8:15-16; 8:23; 8:42-43;11:7-10
Craves God & His Word. 1 Tim.6:4
Differs radically from the heavenly & eternal nature. Lk.20:36; 20:37-38
Has an inner witness to God & righteousness. Threefold. Ro.2:11-15
Has tastes that differ from God's taste. Natural vs. spiritual. Mt.16:21-23
Is imperfect; therefore, unacceptable to God. 1 Tim.2:3-7
Is religious. Acts 17:22; 17:23
Is short of God's glory. Ro.3:23; 7:14-17; 7:18-20
Is spiritually blind. Mk.8:10-13; 2 Cor.3:14-15; 4:3-4;11:3
Opposes God. How. Acts 4:25-28
Struggles for deliverance & for God. Ro.8:28-39
Nature in relation to sin & death.
All men are sinners, ungodly & enemies of God. Ro.5:6-11
Has a seed of corruption & death. (See **CORRUPTION; DEATH**)
Is dead. Already in the process of perishing. 1 Cor.15:50; 2 Cor.5:14-16
Is sinful & depraved. Discussed. Lk.13:1-9; Ro.3:9-20; 7:14-17; 7:18-20
Is "sold as a slave to sin." Ro.7:14-17
Is slave to sin. Ro.3:9
Nature in relation to the world.
Is interrelated & interconnected with his world. Ro.8:19-22
Is part of creation. 1 Cor.6:13-14
Verses. List of. 1 Cor.6:13-14
Needs of **m**. (See **NEEDS**)
How to be right with God. Ro.3:21-26
Origin of **m**.
Of Satan. Jn.8:38; 8:41-47; 8:44; 1 Jn.3:8
Of the earth. Jn.8:23; 8:23-24
Of the physical world & physical dimension of being. Jn.8:23-24
Verses. List of. Jn.8:23-24
Sent into the world by God. Acts 17:26

Privileges of. Life & the beauty & potential of the earth. Lk.20:9
Purpose of. (See **MAN**, Creation of, Purpose)
Discussed. Acts 17:26; 17:27-28; Ph.1:20
What **m**. lives for. Ph.1:20
Reformation. (See **REFORMATION**)
Relationship to Christ.
Fails to understand Christ. Jn.8:25-30
Needs are provided by Christ. Jn.6:1-15; 10:9; 10:10
Reactions to the revelation of Christ. Four revelation. Jn.12:1-11
Rejects the claims of Christ. Six reasons. Jn.5:40-47
Seeks for an earthly deliverer & utopia. Jn.6:26-29; 8:21-24
Some are offended by Christ. View His blood as repulsive. Jn.6:59-71
Some are unattached; some attached; some fruitful. Jn.15:1-8
Relationship to God.
Every child is created by God. Lk.18:16
How all men are related to God. Ro.10:12
Is created in the image of God. Lk.20:25
Is sent into the world by God. Acts 17:26
Is to rule over the world for God. Heb.2:5-13
Is to worship God. Jn.4:23
Owes his existence to God. Lk.13:6-9
Response to Christ.
Attempts to do evil against Christ. Mt.2:13-18
Betrays Christ. How men betray. Mt.26:16
Fallen away from Christ. Fourfold. Mt.13:4-7
Hates & persecutes Christ. Through the ages. Discussed. Jn.15:18-27
Is disturbed by Christ. Reasons. Mt.2:3
Four things. Jn.6:59-71
Reasons. Mt.26:31-32
Oppose Christ. How men oppose Christ. Mt.26:16
Questions the ministry of Christ & questions who He is. Mk.1:27-28
Rebels.
Against God. Mk.12:2; Lk.20:10-12
Wants to rule own life & world. Mt.21:34-35
Rejects.
Do not will to come to Christ. Jn.5:40-41
God's great invitation. Mt.22:1-14
Reason.
Christ is a threat to doing as one wishes. Jn.7:32
Threefold. Mt.23:37
Seeking after Christ. (See **SEEK - SEEKING**)
Seeking after God. (See **SEEK - SEEKING**)
Spirit of **m**. Can live forever. Ro.8:10-11
Spiritually dead. (See **DEATH**)
Born illegitimately. Jn.8:41-47
Can hear & live now. Jn.5:24-26
Condemned already. Jn.3:18-21
Dead because of sin. Ro.5:12; Eph.2:1; Col.2:13
Dies in sin. Jn.8:21-24

Is dead already, in the process of dying & perishing. Jn.3:16; 1 Cor.1:18; 2 Cor.5:14-16

Misunderstands Jesus - tragically. Jn.8:25-30

No life apart from Jesus. Jn.15:1-8

Searches for utopia - in futility. Jn.8:21-24

State of - Future.
A picture of his own hell. Lk.16:22-31
Discussed. Heb.2:5-13
Exists forever. In heaven or hell. Mk.8:36-37
God's plan for **m**. Heb.2:6-8
Lasts forever, eternally. Mt.25:46
Shall bow before Christ as Lord. Ph.2:9-11
World belongs to **m**. Entrusted to **m**. by God. Heb.2:5-8; 12:25-29

State of - Present. (See **MAN**, Depravity; Nature; Origin)
Basic need is not silver & gold, but spiritual. Acts 3:6-8
Condemned. Jn.3:18-21
Discussed.
Deserves to be rebuked. Lk.9:37-45
Fivefold state. Mt.4:16
Life before Christ came. Eph.2:11-12
Life without Christ. Eph.2:1-3
Present & future state. Heb.2:5-13
Wisdom of. 1 Cor.1:17-25
In relation to Christ.
Has no life apart from Jesus. Jn.15:1-8
Is blinded to who Jesus really is. Jn.8:25-30
Is determined by belief in Jesus Christ. Jn.3:36; 5:24
Is known by Christ. Jn.2:25
Receives light from Christ. Jn.1:9
Since Christ came. Life. Eph.2:13-18
In relation to death & judgment.
Lost. (See **LOST, THE**)
Perishing. Jn.3:16-17; 1 Cor.1:18; 2 Cor.5:14-16
Under the wrath of God. Ro.1:18; 2:8; 5:9
In relation to God.
Abandoned by God. Ro.1:24-32
Alienated from God. 2 Cor.5:18-19
Cannot know the things of God. 1 Cor.2:6-13
Created a little lower than the angels. Heb.2:7
Enemy of God. Ro.5:10-11
Given dominion over the world. Mk.12:1
Life without God. Tit.3:3
Rejects God. Mk.12:2-5
Separated from God; division between men. Eph.2:11-12
The natural **m**. 1 Cor.2:14
Welfare of. Determined by concern for righteousness. Lk.10:2
World belongs to **m**. Entrusted to **m**. by God. Heb.2:5-8
In relation to need & searching.
An inner struggle, dissatisfaction. Heb.2:6-8; 4:1-13
Emptiness of. Lk.15:11-24
Harassed; scattered; no shepherd. Mt.9:36
Restless, hungry, fearful. Acts 17:22; 17:23

Searching. Futile search. For Messiah - utopia - heaven. Jn.6:26-29; 8:21-24
Weighed down by several things. Mt.6:25-34
In relation to Satan.
Follows & is enslaved by the devil. Jn.8:38; 8:41-47; 1 Jn.3:8
Under the power of Satan. Eph.2:2-3
In relation to sin & behavior & unbelief.
A case against sinful character. 1 Cor.6:9-11
A reprobate, depraved mind. Ro.1:18-31
A sinner. Ro.5:8-9
A state or condition of darkness. Jn.11:7-10
A state or condition of sin. Jn.8:34-36
Accuses believers. 1 Pt.2:12
All are sinful. Lk.13:1-9
Blind spiritually. Mt.16:1-4; Mk.8:10-13; 2 Pt.1:9
Depraved. Ro.1:24-32
Enslaved by sin. Ro.1:24-32; 3:23; 1 Jn.3:4-9
Half-sincere. Jn.6:26-29
Hypocritical, unbelieving. Jn.12:4-8
Imperfect. Short of what he should be & do. (See **PERFECTION**) Eph.2:1-3
Is short of God's glory. Ro.3:23; 7:14-17; 7:18-20
M.'s word & witness are unacceptable & suspicious. Jn.5:31
Often rejected because of his human condition. Mt.9:20-22
Sinful. Dark sin & God's great forgiveness. Jn.8:1-11
Truth has been hid from **m**. Reasons. Lk.10:21
Wandering in the wilderness. Mt.18:11; Lk.15:4
Without strength, ungodly. Ro.5:6-7
Trials of. (See **TRIALS**)
Value - worth of **m**. (See **GOD**, Love of)
Is known by God, even a man's name. Lk.19:5-6
More important than animals. Mt.12:11
More important than birds. Mt.6:26; 10:29-31; Lk.12:24
More important than religion. Mt.12:9-13; Lk.13:10-17
More important than rules & regulations. Mk.2:23-24
More important than tradition. Lk.14:1-6
Sacred to God. Mt.12:13
Seen in the great love of God & Christ for **m**., in what God & Christ have done for **m**. Ro.8:31-33; 8:34; 8:35-39
Vs. religion. Mt.12:1-8; 12:9-13; 12:10
Weakness of.
Cannot penetrate the spiritual world. Col.2:8
Cannot perfect himself. Gal.2:15-16
Discussed. Mk.14:27-31
Strength & self-sufficiency end up in the grave. 2 Tim.2:1
Will of. (See **FREE WILL; WILL**)

MAN DOOMED TO DESTRUCTION
Antichrist, The. 2 Th.2:3

MAN OF LAWLESSNESS
Antichrist, The. 2 Th.2:4

MAN OF SIN (See **MAN OF LAWLESSNESS**)

MANAEN
Leader of the Antioch church. Acts 13:1

MANAGERS - MANAGEMENT
Discussed. Lk.19:11-27
Parable of the faithful & unfaithful steward. A strong warning - be prepared. Lk.12:41-48
Parable of the laborers in the vineyard. God's glorious grace. Mt.20:1-16
Parable of the pounds. Every man is tested. Lk.19:11-27
Parable of the talents: the steward's duty to work for the Lord. Mt.25:14-30
Parable of the unjust steward: man & money. Lk.16:1-13
Parable of the unmerciful steward. The spirit of forgiveness. Mt.18:21-35
Parable of the wicked tenant: Israel's rejection of Jesus' Messiahship. Mt.21:33-46
Duty. (See **STEWARDSHIP**)
To be a faithful & wise **m**. Lk.12:42
To be faithful. Lk.12:42-48; 1 Cor.4:2
To be forgiving. Mt.18:21-35
To give & support the ministry of Christ. Lk.8:3
To labor diligently in the Lord's vineyard. Mt.20:1-16
To manage & look after God's vineyard. Mt.21:33-46
To use one's gifts & minister to others. 1 Pt.4:10
To use one's talents & increase them. Mt.25:14-30
Essential. Must be faithful or face severe consequences. Mt.21:44; 25:30
Fact. Cannot serve God & money or possessions. Lk.16:13
Judgment of the unfaithful **m**.
To be delivered to the tormentors. Mt.18:34
To be destroyed & have his possessions given to another. Mt.21:41
To be separated from the Lord. Lk.12:46-48
To be stripped of everything & cast into outer darkness. Mt.25:30
To be stripped of everything & slain. Lk.19:20-27
To lose all true riches. Lk.16:11
To lose what was rightfully his own. Lk.16:12
Parable of. Faithful & unfaithful **m**. A warning: be prepared. Lk.12:41-48
Relation with labor. Col.4:1
Reward of the faithful **m**.
To be given a great reward. Lk.19:24-26
To be given just payment. Mt.20:9-10
To be made ruler of the Lord's household. Lk.12:42-44
To be made ruler over many things. Mt.25:21, 23
Who the steward is.
Discussed. Lk.12:41-48; 1 Cor.4:1-2
The manager of the Lord's property. Lk.16:2-3 cp. 16:1-12
The supervisor of laborers. Mt.20:8, cp. 1-16

MANIFEST - MANIFESTATION (See REVELATION; SHOWS HIMSELF)
Meaning. Jn.14:21
To the believer. Very special **m.** of the Lord promised. Lk.3:22; Jn.14:21

MANNA
Discussed. Rev.2:17

MARANATHA
Meaning. The Lord comes. 1 Cor.16:22

MARITAL UNFAITHFULNESS
Caused by.
Partying & failing to separate from the world. Rev.2:20-21
Rejecting & denying the only true & living God. Ro.1:18-32, esp. 29
The heart. Mt.15:19; Mk.7:22-23, esp. 21
Duty.
Not to let **f.** be named even once among us. Eph.5:3
To abstain from **f.** Acts 15:20, 29; 21:25; 1 Th.4:1-8, esp. 3
To avoid **f.** through marriage. 1 Cor.7:2
To be dead to **f.** Col.3:5-7
To flee **f.** 1 Cor.6:18
To repent of **f.** 2 Cor.12:21; Rev.2:21; 14:8
To separate from all fornicators. 1 Cor.5:9-11
Meaning. Mt.19:9; Mk.7:21; 1 Cor.5:9-10; 6:9; 2 Cor.12:19-21; Gal.5:19-21; Eph.5:3; 1 Th.4:3-5; Heb.12:15-17
Results.
Death. Ro.1:29-32, esp. 32
Shall not inherit the kingdom of God. 1 Cor.6:9
Sin of.
Is a characteristic of the world of unregenerate man. Ro.1:18-32, esp. 29
Is a characteristic of whole cities & countries. Jude 7; Rev.17:2, 4; 18:3; 19:2
Is a sin against a person's own body. 1 Cor.6:18
Is a work of the flesh. Gal.5:19
Verses. List of. 1 Cor.5:9-10; 6:13-14

MARK, JOHN
A believer who redeemed himself. Col.4:10
A disciple of Peter. **M.** records Peter's denial. Mt.26:69-75
Deserted Christ at His arrest. Mk.14:51-52
Deserted Paul & Barnabas. Acts 13:13
Discussed. Acts 12:25; 1 Pt.5:13
Greeted by Paul. Phile.1:24
Paul asked for Mark to visit him when he was in prison. 2 Tim.4:11
Was like a son to Peter. 1 Pt.5:13
Was supported by Barnabas against Paul. Acts 15:36-41

MARK OF THE ANTICHRIST (See ANTICHRIST; TRIBULATION GREAT)

MARKETPLACE
Warning. Against displaying oneself in the **m.** Mk.12:38

MARRIAGE - MARRIED
Attitudes toward. Loose attitudes. Mt.5:32
Basis.
Love & obedience. Eph.5:22-33
Only one basis. Mt.5:32
Discussed. Mt.19:1-12; Mk.10:1-12; 1 Cor.7:1-7; Eph.5:22-33
The unmarried, divorced, & mixed **m.** 1 Cor.7:8-16
Duty - Essentials.
Daughter's chastity to be guaranteed. 2 Cor.11:2
Discussed. Mt.19:11
Of husband. Threefold. 1 Pt.3:7
Of wife. To submit herself to her own husband. 1 Pt.3:1-6
To be faithful before God. Lk.1:5-25
To be joined together, to cleave together. Eph.5:31
To focus upon love & subjection to one another. Eph.5:22-23
To give attention to one's spouse. 1 Cor.7:32-35
To give no occasion for reproach by Satan & unbelievers. 1 Tim.5:14
To know that one must control one's own body for one's spouse. 1 Th.4:3-5
To know that one must take care of the needs of one's spouse. 1 Th.4:3-5
To love. Tit.2:4-5
To keep **m.** pure. To keep the bed pure. Heb.13:4
To share one's body. 1 Cor.7:3; 7:4-6
To use **m.** as the basis for preventing immorality. 1 Cor.7:2; 7:8-9
To witness to one's spouse. 1 Pt.3:1-6
Espoused. Engagement before **m.** Discussed. Lk.1:27
Ideal of **m.**
Differs in heaven. Lk.20:34-35
Highest ideal. Concentration upon God. Mt.19:12
In heaven. Love will be perfected. Mk.12:25
Illustrates.
Christ's relationship with His church. Eph.5:22-33
The minister's role to the church. 2 Cor.11:2
Jewish **m.**
Ceremony of. Mt.25:1-13
Steps involved. Three. Mt.1:18
Kinds of. Fourfold. Mt.5:32
Nature of.
Is a creative, logical, & spiritual union. Mk.10:6; 10:7; 10:8; 10:9
Is a spiritual union. Eph.5:31; 5:32
Is one flesh. The spouses own each other's body. 1 Cor.7:3-6
Ordained. By God. Mt.19:5-6; 19:5; Mk.10:6
Problems.
Are serious. Mk.10:10-12
Divorce.
Christian & unbelieving spouse. 1 Cor.7:12-16
Christian couple & divorce. 1 Cor.7:10-11
Questions concerning **m.**
Discussed. 1 Cor.7:1-7; 7:8-16; 7:25-40
Matters to consider in determining if one should **m.** or not. 1 Cor.7:25-40
Relationship between man & woman. 1 Cor.11:2-16
Sex within **m.** 1 Cor.7:1-7

The believing & unbelieving spouse. 1 Cor.7:12-16
The Christian widow & **m.** 1 Cor.7:39-40
The **m.** & unmarried believer contrasted. 1 Cor.7:32-34
The **m.** Christian & divorce. 1 Cor.7:10-16
The unmarried & the widows. 1 Cor.7:8-9
Sanctity of. Mt.19:1-12
Special power is needed in **m.** Mt.19:10-11; 19:11
Symbol - Type of. The binding & intimate relationship between Christ & His church. Eph.5:22-33, esp. 32
Union of.
Cleaving. Mk.10:6; 10:7; 10:8; 10:9
Weakened & broken by adultery. Mt.5:32
When to marry. Discussed. 1 Cor.7:2

MARRIAGE SUPPER OF THE LAMB
Discussed. Rev.19:1-10
Marriage of the Lamb. Mt.25:1-13
Parable of. Rejection of God's great invitation. Mt.22:1-14
Promised. To believers. Meaning. Mk.14:25

MARTHA
And Jesus. A growth in faith. Jn.11:17-27
Discussed. Character of. Lk.10:38-39
Family of. Jn.12:1-2
Home opened to Jesus. Mt.21:17
Sister of Mary. Discussed. Mt.26:6-13

MARTYR - MARTYRDOM
Described. As sacrifices offered to God. Rev.6:9
Discussed. Acts 7:54-60
First martyr. Stephen. Acts 6:8-15
In the end time. Mt.24:9; Rev.6:9-11; 7:9-17; 12:11;14:1-5; 17:6; 18:24
Methods of **m.** listed. Heb.11:35-40
Of Antipas, an early believer. Rev.2:13
Of the end time. Seen in heaven. Rev.6:9-11; 7:1-8; 7:9-17
Reward. Position in heaven before God. Very special. Rev.6:9; 6:9-11; 7:9-17; 7:9-10;7:15-17; 14:1-5
Why believers are **m.** Two reasons. Rev.6:9

MARY, BELIEVER AT ROME
Discussed. Ro.16:6

MARY MAGDALENE
Discussed. Lk.8:2
First to discover the empty tomb. Jn.20:1-10
First to whom Jesus appeared after His resurrection. Mk.16:9-10; Jn.20:11-18
Supported Jesus. Lk.8:2-3
Was given special commission by the Lord after His resurrection. Jn.20:17-18
Witnessed the cross, burial & resurrection of Christ. Mt.27:55-56; 27:61; 28:1

MARY, MOTHER OF JESUS
Acknowledged that she needed a Savior. Lk.1:47-48
An event for all generations. Lk.1:47-48
Embarrassed over Jesus. Reasons. Mk.3:31-32
Humility of. Lk.1:47-48
Magnificent song describing God. Lk.1:46-56
Proclaimed to be blessed. Reasons. Lk.1:45
Special, but still only human. Mk.3:31-32
Submission to God's will. Lk.1:26-38

Virgin. Proof. (See **INCARNATION; VIRGIN BIRTH**) Lk.1:27
Visited Elizabeth, John the Baptist's mother. Lk.1:39-45

MARY, MOTHER OF JOHN MARK
Discussed. Acts 12:12

MARY, SISTER OF MARTHA
And Jesus. The needs of man. Jn.11:28-38
Anointed Jesus.
  A study of love. Mk.14:3-9
  Sacrificed love & faith. Mt.26:6-13
  The picture of a supreme believer. Jn.12:3
Discussed. Mt.26:6-13
  Character of. Lk.10:38-39

MARY, WIFE OF CLEOPAS
Was a witness of the death & resurrection of Christ. Mt.27:55-56, 61; 28:1-11
Was the mother of James the less & Joses. Mt.27:56

MASTER
Duty toward. To submit to one's **m.** 1 Pt.2:18-20
Fact. Cannot serve two masters. Lk.16:13
Kinds of **m.** God & the world. Mt.6:24
Meaning. Mt.8:19
Relation to slaves. Col.4:1
Title of Jesus (epistata). Meaning. Lk.17:11-14

MATERIAL (See PHYSICAL)

MATERIALISM (See MONEY; WEALTH)
Caused by - Source. Distraction. Lk.10:40
Denial of. Essential to follow Christ. Mt.8:19-20
Described.
  As a master. Mt.6:24
  As evil. Reasons. Mt.6:21-23
  As necessary, as niceties, as extravagant. Mt.6:25
Desire for.
  By a people who chose **m.** over Jesus. Mk.5:14-18
  By Matthew. Mk.2:14
Discussed. Mt.6:19-24; Lk.9:23-27; 12:13-21; 1 Tim.6:6-10
  Giving all beyond true necessities demanded by Christ. Mt.19:16-22; 19:23-26; 19:27-30
  Sin of. Lk.16:19-21
  The man of wealth. Condemned by Christ. Lk.12:13-21
  The worldly are more dedicated to **m.** than believers to their pursuits. Lk.16:8
Duty.
  Christian & **m.** Parable of the Unjust Steward. Lk.16:1-13
  Not to be anxious about. Mt.6:25-34; Lk.12:22-34
  Not to be wrapped up in. Mt.6:31-32
  Not to seek **m.**, but to trust God. Lk.12:29-30
  To awaken to righteousness & sin by not giving oneself over to **m.** 1 Cor.15:30-34, esp. 33-34
  To be used for good by helping others. Lk.16:9
  To deny & discipline oneself while on earth. Mt.11:8; 19:16-22; 19:23-26; 19:27-30; Lk.9:23

To know that all belongs to God. Man is a steward of. Lk.16:12
To set one's mind on God, not on materialism. Mt.6:19-24
What to labor for. Jn.6:27-29
Error of. Four errors. Mt.6:26
Judgment of.
  Condemned by Christ. Lk.12:13-21
  Nine reasons listed. Lk.9:26
Meaning. Mt.6:19-20
Misconception - Misunderstanding. One of three great **m.** Lk.16:14-15
Problems with - Dangers of. Mk.10:23-27
  Are evil. Reasons. Mt.6:21-23
  Are insecure. Mt.6:19-20
  Can enslave. Mt.6:25
  Causes loss of life. Meaning, purpose. Mt.6:19-20
  Causes many harmful desires. What **m.** does. 1 Tim.6:9-10
  Causes one to lose oneself. Lk.9:23-27
  Chokes the Word. Lk.8:7, 14
  Determines eternal responsibility. Lk.16:10-12
  Determines whether one inherits eternal life or not. Mt.19:16-22
  Discussed. Mt.19:23-26
  Distracts from the essential. Lk.10:40
  Is focused on by man. Jn.6:30-31
  Often leads to greed & slavery. Acts 16:16-24
  Passes away. Mt.6:25-34
  Perils of. Discussed. Lk.6:20-26
  Used as an excuse for rejecting Jesus. Lk.14:18-20
The passion for wealth. 1 Tim.6:6-10
The rich man. 1 Tim.6:17-19
Vs. being spiritually minded.
  Discussed. Lk.12:13-21
  Seeking **m.** Lk.9:46
Vs. Christ.
  Cannot serve two masters. Lk.16:13
  Ct. Christ. Lk.16:14-15
  Preferred over salvation & Jesus. Lk.8:35-37
Vs. God. Mt.6:19-24
Warning against. Mt.6:19-24
  Craving for more & more. Lk.21:34-35
  Discussed. Lk.9:23-27
Weakness of. Silver & gold cannot save. Acts 3:6-8

MATTHEW - LEVI, THE APOSTLE
Call of. Lk.5:27-32
  Reaching the outcast & sinner. Mk.2:14
Conversion. Discussed. Mt.9:9-13; 9:9
Discussed. Mk.3:18
Humility. Discussed. Mt.10:3-4
Wrote the Gospel of Matthew. Mt. Introd.

MATTHIAS
Chosen to replace Judas as an apostle. Acts 1:23

MATURE - MATURITY
Discussed. Mt.5:48; Heb.7:1-24
Duty.
  To be **m.** by God & Christ. Heb.13:20-21
  To be **m.** even as God is **m.** Mt.5:48
  To be **m.** in every good work. Heb.13:20-21
  To be the believer's great aim. Ph.3:12-13
  To go on to **m.** Heb.6:1

To live in the Word of God. 2 Tim.3:16-17, cp. 2 Tim.2:15; 1 Pt.2:2-3
To **m.** holiness. 2 Cor.7:1
To **m.** one's faith. 1 Th.3:10
To praise God in **m.** Mt.21:15-16
To rely upon the strength of Christ for **m.** 2 Cor.12:9
To seek & pursue **m.** 2 Cor.13:9; Ph.3:12-16
Essential. To live in God's presence. Ph.3:7-11; 3:7-16
Fact.
  Believers do not achieve **m.** on earth. Ph.3:12-16
  Love is the way to **m.** 1 Cor.13:8-12
  Man is not **m.** & cannot secure **m.** Gal.2:15-16
  The person who sets his life apart unto God is perfected forever through Christ. Heb.10:14
Meaning. Jn.17:23; 1 Cor.2:6; Jas.1:3-41 Pt.5:10
Need for **m.**
  By man. Discussed. Heb.7:1-24; 9:9
  Met by Christ. Heb.2:9-10; 5:9; 7:1-24; 7:11-247:25-28; 9:11-14; 11:39-40
  His strength. 2 Cor.12:9
Source - How one is **m.**
  A spiritual union with God & Christ alone. Jn.17:23
  Controlling one's tongue & words. Jas.3:2
  Discussed. Heb.7:11-24, esp. 11-12, 18-19
  Following after **m.** Ph.3:12, cp. 7-16
  Giving all one is & has to Christ & the poor. Mt.19:21, cp. 16-30
  God. Heb.13:20-21; 1 Pt.5:10
  Help from faithful ministers. Eph.4:11-16; Col.1:28; 4:12; 1 Th.3:10
  Hope. Heb.7:19
  Living in Christ's presence. An absolute essential. Ph.3:7-11; 3:7-16
  Love. Col.3:14, cp. 1 Jn.4:17-18
  Not by sacrifice or law. Heb.10:1-4
  Overcoming & conquering trials & temptations. Jas.1:2-4
  Prayer. 1 Th.3:10
  Presenting one's body as a living sacrifice to God. Ro.12:1-2
  Scripture. 2 Tim.3:16-17
  The blood of Christ. Heb.10:1-18; 12:22-24; 13:20-21
  The Holy Spirit. Gal.3:3, cp. 1-5
  The perfect life of Christ. Secured by suffering as a Man upon earth. Heb.2:10
  The perfect sacrifice & death of Christ. Heb.10:1-4, esp., 1-4, 14
  Warning & teaching every person. Col.1:28
  Work & faith. Jas.2:22

MATURITY (See GROWTH, SPIRITUAL; MATURE)

MEANING (See PURPOSE)

MEASURE
Law of. Whatever a person measures will be received back. Jn.12:39-41

MEAT
> Offered to idols. Questions about.
> 1 Cor.8:1-13; 10:14-11:1

MEDIATOR (See **JESUS CHRIST**, Mediator)
> Claimed by Jesus. Jn.12:44-45; 14:6
> Described. In four ways. Jn.14:13-14
> Discussed. Jn.1:51; 12:44-46; 14:6;
> 1 Tim.2:3-7; Heb.4:4-14; 8:6;9:15;
> 1 Pt.2:9; Rev.3:7
> Fact. A human **m.** is no longer needed.
> 1 Pt.2:9
> How Christ became the Mediator. (See
> **JESUS CHRIST**, Death)
>> By becoming a man & bringing us into
>> fellowship with God. 1 Jn.1:1-3
>> By becoming man's advocate.
>> 1 Jn.2:1
>> By becoming the perfect sacrifice for
>> sins. Heb.7:27; 10:1-18
>> By His body becoming the temple of
>> men. Jn.2:18-21
>> By His body, His death, & His resur-
>> rection. Jn.2:18-21; 1 Tim.2:5-6
>> By His coming to earth as the God-
>> Man & dying for man. Ph.2:5-8;
>> Heb.2:14-15
>> By His death. 1 Tim.2:5; Heb.9:15;
>> 12:24-25;1 Jn.2:1-2
>> By shedding His blood. Eph.2:13;
>> Heb.10:19-21
> Meaning. Jn.12:44
> Verses. List of. Mk.1:15
> Work of Christ as Mediator.
>> Appears in the presence of God for us.
>> 1 Tim.2:3-7; Heb.1:3; 7:25; 9:24
>> Intercedes for the believer. Jn.14:13-14
>> Is the perfect sacrifice for sins.
>> Heb.7:27; 10:1-8
>> Makes worship possible. Jn.4:22
>> Provides a better covenant. Heb.8:6
>> Provides an eternal inheritance.
>> Heb.9:15
>> Provides justification & reconciliation
>> with God. Ro.5:6-11, esp. 10
>> Provides salvation through His name
>> alone. Jn.3:17; 4:22; 10:7-8; 14:6
>>> Verses. List of. Jn.3:17; 10:7-8
>> Provides the only Door to God.
>> Jn.10:7-8; 14:6
>> Provides the way to God. Jn.14:6;
>> Eph.2:18

MEDITATE - MEDITATION (See **DE-
VOTION**)
> Duty.
>> To **m.** in the Word of God, letting it
>> abide within. Jn.5:38
>> To **m.** upon the things taught in the
>> Word. 1 Tim.4:15
> Essential. Mt.3:1
>> For preparation & temptation. Mt.4:1
> Verses. List of. Lk.9:36; 10:41-42

MEDO-PERSIA
> Traits of. Will be embodied in the anti-
> christ. Rev.13:2

**MEEK - MEEKNESS--GENTLE - GEN-
TLENESS** (See **GENTLENESS; HU-
MILITY**)
> Christ is **m.** & lowly. Mt.11:29
> Discussed. Tit.3:2

Duty.
> To do good works in a **m.** spirit.
> Jas.3:13
> To dress in a **m.** & quiet spirit.
> 1 Pt.3:4, cp. 2-4
> To receive the Word with **m.** Jas.1:21
Meaning. Mt.5:5; Tit.3:2
Reward. Three rewards. Mt.5:5
Source. Is a fruit of the Spirit. Gal.5:22-23

MELCHIZEDEK
> Priesthood of.
>> Contrasted with Aaron or Levi's
>> priesthood. Heb.7:1-24
>> Type of Christ's priesthood. Heb.5:5-10;
>> 6:18-20; 7:1-24

MELITA
> Island where Paul was shipwrecked.
> Acts 28:1

MEN, ELDERLY (See **MEN, OLDER**)

MEN, OLDER
> How to treat in the church. 1 Tim.5:1

MERCHANT MAN
> Parable of. Mt.13:45-46

MERCIES (See **COMPASSION**)

MERCURY
> False god. Discussed. Acts 14:8-13

MERCY - MERCIFUL (See **COMPAS-
SION**, of Christ; **GOD**, Mercy)
> Basis of.
>> The believer's hope. 1 Pt.1:3; Jude 21
>> The mercies of God. Ro.12:1
> Described.
>> As abundant. 1 Pt.1:3
>> As the return of the Lord Jesus Christ.
>> Jude 21
>> As the supreme law. Mt.12:7
>> As the tender **m.** of our God. Lk.1:78
> Duty.
>> To approach God boldly for **m.**
>> Heb.4:15-16
>> To cry for **m.** Lk.17:12-14; 18:36-38
>> To look for the **m.** of our Lord Jesus
>> Christ, for His return. Jude 21
>> To present one's body as a living sac-
>> rifice to God because of the **m.** of
>> God. Ro.12:1-2
>> To put on **m.** Col.3:12
>> To receive the **m.** of God. 1 Pt.2:10
>> To seek God for **m.** Ro.9:15-18
>> To show **m.** & be cheerful in doing it.
>> Ro.12:8
> Fact. Unbelievers have not obtained **m.**
> 1 Pt.2:9-10
> Gift of. Discussed. Ro.12:6-8, cp.
> Lk.1:76-79
> God desires **m.**, not sacrifice. Discussed.
> Mt.12:7
> How to secure **m.** By coming to God &
> asking God for **m.** Heb.4:15-16
> Meaning. Mt.5:7; Lk.18:13; Eph.2:4-5;
> 1 Tim.1:2; Tit.3:4-5; Jas.3:17-18; 1 Pt.1:3;
> 2 Jn.3
> Need for.
>> Crying for. Mk.10:47
>> Crying for **m.** Saves the desperate.
>> Mt.20:30-32

Neglect of. Causes a man to lose his soul.
> Lk.16:19-21
Of Christ. Purpose. To have **m.**, not sac-
> rifice. Mt.9:12-13
Of God.
> Discussed. Tit.3:4-5
> Seen in election. Ro.9:14-33
> Symbolized. Mt.1:3-6
> Work of. Fourfold. Eph.2:4-7
Parable of. Unmerciful servant.
> Mt.18:21-35
Purpose.
> To show God's great **m.** for sinners.
> 1 Tim.1:15-17
> To stir a person to be faithful to God.
> 1 Cor.7:25
Results.
> Fulfills the promise of salvation made
> to our forefathers. Lk.1:72-73
> Gives a living hope to man. 1 Pt.1:3
> Salvation. Tit.3:4-5
> Seven results. Mt.5:7
Women (four) who received **m.** Mt.1:3

MESSAGE (See **MINISTER**, Preach -
Preaching; **PREACHING**, Message of)
> Duty. To preach because it is believed.
> 2 Cor.4:13
> Essential. Refusing to be silenced or to
> compromise. Acts 4:19-20
> **M.** preached by the early church. Acts
> 2:14-40; 3:12-26; 5:29-42;7:1-53; 8:5-40;
> 9:19-30, 32-35;10:34-43
> **M.** that turned the world upside down.
> Acts 17:1-9
> Surety - Content of.
>> Discussed. 2 Cor.5:17-6:2
>> Peace. Lk.10:5-6
>> Social justice. Lk.3:10-14
>> Stirs the believer to dedicate & to give
>> up his body as a living sacrifice to
>> God. Ro.12:1
>> Summary of Jesus' **m.** Mt.4:17; 5:1-7:29
>> The cross. 1 Cor.1:17
>> The gospel. Mk.1:14-15
>> The kingdom of God. Lk.4:43-44;
>> 8:1; 9:59-60; 10:8-9
>> The **m.** preached to a heathen & su-
>> perstitious people. Acts 14:8-20;
>> 14:22-34
>> The needs of man can be met.
>> Heb.4:16
>> The new covenant, the covenant of the
>> spirit. 2 Cor.3:6-18
>> The points for preaching. Acts 3:12-26
>> The preeminence & power of Christ.
>> Mk.1:7-8; Col.1:18-19
>> What is to be preached. 1 Cor.1:17-25

MESSENGER (See **MINISTER**)

**MESSIAH - MESSIAHSHIP OF JESUS
CHRIST**
> Acknowledged - Proclaimed.
>> By Andrew. Jn.1:35-42
>> By John the Baptist. Jn.1:19-27; 3:27-28
>> By Nathanael. Jn.1:46-49
>> By Peter. Jn.6:66-69
>> By Philip. Jn.1:43-45
>> To be God's appointed **M.** Jn.3:27-28
>> To be greater than religion. Mt.12:1-8
>> To be the Lord of man. Mt.22:43-45
> Belief in. (See **BELIEF; FAITH**)
>> Essential for salvation. Mt.21:32

Claimed.
  By Jesus.
    Confronting death. Mt.26:63-64; Mk.14:62
    In Jerusalem. His major thrust in Jerusalem. Reason. Mk.11:1-12:44
    Is Lord. Mk.12:36-37
    Recognition of. First recognition by Jesus. Lk.2:9-50
    Throughout His ministry. Jn.4:25-30; 4:39-42
    When launching His ministry. Lk.4:16-30
  By Scripture. (See **PROPHECY**, Concerning Christ)
  Some claim to be the light of man, the Messiah & Savior. Jn.1:9
Confession of Jesus as the **M**. (See **CONFESSION; MESSIAH - MESSIAH-SHIP**, Proclaimed)
  By children. Mt.21:15-16
  By evil spirits. Mk.3:11-12
  By John. Mt.3:2-6, 11-12; Mk.1:1-8
  By the disciples. Who Jesus is. Mk.8:27-30
  By the people at the Triumphal Entry. Mt.21:8-11
  C. vs. being ashamed. Mk.8:38
Demonstrated by Jesus.
  Fulfilled prophecy as a warning. Mk.11:1-7
  In Jerusalem. Time & again. Reasons. Mk.11:1-12:44
  In the Triumphal Entry. Mt.21:1-11; Mk.11:1-11;Lk.19:28-40; Jn.12:12-19
Described. (See **MESSIAH**, Names - Titles) Mt.22:41-46; 22:42
Discussed. Mt.1:1; 1:18; 11:1-6; 22:41-46; Lk.9:20; 20:39-44
Exaltation. (See **PROPHECY**, Concerning Christ)
Kingdom of. (See **KINGDOM OF GOD; MILLENNIUM; PROPHECY**, Davidic Heir)
Misunderstood - Misconception of.
  Corrected by Christ. Lk.19:11
  Discussed. Jn.12:12-19
  Earthly **M**. vs. spiritual **M**. Jn.13:36-38
  Entangled idea of. Mk.12:35-37
  False **m**. In last days. Mk.13:21-22
  False vs. true **M**. Mk.8:27-30; 8:31-33;10:35-45; 11:1-11; Jn.12:12-19
  Four misunderstandings. Jn.12:20-36
  Ignorance of. A problem of ambition. Mk.9:33-37
  Jewish concept. Mt.1:1
    Messiah was to do four things. Mt.1:18; Mk.12:35
  Man's concept vs. God's concept. Mk.8:27-9:50; 8:31-33
  Man's concept vs. the true concept. Lk.9:18-22; 22:24-30
  Questioned by John the Baptist. Mt.11:1-6
  Sees Jesus as the Messianic ruler of judgment. Lk.9:52-54
  Sees Jesus only as a great man. Jn.20:25-26
  Sees Jesus only as coming to bring peace. Lk.12:49-53
  Sees Jesus only as the Son of David, a mere man. Mt.22:42
  Thought not to have yet come. Lk.12:54-57
  Thought to be a human, earthly deliverer. Mt.22:42

Thought to only establish an earthly kingdom. Lk.7:18-28; 7:18-20; 19:11;22:67-68
Thought to only involve position & power. Mt.18:1; 21:8-9
World is blind to the Messiah. Mt.11:25-27
Names - Titles.
  God's Servant. Mt.12:18-21
  Immanuel. Mt.1:23
  King. Lk.1:31-33
  Lion of Judah. Rev.5:5
  Messianic King. Lk.7:18-20; 7:21-23
  Priest. Heb.6:20
  Promised seed. Gal.3:16
  Prophet. Mt.21:11
  Root of David. Rev.5:5
  Servant. Mt.12:18
  Son of Abraham. Mt.1:1
  Son of David. Mt.1:1; 1:18; 3:11; 11:1-6; 15:22;22:42; Lk.20:39-47; Jn.1:23
  Son of David (Man) & Lord of David (God). Mk.12:36-37
  Son of God. Acts 13:33
  Son of Man. Mt.20:28
  The Living Stone. 1 Pt.2:4, 7
Origin. Mt.22:42
  Called Lord by David. Mk.12:35-37
  Of man vs. of God. Mk.12:35-37
Predicted. By Scripture. (See **PROPHECY**, Concerning Christ) Mk.12:35; 12:36; 22:43-45
Proclaimed at Jesus' birth.
  By Anna, a prophetess. Lk.2:36-39
  By Simeon, a godly man. Lk.2:25-35
  By the angel to the shepherds. Lk.2:11
Proclaimed before Jesus' birth.
  By Elizabeth. Lk.1:43
  By the angel Gabriel. Lk.1:26-33
  By Zechariah. Lk.1:67-75
Proof that Jesus is the **M**. (See **JESUS CHRIST**, Heals; Power; Works; Related Subjects)
  Final proof of Messiahship. Fourfold. Lk.7:18-28
  Four facts. Lk.20:39-47
  Four logical arguments. Mt.12:22-30
  Fulfilled Scripture. Lk.3:23-38; Jn.1;45
  Great proof. The resurrection. Lk.11:29-36
  Prophecy. (See **MESSIAH**, Prophecies)
  Six proofs. Lk.11:14-28
  The ministry & message of Jesus. Lk.7:18-28
  The power of Christ. Mk.1:25-26
  The resurrection. Jn.16:28
  Work of. Discussed. Mt.11:4-6
Prophecies. (See **PROPHECY**, Concerning Christ)
  Discussed.
    Most verses & their fulfillment. Lk.3:23-38
    N.T. prophecies on Christ's death & their fulfillment. 1 Cor.15:3
    N.T. prophecies on Christ's resurrection & their fulfillment. 1 Cor.15:3
    To be High Priest. Verses & fulfillment. Lk.3:32-38
    To be King. Verses & fulfillment. Lk.3:24-31
    To be the Adamic heir. Verses & fulfillment. Lk.3:32-38

To be the heir of David. Verses & fulfillment. Lk.3:24-31; Acts 13:22-23
To be the Messiah. Verses & fulfillment. Jn.1:45
To be the Messianic ruler during the millennium. Rev.20:4-6
To be the Prophet of God. Verses & fulfillment. Lk.3:38
To be the "seed" of the woman. Fulfilled. Gal.4:4, cp. Gen.3:15
Verses & fulfillment listed. Lk.3:23-38; Jn.1:45; Acts 13:22-23;1 Cor.15:3; 15:4; Rev.20:4-6
Purpose. (See **JESUS CHRIST**, Mission; Purpose)
Search for - Hoped for. Jn.8:56
  By Abraham. Jn.8:56
  Discussed. Jn.6:22-29
  Man's futile search for the Messiah or deliverer - utopia - heaven. Jn.8:21-24
  People pant for. Mt.1:18
  Reasons. Jn.6:14-15, 22-29
Subject of. Five pictures. Jn.4:25-30
Way of God's Messiah vs. man's messiah. Mk.8:31-33
Work of the **M**. To usher in a new age. Lk.16:16

MESSIAH, FALSE (See **MESSIAH - MESSIAHSHIP**, Misunderstood)
  Danger of. Men choose over Christ. Jn.5:43
  Men receive. Jn.5:43
  Prophesied in the last days. Lk.21:8
  Sign of the end time. Mt.24:23-24

MICHAEL, THE ARCHANGEL
  Struggled against Satan & the fallen angels. Rev.12:7-9

MIGHT (See **POWER**)
  Meaning. Eph.6:10-11

MILETUS
  Discussed. Acts 20:13-27
  The city with a notable history in ancient myth. Acts 20:13-16

MILLENNIUM (The Thousand Year Reign of Christ on Earth)
  Description. New order of things. Mt.19:28
  Discussed. Rev.19:11-20:15; 20:4-10
  Coming of Christ as Conqueror. Rev.19:11-16
  Overview of. Rev.11:15; 11:16
  Rebellion of the world at the end of the **m**. Rev.11:18
  Verses. List of. Rev.20:4-6

MILLSTONE
  Discussed. Mk.9:42
  Meaning. Lk.17:2

MINAS
  Meaning. Lk.19:13
  Parable of the **m**. Testing of the Lord's disciples. Lk.19:11-27

MIND (See **ATTITUDE; SELF-DISCIPLINE**)
  Described as.
    A gate to deception & seduction. 2 Cor.11:3
    Reprobate **m**. Ro.1:28

Discussed. Ro.12:2; 2 Tim.1:7
Spiritual struggle & weapons.
2 Cor.10:1-6
Duty - Essential.
Is the major weapon for warfare. 1 Pt.4:1
Must think before building a tower or life. Lk.14:28-32
Not to be double-minded. Jas.1:8
Not to be shaken in m. by world events, nor by the end time. 2 Th.2:1-3
Not to faint in one's m. Heb.12:3
Not to put one's m. on high things, but to be humble. Ro.12:16
To attend upon the Lord without distraction. 1 Cor.7:35
To be armed with the same m. as Christ in facing the trials of life. 1 Pt.4:1-6
To be fully persuaded in one's own m. about social activities. Ro.14:5
To be mentally persuaded of one's behavior before doing questionable things. Ro.14:5
To be of one m. with other believers. 1 Cor.13:11; Ph.1:27; 2:2; 4:2; 1 Pt.3:8
To be of the same m. toward one another. Ro.12:16
To be perfectly joined together in the same m. 1 Cor.1:10
To be unified in one mind with other believers. Ro.12:16
To fix one's m. upon Christ. Heb.3:1
To prepare your m. for action. 1 Pt.1:13
To give undivided attention to one's task. Jn.21:20-23
To glorify God with one m. Ro.15:16
To have a renewed m. Ro.8:5-8; 12:2; Eph.4:23;Heb.8:10-12
To have a willing m. in giving. 1 Cor.8:12
To have one's mind transformed & renewed. Ro.12:2
To keep one's m. on things already learned. Ph.3:15
To keep one's m. sensible. Tit.2:6
To love God with all of one's m. Mt.22:37; Mk.12:30; Lk.10:27
To put on a m. of humility. Col.3:12
To receive the Word of God with a readiness of m. Acts 17:11
To serve the law of God with one's mind. Ro.7:25
To serve with a ready m. 1 Pt.5:1-4, esp. 2
To serve with humility of m. Acts 20:19
To set the m. upon the things of Christ & of heaven. Col.3:1-4
To take on the m. of Christ; to have a m. just like His m. Ph.2:3-5
To think positive thoughts. Ph.4:8-9
To tighten the belt of one's m. 1 Pt.1:13
Evil thoughts. Meaning. Mk.7:21
Fact. Either set on the earth or on God. Mt.6:19-24
Fate of. Discussed. Ro.8:5-8
How to control. Discussed. Ro.12:2
Law of. Meaning. Ro.7:21-23
Meaning. Mt.22:37; Mk.12:29-31; Ro.8:5-8; 2 Tim.1:7
Nature of the natural m. - Of the unbeliever's m. (See MIND, Nature of)
Blinded m. 2 Cor.3:14-15
Focuses upon carnal things, things of the flesh & of the earth. Ro.8:5; Ph.3:19

Is a reprobate m. Ro.1:28
Is alienated from God & stands as an enemy of God. Col.1:21
Is blinded by Satan. 2 Cor.3:14-15; 4:3-4
Is corrupted by Satan. 2 Cor.11:3, cp. 1 Tim.6:5; 2 Tim.3:8
Is defiled. Tit.1:15
Is depraved. Ro.1:28-32
Is fleshly & puffed up. Col.2:18
Is hostile. Ro.8:7; Col.1:21
Is the scene of spiritual warfare. 2 Cor.10:4; 11:3
Is the source of evil desires. Eph.2:3
Is vain, empty. Ro.1:21; Eph.4:17-19
Opens the door to deception & seduction. 2 Cor.11:3
Opens the door to evil thoughts. 2 Cor.10:3
Results. Death. Ro.8:6-7
Nature of the renewed m. - Of the believer's m. (See MIND, Duty)
Can be corrupted & led astray. 2 Cor.11:3; 3:14-15; 4:3-4
Discussed. Eph.4:23
Duties. Listed with references. Ro.12:2
Has the m. of Christ. Experiences life & peace. Ro.8:6
Is pulled to spiritual things by the Holy Spirit. Ro.8:5-8
Is renewed. By Christ. Ro.7:25; 8:5-8; 12:2; Eph.4:23;Heb.8:10-12
Is the area of spiritual warfare. Ro.12:2; 2 Cor.10:3-5
Results.
God's laws are put into one's m. Heb.8:10
God's peace keeps one's m. & heart. Ph.4:6-7
Melts a hard heart. Mk.6:52
Receives life & peace. Ro.8:6
The spirit of a sound m. 2 Tim. 1:7
Verses. List of. Ro.8:5-8
Vs. the carnal & earthly m.
Discussed. Ro.7:21-25; 8:5-8
Example of.
The disciples. Mt.16:5-12
The man of wealth. Lk.12:13-21
The rich young ruler. How a rich man enters heaven. Mt.19:16-22
Verses. List of. Ro.12:2
Of Christ. Meaning. 1 Pt.4:1-6
Proves. God's existence. Ro.1:19

MINDLESS
Message to. Mt.11:16-19
Trait - Characteristic of.
False leaders & teachers within the church. 3 Jn.10
The ungodly & unrighteous. Ro.1:18, 29-32
Unbelievers. Tit.3:3

MINISTER (See BELIEVERS; DISCIPLES; MINISTRY)
Accusation - Criticism Against - Mistreatment of.
A desire to get rid of. Acts 25:2-5; 25:6-7
A list of criticisms. 2 Cor.1:12-22
Comparing one m. with other ministers. 2 Cor.11:5-6
Considering the m. not to be as good as former m. 2 Cor.10:7; 10:9-13

Criticizing & attacking the m. 2 Cor.2:5-11
Criticizing the m.'s appearance, lack of charisma, & poor speaking ability. 2 Cor.10:7; 10:9-13
Discussed. 1 Cor.3:5-9; 4:1-5; 4:6-13; 2 Cor.1:12-2:11; 10:1-13:14;10:7-18
Duty. To forgive divisive persons. 2 Cor.2:5-11
Favoring one m. over another. 1 Cor.1:12
Hurting a m. 2 Cor.1:23-2:4
Is often unloved. 2 Cor.12:15
Persecuting the m. Rejected by the world. (See PERSECUTION) Mt.21:34-35
Questioning the m.'s authority. Mk.6:3
Questioning the m.'s call from God. Gal.1:1; 1:21
Rejecting the m.
How to respond when rejected. Lk.8:40
Reasons. Mk.6:1-6
When a m. is under attack. 2 Cor.1:23-4:2
Appearance - Personal Matters.
Attitude toward dress & appearance. Lk.9:3-5
Need for rest & its dangers. Mk.6:30-34
Attitude toward other m.
Jealousy - envy. Lk.9:46-50
Seeking position. Lk.22:24-30
Authority - Rights of.
Believers are to submit to the authority of the m. 1 Pt.5:5
Discussed. 2 Cor.10:7-18; 13:1-6; Gal.1:1-5
To discipline. 2 Cor.1:23-24
To remit & retain sins. Jn.20:23
To warn & discipline in the spirit of a father. 1 Cor.4:14-21
Call - called.
Discussed. Mt.10:1-4; Mk.3:13-19; Acts13:1-3; Ro.1:1; 1 Cor.3:5-9; 1 Pt.5:2-3
Fact.
Are set forth last. 1 Cor.4:9-13
Great need for m. Acts 11:19-30
Many are called, but few are chosen. Mt.22:14
Saved to m. Mk.1:31
Kinds & types of c.
Call of lay staff. Acts 6:1-7
Call of ministerial staff. Acts 11:22-26
Call to the Word of reconciliation. Committed to the m. 2 Cor.5:19
Commitment & commissioning call. Mt.10:1-4
Three different calls. Mt.10:1-4; 10:1
To a different profession. Mt.4:18-20; 4:21-22
To an obscure place. Jn.7:1-2
To serve in second place. The associate m. Ph.2:19-24
Privilege of being c.
As servant & steward of God's mysteries. 1 Cor.4:1-2
Chosen by God. 2 Cor.1:1-2
Dignity of the call not affected by the sin of other m. Jn.13:19-20
Entrusted & counted worthy. 1 Tim.1:12-17

Entrusted with the gospel.
1 Tim.1:11
Shows that one is trusted by Christ.
Lk.8:23; 1 Tim.1:12
Response to God's **c.**
Must respond in humility. Jn.1:20-22
Must willingly accept God's call.
Not to hesitate. 1 Pt.5:2-3
Reluctant to respond to the call.
Reasons. Lk.5:1-11; 9:57-62
The **c.** accepted or rejected.
Mt.21:28-32
To leave & forsake all, including
employment. Mt.4:21-22
When to begin. Mt.4:12
Source of the **c.**
Christ.
Purposes. Jn.15:16
Who & why. Lk.6:12-19
God
God alone. Gal.1:1
Not of self or men, but of God.
1 Cor.1:1
Ordained by God. 1 Tim.2:7
The steps to God's call. Lk.5:1-11
The Holy Spirit. Acts 6:1-7
Warning.
Must be called by God, not just
choosing a profession. 1 Tim.1:18
Must guard ordination. 1 Tim.5:22
Must heed the personal messages of
Christ. Rev.1:20; 2:1-7; 2:8-11;
2:12-17;2:18-29; 3:1-6; 3:7-13;
3:14-22
Not to enter the ministry as a pro-
fession. 1 Pt.5:2-3
What the minister is called to be.
To be a **m.**, preacher, evangelist.
Eph.3:7-9
To be a servant, a bond-slave to
men. 2 Cor.4:5
To be a servant of God. 1 Cor.3:5
To be an ambassador. Lk.6:13;
2 Cor.5:20
To be enslaved by the gospel. Ro.8:15
To be enslaved to Christ. Ro.1:1-7
To be God's servant & messenger.
Tit.1:1-4
To be like a father to the church.
1 Cor.4:14-21; 4:18-21
To be the messenger of God.
Jn.1:19-27
To go into the world to witness.
Jn.17:17-19
To serve as priests of the gospel.
Ro.15:16
What the **m.** is called *to do*. Dis-
cussed. Eph.3:7-9
Christ, the supreme Minister. Heb.8:1-
9:28
The exalted Minister. Heb.8:1-5
The Minister of the superior covenant.
Heb.8:6-13
The Minister of the tabernacle.
Heb.9:1-14
The Minister of the true tabernacle.
Heb.8:1-5; 9:11-14
Commission - Mission. (See **COMMIS-
SION; MISSION**)
Discussed. Mt.10:5-15; 28:16-20;
2 Cor.12:11-21
Equipped & sent forth. Mk.6:7-13
Overview of the **m.** 2 Cor.2:12-17
The proof of God's **m.** Gal.1:10-2:21
Primary **m.** To preach the cross.
1 Cor.1:17

Source.
Sent by Christ. Sent as Christ was
sent. "Sent" & "send" discussed.
Jn.20:21
Sent by God. To do the will & work
of God. Jn.4:31-35
Sent from God. Jn.1:6
Urgency of. Absolutely essential.
Jn.9:4; Ro.10:14-15
What the **m.** is commissioned to do.
Eight things. Lk.10:1-16
Five things. Great mission.
Lk.5:27-39
Primary duty. To devote himself to
public worship. 1 Tim.4:13
Primary mission. People. Mt.4:15-16
The great task of the **m.** 2 Pt.1:12-15
Three things. Mt.4:15-16; Mk.1:3
To arduously labor for the church.
Col.1:24-29; 1:29
To "be with" Christ, preach, & re-
ceive power. Mk.3:14-15
To center his ministry in the homes.
Lk.9:4
To collect fruit from men for God.
Lk.20:10-12
To complete the sufferings of
Christ. Col.1:24
To fish for men. Mt.4:18-20; 4:21-22
To give light to the world. Mt.5:14-16
To go to the ends of the earth. Acts
1:8
To heal the bruised, not to con-
demn. Mt.12:20
To lead people to glorify God.
2 Cor.4:15
To meet the needs of people.
2 Cor.4:15
To minister & to serve. Mt.20:23-
28; Mk.10:42-45;Lk.4:17-19;
Jn.20:21
To offer people up to God.
Ro.15:16
To preach. Mt.4:17; Lk.24:47-48
First calling. Mk.2:1-2
One's testimony. That one be-
lieves. 2 Cor.4:13
The Word of God. Col.1:25
To salt the earth. Mt.5:13
To seek & save the lost. Mt.18:11-14
Described as.
A shepherd. Lk.11:23; 1 Pt.5:2-3
Athlete. 2 Tim.2:5
Being like a father. 1 Th.2:7-8
To have a father's spirit.
1 Cor.4:14; 4:15
Being like a mother. 1 Th.2:7-8
Companion. In the work of the Lord.
Ph.2:25
Farmer. 2 Tim.2:6
Fellow soldier. Ph.2:25
Good. 1 Tim.4:6-16
Man of God. 1 Tim.6:11
Servants & stewards of God's myster-
ies. 1 Cor.4:1-2
Soldier. 2 Tim.2:3-4
Suffering servants for God & men.
1 Cor.4:9-10; 4:11-13
True. 1 Tim.1:12-17
Discipline of. Discussed. 1 Tim.5:19-20
Discussed. Acts 13:1-3; 1 Tim.3:1-7
A good **m.** Twelve qualities.
1 Tim.4:6-16
A strong & true **m.** 1 Th.2:1-12
A successful ministry. Mt.4:23-25
Called; appointed; changed. Mk.3:13-19

Charge to the young **m.** To be a war-
rior. 1 Tim.1:18-20
Compulsion to preach & minister.
1 Cor.9:16-23
Corrupt **m.** 2 Tim.3:6-9
Discipline required. 1 Cor.9:24-27
Four charges. 1 Tim.5:21-25
Gospel & the **m.** of God. Mk.1:1-8
Ideal **M.** Christ, the Chosen Servant of
God. Mt.12:14-21
In the end time. Jewish **m.**, 144,000 of
them. Rev.7:4-8; 14:1-5
Lessons for **m.** Acts 4:1-22
Qualifications. Tit.1:5-9
Restoring a fallen **m.** 1 Tim.5:22
Spiritual experiences. 2 Cor.12:1-10
Testimony of a true **m.** 1 Tim.1:12-17
The inside look at a **m.** 1 Cor.9:16-23;
9:24-27
The messenger or minister of God.
Ro.15:14-21
Warfare & weapons of. 2 Cor.10:1-6
Who **m.** really are. 1 Cor.3:5-9
Duty - Work. (See **MINISTRY - MIN-
ISTERING** for more discussion)
Activities of. Mt.4:23
Described as. The most difficult task
of all professions. 1 Cor.3:6-7
Discussed. Lk.10:1-16; Acts 18:1-17;
18:18-22;Ro.15:14-21; 15:22-33;2
Cor.4:1-6; 1 Tim.6:11-16;1 Pt.5:1-4
Duty in relation to believers.
Searching questions asked. Lk.14:2
To anoint & pray for the sick.
Jas.5:14-15
To avoid petty arguments & specu-
lations. 2 Tim.2:14-21
To be hospitable, adaptable.
Lk.10:7
To be of one spirit & effort. Source.
Fivefold. Acts 14:1
To be teachable, even by the less
esteemed. Acts 18:26
To be tolerant, accepting. Mk.9:38-41
To exhort & strengthen believers.
Acts 2:40; 11:19-30; 11:22-24;
13:15; 14:22; 15:32; 15:33-34;
18:27; 20:2; 27:22; Heb.3:1-19
To families. Jesus' purpose.
Mt.8:14-17
To feed & shepherd. Jn.21:15-17;
Acts 20:28-31
To shepherd God's flock. 1 Pt.5:2-3
To gather, not scatter the flock.
Lk.11:23
To heal, anointing with oil.
Mt.6:13; Jas.5:14-15
To instruct believers about false
teachers. 1 Tim.4:6
To look after the flock of God.
Acts 20:28
To make disciples. One of the major
duties of the **m.** Acts 13:5-6;
14:21
To shepherd. Eph.4:11
To walk humbly as a brother with
other believers. 1 Cor.1:1
Duty in relation to Christ.
To be surrendered, an instrument of
the Lord. Acts 14:3; Ro.12:1;
1 Cor.6:19-20
To be washed & cleansed by Christ.
Jn.13:6-11
To bear the "dying of the Lord Je-
sus." 2 Cor.4:10-12

To bear witness to Jesus' death &
resurrection. Jn.21:24
To boast in the cross of Christ.
Gal.6:11-18
To complete the sufferings of
Christ. Col.1:24
To exalt Christ & not self. Jn.3:29-30
To honor Jesus Christ. Lk.11:19
To know who Jesus is. Jn.1:20
To receive & heed the messages of
Christ. Rev.1:20; 2:1-7; 2:8-11;
2:12-17;2:18-29; 3:1-6; 3:7-13;
3:14-22
To remember the resurrected Lord.
2 Tim.4:16-18
To talk about Christ, not self-
achievements. Ro.15:17-19
Duty in relation to God.
To deny self & fulfill God's call.
Acts 18:18; 2 Cor.4:10-12
To do the will & work of God.
Jn.4:31-35
To live for God & for God's Word.
Acts 20:32
To surrender to God's will regardless
of circumstances. Acts 10:1-33
Duty in relation to other ministers.
How to treat accusations against
others. 1 Tim.5:19-20
Not to compete with others.
Mt.4:12
Not to ordain others too quickly.
1 Tim.5:22
Not to seek to make an impression
by statistical numbers. Gal.6:12-13
Not to try to be someone else.
1 Cor.3:8
To labor together. 1 Cor.3:5-9
To labor with other **m**. 1 Cor.3:9
To leave judging others up to God.
1 Tim.5:24-25
To receive other **m**. Lk.9:49-50
To step aside for others. Mt.4:12
To welcome traveling **m**., evangel-
ists, prophets, teachers, & mis-
sionaries. 3 Jn.3-4, 5-8
Duty in relation to personal behavior
& example.
Must not fear the face of man.
1 Tim.5:21
Must not pretend, seek, assume.
Jn.1:20-22
Not to be a cheat or thief.
2 Cor.12:13-18
Not to be chargeable to any. Acts
20:33-35
Not to be greedy for position, rec-
ognition, & livelihood.
1 Th.2:5; 2:6
Not to boast in self, but in Christ.
Ro.15:17-19
Not to lose heart. 2 Cor.4:16
Not to lose power. Lk.9:37-40
Not to neglect His gift. 1 Tim.4:14
Not to push oneself forward, but to
be humble. Jn.1:20-22
Not to quit. Ph.2:25-30
Not to try to be someone else.
1 Cor.3:8
To abandon all of self. Acts 20:24
To be a good **m**. 1 Tim.6:6-16
To be a warrior. 1 Tim.1:18-20
To be an example to believers. In
six areas. 1 Tim.4:12
To be consistent & enduring.
2 Cor.6:3-10

To be humble. Vs. being puffed up.
Acts 4:23-24
To be impartial. 1 Tim.5:21-25
To be only a voice for God. Jn.1:23
To be responsible. World's fate at
stake. Mk.6:30
To be strong. 2 Tim.2:1-7
To die daily. 2 Cor.4:10-12
To exercise physically & spiritu-
ally. 1 Tim.4:7-8
To fight & take hold of eternal life.
1 Tim.6:12
To flee lusts & follow after the
Lord. 2 Tim.2:22-26
To focus one's eyes upon the eter-
nal, not upon the physical.
2 Cor.4:17-18
To give all one is & has--all beyond
the necessities. Acts 4:32-37;
1 Cor.4:11-13
To guard against greed.
2 Cor.12:13-18
To have a clear conscience.
2 Tim.1:3
To hold fast in three areas.
2 Tim.1:13-18
To hold fast sound teachings, that
is, the Word of God. 2 Tim.1:13
To keep the commandments of God.
1 Tim.6:13-16
To live a clean & moral life.
1 Th.2:3
To live free of materialism & con-
cern for appearance. Lk.9:3-5
To meditate & to wholly give oneself to the Scriptures. 1 Tim.4:15
To nourish oneself in the faith.
1 Tim.4:6
To pray after preaching. Mk.6:46
To rejoice in weaknesses.
2 Cor.12:7-10
To renew one's inner man day by
day. 2 Cor.4:16
To renounce the things that shame,
disgrace, & are scandalous.
2 Cor.4:2
To rest - to get alone with God.
Acts 14:26-28; 20:13
To take care of one's body.
1 Tim.5:23
To waste no time in empty conver-
sation. Lk.10:4
Duty in relation to personal ministry &
faithfulness.
Day of. Typical day in the life of
Jesus. Lk.4:31-44
Demanding, busy. Mt.4:23
Failure in. Mt.6:2
Faithful **m**. Discussed. Acts 20:1-12;
20:13-27
Faithful vs. unfaithful **m**. Mt.
24:42-51; 25:14-30; Lk.12:35-48
Five duties. 2 Tim.1:6-12
Five points. Tit.1:1-4
Five specific instructions. Mk.6:8-13
Five stern demands. 2 Cor.2:16-17
Five wise lessons. Mk.6:45-52
Four duties. 1 Tim.6:11-16
Heroic Christian **m**. Acts 18:1-17
To be a man of reason & purpose.
1 Tim.4:11
To be an instrument in God's hands.
Ro.15:17-19
To be faithful.
Able to prove one's ministry.
2 Cor.12:13-18

In obscure places. Jn.7:1-2
In preaching the gospel. Acts
17:1-2
To do all things well. Mt.6:31-37
To endure & never quit the minis-
try. 2 Cor.4:17-18
To fulfill the ministry--fill up to the
brim. 2 Tim.4:5
To give undivided attention to one's
own task. Jn.21:20-23
To labor & give, not coveting
worldly wealth. Acts 20:33-35
To labor as faithfully as other **m**.
2 Cor.11:23-31
To labor night & day. 1 Th.2:9
To labor strenuously. 1 Tim.4:10
To pray & minister the Word. Acts
6:4
To receive & heed the messages of
Christ. Rev.1:20; 2:1-7; 2:8-11;
2:12-17;2:18-29; 3:1-6; 3:7-13;
3:14-22
To reject comfort in order to fulfill
God's call. Acts 18:18
To reject false teaching, that is, pro-
fane & old wives fables.
1 Tim.4:7
To reject those who reject Christ.
Lk.9:49-50; Acts 13:46-52; 14:6-7
To serve humbly, esteeming others.
Jn.1:8; 1:27
To serve, ministering to the needful.
Lk.14:12-14
To talk about Christ, not self-
achievements. Ro.15:14
To trust God for money, care.
Lk.10:4
To watch & work for judgment is
coming. Mt.25:14-30
To whom to minister. Lk.10:29-37
To work at secular employment if
needed in order to preach. Acts
18:3; 20:33-35
To work in order to have enough to
give & meet needs. Lk.12:31-34
To work until till Christ returns.
Lk.19:13
To work while it is day before the
night comes. Jn.11:7-10
Twelve duties. 1 Tim.4:6-16
Two duties. 1 Tim.6:20-21
Duty in relation to preaching, the gos-
pel, witnessing, & ministering.
Must sense a compulsion to preach.
Acts 21:1-16
Not to mishandle the Word of God.
2 Cor.4:2
Not to neglect the world. Not to be
cloistered in the church. Mt.5:13
To be stirred over the lost. Acts
17:16
To be unashamed of the gospel.
Ro.1:16-17
To bear witness to Jesus' death &
resurrection. Jn.21:24
To boast in the cross of Christ.
Gal.6:11-18
To concentrate on preaching the
gospel, not eloquence. 1 Th.1:5
To endure abuse for the gospel.
2 Tim.1:6-12
To go into the roads & country
lanes. Lk.14:21-23
To guard himself & his teaching.
1 Tim.4:16
To guard the message. Lk.10:5-6

To heal, anointing with oil.
Mt.6:13; Jas.5:14-15
To labor diligently, for the fields are
ripe unto harvest. Jn.4:35
To leave judging others up to God.
1 Tim.5:24-25
To look after the Word & preach.
Tit.1:2-3
To lose one's life for the sake of the
gospel. Mk.8:34
To meet hopeless & desperate
needs. Mt.9:18-34
To minister at all hours. Mk.1:32
To minister in the home. Lk.9:4
To minister the Word. Lk.1:2
To minister to all men. Acts 10:28
To minister to mixed races
(Samaritans were a mixed race).
Acts 8:5-8, 14-17, 25
To minister to other races. Acts
10:1-48
To nourish a strong faith.
2 Cor.4:13
To open the door of salvation.
Mt.16:19
To persuade people. Acts 13:43;
14:19; 18:4; 19:26
To pray for laborers. Lk.10:2
To preach. (See **MESSAGE;
PREACHING**, Content)
Lk.4:43-44; 8:1; 9:59-60; 10:8-9
Despite trial & opposition. Acts
21:1-16
First calling of the **m**. Mk.2:1-2
First duty of the **m**. Acts 14:21
Honesty. 2 Cor.4:2
Peace by Jesus Christ. Acts
10:34-43
That Jesus is Christ. Acts 18:28
That Jesus is the Son of God.
Acts 9:20, 22
The gospel. 2 Cor.4:5; 1 Th.1:5
The trustworthy message. Tit.1:9
The Word of God. Acts 18:24;
18:25; Col.1:25; 2 Tim.4:1-5
To proclaim forgiveness &
judgment. Jn.20:23
To reach out to help others.
Jn.11:31
To seek the lost. Lk.15:5
To serve & minister. Verses. List
of. Ro.1:1
To share the Word of the Lord
Jesus. Acts 19:20
To sow the seed. How men re-
ceive. Mk.4:1-20
To teach & preach with power.
Lk.4:31-32, 43-44
To teach every man. Col.1:28
To teach the things of salvation
& to teach them diligently.
2 Pt.1:12-15
To testify of God's grace. Acts
20:24
To testify to all. Acts 20:21
To willing hearers. Acts 13:44-52
With compulsion. 1 Cor.2:1-5;
9:16-23
Duty in relation to the church.
Behavior before the church.
2 Cor.12:11-21
Not to ordain others too quickly.
1 Tim.5:22
Not to seek to make an impression
by statistical numbers. Gal.6:12-13
Searching questions asked. Lk.14:2

To accept compensation. Lk.10:7
To arduously labor for the church.
Col.1:24-29; 1:29
To be like a father to the church.
1 Cor.4:14-21
To be people-centered. 2 Cor.3:2;
3:3
To follow up & strengthen
churches. Acts 14:21-28
To guard ordination. 1 Tim.5:22
To guard oneself & the church.
Acts 20:28
To love the church. 2 Cor.11:2
To properly handle church finances.
2 Cor.12:13-18
To struggle in prayer for all believ-
ers & churches worldwide.
Col.2:1
To treat one's congregation gra-
ciously. Ro.15:14
To walk before one's congregation
in humility. Ro.15:14
Duty in relation to the Holy Spirit.
To follow the Holy Spirit. Jn.21:18
Duty in relation to the lost & unbe-
lievers. (See **MINISTER**, Duty in
relation to preaching; Duty in rela-
tion to the world)
Duty in relation to the world.
Not to covet worldly wealth. Acts
20:33-35
Not to neglect the world. Not to be
cloistered in the church. Mt.5:13
To be responsible. World's fate at
stake. Mk.6:30
To be stirred over the lost. Acts
17:16
To have a realistic view of the
world. Mt.6:3-4
To minister to the multitude. Jesus'
purpose. Mt.8:16-17
To turn to willing hearers. Acts
13:46-52
To walk away from rejectors.
Lk.10:10-15
To warn & leave rejectors alone.
Lk.9:4
To warn every man. Col.1:28
Duty of young ministers.
Five duties. 2 Tim.1:6-12
Four duties. 1 Tim.6:11-16
Must not fear the face of man.
1 Tim.5:21
Not to neglect the gift that is in him.
1 Tim.4:14
Of young **m**. Behavior of. Tit.2:7-8
To avoid petty arguments & specu-
lations. 2 Tim.2:14-21
To be a good **m**. 1 Tim.6:6-16
To be a man of reason & purpose.
1 Tim.4:11
To be a strong disciple. Seven traits.
Acts 18:23-28
To be a trusted son. 1 Tim.6:20-21
To be a warrior. 1 Tim.1:18-20
To be an example to believers. In
six areas. 1 Tim.4:13
To be strong. 2 Tim.2:1-7
To fight & lay hold of eternal life.
1 Tim.6:12
To flee lusts & follow after the
Lord. 2 Tim.2:22-26
To fulfill the ministry--fill up to the
brim. 2 Tim.4:5
To guard himself & his teaching.
1 Tim.4:16

To guard ordination. 1 Tim.5:22
To hold fast in three areas.
2 Tim.1:13-18
To hold fast sound words, that is,
the Word of God. 2 Tim.1:13
To instruct believers about false
teachers. 1 Tim.4:6
To keep the commandments of God.
1 Tim.6:13-16
To labor diligently & strenuously.
1 Tim.4:10
Duty toward ministers.
Conditions for receiving **m**. Mk.9:38-41
Has the right to be accepted. Reasons.
2 Cor.10:7-18
How **m**. are to be received. Gal.4:12-20
How teachers are to be treated.
Gal.6:6-10
Must be defended sometimes.
2 Cor.11:16-33; 12:11-21
Not to judge, criticize, or compare
with other **m**. 1 Cor.4:1-5; 4:6-13
To be honored. 1 Tim.5:17-18
To be received & heard. 1 Cor.16:10-11;
2 Cor.11:16-21
To restir affection for true **m**. of God.
Gal.4:12-20
To submit to & follow one's **m**.
1 Cor.16:16
To support & serve with the **m**.
Gal.6:6-10
To welcome traveling **m**., evangelists,
prophets, teachers, & missionaries.
3 Jn.3-4, 5-8
Why the **m**. is to be accepted.
2 Cor.10:7-18
Equipped - Resources of the minister.
Discussed. Mt.12:18; Acts 10:1-33
Eight resources. 2 Cor.4:7-18
Encouraged by God. Acts 28:13-15
Gifts, Spiritual. (See **GIFTS, SPIRI-
TUAL**) Ro.12:3-8; 1 Cor.12:4-11;
Eph.4:11; 4:12-16; 1 Tim.1:6
Given power over evil, over Satan &
evil spirits. Mk.6:7; Lk.9:1
God.
Causes the **m**. to always triumph.
2 Cor.2:14
His compelling motives. 2 Cor.5:11-16
Is a sweet fragrance, very special to
God. 2 Cor.2:15-16
Power. Mt.4:24
Power of Christ within. 2 Cor.12:7-10
Power to do great works. Acts 1:8
Power to heal, anointing with oil.
Mk.6:13; Jas.5:14-15
Prayer. Acts 6:4
Preparation. Sermon on the Mount
given for preparation. Mt.5:1-2
Security is in the hands of God.
Rev.2:1; 3:1
The Holy Spirit & power. Lk.24:44-49;
Acts 1:8
To suffer for Christ. 1 Cor.4:9-10;
4:11-13
Example.
Epaphras--the faithful **m**. of the Co-
lossian church. Col.4:12-13
Interceding in a dispute. Phile.8-21
John the Baptist. Mk.1:1-8
Noah, a **m**. of righteousness. 2 Pt.2:5
Of not quitting. Ph.2:25-30
Of serving in second place. Ph.2:19-24

To save life, not to be religious.
Mk.3:4, cp. 1-5
To seek the lost. Lk.15:5
To serve & minister. Verses. List
of. Ro.1:1
To serve, ministering to the needful.
Lk.14:12-14
To warn & leave rejectors alone.
Lk.9:4
To warn every man. Col.1:28
Duty in relation to personal behavior
& faithfulness.
Demanded. Imperative! Today!
Mt.21:28-32
Demanding, busy. Mt.4:23
Excuses for not **m**. Mt.15:33-34
Faithful vs. unfaithful **m**. Mt.24:42-
51; 25:14-30; Lk.12:35-48
Not to quit. Ph.2:25-30
To arduously labor for the church.
Col.1:24-29; 1:20
To be consistent & enduring.
2 Cor.6:3-10
To be faithful. Acts 1:1-2
To be washed & cleansed. Jn.13:6-11
To endure & never quit the **m**.
2 Cor.4:17-18
To fulfill the **m**.--fill up to the brim.
2 Tim.4:5
To gather, not scatter the flock.
Lk.11:23
To give. Great ethic of the believer.
Mt.5:42
To grasp the opportunity while one
can. Mt.26:10-11
To hold fast one's trust, one's **m**.
2 Tim.1:14
To labor & give, not coveting
worldly wealth. Acts 20:33-35
To labor as faithfully as other **m**.
2 Cor.11:23-31
To labor diligently & strenuously.
1 Tim.4:10
To labor diligently, for the fields are
ripe unto harvest. Jn.4:35
To labor night & day. 1 Th.2:9
To live for God & for God's Word.
Acts 20:32
To look after the *flock* of God. Acts
20:28
To look after the Word & to preach
the Word. Tit.1:2-3
To love the church. 2 Cor.11:2
To **m**. & not live on spiritual highs.
Lk.9:32-33
To **m**. even if tired. Lk.9:11
To seek a verdict of faithfulness.
Mk.7:31-37
To seek opportunity to minister.
Gal.6:10
To share in the **m**. Acts 2:44
To support the **m**. Lk.8:1-3
Two areas. Preaching & minister-
ing. Mt.10:7
Of the elderly. Elderly expected to **m**.
Mk.1:31
Equipped - Resources. Mt.14:15-21
Christ uses one's resources. Mt.14:18-21
Fivefold. Mt.15:29-39
Love. Jn.21:15; 21:15-17
Power.
By prayer & fasting. Mt.17:20-21
To heal. Mt.4:24; 6:13; Jas.5:14-15
Prayer & fasting. Mt.17:20-21
The compelling motives of the **m**.
2 Cor.5:11-16

The **m**. is a sweet fragrance, very spe-
cial to God. 2 Cor.2:15-16
The secret to enduring trials & trouble.
2 Cor.4:7-18
The sustaining, enduring spirit of the
m. 2 Cor.4:7-18
Three things. Jn.13:1-2
Example.
Of not helping the needy. Lk.10:31
Onesiphorus. **M**. to Paul while Paul
was a prisoner. 2 Tim.1:15-18
Gift of **m**. Discussed. Ro.12:6-8
Meaning. Mt.25:34-40; Lk.9:48
Methods of **m**.
Discussed. Mt.10:5-15
To be centered in the home. Lk.9:4;
10:5-6
Two by two. Mt.10:3-4
Ministers. Duty toward. (See **MINIS-
TERS**, Duty Toward)
Of Jesus Christ. Identified with man in
every conceivable experience. Lk.2:40;
Heb.2:17-18; 4:15-16
Place of **m**.
In the church. Acts 14:21-28; 20:28;
1 Cor.4:14-21; 2 Cor.11:2; Col.1:24-29
In the earth. Mt.5:13; 5:14; 5:14-15
Where to minister. Mt.4:23
Where to serve strategically. Mt.4:12-13
Preparation for the **m**.
Launching a new **m**. Mk.1:21-22;
Lk.4:1-2
Training. Must precede service.
Mt.10:1
Problems of the **m**. (See **MINISTER**,
Accusations - Criticism - Mistreatment;
Temptations)
Attacked by religionists who differ.
Lk.19:47-48
Attempts to sidetrack. Lk.4:43-44
Burdened down with work. Lk.10:40
Discouragement. Discussed. Acts
18:9-11
Distracted from the **m**. Lk.10:40
Leaving one's first love. Lk.9:61-62
Looking back. Lk.9:61-62
Stressing spiritual need as an excuse for
no power in the physical. Lk.9:11
Qualifications. (See **MINISTERS**,
Qualifications)
Result - Reward.
A successful ministry. Mt.4:23-25
Discussed. Mt.25:40-42; 1 Pt.5:1; 5:4
Fourfold. Parable of the Seed. Lk.8:4-15
Greatness assured. Mk.10:43-44
Verdict upon. Doing all things well.
Mk.7:31-37
Urgency of. Time limited. Jn.9:4
Verses. List of. Lk.9:11; 9:16-17; 10:29-37;
11:42; 17:7-10

MINT
Described. Mt.23:23

MIRACLES (See **JESUS CHRIST**, Power;
HEALING; MIRACULOUS POWERS)
Duty.
To be common to believers, not sur-
prising. Acts 3:12-13
To be tested by law. Acts 4:5-10
First recorded **m**. Lessons for witnessing.
Acts 3:1-11
How one receives **m**. By faith, not by
works of goodness nor by the law.
Gal.3:5

Of Jesus. Only a few included in the gos-
pels. Jn.20:30-31
Power to heal. Mt.4:24; 6:13; Jas.5:14-15
Purpose.
Are signs to point to Christ. Jn.2:23
Major purpose. Mt.10:1
To demonstrate the glory of Christ.
Jn.2:11
To give opportunity to witness. Acts 5:20
To lead men to believe. Jn.2:9-10; 2:23
To prove that Jesus is the Messiah, the
Son of God. Jn.20:30-31, cp.
Mt.11:2-5
To prove the minister's call.
Ro.15:17-19; 2 Cor.12:12
To stir belief in Christ. Jn.11:41-42;
20:30-31
Response to.
Religionists were confused. Jn.11:47;
Acts 4:13-16
Some believed on the name of Christ.
Jn.2:23
Some were amazed & glorified God.
Lk.5:26; 7:16; 13:13; 17:15
Unbelievers rejected. Jn.12:37-41
Source.
Belief. Faith. Acts 3:16
Christ & His power. Mt.10:1
God & His power. Acts 15:12
Not man, but Christ. Acts 3:12-13
Spirit of God. Mt.12:27-28

MIRACULOUS POWERS
Duty.
To be common to believers, not sur-
prising. Acts 3:12-13
To be tested by law. Acts 4:5-10
First recorded **m**. Lessons for witnessing.
Acts 3:1-11
Gift of. Discussed. 1 Cor.12:8-10
How one receives **m**. By faith, not by works
of goodness nor by the law. Gal.3:5
Of Jesus. Only a few included in the gos-
pels. Jn.20:30-31
Power to heal. Mt.4:24; 6:13; Jas.5:14-15
Purpose.
Are signs to point to Christ. Jn.2:23
Major purpose. Mt.10:1
To demonstrate the glory of Christ.
Jn.2:11
To give opportunity to witness. Acts
5:20
To lead men to believe. Jn.2:9-10;
2:23
To prove that Jesus is the Messiah, the
Son of God. Jn.20:30-31, cp.
Mt.11:2-5
To prove the minister's call.
Ro.15:17-19; 2 Cor.12:12
To stir belief in Christ. Jn.11:41-42;
20:30-31
Response to.
Religionists were confused. Jn.11:47;
Acts 4:13-16
Some believed on the name of Christ.
Jn.2:23
Some were amazed & glorified God.
Lk.5:26; 7:16; 13:13; 17:15
Unbelievers rejected. Jn.12:37-41
Source.
Belief. Faith. Acts 3:16
Christ & His power. Mt.10:1
God & His power. Acts 15:12
Not man, but Christ. Acts 3:12-13
Spirit of God. Mt.12:27-28

MISERY - MISERABLE (See **PITIFUL**)
Caused by.
Being comfortable & self-satisfied.
Rev.3:7
Hoarding riches. Jas.5:1
Hoping in Christ only for this world.
1 Cor.15:9
Rejecting Christ & God's servants.
Mt.21:33-41, esp. 41
Seeking God by law. Ro.6:14-15
Sin, oppression, war. Ro.3:15-18
Fact. If we have hope in Christ only for
this life, we are left without hope & are
most **m.** 1 Cor.15:19
Results.
Stand guilty before God. Ro.3:16, 19
The rich are going to howl because of
the **m.** coming upon them. Jas.5:1
The wicked will be **m.** destroyed.
Mt.21:41
Will be spued out by Christ.
Rev.3:16-17
Trait of. Unbelievers. Ro.3:16, cp. 9-20

MISLEADING OTHERS (See **STUM-
BLING BLOCK**)

MISSION - MISSIONS (See **BELIEV-
ERS; COMMISSION; DISCIPLES;
MINISTERS**)
Beginning of. Picture of **m.** & evangel-
ism. Acts 13:4-13
Call - Called. (See **CALL - CALLED;
MINISTER**, Call of)
By the Spirit. Acts 13:1-3, cp. 11:1-18
Deserted. By John Mark. Acts 13:13
Recommitment to **m.** By John Mark.
Acts 15:37
Dangers - Hindrances to.
Attempts to sidetrack. Lk.4:43-44
Discouragement. Acts 18:9-11
Discussed. Mk.16:14; Lk.10:19-21
Lack of vision. Narrow & traditional.
Acts 11:4-15
Leaving one's first love. Lk.9:61-62
Looking back. Lk.9:61-62
Stressing professionalism. Neglecting
lay witnessing. Acts 2:17-21
Tempted to leave the ministry.
2 Cor.4:7-18; 4:13; 4:14; 4:15;
4:16;4:17-18
Defended by Paul. Gal.2:2
Described. Being sent from God. Jn.1:6
Discussed. Lk.10:1-16
Duty - Essentials.
Are saved to obey & to lead others to
obey. Ro.1:5
Fivefold **m.** Lk.5:27-39
Fourfold. Ro.10:14-15
Great call to world **m.** Mt.28:19-20;
Mk.16:15; Acts 8:1;16:6-11
M. is the first duty of the church.
Rev.3:8
Threefold **m.** Lk.6:17-19
To give light to the world. Mt.5:14-18
To have a world-wide vision. Acts
11:4-15; Ro.15:22-33
To preach. Mt.4:17; Mk.2:1-2
To reach city-dwellers & religionists.
Ro.10:14-15
To reach our homes & friends for
Christ. Gal.1:18-20; 1:20
To reach people. Mt.4:14-15
To reach pioneer areas. Ro.15:20-21
To revive giving to **m.** Ph.4:10-19
To salt the earth. Mt.5:13

To support mission projects.
2 Cor.9:1-7; 9:8-15
Example of. A faithful church in **m.**
Rev.3:8
Journeys.
The first great **m.** to the Gentiles by
Peter. Acts 9:32-11:18
To Athens, the great intellectual &
philosophical city. Acts 17:16-21
To Berea, the receptive city. Acts
17:10-15
To Caesarea. Cornelius. Acts 10:1-33
To Cyprus. Picture of **m.** & evangel-
ism. Acts 13:4-13
To Damascus. Acts 9:19-22
To Ethiopia. Acts 8:27-28
To Europe, the chosen area. Acts
16:6-11
To Galatia. The journey to a far dis-
trict. Acts 13:13
To Iconium, the ancient city. Acts
14:1-7
To Jerusalem by Paul. Acts 9:23-30
To Joppa. Acts 9:36-43
To Judea & Samaria. Acts 8:1-9:31
To Lydda. Acts 9:32-35
To Lystra & Derbe, the frontier towns.
Acts 14:8-20
To Miletus, the city with a notable his-
tory in ancient myth. Acts 20:13-16
To Paphos. Acts 13:6-12
To Perga. Acts 13:13; 14:25
To Philippi, a chief city. Acts 16:12-15
To Pisidian of Antioch, the main city
of South Galatia. Acts 13:14-41
To Ptolemais. Acts 21:7
To Rome. Paul as a prisoner. Acts
23:12-28:31
To Samaria. A great revival. Acts 8:5-25
To the Gentiles. Acts 9:32-11:18
To Thessalonica, a city of first impor-
tance. Acts 17:1-9
Method. Pattern of **m.** Discussed. Acts
14:1-7
Of Christ. Sense of. Mk.1:36-38
Of Paul. His thirty years as a missionary.
Acts 28:25-29
Predicted. The world will be evangelized.
Mk.13:10
Purpose. What **m.** is & is not. Jn.1:7
Response to. Four responses. Acts
13:42-52
Sent forth. (See **COMMISSION; MIN-
ISTERS**, Commission)
Discussed. Lk.9:1-9
To preach, heal & share the power of
Christ. Lk.6:17-19
To the whole world. Mt.28:19-20;
Mk.16:15; Acts 1:8
Source.
Must be sent from the heart of God.
Jn.1:6
Power of the Word. Mk.16:17-18
Support of. Discussed. Ph.4:10-19
Urgency of. Time limited. Jn.9:4
Verses. List of. Mk.1:17-18; 3:14-15
Vision. God's will is a world-wide vi-
sion. Acts 11:4-15
Work of. Discussed. Acts 13:4-13
World-wide **m.** Christ works to enlarge
the fold, to reach out. Jn.10:14-16

MISSIONARIES (See **APOSTLES; MIN-
ISTERS** for more discussion)
Call & traits of early **m.** Acts 13:1-3
Duty. To be adaptable. Lk.10:8-9

Duty toward. To welcome if they are
traveling **m.**, evangelists ,or teachers.
3 Jn.3-4, 5-8
First **m.** ever sent out. By the great
church at Antioch. Acts 13:1-3
First two **m.** were Paul & Barnabas. Acts
13:1-3

MNASON OF CYPRUS
Paul lodged with. Acts 21:16

MOB
Reacted against Christianity. In Ephesus.
Acts 19:21-41
Seized Paul. Acts 21:27-40; 22:1-29

MOCKERY (See **JESUS CHRIST**, Re-
sponse; Rejected)
Of Christ.
At the crucifixion. Mt.27:26-44
By His half-brothers. Jn.7:3-5
Of God. God is not mocked. He will
judge. Gal.6:7-9

MODERATION (See **GENTLENESS**)

MODESTY
In behavior & works. 1 Tim.2:9-10;
1 Pt.3:1-2
In dress. (See **CLOTHING; DRESS**)

MOLECH
False god. Discussed. Acts 7:43

MONEY (See **MATERIALISM;
RICHES; STEWARDSHIP; WEALTH**)
Discussed.
Borrowing. Ro.13:8
Love of. Mt.26:15; 2 Tim.3:2-4
Causes four things. 1 Tim.6:9-10
Fact.
Determined by God. Lk.16:12
Is described as a trust from God.
Lk.16:12
M. is the least trust given to man.
Lk.16:10-12
Misconception - Misunderstanding of.
One of three great misconceptions.
Lk.16:14-15
Purpose. To use for good in helping oth-
ers. Lk.16:9; Eph.4:28
Vs. Christ. Lk.16:14-15
Power of **m.** & the power of Jesus'
name. Acts 16:16-24
Vs. spiritual things. Lk.16:10-12
Vs. trust in God. Lk.21:3
Weakness of. Silver & gold cannot save.
Acts 3:6-8

MONEY, LOVE OF
Meaning. 1 Tim.3:2-3

MONEYCHANGERS
Cast out of the temple. Mt.21:12-16

MORAL UNIVERSE
The universe is **m.** 2 Th.1:6

MORALIST, THE
Discussed. Ro.2:1-16
Judgment of. Ro.2:1-16
Misconception of.
Thinks God is too good to judge.
Ro.2:2-5; 3:5-8
Thinks man is basically good. Ro.2:2-5

MORALS - MORALITY (See JUST - JUSTICE; IMMORALITY; PURITY; RIGHTEOUSNESS)
Discussed.
Sexual purity. 1 Th.4:1-8
To live a **m**. life. 1 Th.4:1-8
Duty.
Not to fellowship with an immoral person. 1 Cor.5:11
Not to look upon a person with lust. Mt.5:27-28
Not to talk or joke about immoral subjects. Eph.5:3-12
Not to touch a woman. 1 Cor.7:1
To dress modestly. 1 Tim.2:9-10; 1 Pt.3:1-6
To live a pure life. Lk.1:27; Tit.2:5
Verses. List of. Lk.1:27
Essential. For God to use. Lk.1:27
Need for. In the midst of an immoral, cesspool society. Ro.1:8
Source of - How one can be **m**.
By knowing God. His putting His laws into one's *mind & heart*. Heb.8:10-11
By putting on the new man. Eph.4:24, cp. 2 Cor.5:17; 2 Pt.1:5-7
By the grace & salvation of God. Eph.2:8-10, cp. 1-10
By the Spirit of God. Ro.8:1-17

MORTIFY (See PUT TO DEATH)

MOSES
Discussed. Acts 7:17-41
Esteem of. By the Jews. Exalted above God. Acts 7:30-38
Facts.
Appeared with Jesus at the Transfiguration. Reason. Mt.17:3
Experienced God's glory. 2 Cor.3:7-16
Not as great as Christ. Heb.3:1-6
Faith of.
A self-denying faith. Heb.11:24-28
Gave up the riches of Egypt & the pleasures of sin for God. Heb.11:24-28
History of.
Place in God's plan. Acts 7:17-41
Summarized. Acts 7:20-44
Illustrates. The devotional life. 2 Cor.3:7
Life of.
Discussed. Heb.3:2
Periods of. Three periods of 40 years. Acts 7:23
Ministry.
Established the sacrificial system. Heb.9:18-22
Mediated the covenant. Heb.9:18-22
Moses' veiled face. 2 Cor.3:13
Parents. Faith of. Loving & protecting. Heb.11:23
Prophecies of. Messiah. Acts 7:30-38
Spirit of. Present in the last days. Rev.11:6
Type - Symbolized - Pictured.
Christ. Acts 7:17-29
Death of Christ. Lifting up the snake in the wilderness. Jn.3:14-15
Vs. Christ. Discussed. Heb.3:1-6

MOST HOLY PLACE
Christ entered once. Heb.9:11-14
Discussed. Heb.9:1-10; 9:15-22; 9:23-28
Entrance into.
By Jesus Christ. Heb.10:19-21
Not by the blood of animals, but by Christ. Heb.9:11-14; 10:19

Purpose for. Heb.9:1-14
Veil or curtain of.
Torn at Christ's death: symbolizes open access to God. Mt.27:50-51
Type. Symbol of Christ's death. Heb.10:19-21

MOTHER
A godly **m**. Lk.1:26-38; 2 Tim.1:5
Duty.
Discussed. Tit.2:4-5, cp. 1 Tim.5:14
Not to be overly ambitious for children. Mt.20:20-28
Not to influence children with evil. Mt.14:6-8
To lead children to salvation. 2 Tim.3:15
To live as the holy & dearly loved chosen person of the Lord. 2 Jn.1-4
To love her children. Tit.2:4
To rear children in the Lord & in His truth. 2 Tim.1:5; 3:15; 2 Jn.1-4
To root children in the Scripture. 2 Tim.3:15; 3:16
To take the lead & to open one's home for prayer. Acts 12:12
Duty toward. (See **CHILDREN**, Duties)
To honor. Eph.6:1-3
To look after & provide for. Jn.19:25-27; 1 Tim.5:3-8

MOTIVE
For giving & doing good. Mt.6:1-4
For prayer. Discussed. Mt.6:5-6
For works. Mt.6:1-4
Kinds of.
Deceptive, covetous **m**. Acts 5:1-11
Pure **m**. vs. impure. Mt.5:8
Ulterior, corrupt **m**. Jn.12:4-8
Of Christ. The joy set before Him. Heb.12:2
Of the believer.
Fear & reverence for God. Heb.11:7
Hope for a heavenly city. Heb.11:8-10
Hope for a heavenly country. Heb.11:13-16
Hope for a heritage. Heb.11:11-12
Hope for deliverance. Heb.11:17-19, 29; 11:31; 11:32-34;11:35-40
Hope for God's promises. Heb.11:21-22; 11:32-40
Hope for reward. Heb.11:24-28
Hope for salvation. Heb.11:7
Hope for some better thing. Heb.11:32-40
Hope for the resurrection. Heb.11:17-19; 11:35-40
Hope for things to come. Heb.11:20
Wrong **m**.
For rejection of Christ. Mk.8:11
Of ambition. Mk.10:36-37
Vs. right **m**. Mt.6:1-4; 6:5-6

MOUNTAIN - MOUNTAINS
Christ & **m**.
Ascended into heaven while on the **m**. Acts 1:9-12
Fasted & was tempted on the **m**. Mt.4:1-8, esp. 8
Prayed on the **m**. Mt.14:23; 26:30, 36-46; Mk.6:46; Lk.6:12; 9:28
Sought refuge, to be alone on the **m**. Jn.3:15

Spent nights there; spent His last week upon earth on the Mount of Olives. Lk.21:37; Jn.8:1
Taught on the **m**. Mt.5:1; 15:29; 24:3; Mk.13:3
Was transfigured on a **m**. Mt.17:1-2
Meaning. Mk.11:22-23
Mount of Olives. (See **GETHSEMANE**)
Power to remove **m**. Meaning. Mt.17:20
Symbolized. Difficulties. Mt.17:20

MOURN
Meaning. Mt.5:4

MOUTH (See SPEECH; TONGUE)
Duty. To be clean-mouthed. Eph.5:4; Col.3:8-9
Sins of. Misusing the **m**. in speech & sexually. Eph.5:4

MOVE TO BOAST
Discussed. Ro.3:27; 3:28
Duty.
No flesh should glory in God's presence. 1 Cor.1:29
Not to glory as though one is self-sufficient. 1 Cor.4:7
Not to glory in men. 1 Cor.3:21
Not to glory in one's call to preach. 1 Cor.9:16-17
Not to glory in the flesh. 2 Cor.11:18
To glory only in the Lord. 1 Cor.1:31; 2 Cor.10:17
To renounce glorying in man. 1 Cor.3:21-23
Results. Glorying in man leavens the whole lump, contaminates the whole person. 1 Cor.5:6
Sin of.
Glorying in self. Cause. Self-centeredness. Ro.3:27
In the Corinthian church. 1 Cor.1:29; 1:31; 3:21; 4:6; 4:7; 4:8; 5:1; 5:2; 5:6; 9:16-17; 2 Cor.10:17; 11:18

MULTITUDE (See CROWD)
Excitement of the **m**. & crowds is not always wise. Mk.6:45
Fed by Christ. Lk.9:10-17
Feeding of.
Followed Christ. By the thousands. Lk.8:4
Why **m**. followed Christ. Mt.20:29

MURDER
Arises from - Source.
Anger. Mt.5:21-22
The flesh - a work of the flesh. Gal.5:19-21
The heart. Mt.15:19
Discussed. Jn.8:48-59; Ro.13:9; 2 Tim.3:2-4
Is the nature of man. Ro.3:15-18
Judgment of.
Excluded from the kingdom of God. Gal.5:19-21, esp. 21. Cp. Ro.1:29-32, esp. 32
Shall not inherit eternal life. 1 Jn.3:15
Meaning. Mt.5:21-26; 5:21-22; Mk.7:21; Ro.1:29; 1 Jn.3:15
Sin of. Committed by man & Satan. Jn.8:44-45

MURMUR - MURMURING (See COMPLAIN, COMPLAINING; GRUMBLING)
Against Christ & His claims. Jn.6:41-43
Caused by.
Anxiety, worry. Lk.10:40
Hate. 1 Jn.3:15
Characteristic - Trait of. False teachers. Jude 16

MUSIC
Duty. To exhort each other in songs.
Col.3:15-17
Exhorted. Result of the Spirit's infilling.
Eph.5:19-21

MUSTARD SEED
Described. Mt.17:20
Discussed. Mt.13:31-32; Mk.4:31;
Lk.13:19
Meaning. Lk.17:5-6
Parable of. Lk.13:18-21
Greatness of Christianity. Mt.13:31-32
Growth of God's Kingdom. Mk.4:30-32

MYSTERY--SECRET
Discussed. Ro.16:25-26; Eph.3:1-13; 3:6
All **m**. listed. 1 Cor.2:7
M. of Babylon the great. Rev.17:5
M. of Christ.
And of the gospel. Ro.16:25
Christ in you. Col.1:26-27; 4:2-3
Of Him & the church. Eph.5:32
The nature of Christ. Col.2:2-3
M. of God.
Committed to ministers. 1 Cor.4:1-2
Completed. Rev.10:3-7
Great day of salvation. Announcement
of. Rev.10:1-11
Of His grace. Eph.3:1-13
Of His will. Eph.1:9-10
To be finished. Rev.10:7
M. of godliness.
Discussed. 1 Tim.3:16
Six facts. 1 Tim.3:16
M. of iniquity, of sin. 2 Th.2:7
M. of Israel. Ro.11:25, cp. Ro.9:1-11:36
M. of the faith. Discussed. 1 Tim.3:9-10
M. of the gospel. Eph.6:18-19
M. of the kingdom of heaven. Mt.13:1-52
M. of the resurrection. 1 Cor.15:51
M. of the seven stars of Revelation.
Rev.1:16, 20
Meaning. Mt.13:1-52; Eph.1:9-10; 3:3-5;
Col.1:26-27

MYTHS
Duty.
Not to pay attention to **m**, false &
speculative teaching. 1 Tim.1:4;
Tit.1:14
To have nothing to do with worldly **m**.
1 Tim.4:7
Fact.
M. arouse questions & doubt instead
of edifying. 1 Tim.1:4
M. destroy godliness. 1 Tim.4:7
M. turn people away from the truth.
2 Tim.4:3-4
People will turn aside to **m**. in the end
time. 2 Tim.4:3-4, esp. 4
Salvation, the power & coming of
Christ, is not a **m**. 2 Pt.1:16
The true minister does not follow nor
proclaim cunningly devised **m**.
2 Pt.1:16
Meaning. 1 Tim.1:4
Results.
Arouse questions & doubt instead of
edifying. 1 Tim.1:4
Destroy godliness. 1 Tim.4:7
Turn people away from the truth.
2 Tim.4:3-4

N

NAIN
City of. Discussed. Lk.7:11

NAKED-NAKEDNESS
Duty.
To clothe & minister to those who are
n., who do not have adequate cloth-
ing. Mt.25:33-36, esp. 36
To feed & clothe the hungry & **n**.
Jas.2:15-16
Fact.
Conversion to Christ leads a person to
clothe his **n**. Mk.5:15, cp. 5:1-20
Evil spirits caused people to strip
themselves **n**. Acts 19:16
John Mark fled the arrest of Christ--
fled **n**. Mk.14:51-52
Judgment is based upon ministering to
the needy & the **n**. Mt.25:31-46,
esp. 36, 38, 43, 44
Paul sometimes had inadequate cloth-
ing. 1 Cor.4:9-13, esp. 11
Peter was **n**. when he was fishing.
Jn.21:7
In the end time.
All things are **n**. & open to God's
eyes. Heb.4:13
God will strip the great capital of the
world & make her **n**. because of her
great sins. Rev.17:16-17
Spiritual **n**.
Meaning. Rev.3:16-17
To strive to be clothed with the righteousness & immortality of heaven lest
we be found **n**. in the day of judgment. 2 Cor.5:2-3

NAME - NAMES
The name of believers. (See **BELIEV-
ERS**, Names - Titles)
Is confessed before God & the angels
by Christ. Rev.3:5
Is known & called out by Christ. Jn.10:3
Is reproached & ridiculed by unbeliev-
ers. Lk.6:22
Is written in heaven. Lk.10:20
Is written in the book of life. Ph.4:3
Shall receive a new **n**. in heaven.
Rev.2:17
Shall receive the **n**. of God & of the
city of God in heaven. Rev.3:12
The name of Christ. (See **JESUS
CHRIST**, Names - Titles)
Duty toward.
To be baptized in the **n**. of Christ.
Acts 2:38; 19:5
To be obedient for His **n**. Ro.1:5
To believe on the **n**. of God's Son.
1 Jn.3:23; 5:13
To call upon the **n**. of Jesus. Mean-
ing. Acts 3:6
To cast out demons in the **n**. of
Christ. Mt.7:22; Mk.16:17
To depart from iniquity if one
names the **n**. of Christ.
2 Tim.2:19
To do all in the **n**. of the Lord.
Col.3:17
To give thanks to His **n**. Heb.13:15
To hazard one's life for the **n**. of
Christ. Acts 15:26
To pray in the **n**. of Christ.
Jn.14:13-14; 15:16; 16:23, 24, 26

To preach forgiveness of sins in His
n. Lk.24:47; Acts 10:43
To preach in the **n**. of Jesus. Acts
9:27, cp. 20
To thank God in the **n**. of Christ.
Eph.5:20
Fact.
A person can be healed in the **n**. of
Christ. Acts 3:6; 16:18
A person is condemned because he
does not believe in the**n**. of Christ,
the Son of God. Jn.3:18
A person is justified in the **n**. of the
Lord Jesus. 1 Cor.6:11
Believers will be hated because of
the **n**. of Jesus. Mt.10:22; 24:9;
Mk.13:13; Lk.21:17
Christ came in the **n**. of His Father,
God Himself. Jn.5:43
Christ has a more excellent **n**. than
all heavenly beings. Heb.1:4
Christ has been given a name above
every **n**. Ph.2:9-10
Many false teachers will come in
His **n**. Mt.24:5; Mk.13:6; Lk.21:8
Some think that they should act con-
trary to the **n**. of Christ. Acts 26:9
The **n**. of Christ is Immanuel, God
with us. Mt.1:23
The **n**. of Jesus was the name given
by God. Mt.1:23; Lk.1:31
The person who believes on His **n**. be-
comes a true child of God. Jn.1:12
The person who believes on His **n**.
receives life. Jn.20:31
The person who is reproached for
the **n**. of Christ receives the spe-
cial glory of God. 1 Pt.4:14
The rich tend to blaspheme the **n**. of
Christ. Jas.2:7
The works of Christ were done in
the **n**. of His Father. Jn.10:25
There is no other **n**. that can save a
person. Acts 4:12
When believers gather together in
His **n**., Christ is in the midst of
them. Mt.18:20
The name of God. (See **GOD**, Names - Titles)
Duty. To honor one's employer so that
the **n**. of God will not be blas-
phemed. 1 Tim.6:1
Fact.
All creation bears the **n**. of God.
Eph.3:15
God keeps believers through His **n**.
Jn.17:11-12
God's **n**. is blasphemed by the sins
of those who profess Christ but do
not live righteously. Ro.2:24
God's **n**. is hallowed. Mt.6:9;
Lk.11:2
God's **n**. was revealed by Christ.
Jn.17:6, 26

NARCISSUS
Believer in Rome. Ro.16:11

NARROW GATE
Vs. the wide gate. Mt.7:13-14

NATHANAEL
Discussed. Jn.1:46-49
Led to the Lord. Jn.1:46-49
Witnesses to Christ: the Son of God, the
King of Israel. Jn.1:46-49

NATIONS (See **CITIZENSHIP; GOVERNMENT**)
Duty. To preach the gospel to all **n.** of the world. Mt.24:14; 28:19-20; Mk.13:10; 16:15; Lk.24:47; Ro.16:26; Acts 1:8. Cp. Rev.14:6
Fact.
All **n.** are blessed by the gospel. Gal.3:8
All **n.** are made of one blood. Acts 17:26
All **n.** shall be deceived by the antichrist & the devil. Rev.18:23; 20:3
All **n.** shall be destroyed in the end time. Rev.16:19
All **n.** shall be judged by Christ Himself. Mt.25:31-32, cp. 33-46
All **n.** shall come & worship before God. Rev.15:4
Believers shall be rewarded with power over the **n.** in eternity. Rev.2:26; 21:24-27
Christ died for all the **n.** of the world. Jn.11:49-53
Christ redeems persons out of every **n.** Rev.5:9
God has suffered all **n.** to walk in their own ways. Acts 14:16
God is Sovereign over all the **n.** Discussed. Acts 17:26
Persons in every **n.** who fear God & works righteousness are acceptable to God. Acts 10:35-36
Severe distress will sweep the **n.** of the earth in the end time. Lk.21:25
The antichrist will have power over all **n.** & peoples of the earth. Rev.13:7-8
The **n.** of the world are crooked & perverse. Ph.2:14-16
Judgment of. Final judgment of nations. Mt.25:31-46
Righteousness vs. sin. Results of. Lk.19:43-44

NATURAL CATASTROPHES (See **END TIME**)

NATURAL MAN (See **CARNAL; FLESH**, Physical World & Dimension; **MAN**)
Discussed. 1 Cor.2:14; Eph.2:1-3
Errors of.
Discussed. Mk.8:32-33
Misunderstands the spiritual dimension. Mk.12:24
Fact.
Man has a consciousness, an inner sense of right & wrong. Ro.1:19-20; 2:14-15
Man's body is a **n.** body: dying, corruptible, dishonorable, & weak. 1 Cor.15:42-43
There is a **n.** body & a spiritual body. 1 Cor.15:44-49
Is sinful & depraved.
By nature. Mk.14:27-31
Cannot receive the things of God's Spirit. 1 Cor.2:14, cp. 1-16
Is like a **n.** brute beast when he teaches false doctrine. 2 Pt.2:12
Is without **n.** affection. Ro.1:28-32, esp. 31
Sins against the **n.** order of nature. Ro.1:26, cp. 18-32

NATURAL SENSES
Vs. spiritual senses. Mt.16:2-3

NATURE (See **EARTH; WORLD**)
Deliverance from. Shall be delivered from corruption. Ro.8:19-22
Discussed. Ro.8:19-22
Good & evil in the world. Jn.12:31
In the end time. (See **END TIME**)
Astronomical eclipse. Rev.8:12
Disasters to be intensified. Lk.21:11
Famine. Rev.6:5-6
Fierce storms. Rev.8:6-7
Meteoric mass. Rev.8:10-11
One third of the fish & of the fishing & shipping industry destroyed. Rev.8:8-9
One third of the water supply destroyed. Rev.8:10-11
One third of the vegetation destroyed. Rev.8:6-7
Pestilence. Rev.6:7-8
Volcanic explosion. Rev.8:8-9
Judgment of. Reasons why. **N.** is imperfect & corruptible. Jn.12:31
Laws governing. Eight laws. Jn.12:39-41
Power over. Christ's power over. (See **JESUS CHRIST**, Power)
State of nature.
Is corruptible; suffering under corruption. Ro.8:19-22
Man sins against **n.**, the natural order of things. Ro.1:26, cp. 18-32
What **n.** reveals & shows. Reveals God. Ro.1:20

NATURE, DIVINE
Discussed. Given to believers. 2 Pt.1:4
Revealed in creation. Ro.1:20

NAZARETH
Discussed. Lk.1:26; Jn.1:46
Hometown of Jesus. Discussed. Mt.2:23
Rejected Christ.
Broke His heart. Jn.4:44
Reasons. Mt.13:53-58; Mk.6:1-6; Lk.4:16-30

NEAR, DRAW (See **DRAW NEAR**)

NECESSITIES (See **HARDSHIPS**)

NEEDLE
Camel passing through. Meaning. Mt.19:24; Mk.10:25
Cp. a rich man. Mk.10:25

NEEDS - NECESSITIES
Attitude toward. Mt.6:25-34
N. & resources. Mk.6:35-44
Right vs. wrong attitude. Lk.9:12
Caused by.
Anxiety. Lk.10:40
Distraction. Lk.10:40
Discussed. Acts 4:32-37
Lesson on **n.** and gratitude. Lk.17:11-19
Times when help is needed. 2 Tim.4:9-18
Duty.
Not to fear **n.** Lk.12:4-12
To be met by believers. Lk.11:42
To be sensitive to **n.** Acts 9:39
To cry for help. Mk.6:47-49
To meet **n.** as world missions go forth. Ro.15:22-33
To meet the **n.** of one's family, then give all else. Acts 4:32
To trust God to take care of **n.** Lk.10:4

Meaning. 2 Cor.6:4-5
Met - Provided for.
By God.
Discussed. Mt.6:25-34; Mk.12:15; Lk.12:22-34; Jn.6:10-13
Proves the love & power of God. Lk.11:29
Seeking to meet **n.** vs. trusting God. Lk.12:29-30
Verses. List of. Jn.6:10-13
By Jesus Christ. Ph.4:11-14
Jesus' purpose & power to meet **n.** Mt.8:14-17
No **n.** that Jesus does not want to meet. Jn.6:1-15; 10:9-10
By man himself.
By necessary work. Discussed. Mt.12:5
By prayer. Mt.6:11; Lk.9:28-36
Each **n.** is a foretaste of the cross. Mt.8:16
Early church met **n.** of all. Acts 4:34-37
How to meet.
By sitting at Jesus' feet. Lk.10:40; 10:41
Five steps. Lk.17:11-14; Acts 3:1-5
Persevering prayer. Mt.7:7-11
Steps for getting help & meeting needs. Mt.20:29-34; Mk.10:46-52; Lk.18:35-43
Must be met by the wealthy. Lk.18:18-23; Acts 4:32
Must be seen by believers. Acts 3:1-5
Must give all above necessities. Acts 4:32
Must have precedence over tradition & ritual. Mt.12:3-4; 12:9-13; Lk.6:1-11
Personal responsibility vs. social responsibility. Mk.6:35-36
Steps to meeting. Acts 4:32
Discussed. What it takes to have **n.** met. Mt.15:21-28
Of men - Of life.
Five great **n.** Jn.11:28-37
For salvation. How the desperate can be saved. Mt.9:18-34; 20:29-34
For the Light of the world. Jn.8:12
Great **n.** Mt.4:23
Meaning. Mt.6:11
Severe, desperate **n.** of life. Jn.4:46-47
Spiritual hunger. Listed. Jn.6:32
To prepare for the Lord. Jn.1:23
Response to. Four **r.** Jn.6:1-15
Social vs. spiritual **n.** Jn.2:3-5
Temptation. To meet needs apart from God. Mt.4:2-4; Lk.4:3-4
Verses. List of. Lk.8:11-15; Ro.8:34
Vs. lust. Mt.12:3-4

NEEDY, THE (See **MINISTERING**, Duty; **POOR - POVERTY**)
Care for. By Jesus. For people in the streets. Mk.1:32-34
Picture of. Described. Verses. Listed. Jn.5:2-4
Seeking Jesus. (See **SEEK - SEEKING**)

NEGLECT - NEGLECTING

Danger of.
Knowing, but not doing. Ro.9:4
Neglecting salvation. Heb.2:1-4
Neglecting the body in the name of religion. Col.2:20-24, esp. 24
Neglecting the invitation of God & of Jesus Christ. Mt.22:1-14
Neglecting to minister to the needy. Mt.25:41-46
Neglecting to prepare for the return of Christ. Mt.25:1-13

Is sin. Described. Lk.16:19-21

Judgment of.
Shall not be allowed into heaven. Mt.25:12
Shall suffer everlasting punishment. Mt.25:46

NEIGHBOR (See LOVE)

Duty.
Not to feed friends & n. but the poor & needy. Lk.14:12-14
To loves one's n. 1 Jn.2:7-11
To love one's n. as oneself. Mt.22:39; Mk.12:31; Lk.10:25-37;Ro.13:8-10
To speak truth with one's n. Eph.4:25

Law governing. Old Testament view. Mt.5:43

Love for. Ministering to. Lk.10:29-37

Who is my n. Lk.10:29-37

NET

Parable of the fisherman's n. Mt.13:47-50

NEUTRALITY (See DOUBLEMINDED; INDECISION)

Fact.
A choice has to be made. Mt.4:10
Cannot be indecisive. Lk.9:57-62; 11:23; 14:18-20
Cannot serve two masters. Lk.16:13; 1 Cor.10:21
Disqualifies a person. Lk.9:61-62
Is impossible to be n. Mt.12:30; 12:33; Mk.9:40
Makes a person unstable in all his ways. Jas.1:8

NEW AGE (See AGE, New)

Ushered in by Christ. Mt.9:14-17

NEW BIRTH (See BORN AGAIN; NEW CREATION; NEW MAN; REGENERATION; SALVATION)

A confrontation with Jesus Christ. Jn.4:30

Discussed. Jn.3:1-15; 2 Cor.5:17-21; Tit.3:5; 1 Pt.1:23; 1 Jn.5:1-5;Rev.5:8-10

Duty - Proof of.
Doing righteousness. 1 Jn.2:28-29; 3:9. Cp. Mt.5:6
Hunger for the Word of God. 1 Pt.2:2-3
Loving one another. 1 Jn.4:7
Obedience. 1 Jn.2:28-29
Three proofs. 1 Jn.5:1-5

Meaning.
Partaker of God's nature. 1 Jn.3:9
Partaker of God's seed. 1 Pt.1:23; 1 Jn.3:9

Nature.
Imperishable. 1 Pt.1:23
Spiritual. Jn.3:4-8; Eph.1:3; 4:24

Result.
Changes a person's life radically. Jn.4:30
Delivers one from continuous sin. 1 Jn.3:9, cp. 3:4-9
Keeps one from sin & Satan. 1 Jn.5:18
Overcomes false spirits. 1 Jn.4:1-6
Overcomes the world. 1 Jn.5:4-5
Stirs love. 1 Jn.4:7

Source - How to secure.
By confession. 1 Jn.4:14-16
By facing the truth of sin. Jn.4:16-18
By God's workmanship. Eph.2:10
By Jesus Christ. Faith in Him. 1 Jn.5:1
By the righteousness of Jesus Christ. 1 Jn.2:29
By the Spirit & water. Jn.3:5
By the Word of God. 1 Pt.1:23
Not by man, but by God. Jn.1:12-13

NEW COVENANT (See COVENANT, NEW)

NEW CREATION - NEW CREATURE (See BORN AGAIN; MIND, Renewed Mind; NEW BIRTH; NEW MAN; REGENERATION; SALVATION)

Demands of. Col.3:5-11

Described.
Several ways. Eph.2:11-18
The great mystery of Christ. Eph.3:1-13

Discussed. Mt.21:43; 2 Cor.5:17-21; 2 Pt.1:4
Basis of. Col.3:1-4
Demands of. Violent demands. Col.3:5-11
Clothing of. Col.3:12-14
Heart of. Col.3:15-17

Meaning.
A complete change of life: old things have passed away, all things have become new. 2 Cor.5:17
Participates in God's nature. 2 Pt.1:4
Partaking of God's seed. 1 Jn.3:9
Seen in Abraham. Ro.4:1-25
Names - Titles - Identity. The seed of Abraham. Gal.3:6-7; 3:8-9

Nature.
A new & an adventuresome life. Mk.2:21-22
A new creation, a new individual. (See NEW MAN) Lk.13:20-21
A new society, a new race. Lk.8:21; Eph.2:11-18; 2:14-15;4:17-19
Are different. 2 Cor.6:11-7:1

Necessary - Essential. Reasons. Mk.14:27-31

Of the world. God's plan for the ages. Jn.4:22

Source.
Christ. Mk.2:21; 2 Cor.5:17
God. Is creating a new people, a new nation, a new race. Lk.8:21; Acts 15:13-21; Eph.2:11-18; 2:14-15; 4:17-19; 1 Pt.2:9
The cross of Christ. Gal.6:14-18

NEW JERUSALEM (See JERUSALEM, NEW & HEAVENLY)

NEW MAN - NEW LIFE--NEW SELF (See BORN AGAIN; MIND, Renewed Mind; NEW BIRTH; NEW CREATION; NEW PERSON; REGENERATION; SALVATION)

Describes. The church & the believer. 1 Cor.5:7

Discussed. Eph.4:20-24; 4:24; Tit.3:5

Duty.
To put on, to be clothed with Christ. Ro.10:11; Eph.4:32;
To renew day by day. 2 Cor.4:16

Clothing of. Eph.4:25-32

How to receive. By the resurrection of Christ. Ro.6:3-5

Law of. Discussed. Ro.7:21-23

Meaning. 2 Cor.4:16; Eph.4:24

Nature.
A new creation, person. Lk.13:20-21; 2 Cor.5:17; Eph.2:11-18; 2:14-15; 4:24; 2 Pt.1:4
Christ-centered, not self-centered. 2 Cor.5:16

Necessary - Essential. Reasons. Mk.14:27-31

Result.
Changes a person radically. Jn.4:30; 2 Cor.5:17
Changes one's master. Ro.6:17-18
Frees from the law. Ro.7:4
Swaps sin for God. Ro.6:17-18

Source.
A confrontation with Jesus Christ. Jn.4:30
A decision for Christ. Ro.6:17-18
God's workmanship. Eph.2:10
The cross of Christ. Gal.6:14-18
The quickening power of the Holy Spirit. Verses. List of. Jn.6:44-46

Ushered in by Christ. Mt.9:14-17

Verses. List of. 1 Cor.5:7

Vs. old person. Eph.4:20-24

NEW NATION

Fact. Believers are being formed into a new & holy n. Lk.8:21; Eph.2:11-18; 2:14-15; 4:17-19; 1 Pt.2:9

NEW PERSON

Basis of. Col.3:1-4

Describes. The church & the believer. 1 Cor.5:7

Discussed. Eph.4:20-24; 4:24; Col.3:1-17; Tit.3:5

Duty.
To put on, to be clothed with Christ. Ro.10:11; Eph.4:32; Col.3:8-11
To renew day by day. 2 Cor.4:16

Clothing of. Eph.4:25-32; Col.3:12-14

How to receive. By the resurrection of Christ. Ro.6:3-5

Law of. Discussed. Ro.7:21-23

Meaning. 2 Cor.4:16; Eph.4:24

Nature.
A new creation, person. Lk.13:20-21; 2 Cor.5:17; Eph.2:11-18; 2:14-15; 4:24; 2 Pt.1:4
Christ-centered, not self-centered. 2 Cor.5:16

Necessary - Essential. Reasons. Mk.14:27-31

Result.
Changes a person radically. Jn.4:30; 2 Cor.5:17
Changes one's master. Ro.6:17-18
Frees from the law. Ro.7:4

Swaps sin for God. Ro.6:17-18
Source.
  A confrontation with Jesus Christ.
    Jn.4:30
  A decision for Christ. Ro.6:17-18
  God's workmanship. Eph.2:10
  The cross of Christ. Gal.6:14-18
  The quickening power of the Holy
    Spirit. Verses. List of. Jn.6:44-46
  Ushered in by Christ. Mt.9:14-17
    Verses. List of. 1 Cor.5:7
  Vs. old person. Eph.4:20-24; Col.3:5-11

NEW TESTAMENT (See **BIBLE**)

NEWNESS OF LIFE
  Meaning. Ro.6:4

NEWNESS OF SPIRIT
  Meaning. Ro.7:6

NICANOR
  One of the first deacons. Acts 6:1-8

NICODEMUS
  Buried Jesus. Fear conquered by Jesus'
    death. Jn.19:39
  Discussed. Jn.3:1-2
  Spoke up for Christ in the Sanhedrin.
    Jn.7:42

NICOLAITANS
  Discussed. A false teaching of worldli-
    ness. Rev.2:5-6

NICOLAS
  One of the first deacons. Acts 6:1-8

NIGER
  A minister in Antioch. Acts 13:1

NINEVEH
  Illustration. Of rejecting Christ. To con-
    demn this generation. Mt.12:41

NOAH
  Days of. Discussed. Cp. Christ's return.
    Lk.17:26-30
  Fact. Saved through the flood. 1 Pt.3:19-22
  Faith of.
    Reverent faith. Heb.11:7
    Vindicated. Heb.11:7
  Salvation of.
    Because of righteousness. 2 Pt.2:5
    Saved by God. 2 Pt.2:5
    Saved in that he feared the world's
      first destruction. 2 Pt.2:5
  Type - Symbol of.
    Salvation. 1 Pt.3:19-22
    The coming judgment. Lk.17:26-30
    The end of the world. Will be like
      Noah's day. Mt.24:37-39

NOBLE - NOBILITY
  A n. people. Discussed. Acts 17:10-15

NOBLEMAN (See **ROYAL OFFICIAL**)
  An official in a king's court. Jn.4:46-47
NOTHING FALSE
  Christ lived a guileless, perfect life.
    1 Pt.2:22
  Meaning. Jn.1:47; 1 Pt.2:1

NOVICE (See **RECENT CONVERT**)

NUMBER 666 OF ANTICHRIST
  Meaning. Rev.13:18

NUNC DIMITTIS
  Song of. By Simeon. Lk.2:29-33

NYMPHAS
  Discussed. Believer of Laodicea.
    Col.4:15

O

OATH - OATHS
  Discussed. Mt.5:33-37; 23:16-22
  Law governing. Mt.5:33-37
  Misuse of. Mt.23:16-22
  Of God.
    To Abraham. Lk.1:73-75
    To all believers. Heb.6:16-20
    To judge the unbelieving & disobedi-
      ent. Heb.3:7-19, esp.11
  Types. Fivefold. Mt.5:33-37

OBEY - OBEDIENCE (See **COMMIT-
MENT; DISOBEDIENCE; FAITH-
FULNESS; PERSEVERANCE**; Also see
the person desired for the obedience of a
particular person; e.g., Parent, Child, etc.)
  Described.
    As obeying of the Word. Ro.2:11-15
    As wise & foolish builders. Mt.7:24-27
  Discussed. Ro.1:5
    Obeys God's Word. 1 Jn.2:5; 5:2-3
    Reasons for remaining loyal, obeying
      God. Acts 5:26-42
    Reluctant o. Lk.5:4-5; 9:57-62
  Duty.
    Not an option if one is a believer.
      Jn.14:15; 14:23; 15:14-15
      Verses. List of. Jn.15:14-15
    To obey the commands of God.
      1 Jn.5:2-3; 2 Jn.2:4
    To o. because God expects obedience.
      Mt.2:13-18
    To o. Christ. 1 Pt.1:2
    To o. God before men. Acts 4:19-20
    To o. God rather than men. Acts 5:29
    To o. leaders. Heb.13:17
    To o. the faith. Acts 6:7
    To o. the truth. Reasons. Gal.5:7-12;
      1 Pt.1:22
    To o. the will of God. Mk.3:34-35
    To o. until Jesus returns. Lk.12:41-48
    To seek & pursue o. 1 Pt.1:14
  Example of.
    Jesus Christ. Makes many righteous.
      Ro.5:9
    Joseph, the father of Jesus. Mt.1:24-25
    Paul. Was o. to God's call. Acts 26:19
    The church. Ph.2:12
  Importance of o. (See **OBEY**, Result)
    Failure to o. results in eternal punish-
      ment. 2 Th.1:7-9
    Is a duty, not a service. Lk.17:7-10
    Is the foundation of discipleship.
      Lk.6:46
    Is the greatest thing in life. To hear the
      Word of God & obey it. Lk.11:27-28
    Means believing: to o. is to believe,
      and to believe is to o. Heb.5:9
    The very purpose of election. 1 Pt.1:1-2

  Meaning.
    Faith means o. Jn.3:36; 4:50; 4:51-53;
      5:5-9; 9:6-7;Acts 2:38; 5:32; Heb.5:9;
      Jas.2:17
      Verses. List of. Jn.4:50
    Synonymous with belief. Jn.3:36;
      Ro.10:16
    To believe. Lk.17:14; Heb.5:9;
      Jas.2:17
  Of Jesus Christ. To God. Mk.11:11
  Proves.
    One lives in God. 1 Jn.3:24
    One's faith. Jn.4:50
    One's love. 1 Jn.5:2-3
    One's profession, love for Christ.
      Jn.14:15, 21, 23-24
  Results.
    Assures that one is a friend of God's
      Son, of Christ Himself. Jn.15:14
    Assures that one is accepted into the
      family of God. Mk.3:34-35
    Assures that one will be especially
      loved by God. Jn.14:23; 15:10
    Frees from sin. Ro.6:17-23
    Perfects love. 1 Jn.2:5
    Proves that one knows God. 1 Jn.2:5
    Purifies the believer. 1 Pt.1:22
    Removes the discipline of God.
      Lk.1:59-66
    Saves one & gives assurance of salva-
      tion. Heb.5:9
    Secures God's approval & blessings.
      Threefold. Lk.3:22
  Reward for. (See **REWARD**)
    Made great in the Kingdom of Heaven.
      Mt.5:19
  Source - Stirred by.
    Love for God & Christ. Jn.14:15;
      14:21; 14:23
    The heart. Ro.6:17
    The Holy Spirit. 1 Pt.1:22
  Verses. List of. Lk.11:27-28; Ro.1:5;
    2:11-15
  Vs. the professing man. 1 Jn.2:4; 2:9

OBJECTIONS
  To ministering. Mt.15:33-34

OBSCENITY
  Duty.
    Not to have any part of anything that is
      f. Eph.5:3-4
    To lay aside all f. Jas.1:21
  Meaning. Eph.5:4
  Results. Keeps one out of the kingdom of
    God. Eph.5:5
  Trait - Characteristic of.
    False teachers. 2 Pt.2:10
    Religionists, hypocrites. Mt.23:27
    Unbelievers, the old man. Ro.6:19

OBSTINATE - OBSTINACY (See **HARD
- HARDNESS OF HEART; UNBE-
LIEF**, Obstinate)

OCCULT
  Fortune-telling. Acts 16:16-17
  Power of. Discussed. Acts 16:16-17

OCCUPY (See **WORK**)
  Meaning. Until Jesus returns. Lk.19:13

OFFEND - OFFENDING - OFFENSE
(See **CAUSING OTHERS TO SIN; FALL AWAY; STUMBLING BLOCK**)
Discussed. Lk.11:44; 17:1-2
Duty.
  Not to be **o.** by persecution & ridicule. Mt.13:21; Mk.4:17; Jn.16:1-4
  Not to do anything that will **o.** a brother. Ro.14:21
  Not to **o.** in anything. 1 Cor.10:32; 2 Cor.6:3
  Not to **o.** in questionable activities. Ro.14:1-23; 1 Cor.8:1-13
  Not to **o.** others. 1 Cor.8:9-11; 10:23-28; 10:29-11:1
  To be without **o.** until the day of Christ. Ph.1:10
  To cut out of one's life all that **o.** Mt.5:29-30; 18:7-9; Mk.9:43-48
  To mark those who cause division & **o.** Ro.16:17-18
Fact.
  Christ died for our **o.** Ro.4:25
  Many will be **o.** because of Christ in the end time. Mt.24:9-10
  The gift of Christ justifies us from many **o.** Ro.5:16
  We all **o.** in many things, especially in word & tongue. Jas.3:2
How. Six ways. Mk.9:42
Judgment of those who **o.** Shall be cast into a furnace of fire. Mt.13:37-42
Meaning. Mt.5:29; 17:27; Mk.14:27; Ph.1:9-10
Steps to correcting. Mt.18:15-20
Verses. List of. Mk.9:42
Warning against **o.** others. Mt.18:5-10; Lk.17:1-2
  If one **o.** in one point, he is guilty of all the law. Jas.2:10
Ways one causes others to sin. Mt.18:15
What **o.** men about Christ.
  Four things **o.** Jn.6:59-71
  His claims. Jn.6:61
  His cross, blood. Jn.6:61; 1 Cor.1:23; Gal.5:11
  His Lordship. Jn.6:62
  His Person & claims. 1 Pt.2:7-8
  His works. Mt.11:1-6, esp. 6; Mt.13:53-58

OFFERING (See **GIVE - GIVING; STEWARDSHIP**)
Discussed. 2 Cor.8:1-15
Fact. Cannot make a person perfect & acceptable to God. Heb.9:9
Meaning. 2 Tim.4:6
The **o.** of poor people. Lk.2:24

OIL
Anointing with **o.** To heal. Mk.6:13; Jas.5:14-15
Symbol of the Holy Spirit & righteousness. Mt.25:1-4, cp. 1 Jn.2:27

OLD MAN (See **OLD PERSON**)

OLD PERSON
Discussed. Ro.6:6-7; Eph.4:20-24; 4:22
Duty.
  To put off the old man. Eph.4:20-24; Col.3:5-11
  To strip off seven things. Eph.4:25-32
Of the believer. Old **p.** has been crucified with Christ. Ro.6:6-7
Sins of. Eph.4:25-32
Vs. the new man. Eph.4:20-24

OLD TESTAMENT (See **BIBLE**)

OLDER MEN AND WOMEN
Authority of. Believers to subject to the authority of **o.** 1 Pt.5:5
Discussed. Ph.1:1; 1 Tim.3:1-7; 5:17-20; Tit.1:5-9
Duty of **o.** 1 Pt.5:1-4
  Discussed. Tit.1:5-9
  To consider & handle problems within the church. Acts 15:6, cp. 15:1-35
  To do a good job, do their work well. 1 Tim.5:17
  To minister to those in need. Acts 11:29-30
  To pray for & minister to the sick. Jas.5:14-15
Duty toward **o.**
  Discussed. 1 Tim.5:17-20
  To ordain **o.**, set them apart. Tit.1:5, cp. Acts 14:23
Example of. Peter. 1 Pt.5:1

OLDER SON
Parable of. Self-righteous religionist. Lk.15:25-32

OLIVE TREE
Discussed. Ro.11:17

OLIVES, MOUNT OF (See **MOUNTAIN**)

OLIVET DISCOURSE
Discussed. Mt.24:1-25:46; Lk.21:5-38

OLYMPAS
Believer of Rome. Ro.16:15

OMISSION
Sin of. Is wickedness. Lk.19:15-23

OMNIPOTENCE (See **GOD**, Power of; **JESUS CHRIST**, Power of)

OMNISCIENCE (See **JESUS CHRIST**, Knowledge - Omniscience)

ONE HUNDRED & FORTY FOUR THOUSAND JEWS OF REVELATION
Discussed. Rev.7:4-8; 14:1-5

ONENESS (See **BROTHERHOOD; FELLOWSHIP; UNITY**)

ONESIMUS
A man greatly changed. Phile.8-21
Discussed. Col.4:9

ONESIPHORUS
Believer who went to Rome to minister to Paul while Paul was a prisoner. 2 Tim.1:16-18

OPPORTUNITY
Duty.
  Must grasp while there is still time. Mt.26:10-11; Mk.14:7; Lk.9:59-60; 10:1-4; Jn.2:3-5; 11:7-10
    Verses. List of. Mk.1:21
  To seize the **o.** while one can. Mk.14:7
Missing an **o.** Four causes. Mk.1:21

OPPOSE - OPPOSITION
To Christ. (See **JESUS CHRIST**, Opposed)
  His reply to those who **o.** Jn.7:32-36
  Reasons. He is a threat to doing as one wishes. Jn.7:32

OPPRESSED, THE
By whom.
  Evil men. Ro.3:15-18
  Satan. Acts 10:38
Delivered by. Christ. Lk.4:16-19
Duty.
  To minister to the **o.** Acts 10:38
  To treat justly; to meet the needs of. Lk.11:42
Jesus heals the **b.**
  The persons **b.** by evil spirits. A rebuke of the present generation. Lk.9:37-45
  The physically, mentally, & spiritually **b.** Lk.4:17-19
Symbol of the defeat of Satan. Ro.16:20
What **c.**
  Satan. 2 Tim.2:26
  Sin. 2 Tim.3:1-9
Who is **c.** Men. Lk.4:18

OPTIMISM - OPTIMISTIC
Faith of. An optimistic but questioning faith. Jn.6:8-9

ORAL LAW (See **SCRIBAL LAW**)

ORDAIN - ORDINATION (See **APPOINT-APPOINTMENT-APPOINTED; PREDESTINATION**)
Discussed. Acts 14:23
Duty.
  Not to **o.** a fallen minister too quickly. 1 Tim.5:22
  Not to **o.** too quickly. 1 Tim.5:22
  To closely guard **o.** 1 Tim.5:22
Meaning. Mk.3:14
Of whom - Of what.
  The ordaining of other things.
    Believers.
      Are **o.** to eternal life. Acts 13:48
      Are **o.** to good works. Eph.2:10
      Are **o.** to receive the hidden wisdom of God. 1 Cor.2:7
    Decrees of the church. Acts 16:4
    False teachers. **O.** to condemnation. Jude 4
    Good works. Eph.2:10
    Support of ministers. 1 Cor.9:14
    The law. Gal.3:19; Ro.7:10
    The tabernacle & the things of worship in the O.T. Heb.9:6, cp. 1-10
    The wisdom of God. 1 Cor.2:7-10, esp. 7
  The ordination to office.
    Apostles. Mk.3:14; Acts 1:21-22
    Deacons. Acts 6:6
    Elders. Acts 14:23; Tit.1:5
    Government leaders. Ro.13:1
    High Priests. Heb.5:1; 8:3
    Ministers. 1 Tim.2:7
    Preachers & teachers. 1 Tim.2:7
  The ordination of Christ.
    As High Priest. Heb.5:1-10
    As the Judge of the living & the dead. Acts 10:42; 17:31
Purpose. To bear fruit. Threefold. Jn.15:16
Source.
  By Christ. Jn.15:16
  God is the One who ordains. 1 Tim.2:7

ORDER--ORDERLY
Duty.
　To do all things within the church decently & orderly. 1 Cor.14:40
　To have the church in such good o. that it stirs joy in other believers. Col.2:5
　To set in o. all things within the church. Tit.1:5
Meaning. Col.2:5
New vs. old order. Lk.16:16; 16:17-18

ORDINANCE (See **BAPTISM; LORD'S SUPPER**, Related Subjects)
Of baptism. Mt.28:19, cp. Mt.3:13-15
Of the Lord's Supper. Mt.26:17-30
Purpose. To serve only as signs of spiritual truth. Ro.4:9-12
Weaknesses of.
　Do not save. Ro.2:25-27
　Wrong way to seek justification. Ro.4:9-12

ORGANIZATION
Essential. In meeting needs. Lk.9:14-15

ORGIES
A study of mob behavior. Acts 18:28-19:15
Against Christianity in Ephesus. Acts 19:21-41
Against Stephen. By students. Acts 6:9-10; 7:54-60
Meaning. Ro.13:13; Gal.5:19-21; 1 Pt.4:3

ORIGIN
Of Christ. (See **JESUS CHRIST**, Nature & Origin)
Of man. (See **MAN**, Nature; Origin)
Of sin. (See **SIN**, Origin)

ORPHAN
Duty toward. To visit & minister to. Jas.1:27

OSTRACIZED
Who was o.
　A woman with a hemorrhage. Mt.9:20
　Tax collectors. Mt.9:9-13

OUTBURSTS OF ANGER
Caused by - Reason.
　Are as vipers, biting, poisonous. Lk.3:7
　Discussed. Ro.1:18-23
　Hard & unrepentant hearts. Ro.2:5; 2:6-10
　Not believing on the Son of God. Jn.3:36
　Sin. Ro.5:1
　Sinful, immoral behavior. Eph.5:6, cp. 3-5
　Sins of the body & mouth. Eph.5:5-6
　Ungodliness & unrighteousness of men. Ro.1:18
Deliverance from. By Christ. Ro.5:8-9; 1 Th.1:9-10; 5:8-10
Described. As drinking the o. of God. Rev.14:8
Discussed.
　God gives man over. Reasons. Ro.1:24
　God's o. in the end time. Rev.6:12-17; 14:10-11; 19:15
　How God shows o. Ro.1:24-32
　Subjects of o. Ro.1:18
　The great day of God's wrath. Rev.6:12-17; 6:16-17
　Why God shows o. Ro.1:18-23

Duty. To flee. Mt.3:7
Fact.
　God shall avenge His elect. Lk.18:6-8
　Is predestined. Ro.9:22-24
Meaning. Jn.3:36; Ro.1:18; Col.3:5-7
Misconception of. Some think God is too good to judge. Ro.2:2-5; 3:5-8
Verses. List of. Ro.1:18

OUTCAST (See **DISCRIMINATION; DIVISION; PREJUDICE**)
Attitude toward.
　By society. Mk.2:16-17
　By the church. Mk.2:15
Called by Christ. Lk.5:27-29
Power to reach. Discussed. Mk.2:13-17
Who was an o. Gentiles. Mt.15:30-31; 15:32

OUTREACH (See **COMMISSION; EVANGELISM; MISSION; WITNESSING**)

OUTWARD APPEARANCE (See **APPEARANCE, OUTWARD**)

OVER-CONFIDENCE (See **SELF-SUFFICIENCY**)

OVERCOME - OVERCOMERS
Discussed. Rev.2:7
Duty.
　Not to be o. by the false teachers of corruption. 2 Pt.2:19
　To o. all & not to be brought into bondage by any. 2 Pt.2:20-22
　To o. evil, not to let evil o. oneself. Ro.12:21
　To o. false teachers by the power of God's Spirit. 1 Jn.4:1-4, esp. 4
　To o. the wicked one. 1 Jn.2:13-14
Fact. God o. all who judge & reject Him. Ro.3:4
How one o.
　By being born of God. 1 Jn.5:4-5
　By believing & trusting the work of Christ.
　　He has o. the devil. Lk.10:20-22, cp. 14-27
　　He has o. the world. Jn.16:33
Reward. (See **REWARD**)
　Not to be blotted out of the Book of Life. Rev.3:4-6
　Not to be hurt by the second death. Rev.2:11
　To be acknowledged & presented to God by Christ. Rev.3:4-6
　To be dressed in white. Rev.3:4-6
　To be given a white stone with a new name written on it. Rev.2:17
　To be given power over the nations. Rev.2:7
　To be given the morning star, Christ Himself. Rev.2:7
　To be made a pillar in the temple of God. Rev.3:12-13
　To be made perfectly secure. Rev.3:12-13
　To eat of the hidden manna. Rev.2:17
　To eat of the tree of life. Rev.2:7
　To inherit all things. Rev.21:7
　To receive God's name. Rev.3:12-13
　To receive paradise. Rev.2:7
　To receive the Lord's new name. Rev.3:12-13
　To receive the name of the New Jerusalem. Rev.3:12-13

OVERSEERS
Discussed. Acts 20:28-31; Ph.1:1; 1 Tim.3:1-7; Tit.1:5-9
Qualifications. 1 Tim.3:1-7
Title of Christ. 1 Pt.2:25

OWNER
Discussed. Mt.24:43-44
Parable of. Mt.24:43-44

OXEN
Yoke of. Meaning. Mt.11:29

P

PALM BRANCHES
Discussed. Jn.12:13
Meaning. Rev.7:9-10

PALM SUNDAY
Meaning. Mk.11:1-11

PALSY - PARALYSIS
Healed by Christ. Mt.4:24; 8:5-13; 9:2-8; Mk.2:1-12; Lk.5:18-26; Acts 8:7; 9:33-35

PAMPER
God does not p. Mt.6:25

PAMPHYLIA
Discussed. Acts 13:13

PAPHOS
Capital of Cyprus. Discussed. Acts 13:6

PARABLE
Meaning. Mk.4:2
Of Jesus Christ. Listed.
　Parables concerning Christ, His deity & mission.
　　Divided kingdom & house. Christ is not of Satan. Mk.3:24-25; Lk.11:17
　　New & old cloth. The new vs. the old life. Mt.9:16; Mk.2:21; Lk.5:36
　　New wine & old bottles. The new vs. the old life. Mt.9:17; Mk.2:22; Lk.5:37-39
　　Strong man who is conquered. Satan is conquered. Lk.11:21-22
　Parables concerning faithfulness & fruitfulness.
　　Branches & vine. Jesus & people. Jn.15:1-8
　　Fruitless fig tree. Bear fruit or perish. Lk.13:6-9
　　Good & corrupt tree. Watch what kind of fruit is borne. Lk.6:43-45
　　Laborers in the vineyard. God's grace. Mt.20:1-16
　Parables concerning Israel.
　　Fruitless fig tree. Bear fruit or perish. Lk.13:6-9
　　Two sons. What it takes to enter heaven. Mt.21:34-35
　　Wicked tenants. God & Israel. Mk.12:1-12
　　Wicked tenants. Israel's rejection of Christ. Mt.21:33-46
　　The overview of world history. Lk.20:9-18
　Parables concerning judgment & punishment.

Dragnet. Separating the bad from the good. Mt.13:47-50

Pounds or ten minas. Testing the disciples. Lk.19:11-27

Rich fool. The man of wealth. Lk.12:13-21

Sheep & goats. Final judgment of the nations. Mt.25:31-46

Talents. Work for judgment is coming. Mt.25:14-30

Wheat & Weeds. The question of evil. Mt.13:24-30; 13:36-43

Parables concerning religionists & self-righteousness.

Older son. Self-righteous religionists. Lk.15:25-32

Parables concerning spiritual growth & discipleship & witnessing.

Afflicted eye. Blind leading the blind. Watch being blind. Lk.6:39

Disciple & the master. Watch the Lord. Lk.6:40

Growing Seed. Growth of believers. Mk.4:26-29

Householder. Devotion, study, sharing. Mt.13:51-52

Lamp. The purpose of seeing. Lk.8:16; 11:33

Under a bushel basket. Truth & man's duty. Mk.4:21-25

Salt. Serving God. Mt.5:13; Mk.9:50; Lk.14:34-35

Supreme example of caring. Mt.18:11-14

Parables concerning the believers' behavior.

Ambitious guest. The importance of humility. Lk.14:7-14

Good Samaritan. Who is my neighbor. Lk.10:25-37

Speck & plank in the eye. Discussed. Lk.6:41-42

Unjust judge. The secret of prayer. Lk.18:1-8

Unjust manager. The Christian & money. Lk.16:1-13

Unmerciful servant. The spirit of forgiveness. Mt.18:21-35

Parables concerning the Christian, the church, the new age, & the Kingdom of God.

Bridegroom. A new life & a new age. Mt.9:15; Mk.2:19-20

Kingdom of God. Lk.13:20-21

Mustard seed.

The growth of Christianity. Mt.13:31-32

The growth of God's kingdom. Mk.4:30-32

The Kingdom of God. Lk.13:18-19

New & old cloth. The new vs. the old life. Mt.9:16; Mk.2:21; Lk.5:36

New wine & old bottles. The new vs. the old life. Mt.9:17; Mk.2:22; Lk.5:37-39

Transforming power of the gospel. Mt.13:33

Lost coin. The lost sinner within the house. Lk.15:8-10

Lost sinner out in the world. Lk.15:1-7

Marriage Feast. Rejection of God's invitation. Mt.22:1-14

Merchant man. Giving up all for Christ. Mt.13:45-46

Narrow door. The way to life is narrow. Lk.13:24

Pearl of great price. Giving up all for Christ. Mt.13:45-46

Pharisee & tax collector. The spirit needed for prayer. Lk.18:9-14

Prodigal son. The lost son. Lk.15:11-24

Sower or farmer. How one receives the gospel. Mt.13:1-9; Mk.4:1-20

The transforming power of the gospel. Mt.13:33

The two foundations. True vs. false discipleship. Lk.6:46-49

Two debtors. The repentant & the self-righteous. Lk.7:40-43

Two sons. What it takes to enter heaven. Mt.21:28-32

Unclean spirit who returns. Reformation. Lk.11:24-26

Wise & foolish builders. Life. Mt.7:24-27

Parables concerning watching & being ready for the Lord's return.

Faithful & wise servant. Being watchful & godly. Mt.24:45-47

Owner of the house. The man who lived without watchfulness. Mt.24:43-44

Steward, faithful & unfaithful. Warning. Be prepared. Lk.12:35-48

Ten virgins. Watch for the Lord's return. Mt.25:1-13

Wicked servant. Being unwatchful & worldly. Mt.24:48-51

Reasons for **p.** Speaking in **p.** Mt.13:10-17; 13:34-35; Lk.8:9-10

Use of **p.** Why Jesus used illustrations. Mk.4:33-34

PARADISE

Discussed. Lk.16:23; 2 Cor.12:4

Promise of. Given to overcomers. Rev.2:7

Where Jesus went when He died. Lk.23:43

Where the thief who died with Jesus went at death. Lk.23:42-43

PARADISE, EARTHLY

Inadequate. Mt.14:34

PARALYZED MAN

Healed by Jesus. Forgiving sin. Mt.9:1-8

PARDON (See FORGIVENESS)

PARENTS (See FAMILY & Related Subjects)

Discussed. Mt.19:13-15; Eph.6:1-4; Col.3:21

Disobedience to.

Discussed. 2 Tim.3:2-4

Meaning. Ro.1:30

Duty.

Influence on children. Mt.2:19-23

Not to provoke children. Eph.6:4

To be faithful before God. Lk.1:5-25

To be godly. Picture of godly **p.** Lk.1:5-25

To bring children to Jesus. Lk.18:15

Prevented. Mk.10:13

To forgive children. Lk.15:17-24

To instill a strong faith in children. 2 Tim.1:5; 3:15

To protect children. Heb.11:23

To provide for children. 2 Cor.12:14

To rear children in the Lord. Lk.2:41-42; Acts 16:15

To rear children in the Scriptures. 2 Tim.1:5; 3:15

To rear children to be obedient. Eph.6:1-4

Touched by Jesus. Should want children touched. Lk.18:15

Toward children. Discussed. Eph.6:1-4

Duty toward parents.

Not to disobey **p.** Ro.1:30

Not to forsake & abandon. Mk.1:20

To care for **p.**

Discussed. 1 Tim.5:4-8

Example. Mt.8:8; Jn.19:25-27

To obey **p.** Eph.6:1-3; Col.3:20

Faith of. Stubborn, helpless, but believing. Lk.8:49-56

Irresponsible or evil **p.**

Do not bring children to Christ. Mt.19:13

Indulge & pamper children. Eph.6:4

Influence of. Worldliness. Mk.6:24-25

Provoke children to anger. Eph.6:4

Verses. List of. Mk.10:14

PARMENAS

One of the first deacons. Acts 6:1-6

PARTAKE - PARTAKER (See SHARED)

What believers are not to **p.** of.

Other men's sins. 1 Tim.5:22

The sinners & sins of the world. Eph.5:7, cp. 1-7

The sins of the cities of the world. Rev.18:4, cp. 1-5

The table of devils. 1 Cor.10:21

The teaching of false teachers. 2 Jn.10-11

What believers are to **p.** of.

Afflictions of the gospel. 2 Tim.1:8

Christ Himself. Heb.3:14

Christ's sufferings. 1 Pt.4:13

Flesh & blood, the same as all men & the same that Christ partook of. Heb.2:14-15

God's holiness. Heb.12:10

God's promise in Christ. Eph.3:6

One another's grace. Ph.1:7

One another's hope. 1 Cor.9:10, cp. 9-11

The chastisement of God. Heb.12:8

The divine nature. 2 Pt.1:4

The freedom & liberty to **p.** of social activities. 1 Cor.8:1-13

The fruits of one's labor. 2 Tim.2:6

The glory that shall be revealed. 1 Pt.5:1

The gospel. 1 Cor.9:23

The heavenly calling. Heb.3:1

The Holy Spirit. Heb.6:4

The inheritance. Col.1:12

The Lord's Supper. 1 Cor.10:16-17

The sufferings & comfort of salvation. 2 Cor.1:5-7, esp. 7

PARTIALITY (See DISCRIMINATION; FAVORITISM; IMPARTIAL; PREJUDICE)

And God.

Does not show **p.** Ro.3:29-30; Gal.2:6

Shows no favoritism. Acts 10:23-33; 10:34-35

Treats all men just alike. Ro.3:29-30; 10:12

Ways all men are related to God. Four ways. Ro.10:12

Discussed. Jas.2:1-13
Duty. Of the minister.
Not to show **p**. 1 Tim.5:21
Not to show **p**. in choosing workers.
Acts 15:36-41
Not to show **p**. in sharing salvation.
Acts 10:34-43
Not to show **p**. to any person, no matter position, power, or importance.
2 Cor.5:16, cp. 12
Not to show **p**. within the church. Jas.2:1-3
Fact. No **p**. with God. Col.3:11
Temptation to show **p**. Discussed. Jas.2:1-13

PARTIALITY, WITHOUT (See FAVORITISM)
Meaning. Jas.3:17-18

PARTYING (See ORGIES; SOCIAL FUNCTIONS)
Caused by. Selfishness & godless independence. Lk.15:11-13
Described.
As drinking & carousing. Mt.24:38
As wild, indulgent living. Lk.15:11-13
Discussed. Lk.21:34-35
Example of.
As suggestive, lustful, drinking.
Mk.6:21-22
Herod. Suggestive, lustful, drinking.
Mk.6:21-22
Of the world. Judgment. Lk.6:24-26
Results. Mt.14:6-8
Drinking & immoral dancing.
Mk.6:21-22
Dulls & makes one unprepared for the Lord's return. Lk.21:34
Makes one an enemy of God. Jas.4:4
Passion & immoral decisions.
Mk.6:21-22

PASSION - PASSIONS (See LUST)
Caused by.
An evil heart. Mt.15:19
Dancing & passion. Mt.14:6-8
False teachers. 2 Pt.2:10-22
Foolish behavior & foolish promises.
Mt.14:6-8
Immoral looking & dressing. Mt.5:27-30
Lusting after the world. 2 Pt.1:4
Not enduring sound doctrine, but **l**. after false teachers. 2 Tim.4:3-4
Satan. 1 Jn.3:8-10
The lust of one's own flesh.
Jas.1:14-15
Characteristics - Traits. Of false teachers.
Jude 16
Deliverance from - Prevention - Cure.
Mt.5:28; 5:30; 2 Pt.1:4
Discussed. Jn.8:44-45; Ro.1:24-25;
1:26-27; Eph.2:1-3; Tit.3:3; Jas.4:1;
4:1-3; 4:2; 1 Pt.2:11
Duty.
Not to fulfill the desires of the flesh.
Eph.2:3
To crucify the flesh with its lusts.
Gal.5:24
To deny worldly **l**. Tit.2:12-13
To flee youthful **l**., the evil desires of youth 2 Tim.2:22
To put off **l**. before it corrupts one.
Eph.4:22-24
To walk in the Spirit & not to fulfill the **l**. of the flesh. Gal.5:16
Judgment of. If a man chooses **l**., God gives him up to his **l**. Ro.1:24-32

Indulgence of. God does not indulge passions. Mt.6:14-15
Meaning. Ro.1:24-25; Gal.5:16-18; 2 Tim.2:22; Jas.1:14-16; 1 Pt.2:11; 4:3
Misconceptions of. Viewed as acceptable & natural. Mt.5:27-30
Problems with.
Are deceitful & lead to corruption.
Eph.4:22
Burdens one with sin. 2 Tim.3:6
Corrupts one. Eph.4:22
Draws one into many foolish & hurtful lusts. 1 Tim.6:9-10
Drowns one in destruction. 1 Tim.6:9-10
Enslaves.
Craves more & more. Mt.24:37-39
Example. Judas' greed. Mt.26:15
Grows & grows. Mt.5:27-30; 26:15
To the corruption of the world.
2 Pt.1:4
Entices, draws one into sin. Jas.1:14-15
Passes away; is not lasting or fulfilling. 1 Jn.2:15-17
Stirs one to fulfill the desires of the flesh. Eph.2:3
Wars against the soul. 1 Pt.2:11
Sin of.
Committed by man & Satan. Jn.8:44-45
If a man chooses **l**., God gives him up to his **l**. Ro.1:24-32
Man walks in the **l**. of the sinful nature. Eph.2:3
Verses. List of. Jn.6:26-27
Vs. need. Mt.12:3-4

PASSOVER
Atmosphere at the **P**. Mt.26:5; Jn.12:12
Commercial, carnival atmosphere.
Mk.14:12
Attendance. Multitudes of pilgrims. Two to three million. Mk.14:12; Jn.12:12
Discussed. Mt.26:17-30; Mk.14:1;
Lk.22:722;19-20
Basis for the Lord's Supper.
Mt.26:17-30; 26:17-19; Lk.22:7-23
Preparation of. Jesus makes secret preparations for the **P**. Reasons. Mk.14:13-17
Symbolized - Pictured. The death of Christ. Mt.26:2; Mk.14:1; Lk.22:1;
1 Cor.5:7; 1 Pt.1:19

PASTORAL EPISTLES
Purpose for writing. 1 Tim.3:14-15

PASTORS (See MINISTERS)

PATARA
City of. Discussed. Acts 21:1-3

PATIENT - PATIENCE (See ENDURANCE; GENTLENESS; PERSEVERE - PERSEVERANCE)
Duty.
Must be strengthened with God's power to be **p**. Col.1:11
To be longsuffering in living for Christ. 2 Tim.3:10-12
To be longsuffering in ministering: preaching, teaching, etc. 2 Tim.4:2
To be longsuffering in persecution.
2 Tim.3:10-12
To be longsuffering in trials. 2 Cor.6:6-7
To put on **p**. Col.3:12
To show forth all **p**. as a pattern for other believers. 1 Tim.1:16
To walk in longsuffering. Eph.4:1-2

Duty - Essential.
Of the elderly.
To be characterized by **p**. Tit.2:2
To be sound in faith, love, & **p**.
Tit.2:2
Of the minister. To be **p**. 1 Tim.3:3;
2 Tim.2:24
To add **p**. to one's faith. 2 Pt.1:5-7
To be **p**. in continuing to do good works. Ro.2:6-7
To be **p**. in persecution & trials.
2 Th.1:4; 1 Pt.2:20
To be **p**. in standing against false teachers. Rev.2:2
To be **p**. in the hope of the Lord Jesus Christ. 1 Th.1:3
To be **p**. in waiting for one's eternal salvation. Ro.8:23-25
To be **p**. toward all men. 1 Th.5:14
To follow after love & **p**. 1 Tim.6:11
To minister in **p**. 2 Cor.6:4; 12:12;
2 Tim.3:10-11
To pray for strength to be **p**. Col.1:9-11,
esp. 11
To run with **p**. the race set before one.
Heb.12:1
To wait upon God. Jn.11:6
Example of.
Abraham. The **p**. needed to endure.
Heb.6:13-15
The prophets & Job. Perseverance needed to combat temptation & trials. Jas.5:10-11
The farmer. Perseverance needed to wait for the Lord's return. Jas.5:7-8
Meaning. 2 Th.1:4; 2 Tim.3:10-11;
Jas.1:3-4; 2 Pt.1:5-7
Meaning. 2 Cor.6:6-7; Gal.5:22-23;
Eph.4:1-2; Jas.5:7
Of God.
God endures with much **p**. the vessels of wrath. Ro.9:22
The **p**. of the Lord means salvation.
2 Pt.3:15
Why God is **p**. with men. Ro.2:4; 2 Pt.3:9; 3:15-16
Proves.
That one has truly been called of God.
1 Tim.1:16
That one walks worthy of God.
Eph.4:1-2
Source of. The Holy Spirit. Gal.5:22-23
Reasons. God knows the exact time, the best time to act. Jn.11:6
Result.
Determines one's reward. Ro.2:7
Glory, honor & immortality. Ro.2:6-7
Inherits the promises. Heb.6:12; 10:36
Joy. Col.1:11
Keeps & saves one's soul. Lk.21:19
Source.
An honest & good heart. Lk.8:15
God. Ro.15:5; 2 Th.3:5
God's power. Col.1:11
Hope. Ro.8:25
The Holy Spirit. Gal.5:22-23
The trials & testing of one's faith.
Ro.5:3-5; 12:12; Jas.1:2-4
The Word of God, the Scriptures.
Ro.15:4

PATMOS
Discussed. Rev.1:9
The island from which the Revelation was written. Rev.1:9

Was not ashamed of the gospel.
Three reasons. Ro.1:16-17;
2 Tim.1:6-12
Ministry in relation to witnessing &
evangelism & preaching.
A mature witness. Ph.1:12-19
Beginnings of Paul's witness. Acts
9:19-22
Face set for Jerusalem. To bear wit-
ness for Christ. Acts 20:13
Final journey & witness. Acts
23:12-28:31
Journeys.
Listed. Gal.1:17-24
Places of ministry & time at
each. Acts 9:23
Love for Israel, for his own people,
the Jews. Acts 21:1-16; 28:17-22;
Ro.9:1-3
Message preached. Mentioned. (See
GOSPEL OF PAUL) Acts
28:23-24
The only complete message of
Paul in the Scriptures. Acts
13:14-41
Strong compulsion to preach.
Acts 21:1-16, esp. 13-14
Testimony & message. Acts
26:19-23
What Paul preached. Acts 9:19-22
Method of world evangelism. Dis-
cussed. Acts 13:14-16; 13:46-
47;19:21-23; 28:16-31
Preaching of Paul. 1 Cor.2:1-5
Strategy for world evangelism.
Acts 13:14-16; 13:46-47; 19:21-
23, 28:16-31
Turned to the Gentiles. Acts 13:42-52;
22:21; 28:25-29
Vision of Macedonia. Acts 16:6-11
Witness reached to the palace of
Rome. Ph.1:13; 4:22
Mission of.
First great mission. Acts 13:1-14:28
Second great **m**. to Europe. Acts
15:36-18:22
Third great **m**. Acts 18:23-21:16
Third **m**. Last part outlined. Acts
20:1-2
To Rome. As a prisoner. Acts 23:12-
28:31
To the world. Third great **m**. Acts
18:23-21:16
Spiritual experiences of.
An eye-witness of Christ in glory.
1 Cor.15:8-10
Discussed. 2 Cor.12:1-10
Had the gift of tongues. 1 Cor.14:15-20
Jesus appeared to Paul after His resur-
rection. 1 Cor.15:8-10
Received special revelations. Eph.3:1-5;
Col.1:25-27
Was caught up into heaven.
2 Cor.12:2-6
Sufferings - Trials of.
Discussed. Acts 18:9-11; 1 Cor.4:9-10;
4:11-13; 2 Cor.6:3-10; 11:23-31;
2 Tim.3:11-12
Legal trial.
Before Felix. What real worship is.
Acts 24:1-21
Before Festus. Pictures of all kinds
of men. Acts 25:1-27
Seven legal trials. Acts 28:17-22
Listed. 2 Cor.1:8-10

Overcame **s**., conquered & triumphed
over **s**.
Conquered his **s**. through Christ.
Ph.1:12-14
Was encouraged by God. Acts
23:11
Was faithful despite **s**. Acts 28:30-31
Proves there is to be a resurrection of
the dead. 1 Cor.15:30-32
Sufferings caused by personal afflic-
tion & emotions.
Faced discouragement. Acts 18:9-11
Had a thorn in the flesh. Acts 13:13
Reached a breaking point. Acts
23:11
Was extremely taxed & strained.
Acts 23:11
Sufferings caused by the church's failure.
Considered Paul unimpressive.
1 Cor.2:3
Deserted by all when imprisoned.
2 Tim.1:15-18
Rejected & feared by believers.
Acts 9:26-30
Sufferings caused by the world & re-
ligionists.
Assaulted. Acts 14:5
Called insane by King Agrippa.
Acts 26:24-27
Faced mob uprisings against.
2 Cor.6:4-5
Faced some terrible trials in Cor-
inth. 1 Th.3:7-10
Fought with beasts at Ephesus.
1 Cor.15:30-32
Had attempts made on his life. Acts
9:23-30, 29; 23:12-24
Seized by a mob. Acts 21:27
Shamefully treated. 1 Th.2:2
Stoned. Acts 14:18-20
Stood before a crazed mob. Acts
22:1-21
Sufferings of imprisonment.
A prisoner for five years. Acts
22:27
Beaten & jailed. Acts 16:19-24
His imprisonment. 2 Cor.6:4-5;
Ph.1:12-14
Sufferings of nature or natural forces.
Shipwrecked. Delivered, saved by
God. Acts 28:1-15
Snakebitten. Delivered, saved by
God. Acts 28:3-5
Testimony.
Of his conversion experience.
1 Cor.15:8-10; Gal.1:10-24;Ph.3:4-16
Triumphant at the end of life.
2 Tim.4:6-8
Trials before civil courts.
Before the Sanhedrin. Acts 22:30-
23:11
Charges against. Acts 24:5-6
Claimed to be a Roman & to have the
right to a Roman trial. Acts 22:25-29
Listed. Acts 28:17-22
Trial four - before King Agrippa. Acts
25:13-27; 26:1-32
Trial one - defense before Felix. Acts
24:1-21
Trial three - before Festus. Acts 25:1-12
Trial two - before Felix. Acts 24:22-27
Writings of.
A painful letter written to the Corin-
thian church. 2 Cor.2:4
Are true. 2 Cor.1:13-14; 1:18-20

Authenticity of his epistles.
1 Cor.16:21
Came by a revelation from the Lord
Jesus. Gal.1:11-12
Contain some things difficult to un-
derstand. 2 Pt.3:15-16
Counted as Scripture by the early
church. 2 Pt.3:15-16
Given special revelations. Eph.3:1-5;
Col.1:25-27
Reveal the revelation of God's grace,
the mystery of Christ. Eph.3:1-13;
Col.1:25-27
Twisted by some. Two doctrines in
particular. 2 Pt.3:15-16
Were the commandments of God.
1 Cor.14:37

PAYBACK
Discussed. 2 Th.1:6

PEACE (See RECONCILIATION)
Discussed. Jn.14:27; Col.3:15;
Heb.12:141 Pt.3:8-9; 2 Pt.3:14
Duty.
Is the great duty of believers.
Heb.12:14
To follow after the things that make **p**.
Ro.14:19
To go on to **p**. Heb.6:1
To know that **p**. is not always possible.
Ro.12:18
To let **p**. rule in one's heart. Col.3:15
To live in **p**. Two qualifications.
Mk.9:50; Ro.12:18; 2 Cor.13:11
To live in **p**. with one's spouse.
1 Cor.7:15, cp. 10-16
To make **p**. Jas.3:18
To obey all authority that one may
lead a quiet & peaceable life.
1 Tim.2:2
To preach peace. Mk.9:50; Lk.10:5-6;
Acts 10:36
To seek & pursue peace. 2 Tim.2:22;
1 Pt.3:11
Fact.
The distinctives of believers. Ph.1:1-2
The possessions of the believer.
2 Th.3:16
To be taken away & destroyed by the
antichrist. Rev.6:3-4
Kinds of.
Brotherly **p**. Ro.14:19; 2 Tim.2:22
Civic **p**. Tit.3:1-3
Social **p**. Ro.12:18; Heb.12:14;
1 Pt.3:11
Spiritual, inward **p**. Jn.14:27
Lack of. Caused by. Sin & the depraved
nature of man. Ro.3:15-18
Meaning. Jn.14:27; Gal.1:3; 5:22-
23;Eph.2:14-15; Col.3:15; 1 Th.1:1;
1 Tim.1:2; 2 Pt.1:2; 2 Jn.3;Rev.1:4
P. with God. Ro.5:1
Misconception of. Men have no need to
make "peace with God." Lk.12:58-59
Results.
Are blessed. Mt.5:9
Bear the fruit of righteousness.
Jas.3:18
Heart & mind, spirit & soul are kept &
preserved by God. Ph.4:6-7, esp. 7;
1 Th.4:23
Please God. Ro.8:5-8, esp. 8
Proves that one belongs to the king-
dom of God. Ro.14:17

Receives the very special presence of God. 2 Cor.13:11; Ph.4:9
Solves & erases confusion. 1 Cor.14:33
Will be without spot & blameless before Christ in the day of judgment. 2 Pt.3:14
Secret of. Discussed. Ph.4:1-9
Source - How one secures peace. Jn.14:27; Rev.1:4
  A gracious gentleness. Ph.4:5
  A new creation. Col.3:9-11
  Agreement & unity. Ph.4:2-3
  Christ.
    Came to bring **p.** Mk.11:1-7; Lk.2:14
    His blood brings reconciliation. Eph.2:14-15; Col.1:20
    His presence & power. Mk.4:35-41; Jn.14:27; 2 Th.3:16
    His resurrection brings triumphant **p.** Jn.16:33
    Is the Lord of peace. 2 Th.3:16
  Doing good works. Ro.2:10
  Faith & justification. Ro.5:1
  God.
    God is the God of peace. Ro.15:33; 16:20; 2 Cor.13:11; Ph.4:9; 1 Th.5:23; Heb.13:20
    P. comes from God. Ro.1:7; 1 Cor.1:3; 2 Cor.1:2; Gal.1:3; Eph.1:2; Ph.1:2; Col.1:2; 1 Th.1:1; 1 Tim.1:2; 2 Tim.1:2; Tit.1:4; Phile.3; 2 Jn.3
    The Author of **p.** 1 Cor.14:33
  Holy Spirit. Gal.5:22-23, cp. Ro.14:17
  Keeping one's mind on spiritual things. Ro.8:5-7, esp. 6
  Positive thinking. Ph.4:8-9
  Prayer, agonizing prayer. Mt.26:45; Ph.4:6-7
  Rejoicing. Ph.4:4
  Standing firm. Ph.4:1
  The gospel. Is the gospel of **p.** Ro.10:15

PEACE-LOVING
  Meaning. Mt.5:9
  Vs. troublemakers. Mt.5:9

PEACE, SOCIAL
  Duty. To be at peace with men if possible. Ro.12:18; Heb.12:14; 1 Pt.3:11

PEACEABLE (See **PEACE-LOVING**)

PEACEABLE, TO BE; QUARREL-SOME
  Discussed. Tit.3:2
  Meaning. 1 Tim.3:2-3

PEACEMAKERS (See **PEACE-LOVING**)
  Meaning. Mt.5:9
  Vs. troublemakers. Mt.5:9

PEARL
  Parable of great price. Mt.13:45-46

PENALTY
  Of sin. Is death. Jn.8:21-22

PENITENCE (See **CONFESSION; FORGIVENESS; REPENTANCE**)

PENTECOST
  Coming of the Holy Spirit. Acts 2:1-13; 2:1-4
  Feast of. Acts 2:1

PEOPLE (See **MAN; WORLD**)

PERDITION (See **DESTROY - DE-STRUCTION; JUDGMENT**, Who is to be judged)
  Meaning. 2 Th.2:4, cp. 3. Cp. Mt.10:28; 2 Th.1:9
  Who goes into **p.**
    Judas Iscariot. Jn.17:12
    The antichrist. 2 Th.2:3
    The ungodly. 2 Pt.3:7
    Those who covet, indulge in, & waste wealth. 1 Tim.6:9
    Those who persecute believers. Ph.1:28
    Those who shrink & draw back. Heb.10:37-38

PERFECT - PERFECTION (See **EQUIP - EQUIPPED; MATURE; RESTORE**)
  Discussed. Mt.5:48
  Duty.
    To be **p.** even as God is **p.** Mt.5:48
    To be **p.** in every good work. Heb.13:20-21
    To be the believer's great aim. Ph.3:12-13
    To go on to **p.** Heb.6:1
    To live in the Word of God. 2 Tim.3:16-17, cp. 2 Tim.2:15; 1 Pt.2:2-3
    To **p.** holiness. 2 Cor.7:1
    To **p.** one's faith. 1 Th.3:10
    To praise God in **p.** Mt.21:15-16
    To rely upon the strength of Christ for **p.** 2 Cor.12:9
    To seek & pursue **p.** 2 Cor.13:9; Ph.3:12-16
  Essential. To live in God's presence. Ph.3:7-11; 3:7-16
  Fact.
    Believers do not achieve **p.** on earth. Ph.3:12-16
    Love is the way to **p.** 1 Cor.13:8-12
    Man is not **p.** & cannot secure **p.** Gal.2:15-16
    The person who sets his life apart unto God is perfected forever through Christ. Heb.10:14
  Meaning. Jn.17:23; Jas.1:3-4
  Need for **p.**
    By man. Discussed. Heb.7:1-24; 9:9
    Met by Christ. Heb.2:9-10; 5:9; 7:1-24; 7:11-247:25-28; 9:11-14; 11:39-40
      His strength. 2 Cor.12:9
  Source - How one is **p.**
    A spiritual union with God & Christ alone. Jn.17:23
    Controlling one's tongue & words. Jas.3:2
    Discussed. Heb.7:11-24, esp. 11-12, 18-19
    Following after **p.** Ph.3:12, cp. 7-16
    Giving all one is & has to Christ & the poor. Mt.19:21, cp. 16-30
    God. Heb.13:20-21; 1 Pt.5:10
    Help from faithful ministers. Eph.4:11-16; Col.1:28; 4:12; 1 Th.3:10
    Hope. Heb.7:19

Living in Christ's presence. An absolute essential. Ph.3:7-11; 3:7-16
Love. Col.3:14, cp. 1 Jn.4:17-18
Not by sacrifice or law. Heb.10:1-4
Overcoming & conquering trials & temptations. Jas.1:2-4
Prayer. 1 Th.3:10
Presenting one's body as a living sacrifice to God. Ro.12:1-2
Scripture. 2 Tim.3:16-17
The blood of Christ. Heb.10:1-18; 12:22-24; 13:20-21
The Holy Spirit. Gal.3:3, cp. 1-5
The perfect life of Christ. Secured by suffering as a Man upon earth. Heb.2:10
The perfect sacrifice & death of Christ. Heb.10:1-4, esp., 1-4, 14
Warning & teaching every person. Col.1:28
Work & faith. Jas.2:22

PERFECTER
  Title of. Jesus Christ. Heb.12:2

PERGA
  Discussed. Acts 13:13

PERGAMOS
  Church of.
    One of the seven churches of Revelation. Rev.2:12-17
    Represents the worldly church. Rev.2:12-17
    Discussed. Rev.2:12-17

PERILOUS TIMES (See **TERRIBLE TIMES**)

PERISH - PERISHING
  Cause of.
    Natural heritage - bearing perishable seed. 1 Pt.1:23
  Deliverance - Escape from
    By being born again. 1 Pt.1:23
    By being redeemed. 1 Pt.1:18-20
    By believing in Christ. Jn.3:16-17
    By God's will. Wills that no one **p.** Mt.18:14
    By repentance. Lk.13:1-5
    By the believer's endurance & the promise of Christ. Lk.21:18-19
    By the death of Christ. Jn.3:14-15
    By the power of Christ & God. Jn.10:27-29
    By the resurrection of Christ. 1 Cor.15:16-19
    Not by perishable things. 1 Pt.1:18-20
  Discussed. 1 Cor.1:18
  Meaning. Jn.3:16; 2 Cor.4:3-4; 2 Th.1:9
  The things that **p.**
    Children can **p.** Mt.18:12-14, esp. 14
    False teachers shall **p.** 2 Pt.2:12, cp. 1-22
    Food **p.** Jas.1:11
    Gold perishes, but faith tried by fire does not **p.** 1 Pt.1:7
    The followers of antichrist shall **p.** 2 Th.2:10
    The heavens & the earth shall **p.** Heb.1:10-12, cp. 2 Pt.3:10-13
    The human body is **p.**, in a process or state of **p.** 2 Cor.4:16
    The human soul & body can **p.** in hell. Mt.10:28

The members of the body can **p.** in hell. Mt.5:29-30

The outward man **p.** 2 Cor.4:15

The rich man in his covetous ways shall **p.** Jas.1:11

The rituals, ceremonies, & rules of religion **p.** Col.2:20-23, esp. 22

The unsaved are **p.** even now. 1 Cor.1:18; 2 Cor.2:15

The world of Noah perished in the flood. 2 Pt.3:5-7

Those who do not repent shall **p.** Lk.13:3, 5

Those who follow false teachers shall **p.** Jude 11

Those who reject the cross of Christ shall **p.** 1 Cor.1:17-18, 23-24

Those who sin without law & those who sin in the law shall **p.** Ro.2:12

Those who take up the sword shall **p.** Mt.26:52

Vs. imperishable. 1 Pt.1:23

Who the **p.** are. Discussed. 2 Th.2:10

PERJURY (See **WITNESS OF MAN; LYING**)

PERMISSIVE - PERMISSIVENESS
Results. Upon a church. Rev.2:18-29

PERPLEXED
Meaning. 2 Cor.4:7-9

PERSECUTION - PERSECUTORS (See **PAUL**, Sufferings & Trials)
By whom.
Family. Reasons. Mt.10:21; 10:35-37; Mk.13:12-13
Religionists. Jn.16:1-6
Secular & religious leaders. Mk.13:9; Acts 5:17-18
The government or civil authorities. 1 Pt.2:13-17
The world. Mt.21:34-35; Jn.15:18-27
Three groups. Mt.10:17-18
Deliverance from - How to stand against & overcome in **p.**
Answer to. Given by Jesus. Jn.7:6-9
Attitude under. Lk.6:20-23; 6:27-31
By arming oneself with the attitude of Christ. 1 Pt.3:13-17; 4:1-6
By being a man of conviction. Acts 4:23-31
By being miraculously delivered. Acts 5:19-20; 12:1-25
By endurance. Mk.13:13; 1 Cor.4:12
By fleeing from **p.** Mt.10:23
By God.
God's pattern for deliverance. Acts 12:1-25
His deliverance. Acts 9:31
Three ways. Acts 5:41
By not fearing. Reason. Lk.12:11-12
By not worrying. Reasons. Mt.10:19-20
By knowing how to handle terror. Ph.1:28-30
By knowing that God gives His very special presence in **p.** Ph.3:10
By knowing that God's will & the gospel cannot be defeated. Acts 5:33-40
By praying unceasingly. Mt.5:44; Acts 12:5
By supernatural protection & strength. Mk.13:11

By trusting God to give one the words to say & the right defense. Lk.12:4-12
Deliverance promised. Acts 14:21-28
How to be secure through **p.** 1 Pt.1:1-12
How to handle or conquer **p.** 1 Pt.3:13-4:19
Three ways. Acts 5:19-21
To bless persecutors. Ro.12:14
Triumph over **p.** Acts 4:23-31
What to fear & not to fear. Mt.10:24-33; Lk.12:1-12; 12:13-21
Described.
As a reward. Mk.10:30
As the glow of God's glory. 1 Pt.4:14
Attitude to **p.** (See **PERSECUTION**, Duty)
Sheep in the midst of wolves. Lk.10:3
Discussed. Mt.10:16-23; 10:24-33; Mk.13:9;Lk.6:20-23; 6:27-31; 21:12-19, 1 Pt.4:1-6
Men doing evil against believers. Mt.5:10-12
The picture of a model church under **p.** 2 Th.1:1-5
Duty. (See **PERSECUTION**, Deliverance)
Discussed. 1 Pt.4:12-19
How to treat persecutors. Ro.12:14-21
Not to be ashamed to suffer for being a Christian. 1 Pt.4:16
Not to be terrified by **p.** Reasons. Ph.1:28-30
To continue serving despite **p.** 1 Cor.4:11-13
To endure. Mt.10:22
To endure for the gospel. 2 Tim.1:6-12; 3:11-12
To flee **p.** Mt.10:23
To keep one's conscience clear in **p.** 1 Pt.3:16-17
To pray for deliverance. 2 Th.3:1-2
To pray for persecutors. Mt.5:44
To rejoice in **p.** Mt.5:12
To share in the sufferings of Christ. Ph.3:10
To stand firm for Christ despite **p.** Rev.2:9; 2:13
To stand up under the painful trial of **p.** 1 Pt.4:12-19
Example of. Acts 4:1-3, 13-22; 5:17-42; 6:9-15;7:54-60; 8:1-4; 9:23-30; 12:1-23; 15:1-2, 5; 16:3, 19-24; 17:5-9, 13-14, 15-16, 19-20; 18:5-6, 12-17; 19:9
The church.
At Thessalonica. 1 Th.2:1-12; 2 Th.1:6
Discussed. Rev.2:9; 2:13
The early church & believers.
By Saul of Tarsus. Violent **p.** Acts 8:1-4; 9:1-2
Discussed. 1 Pt.1:1-2; 1:13-16
First martyr. Acts 7:54-60
First **p.** Acts 4:1-22
First political **p.** Acts 12:1-25
God delivered the early church from **p.** Acts 9:31
Of bearing **p.** then backsliding. Rev.2:12-17
Picture of **p.** Acts 5:12-25
Picture of a model church under **p.** 2 Th.1:1-5
Recipients of the letter of I Peter. 1 Pt.1:1; 1:13-16
Severe **p.** Acts 12:1-25
The prophets. By Israel. Acts 7:42-53

Fact.
God gives a glow of His glory to persecuted believers. 1 Pt.4:14
Is a sign of coming judgment. 2 Th.1:5
Fear of.
Causes several things. Mt.10:28
Reasons for not fearing. Mt.10:28; Lk.12:11-12
In the end time. Discussed. Lk.21:12-19
Judgment of. To be great. Discussed. Mt.10:26-27; 23:34-36; 2 Th.1:6-12
Kinds - Methods - Types. Mt.5:10-12
Discussed. 1 Th.3:3-5
Excommunicated - forbidden to worship. Jn.16:2
Hatred. Mt.10:22; Jn.15:18; Jn.17:14-16
Killing. Mt.10:21; Jn.16:2
Mockery, ridicule. Jn.7:6-9
Tried before civil courts. Mt.10:17-18
Various methods. Mt.10:24-33
Meaning. Mt.5:10-12
Purpose of - Why believers are **p.**
Are considered evil doers. 1 Pt.2:12; 3:16
Are identified with Christ. Jn.15:20
Are not of the world, but separated from the world. Jn.15:19
Are thought to be strange. 1 Pt.4:4-5
Because believers live godly lives & godliness convicts the world. 2 Tim.3:12
Because men are offended by the cross. Gal.5:11; 6:12
Because men are sinful. Jn.15:24; Gal.4:29; 1 Th.2:15-16
Because men hate God & Christ. Jn.15:23-24
Because religionists are deceived. Think they know God but do not. Jn.16:2
Because the world does not really know God or Christ. Jn.15:21; 16:3; 1 Jn.3:1
Discussed. Mt.10:16; Jn.15:19-24; 17:14-16;1 Th.3:3-5
For bearing the believer's hope. 1 Pt.3:15
For bearing the name of Christ. 1 Pt.4:14
For evil works. 1 Pt.3:13-14
For misbehavior. 1 Pt.4:15
For preaching the resurrection. Acts 4:2-4
For righteousness' sake. 1 Pt.3:13-17
Four reasons. Mt.5:10-12
God uses for a greater witness. Verses. List of. Jn.11:55-57
Seven reasons. Acts 5:12-16
Response to. (See **PERSECUTION**, Deliverance From - How to Stand Against)
By Christ. Jn.11:54
Encouragement not to fear. Mt.10:24-33; 10:28
Four things believers must do. Mt.5:10-12
Three reasons to rejoice in **p.** Mt.5:12
To rejoice in **p.** Mt.5:12
Results - Privileges of.
Assures the Lord's very special presence. Ph.3:10
Causes laymen to scatter & spread the gospel. Acts 8:1-4; 11:19-30
Fills up & completes the sufferings of Christ. Mk.10:30
Gives one a share in the sufferings of Christ. Mt.10:24-25

God instills within the believer the very glow of His glory. 1 Pt.4:14
Matures a church. 2 Th.1:3-5
Proves a person's faith--that he is worthy of heaven. 2 Th.1:5
Reveals the evil nature of the world. Mt.5:10-12
Verses. List of. Mk.10:30; Lk.10:3
Warning - Predicted. Mt.10:16-23; Mk.13:9
    Discussed. Acts 14:21-28
    Friends will forsake & enemies will be fierce. Lk.22:33-37
    Is to be expected. Lk.20:10-12
    True believers shall suffer. Jn.21:18-19; 2 Tim.3:12
    Will be severe in the end time. Mk.13:9
Who is p.
    Believers. Lk.13:31-33; Jn.4:44; 15:18-27;16:1-6
    God's messengers. Mt.21:34-35; Mk.12:2; 12:3-5
    Jesus Christ.
        By Herod, the state or government. Lk.13:31-33
        By the world. Jn.15:18-27
    Prophets.
        By religionists. Lk.13:34
        Present day prophets. Mt.23:34-36

PERSEVERE - PERSEVERANCE - PERSISTENCE (See **ENDURANCE; STEADFASTNESS**)
Discussed. 2 Tim.1:13-18
Duty to **p.**
    In faith. Essential. Lk.8:49-56; Jn.4:48-49
    In persecution. (See **PERSECU-TION**) 1 Th.3:3-5
    In prayer. Meaning. Mt.7:7; Lk.11:5-10
    In seeking forgiveness. Mk.2:3-4
    In seeking healing. Lk.17:12-14; 18:39
    In seeking Jesus. Lk.18:39; 19:3-4
    Must be strengthened with God's power to be **p.** Col.1:11
    Must not faint. Gal.6:9
    To be longsuffering in living for Christ. 2 Tim.3:10-12
    To be longsuffering in ministering: preaching, teaching, etc. 2 Tim.4:2
    To be longsuffering in persecution. 2 Tim.3:10-12
    To be longsuffering in trials. 2 Cor.6:6-7
    To endure the chastening of God. Heb.12:5-7
    To maintain military discipline. Col.2:5
    To **p.** for the gospel. 2 Tim.1:6-12
    To **p.** in hope, for God's help. Jn.4:46-47
    To put on **p.** Col.3:12
    To show forth all **p.** as a pattern for other believers. 1 Tim.1:16
    To stand against the devil & his strategies. Eph.6:10-20
    To stand firm against persecution. Ph.1:28-30
    To stand firm, striving for the gospel. Ph.1:27
    To walk in longsuffering. Eph.4:1-2
Duty - Essential.
    Of the elderly.
        To be characterized by **p.** Tit.2:2
        To be sound in faith, love, & **p.** Tit.2:2
    Of the minister. To be **p.** 1 Tim.3:3; 2 Tim.2:24
    To add **p.** to one's faith. 2 Pt.1:5-7

To **p.** in combating all temptations & trials. Ro.5:3-5; Jas.5:7-11
To **p.** in continuing to do good works. Ro.2:6-7
To **p.** in keeping one's eyes fixed upon the return of Christ. 2 Th.3:5; Jas.5:7-8; 5:7-11
To **p.** in persecution & trials. 2 Th.1:4; 1 Pt.2:20
To **p.** in standing against false teachers. Rev.2:2
To **p.** in the hope of the Lord Jesus Christ. 1 Th.1:3
To **p.** in waiting for one's eternal salvation. Ro.8:23-25
To **p.** toward all men. 1 Th.5:14
To follow after love & **p.** 1 Tim.6:11
To minister in **p.** 2 Cor.6:4; 12:12; 2 Tim.3:10-11
To pray for strength to be **p.** Col.1:9-11, esp. 11
To run with **p.** the race set before one. Heb.12:1
To wait upon God. Jn.11:6
Example of.
    A blind man. Steps for getting help. Mk.10:46-52
    A government official. Stages of faith. Jn.4:44-54
    A man with palsy. The hope of **p.** for healing. (See **JESUS CHRIST,** Heals) Lk.5:18-20
    A rejected woman. Caring for the rejected. Mk.7:24-30
    Abraham. The **p.** needed to endure. Heb.6:13-15
    Anna. Hoping for salvation, for the Messiah. Lk.2:36-38
    Blind Bartimaeus. Crying for mercy. Lk.18:35-43
    The farmer. Perseverance needed to wait for the Lord's return. Jas.5:7-8
    The prophets & Job. Perseverance needed to combat temptation & trials. Jas.5:10-11
    Two blind men. The cry for sight. Mt.9:27-31
Meaning. Col.1:11; 2 Th.1:4; 1 Tim.3:2-3;2 Tim.3:10-11; Jas.1:3-4; 2 Pt.1:5-7
Meaning. Mt.7:7; Lk.11:8; Acts 2:42; 2 Cor.6:6-7; Gal.5:22-23; Eph.4:1-2; 2 Tim.3:10-11; 4:2; Jas.5:7
Of God.
    God endures with much **p.** the vessels of wrath. Ro.9:22
    The **p.** of the Lord means salvation. 2 Pt.3:15
    Why God is **p.** to men. Ro.2:4; 2 Pt.3:9; 3:15-16
Proves.
    That one has truly been called of God. 1 Tim.1:16
    That one walks worthy of God. Eph.4:1-2
Reasons. God knows the exact time, the best time to act. Jn.11:6
Result.
    Determines one's reward. Ro.2:7
    Glory, honor & immortality. Ro.2:6-7
    Inherits the promises. Heb.6:12; 10:36
    Joy. Col.1:11
    Keeps & saves one's soul. Lk.21:19
Results - Why **p.**
    Assures God's presence. 2 Tim.4:16-18

God stands by the believer when others forsake. 2 Tim.4:16-18
Assures healing & forgiveness. Mt.9:1-8
Assures salvation. Mt.10:22
Demonstrates faith. Mk.2:4
Discussed. 2 Tim.2:8-13
Fivefold. Mk.10:48
Is the secret of prayer. Lk.18:1-8
Saves the desperate. Mt.9:29-34; 20:29-34
Secures more & more. Lk.8:18
Secures the answer to one's needs. (See Examples, above) Mk.10:48; Lk.11:5-10; 11:8
Why Jesus demands **p.** Lk.17:11-14
Will be rewarded with eternal life. Gal.6:8-9
Source.
    An honest & good heart. Lk.8:15
    Counting all things lost. Ph.3:7-11
    Counting oneself as imperfect. Ph.3:12-16
    Denying self-righteousness. Ph.3:4-6
    God. Ro.15:5; 2 Th.3:5
    God's power. Col.1:11
    Guarding oneself. Ph.3:1-3
    Hope. Ro.8:25
    The Holy Spirit. Gal.5:22-23
    The trials & testing of one's faith. Ro.5:3-5; 12:12; Jas.1:2-4
    The Word of God, the Scriptures. Ro.15:4
Source of. The Holy Spirit. Gal.5:22-23
    Putting on the armor of God. Eph.6:10-20
Verses. List of. Jn.8:31

PERSIA
Traits of. Will be embodied in the antichrist. Rev.13:2

PERSIS
Believer in Rome. Ro.16:12

PERSUADE - PERSUASION
Duty - Essential.
    Not to be almost **p.** of Christ, but fully **p.** Acts 26:28
    To be fully **p.** that we do not cause others to stumble over the social activities we take part in. Ro.14:5, cp. 1-23
    To be **p.** of God's promises. Ro.4:20-22; Heb.11:13
    To be **p.** that God is able to keep that which we commit to Him against the day of judgment. 2 Tim.1:2
    To be **p.** that nothing can separate us from the love of God. Ro.8:38-39
    To **p.** all men that Jesus is the Christ. Acts 18:4-5; 28:23
    To **p.** believers to continue in the grace of God. Acts 13:43
    To **p.** men because of the terror of the Lord. 2 Cor.5:11
    To preach. Preaching must **p.** Acts 18:4
Fact. Many refuse to be **p.** of God's Word. Refuse even though One has risen from the dead. Lk.16:31

PERVERSE
Generations of men are **p.** Mt.11:16-19
Meaning. Mt.17:17; Lk.9:41

PESSIMISM
Discussed. Jn.6:7
There is a **p.** of faith. Discussed. Jn.6:7

PHOEBE
Her home church. Acts 18:18

PHOENICIA
A country northwest of Palestine that bordered the Mediterranean Sea. Acts 11:19; 15:3; 21:2

PHRYGIA
A large province of Asia Minor visited by Paul at least twice. Acts 16:6; 18:23

PHYGELLUS
Forsook Paul. 2 Tim.1:15

PHYLACTERIES
Described. Mt.23:5

PHYSICAL
P. senses. Vs. spiritual senses. Mt.16:2-4
Weakness of the p. Cannot penetrate the spiritual. Col.2:8

PHYSICAL FOOD
Vs. spiritual food. (See **HUNGER, SPIRITUAL; SATISFACTION, SPIRITUAL**)
Jn.4:31-35

PHYSICAL WORLD & DIMENSION
(See **CORRUPTION**)
Is corruptible, wasting away. (See **CORRUPTION**, Meaning; **MAN**, Nature)
Is the only world & dimension seen & known by man. Jn.8:14; 8:15-16; 8:23; 8:42-43;11:7-10
Meaning. Mt.6:19-20; Acts 2:27; 13:32-37; 2 Pt.1:4
Decaying, aging, deteriorating. Mt.6:19-24
Flesh & blood which wastes away. 1 Cor.15:50-58
Flesh withering, falling away, dissolving. 2 Cor.5:1-4
Mortal--mortality. 2 Cor.5:1-4
Physical death. 1 Cor.15:42-49
The natural world & body. 1 Cor.15:35-49; Jude 10, cp. 8-10
The world passing away. 1 Jn.2:17
Seed of.
In the world. Jn.12:31
Is within the world. 2 Pt.1:4
Physical vs. spiritual dimension. Jn.8:23
Vs. the spiritual dimension. Jn.8:14; 8:15-16; 8:23; 8:42-43;11:7-10; 2 Cor.4:17-18

PILATE, PONTIUS
Compromised with the crowd. Lk.23:13-25
Discussed. Mt.27:11-25; Mk.15:1-15; Lk.3:1-2;Jn.18:28
Governor of Judea (A.D. 26-36). Lk.3:1
Picture of a morally weak man. Mk.15:1-15
Trial of Jesus.
Indecisive compromise. Jn.18:28-19:15
Shirking duty. Lk.23:1-7
Superstitious. Jn.19:8-11

PILGRIMS (See **ALIENS**)
Duty of.
To abstain from fleshly lusts. 1 Pt.2:11-12
To endure seeking the unseen, heavenly kingdom. Heb.11:13-16
To journey upon earth as in a strange country, looking for the city of God-- all by faith. Heb.11:8-10

PISIDIA
A district in Asia Minor visited by Paul at least twice. Acts 13:14; 14:24

PISIDIAN OF ANTIOCH
Church at **A.**
Became the center of world-wide missions. Acts 13:1
Great church. Reasons. Twofold. Acts 13:1
Leadership of. Five leaders. Acts 13:1
Where believers were first called Christians. Acts 11:26
City of. Discussed. Acts 11:19-30
Discussed. Acts 11:19-30
False teachers arose in **A.** Acts 15:1-5
First great Gentile church. Acts 11:19-30
Home of one of the first deacons-- Nicolas. Acts 6:1-7
Launched the first great missionary thrust into the world. Acts 14:26-28
Paul & Barnabas were ministers of **A.** Acts 11:22-26
Paul was commissioned by **A.** Acts 13:1-3; 15:35-41
Sent out the very first missionaries. Acts 13:1-3

ANTIOCH OF PISIDIA
Discussed. Acts 13:14

PITIFUL
Caused by.
Being comfortable & self-satisfied. Rev.3:7
Hoarding riches. Jas.5:1
Hoping in Christ only for this world. 1 Cor.15:9
Rejecting Christ & God's servants. Mt.21:33-41, esp. 41
Seeking God by law. Ro.6:14-15
Sin, oppression, war. Ro.3:15-18
Fact. If we have hope in Christ only for this life, we are left without hope & are most **m.** 1 Cor.15:19
Meaning. Rev.3:16-17
Results.
Stand guilty before God. Ro.3:16, 19
The rich are going to howl because of the **m.** coming upon them. Jas.5:1
The wicked will be **m.** destroyed. Mt.21:41
Will be spued out by Christ. Rev.3:16-17
Trait of. Unbelievers. Ro.3:16, cp. 9-20

PITY (See **COMPASSION**)
Duty. To have compassion. Lk.10:31-32;1 Pt.3:8, cp. Mt.18:29-30;

PLAN - PLANS - PLANNING
Duty.
Not to **p.** without God. Lk.12:16-21; Jas.4:13-17
To lay detailed **p.** in building one's life. Lk.14:28-33
Of the ministry. Discussed. Mt.10:5-15; 10:12-15
Redirected by the Holy Spirit through restraint. Acts 16:6-7

PLANK
Parable of. Watch hypocrisy & criticizing. Lk.6:41-42

PLEASURE - PLEASURE-SEEKERS
(See **SOCIAL FUNCTIONS; WORLDLY - WORLDLINESS**)
Caused by. Selfishness; godless independence. Lk.15:11-13
Discussed. Acts 17:18; 2 Tim.3:2-4; Tit.3:3;Jas.4:1; 4:1-3; 4:2
Kinds of **p.**
The **p.** of material wealth & possessions. Lk.12:13-21, esp.19; Jas.5:5, cp. 1-7
The **p.** of partying & of lust & sex. Tit.3:3; 2 Pt.2:13-14
The **p.** of sin. Ro.1:29-32
The **p.** of the world & flesh. Lk.8:14; Tit.3:3; 1 Jn.2:15-16
Of the world. Judgment. Lk.6:24-26
Questionable. Discussed. Ro.14:1-23; 1 Cor.8:1-13
Results.
Chokes the Word of God out of a person. Lk.8:11-15
Death. 1 Tim.5:6
Lasts only for a season, a short time. Heb.11:25
Verses. List of. Lk.8:11-15
Sin of. 2 Pt.2:13

POLLUTION
What defiles a man. Mt.15:1-20

POOR - POVERTY (See **NEED - NECESSITIES**)
Discussed. God's provision for the believer. Mt.6:25-34; Lk.12:22-34
Duty - Essential.
To follow Christ in ministering to the **p.** Mt.8:19-20
To help the poor & lonely. Ro.12:16
To treat all men justly, meeting their needs. Lk.11:42; 14:12-14
Verses. List of. Lk.11:42
Example: being poor yet faithful to Christ. Rev.2:8-11
Facts.
Jesus was **p.** Mt.2:19-23
Not a disgrace. Mt.2:19-23
Meaning. Lk.21:3
Of believers. Discussed. Rev.2:9
Special objects of the Messiah's ministry. Mt.11:4-6

POOR IN SPIRIT - POVERTY, SPIRITUAL
Meaning. Mt.5:3; Lk.6:20-23; Rev.3:16-17

POOR, OFFERING OF THE
The offering made by Jesus' parents. Lk.2:24

POSITION (See **AMBITION**)
Seeking.
Discussed. Mt.18:1-4; Mk.10:35-45
Love of position is wrong. Mt.23:5; Lk.11:43; 14:7-11
The problem of ambition. Mk.9:33-37

POSITIVE THINKING (See **MIND**)
Discussed. Ph.4:8-9

POSSESSIONS (See **MATERIALISM; WEALTH; WORLDLINESS**)

POUNDS (See **MINAS**)
Meaning. Lk.19:13
Parable of the **p.** Testing of the Lord's disciples. Lk.19:11-27

POWER - POWERFUL (See JESUS CHRIST, Power)

Difference between p. & authority. Lk.9:1
Discussed. Lk.10:17-20; Acts 1:8; 6:8
  P. of faith. Mk.11:22-23
  P. of the Holy Spirit. Ro.8:1-17
Duty.
  P. is to be the believer's great aim.
    Ph.3:10-11
  To know & experience the p. of God
    day by day. Eph.1:19-21
  To know the p. of Christ & His resur-
    rection. Ph.3:10-11
  To possess God's p. Col.1:11
  To possess great power. Lk.10:17-20
  To preach the gospel in power.
    1 Th.1:5-10
  To rejoice in salvation, not power.
    Lk.10:20
  To seek p. The problem of ambition.
    Mk.9:33-37; 10:35-45
Essential - Need for.
  P. to overcome sin & struggling.
    Ro.8:1-17
  P. to save. Ro.1:16-17
Lack of - Problems.
  Many stress spiritual need over physi-
    cal need because of no p. Lk.9:11
  Misuse of p. Lk.22:49-50
  Reasons why one does not have p. &
    the results. Mk.9:18; Lk.9:37-40
  Rejoicing in p. instead of salvation.
    Lk.10:20
  Seeking p. for selfish ends - to be
    great. Lk.9:46-48; 22:24-30
  Tempted to secure p. by compromise.
    Lk.4:5-8
  Tempted to seek p. Mt.4:3
Meaning. Jn.2:23; Eph.3:16; 6:10-11
  Discussed. Eph.1:19-23
Of faith.
  Discussed. Heb.11:4-5
  Great power of faith. Mt.17:14-21;
    Lk.17:5-6
  P. to remove mountains. Mt.17:20;
    Mk.11:22-23
Of God. (See GOD, Power of)
Of Jesus. (See JESUS CHRIST, Power of)
Of the Holy Spirit. (See HOLY SPIRIT,
  Power of)
Purpose.
  Discussed. Mt.11:4-6; 21:17-22
  To carry the gospel to the whole
    world. Mt.28:18-20; Acts 1:8
  To control evil spirits. Mk.6:7
  To control fear & nature. Mt.8:23-27
  To defeat Satan & enemies. Lk.9:1;
    9:42-43; 10:17-20; 10:18; 10:19
  To direct p. against evil. Mt.10:1
  To equip & give assurance. Mt.10:1
  To exercise p. over the whole man.
    Mt.4:24
  To heal. (See HEAL - HEALING)
    Mt.4:24
  To receive & reject men. Mt.8:5-13
  To remove mountains. Meaning.
    Mt.17:20
  Twofold. Mt.10:8
Results.
  Led some to believe. Jn.2:23
  Powerful preaching. 1 Cor.2:4
  Spiritual rest. Heb.4:11-12
  What God's p. gives us. 2 Pt.1:3

Source.
  A given power. Mt.10:1
  Being with Jesus. Acts 4:13-14
  Discussed. Mk.1:35-39; Acts 9:40-41
  Faith, belief. Acts 3:16; Eph.1:19
  God. Ro.1:16-17; Col.1:11;
    Eph.1:19-23; Jude 24-25
  Not man, but Christ. Acts 3:12-13
  Preaching the cross. 1 Cor.1:22-24,
    esp. 24
  Preaching the gospel. Ro.1:16;
    1 Th.1:5
  Teaching God's Word. Heb.4:12
  The Holy Spirit. Lk.24:44-49; Acts
    1:8; 1 Cor.2:4; Eph.3:20
  Verses. List of. Mk.3:14-15; Ro.5:6-7

POWER OF DARKNESS
Identified. Satan. Lk.22:53

POWERLESS
Meaning. Ro.5:6-7

POWERLESSNESS
Caused by.
  Lack of faith & a wayward heart.
    Lk.9:37-45; 9:43-45
  Spiritual immaturity & p. Mk.9:14-29
  Unbelief. Mt.17:14-21; 17:19-20
Discussed. Mt.17:14-21
Of man. Cannot save himself. Ro.5:6-7
Results. Discussed. Mt.17:15-16;
  Mk.9:18
Warning against. Christ warns.
  Mt.17:17-18

PRAETORIAN GUARD
Of Rome. Discussed. Ph.1:12-14

PRAISE (See PRAYER; THANKSGIV-ING; WORSHIP)
Discussed. Lk.14:7-14
Duty.
  To endure trials & temptations so that
    one's faith will be to the p. & honor
    of God. 1 Pt.1:6-7
  To faithfully preach & minister so that
    God will be glorified & p. forever.
    1 Pt.4:11
  To offer the sacrifice of p. to God.
    Heb.13:15
  To p. God despite circumstances, even
    if in prison. Acts 16:25
  To p. God for miracles of healing.
    Lk.18:43; Acts 3:8-9
  To p. God for the fruits of righteous-
    ness. Ph.1:11
  To p. in order to conquer afflictions.
    Jas.5:13
  To p. the glory of God's grace &
    glory. Eph.1:6, 12, 14
  To sing p. in the midst of the church.
    Acts 2:47; Heb.2:12
Example of. Heavenly p. Rev.19:1-6
Meaning. 1 Pt.2:9
Purpose. P. is the very reason believers
  are saved. 1 Pt.2:9
To God.
  Discussed. Ph.4:20
  Some love the p. of men more than the
    p. of God. Jn.12:43
  What to p. God for. Rev.7:11-12

PRAY - PRAYER - PRAYING
And the Holy Spirit. Discussed. Ro.8:23-27
Answers to.
  Answers in two ways. Mt.7:8
  Assured. Mt.7:7-11; Lk.11:11-13
  Clearly seen. Mt.6:6
  Conditional. Mk.11:20-26
    Discussed. Mk.11:20-26
    Must forgive others. Mt.6:12; 6:14-
      15; Mk.11:25; Lk.11:4, cp. Mt.5:7
    Must p. according to God's will.
      Discussed. 1 Jn.5:13-15
    Three conditions. 1 Jn.5:13-15
  P. is the source for receiving all things.
    Jas.4:2
  The reason why God sometimes delays
    the answer. Lk.18:6-8
  The very reason God chooses us is to
    answer our prayer. Lk.18:6-8
  Why Jesus answers p. Jn.14:13-14
  Why God does not always answer p.
    Lk.11:5-10
Bold p.
  In time of need. Heb.4:14-16
  To boldly enter the holiest of God's
    presence. Heb.10:19-21
Described. As access into God's pres-
  ence. Jn.16:23-24
Discussed. Mt.6:5-6; 6:7-8; Lk.11:1-13;
  18:1-8; 18:9-14; Ro.1:9; Ph.4:6-
  7; Col.4:2-4; 1 Tim.2:1-8; 1 Jn.5:13-15
  Great subject of p. Lk.11:1-13
  The model p. of Jesus. Lk.11:2-4
  What believers should p. every day.
    Mt.6:9-13; Eph.3:14-21
Duty.
  Is commanded. Several verses.
    Mt.6:5-6
  Is the first duty of the church.
    1 Tim.2:1-8
  To approach God boldly. Heb.4:15-16
  To boldly enter the holiest of God's
    presence. Heb.10:19-21
  To continue, to give constant attention
    to p. Ro.12:12
  To draw near God with assurance.
    Heb.10:22
  To pray.
    Prayers that should be prayed daily.
      Eph.3:14-21
    The daily prayer of Paul. Eph.3:14-21
    The Lord's pattern for prayer.
      Mt.6:9-13
  To p. all through life. Lk.3:21
  To p. constantly. Lk.2:37; 3:21
  To p. for all men to be saved.
    1 Tim.2:3-7
  To p. for all rulers. 1 Tim.2:2
  To p. for deliverance from persecu-
    tion. 2 Th.3:1-2
  To p. for leaders. Heb.13:18-19
  To p. that the message of the Lord
    may spread rapidly & be honored.
    2 Th.3:1-2
  To p. in the Spirit. Jude 20-21
  To p. night & day.
    Commanded. 1 Th.3:10; 1 Tim.5:5
    To arise early in the morning & p.
      Mk.1:35
    To p. always. Acts 10:2
    To p. continually. 1 Th.5:17
    To serve God with fastings & p.
      night & day. Lk.2:37
    To p. seeking to be re-strengthened.
      Lk.4:42

To **p.** to be healed when seriously sick. Jas.5:14-15

To **p.** to conquer afflictions. Jas.5:13

To **p.** while being baptized. Lk.3:21

To struggle in **p.** for all believers & churches world-wide. Col.2:1

To watch & **p.** for the end time. Lk.21:34-36

To watch, stay alert, and pray. 1 Pt.4:7

Verses. List of. Ro.1:9

Essentials.
Discussed. Mk.11:25-26

Few words--many words are not necessary. Mt.6:7

For personal preparation. Mt.14:22-33

For teaching & making disciples. Lk.9:18; 9:28

Five basic essentials.
According to God's will. Jn.5:14-15

Faith. Mt.21:22; Mk.11:24; Heb.11:6;Jas.1:6-7

Forgiveness. Mt.6:14-15

Perseverance. Mt.7:7-8; Lk.18:1; Eph.6:18;Col.4:2; 1 Th.5:17

Purity - cleanliness - obedience. Jas.4:3; 1 Jn.3:22

In facing trials. Lk.9:28

Three essentials. Mt.6:6

To have set times for **p.**; much time is essential. Acts 3:1

What it takes to receive things of God. Mt.15:21-28

Examples of precious **p.** meetings.
A church **p.** for Peter's deliverance from prison. Acts 12:5

A whole church escorted Paul out of town & **p.** Acts 21:5

Epaphras. Labored fervently in **p.** for the church. Col.4:12-13

Lydia & other ladies beside a river in Philippi. Acts 16:12-13

Paul & Silas in jail. Acts 16:25

Paul & the Ephesian elders. Acts 20:17, 36-38

Pentecost. Acts 2:1-4

Peter & the church after the first persecution. Acts 4:23-31

Peter in being prepared to go to Cornelius. Acts 10:9-10

Peter raising Dorcas from the dead. Acts 9:40

Stephen during his martyrdom. Acts 7:59-60

The church **p.** before sending out the first missionaries. Acts 13:1-3

The disciples in the upper room right after the Lord's ascension. Acts 1:12-14

The early church. Was steadfast in **p.** Acts 2:42

Fact.
P. is offered upon the golden altar in heaven. Rev.8:2-4

P. is the source for receiving all things. Jas.4:2

Hindrances to - Failure in **p.**
An unforgiving spirit. Mt.6:14-15

Empty repetition. Mt.6:7-8

Family problems. 1 Pt.3:7

Hypocritical **p.** Mt.6:5

Just failing to **p.** Mt.26:40-41; Mk.14:34

Long **p.** Mt.6:7; Mk.12:40

P. to oneself only. Lk.18:11-12

P. with the wrong motive. Mt.6:5-6

Self-righteousness. Lk.18:11-12

Spouses failing to honor & respect one another. 1 Pt.3:7

Talking about **p.**, but not **p.** Ro.1:9

Today's problem twofold. Mt.6:7

Weaknesses. Helped by the Holy Spirit. Ro.8:23-27

How to pray
Being specific & making definite requests. Ph.4:6-7

By approaching God as our Father. Mt.7:11

By obeying God's commands. 1 Jn.3:22

Discussed. Mt.6:9-13
The disciples asked how to **p.** Lk.11:1-13

In secret; in one's room. Mt.6:6

In the name of Jesus. Meaning. Jn.14:13-14

Joined together, agreeing. Mt.18:19; Acts 1:14

Kneeling down. Acts 7:60; 9:40; 21:5

Man's part & God's part. Lk.11:5-10

Must first forgive others. Forgiveness is the basic principle of **p.** Mt.6:14-15

Overcoming the sinful nature, distractions, & wandering thoughts. Ro.8:23-27

Persevering. Mt.7:8-11; Acts 1:14; Jas.5:16-18

Powerful & effective, intensely. Helped by the Holy Spirit. Ro.8:23-27; Jas.5:16-18

Praising God for deliverance. Acts 4:23-31

The prayer of great purpose. Jn.11:41-42

The spirit needed for **p.** Lk.18:9-14

Three great rules. Mt.6:7-8

In the end time.
Believers will **p.** for vindication. Rev.8:2-4

Prayer will stir God to judge the world. Rev.8:2-4

Kinds of **p.**
Bold **p.** Heb.4:14-16; 10:19-21

Chance **p.** vs. persistent **p.** Mt.15:23-24

Confession **p.** 1 Jn.1:9

Different kinds of **p.** 1 Tim.2:1

Fellowship **p.** vs. concentrated **p.** Lk.6:12

Four kinds. Ph.4:6-7

Intercessory **p.** Meaning. Eph.6:18-19; Col.4:2-4; 1 Tim.2:1;Jas.5:15

Persevering **p.** (See **PRAYER**, Persevering)

Self-righteous vs. humble **p.** Of Pharisee & Tax collector. Lk.18:10-14

Supplication **p.** Meaning. 1 Tim.2:1

Thanksgiving **p.** 1 Tim.2:1

Lack of. (See **PRAYERLESSNESS**)

Meaning. Talking & sharing with God. Mt.6:5-6

Model **p.** of Jesus. Mt.6:9-13

Of Jesus. (See **JESUS CHRIST**, Prayer Life)

Of Paul. Great **p.** for the church & believers. Eph.3:14-21

Perseverance in.
Discussed. Lk.11:5-10

Is the secret of prayer. Lk.18:1-8

Meaning. Mt.7:7

Saves the desperate. Mt.20:21-34; 20:31-32

Verses. List of. Lk.9:28; 11:5-10; 11:11-13

Why Jesus demands perseverance in **p.** Two reasons. Lk.17:11-14

Purpose. (See **PRAYER**, Duty; What to pray for)
To bear fruit. Jn.15:16

To have one's needs met. Mt.6:8

To minister. Mt.17:14

Requests of. Great requests. Col.1:9-11

Results - Work of.
Answers to. (See **PRAYER**, Answers to)
Why Jesus **a.** prayer. Jn.14:13-14

Assurance of. 1 Jn.5:14-15

Delivers & saves the believer. Ro.8:23-27

Erases anxiety. Ph.4:6-7

Fills one with the Spirit. Acts 4:31

Is the answer to receiving things from God. Jas.4:2

Is the supernatural resource. Eph.6:18-20

Peace & release. Mt.26:45; Ph.4:6-7

Power--great power for ministry. Mt.17:20; 21:21-22

Protects against temptation. Lk.22:40, 46

The very reason God chooses us. To answer our **p.** Jn.15:16

Source.
The love of God. Jn.16:25-27

The resurrection of Christ. Jn.16:23-24

Verses. List of. Ro.1:9

What to **p.** for. (See **PRAYER**, Duty; Purpose)
A good conscience. Heb.13:18

A safe reunion. Heb.13:19

All believers. Eph.6:18; Jas.5:16

Boldness. Acts 4:29; Eph.6:19; Ph.1:19-20

Discussed. Mt.6:9-13

For believers to be preserved blameless until the day of Christ. 1 Th.5:23

For the love of believers to increase & grow. Ph.1:19

For unbelievers to be reconciled to God. 2 Cor.5:19-20

Great things, even healing. Lk.18:39

Great works. Jn.14:12-14

Help in time of need. Heb.4:15-16

Laborers. Mt.9:37-38; Lk.10:2

Maturity. Eph.3:14-21

Ministers. Eph.6:19; 1 Th.5:25; 2 Th.3:1; Heb.13:18

Nine things Christ said to pray. Mt.6:9-13

Persecutors. Mt.5:44; Lk.16:27

Renewed strength. Lk.4:42

Six things Paul prayed. Eph.3:14-21

The brother who sins. 1 Jn.5:16

To be delivered from temptation. Mt.26:41

To be healed. Jas.5:14-15

To conquer afflictions. Jas.5:13

When to **p.**
After ministry. Mk.6:46

Always--all day long. Acts 10:2; 1 Th.3:10; 1 Tim.5:5

As history's climax draws near. 1 Pt.4:7

At meals. Listed. Mt.14:19; Mk.6:41; Jn.6:11;Acts 27:35

At three significant times. Lk.9:18-19

In the early morning. Mk.1:35

When facing death. Lk.23:42

When one is sick. Jas.5:14-15

Where to **p.** - Places.
Among believers beside a river. Acts 16:13

Among believers on a beach. Acts 21:5

Discussed. Mt.6:5-6
In churches & on streets. Mt.6:5
In groups. Mt.18:19-20
In one's closet, in secret. Mt.6:6
In one's home. Acts 10:1-3, 20; 12:12
In the church--publicly. Acts 1:14
In the temple. Mt.21:12-16
On the mountain top. Mt.14:22-33
Peter & John entered the temple for p.
Acts 3:1
Who is to p.
The church: its first duty. 1 Tim.2:1-8
The righteous. 1 Pt.3:10-12

PRAYERLESSNESS
Caused by. Temptation & trials. Jas.4:3

PREACH - PREACHING (See MINISTER; PROCLAIM-PROCLAIMING; WITNESSING)
Call to. (See CALL - CALLED)
Enabled by the Holy Spirit. 1 Pt.1:12
P. is the first call of the minister.
Mk.2:1-2; Lk.8:1
Conditions. For receiving messengers, preachers. Mk.9:38-41
Described.
As a voice crying, "Prepare." Jn.1:23
As sowing seed. How men receive the Word of God. Mt.13:3; Mk.4:1-20
Discussed. Lk.8:1; 1 Cor.2:1-5; 2 Tim.4:1-5
Four Greek words used for p. & witnessing. Acts 11:19-30
To p. baptism of repentance. Lk.3:3
To. p. the good news. Lk.3:18, 16:16
To p. the good news to the poor. Lk.4:18, 7:22
To p. the gospel. Lk.9:6, 20:1
To p. His name. Lk.24:47
Duty.
A strong & true minister p. the gospel. 1 Th.1:5-10; 2:1-12
Are obligated, indebted to p. Ro.1:14-15
The charge to p. Acts 14:1; 2 Tim.4:1-5
The first task of the minister. Acts 14:21
To be a pattern & example of good works. Tit.2:7-8
To center in the Scripture. Acts 17:1-2; 18:24; 18:25
To exalt Christ & not self. Jn.3:29-30
To fear p. another Jesus. 2 Cor.11:4; Gal.1:8-9
To please God, not man. Not to use flattering words, be greedy for position or livelihood. 1 Th.2:5-6
To preach. Tit.1:2-3; 1:9
To p. boldly. 1 Th.2:2
To p. in the power of the Holy Spirit. 1 Cor.2:4; 1 Th.1:5
To p. peace. Lk.10:5-6
To p. social justice. Lk.3:10-14
To p. the gospel. To p. the gospel as it should be preached. 1 Th.1:5
To p. the kingdom of God. Lk.9:59-60; 10:8-9
To proclaim the grace of God through every means of speech. Tit.2:15
To reason & persuade. Acts 18:4
To sense the urgency of p. Acts 17:16; 18:4; Ro.1:14-15
Errors of. Mentioned. Mt.9:35
Essential.
A preacher must focus upon the cross. 1 Cor.1:17-25

Must focus upon the cross. 1 Cor.1:23
Must have a compulsion to p. Discussed. 1 Cor.9:16-23
Must have a preacher to p. Ro.10:14-15
Kinds.
Christ-centered p. Mk.16:15; 1 Cor.1:17-25
Divisive & envious p. Ph.1:15-16
Empty p. Trait of false teachers. Jude 16
God ordained p. 1 Cor.2:7
Gospel p. 1 Cor.1:17-18; 9:16; Gal.1:6-9
Human p. - Man-made p. 1 Cor.2:4
Perverted & false p. Gal.1:6-9
Powerless p. 1 Cor.1:17
Spirit led p. 1 Cor.2:4-5; 2:13
Meaning. Mt.9:35; Mk.3:14; Lk.8:1; 2 Tim.4:2
Message of.
Danger. Can be emptied of its power. Ways. 1 Cor.1:17
Kingdom of God. Lk.4:43-44
Preached by Jesus. Mt.4:17; 5:1-7:29; Mk.1:14-15
Sound p. What it is. 1 Cor.2:1-5
Subject - Content of. Acts 2:14-40; 3:12-26; 4:8-12, 20;5:29-32, 42; 7:1-53; 8:25, 32-35;9:20, 22; 10:34-43; 13:14-41; 14:7; 15:35; 16:30-32; 17:3, 11, 13, 22-34; 18:28; 19:8; 20:21; 1 Cor.1:17-25
Discussed. Acts 2:14-24; 2:15-36; 9:20; 10:34-43; 13:14-41; 2 Cor.5:17-6:2
Peace. Lk.10:5-6
Social justice. Lk.3:10-14
The cross. 1 Cor.1:17
The good news of the gospel. Mk.1:14-15
The Kingdom of God. Lk.4:43-44; 8:1; 9:59-60; 10:8-9
The message to a heathen & superstitious people. Acts 14:8-20; 17:22-34
The New Covenant, the covenant of the Spirit. 2 Cor.3:6-8
The pattern of p. Acts 14:1-7
The points for p. Acts 3:12-26
The preeminence & power of Christ. Mk.1:7-8; Col.1:18-19
What is to be preached. 1 Cor.1:17-25
Summary of Jesus' message. Mt.4:17; 5:1-7:29
The wisdom of words vs. the power of the cross. 1 Cor.1:17
Mission.
Of believers. Mt.4:17; Mk.1:36-38; 1:39
Of Christ. Mt.4:17; 11:4-6; Mk.1:36-38; 1:39; 2:1-2; Lk.4:17-19
P. of Paul. His only complete message in Scripture. Acts 13:14-41
P. of the early church.
Focused on the resurrection. Acts 2:25-36
Points for p. Acts 3:12-26
To a heathen & superstitious people. Acts 14:8-20; 17:22-34
Response to.
Counted as foolish by the lost. 1 Cor.1:17
Counted as the power of God by the saved. 1 Cor.1:17
Discussed. Mt.13:1-9
Fourfold response. Lk.8:4-15; Acts 13:42-52

How men receive the gospel. Mt.13:1-9
Discussed. Acts 11:19-30
Refuse to hear. Lk.6:27-31
Rejected. Lk.4:22-30
Ridiculed. Acts 17:18
Some repent, some reject. Lk.11:32
Unbelief. Does not benefit the hearer. Heb.4:2
Results.
Is rejected. And rejecters are to be rejected. Acts 13:46-48, 50-51
Provides the answer to division. 1 Cor.2:1-5
Stirs the people. But the excitement of the crowd is not always wise. Mk.6:45
Triumphs. 2 Tim.4:6-8
Turns the world upside down. Acts 17:1-9
Vs. tongues. 1 Cor.14:1-25
Where to p.
Everywhere. Mk.16:20
In houses & homes. Acts 5:42
In the public worship centers: the church, synagogues, & temples. Mk.1:39; Lk.4:44; Acts 5:42; 9:20; 13:5
In the towns & cities. Mt.11:1; Mk.1:38; Acts 15:21
On city streets & in the open air. Acts 14:8-9
To all nations, the whole world. Mk.16:15; Gal.1:16; 2:2; Eph.3:8; 1 Tim.3:16
To individuals. (See WITNESS - WITNESSING)
To the poor. Mt.11:5

PREACHER (See HERALD, A; MINISTER)
Meaning. Who a p. is. 2 Tim.1:11-12

PREACHER'S OUTLINE & SERMON BIBLE
Purpose. Discussed. Heb.6:4-8; Rev.4:4; 20:1-3; Dedication Page

PREDESTINATION (See CHOSEN; ELECTION; FOREKNOWLEDGE; FORE-ORDAINED)
Described. As those whom God gives to Christ. Jn.6:37; 6:39; 6:44-46
Determined by. Eight laws. Jn.12:39-41
Discussed. Jn.6:37; 6:39; 6:44-46; Acts 13:48;Ro.9:7-13; 9:14-24
Fact.
God has the right to show mercy & justice as He wills. Ro.9:14-33
God puts up with evil men in order to share His glory with believers. Ro.9:22-24
Meaning. Acts 2:23; 4:25-28; Ro.8:29; Eph.1:5-6
Purpose. 1 Pt.1:2
That believers might be adopted as children of God. Eph.1:3-4
That believers might be called, justified, & glorified. Ro.8:30
That believers might be delivered from the most severe circumstances & extreme experiences. Ro.8:28, 35-39
That Christ might have many brothers & sisters. Jn.6:39; Ro.8:29
To give perfect assurance & security to the believer. Jn.6:37; 6:39; 10:27-29; Ro.8:28-39

Who.
A line of people to receive God's glory. Ro.9:22-24
Believers. Ro.8:28-39; Eph.1:5-6
Discussed. 1 Pt.1:18-20
Paul. Before his birth. Gal.1:15-16
The chosen people of God. Jn.15:12-17; Eph.1:5-6; 1 Pt.1:2
Unbelievers. Appointed to unbelief. 1 Pt.2:7-8

PREEMINENCE (See **JESUS CHRIST**, Deity)

PREEXISTENCE
Of Christ. (See **JESUS CHRIST**, Preexistence)

PREGNANT WOMAN, THE UNNAMED
Discussed. Rev.12:1-17

PREJUDICE (See **BARRIERS; BIGOTRY; DISCRIMINATION; FAVORITISM; PARTIALITY**)
Broken down - Abolished.
All barriers are broken down by Christ. Gal.3:28
By Christ's ministry. Mt.15:21-28; 15:29; 15:30-31;Mk.7:24-30; Lk.17:15-19;Eph.2:13-18
By compassion. Lk.10:29-37
By receiving all. Ro.15:7-12
By witnessing. Jn.4:1-42
Discussed. Acts 10:1-48; Ro.12:14-21
Steps to. Mk.7:24-30
Caused by.
Being of a different nationality. Mk.7:25-26
"Elitist" groups. Lk.9:49-50
Judging others. Ro.14:4; 14:13; 1 Cor.4:5; Jas.4:12
Racial differences. Mt.15:21-28; Jn.4:5
Religious beliefs. Jn.9:28-34; Acts 9:1-2
Self-righteousness. Lk.18:9
Sin. Mt.6:14; 6:15
Wealth & social position. Jas.2:1-6
Discussed. Receiving & rejecting men. Mt.8:5-9
Duty.
Of the minister. Not to show **p**. 1 Tim.5:21
To receive everyone; no discrimination. Ro.15:7-12
Example of.
Nathanael. Jn.1:46
Religionists. Jn.9:28-34
The disciples toward the Samaritans. Jn.4:27
Fact. No **p**. with God. Acts 2:17-21
How to overcome.
By faith. 2 Pt.1:1
By following Jesus' example. Jn.4:27
By Jesus Christ. Gal.3:28
Jew vs. the Gentile. Example. Mt.15:23-28
Jews.
Barricaded the Gentiles from God. Eph.2:11-12
Vs. the Gentiles. One race vs. another. Eph.2:11-12
Results.
Casts harsh insults against people. Mk.7:27; Jn.8:48-50
Persecution. Jn.9:28-34; Acts 7:54-60; 9:1-2
Prevents compassion. Lk.10:29-37

PREPARE - PREPARED - PREPARATION (See **COMMITMENT; CROSS - SELF-DENIAL; DEDICATION; DEVOTION**)
Discussed. Mt.10:1
Essential.
Before ministry & service. Mt.10:1
To be tried & proven. Lk.4:1-2
To **p**. the way for the Lord. Mk.1:3-5; 1:3
In season, out of season. Meaning. 2 Tim.4:2
Spiritual **p**.
Must be **p**. for service. 2 Tim.2:21
Must be **p**. for the Lord. Lk.1:17
Must **p**. for Jesus' coming. Lk.3:4-6
Must **p**. the way of the Lord. Mt.3:3; Mk.1:2-3; Lk.3:4; 7:27
Must seek the power of the Lord's presence. Mt.14:22-33
Needed after being disciplined by God. Lk.1:23-25
The things being **p**. for the believer.
A heavenly city, the new Jerusalem. Heb.11:16; Rev.2:2
A kingdom. Mt.25:34
A place, an eternal mansion in heaven. Jn.14:2-3
A place of position & authority in eternity. Mt.20:23; Mk.10:40
The Great Marriage Supper of the Lamb. Mt.22:1-14
The revelation of the riches of God's glory. Ro.9:23, cp. Eph.2:4-7, esp. 7
Things above & beyond what we can ask or even think. 1 Cor.2:9, cp. Eph.3:20
The things **p**. for the unbeliever.
Hell. Mt.25:41
The great invitation of God to be saved. Mt.22:1-14

PRESBYTERY
Duty. The **p**. is to lay hands upon those who are being ordained. 1 Tim.4:14

PRESENCE (See **INDWELLING PRESENCE**)

PRESSURE
Caused by. Deliverance from. Jn.4:16-18; Ph.4:6-7
Discussed. Mt.11:28-30

PRESTIGE
Fearing the loss of. Jn.11:47-48

PRESUME - PRESUMPTION
Sin of. Discussed. 2 Pt.2:10
Warning against.
Not to live a hypocritical life presuming that Christ is not the Son of God & that man determines his own destiny. 2 Pt.2:1, 10
Not to **p**. that life goes on & on & make plans without God. Lk.12:16-21; Jas.4:13-15
Not to **p**. upon Christ, not to tempt Him. 1 Cor.10:6-11, esp. 9

PRETEND - PRETENDING - PRETENSION (See **PROFESSION, FALSE;HYPOCRISY**)
Denial of **p**. Do not know Christ. Mt.26:69-70

PRIDE (See **ARROGANCE; BOASTING; GLORYING IN MAN; SELF-SUFFICIENCY**)
Caused by.
Ambition. Lk.9:46-50
Conceit-given responsibility too soon. 1 Tim.3:6
Boasting in one's knowledge. 1 Cor.8:2
Comparing & judging ministers. 1 Cor.4:6
Discussed. Lk.7:39
Evil heart. Mk.7:20-22
Feeling oneself is better than others. Ro.2:19; 12:16
Loving the preeminence, the desire to be first. 3 Jn.9-11
Religion of works. Col.2:20-23; 2:23
Roots & heritage. Mt.23:29-33
Seeking attention & recognition. Mt.6:2
Self-centeredness. Ro.3:27
Self-righteousness. Lk.18:11-12
Self-sufficiency. Lk.10:21; 18:9
Selfishness & self-glorying. Ph.2:3-4
Spiritual superiority. "But for the grace of God, there go I." Mt.8:4
Wealth. Creates the "big I." Mt.19:23; Mk.10:24
Works. Ro.4:1-3
Worldliness - the world. 1 Jn.2:15-16
Described.
As believing one is good enough to be acceptable to God. Lk.3:8; 7:39; 18:9
As puffed up air bags. 1 Cor.4:6
As saying, "But for the grace of God, there go I." Mk.1:44
As the pride of life. 1 Jn.2:15-16
Discussed. Lk.14:7-14; Ro.1:22-23; 3:27; 3:28
Fact. No man is better than another man-- not spiritually. Gal.6:3
Judgment of. Lk.6:24-26
Abased. Mt.23:12
Death. Lk.12:16-20
Excluded from heaven. Mt.19:23-26
Meaning. 1 Cor.13:4-7
Overcome by.
Acknowledging one's sinfulness. Lk.18:10-14
Faith. Ro.3:27-31
Humility. Ph.2:3-4; Col.3:12
Not loving the world. 1 Jn.2:15-16
Serving & giving quietly. Mt.6:3-4
Serving others. Mt.20:26-28
Submitting to others. 1 Pt.5:5-7
Results of **p**.
Boasting. Jas.3:3-5; 4:16
Causes one to act superior, self-sufficient, & super-spiritual. 1 Cor.4:7; 4:8
Causes one to seek the approval & honor of men. Jn.5:44
Causes one to seek position. Lk.14:7-11; 19:14-27
Causes one to seek recognition. Lk.14:12-14; 19:14-27
Causes one to turn from God to idols. Ro.1:22-23
Conceit. Ro.12:16; 1 Cor.8:2
Elevating oneself over others. Ro.2:19; 11:18; 12:16
God's resistance. Jas.4:5-6
Idolatry. Ro.1:22-23
Strife. Ph.2:3-4
To be condemned with the devil. 1 Tim.3:6
Verses. List of. Jn.5:44; 8:33

Sin of **p.**
  Discussed. Boasting what one has and does. 1 Jn.2:15-17
  The false minister. What he take **p.** in. 1 Tim.6:4
  The sin of the Corinthian church. 1 Cor.4:6; 4:7; 4:8; 5:1; 5:2; 5:6
  The sin of the religionists. Ro.3:27-31
Source. Man's claim to be too wise to believe in God. Ro.1:22-23
Verses. List of. Lk.10:21; 14:11
Vs. humility. Mt.18:1-4; Acts 4:23-24
Vs. the cross of Christ. 1 Cor.1:17-25
Warning against. (See **PRIDE,** Judgment of)
Religious **p.** Mt.23:1-12
To be scattered, lost. Lk.1:51-53

PRIEST - PRIESTS (See **HIGH PRIEST**)
Discussed. Acts 4:1; 1 Pt.2:9
Division of **p.** in Christ's day. Lk.1:5
Names of some **p.** Lk.1:5
  Zecharias, John the Baptist's father. Lk.1:5
Privilege of. Burning incense considered the highest privilege of the **p.** Lk.1:8-10
Some believed in Jesus Christ. Acts 6:7; 15:5; 18:8, 17

PRIESTHOOD
Discussed. 1 Pt.2:9
Need for. Felt by men throughout history. 1 Pt.2:9
P. of believers.
  Are a royal priesthood. 1 Pt.2:9
  Are being built into a holy priesthood. 1 Pt.2:5
  Are made a kingdom & priests. Rev.1:5-6; 5:10; 20:6
  Discussed. 1 Pt.2:9
  Duty. (See **SACRIFICE,** Duty)
    To present one's body as a living sacrifice to God. Ro.12:1-2
    To sacrifice oneself to do good & to give. Heb.13:16
  Purpose. To offer up spiritual sacrifices. 1 Pt.2:5
P. of Christ. (See **JESUS CHRIST,** Priesthood of)
  Jesus Christ is the supreme Priest of heaven. Heb.8:1-5
  Qualifications of. Heb.8:1-5
P. of Melchizedek. Type of Christ's **p.** Heb.7:1-24
P. of men.
  Discussed. Heb.5:1-10; 7:1-24; 8:1-9:28; 1 Pt.2:9
  Weakness & insufficiency of. Discussed. Heb.5:1-10; 7:1-24; 8:1-9:28
Problem. Deteriorated down through the years. Lk.20:19-21

PRIESTLY OFFICE OF CHRIST (See **JESUS CHRIST,** Priesthood of; Priestly office)

PRINCE OF PEACE (See **JESUS CHRIST**)

PRINCE OF THIS WORLD (See **SATAN**)

PRINCIPALITIES (See **ANGELS; EVIL SPIRITS; GOVERNMENT; SATAN**)

PRISCILLA
A lady believer. Discussed. Acts 18:2
Paul sent greetings to Priscilla while he was a prisoner. 2 Tim.4:19

PRISONERS
Believers imprisoned.
  Aristarcus. The believer who stood as a companion in trials. Col.4:10
  Believers. How God uses persecution. Acts 8:3
  John the Baptist. The godly vs. the immoral. Mt.14:3-4
  Paul & Silas. The power of sin & money & of Jesus' name. Acts 16:23
  Peter. God's pattern for deliverance. Acts 12:1-4
  The disciples. A picture of abuse. Acts 5:17-18
Ministry to. Discussed. Heb.13:3

PRIVILEGE (See **BELIEVERS,** Privileges of; **BLESSINGS; REWARDS**)
Degrees of. Determines judgment. Mt.11:20-24
Discussed. Lk.10:21-24

PROBLEMS (See **TRIALS**)
Answer to.
  Faith. Mt.17:20
  The love of God. Ro.8:28-39, esp. 38-39
Caused by.
  Circumstances of life. 1 Cor.7:17-24
  Trials & storms of life. Jn.6:17-19
Deliverance from. Jn.14:1-3
Verses. List of. Jn.6:17-19

PROCLAIM - PROCLAIMING
Call to. (See **CALL - CALLED**)
  Enabled by the Holy Spirit. 1 Pt.1:12
  P. is the first call of the minister. Mk.2:1-2; Lk.8:1
Conditions. For receiving messengers, preachers. Mk.9:38-41
Described.
  As a voice crying, "Prepare." Jn.1:23
  As sowing seed. How men receive the Word of God. Mt.13:3; Mk.4:1-20
Discussed. Lk.8:1; 1 Cor.2:1-5; 2 Tim.4:1-5
  Four Greek words used for **p.** & witnessing. Acts 11:19-30
  To **p.** baptism of repentance. Lk.3:3
  To. **p.** the good news. Lk.3:18, 16:16
  To **p.** the good news to the poor. Lk.4:18, 7:22
  To **p.** the gospel. Lk.9:6, 20:1
  To **p.** His name. Lk.24:47
Duty.
  A strong & true minister **p.** the gospel. 1 Th.1:5-10; 2:1-12
  Are obligated, indebted to **p.** Ro.1:14-15
  The charge to **p.** Acts 14:1; 2 Tim.4:1-5
  The first task of the minister. Acts 14:21
  To be a pattern & example of good works. Tit.2:7-8
  To center in the Scripture. Acts 17:1-2; 18:24; 18:25
  To exalt Christ & not self. Jn.3:29-30
  To fear **p.** another Jesus. 2 Cor.11:4; Gal.1:8-9
  To please God, not man. Not to use flattering words, nor to covet position or livelihood. 1 Th.2:5-6

To preach. Tit.1:2-3; 1:9
To **p.** boldly. 1 Th.2:2
To **p.** in the power of the Holy Spirit. 1 Cor.2:4; 1 Th.1:5
To **p.** peace. Lk.10:5-6
To **p.** social justice. Lk.3:10-14
To **p.** the gospel. To **p.** the gospel as it should be preached. 1 Th.1:5
To **p.** the kingdom of God. Lk.9:59-60; 10:8-9
To proclaim the grace of God through every means of speech. Tit.2:15
To reason & persuade. Acts 18:4
To sense the urgency of **p.** Acts 17:16; 18:4; Ro.1:14-15
Errors of. Mentioned. Mt.9:35
Essential.
  A preacher must focus upon the cross. 1 Cor.1:17-25
  Must focus upon the cross. 1 Cor.1:23
  Must have a compulsion to **p.** Discussed. 1 Cor.9:16-23
  Must have a preacher to **p.** Ro.10:14-15
Kinds.
  Christ-centered **p.** Mk.16:15; 1 Cor.1:17-25
  Divisive & envious **p.** Ph.1:15-16
  Empty **p.** Trait of false teachers. Jude 16
  God ordained **p.** 1 Cor.2:7
  Gospel **p.** 1 Cor.1:17-18; 9:16; Gal.1:6-9
  Human **p.** - Man-made **p.** 1 Cor.2:4
  Perverted & false **p.** Gal.1:6-9
  Powerless **p.** 1 Cor.1:17
  Spirit led **p.** 1 Cor.2:4-5; 2:13
Meaning. Mt.9:35; Mk.3:14; Lk.8:1; 2 Tim.4:2
Message of.
  Danger. Can be emptied of its power. Ways. 1 Cor.1:17
  Kingdom of God. Lk.4:43-44
  Preached by Jesus. Mt.4:17; 5:1-7:29; Mk.1:14-15
  Sound **p.** What it is. 1 Cor.2:1-5
  Subject - Content of. Acts 2:14-40; 3:12-26; 4:8-12, 20;5:29-32, 42; 7:1-53; 8:25, 32-35;9:20, 22; 10:34-43; 13:14-41; 14:7; 15:35; 16:30-32; 17:3, 11, 13, 22-34; 18:28; 19:8; 20:21; 1 Cor.1:17-25
    Discussed. Acts 2:14-24; 2:15-36; 9:20; 10:34-43; 13:14-41; 2 Cor.5:17-6:2
    Peace. Lk.10:5-6
    Social justice. Lk.3:10-14
    The cross. 1 Cor.1:17
    The good news of the gospel. Mk.1:14-15
    The Kingdom of God. Lk.4:43-44; 8:1; 9:59-60; 10:8-9
    The message to a heathen & superstitious people. Acts 14:8-20; 17:22-34
    The New Covenant, the covenant of the Spirit. 2 Cor.3:6-8
    The pattern of **p.** Acts 14:1-7
    The points for **p.** Acts 3:12-26
    The preeminence & power of Christ. Mk.1:7-8; Col.1:18-19
    What is to be preached. 1 Cor.1:17-25
  Summary of Jesus' message. Mt.4:17; 5:1-7:29
  The wisdom of words vs. the power of the cross. 1 Cor.1:17

Mission.
Of believers. Mt.4:17; Mk.1:36-38; 1:39
Of Christ. Mt.4:17; 11:4-6; Mk.1:36-38; 1:39; 2:1-2; Lk.4:17-19
P. of Paul. His only complete message in Scripture. Acts 13:14-41
P. of the early church.
Focused on the resurrection. Acts 2:25-36
Points for **p**. Acts 3:12-26
To a heathen & superstitious people. Acts 14:8-20; 17:22-34
Response to.
Counted as foolish by the lost. 1 Cor.1:17
Counted as the power of God by the saved. 1 Cor.1:17
Discussed. Mt.13:1-9
Fourfold response. Lk.8:4-15; Acts 13:42-52
How men receive the gospel. Mt.13:1-9
Discussed. Acts 11:19-30
Refuse to hear. Lk.6:27-31
Rejected. Lk.4:22-30
Ridiculed. Acts 17:18
Some repent, some reject. Lk.11:32
Unbelief. Does not benefit the hearer. Heb.4:2
Results.
Is rejected. And rejecters are to be rejected. Acts 13:46-48, 50-51
Provides the answer to division. 1 Cor.2:1-5
Stirs the people. But the excitement of the crowd is not always wise. Mk.6:45
Triumphs. 2 Tim.4:6-8
Turns the world upside down. Acts 17:1-9
Vs. tongues. 1 Cor.14:1-25
Where to **p**.
Everywhere. Mk.16:20
In houses & homes. Acts 5:42
In the public worship centers: the church, synagogues, & temples. Mk.1:39; Lk.4:44; Acts 5:42; 9:20; 13:5
In the towns & cities. Mt.11:1; Mk.1:38; Acts 15:21
On city streets & in the open air. Acts 14:8-9
To all nations, the whole world. Mk.16:15; Gal.1:16; 2:2; Eph.3:8; 1 Tim.3:16
To individuals. (See **WITNESS - WITNESSING**)
To the poor. Mt.11:5

PROCRASTINATION (See **EXCUSES; SLOTHFULNESS**)

PROCURATOR
Discussed. Mt.27:11-25

PRODIGAL SON
Parable of. Lost son. Lk.15:11-24

PROFANE (See **ABUSIVE; GODLESS**)
Meaning. Heb.12:15-17

PROFANITY (See **CURSING**)
Discussed. Mt.5:33-37; Ro.3:13-14

PROFESSION, FALSE - PROFESSION ONLY (See **HYPOCRISY**)
Danger of religionists. Mt.3:7-10
Described as.
Betrayal, apostasy, counterfeit. Jn.13:18-19
Big "I." Mt.7:21
Birds lodging in Christianity. Mt.13:31-32
By the path. Mt.13:4
Dramatic conversion. Often lacks depth. Lk.8:11-15
Path--wayside, hard soil. Mt.13:4, 19
Rocky soil. Mt.13:5-6, 20-21
Weeds. Unregenerate. Mt.13:25, 38-39
Thorns. Mt.13:7, 22
Discipline of. (See **CHURCH DISCIPLINE**)
Discussed. Mt.7:21-23; Ro.2:17-29 Jas.2:14-26; Rev.2:5-6; 3:16-17
Claiming to know God but not obeying God's commands. 1 Jn.2:4
Dramatic conversion, but false. Mt.13:5-6, 20-21
Four **f**. professions. Mt.16:13-14
Professing to know God but not loving one's neighbor. 1 Jn.2:7-11
Two kinds of people. Mt.7:21-23
Error -Misconceptions of.
Attends church, but sits off to the side. Lk.8:11-15
Claims to know God, but does not really know Him. Jn.8:41; 8:54-59; 1 Cor.5:11
Discussed. Jn.2:23; 2:24
Does not do God's will. Mt.7:21
Fails to see Christ. Mt.7:21
Lacks conviction against error & evil. Mk.3:5
One can become righteous on his own. 1 Jn.1:10-2:2
One can know God & walk in sin. 1 Jn.1:6-7
One is not totally sinful & depraved. 1 Jn.1:8-9
Professing yet hating one's brother. 1 Jn.2:9
Professing yet loving the world. 1 Jn.2:15-17
Professing yet not obeying God's commands. 1 Jn.2:4
Refuses to accept Jesus as the Messiah. Mk.7:6
Rejecting God & professing one's own wisdom & thoughts of God. Ro.1:22-23
Self-righteousness vs. Christ's righteousness. Mt.7:22
The error of religionists. Ro.2:17-29
The reasons why people follow Christ. Lk.7:11
Thinking that being a spectator is enough. Mt.3:7-10
Thinking that one is the light to men. Jn.1:9
Thinking that profession is enough. Lk.6:46
Thinking that profession only is adequate. Mt.9:4-7

Example of. (See **APOSTASY; DENY - DENIAL**)
Three examples of failing to count the cost. Lk.9:57-62
Within the church. Rev.2:9
Fact. Does not save a person. Acts 2:38
Identified. (See **PROFESSION, FALSE**, Described as)
As false religion. Mt.21:28-32
As persons who have the privileges of the gospel. Lk.13:26
As resting under the church's umbrella. Mk.4:30-32
As tares - growing with the wheat. Mt.13:24-30
Judgment.
Discussed. Mt.7:23; Lk.10:10-15
False **p**.
Will be rejected by Christ. Mt.7:23
Will be seen, examined, & condemned. Mk.11:12-14
Will make a threefold plea in the day of judgment. Mt.7:22
The **p**. of intellectual pride will be judged. Mt.11:25-27
Kinds. Materialistic **p**. Jn.6:14-15
Meaning. Mt.7:21
Results in.
Being denounced. Mt.21:28-32
Deception. Mk.11:13
False religion. Mt.21:28-32
Honoring oneself. Mt.7:21
Hypocrisy. Mt.23:25-28
Making one a liar. 1 Jn.4:20-21
Misjudging. Mt.11:16-19
Not continuing on in following Christ. Jn.8:31
One's life being condemned. Mk.11:12-14
Verses. List of. 1 Cor.5:11
Vs. action. Mt.9:4-7
Vs. true confession. Discussed. Mk.8:27-30
Warning against. Discussed. Mk.11:12-14
What it takes to enter God's kingdom. Mt.21:28-32

PROFESSION, SPIRITUAL OR RELIGIOUS (See **CONFESSION**)
Duty.
To consider the High Priest of our **p**. Heb.3:1
To hold fast our **p**. in Christ. Heb.4:14; 10:23
To lay hold on eternal life & to make a good **p**. 1 Tim.6:11-12
To profess godliness & to live godly. 1 Tim.2:9-10
To profess the gospel of Christ. 2 Cor.9:13
Essential **p**. Jesus is the Messiah. Mk.8:27-30
Kinds. Three **p**. Jn.6:66-71
Misconception. (See **PROFESSION, FALSE**)
Steps required in **p**. Discussed. Mk.10:46-52
True **p**.
Discussed.
Keeps God's Word. 1 Jn.2:5
Loves one's neighbor. 1 Jn.2:7-11
Kind of heart. Lk.8:11-15
Love proves. 1 Jn.2:15-16

MASTER SUBJECT INDEX

PROMINENCE
Love of. Is wrong. Lk.11:43

PROMISE - PROMISES (See **REWARD**)
Age of p. vs. the age of God's kingdom. Lk.7:28
Described as. (See **REWARD**)
Duty. Threefold. Ro.9:4
Promises to the believer.
The **p**. are based upon & rooted in Christ. 2 Cor.1:20; 2 Tim.1:1
The **p**. concerning the Holy Spirit.
His guidance. Jn.16:13
His presence. Jn.14:16-17
His teaching. Jn.14:26
The **p**. of prayer. (See **PRAYER**)
The **p**. of provision & care.
Abundance of life. Jn.10:10; 1 Pt.3:10
All things will be worked out for good. Ro.8:28; 2 Cor.4:17; 12:9
Comfort. Mt.9:22; Jn.14:18; 2 Cor.1:3-4
Daily provisions. If we seek God first. Mt.6:33
Deliverance from temptation. 1 Cor.10:13; 2 Pt.2:9
Peace. Jn.14:27; 16:33
Power to witness. Acts 1:8; 2 Tim.1:7
Protection & deliverance from every evil work. Mt.10:30-31; Jn.17:11; 2 Tim.4:18
Spiritual blessings & gifts. Lk.11:13
Spiritual rest. Mt.11:28
Strength. 2 Cor.12:9; Eph.1:18-19; 3:20; Col.1:11
To the persecuted believer. 1 Pt.3:13-14
Wisdom. Lk.21:15; Jas.1:5
The **p**. of rewards. (See **REWARDS**)
The **p**. of salvation & eternal life.
Conditional.
Must believe. Jn.5:24-25; 11:25-27
Must endure to the end. Mt.10:22
Forgiveness & spiritual cleansing. Mt.6:14; Acts 5:31; Eph.1:7; Heb.9:14; 1 Jn.1:7; 1:9
Made a partaker of God's divine nature. 2 Pt.1:4
Open to all men everywhere. Eph.3:6
Protection & deliverance from death. 2 Cor.1:10; Heb.2:14-15
The Lord's return. Jn.14:1-3
Surety of.
Are always fulfilled on time. Acts 7:17; Gal.4:4-7
Guaranteed & assured. Ro.4:20-21; 2 Cor.1:20; Heb.6:16-18
Is confirmed by Christ. Ro.15:8
Never voided or broken. Ro.3:3-4
Not broken by Israel's rejection. Ro.9:6
Verses. List of. Mk.16:7
To whom God makes p.
To believers. (See **PROMISES**, Promises to believers)
To children. 2 Tim.3:15-16
To families. Acts 2:39; 16:31; Eph.6:1-3; 1 Tim.2:9-15
To Israel. Ro.9:4
To laborers. Will do great works & greater than Christ. Jn.14:12

To the afflicted. 2 Cor.4:17
To the humble. Lk.14:11; Jas.4:6; 1 Pt.5:5-6
To the meek. Mt.5:5; Jas.1:21
To the merciful. Mt.5:7
To the obedient. Lk.11:28; 14:23; 15:10
To the peacemakers. Mt.5:9
To the pure in heart. Mt.5:8
To the troubled. Jn.14:1-3
To the weak. 2 Cor.12:9
To the younger son. Why God usually chose the younger son over the oldest to receive the **p**. of God. Ro.9:13
To those persecuted for righteousness. Mt.5:10-12
To those who forgive others. Mt.6:14
To those who give consistently. Lk.6:38; 2 Cor.9:7
To those who hunger after righteousness. Mt.5:6
To those who minister. Mt.25:31-40
To those who mourn. Mt.5:4
To those who repent. Acts 2:38; 3:19
To those who sorrow over the dead. 1 Th.4:13-18; Rev.21:4

PROMISED LAND
Described. As inheriting the world. Ro.4:13
Discussed. Acts 7:2-8
Type-Symbol of.
An eternal inheritance. Acts 7:2-8
Heaven. Heb.11:10; 11:13-16
New heaven & earth. Ro.4:13

PROOF - PROOFS
Discussed. Mt.4:3-11

PROPERTY
Damage to. Discussed. Mt.5:39-41

PROPHECY
Curiosity in. Causes distraction from one's duty. Jn.13:36-38
Discussed.
All the **p**. in the N.T. on the death of Christ & their fulfillment. Mt.17:23
All the **p**. in the N.T. on the resurrection of Christ & their fulfillment. Mt.17:23
Chart of the **p**. of the O.T. & their fulfillment in the N.T. Jn.1:45
The place of **p**. in the early church services. 1 Cor.14:26-40
Duty. Not to treat prophecies with contempt. 1 Th.5:20
Elements of **p**. Mt.1:22
Gift of.
Contrasted with tongues. 1 Cor.14:1-25; 14:26-40
Discussed. 1 Cor.12:8-10
Meaning. (See **ANTICHRIST**)
P. *concerning* Christ.
A Savior - Jesus. Acts 10:38; 13:23
Discussed.
Chart of the **p**. of the O.T. & their fulfillment in the N.T. Jn.1:45
Most verses & fulfillment. Lk.3:24-38
N.T. prophecies on Christ's death & their fulfillment. 1 Cor.15:3
N.T. prophecies on Christ's resurrection & their fulfillment. 1 Cor.15:4

To be High Priest. Verses & fulfillment. Lk.3:32-38
To be King. Verses & fulfillment. Lk.3:24-31
To be the Adamic heir. Verses & fulfillment. Lk.3:32-38
To be the heir of David. Verses & fulfillment. Lk.3:24-31; Acts 13:22-23
To be the Messiah. Verses & fulfillment. Jn.1:45
To be the Messianic ruler during the millennium. Rev.20:4-6
To be the Prophet of God. Verses & fulfillment. Lk.3:38
To be the "seed" of the woman. Fulfilled. Gal.4:4; cp. Gen.3:15
Verses & fulfillments listed. Lk.3:23-38; Jn.1:45; Acts 13:22-23; 1 Cor.15:3; 15:4; Rev.20:4-6
Events & fate of the child's life foretold. Lk.2:25-35
Fulfillment is sure. Lk.18:31
His betrayal by Judas. Acts 1:16, 20
His death & resurrection in the Gospel of John. Jn.20:20
His death & resurrection. All **p**. in John. Jn.20:20
His destiny. Death, resurrection, & ascension. Jn.7:33-34
His exaltation. Predicted by David. Lk.20:42-44
His Messiahship. Lk.4:17-19
His ministry. Lk.7:22
His Person & ministry. Lk.1:67-80
His resurrection. Acts 2:25-31; 13:32-37
P. by David. Acts 2:25-31
His return. (See **JESUS CHRIST**, Return) Acts 15:16
List of the **p**. & their fulfillments. Jn.1:45
P. by Moses. Acts 3:22
P. by Samuel. Acts 3:24
Work of. To reverse the order of five things. Lk.1:51-53
P. concerning Gentile believers. Acts 13:47; 15:16-17
P. concerning Jerusalem. Lk.21:5-8; 21:20-24
P. concerning John the Baptist. Forerunner. Mk.1:2
P. concerning Pentecost. Acts 2:16-21
P. concerning persecution. Mt.10:16-23; Acts 4:25-28
P. concerning the antichrist. Chart of the **p**. of Revelation with Daniel's **p**. Rev.13:1; 13:2
P. concerning the end time. (See **END TIME**)
A book of things hereafter - of destiny. Rev.4:1-5:14
A special blessing promised to the hearer of Revelation. Rev.1:3
Foretold the world's end. 2 Pt.3:1-7
Is scoffed at. 1 Cor.15:12; 2 Pt.3:3-13
Prophetic word to be proclaimed in the last days. Rev.10:8-11
Vision four of the Revelation. Rev.21:9-22:21
Vision one of the Revelation. Rev.1:9-3:22
Vision three of the Revelation. Rev.17:1-21:8
Vision two of the Revelation. Rev.4:1-16:21
P. concerning the gift of the Holy Spirit. Acts 2:17-21

P. fulfilled *by* Christ.
  All the **p.** in the N.T. on the death of Christ & their fulfillment. Mt.17:23
  All the **p.** in the N.T. on the resurrection of Christ & their fulfillment. Mt.17:23
  Chart of **p.** & their fulfillment. Lk.3:23-38; Jn.1:45
  Christ.
    Person & work. Mt.4:12-17; 5:17-18; 12:17-21
    Shiloh to come. Lk.2:1-24
  Deliberately fulfilled. Triumphal Entry. Mt.21:1-11; 21:2-5
  Fulfilled in Jesus' childhood. Mt.2:15
  Fulfilled in Jesus' ministry. Mt.11:5
  His being called a Nazarene. Mt.2:23
  His being called out of Egypt. Mt.2:13-23
  His being the seed of Abraham. Acts 3:25
  His birth. Mt.1:22-23
  His death. Lk.18:31-34; Acts 2:23; 4:25-28;8:32
  His mission. Mt.4:14-16
  His resurrection. Acts 2:25-36
  His sacrifice. 1 Pt.1:11-12
  Israel. Scepter passed from Judea. Five proofs. Lk.2:1-24
  List of the **p.** concerning Christ & their fulfillment. 2 Pt.1:19-21
  Must be fulfilled. Lk.18:31; 24:44-49
  Rejected - Unbelief in. Leads to the rejection of Christ. Jn.5:45-46
  Results of **p.** Proves salvation, the deity of Christ, & the Word of God. 2 Pt.1:19-21
  Surety of. Is of no one's own interpretation. 2 Pt.1:19-21

PROPHECY, GIFT OF
  Discussed. Ro.12:6-8; Eph.4:11
  P. & tongues.
    Ct. tongues. 1 Cor.14:1-5
    Effect upon unbelievers. 1 Cor.14:21-25
    The place of **p.** in the church. 1 Cor.14:26-40
    The place of tongues in the church. 1 Cor.14:26-40
  Purpose of. 1 Cor.14:1-5, 21-25; Eph.4:12-16
  To be tested by Jewish law. Acts 4:5-10
  View of. People thought **p.** was the highest call. Jn.9:16-17
  Work - exercise of. Predicted Timothy's call to the ministry. 1 Tim.1:18

PROPHET (See **PROPHECY**, Gift of)
  Call of. Purpose. To proclaim & predict God's great salvation. 1 Pt.1:10
  Christ is the **P.** of God. Verses of prophecy & fulfillment. Lk.3:38
  Discussed. Mt.11:9; Acts 11:27; Ro.12:6-8; Eph.4:11
  Honor of. A prophet is not without honor except in his own country. Jn.4:44
  Inspiration of.
    Discussed. 1 Pt.1:10-12
    The **p.** himself. Sought to understand his prophecies. 1 Pt.1:10-12
  Meaning. Mt.11:9; Eph.4:11
  Principles governing. Threefold. Lk.6:27-31
  Purpose. Eph.4:12-16

PROPHET OF REVELATION, FALSE
  Chief officer of the antichrist. Rev.13:11-18
  Discussed. Rev.13:11-18

PROPHETIC OFFICE (See **JESUS CHRIST**, Prophetic Office)
  Transferred to Christ. Mt.17:3

PROPHETS, FALSE (See **FALSE TEACHERS**)
  Discussed. 2 Pt.2:1-9
  In the last days. Predicted: will intensify. Lk.21:8
  Where they are. In the church. 2 Pt.2:1

PROPITIATION (See **ATONEMENT; ATONING SACRIFICE**)
  Discussed. Lk.18:13; Heb.2:17-18; 1 Jn.2:1-2;2:2
  Source.
    The sacrifice & death of Christ. 1 Jn.4:9-11

PROSELYTE (See **CONVERT**)
  Many sought to know the Lord. Acts 13:42-45
  To Judaism. Discussed. Mt.23:15

PROTECTS
  Meaning. Ro.15:1-3
  Of trials. Meaning. 1 Cor.13:4-7

PROSTITUTE (See **ADULTERY; IMMORALITY**)
  Repented. Was saved. Lk.7:37-38

PROTECT
  Duty.
    To keep oneself from idols. 1 Jn.5:21
    To keep oneself from sin. 1 Jn.5:18
    To keep oneself in the love of God. Jude 21
    To keep oneself pure. 1 Tim.5:22
    To keep oneself unspotted from the world. Jas.1:27
    To keep the commandments of God. Mt.19:17
    To keep the faith. 2 Tim.4:7
    To keep the Lord's commandments. Jn.14:21; 15:10, 14; 1 Jn.5:2
    To keep the trust, the gift of God--that which God has entrusted to oneself. 1 Tim.6:20
    To keep the words of the Book of Revelation. Rev.22:7, 9
    To keep this commandment: fight the good fight of faith & lay hold on eternal life. 1 Tim.6:11-14
    To strive to keep the unity of the Spirit. Eph.4:1-3, esp. 3
  Meaning. 2 Th.3:3-5
  Reward.
    Will abide in the love of Christ. Jn.15:10, 14
    Will be blessed. Rev.1:3; 22:7
    Will be blessed & given rest forever & ever. Rev.14:13
    Will be loved by God & Christ. Jn.14:21
    Will enter into life. Mt.19:17

PROUD (See **ARROGANT; PRIDE**)
  Meaning. 1 Cor.13:4-7;

PROVE - PROVED (See **TEST; TRIED**)
  Duty.
    To be proven before being ordained as a deacon. 1 Tim.3:10
    To examine & **p.** oneself, whether one be in the faith. 2 Cor.13:5
    To **p.** one's own work. Gal.6:4
    To **p.** the good will of God. Ro.12:1-2, esp. 2
    To **p.** the sincerity of one's love. 2 Cor.8:8-9

PROVIDENCE (See **GOD**)

PROVISION, DIVINE (See **CARE; PROMISES**, To the believer)
  Source. God. Verses. List of. Jn.6:10-13

PROVOKED (See **ANGER; WRATH**)

PRUDENCE - PRUDENT (See **UNDERSTANDING**)_
  Of the world. Truth hid from. Lk.10:21

PSYCHOLOGY
  Weakness of. 2 Tim.3:6-9

PUBLICAN (See **TAX COLLECTOR**)

PUBLICITY
  Reasons for not seeking. Christ's reasons. Mt.12:16

PUDENS
  Believer in Rome. Visited Paul in prison & knew Timothy. 2 Tim.4:21

PUFFED UP (See **PROUD**)

PUNISHMENT (See **FIRE; HELL; JUDGMENT; LAKE OF FIRE; VENGANCE**)
  Caused by.
    A desire to live as one wishes. Mk.6:24-25
    Being hurt by the sin of a loved one. Jn.8:3-6
  Duty. Not to take **p.** Three reasons. Ro.12:19-21
  Meaning. Lk.21:22; 2 Th.1:9
  Of judgment. Described. Ro.2:6-10

  Of the wicked. In eternity. Ro.2:6-10
  Results.
    God takes **p.** on the persecutors of His followers. Lk.18:6-7
    Verses. List of. Lk.21:22
  Warning.
    Evil men will suffer the **p.** of eternal fire. Jude 7
    God will take **p.** Ro.12:19; 2 Th.1:8

PURE - PURITY (See **MORALS - MORALITY**)
  Duty.
    Of wives. 1 Pt.3:2
    The church must clean out all leaven of sin--in **s.** & truth. 1 Cor.5:8
    To approve the best things in order to be **s.** & blameless. Ph.1:10
    To be an example in **p.** 1 Tim.4:12

To be **p**. from the blood of all men--by witnessing. Acts 20:26

To have a **p**. mind that is focused upon the Scriptures. 2 Pt.3:1

To hold the faith with a **p**. conscience. 1 Tim.3:9

To keep a **p**. body. Heb.10:22

To keep oneself **p**. 1 Tim.5:22

To keep oneself unspotted from the world. Jas.1:27

To live in holiness & godly **s**. 2 Cor.1:12

To live with a pure conscience. 2 Cor.1:12

To love in **s**. & to show it. 2 Cor.8:8, cp. 1 Jn.3:18

To preach & teach the Word of God in **s**. 2 Cor.2:17, cp. 1 Th.2:3-4

To serve God with a **p**. conscience. 2 Tim.1:3

To show **s**., purity in doctrine. Tit.2:6-7

To think only upon the things that are **p**. Ph.4:8

Fact.

All things are **p**. Ro.14:20

To the pure all things are **p**., but to the impure all things are impure. Tit.1:15

Meaning. Mt.5:8; 2 Cor.1:12; 6:6-7; Ph.1:9-10; 2:15; Jas.3:17-18; 1 Pt.2:2-3

Of morality. (See **MORALITY**)

Of the heart. Seeking. Jn.3:22-26

Perfect **p**. Impossible. Mt.5:8

Results of **p**.

Cleanses the mind & conscience. Tit.1:15

Gives one a pure religion. Jas.1:27

Love, a good conscience & an un-soiled conscience. 1 Tim.1:5-6

Source.

God's wisdom. Jas.3:17

Keeping one's heart on the Lord's return. 1 Jn.3:2-3

The heart. Mt.23:25-26

PURIFY

How to be purified. By confession. 1 Jn.1:9

PURPOSE (See **CALL - CALLED; MIS-SION**)

Earthly **p**. vs. spiritual **p**. Mt.6:19-20

P. of all things. God's glory. 1 Pt.4:11

P. of Christ. (See **JESUS CHRIST**, Purpose)

P. of God.

Discussed. Ro.8:29; 9:6-13; 9:14-33; 2 Tim.1:8-10

Focuses upon.

Christ. Eph.2:7; 3:10-12, cp. Acts 2:23; 4:25-28

Eternity. Eph.3:11

Salvation. Ro.8:28

For all things. Eph.1:3-23

For believers.

Eternally set. Ro.9:10-13; Eph.1:3-14

Predestined to be fulfilled. Eph.1:3-14

Saved for good works. Eph.2:10

His plan for the ages. Jn.4:22

His purpose is eternal. 2 Tim.1:8-10

P. of man. (See **MAN**, Creation, Purpose of; **MAN**, Purpose of)

P. of the believer.

Discussed. Ph.1:20-26

Not to focus one's **p**. upon fleshly desires & plans. 2 Cor.1:17

To be committed to Christ & His mission. 2 Tim.3:10-11

To be conformed to the image of Christ. Ro.8:29

To be focused upon spiritual **p**. no matter the cost. 2 Tim.3:10-11

To bear fruit. Lk.13:6-9

To do good works & to glorify God. Mt.5:14-16

To give light to the world. Mt.5:14-16

To have one's spirit focused upon evangelism & ministry. Acts 19:21-25

To heal the bruised, not condemn them. Mt.12:20

To live *is* Christ. Ph.1:21

To magnify Christ. Ph.1:20

To obey God & share in Christ's blood. 1 Pt.1:2

To show forth the praises of God. 1 Pt.2:9

To subdue the earth. Ro.13:9

Why God created man. Jn.4:23-24; 4:23

P. of the Holy Spirit. (See **HOLY SPIRIT**, Work of)

Without **p**.

Being blind.

Hate blinds one to real **p**. in life. 1 Jn.2:11

Not seeing God's **p**. Mt.11:25-27

Not seeing one's **p**. 2 Pt.1:9

Many just do not know their **p**. on earth. Mt.4:12-17

What causes. 2 Pt.1:9

PUT INTO EFFECT

Meaning. 1 Cor.9:16-17; Eph.1:9-10; 3:1-2

Old vs. New **p**. Lk.16:16; 16:17-18

PUT ON - SPIRITUAL CLOTHING

Duty.

To put on Christ. Discussed. Ro.13:14

To put on seven things. Ro.13:14

To put on the new man. Eph.4:20-24; Col.3:8-11

PUT TO DEATH

Meaning. Ro.8:12-13; Col.3:5-7

PUTEOLI

Discussed. Seaport of Italy. Acts 28:13

Q

QUARREL (See **ARGUE - ARGU-MENTS; DIVISION; STRIFE**

Caused by.

Arguing over ministers, which one is better. 1 Cor.1:11-16, esp. 11

Biting & devouring one another. Gal.5:15

Differences of conviction. Acts 15:36-41

Discussed. Acts 15:36-41; 1 Tim.4:7; 6:20-21; 2 Tim.2:14; 2:16-18; 2:23; 2:24-26; Tit.3:2

Duty.

Must not **q**. 2 Tim.2:24-26

To do nothing through strife or **q**. Ph.2:3-4

To put off the clothing of **q**. Eph.4:31; Col.3:13

To turn away from. Tit.3:9

Honest **q**. Study of. Acts 15:36-41

Meaning. Ro.2:8; 1 Cor.1:11

Results - Signs of being **c**.

A great sense of unworthiness. Lk.5:8

A pricking, convicting, bothersome conscience & heart. Acts 9:5

Obedience. Doing what Christ demands. Acts 9:5-6, cp. 1-11

Reaction, a defensive attitude. Jn.20:24-25, cp. 26-29

Trembling, but rejecting & becoming harder. Acts 24:24-25

Source - Caused by.

Genuine differences. Acts 15:36-41

Lust. Jas.4:1-2

Self-seeking. Mt.20:20-28

Sin. Mk.6:17-19

Verses. List of. Ro.2:8

QUARTUS

A Corinthian believer, a strong brother in the Lord. Ro.16:23

QUEEN OF SHEBA

Example. Of seeking the truth. Lk.11:31

QUEEN OF THE SOUTH

Example. Of great wisdom. Mt.12:42

QUENCH - QUENCHING

Faith quenches persecution. Heb.11:34

Not to **q**. the Spirit within one's heart & life. 1 Th.5:19

QUESTION - QUESTIONING

A **q**. disciple. Assurance given. Mt.11:1-6

About Christ. (See **JESUS CHRIST**, Related Subjects)

Cause. Unbelief. Jn.7:20-24; 7:25-31

Is an attempt to discredit Christ. Mt.22:15-22

Is illogical & inconsistent. Jn.12:37-41

Q. the Lord's deity. Lk.7:18-28; Jn.18:33-37

About the end time. Mt.24:1-4; Acts 1:6-7

About who is greatest in the kingdom of heaven. Mt.18:1-4

Answer to. Discussed. Mt.11:7

Discussed. Questioning, yet still believing. Mt.11:2-3

QUICKEN - QUICKENING (See **RES-URRECTION, SPIRITUAL**)

Meaning. Eph.2:4-5

Seeing & understanding the gospel as never before. Jn.6:44-46 Results.

Abundant & eternal life. Jn.5:21

Salvation. Eph.2:4-7

Source.

Christ. 1 Cor.15:45

God.

Because He loves us. Eph.2:4-5

God quickens all things. 1 Tim.6:13

God & Christ. Quickens the dead. Jn.5:21

The Holy Spirit. Quickens the Words of Christ to the heart of man. Jn.6:63-64

Who is **q**.

The spiritually dead. Jn.5:21

Those who are "dead" in sins. Eph.2:4-5

QUIET - QUIETNESS
Duty - Essential. Mt.3:1
    To be still in the presence of God.
      Lk.9:36; 19:40-52
    To clothe one's marriage with a meek
      & **q**. spirit. 1 Pt.3:4
    To clothe oneself with a meek & **q**.
      spirit. 1 Pt.3:4
    To conquer temptation. Mt.4:1
    To live a **q**. life 1 Th.4:11
    To work in **q**. 2 Th.3:12
    Verses. List of. Lk.9:36

QUIET TIME (See DEVOTIONS)
Essential. To have needs met. Lk.18:39
Inconsistent. Reasons. Mt.6:6

R

RABBI - RABBONI
Meaning. Jn.20:14-16

RACE, CHRISTIAN (See CHRISTIAN RACE)

RACHEL
Prophecy concerning. Fulfilled. Mt.2:17-18

RACIAL SLUR (See PREJUDICE)
An insult against Christ. It is not worthy
    of comment or attention. Jn.8:48-50

RAGE
Meaning. Acts 4:25-28

RAHAB
Faith of.
    A saving faith. Heb.11:31
    Proved her faith by deeds. Jas.2:25-26
Saved by God. Mt.1:5

RAILING - RAILER (See SLANDER)
Duty.
    Not to fellowship with a railer.
      1 Cor.5:11
    Not to rail, even when railed against.
      1 Pt.3:9
Trait of.
    False teachers. 2 Pt.2:10-12
    Unbelievers. Mk.15:29-32; Lk.23:39

RAISING THE DEAD (See DEAD, Raised)

RANSOM (See REDEEM - REDEMPTION)
Discussed. 1 Cor.6:20
Meaning. Mt.20:28; Mk.10:45
Verses. List of. Mk.10:45; 1 Cor.6:20

RAPTURE (See JESUS CHRIST, RETURN)

RASH
Example of.
    A foolish traveler. Lk.10:29-37
    A mob reacts recklessly or rashly
      against the gospel. Acts 19:35-41
Meaning. 2 Tim.3:2-4

RASHNESS (See RECKLESS)

RATIONALISM - RATIONALISTS (See PHILOSOPHY; REASON - REASONING)
Arguments that corrupt. Mt.23:13-36
Prospects for the gospel. Acts 17:18
Three basic misconceptions of man. (See
    MAN, Errors - Mistakes of; Misconceptions) 1 Jn.1:6-2:2
To avoid. Discussed. 2 Tim.2:14-21

RAVENS
Fed by God. Lk.12:24

READY - READINESS (See JESUS CHRIST, Returns)
Duty.
    To be **r**. always to give an answer to
      every man for one's hope. 1 Pt.3:15
    To be **r**. to do every good work.
      Tit.3:1
    To be **r**. to do good & to give.
      1 Tim.6:17-19, esp. 18
    To be **r**. to enter heaven when all things
      are prepared. Mt.22:1-14, esp. 4, 8
    To be **r**. to exercise discipline in the
      church. 2 Cor.10:6
    To be **r**. to preach the gospel. Ro.1:15
    To be so dedicated--to have served &
      ministered so much--that one is **r**. to
      be offered to God. 2 Tim.4:6-8, esp. 6
    To follow through when the heart is **r**.
      & prepared. 2 Cor.8:11
    To prepare & make **r**. a people for the
      Lord. Lk.1:17
    To receive the Word with **r**. of mind.
      Acts 17:11
    To watch for the Lord's return.
      Lk.12:35-48
    To willingly serve & feed the people
      of God. 1 Pt.5:2-3
Facts.
    God is ready to judge both the living
      & the dead who live worldly & uncommitted lives. 1 Pt.4:4-5
    The believer's salvation is **r**. to be revealed in the last time. 1 Pt.1:5
    The old covenant is **r**. to pass away.
      Heb.8:13
    The things in the church that are **r**. to
      die are not hopeless. They can be
      strengthened--Christ demands it.
      Rev.3:2

REAL - REALITY
Jesus, The **R**. Jn.1:9
Source. Jesus Christ. Col.2:9-10

REAP - REAPING (See WITNESSING)
Fact.
    The reaping of God's care.
      The birds of the air do not **r**., &
        God cares for them. Of how much
        greater value are believers.
        Mt.6:26; Lk.12:24
    The reaping of judgment.
      The tares or unbelievers of the earth
        shall be **r**., gathered, & burned.
        Mt.13:30, 37-42
      The time is coming when the sickle
        of God shall **r**. the harvest of the
        earth. Rev.14:15-16
    The reaping of reward.
      A man reaps exactly what he sows.
        Jn.12:39-41; Gal.6:7-9

The person who **r**. souls shall receive great wages, that of eternal
    life. Jn.4:35-38
The person who sows little shall **r**.
    little, & the person who sows
    much shall **r**. much. 2 Cor.9:6
The reaping of souls.
    The fields of souls are ripe for harvest. Jn.4:35-38
The reaping of unjust treatment.
    The cries of the reaper or laborer
      who is treated unjustly shall be
      heard by God. Jas.5:4
Law of. A person **r**. what he sows.
    Gal.6:7-9

REASON - REASONING - REASONABLE (See PHILOSOPHY; RATIONALISM; SUBMISSIVE; WISDOM, Of Men)
Errors - Failures of.
    Cannot save man. 1 Cor.2:5; 2:6; 2:7-9;
      Col.2:8. Cp. Ro.1:18-32
    Is sometimes based upon false beliefs.
      Mk.2:6-12
    Is used by men to escape the truth.
      Mk.11:29-33
Essential.
    In life. Must do the only reasonable
      thing: commit one's body & service
      as a living sacrifice to God. Ro.12:1-2
    In preaching & witnessing. Must be
      sound, logical. Acts 18:4, 19; 24:25,
      cp. Acts 17:2
Proves. God's existence. Ro.1:19

REBELLION (seditions) (See DISSENSIONS; REJECTION; UNBELIEF)
Against government. Discussed. Ro.13:1-7
Against the Lordship of Christ.
    Mt.12:14-16
Characteristic - Trait. Of false teachers.
    Jude 8, 11
Discussed. Lk.11:44; 17:1-2; Heb.5:11-
    6:3; 2 Pt.1:10
Duty.
    Not to **f**. by persecution & ridicule.
      Mt.13:21; Mk.4:17; Jn.16:1-4
    Not to do anything that will make a
      brother **f**. Ro.14:21
    Not to **f**. in anything. 1 Cor.10:32;
      2 Cor.6:3
    Not to **f**. in questionable activities.
      Ro.14:1-23; 1 Cor.8:1-13
    Not to cause others to **f**. 1 Cor.8:9-11;
      10:23-28; 10:29-11:1
    To be without **f**. until the day of
      Christ. Ph.1:10
    To cut out of one's life all that **f**.
      Mt.5:29-30; 18:7-9; Mk.9:43-48
    To mark those who cause division & **f**.
      Ro.16:17-18
Fact.
    Christ died for our **f**. Ro.4:25
    Many will be **f**. because of Christ in
      the end time. Mt.24:9-10
    The gift of Christ justifies us from
      many **f**. Ro.5:16
    We all **f**. in many things, especially in
      word & tongue. Jas.3:2
How. Six ways. Mk.9:42
In the end time. Discussed. 2 Th.2:3;
    1 Tim.4:1-2; 2 Tim.3:1-5
Judgment of those who **f**. Shall be cast
    into a furnace of fire. Mt.13:37-42

Meaning. Mt.5:29; 17:27; Mk.14:27; 2 Cor.6:3; Ph.1:9-10; Heb.6:6;
Precautions against. Six precautions. Heb.6:9-20
Steps to correcting. Mt.18:15-20
Verses. List of. Mk.9:42
Warning against **f.** others. Mt.18:5-10; Lk.17:1-2
   If one **f.** in one point, he is guilty of all the law. Jas.2:10
Ways one causes others to sin. Mt.18:15
What **f.** men about Christ.
   Four things **f.** Jn.6:59-71
   His claims. Jn.6:61
   His cross, blood. Jn.6:61; 1 Cor.1:23; Gal.5:11
   His Lordship. Jn.6:62
   His Person & claims. 1 Pt.2:7-8
   His works. Mt.11:1-6, esp. 6; Mt.13:53-58

REBIRTH
Described. A new life & religion. Mk.2:21; 2:22
Discussed. Jn.3:1-15; 2 Cor.5:17
Duty.
   Not to be conformed to this world, but renewed. Ro.12:2
   To be renewed in knowledge, in the very image of God. Col.3:10
   To be transformed by renewing our minds. Ro.12:2
   To **r.** the inner man day by day. 2 Cor.4:16
How to be renewed.
   By putting on the new man. Col.3:10
   By regeneration & renewing of the Holy Spirit. Tit.3:5
   By renewing our minds. Ro.12:2; Eph.4:23
Meaning. Mt.19:28; Jn.3:1-15
Result.
   Changes a person's life radically. Jn.4:30; 2 Cor.5:17
   Salvation. Tit.3:5
Reward. Predicted by Christ. Lk.22:30
Source.
   God. His mercy. Tit.3:5
   The creative power of Christ. Jn.2:3-5; 2:6-8
Vs. reformation. Mt.12:43-45; Lk.11:24-26

REBUKE - REBUKED (See FAULT, WITHOUT)
By Jesus Christ. (See **HEAL - HEAL-ING; JESUS CHRIST,** Power Of)
   He **r.** & chastens the irresponsible & sinning believer. Heb.12:5
   He **r.** disease. Lk.4:39
   He **r.** His disciples for being worldly & carnal. Mk.8:27-33, esp. 33; Lk.9:55-56, cp. 51-56
   He **r.** nature & delivers men. Mt.8:26; Mk.4:39; Lk.8:24
   He **r.** sickness & evil spirits. Mt.17:14-21; Lk.4:38-39
   He **r.** the devil & evil spirits & sets people free. Mt.17:18; Mk.1:25; 9:25; Lk.4:35; 9:42
   He **r.** those He loves. Rev.3:19
Duty.
   Not to despise the rebuke of the Lord. Heb.12:5-7
   Not to **r.** an elder, but appeal to him as a father. 1 Tim.5:1

To be without **r.** in the midst of a crooked & perverse nation. Ph.2:15
To call upon the name of the Lord in rebuking Satan. Jude 9
To **r.** & convict people. Tit.2:15
To **r.** a faithless & perverse generation. Lk.9:41
To **r.** a judgmental spirit. Lk.9:55-56
To **r.** false teachers. Tit.1:13-14
To **r.** hypocritical living. Mt.3:7-10; Gal.2:11-13
To **r.** sinning brothers. Lk.17:3-4
To **r.** those who resist the Holy Spirit. Acts 7:51
To **r.** those who sin before all. 1 Tim.5:20
To use the Word of God to **r.** people. 2 Tim.3:16; 4:2
To willingly receive the **r.** of the Lord. Heb.12:5-7
Meaning. 1 Tim.5:1; 2 Tim.4:2

REBUKE, WITHOUT

RECEIVE (See WELCOME)
Duty.
   Not to **r.** the grace of God in vain. 2 Cor.6:1
   Not to touch any unclean thing & God will **r.** one. 2 Cor.6:17-18
   To be faithful in feeding the people of God & one shall **r.** a crown of glory. 1 Pt.5:2-4
   To do the will of God that one might **r.** the promise. Heb.10:36
   To endure temptation that one may **r.** the promise of life. Jas.1:12
   To humbly **r.** the Word which is able to save one's soul. Jas.1:21
   To keep God's commandments so that we can **r.** the answers to our prayers. 1 Jn.3:22
   To **r.** a spiritual inheritance. Acts 26:18
   To **r.** Christ Jesus the Lord. Col.2:6
   To **r.** forgiveness of sins. Acts 10:43; 26:18
   To **r.** one another even as Christ received us. Ro.15:7
   To **r.** one's reward. Through diligent labor. 1 Cor.3:8; 3:13-15; 2 Jn.8
   To **r.** others. Lk.9:49-50
   To **r.** the answer to prayer. Through asking, believing, & living an obedient life. Mt.21:22; Mk.11:24; Jn.16:24; 1 Jn.3:22
   To **r.** the Holy Spirit. Through faith & baptism. Acts 2:38
   To **r.** the Word of God & bring forth fruit for God. Mk.4:20
   To **r.** the Word of God which is able to save our soul. Jas.1:21
   To **r.** those weak in the faith. Ro.14:1
   To watch & examine ourselves that we **r.** a full reward. 2 Jn.8
Facts.
   A doubleminded person shall not **r.** anything of the Lord. Jas.1:5-8, esp. 7
   A person can **r.** nothing unless it is given by God. Jn.3:27; 1 Cor.4:7
   A person prays & asks & does not **r.** because he asks amiss; he asks to consume it upon his lusts. Jas.4:2-3
   Believers **r.** power after the Holy Spirit is come upon them. Acts 1:8

Believers who forsake all for Christ shall **r.** a hundredfold from God. Mt.19:28-29; Mk.10:29-30
Christ is coming again to **r.** all believers to Himself. Jn.14:2-3
Faithful believers shall **r.** the reward of the inheritance. Col.3:23-24
False teachers shall **r.** the reward of their unrighteousness. 2 Pt.2:13
God sent His Son to redeem us that we might **r.** the adoption of sons. Gal.4:3-5
Hypocritical religionists shall **r.** the greater damnation. Mt.23:14; Mk.12:40; Lk.20:49
In the day of judgment everyone shall **r.** the things done in his body, whether good or bad. 2 Cor.5:10
It is more blessed to give than to **r.** Acts 20:35
The heavens have **r.** Christ until the restoration of all things. Acts 3:19-21
The Lord alone is worthy to **r.** all power, glory & honor. Rev.4:11; 5:12
The world cannot **r.** the Holy Spirit of God. Jn.14:16-17
Those who do wrong shall **r.** for the wrong they have done, & there is no respect of persons with God. Col.3:25
Those who **r.** God's ministers & people shall receive an equal reward with them. Mt.10:40-42
Unbelievers **r.** more & more enslavement to sin. Ro.1:26-27
Whatever good thing a person does, the same shall be **r.** of the Lord. Eph.6:8
Wrong-doers shall **r.** for the wrong they have done. Col.3:24-25
Meaning. Ro.15:7-12

RECENT CONVERT
Meaning. 1 Tim.3:6

RECEPTIVE - RECEPTIVITY (See JE-SUS CHRIST, Response to)
Duty. To be **r.** to Christ. Jn.4:45

RECKLESS - RECKLESSNESS (See RASH)
Example of.
   A foolish traveler. Lk.10:29-37
   A mob reacts recklessly or rashly against the gospel. Acts 19:35-41
Meaning. 2 Tim.3:2-4

RECKON (See CREDITED; SETTLE-MENT)
Meaning. Mt.18:24; 2 Cor.5:18-19

RECOGNITION (See PRIDE; SELF-RIGHTEOUSNESS; SELF-SEEKING)
Discussed. Mt.6:1-4
Human **r.** fails. Mt.6:5
Seeking **r.** Discussed. Lk.11:43; 14:7-14; 19:14-27;Jn.5:44; 3 Jn.9-11

RECOMPENSE (See PAYBACK; RE-TALIATION; REVENGE)

RECONCILE - RECONCILIATION
(See **JESUS CHRIST**, Death, Sacrifice;
**JUSTIFICATION; PROPITIATION;
REDEMPTION**)
Discussed. Lk.15:20-24; Ro.5:10;
2 Cor.5:18-19; Eph.2:16-17; Col.1:20-23
Duty.
To be **r.** to God. 2 Cor.5:19-21
To be **r.** to one's brother. Mt.5:23-24
To be **r.** to one's spouse. 1 Cor.7:10-11
Meaning. Ro.5:10; 2 Cor.5:18-19;
Eph.2:16-17
Message of. Eph.1:9-10
Purpose of. Col.1:23
Results.
Brings peace with God. Jn.14:27;
Ro.5:1; Eph.2:16-17; Col.1:20
Creates one body of people, a true
peace & brotherhood. Eph.2:16-17
Frees a person from sin. Heb.2:17-18
Gives a person the ministry of **r.**
2 Cor.5:18
Restores a person. Lk.15:22-24
Source.
Christ's blood. Col.1:20
Christ's death. Ro.5:10; 2 Cor.5:18;
Heb.2:14-18
Christ's priesthood. Heb.2:17-18
The cross. Eph.2:16; Col.1:20
Steps to. Correcting divisiveness.
Mt.18:15-20
Verses. List of. Ro.5:10
Who needs **r.** Man needs **r.** not God.
1 Jn.2:1-2

RECREATION (See **SOCIAL FUNC-
TIONS**)
Questionable **r.** Discussed. 1 Cor.8:9-11;
10:4-11:1

REDEEM - REDEMPTION
Assurance of. God will complete what He
began. Ph.1:6
Described.
As eternal **r.** Heb.9:11-14; 9:15
As the day of **r.** Eph.4:30
Discussed. 1 Cor.6:20; 2 Cor.5:21;
Eph.1:7; Col.1:14; 1 Tim.2:3-7;
Tit.2:11-15; 2:14; Heb.9:11-14; 9:15;
1 Pt.1:18-20
Meaning. Mt.20:28; Ro.3:24;
Gal.3:13-14; 1 Pt.1:18-20
Message. Verses. List of. Lk.2:38
Purpose - Results.
To adopt. Gal.4:4-7
To assure believers of heaven.
Rev.14:1-5, esp. 3-4
To bring righteousness & justification
to man. Ro.5:8-9; 5:10-11
To bring the blessings of Abraham to
the Gentile--all people. Gal.3:13-14
To cleanse the conscience. Heb.9:11-14
To deliver man from an empty life &
empty tradition & religion.
1 Pt.1:18-20
To forgive sins. Col.1:14; Tit.2:14
To free man from the curse of the law,
the bondage to sin & death.
Gal.3:13-14
To free man from the law. By Christ's
death. Ro.7:4
To give faith & hope in God.
1 Pt.1:18-21 esp. 21
To justify man. Ro.3:24

To purify a special people, a people
who would be God's very own pos-
session. Tit.2:14, cp.
1 Cor.6:19-20
To redeem man. 1 Tim.2:3-7
To save all creation. Ro.8:18-27
Source.
Christ. 1 Tim.2:3-7
Christ becoming a man. Gal.4:4-7
Christ being made a curse for man.
Gal.3:13-14
God. Lk.1:68
God's grace. Ro.3:24
The blood of Christ. Ro.3:24-26;
Heb.9:11-14; 9:15;1 Pt.1:18-20
The death of Christ. Mk.9:31;
Lk.2:38; Ro.5:6-7;Rev.1:5-6; 5:9
The Holy Spirit. Seals believers until
the day of **r.** Eph.4:30
Stages of **r.** Future. Is eternal. Lk.21:28
Verses. List of. Mk.9:31; 10:45;
Ro.3:24; 1 Cor.6:20

REFORMATION
Discussed. Mt.12:43-45
Inadequate. Corrupts even more.
Lk.11:24-26
Vs. regeneration. Lk.11:24-26

REFUSE - REFUSING
Discussed. The danger of **r.** to hear Jesus
Christ--of shutting one's ear to the cry
of His blood. Heb.12:25-29
Duty.
Not to **r.** God. Heb.12:25
Not to **r.** godly leadership. Acts 7:35-36
To **r.** speculations that differ from the
Word of God. 1 Tim.4:7
To **r.** the world & pleasures of sin.
Heb.11:24-25
Meaning. Heb.12:25

REGENERATION--RENEWAL (See
**BORN AGAIN; NEW BIRTH;
QUICKENING; REBIRTH; RE-
NEWAL; SALVATION**)
Described. A new life & religion.
Mk.2:21; 2:22
Discussed. Jn.3:1-15; 2 Cor.5:17; Tit.3:5
Duty.
Not to be conformed to this world, but
renewed. Ro.12:2
To be renewed in knowledge, in the
very image of God. Col.3:10
To be transformed by renewing our
minds. Ro.12:2
To **r.** the inner man day by day.
2 Cor.4:16
How to be renewed.
By putting on the new man. Col.3:10
By regeneration & renewing of the
Holy Spirit. Tit.3:5
By renewing our minds. Ro.12:2;
Eph.4:23
Meaning. Mt.19:28; Jn.3:1-15
Result.
Changes a person's life radically.
Jn.4:30; 2 Cor.5:17
Salvation. Tit.3:5
Reward. Predicted by Christ. Lk.22:30
Source.
God. His mercy. Tit.3:5
The creative power of Christ. Jn.2:3-5;
2:6-8
Vs. reformation. Mt.12:43-45; Lk.11:24-26

REJECT - REJECTED - REJECTION
(See **REBELLION; UNBELIEF**)
Answer to. Mt.9:20-22
Described. Mk.7:24-30
Duty.
To care for **r.** people. Mt.9:20-22; 9:20
To **r.** all divisive & heretical people.
Tit.3:10-11
To turn away from **r.** Lk.10:10-15;
Acts 13:46-52
To warn man, then leave him alone.
Lk.9:3-5
Judgment.
Causes Christ to turn away. Mt.9:1
Causes the Holy Spirit to turn away.
Mt.12:14-16
Jesus leaves & never returns. Mt.9:1
Judicial blindness & **r.** by God.
Mt.13:13-15
Of rejecters. Lk.10:10-15
To be judged in the last days--by the
words of Christ. Jn.12:47-48
To be rejected & turned away from.
Acts 13:46-52; 14:6-7
To be rejected, cursed, & burned.
Heb.6:7-8
Rejection of Christ. (See **JESUS
CHRIST**, Response to; Unbelief)
By the citizens of the world.
Lk.19:14; Jn.1:10-11
By unbelievers. 1 Pt.2:7-8
His claims to be Messiah. Lk.4:24-27
His cross. Lk.2:34-35
Warning against. Three reasons.
Heb.12:25-29
Will not always contend with man.
Lk.4:28-30
What it is that man rejects.
God's great invitation. Time & again.
Mt.22:1-14
Jesus Christ. (See **REJECTION**, Of Christ)
The commandments of God. Mk.7:9
The gospel.
By Herod. Lk.23:8
Hardened to. Mt.13:4, 19
Men. Often **r.** because of their cir-
cumstances. Mt.9:20-22; 9:20
The Word of God. Various persons **r.**
the Word. Mt.13:4-7
Who **r.** Several rejecters described.
Mt.22:5-6
Why men reject. Many reasons.
Mt.19:22; 22:3-4

REJOICE - REJOICING (See **BEING
GLAD; JOY**)
Duty. To **r.**
Always. 1 Th.5:16
In God our Savior. Lk.1:47-48
In God's work within one's life. Jas.1:9-
11
In hope. Ro.12:12
In receiving faithful believers.
Ph.2:29-30
In sorrow & trials. 2 Cor.6:10
In suffering. 1 Pt.4:12-13
In the fact that one's name is written in
heaven, in the Book of Life.
Lk.10:20
In the joy of others. Ro.12:15
In the Lord. Ph.3:1; 4:4; 1 Th.5:16
In the salvation of the lost. Lk.15:5-6;
15:9
In the words & teachings of Christ.
Jn.15:11
In trial & persecution. Acts 5:41; 16:25

Meaning. Lk.10:21; Jn.14:28-28
Of Jesus. Lk.10:21

RELATIONSHIPS (See **BROTHER-HOOD**)
Discussed. Spirit & discipline of **r.**
1 Tim.5:1-2
Man & woman. Discussed. 1 Cor.11:2-16

RELIGION (See **CEREMONY; RELIG-IONISTS; RITUAL**)
Christ used established **r.** Mk.1:39
Conflicted with Jesus. Reasons.
Mt.12:1-8; 12:9-13; 12:10
Described. Rev.17:1-6
Myths or the commands of those who
reject the truth. Tit.1:13-14
Ritual, tradition. Mk.7:1-13
Rules & regulations. Mk.2:23-28; 3:1-6;
Lk.5:30-35
False approach to **r.**
By astrology. Col.2:8-10
By spirits. Col.2:18-19
By visions. Col.2:18-19
Godless. Described. Rev.14:8
In the end time.
Apostate. Will be destroyed by God.
Rev.14:8
Discussed. To be corrupt. 2 Tim.3:1-9
World-wide **r.**
To be enforced by the antichrist.
2 Th.2:4
Worship of the state. Rev.12:1-2;
13:4-8; 13:13-17; 17:1-6; 17:7-18
Jewish. (See **JUDAISM**)
Jews offered a moral **r.** for Jesus' day.
Acts 16:14
Laws of. Jewish laws. Mt.12:1-8
Need.
To be redeemed from empty **r.**
1 Pt.1:18-20
To be straightened out. Jn.1:23
To know that Christ is greater than **r.**
Mt.12:1-8
To know that man is greater than **r.**
Mt.12:9-13
To know that **r.** is less important than
man. Lk.6:1-11; 13:10-17; 14:1-6
To know that **r.** is superseded by sav-
ing life. Lk.6:6-11
To know that the mechanics of **r.** are
replaced by Christ. Mt.9:16-17; 9:16
To know that the need has precedence
over **r.** Mt.12:5; Lk.6:1-11
Of feelings. Sensationalism. Temptation
of. Lk.4:9-12
Of the ancient world. Corrupt. Acts 16:14
Old vs. new religion. Mt.9:16-17
Problem with - Weaknesses of - Errors
of.
Discussed. Mt.23:1-12; Col.2:20-23;
Heb.13:9-11
Accusation against. Nine **a.**
Mt.23:13-36
Evils of. Mk.8:14-21
Four terrible things. Mt.27:1-5
Fourfold problem. Mt.12:10
In relation to man.
Deceives & defiles man. Mt.15:1-9
Has a misconception of man. Thinks
that **r.** is righteousness. Mt.21:31
Imposes rules & regulations upon
men. Mt.23:4
Is inconsistent & deceptive.
Mt.27:6-10
Is orthodox, but without love.
Rev.2:1-7

Is placed before compassion.
Lk.10:29-37
Many are attached to **r.** Mt.9:16
Puts religion before man. Mt.12:1-8;
12:9-13; 12:10
Rejects people because of their cir-
cumstances. Mt.9:20-22
Should a believer stay in a church
with problems. 1 Cor.7:18-19
Stresses reformation. Mt.12:43-45
In relation to other religions.
Seeks to destroy the ministry of
those who differ. Lk.19:47-48
Its tendency to be institutional, human-
istic, & man-centered.
Emptiness of. Mk.7:1-13
Has a tendency to become institu-
tionalized. Lk.6:1-11; 10:29-37
Is a creation of man's mind. (See
IDOLATRY) Gal.4:8; 4:9-11;
Col.2:20-23
Is dead **r.** Tries to meet the needs of
the world. Jn.5:10-12
Is false profession. Mt.21:28-32
Is formal, institutional **r.** Discussed.
Jn.1:23
Is humanistic **r.** Mt.13:33
Is man-made **r.** Mk.7:1-13
Is powerless. Has a form of godliness,
but denies the power. 2 Tim.3:5
Is self-righteousness. Ph.3:4-16
Is spiritually blind. Mk.8:10-13
Is the wrong way to seek God's ac-
ceptance & justification. Ro.4:9-12
Stresses form & ritual over people.
Lk.13:14-16; 14:3
Stresses ritual & ceremony.
Heb.13:9-11
Thinks that ritual saves. Ro.2:25-27
Purpose. To serve, not master man.
Mk.2:25-27
Teaching of. (See **TEACHING, FALSE**)
A creation of man's mind & imagination.
Mt.13:57; Acts 17:29; Ro.1:22-23;
1:24-25; Gal.4:8; 4:9-11; Col.2:20-23;
2 Pt.1:16
Discussed. Mt.16:12
Stresses ritual, tradition. Mk.7:1-13
Stresses rules & regulations.
Mk.2:23-28; 3:1-6
True **r.**
Christ is greater than **r.** Mt.12:1-8
Discussed. Col.2:12; 2:16-17; Jas.1:27
Is inward, of the spirit, of the heart.
Ro.2:28-29
Is not ritual & ceremony, rules &
regulations. Mk.2:23-24; Lk.6:1-11;
10:29-37;13:14-16; 14:3; Ro.2:25-27;
3:3-4; 1 Cor.7:18-19; Gal.4:1-3
Is redeemed from empty **r.** 1 Pt.1:18-20
Is to be unspotted & separated from
the world. Jas.1:27
Is to visit the orphans & widows. Jas.1:27
Stresses renewal. Mt.12:43-45
Stresses that it takes more than **r.** to
enter heaven. Mt.21:31; 21:32
Stresses that man is greater than **r.**
Mt.12:9-13; Lk.13:10-17; 14:1-6
Stresses that need supersedes **r.**
Mt.12:5; Lk.6:1-11
Stresses the inner person. Mt.15:1-20
What true **r.** really is. Five things.
Mk.3:1-6
Vs. Christ. Mt.12:1-8; 12:9-13;
12:10;Col.2:11-12
Vs. love. Mk.12:31

Vs. man. Mt.12:1-8; 12:9-13; 12:10;
Lk.14:3
Vs. renewal. Mt.12:43-45
Vs. the state, government. Mk.12:13-17;
Lk.20:19-26
Warning against **r.** Mt.23:1-12
Fails to meet the needs of man.
Ph.3:4-16

RELIGION, FALSE (See **TEACHING, FALSE**)

RELIGION, STATE
In the end time.
Apostate. Will be destroyed by God.
Rev.14:8
Discussed. To be corrupt. 2 Tim.3:1-9
World-wide **r.**
To be enforced by the antichrist.
2 Th.2:4
Worship of the state. Rev.12:1-2;
13:4-8; 13:13-17; 17:1-6; 17:7-18

RELIGIONISTS (See **JUDAIZERS;
PHARISEES; TEACHERS OF THE
LAW; SADDUCEES; HERODIANS;
ELDERS**)
Accusations against.
Nine **a.** Mt.23:13-36
Seven charges. Lk.11:37-54
Beliefs of. Strong, steeped in. Mt.12:10
Described as.
Fools. Lk.11:39-41
Self-righteous. Lk.11:39-41; 15:25-32
"Vipers." Meaning. Mt.3:7
Discussed. Ro.2:17-29; Gal.2:3-5; 2:4;
2:11-13; Jas.2:14-26
Fact.
Are prospects for the gospel. Reasons.
Acts 17:17
Object to God's judgment. Ro.3:1-8
Some are converted. Acts 6:7; 18:8, 17
Meaning. Ro.2:17-29
Need.
Spirit needed by **r.** Lk.18:9-14
To become a true **r.** Ro.2:28-29
Opposed Christ.
Discussed. Mt.12:10; 16:21; 17:22
How the **r.** opposed Christ.
Accused Christ.
Of being demon possessed.
Mk.3:22-30; Lk.11:14-16
Of opposing religion. Reasons.
Jn.7:20-24
Arrested Christ. Four pictures of
commitment. Mt.26:47-56
Hunted Christ down. Jn.11:57
Initiated Christ's death. Jn.18:28-
19:15
Mocked Christ upon the cross.
Mt.27:42-43
Murmured against Christ's claim.
Jn.6:41-43
Persecuted Christ. Jn.5:16
Plotted against Christ. Jn.12:19
Plotted the death of Christ.
Mt.16:21; 26:3-5; Jn.5:16, 17-18;
7:1-2; 8:39-40; 8:54-59; 10:31-33,39
Plotted to kill Lazarus, the evidence
of Christ's deity. Jn.12:10
Put Christ on trial. (See **JESUS
CHRIST**, Trials)
Questioned Christ. (See **JESUS
CHRIST**, Challenged)
His source of power. Lk.11:14-16
Rejected Christ. Reasons. Mk.11:33

MASTER SUBJECT INDEX

Sent an investigating committee to
observe Christ. Lk.5:17
Sought to kill Christ even as they had
killed the prophets. Lk.11:47-51
Tried to discredit Christ. Mk.10:1-4;
11:27-33
Response of Christ to r. opposition.
Mt.22:41-46; 23:13-36
Why the r. opposed Christ.
Considered Christ a rabble-rouser.
Jn.7:32-36
Feared the loss of their position,
esteem & livelihood. Mt.12:1-8;
12:10; 16:12;21:23; 22:15-22;
22:23-33;22:34-40; 23:1-12
For allowing His disciples to work
on the Sabbath. Mk.3:1-6
For associating with outcasts & sin-
ners. Mk.2:13-17
For breaking ceremonial law. Mk.3:4
For breaking tradition. The Scribal
law. Mt.12:1-8; 12:9-13; 12:10;
15:1-20;15:6-9; 16:1-12; Mk.2:23-
24; 3:1-6; 7:1-13; Lk.6:1-5
For driving out demons. Mk.3:22-30
For forgiving sins. Mk.3:6-7
For healing on the Sabbath.
Mk.3:1-6
For not fasting, not keeping the rit-
ual of f. Mk.2:18-22
Four reasons why the r. opposed
Christ. Mk.14:1-2
Reasons. Lk.13:14; 22:2; Jn.5:16
Several events of the last week of
Christ's life. Mk.3:22; 11:27
Were confused over Christ. Jn.6:52-53
Were insanely angry & vengeful
against Him. Lk.6:1-11
Opposed the early church.
Feared the church. Reasons. Acts 4:2-4
Feared the loss of position, livelihood.
Acts 4:2-4
Opposed the gospel. Reasons. Envy, jeal-
ousy, fear. Acts 17:5
Privileges of. Lk.15:31-32
Have the Word of God. Ro.3:1-2
Problem with - Errors of.
Fact.
Some cared for Jesus. Lk.13:31
Five problems. Lk.14:1-6; 15:25-32
Four problems. Mt.12:10; Mk.14:1-2
In relation to God & Christ & Scrip-
ture.
Are confused & perplexed over
Christ. Jn.6:52-53
Are ignorant of Christ's coming.
Mt.2:3-6
Are in the church, but not planted
by God. Mt.15:12-14
Are not of God. Mt.15:12-14
Corrupt God's Word. Mt.12:1-2;
Lk.11:52; 13:14
Misinterpret the words of Christ.
Jn.6:52-53
Miss the truth of Christ. Reasons.
Mk.12:36-37
Plunder the way of God. Lk.11:39-41
Seek signs for proof. Mk.8:10-13
In relation to life & behavior.
Are greedy. Lk.16:14-15
Are hypocritical. Cp. leaven. Lk.12:1-3
Can fail & fall. Jn.7:20-24
Change their appearance & seek
recognition & position. Mt.23:5
Commit sins. Common to leaders.
Listed. Acts 4:5-10

Do not understand repentance.
Lk.15:28
Love the praise of men more than
the p. of God. Jn.12:42-43
Oppose Christ. "Sat by"; critical;
refused to participate. Lk.5:17
Their life is warped. Lk.13:14
Their prayer is a prayer of religion.
Lk.18:9-14
In relation to others.
Often become witch hunters. Acts
21:20-26
Persecute believers. Jn.16:1-6
Place form & ritual before people in
need. Mk.2:23-24; Lk.6:1-11;
10:29-37;13:14-16; 14:3
Seek to destroy the ministry of
those who differ. Lk.19:47-48
Their attitude toward the sinner &
outcast. Mk.2:16-17
In relation to righteousness & salva-
tion & religion.
Are in the field of religion, but not
in the house of salvation.
Lk.15:25
Are incorrectly thought to be
genuine. Lk.20:45-47
Are self-righteous. Lk.16:14-15;
18:9-14
Five faults. Lk.7:36-50; 15:25-32
Many faults. Lk.11:37-54
Not acceptable to God.
Lk.11:39-41
Resting in false security.
Ro.11:6-10
Are social r. Mt.6:14-15
Argue against a heart religion.
Ro.3:1-8
Have an inadequate religion. Ex-
ample of. Herod. Mk.6:20
Have some righteousness, but not
enough for heaven. Mt.5:20
Honor the past & its heritage, but
neglect the present. Lk.11:47-51
Know the truth but fail to confess it.
Jn.12:42-43
Lack one central thing: faith.
Lk.15:29
Mistakes of. In seeking acceptance
with God. Mt.5:20; Ro.10:1-3
Stress ritual. Gal.5:1-6
Stress rules & regulations. Lk.5:30-35
Strict vs. loose religion. Mt.5:17-18
Several problems. Lk.20:45-47
Ten problems. Ro.2:17-29
Teaching of. (See TEACHING, FALSE)
Errors of. Mt.16:12
Evil & dangers of. Mk.8:14-21
Vs. Jesus. (See RELIGIONISTS, Op-
posed Christ, above)
Warned - Fate of.
Beware of some things. Mk.12:38-40
Dangers confronting. Mt.3:7-10
God's case against. Ro.2:17-29
Nine accusations made by Christ
against r. Mt.23:13-36
Seven charges made by Christ against
r. Lk.11:37-54
Who r. were. Discussed. Jn.5:10; 5:15-16

RELIGIOUS LIFE
Activities of. Mt.7:21

RELUCTANCE
Illustration of r. to obey. Lk.5:4-5

REMAIN - REMAINING (See **ABIDE**)

REMARRIAGE
Discussed. Mk.10:1-12; 10:10-12

REMEMBER - REMEMBERING
Duty.
To always r. some things. List of.
2 Pt.1:12, cp. 5-15
To r. Lot's wife. Flee the things &
judgment to come & do not look
back. Lk.17:26-32
To r. ministers. 1 Cor.4:17
To r. one's love for Christ. Rev.2:5
To r. that Jesus Christ was raised from
the dead. 2 Tim.2:8
To r. that mockers will come who
walk after their own lusts. Jude 17
To r. that one shall be persecuted if
one really follows Christ. Jn.15:20;
16:1-4
To r. that the world, both heaven &
earth, are to be destroyed & remade.
2 Pt.3:1-14
To r. that there are false teachers deceiving people. 1 Tim.4:6, cp. 4:1-5
To r. the "great things" of God.
1 Pt.1:12, cp. 1:5-15
To r. the Lord's Supper. Lk.22:19, cp.
22:15-20
To r. the message of the Word of God.
2 Pt.3:1-2
To r. the teaching on the return of Christ
& the end time. 2 Th.2:5, cp. 1-5
To r. the teachings of Scripture.
2 Tim.2:14
To r. the words of the Lord Jesus, "It
is more blessed to give than to re-
ceive." Acts 20:35
To r. those in authority who preach &
teach the Word. Heb.13:7
To r. those in prison. Heb.13:3
To r. what God has done for one.
Jn.5:13-14
Source of r. - How believers can r.
By making a diligent effort to r.
Heb.10:32
Preaching & teaching by faithful min-
isters. 1 Tim.4:6; 2 Tim.1:6; 2:14;
2 Pt.1:12-13; Jude 5
Scripture. 2 Pt.3:1, cp. Acts 17:11;
1 Cor.10:6
The Holy Spirit. Jn.14:26

REMISSION OF SINS (See **FORGIVE-
NESS**)
Discussed. Mt.26:28
Duty. To preach r. of sins. Lk.3:3;
24:47-48
How one receives.
By believing in Christ. Acts 10:43
By repentance & baptism. Lk.3:3;
Acts 2:38
Through the blood of Christ.
Mt.26:28; Ro.3:25; Heb.9:22
Results.
Salvation. Lk.1:76-79
The righteousness of God is declared.
Ro.3:25-26

REMNANT
Of Israel. (See **ISRAEL**, Remnant;
JEWS, Remnant)

170

REMORSE (See **CONFESSION; CONTRITION; REPENTANCE**)
Illust.
A man in hell. Lk.16:23-24
Esau. Heb.12:16-17
Judas. Mt.27:3-5
Peter. Mt.26:75

REPHAN
False god. Discussed. Acts 7:43

RENEW - RENEWAL (See **CONVERSION; REGENERATION**)
Described. A new life & religion.
Mk.2:21; 2:22
Discussed. Jn.3:1-15; 2 Cor.5:17; Tit.3:5
Duty.
Not to be conformed to this world, but renewed. Ro.12:2
To be renewed in knowledge, in the very image of God. Col.3:10
To be transformed by renewing our minds. Ro.12:2
To r. the inner man day by day.
2 Cor.4:16
How to be renewed.
By putting on the new man. Col.3:10
By regeneration & renewing of the Holy Spirit. Tit.3:5
By renewing our minds. Ro.12:2; Eph.4:23
Meaning. Mt.19:28; Jn.3:1-15
Result.
Changes a person's life radically. Jn.4:30; 2 Cor.5:17
Salvation. Tit.3:5
Reward. Predicted by Christ. Lk.22:30
Source.
God. His mercy. Tit.3:5
The creative power of Christ. Jn.2:3-5; 2:6-8
Vs. reformation. Mt.12:43-45; Lk.11:24-26

REPENT - REPENTANCE (See **CONVERSION; SALVATION**; Related Subjects)
Baptism of repentance. Meaning. Lk.3:3
Discussed. Mt.4:17; Lk.15:11-24; Acts 17:29-30; 2 Pt.3:9
Door of r. thrown open to the Gentiles. Acts 11:16-18
Not understood by religionists. Lk.15:28
Repentance of a fallen minister. 1 Tim.5:22
Duty.
Called to r. Lk.3:3; Acts 2:38; 3:19; 8:22
God commands all men everywhere to r. Acts 17:30-31
To call sinners to r. Lk.5:30-32; 24:47
To preach r. Mk.1:15
To repent. Rev.2:5; 2:16; 2:21; 3:3; 3:19
To r. from compromising - idolatry. Rev.2:20-29
To r. from deadness. Rev.3:2-6
To r. from losing one's first love. Rev.2:4-7
To r. from lukewarmness. Rev.3:15-22
To r. from worldliness. Rev.2:14-17
To r. of denying Christ. Mt.26:75
To turn to God from idols. 1 Th.1:9-10

Essential.
An attitude of r. vs. self-righteousness. Lk.7:36-50
Great need for all to r. Lk.13:1-9
Man is without excuse if he does not r. Lk.11:30-32
Must r. for restoration. Lk.15:20-21
Must r. For salvation. Acts 2:38
Reasons why r. is essential. Mk.1:15
Repentance must accompany faith. Mk.1:15
What it takes to enter God's kingdom. Mt.21:28-32
Example of - Illustrated.
Finding a great treasure. Mt.13:44
Nineveh. Mt.12:41
Peter. Mk.14:72; Lk.22:60-62
Zacchaeus. A true repentance. Lk.19:7-8
Facts. Is impossible to r. of falling away. Heb.6:3-8
False repentance.
Is sorrow & regret, not a change of life. Mt.27:1-5; Heb.12:16-17
Is verbal r. only. Mt.3:7-10
Is wrong r. & human religion. Picture. Mt.27:1-10
Godly vs. worldly sorrow. 2 Cor.7:10
Meaning. Acts 17:29-30; 2 Pt.3:9
A changed life. Lk.19:7-10
Godly vs. worldly sorrow. 2 Cor.7:10
Turning to God & doing good works. Acts 3:19; 26:19-21
Message of r.
To be the subject of preaching. Acts 20:21
Was the message of Jesus Christ. Mt.4:17
Was the message of John the Baptist. Mt.3:2-6
Refusal to r.
A last chance given Judas. Jn.13:21-26
Results in perishing. Lk.13:2-5
Repentance in the last days.
Failure to repent will lead to judgment. Rev.9:20-21
Many will not repent in the last days. Rev.9:20-21
Results of repentance.
Bears fruit. Mt.3:8; Lk.3:8
Forgiveness of sins & of wickedness. Mk.1:4; Acts 2:38; 3:19; 8:22
Good works. Acts 26:19-20
Joy. Lk.15:5-7; 15:9-10
Life. Acts 11:18, cp. 17-18
Proves the deity of Christ. Lk.20:6
Restores a person into fellowship with God. Lk.15:22; 15:30
Salvation. 2 Cor.7:10
The gift of the Holy Spirit. Acts 2:38
Times of refreshment from the Lord. Acts 3:19
Source of r.
Christ. His very purpose for coming to earth was to call men to r. Mt.9:13; Mk.2:17; Lk.5:32
Christ the Savior. Acts 5:30-31
Conviction of sin. Acts 2:37-38
Godly sorrow, not just sorrow. 2 Cor.7:10
God's longsuffering. 2 Pt.3:9, 15
Is the gift of God. Acts 11:18
Verses. List of. Mk.1:3-5; 1:15; Lk.11:31-32; 15:20-21; 22:60-62
Worldly vs. godly repentance. Lk.18:9-14

REPETITION
In prayer. Problem with. Mt.6:7

REPORTING
Time for r. essential. Lk.9:10

REPROACH - REPROACHING
Duty.
Must have a good testimony before being ordained lest one fall into r. 1 Tim.3:7
To bear the r. of Christ. Heb.13:13-16, esp. 13
To consider the r. of Christ of greater value than the riches of the world. Heb.11:24-28, esp. 26
To have a good testimony among the unsaved. 1 Tim.3:7
To labor & suffer reproach so that all men can be saved. 1 Tim.4:10
To stand up under r. for the name of Christ. 1 Pt.4:14
Who is reproached.
Disciples, believers. Lk.6:22
Faithful believers who long for heaven. Heb.10:32-34
Hypocrites, those who live unholy lives. Ro.2:24; 1 Tim.5:14; 2 Pt.2:2
Mature believers. Ro.15:1-3, esp.3

REPROBATE (See **APOSTASY; BACKSLIDING; DENIAL; FAILED THE TEST**)
Described. 2 Tim.3:1-9, esp.8

REPRODUCTION
Law of. Discussed. Mk.4:32

REPROOF - REPROVE (See **CORRECT; REBUKE**)
Duty.
To r. the works of darkness. Eph.5:1-14
To use the Word of God to r. 2 Tim.3:16; 4:2
What reproves a person.
Believers r. the works of darkness. Lk.3:19; Eph.5:11-13
Christ. Lk.9:41; 9:55-56; Jn.6:27-29; 7:7; Rev.2:16
God. Heb.12:5-7
God's Word. 2 Tim.3:16
Light. Jn.3:19-20; Eph.5:13
Preaching. Lk.3:18-19; 2 Tim.4:2
The Holy Spirit. Jn.16:8-11

REPUTATION (See **TESTIMONY**)
Danger - Warning.
Against being a friend with the world. Makes one an enemy of God. Jas.4:4
Not to compromise in order to be accepted. Lk.6:26
Duty.
To be known as a person of the gospel. 2 Cor.8:18
To have a good r. among all. Acts 10:22; 16:15; 3 Jn.12

REQUESTS
Meaning. Ph.4:6-7; 1 Tim.2:1

RESIST - RESISTANCE
Discussed. Mt.5:38; 5:39-41; 5:42
Duty.
Not to resist & fight against being persecuted for Jesus' name. Mt.5:39
Not to resist authority. Ro.13:2
Not to resist the Holy Spirit. Acts 7:51
To resist temptation & sin. Heb.12:4
To resist the devil. Jas.4:7, cp.
Eph.4:26-27; Eph.6:11;1 Pt.5:8-9
Facts.
God resists the proud. Jas.4:6; 1 Pt.5:5
False teachers resist the truth.
2 Tim.3:8
People, generation after generation, resist the Holy Spirit. Acts 7:51
Persecutors cannot r. the wisdom & words of believers. Lk.21:15;
Acts 6:10
Meaning. Jas.4:7; 1 Pt.5:9

RESISTING AN EVIL PERSON
Meaning. Mt.5:38-42

RESOURCES (See **PROMISES**, To the believer)
Attitude toward.
Fivefold. Mk.6:37-44
Right vs. wrong. Lk.9:12
Described - Listed.
Power. (See **POWER**) Lk.10:17-20
Privileges. (See **PRIVILEGES**)
Lk.10:21-24
Provision of necessities. (See **NEEDS - NECESSITIES**) Lk.12:22-34
Duty.
To labor until Jesus returns.
Lk.19:15-23
To surrender to Christ.
Mt.14:18-21
Limited r. Attitudes toward. Jn.6:8-9;
6:10-13

RESPECT (See **HONOR; OBEDIENCE**)
To r. all men. 1 Pt.2:17
To r. the king. 1 Pt.2:16-27

RESPECTABILITY
Inadequate for salvation. Mk.10:19-20

RESPECTABLE
Meaning. 1 Tim.3:2-3

RESPECTER OF PERSONS (See **FAVORITISM; PARTIALITY**)

RESPONSIBILITY (See **BELIEVERS**, Duty; **MINISTERS**, Duty; & Related Subjects)
Determines destiny - reward. Mt.13:8;
25:19-30; Lk.16:10-12;19:15-23; 19:15
Duty. To be r. for the world & the church. Mt.21:33
Failure in r. Pilate attempted to shirk r.
Mt.27:24; Lk.23:6-7

REST - RELAXATION, PHYSICAL
Believers r. Discussed. Heb.4:1; 4:2; 4:3
Duty.
Not to r. when we should be praying.
Mt.26:45-46
To allow interruptions sometimes.
Mk.7:25-26
Meaning. Heb.4:1
Need for.
Dangers of. Mk.6:30-34

Sought by Jesus for preparation.
Mk.7:24
Proof of. Six proofs. Heb.4:3-10
Source. Jesus. Power to bring r. & peace.
Mk.4:35-41
Time for r. essential. Mk.6:31-32;
Lk.9:10
Verses. List of. Lk.9:10

REST, HEAVENLY
Described. Five things. Rev.6:11

REST, SPIRITUAL & ETERNAL
Believer's rest. Heb.3:11, 18-19; 4:1;
4:1-13
Discussed. Heb.3:18-19; 4:1-13
Believers will receive eternal rest.
Rev.6:11; 14:13
Duty. To fear lest we miss God's rest.
Heb.3:11; 3:18-19; 4:4-13
Essential. Time for spiritual renewal & r.
Lk.9:10
Fact. Israel did not enter God's rest.
Heb.3:7-19, esp. 18-19; 4:1-13
How to secure.
Being assured of Jesus' return.
2 Th.1:7
Facing & renouncing sin. Jn.4:16-18
Meaning. Mt.11:28-30; Heb.4:1
To tabernacle, pitch a tent upon the hope for r. Acts 2:25-31
Source.
Hope. Acts 2:25-31
The presence & power of Christ.
Mk.4:35-41
Verses. List of. Lk.9:10
Vs. pressure & burdens. Mt.11:28-30

RESTITUTION
Duty. To make r. Zacchaeus. Lk.19:7-8
Made by Judas, but too late. Mt.27:1-5

RESTLESS - RESTLESSNESS
Caused by. Sin & sinful acts; a depraved nature. Ro.3:15-18

RESTORATION (See **CONFESSION; FORGIVENESS; REPENTANCE; SALVATION**)
Discussed. Lk.15:20-21; 22:61-62;
Gal.6:1-5
Of all things. Acts 3:21
Duty. To seek r. after sin. Lk.1:20-21;
22:61-62
Of a fallen minister. Discussed.
1 Tim.5:22

RESTORATION OF ISRAEL (See **ISRAEL**, Restoration)

RESTORE
Meaning. 1 Pt.4:3

RESTRAINT - RESTRAIN (See **GOD**, Power; Providence - Sovereignty; **POWER**)

RESURRECTION
Assurance of - Surety of.
Christ assures. Jn.5:28-30; 6:39-40,
44, 54, 58;Ro.8:10; 1 Cor.15:20-28
Discussed. Mt.22:31-32; Jn.11:25-27;
Ro.8:10-11; 8:11
Some taken - some left. Lk.17:34-37
The gospel demands 1 Cor.15:1-11

The resurrection of Christ assures.
1 Cor.6:14; 15:20-28
Verses. List of. 1 Cor.6:13-14
Body of.
A change in man's body is needed.
1 Cor.15:50-58
Discussed. Jn.21:1
Will be conformed to the image of Christ. Ro.8:29
Will be made blameless by God.
1 Th.5:23
Will be made into a glorious body just like the body of Christ. Ph.3:21
Comes by.
Being drawn by God. Jn.6:44
Faith in Christ. Jn.6:39-40
Partaking of Christ. Jn.6:54
Denied.
By the liberal minded. Acts 23:6-10;
23:8
Consequence. 1 Cor.15:12-19
Discussed. 1 Cor.15:12-19
Is spiritualized by false teachers.
2 Tim.2:16-18
Reasons why the r. is denied.
Mk.12:19-23; 12:24
Scoffed at.
By philosophers & unbelievers.
Acts 17:32, cp. 2 Pt.3:3-4, cp.
1 Cor.15:12-20
By religionists. Mt.22:23-33
Described as. Heavenly citizenship.
Ph.3:20-21
Discussed. Mt.22:23-33; 22:31-32;
Mk.12:18-27; Lk.20:27-38;Jn.5:28-30;
11:25-27; 14:3;1 Cor.13:4-7; 15:1-58;
15:29-34;15:35-49; 15:50-58;
1 Th.4:13-5:3; Rev.20:4-6; 20:13
Kind of body believers will receive.
Ro.8:29; 1 Cor.15:35-49; 15:50-58;
Ph.3:21; 1 Th.5:23
Effects of.
A day of reward. Lk.17:34-37
Is precious. To be with the Father & know the Father. Jn.14:6
The body shall be changed.
1 Cor.15:35-58; Ph.3:20-21
The r. will usher in a just judgment.
Jn.5:28-30
The world of the r. differs from this world. Lk.20:27-38
Events of. Order of.
Discussed. 1 Th.4:13-5:3
Shall be r. wherever & however many places the dead lie. Jn.14:3
Hope for.
Stirs faithfulness. 2 Cor.4:14
Sustains the minister. 2 Cor.4:14
How the dead are raised.
By a great summons. Mt.24:29-31;
1 Th.4:16-17, cp. 13-18
By the great compassion of Christ.
Lk.7:12-13
By the great power of Christ.
Lk.7:14-15; Jn.5:28-30
By the Holy Spirit. Ro.8:11
By the power of God. Mt.22:29;
1 Cor.6:14
Shall be r. wherever & however many places the dead lie. Jn.14:3
Nature. Discussed. Mt.22:30; Mk.12:25;
1 Cor.15:42-44; 15:50-54; Ph.3:20-21
Of Jesus Christ. (See **JESUS CHRIST**, Resurrection)
Of unbelievers.
Discussed. Rev.20:13

Of the just & the unjust. Jn.5:28-30;
Acts 24:15
Proof of. Discussed. Mk.12:18-27;
1 Cor.15:1-58
Questioned. Discussed. Mk.12:18-27;
1 Cor.15:1-58
Stages of the r.
Future.
At the end of the Millennium.
Rev.20:13
At the last day. Jn.5:25; 6:39-40, 44,
54, 58; 11:25;1 Cor.15:51-52; 2
Cor.4:14;1 Th.4:13-5:3; Rev.20:4-6
Of the just & the unjust. Jn.5:28-30;
Acts 24:15
When Christ returns. 1 Th.4:13-18
Past.
Christ r. a widow's son at Nain.
Lk.7:11-17
Christ r. Lazarus. Power over death.
Jn.11:43-44
Christ r. the daughter of Jairus.
Mt.9:23-25
Some believers were r. at Christ's
death. Mt.27:52
Present. Believers are already r. in
Christ. Eph.2:6
Two witnesses shall be r. in the last
days. Rev.11:3-13
Type. Symbol of. By Abraham sacrific-
ing Isaac. Heb.11:17-19
Verses. List of. Mt.22:31-32; Mk.12:24;
Lk.14:12-14; Jn.5:28-30; Ro.8:10-11

RESURRECTION, SPIRITUAL (See QUICKENING)
Duty.
To arise from spiritual death. Eph.5:14
To know the power of Christ's r.
Ph.3:10-11
To seek those things above, the things
of Christ. Col.3:1
To yield oneself to God as much as
those who are alive from the dead are
yielded. Ro.6:13
How one experiences the spiritual r.
By faith in the power of God. Col.2:12
By hearing the Word of Christ.
Jn.5:24-25
By the Holy Spirit. Ro.8:11
By the life of Christ. Jn.5:24-26, esp. 26
By the light of Christ. Eph.5:14
By the r. of Christ. Eph.2:6; Col.2:12
Nature.
Is a spiritual r. from spiritual death,
from being dead to God. Jn.5:21;
Eph.2:1-10; Col.2:12-13
One is risen to live a new life. Ro.6:3-5
One is spiritually made alive to God.
Lk.15:24
One is spiritually r. with Christ, iden-
tified with the r. of Christ. Col.2:12
One's mortal body is spiritually quick-
ened, made alive spiritually. Ro.8:11
Results.
Assures being resurrected from the
dead. Ro.6:3-10; 8:11; Ph.3:10-11
Gives life, both abundant & eternal
life. Jn.5:24-25
Places the believer in heavenly places
in Christ. Eph.2:6

RETALIATION - RESISTANCE (See HATE; REVENGE; VENGEANCE)
Discussed. Mt.5:38; 5:39; 5:40; 5:41;
5:42;1 Pt.3:9

Duty. Not to r. Ro.12:17; 12:19-21
Fact. Is rebuked. Reveals a spirit contrary
to Christ. Lk.9:55-56

RETRIBUTION (See JUDGMENT)

RETURN OF JESUS CHRIST (See JE-SUS CHRIST, Return)

REVEALED - REVELATION (See JE-SUS CHRIST, Revelation)
Discussed. Eph.1:17-18
All things shall be r. Nothing hid.
Lk.8:17
God's Word is r. through preaching.
Tit.1:3
Twelve mysteries r. in Scripture.
1 Cor.2:7
Insight into revelation is given.
Only to true believers. Mt.13:10-17;
Lk.10:21
To Paul & others. Eph.3:2-5
To prophets. 1 Pt.1:10-12
To those who continue in the Lord's
words. Jn.8:31-32
Meaning. Jn.14:21; Eph.1:17-18
Rejected by. Unbelievers. Jn.12:37-41
Source of revelation.
God. Eph.1:9-10
Jesus Christ. (See REVELATION, Of
Christ) Jn.8:26; 12:49; 14:10;
17:8;Gal.1:11-12
The Holy Spirit. 1 Cor.2:9-13, cp.
Jn.16:13
The revelation of Christ.
God's great love. Jn.3:16-17
His creative power to meet man's
need. Jn.2:1-22
His glory. Jn.2:11
His knowledge of all men. Jn.2:23-25
His Supremacy over God's House.
Jn.2:12-22
Reactions to. Four r. Jn.12:1-11
The Answer to man's great hunger.
Jn.6:22-29
The Bread of Life. Jn.6:1-71
The Deliverer from fear. Jn.6:16-21
The Embodiment of God. Jn.14:8-14
The Great Minister & His legacy.
Jn.13:1-16:33
The Living Water. Jn.4:1-14
The New Master. Jn.3:22-36
The Object of Faith. Jn.4:43-54
The Provision for human needs.
Jn.6:1-15
The Resurrection & the Life. Jn.11:1-
12:11
The Son of God. Various r. Jn.2:1-3:21
The Spokesman, the R. of God.
1 Cor.3:18-20
The Suffering Savior. Jn.18:1-19:42
The Supreme r. Jn.14:6-7
The way of life. Acts 2:25-31
The Way, the Truth, & the Life.
Jn.14:6-7
The Word. Jn.1:1
Verses. List of. Jn.14:6
Witnesses to the r. of Christ. Jn.1:1-51
The revelation of God.
By Christ.
Not left in the dark, groping after
God. Jn.14:6-7; 14:9; Col.2:9-10;
Tit.3:4-5
Revealed the truth of God & of
God's Word to man. 1 Cor.3:18-20

God gave more than words. He gave a
life to live the truth out before man,
Christ Himself. Jn.12:37-41, cp.
Jn.1:1
God has not left man to grope & grasp
after Him. He is love & has r. Him-
self. Col.2:9-10
God is not distant & far off. Jn.14:9
God is seen through nature. Acts
14:14-18; 17:24-25; Ro.1:20
God's Person is unseen. Has never
been seen by man. Seen only by
Christ. Jn.1:18; 5:37-38
Is Jesus Christ. Jn.1:18; 3:13; 3:31;
8:19; 12:45;14:6-7; 14:9; 16:5;
1 Cor.3:18-20; Col.2:9; 1 Tim.3:16;
Heb.1:1-3; 2:9-13
The supreme r. of God. Jesus Christ.
Heb.1:1-4:13
Verses. List of. Jn.5:37-38
The revelation of several things.
God's grace. Eph.3:1-6
God's great love. 1 Jn.4:9-11
God's wisdom. Discussed. 1 Cor.2:6-13
Man's condemnation. Jn.3:18-21
The church. Mt.16:13-20
The eternal God. 1 Jn.1:1-4
The gospel. Given to Paul by Christ.
Gal.1:11-12
The life (Christ) entered history.
1 Jn.1:2
The mystery of Christ. Ro.16:25-26;
Eph.3:3-6
The new birth. Jn.3:1-15
The new creation. Eph.3:3-6
The spiritual world. By Christ only.
Lk.10:22
Twelve mysteries r. in Scripture.
1 Cor.2:7

REVEL - REVELLING (See ORGIES)

REVELATION, THE BOOK OF
Discussed. Rev.22:6-21
Epistle of. Given by Jesus Christ, not
John. Rev.1:1-3
Is the Revelation of Jesus Christ. His per-
son. Rev.1:9-20
Meaning. Rev.1:1-3
Message of.
Eleven stirring facts. Rev.22:6-21
Is said to be the Word of God.
Rev.1:1-3
Setting for. Rev.1:9-10
The outline of the Book of Revelation.
Rev.1:19
Visions of.
First vision. Rev.1:9-3:22
Fourth vision. Rev.21:9-22:21
Second vision. Rev.4:1-16:21
Third vision. Rev.17:1-21:8

REVENGE - REVENGEFUL (See RE-TALIATION; VENGEANCE)
Answer to - Remedy for - Solution to re-
venge.
Blessing those who persecute.
Ro.12:14
Giving to those who demand & abuse.
Mt.5:38-42
Just refusing to take r. Leaving judg-
ment in God's hands. Ro.12:19-21
Love & mercy. Lk.6:35-36

Caused by.
Being hurt by the sin of a loved one.
Jn.8:3-6
Doing evil against society. Ro.13:3-5
Reacting against God & God's mes-
senger. Mk.6:16-23, esp. 18-19; Act
5:33;7:54, 59; 23:12
Rejecting God & not obeying the gos-
pel of Christ. 2 Th.1:7-8
Discussed. Mt.5:38; 5:39-41; 5:42
Duty. Not to seek revenge. Mt.5:38;
5:39-41; 5:42; Lk.9:55-56
Fact. God & God alone has the right to
take **r**. Ro.12:19; Heb.10:30
Reasons for **r**. Threefold. Mk.6:24-25

REVERENCE (See HONOR, Of God; WORSHIP)
Duty.
To **r**. Christ. Mt.8:2; 15:25; Mk.5:22-23;
7:24-25; Jn.9:35-38
To **r**. God. 1 Pt.1:17-21; 1:17
To **r**. God's house, the temple &
church. Mt.21:13
To **r**. husbands. Wives are to **r**. Eph.5:33
To **r**. parents. Eph.6:1-3; Heb.12:9
For Christ.
God expects man to **r**. Christ.
Mt.22:37
God will force every person to **r**.
Christ in the day of judgment.
Ph.2:9-11
For God. Discussed. 1 Pt.1:17-21; 1:17

REVILE - REVILER (See SLANDERS)
Duty.
Not to be a **r**. 1 Cor.6:9-11
To bless when **r**. 1 Cor.4:11-13
To suffer being reviled even as Christ
did. 1 Pt.2:21-24
Of what.
Believers. Mt.5:11-12; 1 Pt.2:21-24
Christ upon the cross. Mt.27:39-44;
1 Pt.2:21-24, esp. 23
Results. The **r**. shall not inherit the king-
dom of God. 1 Cor.6:9-10

REVIVE - REVIVAL (See QUICKEN - QUICKENING; RENEW - RENEWAL)
Discussed. 2 Cor.7:2-16
A study in **r**. Acts 8:5-25
Duty. (See REPENT)
Essentials for **r**. A faithful minister.
2 Cor.7:2-5
Example of.
Christ & all Israel. Lk.7:16-17; 8:4
Christ & the Samaritans. Labor for
God & results will follow. Jn.4:1-42,
esp.39-42
John the Baptist & all Israel. A mes-
sage for all ages. Lk.3:1-6; 3:7-20
Paul at Antioch of Pisidia. Various re-
sponses to the gospel. Acts 13:42-52,
esp. 48-49
Paul at Antioch of Syria. God's pattern
for all churches. Acts 11:19-30
Paul at Corinth. An indisputable
Christian. Acts 18:1-17, esp. 8
Paul at Ephesus. Lessons on salvation
& revival. Acts 19:1-20, esp. 18-20
Pentecost. The imperatives for salva-
tion. Acts 2:1-40, esp. 37-40
Peter at Lydda. Making men whole.
Acts 9:32-35
Philip & the Samaritans. A study in **r**.
Acts 8:5-25

The Corinthian church. 2 Cor.7:2-16
False vs. true **r**. Lk.8:4-15
Lessons on **r**. Discussed. Acts 19:1-20
R. in the end time. Rev.7:1-8; 7:9-17
Thousands followed Christ. Lk.8:4
Widespread **r**. throughout Israel. Lk.3:1-20;
7:17

REWARD - REWARDS (See SPIRITUAL INHERITANCE)
Basis - Based upon.
Faith. Ro.4:13, cp. 4:4-5, 16
God's grace. Mt.20:11-14; Ro.4:16
Justice. God is just, not unjust in giv-
ing **r**. Mt.20:8-16; 20:11-14
Righteous acts & deeds. Rev.19:7-8
What one does within his body.
2 Cor.5:10
Works. Faithful works. Mt.16:27;
25:31-46; Lk.19:11-27;Ro.2:10;
1 Cor.3:8; 2 Cor.5:10;Eph.6:8;
1 Pt.1:17; Rev.19:7-8;20:12;
21:24-27; 22:1-5; 22:12
Crown.
Of glory. 1 Pt.5:4
Of incorruption. 1 Cor.9:25
Of life. Jas.1:12; Rev.2:10
Of righteousness. 2 Tim.4:8
Of the soul-winner. 1 Th.2:19-20
Degrees of rewards. Mt.13:8; 20:23-28;
25:20-30;Lk.12:44; 16:12; 19:15-28
The great vs. the chief. Mk.10:40
Discussed. Mt.19:27-30; Ro.8:17;
Eph.1:3-14;2:4-7
List of heavenly rewards. Lk.16:10-12;
Ro.8:17; 1 Cor.3:13-15; Tit.3:6;
1 Pt.1:4; Rev.14:13
Six significant **r**. for being faithful.
Jn.4:36-38
How to secure - Duty.
Accepting one's call & laboring.
Mt.20:1-7
Being faithful & responsible.
Lk.10:15-28; 16:10-12; 22:28-30
By diligently seeking God. Heb.11:6
By not seeking recognition, but labor-
ing quietly. Mt.6:1; Col.3:22-24
By receiving ministers. Mt.10:40-42
Enduring trials & temptation.
1 Pt.1:6-9
Giving all one is & has. Lk.18:18-30
Laboring diligently. Lk.19:15-26
Leaving all & following Christ.
Mk.10:28
Looking to Christ, the supreme exam-
ple. Ph.2:9-11
Looking to one's **r**. Ph.3:20-21
Ministering. Lk.9:48
Ministering in Christ's name. Mk.9:41
Ministering to & welcoming others.
Mt.10:40-42
Not by fleshly works & energy.
Mt.20:11-14
Obedience. Lk.6:35-36
Seekers & achievers receive more &
more. Mt.13:10-11
Seeking. Mk.10:28-31
Staunch labor. 1 Cor.15:58
Suffering & enduring the sufferings
for Christ. Mt.5:11-12; Ro.8:16-17;
2 Tim.2:12; Heb.10:34;
11:26;Rev.20:4
Using one's gifts faithfully. Mt.25:14-30
Watching so that we will not lose our
r. 2 Jn.8

Welcoming people. Threefold.
Lk.9:48
In the New Jerusalem. Discussed.
Rev.21:24-27; 22:1-5
Misconception of. Seeking **r**. are thought
to be mercenary. Mk.10:28-31
Of martyrs. Discussed. Rev.7:15-17
Of the Apostles. To sit upon thrones.
Mt.19:27-28
Promised. In both this life & in the next
life. Four **r**. Mt.19:29; Mk.10:29
Results. Last shall be first; first shall be
last. Mt.20:16
Verses. List of. Lk.16:10-12; Ro.8:17;
1 Cor.3:13-15; Tit.3:6; Rev.14:13
What the rewards are.
Rewards dealing with inheritance or
wealth.
A great **r**. Mt.5:12; Lk.6:35
A house, building, mansion.
Jn.14:1-3; 2 Cor.5:1-4
All the things of heaven yet to
come. Heb.11:20
An inheritance. Mt.25:34; 1 Pt.1:3-5
Being made a joint heir with Christ.
Ro.8:16-17; 8:17; Rev.1:5
Great riches. Heb.11:26
Heavenly riches. Lk.16:12
Inheriting a continuing city.
Heb.13:13-14
Inheriting the world. Ro.4:13
Material & spiritual **r**. Mt.19:29
Possessing all things. 1 Cor.3:21-23
Receiving a hundredfold & eternal
life. Mt.19:27-30
The heavenly city. Heb.11:10
The heavenly country. Heb.11:13-16
The heavenly Jerusalem.
Heb.12:22
The inheritance of all of God's pos-
sessions. Heb.11:8-9
The Promised Land, heaven. Acts
7:2-8
Wages paid. Mt.20:8-16
Rewards dealing with nature or state
of being.
A full reward. 2 Jn.8
A glorious incorruptible body.
1 Cor.15:35-49; 15:50-58
All needs met. Rev.7:16
An abundant **r**. Lk.18:28-30
An rich welcome into heaven. 2
Pt.1:11
Being filled. Mt.5:6
Being in glory. Verses. List of.
Jn.17:24
Being translated into the Kingdom
of God. Col.1:13
Being transported into heaven.
2 Tim.4:18
Clothed in white raiment. Rev.3:4-5
Comfort. Mt.5:4
Crown of glory. 1 Pt.5:4
Crown of incorruption. 1 Cor.9:25
Crown of life. Jas.1:12; Rev.2:10
Crown of rejoicing. 1 Th.2:19-20
Crown of righteousness. 2 Tim.4:8
Crown of soul-winning. 1 Th.2:19-20
Deliverance from death. Heb.11:19
Deliverance from the second death.
Rev.2:10
Eternal inheritance. An eternal exis-
tence of life. Eph.2:11-13
Fivefold **r**. Ro.2:6-10
Glorified. Eternal glory. Ro.8:30

Living in a place where there is no more curse. Rev.20:3

Made a citizen of God's kingdom. Lk.9:27; 22:29-30

Made a citizen of Kingdom of Heaven. Mt.5:3; 5:10-12; Lk.22:28-30

Made a citizen of the New Jerusalem, the capital of the new heavens & earth. Rev.21:9-22:5

Made immortal. 2 Tim.1:10

New heavens & earth. Rev.21:1-22:5

No more hunger. Rev.7:16

No more tears. Rev.7:17

No more thirst. Rev.7:16

Partaking of the hidden manna. Rev.2:17

Partaking of the river of life. Rev.22:1

Partaking of the tree of life, paradise. Rev.2:7; 22:2

Protection from scorching heat & sweat. Rev.7:16

Rest. Heb.4:1; 4:9; Rev.14:13

Resurrection of the body. Heb.11:19; 11:35

Righteousness. 2 Cor.5:21; Heb.1:8-9

Seeing the New Jerusalem. Rev.21:2

Sharing equally with Christ. Heb.2:11-13

To receive glory. Ro.8:18; 2 Cor.4:17; 2 Tim.2:10;1 Pt.5:1

Utopia - all things provided. Rev.7:15-17

Rewards dealing with the personal relationship between God & Christ & believers.

Adopted as brothers of Christ. Heb.2:11-13

Beholding Jesus' glory. Jn.17:24

Being made kings & priests. Rev.5:10

Being shown the riches of God's grace throughout all of eternity. Eph.2:7

Being where Jesus is. Jn.12:26; 17:24

Children of God. Mt.5:9

Equal with Christ. Jn.16:15

Face to face with God. Ro.8:34

Given the name of God. Rev.3:12

Given the name of the city of God. Rev.3:12

Given the name of the Lord. Rev.3:12

Leadership of God. Rev.7:17

Mercy. Mt.5:7

Name will be kept in the Book of Life. Rev.3:5

Part of the great family of believers. Heb.11:11-12

Placed before the throne of God. Rev.7:9

Presence of God & Christ. Mt.10:40-42

Presented without fault- by God's power. Jude 24-25

Seeing God. Mt.5:8

Surrounding the throne of God. Rev.7:9-13; 20:4

The morning star - Christ Himself. Rev.2:28

Three things. Mt.5:3; Lk.6:35-36

Will be with Christ in glory. Jn.17:24; 2 Cor.5:8; Ph.1:23;Col.3:4; 1 Th.4:17

Rewards dealing with work or position or rule.

Being honored. Jn.12:26

Being made a kingdom & priests. Rev.5:10

Being made ruler over God's property. Mt.24:45-47

Being publicly rewarded. Mt.6:4; 6:6; 6:18

Exaltation. If one humbles himself. 1 Pt.5:5-7

Given authority & power over nations. Rev.2:26-27

Given judgment over the world & angels. 1 Cor.6:2-3

Given responsibility over many things. Mt.25:20-23

Given rulership & joy. Mt.25:20-23

Judged great in the Kingdom of Heaven. Mt.11:11; Lk.6:20-23

Receiving a great kingdom. Heb.12:28

Receiving reciprocal r. equal to one's labor. Mt.10:40-42; Lk.6:35-36; 6:37-38;Eph.6:8

Recognition of men. Mt.6:2

Reigning forever & ever. Rev.22:5

Reigning on earth. Rev.5:10; 20:4-6

Ruling & reigning. Mt.19:28; Lk.22:28-30; 22:30;1 Cor.6:2-3; Rev.14:13; 20:4-6;21:24-27; 22:5

Ruling & reigning & serving Christ forever. Rev.14:13; 2:24-27

Sitting upon thrones. Mt.19:27-28; Lk.22:28-30

Work & responsibility. To serve God night & day. Rev.7:15

REWARD OF UNBELIEVERS (See **JUDGMENT**)

RHODES

City of. Discussed. Acts 21:1-3

RICH - RICHES (See **MONEY; TREASURE, SPIRITUAL; WEALTH**)

Desire for. By Matthew. Mk.2:14

Discussed. Mt.19:16-30; Mk.10:17-22;Lk.18:18-23; Jas.5:1-6

How a rich man enters the kingdom of heaven. Mt.19:16-22

The danger of r. Mt.19:23-26

The parable of the rich fool. The man of wealth. Lk.12:13-21

The reward for believers. Mt.19:27-30

The rich man & Lazarus. The self-indulgent vs. the man of faith. Lk.16:19-31

The secret to contentment. 1 Tim.6:6-10

Duty toward riches.

Discussed. The charges to the rich man. 1 Tim.6:17-19

To be totally committed to helping others. Acts 4:32

To count the possession of Christ greater riches than the r. of the world. Heb.11:26

To fear death & not trust in r. Lk.12:20

To give all beyond one's necessities to meet the needs of the world. Acts 4:32

To give even when one is poor. 2 Cor.8:1-5

To keep one's mind focused upon the provision & riches of God. Mt.6:33; Ph.4:19

To trust God, not r. Lk.21:2

Facts.

Hoarding condemns one. Mt.19:21-22

It is easier for a camel to go through the eye of a needle than for a r. man to enter heaven. Mt.19:24

R. are not a permanent possession. Someone else gets. Lk.12:20-21

Some r. people did turn to Christ. Listed. Mt.19:26

The rich are doomed if they do not meet the needs of the world. Lk.18:18-30

The rich die just as everyone else. Lk.12:20

The rich often neglect needs. Lk.18:18-30

Judgment of the rich.

To be barred, excluded from heaven. Mt.19:23; 19:24

To be destroyed. Ph.3:18-19

To be stripped & emptied. Lk.1:51-53

To face destruction & perdition. 1 Tim.6:9-10

To suffer perdition. Heb.10:39

To suffer the vengeance of God. 2 Th.1:7-9

Meaning. Mk.10:23

Who are the r. Mt.19:23

Misconceptions of riches.

R. are a sign of God's blessings. Mt.19:25

R. are worth more than Christ & heaven. Mt.19:16-22; 19:23; 19:24

R. make one secure. Lk.12:19-20; 1 Th.5:3, cp. Mt.6:33

True treasure is r. on earth. Mt.6:19-21; 19:21; Lk.12:33-34

R. vs. God. Cannot serve two masters. Lk.16:13

R. young ruler. Mt.19:16-22

Results of being rich. Four significant results. 1 Tim.6:9-10

Saved - Salvation of. How the r. are saved.

How a r. man can be saved. Mt.19:16-22; Mk.10:21-22; 10:27

The man of wealth. Lk.12:13-21

Zacchaeus. Lk.19:1-10

Verses. List of. Lk.6:24-26; 8:11-15; 12:20-21

Warning - Danger of riches.

Discussed. Mt.19:23-26; Acts 2:44-45

Lust for. What r. cause. Acts 16:16-24

Three dangers. 1 Tim.6:17-19

Warning against riches.

Are deceitful & make a person unfruitful. Mt.13:22

Cause a person to reject Christ. Lk.18:18-30

Choke the life out of a person. Lk.8:11-15, esp. 14

Discussed. Lk.6:24-26; Jas.5:1-6

Hoarding & banking. Mt.19:21-22; Jas.5:1-6

Must not choose r. over Jesus. Mk.10:23-27

R. are uncertain. 1 Tim.6:17

RICH FOOL
Parable of. Man of wealth. Lk.12:13-21

RICH MAN & LAZARUS
The self-indulgent vs. a man of faith. Lk.16:19-31

RICH, THE (See RICH - RICHES; WEALTHY, THE)
Discussed. Jas.1:9-11

RICH YOUNG RULER
How a r. man enters heaven. Mt.19:16-22
Problem of eternal life. Mk.10:17-22
The cost of eternal life. Lk.18:18-30

RID YOURSELF
Meaning. Eph.4:20-24; Col.3:8-11; Heb.12:1; 1 Pt.2:1-3

RIDICULE (See MOCKERY)

RIGHTEOUS - RIGHTEOUSNESS (See GODLY - GODLINESS; JUSTICE)
Armor of.
  Breastplate of. Eph.6:14-17
  Discussed. 2 Cor.6:6-7
Crown of. Discussed. 2 Tim.4:8
Described. As the golden rule. The summit of ethics. Mt.7:12
Discussed. Mt.5:6; Ro.1:17; 3:21-26; Gal.2:15-16; 3:19-22
Duty - Essential.
  One's r. must exceed the r. of religionists. Mt.5:20
  To awake to r. & not sin. 1 Cor.15:34
  To be clothed in r. Mt.22:11-14
  To be clothed with the r. of Christ. Rev.3:18-20
  To be convicted of r. Jn.16:8-11
  To be filled with the fruits of r. Ph.1:11
  To be made (created into) the r. of God in Christ. Created into a new man. 2 Cor.5:21; Eph.4:24
  To be skillful in the Word of r. Heb.5:13
  To do the deeds of r. Rev.19:7-8
  To do to others what one would want done to oneself. Mt.7:12
  To follow after r. 1 Tim.6:11
  To hunger & thirst for r. Mt.5:6
  To know that it is time to live a r. life. Lk.12:54-57
  To live a r. life. Lk.1:68-75; 1 Jn.2:29
  To live a r. life, keeping one's eyes on the return of Christ. Tit.2:12-13
  To possess the name of *the righteous.* Mt.25:37, 46
  To put on the breastplate of r. To protect the heart with r. Eph.6:14
  To receive the r. of Christ. Rev.19:7-8
  To seek r. first. Mt.6:33
Fact.
  Fulfilled in the symbol of Jesus' baptism. Mt.3:13
  Man is not righteous & cannot earn r. Gal.2:15-16; 3:19-22
  Meaning. Lk.6:20-23; Ro.1:17; Eph.5:9;1 Tim.6:11; Tit.2:12-13; 2 Pt.1:1
    Christ Himself is the r. of God. Ro.3:21-22; 10:4; 1 Cor.1:30; Ph.3:9; 1 Jn.2:1
    Sins are not counted against a r. person. Ro.4:6-8
    The seal or sign of right standing with God. Ro.4:9; 4:10

Need for righteousness.
  Discussed. Ph.3:9; 3:7-16
  Man misses God's righteousness. Ro.10:1-11
  Man needs to be clothed in righteousness. Mt.22:11-14
  One can touch the r. of the law & still miss God's r. Ph.3:6, cp. 3:7-11
  R. is misunderstood by Israel. Ro.10:1-11
  Sin makes the r. of God an utter necessity. Ro.3:22-23
  The r. of religion is not enough to enter heaven. Mt.5:20; Ro.10:3
  The way to be right with God. Ro.3:21-26
Purpose. To declare God's r., His justice. Ro.3:25-26
Results of being made righteous in Christ.
  One inherits the kingdom of God. Mt.25:33-40, esp., 34, 37
  One is created into a new man. Eph.4:24
  One receives a crown of r. 2 Tim.4:8
  One shines forth as the sun with the glory of God. Mt.13:43
  Proves that one is a child of God. 1 Jn.3:10-17
  Proves that one is born of God. 1 Jn.2:28-29; 3:6-7
    To be given all the necessities of life. Mt.6:33
  R. is fulfilled in one's life. Ro.8:2-4
Self-righteousness. Vs. the righteousness of another. Mt.5:3
Source of righteousness.
  Abiding, continuing in Christ. 1 Jn.2:29
  Discussed. 2 Cor.5:21
  Faith in Christ. Ro.3:22
  God. Seen in Abraham. Ro.4:1-25; 4:1-3
  Jesus Christ. Ro.3:21-22; 10:4; Ph.3:9; 1 Jn.2:1
  Not by the law. Ro.3:21-22; 10:4
  Not inherited. Mt.3:7-10
  Rejecting self-righteousness. Ph.3:4-6
  The Spirit of God. Ro.8:2-4
The righteousness of God.
  Discussed. Ro.10:1-11
  God ended securing righteousness by law & doing good. Through Jesus Christ. Ro.10:4
  God is opposed to man's r. Ro.10:5
  God's r. is Jesus Christ. Ro.3:21-22; 10:4; Ph.3:9; 1 Jn.2:1
  R. is the very nature of God. Jn.17:25
Vs. self-righteousness. Discussed. Lk.11:39-41; Ro.4:9-12

RIGHTEOUSNESS, CROWN OF
Meaning. 2 Tim.4:8

RING
Pictures authority. Lk.15:22

RIOT - RIOTING (See MOB, Riot; ORGIES)
A study of mob behavior. Acts 18:28-19:15
Against Christianity in Ephesus. Acts 19:21-41
Against Stephen. By students. Acts 6:9-10; 7:54-60

RIOTOUS LIVING (See WILD LIVING)
Defined. Lk.15:12-13
Duty. Not to walk in r., drunkenness & immorality. Ro.13:13

RISE - RISEN (See JESUS CHRIST, Resurrection)

RITUAL (See CEREMONY; RELIGION)
Problem with.
  Does not make men acceptable to God. Ro.2:25-27
  Does not save. Acts 15:1-3; 15:24; Ro.2:17-29;4:11
  Enslaves a person. Gal.4:9-11
  Placed before people & their needs. Mk.2:23-24; 3:1-6; Lk.6:1-11; 10:29-37; 13:14-16; 14:3
  Rituals are not the way to God. Ro.2:25-27; 1 Cor.7:18-19;Gal.4:1-3; 4:9-11
  Rituals are the wrong way to seek justification. Ro.4:9-12; Gal.3:1-4:7; 4:8-5:12
  Should a believer stay in his old church after conversion. 1 Cor.7:18-19
  Signs & symbols only. Ro.4:11
Purpose of rituals. To serve, not master man. Mk.2:25-27
Vs. Christ. Discussed. Col.2:20-23
Weakness of rituals.
  Discussed. Col.2:20-23
  Stressed over Christ. Heb.13:9-11

RIVALRY (See JEALOUSY)

ROADS
Of ancient days. Discussed. Mk.1:3

ROB - ROBBERY (See STEALING)

ROBE
Pictures honor & sonship. Lk.15:22

ROBES, WHITE
Meaning. Rev.7:9-10; 7:13-14

ROCK
Duty. To build one's life upon the solid foundation of a r. Mt.7:24-27
Symbol - Type of. The confession of Christ. Mt.16:18
The Lord is not a lifeless r., but a "living stone." Mt.7:24-25

ROCK OF OFFENSE (See ROCK THAT MAKES THEM FALL)

ROCK THAT MAKES THEM FALL
Name - Title. Of Christ. Many stumble over. Ro.9:32-33

ROME, ANCIENT
Church at Rome. Ro. Introd.
Discussed. Ro. Introd., cp. Acts 16:12-40; 28:13-15; 28:13; 28:16-31;
Paul & Rome.
  Longed to evangelize Rome. Acts 19:21
  Was taken to Rome as a prisoner. Acts 28:16-17
  Wrote the church at Rome. Ro.1:7
Symbolic name of. Babylon. 1 Pt.5:13
Traits of. Will be embodied in the antichrist. Rev.13:2

ROOT OF DAVID
Name for the Messiah. Rev.5:5

ROOTS (See **HERITAGE**)
Honoring, relying upon. Mt.23:29-33

ROYAL OFFICIAL
An official in a king's court. Jn.4:46-47

RUDE - RUDENESS
Meaning. 1 Cor.13:4-7

RUDIMENTS (See **BASIC PRINCIPLES**)

RUFUS
Son of Simon of Cyrene who bore Jesus'
cross. Mk.15:21; Ro.16:13

RULERS (See **JESUS CHRIST**, Opposed;
Response to; **RELIGIONISTS**, Opposed
Christ)
Duty toward.
To obey God rather than men. Acts 5:29
To pray for all **r**. 1 Tim.2:2
To submit & obey **r**. Tit.3:1;
1 Pt.2:13-17
Of government. Discussed. Ro.13:1-7
Opposed Christ. Wanted nothing to do
with Him. Jn.7:45-53
Sins of. Common to civil **r**. Acts 4:5-10

RULES & REGULATIONS (See
**CEREMONY; RELIGION; RELIG-
IONISTS; RITUAL; SCRIBAL LAW**)
Criteria to break. Mt.12:3-4
Deliverance from. Wiped out by Christ.
Eph.2:13-18
Described as. Heavy burdens. Mt.23:4
Facts about rules.
Are not to be put before man's wel-
fare. Mk.2:23-24; 3:1-6
Are to be subject to Christ. Mk.2:23-28
Inward purity is more important than
ceremony. Lk.11:37-39
Superseded by need. Lk.6:1-11;
13:10-17; 14:1-6
Problem with.
Emptiness of. Mk.7:1-13
Enslaves. Gal.4:9-11
Stands against the gospel. Gal.2:1-10
The wrong way to seek justification.
Ro.4:9-12
R. are placed upon men's shoulders. Four
ways. Mt.23:4
Vs. Christ. Col.2:16-17; 2:20-23
Weakness of. Discussed. Col.2:20-23

RULING & REIGNING (See **LEAD-
ERRSHIP; REWARDS**)
Reward of believers. For faithfulness.
Lk.12:41-48

RUNNER, ATHLETIC
Illustrates the Christian race. 1 Cor.9:24-27

RUTH
Saved by God. Mt.1:3

RUTHLESS
Meaning. Ro.1:31

S

SABBATH - SUNDAY
Authority over. Christ has **a**. over. Mk.2:28;
Lk.6:5; Jn.5:1-16; 9:14,cp. 1-41
Discussed. Mt.12:1; 12:12; Lk.6:1

Understanding the **S**. Mk.2:23-28
Duty.
To do good works on the **S**. Mt.12:12;
Mk.6:2; Jn.7:23; 9:14
To pray on the **S**. Acts 16:13
To teach on the **S**. Mk.6:2; Acts 17:2
Fact. Need supersedes the **S**. Lk.6:1-11
Laws governing.
Broken by Christ. Mt.12:1-8; 12:9-13
Broken by the disciples. Mk.2:23-24
Not allowed to heal or help on the **S**.
Mt.12:10
The Jewish **l**. Mt.12:1-8; 12:10
Meaning. Mt.12:12
True meaning of the **S**. Mk.2:23-28
Messiah is greater than the Sabbath.
Mt.12:1-8
Misusing - abusing the **S**.
Condemned by Christ. Lk.13:14-16
Understanding the **S**. Mk.2:23-28
Purpose.
Discussed. Mt.12:5; 12:12
The **S**. was made for man. Mk.2:27
To serve man. Mk.2:25-27
Sunday - the first day of the week.
Called the Lord's Day. Rev.1:10
Christ arose on Sunday. Mk.16:9;
Lk.24:13-15; Jn.20:19
Paul preached on Sunday, the first day
of the week. Acts 20:7
The early church worshipped on Sun-
day. Acts 20:7; 1 Cor.16:1-2
Was the day right after the Sabbath.
Mt.28:1; Mk.16:1-2
Working on **S**. Discussed. Mt.12:5;
12:12

SACRIFICE, SPIRITUAL (See **COM-
MITMENT; CROSS - SELF-DENIAL;
DEDICATION**)
Duty.
Mercy required, not **s**. Discussed.
Mt.12:7
To offer the **s**. of praise to God con-
tinually. Heb.13:15
To offer up spiritual **s**. to God.
1 Pt.2:5
To present one's body as a living **s**. to
God. Ro.12:1
To **s**. all we are & have. Mt.19:21-22;
19:23-26; 19:27-30;Lk.14:28-33
To **s**. our lives to bear witness.
Ph.2:17-18
Idea of. **S**. is present in all of man's en-
deavors. Acts 14:8-13
Meaning. 2 Tim.4:6
Of Christ. (See **JESUS CHRIST**, Death,
Sacrifice; **SACRIFICES**, Christ's sacrifice)
Cost of. Jn.3:16
Died as our **s**. Ro.5:6-7
Purpose.
To offer up spiritual sacrifices to God.
1 Pt.2:5
To secure favor & blessings. Acts
14:8-13
Vs. common sense. Mt.26:8-9; Mk.14:6

SACRIFICES - SACRIFICIAL SYSTEM
Christ's **s**. Vs. the old **s**.
Description. Heb.9:11-14 9:15-22
Discussed.
Christ is the Lamb of God. Jn.1:29-30
Is a better way. Heb.9:11-14; 9:15-22
To be our Passover, the very means by
which God's wrath can pass over us.
1 Cor.5:7

To bear sin. Heb.9:28
To cleanse the unclean. Heb.9:13-14
To deliver from this present evil
world. Gal.1:4
To die to reconcile us to God. Ro.5:10
To enter God's presence for man.
Heb.9:23-24
To enter heaven for man. Heb.9:23-24
To give His life as a ransom for many.
Mt.20:28
To give His life as an offering & as a
sacrifice to God. To please God & to
please Him perfectly. Eph.5:2
To obtain eternal redemption.
Heb.9:12-14
To purge conscience. Heb.9:14
To put away sin. Heb.9:25-26; 9:27-28,
cp. 24-28
To redeem & purify us to be His very
special people. Tit.2:14
To redeem us from the curse of the
law. Gal.3:13
To take away the old **s**. & to establish
the new. Heb.9:1-14; 9:23-28; 10:8-10;
13:12-16
To wash us from our sins. Rev.1:5
Was offered once for all. Heb.7:27;
9:12; 9:24-26; 10:10;10:14; 10:17-18
Was the **s**. of Himself. Heb.9:14; 9:28
Witnesses to by the Holy Spirit.
Heb.10:15-18
Discussed. Heb.7:25-28; 8:1-5; 9:1-14;
9:15-22; 9:23-28; 10:1-18; 13:9-16
Function.
To be an earthly pattern of heavenly
things. Heb.9:23-28
To point to the cleansing of all things
by blood. Heb.9:18-22
To point to the heavenly, spiritual
priesthood. Heb.8:1-5
To point to the tabernacle, the heav-
enly worship not made with hands.
Heb.9:11-14
To provide a shadow of the real image
of things to come. Heb.10:1-18
Of the O.T. The sacrifices were called the
sacrificial "Bread of God." A type of
Christ. Jn.6:33
Problem with the old **s**.
Could not cleanse the conscience.
Heb.9:9
Could not perfect conscience.
Heb.9:9-10
Could not perfect man. Heb.9:9
Could not remove sin or perfect man.
Heb.7:25-28; 9:1-10; 9:11-14;10:1-18
Gave no pleasure to God. Heb.10:5-10
Left a consciousness of sin. Heb.10:3,
cp. 1-4
Purified only the flesh. Heb.9:11-14
Required a better **s**. than the sacrifice
made by man. Heb.9:23-28
Were only a shadow of things to come,
not the image. Heb.10:1-18, cp. 8:3-5
Were only a type of Christ. Heb.9:8-
10, cp. 11-14; 9:23-28
Were only made with hands--only fig-
ures of the true. Heb.9:23-24
Were only material **s**. & ordinances.
Heb.9:10, cp. 1-10
Were only patterns of heavenly things.
Heb.9:10, cp. 1-10; 9:23-28
Were powerless. Heb.9:25-26; 10:1-4
S. was fulfilled in the death of Christ.
Col.1:20

SADDUCEES (See **RELIGIONISTS**)
Attacked - Opposed.
Christ. Mt.16:1-12; 22:23-33
Cooperated with the Pharisees. Discussed. Mt.16:1-12; 22:34-40
John the Baptist. Mt.3:7-12
The apostles: a picture of abuse. Acts 5:17-25; 5:26-42
Belief about signs. Mt.16:13-20
Ct. Pharisees. Acts 23:8
Discussed. Lk.20:27; Acts 23:8
Liberal minded.
Their liberal beliefs. Mt.22:23-33; 22:23-28
Their liberal position caused two things. Mk.12:22-33
They questioned & denied.
The resurrection. Lk.20:27-38; 20:27; Acts 4:1-4; 23:8
The supernatural. Lk.20:27; Acts 23:8
Paul sets **S**. beliefs against the Pharisees. Acts 22:30-23:11
Teaching. Errors of. Mt.16:5-12

SADNESS
Answer to. Christ, the risen Lord. Lk.24:15-27
Caused by. Hopes dashed. Lk.24:13-14; 24:15-27

SAFETY (See **SECURITY**)

SAINTS (See **BELIEVERS; FAITHFUL BROTHERS-HOLY BROTHERS**)
Discussed. Acts 9:32; 1 Cor.1:2; 1 Pt.1:15-16
Meaning. 1 Cor.1:2; Ph.1:1

SALAMIS
City of. Discussed. Acts 13:5

SALOME
Mother of James & John. Mt.20:21
Saw the empty tomb of Jesus. Mk.16:1-8

SALT
Discussed. Mt.5:13; Mk.9:49; 9:50
Must be salted with salt, pure & useful. Mk.9:50
Must let speech be seasoned with salt, that is, with grace, being very gracious. Col.4:6
Fact. Cursing burns just like salt water. Jas.3:12
Symbol - Type.
Of discipleship, self-denial. Lk.14:34-35
Of judgment. Salted with fire. Mk.9:49

SALVATION - SAVED (See **DELIVERANCE; JUSTIFICATION; REDEMPTION**; Related Subjects)
Abundant **s**. (See **SALVATION**, Blessings of)
A **s**. that gives one an abundance of six things. Ro.5:15-18
A **s**. that gives one life abundant. Jn.10:10
A **s**. that saves one to the uttermost. Heb.7:25
Assurance of **s**. (See **ASSURANCE**) Lk.17:19
Are assured through persecution. 1 Pt.1:1-12
Are kept by the power of God. 1 Pt.1:5
Believers are heirs of **s**. Heb.1:14
Chosen & appointed by God Himself. 1 Th.5:9; 2 Th.2:13

God will complete the work He has begun. Ph.1:6
God's oath assures. Heb.6:16-20
The account of **s**. is sure. 2 Pt.1:19-21
The record of **s**. is assured. 1 Jn.5:6-12
What **s**. is & does. Tit.3:4-7
Blessings of.
Abundance of six things. Ro.5:15-18
Christ heals both soul & body. Mt.14:36
S. brings assurance. Jn.6:37-40
S. bring joy. Mt.18:13; Jn.1:45
S. brings seasons of refreshing. Acts 3:19
S. causes heavenly beings to stand in stark amazement. Eph.3:10-12
S. changes masters, not just behavior. Ro.6:17-18
S. gives one a position of authority. Lk.15:22-24
S. gives one an abundant life. Jn.10:10
S. gives the privilege of being chosen & appointed by God Himself. 1 Th.5:9; 2 Th.2:13
S. is forgiveness & receiving of the Holy Spirit. Acts 2:38
S. leads to discipleship. Mt.20:34
S. makes one whole. Meaning. Acts 4:9
S. opens one's eyes. Jn.9:1-7
S. saves & hides a multitude of sins. Jas.5:19-20
S. saves one to the uttermost. Heb.7:25
S. swaps sin for God. Ro.6:17-18
The saved will know the truth & be set free. Jn.8:32
Cost of. (See **JESUS CHRIST**, Death; Sacrifice)
To God. Jn.3:16
Day of **s**.
Final triumph over evil. Great announcement of. Rev.10:1-11
When one is **s**. "Now" is the day of **s**. 2 Cor.6:2
Deliverance of.
From all the evil forces of the universe. Six forces. Rev.5:5
From condemnation. Jn.3:18; 3:18-21; 5:24; 8:1; 8:34, cp.1 Jn.3:18-21
From darkness. The light of life. Jn.8:12-13
From death. Jn.5:24-25; 8:48-59; 8:51
From fear. Jn.6:20-21
From perishing. Jn.3:14-15; 3:16
From Satan's power. Heb.2:14-15
From sin. Ro.6:17-18; 7:14-17
From sin & its dominating power. Ro.6:14-15
From sin, death, & hell. Cure is now available. Acts 1:8; Eph.1:7
From struggling. By the Spirit. Ro.8:1-39
From the severest circumstances & most extreme experiences. Ro.8:35-37
From the wrath of God. Ro.5:9
From trouble. Fivefold deliverance. Jn.14:1-3
Is a conversion experience. Mk.1:25-26
List of things delivered from. Lk.9:47
Meaning & results. Mt.1:21
Sets one free from five things. 2 Cor.3:17-18
The difference between a liberator & a deliverer. Lk.22:19-20
Through persecution. 1 Pt.1:1-12

Described.
As a new birth. One must go through the new birth. Jn.3:1-15
As being healed. Mt.14:36
As good ground. Fruit-bearing. Mt.13:8, 23
As living water. One must drink. Jn.4:10-14
As so great a **s**. One must experience. Heb.2:3-4
As the bread of life. One must eat. Jn.6:30-36; 6:47-51
As the helmet of **s**. One must put on. Eph.6:14-17
As the perfect **s**. Heb.7:25-28
Discussed. Jn.1:12-13; 14:1-3; Ro.1:16; 1:16-17; Eph.2:8-10; 2:13-18; 2 Th.2:13-17; Tit.2:11-15; 3:4-7; Heb.7:25; 1 Pt.1:10-12
Four key questions. Gal.3:1-5
God's eternal plan. Jn.4:22
Lessons on. Acts 19:1-20
Preparation for **s**; cry for **s**; proclamation & fruits of **s**. Acts 16:25-40
Questions about **s**. Great Jerusalem Council answers. Acts 15:1-35
Receiving & rejecting men. Mt.8:5-13
Stages of **s**. 1 Cor.1:18
Stages of spiritual sight. Jn.9:8-41
The final triumph over evil. Overall view. Rev.11:14-19
The wonder of **s**. 1 Pt.1:10-12
What **s**. is & does. Tit.3:4-7
Duty. (See **SALVATION**, How One is Saved; Related Subjects)
Must do the works of salvation. Heb.6:9
Must look for the second coming of Christ. Heb.9:28
Must not neglect or drift away from **s**. Heb.2:1-4
The duties of **s**. 2 Pt.1:5-7
The great task of pastors in **s**. 2 Pt.1:12-15
To carry the message of **s**. to all. Mk.1:36-39
To pray for the **s**. of all men. 1 Tim.2:1-8
To rejoice not in power but in **s**. Lk.10:20
To remember **s**. & not forget one's **s**. experience. Jn.5:13-14
To stand firm & cling to the Word of God. 2 Th.2:15
To struggle to enter the narrow door of **s**. Lk.13:24
To work out one's own **s**. Ph.2:12-18
Two choices. Mt.7:13-14
Error - Misconceptions.
Believing that **s**. is by heritage, godly parents, & forefathers. Jn.8:33
Thinking that a changed life necessarily **s**. Acts 2:38
Thinking that a spectacular, dramatic experience delivers. Jn.14:8
Thinking that baptism necessarily **s**. Acts 2:38
Thinking that man can save man. Mt.19:26
Thinking that one can approach God in one's own way. Lk.11:39-41
Thinking that one can wait & be saved later. Reasons. Mt.8:25; Lk.13:25
Thinking that one is saved by baptism, joining the church, etc. 1 Jn.3:5
Thinking that profession of faith necessarily **s**. Acts 2:38

Essential. **S**. must be a free gift. Seven reasons why. Eph.2:8-9
Fact.
Being **s**. is not assured. Mt.18:13
Even the saved are barely **s**. 1 Pt.4:17-18
Few are actually ever saved. Lk.13:24
God has no favorites. **S**. is available to all men. Col.1:26-27
Jesus seeks every single person. Mt.18:11; 18:12
One can act too late to be saved. Lk.13:25
S. is already an accomplished fact. Eph.2:6
S. is free. Ro.3:24; Rev.22:17
S. is not a fable. 2 Pt.1:16
S. is not inherited. Mt.1:7-10; 3:7-10
S. is universal, offered to everyone. Lk.3:6; Jn.6:33; Acts 2:21;Ro.5:18; 10:13; 1 Tim.2:4;Tit.2:11-12; 2 Pt.3:9
S. was revealed to the O.T. prophets. 1 Pt.1:10-12
S. will be consummated when Christ returns. Heb.9:28
The gate to **s**. will be closed in the last days. Rev.15:8
False **s**. (See **HYPOCRISY; PROFESSION, FALSE**)
How man seeks to meet his needs. 2 Pt.1:16
How one is saved - Conditions - Source.
A person is saved by the act of Christ.
By Christ alone. Acts 4:5-10; 4:11-12
By Christ, the Author of **s**. Heb.5:9
By Christ, the Bread of life. Jn.6:30-36; 6:52-58
By Christ, the Mediator. 1 Tim.2:3-7
By Christ, the only door into God's presence. Verses. List of. Jn.10:7-8; 10:9
By Christ's bitter sufferings. Heb.5:5-10
By Christ's second coming. Heb.9:28
By Jesus Christ. Ro.5:19-21
By the death & resurrection of Jesus Christ. Ro.4:23-25
By the death of Christ. Jn.3:14-15
By the life of the living Lord, the Intercessor, the Mediator. Ro.5:10-11
Discussed. Jn.3:17; 1 Tim.1:15-16; 2 Tim.1:8-10; Heb.2:10; 5:9; 7:11-24; 2 Pt.1:1-4
Christ alone opens & shuts the door. Rev.3:7
Christ knocks on the door of man's heart. Rev.3:18-20
Christ took away sin. 1 Jn.3:5
Eagerness of Christ to save. Jn.1:38-39
Christ alone is the Way to God. Jn.14:4-7
Christ alone saves.
Discussed. Tit.3:7
The world feels that this is a narrow view of **s**. Jn.16:1-6
Christ is the Light of the world. Jn.8:12-13
Christ is the Mediator of **s**. (See **JESUS CHRIST**, Mediator)
One must be covered by the blood of Christ. 1 Pt.1:2
S. is the mission of the Lord. Lk.9:51-56

The initiative of **s**. comes from Christ. Jn.1:43-44
The revelation of Christ is necessary for **s**. Lk.10:22
A person is saved by the act of God.
By God our Savior. 1 Tim.1:1; 2:3-7
By God recreating a person. Through the new birth. Mk.4:27; Eph.2:8-10
By God's act & grace. Acts 2:39; 15:7-11
By God's call. Acts 2:39
By God's gift. Jn.3:16; 4:10; Ro.6:23; 8:32;2 Cor.9:15; Eph.2:8-9
By God's grace.
Bothers some people. Two reasons. Ro.6:1
Discussed. Acts 15:11; Ro.3:23-24; Eph.1:7;2:8-9; Tit.2:11; 3:7
Through faith. Eph.2:8-10
By God's great invitation. Mt.22:1-14
By God's great promise. Ro.10:13
By God's inward working. Ro.2:28-29
By God's longsuffering, patience. 2 Pt.3:9; 3:15-16
By God's love. Jn.3:16-17
By God's mercy. Eph.2:4-9; Tit.3:4-5
By God's power. Ro.1:16-17
God alone **s**. Men rebel against. Jn.6:65
God elects men to **s**. 1 Pt.1:1-2
God makes the believer alive. Eph.2:1-7
God's part & man's part. Jn.6:44-46; Acts 3:16
One is not **s**. by ritual or ceremony, but by the grace of God. Acts 15:1-3
One must be drawn to God. Jn.6:44-46
One must be stirred by God to believe. Acts 3:16
One must open his heart to God. Acts 16:14
A person is saved by the act of man.
Approaches that lay hold of Jesus. Mk.5:21-43
Argument over how one is **s**. Acts 15:4
Attitudes needed for **s**. Mt.14:36
By a faith that works & lives. Jas.2:14-26
By being "*in* Christ." Ro.8:1
By belief, not by works. Jn.6:22-29
By believing & continuing in Christ. Jn.8:31-32; Heb.10:39
By believing God's promise. Ro.9:7-13
By believing that God raised Christ from the dead. Ro.10:9-10
By believing the "message," the gospel. Ro.10:16-17
By building wisely & not foolishly. Mt.7:24-27
By calling on the name of the Lord. Acts 2:21; Ro.10:13
By coming to Christ, the living stone. 1 Pt.2:4-8
By crying for mercy. Lk.18:13
By doing the works of Abraham. Jn.8:39-40
By enduring, standing firm to the end. Mt.10:22; Mk.13:13

By faith. Lk.7:50; 17:19; 18:42; Heb.11:7
By following Christ's great suffering. 1 Pt.2:21-25
By giving all one is & has. Mk.10:21-22; 10:27
By having more righteousness than a religionists. Mt.5:20
By hearing the voice of Christ. Jn.10:4-5
By making restitution. Lk.19:8-10
By prayer & the Holy Spirit. Ph.1:19
By receiving the Word of God. 2 Tim.3:15; Jas.1:21
By repentance. Lk.19:8-10
By repentance & belief. Mk.1:15
By the faith of friends. Mt.9:2
By the stirring of hearts. Jn.8:31
By working out one's own **s**. Ph.2:12-13
Costs everything. Matthew illustrates. Mk.2:14
Faith vs. works. Offends man. Jn.6:63-64; 6:65
God's part & man's part. Jn.6:44-46; Acts 3:16
How one partakes of **s**. Jn.6:41-51
How to be right with God. Ro.3:21-26
Man cannot save man. Mt.19:26; Acts 4:11-12
Man has two choices. Broad & narrow. Mt.7:13-14
Man is not **s**. by corruptible things. 1 Pt.1:18-20
Man is not **s**. by heritage, parents, race, or institution. Ro.3:1-2; 9:6-13
Man is not **s**. by man himself. Reasons. Mt.19:26; Acts 4:11-12
Man is not **s**. by respectability. Mk.10:19-20
Man is not **s**. by ritual or religion, but by Christ. Ro.2:28-29; Col.2:11-12
Man is not **s**. by silver & gold. Acts 3:6-8
Man is not **s**. by the love of Christ alone. Christ's love is not enough to save man. Mk.10:21
Man is not **s**. by works. (See **JUSTIFICATION; WORKS**) Acts 15:1-35
Man is not **s**. by works & law, but by the righteousness of Christ. Gal.2:15-16; 2:16
Man rebels against being disregarded as the source of **s**. Jn.6:63-64
Must face the fact of sin. Jn.4:16-18
Must fear God & work righteousness. Acts 10:34-35
Must follow Christ. Jn.8:12-13
Must hunger for **s**. Lk.15:1-3
Must know God. Jn.7:16-19
Must lose one's life. Means saving one's life. Mt.16:25
Must love. Lk.7:47
Must repent & be baptized. Discussed. Acts 2:38
Must seek after Christ. Mt.5:6; 18:11-14
The confession of Christ.
Confessing vs. denying Christ. Mt.10:32-33
Confession needed. Great **C**. Who Jesus is. Mk.8:27-30

Discussed. Mt.16:13-17;
Ro.10:9-10
The requirements for **s**. Mk.10:17-22
The steps to **s**. Twofold. Mt.19:26
What it takes to receive things of
God. Mt.8:2; 15:21-28
What **s**. is not. Acts 16:31-33
What **s**. takes. Mt.9:27-31
Who shall enter heaven. Mt.7:21-23
Willingness is not enough.
Mt.8:19-20
Work vs. self-denial. Lk.6:32-34
Wrought by godly sorrow.
2 Cor.7:10
A person is saved by the act of Scrip-
ture & the gospel.
By the gospel. Ro.1:16-17
The declaration of James. Acts
15:13-21
The declaration of Paul. Acts 15:8
The declaration of Peter. Acts 15:7-11
The great declaration of **s**. Acts
15:6
The great decree of **s**. Acts 15:23-35
The three essentials involved in **s**.
Acts 24:24-25
The word of **s**. Is Jesus. Acts 13:23-28
Discussed. Lk.13:22-30; Ro.10:8-10;
Eph.2:6
Fourfold. Ro.8:23-27
How a rich man enters heaven.
Mt.19:16-22
How a rich man is **s**. Mt.19:16-22
Peter's great confession. Mt.16:13-20
S. in the end time. Rev.7:1-17;
11:1-13; 14:1-7
S. is from the Jews. Jn.4:22
Spiritual satisfaction. Jn.6:30-36
Steps to **s**.
Being made whole. Mt.8:2; 9:18-34;
14:34-36
Discussed. Mk.6:53-56; 10:46-52
Five steps. Lk.18:35-43
Steps involved in **s**. Discussed.
Acts 9:4-5; Ro.10:16-17
Stirred. By the judgment of God.
Acts 13:12
Three steps. Mt.8:19-20; Lk.18:40-42
Illustrated. By Onesimus. Phile.1:10-16
Meaning. Mt.1:21; Ro.1:16
Plan of. God's eternal plan. Jn.4:22
Proof of - Evidence of salvation.
Discussed. 2 Pt.1:16-21; 1:16
Four proofs. 1 Jn.5:1-21
Scripture. 2 Pt.1:19-21
Seven tests. 1 Jn.2:3-29
Sinning proves one does not know
God. 1 Jn.3:4-9
Six tests. 1 Jn.3:1-4:21
The Holy Spirit. Acts 19:1-9
Purpose of.
Are **s**. to obey & to lead others to
obey. Ro.1:5
Created by God to do good works.
Eph.2:10
The ultimate purpose. Eph.2:7
Response to salvation. Rejected.
Almost persuaded. Acts 26:24-32
Four responses. Acts 13:42-52
If neglect **s**., one cannot escape.
Heb.2:3; 12:25
Judgment of those who reject will be
terrible. Lk.10:10-16
Making excuses. Three excuses.
Lk.14:18-20

Many are invited but few are chosen.
Reasons. Mt.22:11-14
Putting off, procrastinating. Acts 24:25
Reasons why men reject Christ. Mt.8:23
Rejecting the words of Christ. Mt.7:26-27
To reject **s**. is illogical. Jn.12:37-41
Warning.
One can act too late. Lk.13:25
One can become hardened to the
gospel. Acts 28:27
Results of.
Blessings. (See **SALVATION**,
Blessings of)
Deliverance. (See **SALVATION**, De-
liverance of)
Discussed. Jn.6:52-58
Five results. Ro.1:16
The saved receive five resources.
2 Th.2:16-17
Salvation in Second Peter.
The great duties of **s**. 2 Pt.1:5-7
The great gift of Christ in **s**. 2 Pt.1:1-4
The great promises of **s**. 2 Pt.1:8-11
The great proof of **s**. 2 Pt.1:16-18
The great **s**. of God. 2 Pt.1:1-21
The great task of ministers in **s**.
2 Pt.1:12-15
Seeking. (See **SEEK - SEEKING**)
By the lost who have never heard of
Christ. Acts 10:1-6; 10:1-8
By the lost who see the delivering
power of God. Acts 16:30
God reaches any man who truly seeks.
Acts 10:30-33
Must seek by the cross. 1 Cor.1:17-25
Must seek today. Now is the day of **s**.
2 Cor.6:2
The response of Christ to those who
seek. Fourfold. Mt.9:20-22
Who God calls. Those who seek.
1 Cor.1:26-31
Why not seek earlier. Mt.8:25
Stages of. Past, present, & future **s**.
Jn.9:8-41; 1 Cor.1:18
The way of salvation.
Is changed. Heb.7:11-24
Old vs. new **s**. Heb.12:18-24
Who is **s**.
A businesswoman can be **s**. Acts
16:12-15
Anyone can be **s**.
Christ turns no one away. Lk.4:40
"Many" shall come. Predicted. Mt.8:11
No matter how great a sinner. Mk.3:28
People from all nations. Lk.13:29-30;
14:21-23
The desperate. Mt.9:18-34; 14:15-21;
15:29-39; 20:29-34
The evil possessed. Mt.8:28-34
The first European convert. Acts
16:12-15
The Gentiles. The door is opened to
the Gentiles. Discussed. Acts
10:1-48; 10:28-29; 15:13-21
The helpless. Lk.4:38-39; 4:40
The hopeless & desperate. Mt.9:18-34
The most defiled. Mt.8:1-4
The most enslaved & helpless.
Mk.1:23-28
The most rejected. Mk.7:24-30
The most unclean. Mk.1:40-45;
Lk.4:33-37
The most wild & mean. Mk.5:1-20
The outcast & sinner. Mk.2:13-17;
Lk.5:27-29

The person who believes. Jn.3:16
The rude. Mt.9:2
The sick. Mk.1:29-31; 1:32-34
The sinner. Mt.9:1-8; 9:9; 9:9-13;
Lk.18:13
The socially rejected. Mt.8:5-13
The untouchable. Lk.5:12-16
Who receives **s**. Jn.6:59-71
Whosoever. Ro.10:13
Who is not **s**.
Church members who practice sin.
1 Cor.6:9-11
Discussed. Lk.13:26
Unbelievers of so-called Christian na-
tions or certain fellowships. Lk.13:26

SAMARIA
Believers must witness in **S**. Acts 1:8
Churches were founded in **S**. Acts 9:31
Discussed. Lk.10:33; Jn.4:4
Revival in **S**. Led by Philip. A study in
revival. Acts 8:5-25

SAMARITAN, GOOD
Parable of. Supreme questions of life.
Lk.10:25-37

SAMARITANS
Discussed. Lk.10:33; Jn.4:4
Received the Holy Spirit. Discussed.
Acts 8:14-17
Rejected Christ. Reason. Lk.9:52-54

SAMSON
Faith of. Discussed. Heb.11:32

SAMUEL
Faith of. Discussed. Heb.11:32
Was a prophet of God. Acts 3:24

SANCTIFY - SANCTIFICATION
Discussed. Ro.7:14-25; 1 Cor.1:2;
1 Pt.1:15-16
Duty.
To guard against evil associations
which corrupt. 1 Cor.15:33
To live a clean life. 1 Cor.6:11
To live a moral & pure life. 1 Th.4:1-8
To purge oneself from bad behavior.
2 Tim.2:20-21
To sanctify all things by the Word of
God & prayer. 1 Tim.4:4-5
Meaning. Jn.17:17; 1 Cor.1:2; Ph.1:1;
1 Pt.1:2; 1:15-16
Of believers.
How & why believers must be sancti-
fied. Jn.17:17-19
Strong vs. weak believers. Ro.14:1-23
Struggle for **s**. Ro.7:14-25
The way for believers to be free from
sin. Ro.6:1-23
Principles of. Discussed. Ro.14:23
Questionable functions. Discussed.
Ro.14:1-23; 1 Cor.8:1-13
Source - How one is sanctified.
By Christ. 1 Cor.1:30; Heb.2:11-13
By God. 1 Th.5:23
By the death & blood of Christ.
Heb.9:14; 10:10, cp. 5-10; 13:12
By the Holy Spirit. 1 Pt.1:2
By the truth. Jn.17:17-19
By the Word of God & prayer.
Eph.5:26; 1 Tim.4:4-5

SANCTUARY
And worship. Earthly s.
    Discussed. Heb.9:1-10
    Weakness of. Heb.9:1-10
Heavenly s.
    Contrasted with the earthly s.
    Heb.9:1-14
    Discussed. Heb.9:1-14
Of heaven. The minister of the heavenly
    s. is Jesus Christ. Heb.8:2; 8:3; 8:4-5

SAND
Building upon. What s. is. Mt.7:26-27

SANHEDRIN (See RELIGIONISTS)
And Jesus.
    Met to formulate charges against
        Christ. Mk.15:1
    Opposed & condemned Christ. Prede-
        termined His guilt. Mt.21:23;
        26:57
    Sent an investigative delegation to in-
        vestigate Jesus. Mk.2:6-7
    Tried Jesus. For treason. Weak &
        strong character. Mk.14:53-65
Discussed. Mt.26:59; Jn.11:47;
    Acts 4:5-6

SANITY
Source of s.
    Being delivered from madness by con-
        version to Christ & committing one's
        life to making Christ known. Acts
        26:9-32, esp. 11, 24
    God. 2 Tim.1:7; 1 Pt.5:10
    Prayer & the peace of God.
        Ph.4:6-7
    The power of Christ. Lk.8:34-35

SAPPHIRA
Discussed. Acts 5:1-11

SARAH
Bore a son late in life. Heb.11:11-12
Faith of. An impossible faith.
    Heb.11:11-12
Type - Symbol of. Grace & righteousness
    by faith. Gal.4:21-31
Wife of Abraham. Example of. A godly
    wife. 1 Pt.3:4-6

SARCASM (See MOCKERY)
Example of. The brothers of Jesus were
    sarcastic to Him. Jn.7:3-5

SARDIS
Church of.
    Discussed. Rev.3:1
    One of the seven churches of Revela-
        tion. Rev.3:1-6
    Represents the church with reputation,
        but dying. Rev.3:1-6
City of. Rev.3:1-6

SATAN
Children of.
    The unloving. 1 Jn.3:10
    The unrighteous. 1 Jn.3:10
    Unbelievers. Jn.8:41-47
Defeated - Destroyed - Victory over.
    By the believer.
        Crushed by the believer. Ro.16:20
        By the works of the believer.
            Lk.10:17-18
        Crushed by the believer. Ro.16:20
    By Christ.

Satan had nothing in Christ.
    Jn.14:30-31
Satan has been cast out by the cross.
    Jn.12:31-33; 12:31; 14:30-31
Satan has been defeated in four
    ways. Lk.11:21-22
Satan has been defeated in six areas.
    Lk.10:18
Satan has been destroyed by Christ.
    Heb.2:14-15; 1 Jn.3:8
Satan is bound by Christ. Mk.3:27
Satan is condemned & judged by
    the cross. Jn.16:11
Satan's house has been spoiled by
    Christ. Mt.12:25-26; 12:29;
    Mk.3:27
Satan's power has been broken by
    Christ. Jn.12:31; Rev.12:9
Satan's power over death has been
    destroyed by the death of Christ.
    Heb.2:14-15
The purpose of Christ was to de-
    stroy s. Lk.9:1; 9:42-43; 10:18
The works of Satan have been de-
    stroyed by Christ. 1 Jn.3:8
Described as.
    A dragon. Rev.12:3-4
    A roaring lion. 1 Pt.5:8
    A star. Rev.9:1
    An enemy. 1 Pt.5:8
    An exalted being with great authority.
        A ruler. Rev.12:3-4
    The father of man. Jn.8:38
    The father of unbelievers. Jn.8:41-47
Discussed. Jn.8:38; 8:44-45; 2 Cor.4:4;
    1 Pt.5:8-9; Rev.12:3-4; 12:9
Existence of.
    Christ taught that Satan exists.
        Mt.13:19; Lk.11:17-18;
        Jn.8:44; 12:31; 13:38-39; 14:30
    Fell by pride. (See SATAN, Origin of)
        1 Tim.3:6, cp. Rev.9:1
    Satan is not a mistaken notion of
        man's imagination. Lk.11:17-18
    Unbelief in Satan Eph.6:12
Fate of.
    Cast into the lake of burning sulfur.
        Mt.25:41; Rev.20:7-10
    Will be bound & removed from the
        earth. Rev.20:1-3
Hour of. Meaning. Lk.22:53
How to combat & overcome.
    By forgiving others when they do
        wrong to us. 2 Cor.2:10-11
    By putting on the armor of God.
        Eph.6:10-13, cp. 14-18
    By resisting. Do not give place to the
        devil. Eph.4:27; Jas.4:7; 1 Pt.5:8-9
    By the blood of Christ. Rev.12:10-11
    By the keeping power of Jesus Christ.
        1 Jn.5:17-18
    By the new birth. 1 Jn.5:17-18
    Preventions against. Fourfold.
        Lk.22:31-38
    Through Christ. Heb.2:14-15
    Warning against. Attacks of Satan
        Lk.22:31-38
In the end time.
    Rebels against God. The final rebel-
        lion. Rev.11:18
    Will accuse believers. Rev.12:10
    Will attack the earth & the remnant of
        Israel. Rev.12:9, 17
    Will be bound & removed. Rev.20:1-3
    Will be cast into the lake of burning
        sulfur. Rev.20:10

Will be cast out of heaven to earth.
    Rev.12:7-9
Will be released at the end of the Mil-
    lennium. Rev.20:7-10
Will be worshipped world-wide.
    Rev.13:4, 8
Will give power to the antichrist.
    Rev.13:4-8
Will show terrible wrath. Rev.12:12,
    17
Will wage a war in heaven. Rev.12:1-
    17; 12:3-4; 12:7-9;12:13-14
Will wage war against the remnant of
    Israel. Rev.12:17
Names & Titles.
    Abaddon. Rev.9:11
    Accuser. Rev.12:10
    Adversary. Mt.16:21-23; 1 Pt.5:8
    Ancient serpent. Rev.12:9
    Angel of light. 2 Cor.11:14
    Apollyon. Rev.9:11
    Beelzebub. Mt.12:24
    Belial. 2 Cor.6:15
    Devil. Rev.12:9; 20:2
    Dragon. Rev.20:2
    Evil One. Jn.17:15
    Father of man. Jn.8:44, cp. 42-44;
        1 Jn.3:8
    Father of sin. Jn.8:44, cp. 42-44
    God of this world. 2 Cor.4:4
    King, the angel of the Abyss.
        Rev.9:11
    Power of darkness. Lk.22:53
    Prince of the devils. Mt.12:24
    Prince of the power of the air. Eph.2:2
    Prince of this world. Jn.12:31; 14:30
    Satan. 1 Th.2:18; Rev.12:9; 20:2
    Slanderer, accuser. 1 Pt.5:8
    Star. Rev.9:1
    Tempter. 1 Th.3:5
    Wicked one. 1 Jn.2:13
Nature of. (See SATAN, Names & Titles;
    Power of; Work of)
    Does not act against his n. Mk.3:22-26;
        Jn.8:44
    Nature. (See SATAN, Work of)
        Discussed. 2 Cor.4:4; 11:13-15;
        1 Pt.5:8
    Opposed to Christ. Mk.5:6-7
    Spiritual, darkness, & wickedness.
        Eph.6:12
Origin. Discussed. Rev.9:1; 9:11; 12:3-4;
    12:9
Power of.
    Blinds the minds of unbelievers.
        2 Cor.4:3-4
    Broken & judged by the cross. Jn.16:11
    Broken by Christ. Rev.12:9
    Broken by God's Word. Mt.17:17-18
    Enters & possesses the bodies of men.
        Lk.22:3
    Is giving birth to & growing a family
        of people. Jn.8:44; Acts 13:10;
        1 Jn.3:10
    Is strong, but Jesus is stronger.
        Lk.11:21-22
    Over death.
        How Satan controls death.
            Heb.2:14-16
        Is destroyed. Heb.2:14-16
    Raises up evil men. 2 Th.2:9
    Rules up men. Acts 26:18; 1 Jn.3:10
    Rules over principalities, powers, rul-
        ers, spiritual wickedness. Eph.6:12
    Rules over the power of the air.
        Eph.2:2

Rules over the world. Lk.4:6;
Jn.12:31; 14:30; 2 Cor.4:4
Purpose.
Discussed. 1 Pt.5:8; Rev.12:3-4; 12:9
To hurt & cut the heart of God.
Lk.11:17-18; 22:31; Jn.12:31;
1 Pt.5:8; Rev.12:3-4; 12:9
To oppose God.
By begging permission to tempt
man. Lk.22:31
Is the enemy of God. Mt.13:27-30
Thirty-four ways. Lk.22:3
Satanic forces. Described. Eph.6:12
Vs. religion. Some religious groups are
called the "synagogue of Satan."
Rev.2:9; 3:9
Work - strategy of.
A threefold work. Jn.8:38
Afflicts people with disease. Lk.13:16
Attacks new converts. Mk.1:12
Blinds the minds of men to the gospel.
2 Cor.4:4
Causes believers to be cast into prison.
Rev.2:10
Controls the world. 1 Jn.5:19
Destroys man & the work of God.
Lk.11:17-18
Destroys the bodies of people. Lk.9:42
Devours people. Discussed. 1 Pt.5:8
Discussed. Eph.6:11; Rev.12:3-4; 12:9
Charges believers with sin. Accuses
them before God. Jn.12:31;
1 Pt.5:8; Lk.1:17-18;22:31
Disguises his messengers as light.
2 Cor.11:13-15
Ensnares people. 1 Tim.3:7
Enters & stirs people to do evil.
Jn.13:2, 27
Fills man's heart with worldliness.
Acts 5:1-4
Has attempted down through history to
destroy the seed of Israel. Chart of
attempts. Rev.12:3-4
Hinders the gospel & believers.
1 Th.2:18
How Satan operates. Mt.13:25, 38-39
Hurts & causes pain to God.
Lk.11:17-18; 22:31; Jn.12:31;
1 Pt.5:8; Rev.12:3-4; 12:9
Influences the church. Rev.2:14-15; 2:24
Is destroyed by the death of Christ.
1 Jn.3:8
Leads believers into the depth of sin.
Rev.2:24
Makes men insane, wild & fierce.
Lk.8:26-29
Opposes God.
Discussed. 1 Pt.5:8; Rev.12:3-4; 12:9
Is the enemy of God. Mt.13:27-30
Seeks to hurt & cut the heart of
God. Lk.11:17-18; 22:31; Jn.12:31;
1 Pt.5:8; Rev.12:3-4; 12:9
Thirty four ways. Lk.22:3
Vs. God. Begs permission to tempt
men. Lk.22:31
Possesses evil men. Jn.13:27-30
Removes the Word of God sown in the
heart of the unbeliever. Mk.4:15
Rules the world. Jn.12:31
Seduces & deceives. 2 Cor.11:3;
11:14; Rev.20:7-8
Seduces men through evil spirits.
1 Tim.4:1-2
Seeks to gain an advantage.
2 Cor.2:10-11

Seeks to get an advantage over believ-
ers. 2 Cor.2:11
Seeks worship. Mt.4:8-10, cp.
2 Th.2:3-4
Sets up his seat of authority over cit-
ies. Rev.2:13
Sins & has sinned from the beginning.
1 Jn.3:8
Snares & captures men. 2 Tim.2:26,
cp. 22-26
Sows evil men among believers. Sows
the weeds among the wheat.
Mt.13:25, 38-39
Stops & weakens the growth of
churches. 1 Th.2:18
Strategy. Discussed. Acts 5:1-4
Tempts people. Mt.4:1
Tempts the followers of Christ. Rea-
sons. Lk.22:31
Uses anger. Eph.4:26-27
Uses the Scripture, but perverts it. Mt.4:6
Works in the disobedient. Eph.2:1-3

SATANIC FORCES (See **EVIL SPIRITS**)

SATISFACTION, SELF (See **SLOTHFUL**)

SATISFACTION, SPIRITUAL (See
**FULNESS, SPIRITUAL; HUNGER,
SPIRITUAL; LIFE**)
Discussed. Involves fifteen things. Jn.6:55
Source.
God & His Word, not physical food.
Lk.4:3-4
Jesus Christ.
The Bread of life. Lk.13:20-21;
Jn.6:30-36; 6:41-51;6:52-58
The living water. Jn.4:10-14; 7:37-39
Verses. List of. Jn.10:9
Verses. List of. Jn.6:34-35; 6:55

SAUL OF TARSUS (See **PAUL THE
APOSTLE**)
Name of Paul the apostle before his con-
version. Acts 7:58; 8:1, 3; 9:22

SAVAGE - SAVAGERY (See **BRUTAL**)
Fact. To be severe in the last days.
Rev.6:7-8

SAVIOR (See **JESUS CHRIST**, Death;
SALVATION)
Christ as Savior.
Called the Savior. Lk.2:11; Jn.4:42;
Acts 5:31; 13:23;Eph.5:23; Ph.3:20;
2 Tim.1:10;Tit.1:4; 2:13; 3:6;
2 Pt.1:1, 11;2:20; 3:2, 18; 1 Jn.4:14
Mission & works as Savior.
Not to judge the world, but to save
it. Jn.12:47 cp. Jn.3:17-18
To abolish death & make life &
immortality known to man.
2 Tim.1:10
To be the Savior of the world.
1 Jn.4:14
To become the author of eternal
salvation. Heb.5:9
To deliver man from the pollutions
of the world. 2 Pt.2:20
To give repentance & forgiveness
of sins. Acts 5:31
To make it possible for believers to
have an abundant reception into
God's kingdom. 2 Pt.1:10-11
To make men heirs of eternal life.
Tit.3:4-7, esp. 7

To provide righteousness for man.
2 Pt.1:1
To redeem men & purify a special
people for Himself. Tit.2:14
To save sinners. 1 Tim.1:15
To save the church, a body of be-
lievers. Eph.5:23
To save to the uttermost. Heb.7:25
To seek & save the lost. Mt.18:11-14;
Lk.19:10
God as Savior.
Called the Savior. Lk.1:47; 1 Tim.1:1;
2:3; Tit.1:3; 2:10; 3:4; Jude 25
Mission & work as Savior.
To be the Savior of all men, espe-
cially of believers. 1 Tim.4:10
To bring salvation to all men.
Tit.2:10-14
To call men to the ministry. 1 Tim.1:1
To give believers the glorious
privilege of serving Him.
Lk.1:46-48
To present man faultless before
Him. Jude 24-25
To save men. 1 Tim.2:3-6
To share His Word of salvation &
the hope of eternal life. Tit.1:1-3
To shower His kindness & love
upon man. Tit.3:4-7
Meaning. Discussed. Jn.4:42
Title.
Of Christ. Jn.4:42; 2 Tim.1:10
Of God. Jn.4:42

SCANDAL - SCANDALOUS SINS (See **SIN**)
Discussed. Lk.18:11-12
Within the church.
A case of apostasy, of denying Jesus
Christ. 1 Jn.2:18-23; 4:1-3
A case of false teaching. 2 Pt.2:1-22;
Jude 4-16
A case of immorality. 1 Cor.5:1-13
A case of misbehavior, of not working &
mooching off the church. 2 Th.3:6-12
A case of opposing the minister &
seeking the preeminence. 2 Jn.9-10

SCATTERED (See **HELPLESS**)

SCHEME - SCHEMING (See **DECEPTION**)
Of Satan. Meaning. Eph.6:11

SCHOLAR
Attracted to Christ. Mt.8:19-20

SCIENCE
Christ possesses all the treasures of wis-
dom & knowledge. Col.2:3
False s. 1 Tim.6:20-21
The depth of the wisdom & knowledge of
God are unsearchable & can never be
completely discovered. Ro.11:33-36
Weakness of. 2 Tim.3:6-9

**SCOFF - SCOFFERS - SCOFFING -
SCORN**
Characteristic - Trait. Of false teachers.
Jude 9-10
Reasons. Threefold. Mt.13:53-54
Work of.
Scoff at Jesus Christ & His resurrec-
tion. Acts 17:18
Scoff at the resurrection of believers.
1 Cor.15:12, cp. 12-58
Scoff at the return of Christ & the
judgment of the world. 2 Pt.3:1-7;
3:8-10

SCOURGE - SCOURGING (See **BEAT-INGS; FLOG-FLOGGING**)
Discussed. Mt.27:26-38; Jn.19:1
Meaning. Lk.18:32-33
Of Christ. Discussed. Mt.27:26-38
Of cords. Meaning. Jn.2:15
Of Old Testament believers. Heb.11:36
Of Paul. 2 Cor.6:4-5; 11:24-25
Predicted that believers will suffer **s.** Mt.10:17

SCRIBAL LAW (See **CEREMONIAL LAW; RELIGION; RITUAL**)
Condemned by Christ. Mt.5:17-18; 5:17-20; 5:17-48
Described. Six hundred laws. Mt.22:36
Discussed. Lk.6:2; 6:7
Importance of. Considered more important than God's law. Lk.11:45
Vs. Jesus.
　Accused Christ of devil possession. Mk.3:22-30
　Opposed Christ. (See **JESUS CHRIST**, Opposed; Response to; **RELIGIONISTS**, Opposed Christ) Lk.5:17; 6:7; 20:1-8
　Plotted Christ's death. Lk.22:1-2; 23:10
Vs. Jesus.
　Accused Christ of devil possession. Mk.3:22-30
　Opposed Christ. (See **JESUS CHRIST**, Opposed; Response to; **RELIGIONISTS**, Opposed Christ) Lk.5:17; 6:7; 20:1-8
　Plotted Christ's death. Lk.22:1-2; 23:10

SCRIPTURE (See **BIBLE; WORD OF GOD**)
Christ's use of. Mt.4:4
　Taught the **S.** Covered the prophecies about Himself book by book. Lk.24:18-32, esp. 25-27
Discussed. 2 Tim.3:14-17; 3:16
　Books & contents of. 2 Pt.1:19-21
　The gospel of the **S.** Ro.1:1-4
Duty. (See **SCRIPTURE**, Study of)
　Not to tamper with. Mt.12:1-3; 23:1-2; 2 Cor.4:2;Rev.22:18-19
　To heed. Mt.4:14
　To let the Word of God dwell within. Col.3:16
　To live & continue in the **S.** 2 Tim.3:14-17
　To preach. Acts 17:11, 13; 18:28; 2 Tim.4:2
　To rear children in the **S.** 2 Tim.1:5
　To study. (See **SCRIPTURE**, Study of)
Fulfilled - Fulfillment. (See **PROPH-ECY**, Fulfilled by Christ)
History of. Discussed. 2 Pt.1:19-21
Inspiration of.
　Belief in. Paul believed all **S.** Acts 24:14-16; 26:22-23
　Discussed. Ro.1:1-4; 2 Tim.3:16; 1 Pt.1:10-12
　Facts about.
　　S. cannot be broken. Jn.10:34-36
　　S. is to govern life & behavior. Lk.4:4, 8, 12
　　S. is word for word inspiration. Gal.3:16. Cp. Mt.2:1-8; Lk.4:16-21, esp. 21
　　S. shall never pass away. Mt.24:35
　　S. was Christ speaking in men. 2 Cor.13:3, cp. Gal.1:4-12; 2 Pt.3:15-16, cp. 1 Pt.1:10-11

　　S. was God-breathed. 2 Tim.3:16
　　S. was God speaking through the prophets in many dif- ferent ways. Heb.1:1
　　S. was the Holy Spirit speaking through men. Acts 1:16; 2 Pt.1:21
Is called the Word of God. Acts 17:11, 13
Is infallible. **S.** cannot be broken. Jn.10:35
Is not a cleverly invented story. 2 Pt.1:16
Is not to be tampered with. Mt.12:1-3; 23:1-2; 2 Cor.4:2; Rev.22:18-19
Is revealed only by God's Spirit. 1 Cor.2:10-13
Is understood only by believers. 1 Cor.2:10-13
Paul's signature was a sign of authen- ticity. 1 Cor.16:21
Paul's writings are said to be the commandments of God. 1 Cor.14:37
The prophets searched to understand the **S.** 1 Pt.1:10-12
Interpretation of.
　How the **S.** are to be handled. 2 Cor.4:2
　Is not of one's own interpretation. 2 Pt.1:20-21
　Is revealed only by God's Spirit. 1 Cor.2:10-13
　Is understood only by believers. 1 Cor.2:10-13, cp. 1 Pt.1:10-11
　Is understood only by the Holy Spirit. Jn.12:16; 1 Cor.2:10-13, esp. 11,13
　Some minds are blinded from under- standing. 2 Cor.3:14-15; 4:3-4
Message of. (See **MESSAGE**)
　Discussed. Ro.1:1-4, esp. 2
　Preached & taught. Acts 17:2; 17:11, 13; 18:28
Misuse of.
　By adding to & taking away from. Discussed. Mt.23:1; 2 Cor.4:2; Rev.22:18-19
　By not studying or learning the **S.** Not letting **S.** form the basis of one's be- liefs. Mt.22:23-29
　By twisting **S.** Misinterpreting it. Mt.4:6; Lk.4:11; 11:52; 2 Pt.3:16
　Example. Satan. Lk.4:11
Old Testament. Written as an example-- for instruction. 1 Cor.10:11
Prophecies of. (See **PROPHECY**)
Purpose of - Why God gave the **S.**
　Discussed. 2 Tim.3:16
　For our learning & to stir us. Ro.15:4
　To assure eternal life. 1 Jn.5:13-15
　To bear witness to Christ. Jn.5:39
　To enable the believer. 2 Tim.3:15-17
　To stir belief. 1 Jn.5:13-15
Study of.
　How to study & understand. Dis- cussed. Jn.12:16
　Must compare Scripture with **S.** 1 Cor.2:12-13; 2 Pt.1:19-21
　Must depend upon the Holy Spirit to re- veal the meaning of **S.** 1 Cor.2:10-13
　Must learn the **S.** for doctrine, reproof, conviction, & instruction in righteous- ness. 2 Tim.3:16
　Must listen to other teachers. Acts 8:30-38
　Must reason out the **S.** Acts 17:2-3
　Must rightly divide the **S.**, analyze & accurately handle it. 2 Tim.2:15

Must search & study the **S.** diligently. Jn.5:39
Must study & learn the **S.**, for it leads to salvation. 2 Tim.3:15
Must study for **S.** was written for our learning. Ro.15:4
Must study the **S.** to see if the things claimed are true. Acts 17:11, 13
To study the **S.** daily. Acts 17:11
View of.
　By humanists. Prejudice against. Acts 17:11
　Paul's view. Ro.1:1-7
Witness of. Only witness needed is **S.** Lk.16:29-31
Work of - Effects of **S.**
　Assures answered prayer. 1 Jn.5:13-15
　Creates a strong fellowship--if one studies the **S.** Ro.15:4
　Gives a special blessing. Promised to the hearer of Revelation. Rev.1:1-3
　Grows a person. Acts 20:32
　Instructs, reproves, indoctrinates, & corrects a person. 2 Tim.3:16
　Leads to belief in Jesus. Acts 17:11-12
　Makes one approved before God. 2 Tim.2:15
　Proves salvation. 2 Pt.1:19-21
　Proves that justification is by faith. Gal.3:6-14
　Shows that Jesus is the Christ. Acts 17:11; 18:28
　Stirs belief. 1 Jn.5:13-15
　Stirs belief that Jesus is the Christ, the Son of God. Jn.20:31; Acts 17:2-3; 18:28

SEA OF GALILEE
Discussed. Mk.1:16; Lk.8:22

SEA OF GLASS
In front of God's throne. Discussed. Rev.4:5-6

SEAL
Believers are to set their **s.** to Christ. Jn.3:33
God set His **s.** & witness to Christ. Jn.6:27
Meaning. Jn.3:33; 2 Cor.1:21-22
Of the Holy Spirit. Guarantees & assures the believer's hope. Ro.5:3-5; 5:5
Source. The Holy Spirit is the believer's seal & security. 2 Cor.1:22
Meaning. Jn.3:33; 2 Cor.1:21-22
Of the Holy Spirit. Guarantees & assures the believer's hope. Ro.5:3-5; 5:5
Source. The Holy Spirit is the believer's seal & security. 2 Cor.1:22

SEAL JUDGMENT OF REVELATION
Discussed. Events preceding the great tribulation. Rev.6:1-7:17
Fifth **s.** Picture of all the slain martyrs. Rev.6:9-11
First four **s.** Four horsemen of the Apocalypse. Rev.6:1-8
Seventh **s.** Awesome preparation for judgment. Rev.8:1-5
Sixth **s.** The great day of God's wrath begins. Rev.6:12-17

SEAL OF GOD
Fact. Will protect believers in the great revelation against God's judgment. Rev.7:2-3
Meaning. Rev.7:2-3

SEASONS (See **DATES**)

SECOND CHANCE
Given to Judas. Mk.14:18-20
No second **c.** in hell. Lk.16:26, 30

SECOND COMING (See **JESUS CHRIST**, Return)

SECOND DEATH (See **DEATH, SECOND**)

SECOND PLACE
Called to serve in second place. Ro.16:21; 16:22

SECRET - SECRECY (See **EXPOSURE - EXPOSED**)
Secret sins.
Are known by God. Jn.1:47-48; 2:24-25; 5:42; 13:19-20; Ro.2:2-5; 2:16
Called works of darkness. Eph.5:11; 1 Th.5:7
Impossible to hide. Lk.8:17
Warning against. Eph.5:12
Will be exposed by God. Lk.8:17; 12:2; 1 Cor.4:5
Secrets of man. Man tries to hide four things. Lk.8:17

SECULAR WORK (See **BUSINESS; EMPLOYMENT**)

SECULARISM
In the end time. Discussed. Rev.13:4-8; 14:8; 14:9; 17:2; 18:2-7
View of the state. Discussed. Lk.20:22

SECUNDUS
A believer in the Thessalonica church. Discussed. Acts 20:4-6

SECURITY (See **ASSURANCE** for major discussion)
Comes by - Source. (See **ASSURANCE**, Comes by)
Danger - Warning.
Against false **s.** & over-confidence. 1 Cor.10:1-13
Against false **s.** Stumbling & sleeping. Ro.11:6-10
Teaching with inadequate understanding. 1 Cor.10:1-13
Discussed. Jn.6:37-40; 10:9; 10:27-29; 17:9-19;Ro.8:28-39; 2 Th.2:13; 1 Pt.1:5;1:3-6
Eternal **s.** 1 Jn.5:16
In the end time. God will seal believers in the great tribulation. Rev.7:2-3; 9:4-5
Meaning.
Eternal life guaranteed. 2 Cor.1:21-22
Being clothed with immortality. 2 Cor.5:3
Purpose. To present the believer blameless. 1 Cor.1:8
Verses. List of. Jn.6:39; 10:9

SEDITIONS (See **DISSENSIONS**)

SEDUCE - SEDUCTION (See **ASTRAY; DECEPTION**)
Discussed. Col.2:4; Rev.2:20
Duty. To fear **s.**, having one's mind corrupted. 2 Cor.11:3
Of false teaching.
The false teaching of Balaam. Rev.2:14-15
The false teaching of evil spirits. 1 Tim.4:1
The false teaching of Jezebel. Rev.2:20-21
The false teaching of the Nicolaitans. Rev.2:5-6
Will increase more & more. 2 Tim.3:13
Things that **s.** Discussed. 2 Cor.11:1-15

SEE - SEEING (See **SPIRITUAL SIGHT - UNDERSTANDING**)

Meaning. Heb.12:25-29

SEE TO IT
Duty.
To **s.** of being led astray. 2 Pt.3:17
To **s.** of covetousness. Lk.12:15
To **s.** of divisive & conniving religionists. Ph.3:2
To **s.** of false philosophy. Col.2:8
To **s.** of false teachers. Mt.7:15
To **s.** of five things. Mk.12:38-40, cp. Lk.20:45-47
To **s.** of men, for they will persecute believers. Mt.10:17
To **s.** of the false teaching of religionists. Mt.16:5-11, cp. Mk.8:15; Lk.12:1
To **s.** of unbelief. Acts 13:40-41
Meaning. Mt.7:15; Mk.8:15; Col.2:8

SEED
Parable of the growing **s.** Growth of believers. Mt.13:1-9; 13:31-32; Mk.4:26-29
Symbolic of.
Christ's death. Jn.12:24
The burial & resurrection of the believer's body. 1 Cor.15:35-49
The **S.** & the Sower. How the Word is received. Mk.4:1-20
The sowing of spiritual things. 1 Cor.9:11

SEED, THE PROMISED
Identified as.
Christ. Gal.3:16, cp. 3:6-29
The children of Abraham. Gal.3:6-7; 3:8-9; 3:29
The true believers of Israel. Ro.9:29
Those born of the Word of God. 1 Pt.1:23
Promised to Abraham. Ro.4:1-25

SEEK - SEEKING (See **PERSEVERANCE**)
Answer to **s.** The cross. 1 Cor.1:22-24
Christ seeks man - Christ the seeking Savior.
As Savior. Compared to a Shepherd. Five facts. Mt.18:12
Came to **s.** & save that which is lost. Lk.19:10
Extends the invitation & takes the initiative with all who **s.** Him. Jn.1:38-39
Goes to any limit. Jn.1:43-44
His very purpose. Mt.20:28; Lk.19:10
Knocks on the door of man's heart. Rev.3:18-20
S. & questions man. Mk.12:35
S. all who go astray. Mt.18:12
S. every lost sheep until He finds it. Lk.15:4
S. for followers. Jn.1:43
Will not always **s.** & contend with men. Lk.4:28-30
Duty.
To **s.** Christ despite all difficulties. Lk.11:31-32
To **s.** Christ with fervor. Mk.3:7-8
To **s.** God & His kingdom first. Mt.6:33
To **s.** heaven. Heb.11:14
To **s.** peace. 1 Pt.3:11
To **s.** the Lord. Acts 17:27
To **s.** things in prayer. Lk.11:9-10
To **s.** to enter the narrow door. Lk.13:24
To **s.** treasure in heaven. Lk.12:31-34; 16:9; 18:18-23

To **s.** wisdom despite all difficulties. Lk.11:31-32
Law of seeking. Mt.13:12
Man seeks Christ.
Duty.
Must give up all in order to **s.** Christ. Mt.13:44; 13:45-46
Must know about Christ before one can **s.** Mt.14:35
Must **s.** the special presence of Christ. Mk.2:20
Fact.
Christ is approachable any day or hour. Mk.1:32
Man searches for utopia, for an *earthly* messiah. Jn.6:26-29; 8:21-24
Great application. Mt.12:42
How to **s.** Mk.5:21-43; 6:55
In desperation - persistence. Lk.18:35-43; 19:3-4
Reasons for seeking Christ. Mt.8:18-22; Mk.3:20; Jn.12:9
Steps to **s.** Christ & being made whole. Mt.14:34-36
Verses. List of. Mk.2:20
When to seek Christ. Two special times. Mk.2:19
Who can seek Christ.
All men are to **s.** Christ. Symbolized in some Greeks who sought Christ. Four misunderstandings. Jn.12:20-36
The desperate, the blind. Mk.10:46-52; Lk.18:40-42
The empty, lonely, & lost. Lk.19:1-10
The half-sincere. Traits of. Jn.12:9
The helpless. Mk.2:1-5
The man needing help for a loved one. Lk.7:4
The most unclean. Mk.1:40
The most untouchable. Lk.5:12-16
The ruler, but he must repent. Acts 24:24-25
The soldier who rejects false gods. Lk.7:4
The wise men or magi. Mt.2:1-11
Man seeks God.
Cannot discover or find God.
By human reason. Revelation necessary. 1 Cor.3:18-20
By worldly wisdom. 1 Cor.2:6-13
Example of.
Desperate **s.** Acts 13:42-45
The lost who have never heard of Christ. Acts 10:1-6
Fact.
None **s.** God. Ro.3:10-12
Seeking prepares one's heart for receiving Christ. Jn.4:45
How man seeks God.
Through astrology. Col.2:8
Through law. Col.2:11-12; 2:16-17
Through philosophy. Col.2:8
Through religion. Col.2:1-12; 2:16-17
Through ritual. Col.2:16-17
Through rules. Col.2:16-17
Through spirits or angels. Col.2:18-19
Through visions. Col.2:18-19
Man seeks life.
How to secure. Mk.2:20
S. utopia; life; a deliverer. Mk.8:27-9:50; Jn.6:26-29; 8:21-24
Man seeks the things of the world.
Life. Mk.2:20; Lk.17:33
Selfish things. Ph.2:21
The necessities of life. To meet basic needs. Mt.6:25-34

Man seeks truth. Some are prejudiced against man seeking truth in the Bible. Acts 17:11
Meaning. Mt.6:33
Results.
 God meets the need of the seeker. Mt.2:11
 The seeker secures more & more. Lk.8:18
Verses. List of. Lk.11:31-32

SEGREGATION (See **BIGOTRY; DIS-CRIMINATION; PREJUDICE**)
Discussed. Acts 10:1-33

SELF - SELFISH - SELFISHNESS
Answer to.
 Bearing the fruit of the Spirit. Gal.5:22-26
 Humility. Looking out for the interests of others. Ph.2:3-4
 Love. 1 Cor.13:5
 Seeking the welfare of others. 1 Cor.10:24
 Walking in the Spirit. Gal.5:13-16, esp. 16
Caused by.
 Big "I." Mt.7:21; Lk.12:15-19
 "Give me" philosophy. Lk.15:11-13
 Indwelling evil. Ro.7:14-25, esp. 21-23
 Lust. Jas.4:1-2
 Sinful nature. Ro.3:10-12
 Wealth. Creates the "big I." Mt.19:23
 Worldliness & indulgence & extrava-gant living. Lk.16:19-31
Discussed. Lk.15:11-13
 A sign of a godless society. 2 Tim.3:2-4
 A sign of the end time. 2 Tim.3:2-4
Growth of. Step by step. Mt.8:28-31
Meaning. 1 Cor.13:4-7
Results.
 Causes conflict & divisiveness. Gal.5:13-15; Ph.2:3-4
 Causes one to lose his soul. Lk.16:19-31
 Causes one to reject & oppose Christ. Jn.11:47-48
 Causes unbelief. Jn.11:47-48
 Judgment. Lk.12:16-21
 Provokes others & envies others. Gal.5:26
Sins of.
 Discussed. Lk.12:11-19
 Listed. Mt.18:3
 Seeking greatness. Wrong ambition. Lk.9:46
Verses. List of. Lk.12:11-19; Jn.11:47-48

SELF-CENTERED
Caused by. Depraved nature. Mk.14:27-31
Discussed. Ro.3:27; 3:28
Reaction to being offended. Mt.18:15-17

SELF-CONDEMNATION (See **CON-SCIENCE**)
Caused by.
 Judging others & being guilty of the same things. Ro.2:1
 Knowing that one is guilty of wrong & evil. Jn.8:7-11
 The conviction of one's heart. 1 Jn.3:20

SELF-CONFIDENCE (See **SELF-SUFFICIENCY**)

SELF-CONTROL - SELF-CONTROLLED (See **DISCIPLINE; MIND; TEMPERANCE**)
Discussed. 1 Cor.6:12; 1 Pt.1:13
Duty.
 Believers are not to be drunk but self-controlled. 1 Th.5:6-8
 Believers are to live **s.** lives, that is, disciplined, & temperate lives. Tit.2:12-13; 1 Pt.1:13
 Ministers & their wives are to be blameless, **s.**, & never drunk. 1 Tim.3:2, 11; Tit.1:8
 The aged are to be **s.** & never drunk. Tit.2:2-3, 5
 The elderly in particular are to give special attention to self-control. Tit.2:2
 To add temperance, self-control to one's faith & life. 2 Pt.1:5-7, esp. 6
 To control one's words & tongue. Jas.3:2
 To control oneself. 1 Cor.9:25
 To control sin & lust. Ro.6:12
 To fight with determination. 1 Cor.9:26
 To guard against disqualification. 1 Cor.9:27
 To run, to press for the prize. 1 Cor.9:24
 To run with certainty. 1 Cor.9:26
 To strive for the mastery. 1 Cor.9:25
 To subject one's body. 1 Cor.9:27
 Women's minds are to be **s.** 1 Tim.2:9
 Young men & women's minds are to be **s.** Tit.2:4-7
Essential. Great control required. 1 Cor.9:23-27
Fact.
 Preaching self-control convicts people. Acts 24:25
 The disciplined & self-controlled are prospects for the gospel. Acts 17:18
Meaning. Gal.5:22-23; 1 Tim.3:2-3; Tit.2:4-5; 1 Pt.1:13; 2:1; 4:7; 5:8-9; 2 Pt.1:5-7
Verses. List of. 1 Cor.6:12
Warning.
 Must be **s.** & guard against pride, not thinking too highly of oneself & one's gifts. Ro.12:3
 Must be **s.** & pray & watch for the end of all things. 1 Pt.4:7
 Must be **s.**, watching for the Lord's re-turn. 1 Th.5:1-9, esp. 6-8. Cp. Tit.2:12-13
Without self-control. Meaning. 2 Tim.3:2-4

SELF-CONTROL, WITHOUT
Meaning. 2 Tim.3:2-4, esp. 3

SELF-DECEPTION (See **DECEIVE - DECEPTION**)

SELF-DENIAL (See **CROSS, DAILY**)
Discussed. Mt.10:38; Lk.9:23
 Terms of discipleship. Lk.9:23-27
Duty.
 Must give all one has to follow Christ. Lk.18:18-30
 To abstain from all appearance of evil. 1 Th.4:22
 To abstain from fleshly lusts. 1 Pt.2:11; 4:2
 To count all things loss for Christ. Ph.3:8

To count oneself dead to sin. Ro.6:1-10; 6:11-13; 6:14-23
 To deny oneself even as Christ did. 1 Pt.4:1
 To deny the body & keep it under control. 1 Cor.9:27
 To deny ungodliness & worldly lusts. Tit.2:12-13
 To die daily. 2 Cor.4:10
 To die to self. 2 Cor.4:12
 To forsake all to follow Christ. Mt.10:28; Lk.5:11; 5:27; 14:33
 To give oneself--all that one is & has--is essential for salvation. Mt.19:21-22; 19:23-26
 To make no provision for the flesh. Ro.13:14
 To put Christ first. Lk.14:26
 To sacrifice all for the sake of others. 1 Cor.10:23-28
 To sacrifice questionable social func-tions for others. Ro.14:1-23; 1 Cor.10:23-28
 Warning. The great danger of not giving all one is & has to Christ. Mt.19:23-26
Essential.
 For salvation. Mt.19:21-22; 19:23-26
 Self-denial is the cost of discipleship. Discussed. Mk.1:6; Lk.9:23; 9:57-58
 To follow Christ. Mt.8:19-20
Example. John the Baptist. Mk.1:6
Meaning.
 Discussed. Lk.9:23
 Not shirking duties & families. Mt.19:27
Result.
 Infuses life to others. 2 Cor.4:12
 Rewards. Great & glorious. Mt. 19:27-30; Lk.18:28-30

SELF-DEPENDENCY (See **SELF-SUFFICIENCY**)

SELF-DISCIPLINE
Described as.
 A gate to deception & seduction. 2 Cor.11:3
 Reprobate mind. Ro.1:28
Discussed. Ro.12:2; 2 Tim.1:7
 Spiritual struggle & weapons. 2 Cor.10:1-6
Duty - Essential.
 Is the major weapon for warfare. 1 Pt.4:1
 Must think before building a tower or life. Lk.14:28-32
 Not to be double-minded. Jas.1:8
 Not to be shaken in **s.** by world events, nor by the end time. 2 Th.2:1-3
 Not to faint in one's mind. Heb.12:3
 Not to put one's mind on high things, but to be humble. Ro.12:16
 To attend upon the Lord without dis-traction. 1 Cor.7:35
 To be armed with the same mind as Christ in facing the trials of life. 1 Pt.4:1-6
 To be fully persuaded in one's own mind about social activities. Ro.14:5
 To be mentally persuaded of one's be-havior before doing questionable things. Ro.14:5
 To be of one mind with other believ-ers. 1 Cor.13:11; Ph.1:27; 2:2; 4:2; 1 Pt.3:8
 To be of the same mind toward one another. Ro.12:16

SERAPHIM
Discussed. Rev.4:6-9

SERGIUS PAULUS
Roman official. Desired to hear the gospel. Acts 13:7

SERMON ON THE MOUNT
Discussed. Mt.5:1-7:29
Given to prepare the disciples. Mt.5:1-2

SERPENTS--SNAKES (See **SNAKES**)
Discussed. Mt.10:16
Paul healed of a s. bite. Acts 28:1-6
Symbolized - Type of.
    Jesus' death. Lifted up by Moses.
    Jn.3:14-15
    Satan. Rev.20:2
    Wisdom. To be wise or shrewd as a s.
    Mt.10:16

SERVANT - SLAVES
Applied to.
    The believer.
        Is a s. Lk.17:7-10
        Is to be a s. of righteousness.
        Ro.6:16-23
    The sinner. Is a s. of sin. Jn.8:34;
    Ro.6:16, 20
Discussed. Ro.1:1; Tit.1:1; 2 Pt.1:1
Duty. To serve. Lk.17:7-10
Ideal s. Christ, the Chosen Servant of
    God. Mt.12:14-21; 20:28; Lk.22:27;
    Jn.13:4-5; Ph.2:7
Nature. Humility. Lk.17:7-10

SERVANT, FAITHFUL & WISE
Parable of. Mt.24:45-47

SERVE - SERVICE (See **BELIEVER;
MINISTRY - MINISTERING; WORK
- WORKS**)
Conditions - Prerequisite for s.
    A realistic view of the world. Mt.7:3
    Being washed & cleansed. Jn.13:6-11
Described. As service ministries.
    Ro.16:22
Discussed. Ro.1:1; 1:9; 6:16-23
    Subject of. Labor for God. Jn.4:31-42
Duty.
    Must serve either God or the world.
        Cannot serve two masters. Mt.6:24;
        Lk.16:13
    To be faithful until Christ returns.
        Lk.12:41-48
    To do all things well. Mk.7:31-37
    To work until Christ returns. Lk.19:13
    To s. God & not sin. Ro.6:16-23
    To s. in humility & brokenness. Acts
        20:18-19
    To s. others in love. Gal.5:13
    To s. the Lord diligently not slothfully.
        Ro.12:11
    To s. while opportunity exists.
        Mt.26:10-11
    To s. with good will. Eph.6:7
    To s. with reverence & godly fear.
        Heb.12:28
Example. A man who helps much. 3 Jn.5-8
Failure in. Can know four things. Mt.6:33
How to s.
    A demonstration of royal s. Washing
        the disciples' feet. Jn.13:1-17
    Five wise lessons. Mk.6:45-52
Meaning. Mt.6:1; Ro.1:9

Reward. (See **REWARD**)
    Reward is assured. Mt.10:42; Jn.4:36
    Service determines one's degree of
        reward. Lk.19:15-23
    To be counted as great. Mk.10:43-44
    To be given an eternal service & rule in
        the new heavens & earth. Rev.22:3-5
    To be given the inheritance of God.
        Col.3:23-24
    To be honored by God Himself Jn.12:26
    To be where Christ is. Jn.12:26
    Will be acceptable to God. Ro.14:18
    Will be counted as the greatest, the
        chief by God. Mt.20:23-28
Stirred - Motivated by.
    Jesus Christ. Ro.1:1-7
    The gospel. Ro.1:8-15
    The hope of eternal service. Rev.22:3-5,
        esp. 3
Verses. List of. Lk.17:7-10

SERVICE MINISTRIES
Described. Ro.12:6-8; 1 Cor.12:8-10;
    Eph.4:11

SET PURPOSE
Determined the death of Christ. Acts
    2:23; 4:25-28
Discussed. Acts 2:23
Duty.
    To declare the whole c. of God. Acts
        20:27
    To hear the c. of God. Rev.3:18
Is immutable, unchangeable. Heb.6:17-18
Is rejected by some. Lk.7:30
Meaning. Acts 2:23; 4:25-28

SETTLE (See **STEADFAST**)

SETTLEMENT
Meaning. Mt.18:24; Ro.4:6-8; 4:9; 4:22;
    6:11; 2 Cor.5:18-19

SEVEN SPIRITS OF GOD
Described. Rev.1:4; 3:1; 4:5; 5:6

SEVEN STARS OF REVELATION
Ministers of the seven churches in the
    Revelation. Rev.1:16, 20

SEVENTIETH WEEK
Of Daniel. Discussed. Mt.24:15

SEVENTY DISCIPLES
Of the Lord. Sent forth. Lk.10:1-16;
    10:17-20

SEX (See **ADULTERY; FORNICATION;
IMMORALITY; LUST**; Related Subjects)
Discussed. 1 Cor.6:12-20
Purpose. Threefold. Mt.5:27-30
Right vs. wrong use of. Mt.5:27-30

SEXUAL IMMORALITY
Caused by.
    Partying & failing to separate from the
        world. Rev.2:20-21
    Rejecting & denying the only true &
        living God. Ro.1:18-32, esp. 29
    The heart. Mt.15:19; Mk.7:22-23, esp. 21

SEXUAL IMMORALITY
Caused by.
    Partying & failing to separate from the
        world. Rev.2:20-21
    Threefold. Mt.5:27-30

Described. As several things. Eph.5:3;
    5:4; 5:5
Discussed. Mt.5:27-30; Ro.13:9;
    1 Cor.5:1-10
Duty.
    Not to fellowship with immoral persons. 1 Cor.5:11
    Not to let s. be named even once
        among us. Eph.5:3
    Not to look upon a person with lust.
        Mt.5:27-28
    Not to talk or joke about s. Eph.5:3-12
    Not to touch a woman. 1 Cor.7:1
    To avoid i. through marriage. 1 Cor.7:2
    To dress modestly. 1 Tim.2:9-10;
        1 Pt.3:1-6
    To keep a pure body. Heb.10:22
    To live a pure life. Lk.1:26; 1 Th.4:3-7;
        Tit.2:5
    To abstain from s. Acts 15:20, 29;
        21:25; 1 Th.4:1-8, esp. 3
    To avoid s. through marriage.
        1 Cor.7:2
    To be dead to s. Col.3:5-7
    To flee s. 1 Cor.6:18
    To repent of s. 2 Cor.12:21; Rev.2:21;
        14:8
    To separate from all fornicators.
        1 Cor.5:9-11
Example of.
    At a party held by Herod. Suggestive
        dancing. Mk.6:21-22
    Woman. Repents & is saved. Lk.7:36-50
In the church.
    A case of public incest. 1 Cor.5:1-13
    Moral laxity. 1 Cor.5:1-6:20
Meaning. Mt.5:28; Mt.19:9; Mk.7:21;
    Ro.13:13; 1 Cor.5:9-10; 6:9; 2
    Cor.12:19-21; Gal.5:19-21; Eph.5:3;
    1 Th.4:3-5; Heb.12:15-17
Misconception of. Is acceptable & excusable. Mt.5:27-30
Prevention - cure. Discussed. Mt.5:28;
    5:30
Results.
    Causes God to give man over to s.
        Ro.1:26-27
    Cheats a brother. To be avenged by
        God. 1 Th.4:6-8
    Death. Ro.1:29-32, esp. 32
    Results. Four results. 1 Th.4:6-8
    Shall not inherit the kingdom of God.
        1 Cor.6:9
Sin of.
    Is a characteristic of the world of unregenerate man. Ro.1:18-32, esp. 29
    Is a characteristic of whole cities & countries. Jude 7; Rev.17:2, 4; 18:3; 19:2
    Is a sin against a person's own body.
        1 Cor.6:18
    Is a work of the flesh. Gal.5:19
Verses. List of. Ro.13:9; 1 Cor.5:9-10; 6:13-14

SEXUAL IMPURITY
Attitude toward. By the church. Mk.2:15
Deliverance - Cleansing. Discussed.
    Mk.1:40-45
Duty.
    Not to touch any s. thing, but to live a
        separated life. 2 Cor.6:17-18
    To guard against doing the things that
        people consider s. Ro.14:13-15, esp.
        14
    To live a moral & clean life. 1 Th.4:6-8
    To put to death s. Col.3:5-7

Meaning. Ro.1:24-25; 2 Cor.12:19-21;
Gal.5:19-21; Eph.4:17-19; 5:5

SEXUAL SIN
Caused by.
  Partying & failing to separate from the
    world. Rev.2:20-21
  Rejecting & denying the only true &
    living God. Ro.1:18-32, esp. 29
  The heart. Mt.15:19; Mk.7:22-23, esp. 21
Duty.
  Not to let **s.** be named even once
    among us. Eph.5:3
  To abstain from **s.** Acts 15:20, 29;
    21:25; 1 Th.4:1-8, esp. 3
  To avoid **s.** through marriage.
    1 Cor.7:2
  To be dead to **s.** Col.3:5-7
  To flee **s.** 1 Cor.6:18
  To repent of **s.** 2 Cor.12:21; Rev.2:21; 14:8
  To separate from all fornicators.
    1 Cor.5:9-11
Meaning. Mt.19:9; Mk.7:21; 1 Cor.5:9-
  10; 6:9; 2 Cor.12:19-21; Gal.5:19-21;
  Eph.5:3; 1 Th.4:3-5; Heb.12:15-17
Results.
  Death. Ro.1:29-32, esp. 32
  Shall not inherit the kingdom of God.
    1 Cor.6:9
Sin of.
  Is a characteristic of the world of un-
    regenerate man. Ro.1:18-32, esp. 29
  Is a characteristic of whole cities & coun-
    tries. Jude 7; Rev.17:2, 4; 18:3; 19:2
  Is a sin against a person's own body.
    1 Cor.6:18
  Is a work of the flesh. Gal.5:19
Verses. List of. 1 Cor.5:9-10; 6:13-14

SHAME - SHAMEFUL (See **GUILT**)
Caused by.
  False teachers. Jude 13
  Worldliness & earthly things. Ph.3:18-19
Duty.
  Not to be ashamed of the gospel of
    Christ. Ro.1:16
  Not to even talk about shameful, sinful
    things. Eph.5:12
  Not to **s.** believers by ignoring them.
    1 Cor.11:22
  Not to sin, do shameful things.
    Ro.6:21-23, cp. 16-21
  To have one great hope, to be un-
    ashamed before Christ. Ph.1:20
  Many have no shame of sin & take pleas-
    ure in it. Ro.1:24-32, esp. 26-27, 32
  Some foam at the mouth as though cast-
    ing up their shame. Jude 13
  Some glory in their shame. Ph.3:18-19

SHAMEFUL LUSTS
Meaning. Ro.1:26-27

SHAMMAI SCHOOL
Conservative school of thought in
  Christ's day. Mt.19:1-12; Mk.10:1-12

SHARED
Meaning. Heb.6:4-5
What believers are not to **p.** of.
  Other men's sins. 1 Tim.5:22
  The sinners & sins of the world.
    Eph.5:7, cp. 1-7
  The sins of the cities of the world.
    Rev.18:4, cp. 1-5
  The table of devils. 1 Cor.10:21
  The teaching of false teachers.
    2 Jn.10-11

What believers are to **p.** of.
  Afflictions of the gospel. 2 Tim.1:8
  Christ Himself. Heb.3:14
  Christ's sufferings. 1 Pt.4:13
  Flesh & blood, the same as all men &
    the same that Christ partook of.
    Heb.2:14-15
  God's holiness. Heb.12:10
  God's promise in Christ. Eph.3:6
  One another's grace. Ph.1:7
  One another's hope. 1 Cor.9:10, cp. 9-11
  The chastisement of God. Heb.12:8
  The divine nature. 2 Pt.1:4
  The freedom & liberty to **p.** of social
    activities. 1 Cor.8:1-13
  The fruits of one's labor. 2 Tim.2:6
  The glory that shall be revealed. 1 Pt.5:1
  The gospel. 1 Cor.9:23
  The heavenly calling. Heb.3:1
  The Holy Spirit. Heb.6:4
  The inheritance. Col.1:12
  The Lord's Supper. 1 Cor.10:16-17
  The sufferings & comfort of salvation.
2 Cor.1:5-7, esp. 7

SHARING (See **MINISTRY - MINIS-
TERING**)
Duty. To share the Old & New Testa-
  ment. Mt.13:52

**SHARP DOUBLE-EDGED SWORD,
THE**
Meaning. Word of God. Rev.2:12

SHEBA, QUEEN OF
Example of seeking great wisdom.
  Mt.12:42
Illustrates how Christ should be sought
  despite great difficulty. Lk.11:30-32
Sought great wisdom. Mt.12:42
To testify against this generation. Mt.12:42

SHEEP
Describes. The lost world. Mt.9:36; Mk.6:34
Discussed. Jn.10:4-5
Needs of the sheep.
  A good Shepherd. Jn.10:1-6; 10:4-5;
    10:11-21; 10:27-29
  A place of safety. Jn.10:1; 10:7-10
  Only one gate into the sheepfold. Christ
    Himself. Jn.10:7-8
Parable. Of the lost **s.**
  The lost sinner out in the world.
    Lk.15:1-7
  The saved & the lost facing judgment.
    Mt.25:31-47
  The supreme example of caring.
    Mt.18:11-14
Symbol - Type of.
  Believers. Jn.10:1-21
  Believers in facing judgment.
    Mt.25:31-33
  Jesus Christ as the Lamb of God. Jn.1:29
  The church. Acts 20:28
  The lost of Israel. Mt.15:24
  Unbelievers--the lost. Mt.9:36; 15:24; 18:12
Traits of.
  Discussed. Mk.6:34; Jn.10:4-5; 10:27-29
  How **s.** get lost. Lk.15:4
Vs. the goats. Those who are lost.
  Mt.15:31; 25:31-46
Vs. the wolf. Those who persecute.
  Mt.10:16; Lk.10:3
Vs. the wolves, false teachers. Acts
  20:28-29

SHEEPFOLD (See **SHEEP PEN**)
Discussed. Jn.10:1
Fact.
  Believers shall be glorified forever.
    2 Th.1:10; 1 Pt.5:4; 5:10; Col.3:4
  To be manifested at the return of
    Christ. Mt.24:29-31; 25:31-46;
    2 Th.1:7-10

SHEKINAH GLORY
Described. Seen in Christ.
  At His birth. Lk.2:8-18
  At His transfiguration. Lk.9:32-33;
    2 Pt.1:16-18
Discussed. Mt.17:5-8; Jn.1:14; Ro.9:4
Duty. To experience the transforming
  power of God's Shekinah glory.
  2 Cor.3:18; 4:6
History of. Ro.9:4
Meaning. Ro.9:4; 2 Cor.4:6

SHELTER
Duty. Not to worry about **s.**; God provides. Mt.6:26, cp. 25-34; Lk.12:22-34

SHEPHERD
At the birth of Christ. Lk.2:8-12;
  2:15-18; 2:20
Described. By Isaiah 40:1. 1 Pt.2:25
Discussed. Jn.10:1-6; 10:2-3; 10:7-10;
  10:11-21; 1 Pt.2:25; 5:2-3
Duty.
  Discussed. Jn.10:2-3; 1 Pt.2:25
  To gather not to scatter the sheep.
    Lk.11:23
  To seek any sheep that is lost. Five
    facts. Mt.18:12
  What happens to sheep if there is no **s.**
    Mk.6:34
False.
  Discussed. Jn.10:1; 10:11-13
  Vs. the true **s.** Jn.10:1-6; 10:11-18
Meaning. 1 Pt.5:2-3
Reputation of. Base, irreligious. Lk.2:8-12
Title of.
  Christ. Four descriptions. Jn.10:11-21
  The elder or minister or leader.
    Mt.9:36; 1 Pt.5:1-4
Traits - Characteristics of.
  Discussed. Jn.10:2-3; 10:14-16
  The supreme example of caring.
    Mt.18:11-14

SHEWBREAD (See **CONSECRATED
BREAD**)
Discussed. Mt.12:3-4; Lk.6:3-4
Type - Symbol of. Christ. Jn.6:47-51,
  esp. 48

SHIPWRECK
Of Paul.
  Involved in three **s.** 2 Cor.11:25
  On the way to Rome. Acts 27:1-44;
    28:1-15
  Symbol - Type of. Faith being **s.**
    1 Tim.1:18-20

SHOES
Symbol of.
  A free man. Lk.15:22
  Loosening a man's **s.** is a symbol of
    humility. Mk.3:16
  The believer's warfare in carrying forth
    the gospel. Eph.6:15, cp. 6:10-20

Proves one does not know God.
1 Jn.3:4-9
Proves one's depravity. Jn.8:34-36;
8:41-47
Secret s. (See **SIN**, Exposed)
Results. Misleads others. Lk.11:44
To be exposed. Lk.12:1-3
Source. (See **SIN**, Caused by)
The heart within man. Mt.23:28
Symbolic - Type of. Leprosy. Mt.8:1-4;
Mk.1:40-45; Lk.5:12-16
Unpardonable **s.** Blasphemy against the Holy
Spirit. Mt.12:31-32; Mk.3:29-30; Lk.12:10
Vs. Liberty. (See **LIBERTY, CHRIS-
TIAN**)
Warning against. (See **JUDGMENT**)
Continuing in **s.** Will cause a worse
thing to fall upon oneself. Mk.1:43
Offending a child. Mt.18:5-10
Work of. (See **SIN**, Acts of Sin)

SIN AND SUFFERING
Sin does not cause suffering. Jn.9:1-3
Sin is thought to be the cause of suffer-
ing. Lk.13:1-9
Suffering is not always due to sin.
Lk.13:1-9; Jn.9:1-3

SIN, MAN OF (See **LAWLESSNESS,
MAN OF**)

SIN, UNPARDONABLE
Discussed. Mt.12:31-32; Mk.3:29-30;
Lk.12:10

SIN THAT LEADS TO DEATH
Discussed. 1 Jn.5:16

SINAI, MOUNT
Mentioned. Acts 7:30; Gal.4:24-25;
Heb.12:18

SINCERE - SINCERITY (See **PURE**)
Duty.
The church must clean out all leaven
of sin--in **s.** & truth. 1 Cor.5:8
To approve the best things in order to
be **s.** & blameless. Ph.1:10
To desire the **s.**, pure milk of God's
Word. 1 Pt.2:2-3
To live in holiness & godly **s.**
2 Cor.1:12
To love in **s.** & to show it. 2 Cor.8:8,
cp. 1 Jn.3:18
To preach & teach the Word of God in
s. 2 Cor.2:17, cp. 1 Th.2:3-4
To show **s.**, purity in doctrine. Tit.2:6-7
Meaning. 2 Cor.1:12; 1 Tim.3:8; Jas.3:17-18

SINFUL DESIRES
Described. List of acts of the sinful na-
ture. 1 Pet.2:11
Discussed. 1 Pet.2:11
Meaning. 1 Pet 2:11
Works of. Wars against the soul. 1 Pet.2:11

SINFUL NATURE
Caused by.
Corrupt motives. Jn.6:26-27
Failure to see the cross. Lk.22:33-37
Living after the sinful nature. Ro.8:12-13
Twofold. Jn.13:36-38
Commitment of the **s.** Mt.26:51-52
Deliverance from.
By Christ.
By condemning sin in the **s.** Ro.8:3
By His conquest of the **s.** Jn.1:14

By His death. Eph.2:14-18, esp. 15-
16; Col.1:22; Heb.2:14-16; 9:13-
14; 10:19-20; 1 Pt.3:18
By His giving His **s.** for the life of
the world. Jn.6:51
By His power over all **s.** Jn.17:2
By His reconciliation. Eph.2:11-18;
Col.1:22
By His resurrection. Acts 2:30-31;
Ro.1:3-4
By His suffering in the **s.** for us.
1 Pt.4:1
By condemning sin in the **s.** Ro.8:3
By confessing that Christ has come to
earth in the **s.** 1 Jn.4:2-3; 2 Jn.7
By God.
By His being manifested, revealed
in the flesh. 1 Tim.3:16
By His power over all **s.** Jn.17:2
By partaking of the **s.**, of the life of
Christ. Jn.6:54-56
By the Holy Spirit. By walking in
Him. Gal.5:16
Deliverance from **s.** - How to conquer.
Abstaining from fleshly lusts.
1 Pt.2:11-12
Being spiritual minded. 2 Cor.10:5
By prayer. Prayer for a **s.** church.
2 Cor.13:7-10
By taking certain precautions against
s. Can become weighted down.
Heb.6:9-20; 12:1
By the power of the Spirit. Ro.8:1-17;
8:12-13
Discussed. 2 Cor.10:3-5
Doing no evil. 2 Cor.13:7
Fighting & warring against **s.**
2 Cor.10:3-5
Praying and fasting. Mk.9:28-29
Purging out **s.** 1 Cor.5:7
Watching and standing fast.
1 Cor.16:13
Discussed. Ro.7:14-17; 7:18-20; 1
Cor.2:14-3:1-4, 14; Gal.5:16-21;
1 Pt.2:11; Heb.5:11-6:3
Being corrupted under a man's minis-
try. Rev.3:14-22
Better to be cold than lukewarm.
Rev.3:15
Duty.
Not to fulfill the lusts of the **f.**
Gal.5:16-21
Not to give ourselves over to immor-
ality & strange **f.** (unnatural
sexual acts). Jude 7
Not to judge people by the **f.** Jn.8:15
Not to live after the flesh. Ro.8:12
Not to live any longer after the lusts of
the **f.** 1 Pt.4:2
Not to set one's mind on the **f.** Ro.8:5
Not to sow to our **f.** Gal.6:8
Not to use our liberty in Christ as an
opportunity for the **f.** to sin.
Gal.5:13
Not to use the weapons of the **f.** in the
spiritual struggle of life. 2 Cor.10:3-5
Not to walk after the flesh. Ro.8:1-4
To abstain from the **f.** 1 Pt.2:11-12; 4:3
To be cleansed from all filthiness of
the **f.** 2 Cor.7:1
To combat the desires of the sinful na-
ture. Gal.5:16-21
To complete the sufferings of Christ in
our **f.** Col.1:24
To control the **f.**
By having no confidence in. Ph.3:3

By seeking reconciliation when of-
fended. Mt.18:15-17
By struggling against. Ro.8:23-27
To crucify the sinful nature with its af-
fections & desires. Gal.5:24
To hate even the garments spotted by
the **f.** Jude 23
To have no confidence in the **f.** Ph.3:3
To live a crucified & sacrificial life in
the **f.** Gal.2:20
To make no provision for the **f.**
Ro.13:14
To manifest the life of Jesus in our **f.**
2 Cor.4:11
To mortify, put to death, the **f.**
Ro.8:12-13
To purify the **f.** by the blood of Christ.
Heb.9:13-14
To put away the filth of the **f.**
1 Pt.3:21
To put off the old garment of the **f.**
Mk.2:22
To put off the sins of the **f.** Col.2:11
To turn away from the sinful nature &
turn to Christ. Gal.5:24
Illustrated.
Barnabas' compromise. Gal.2:11-13
Peter's weakness. Lk.22:31-34;
Gal.2:11-13
Meaning. Jn.1:14; Ro.7:5; 8:5-8;
Eph.2:3; 1 Pt.2:11
Spiritual immaturity. 1 Cor.3:1-4;
Heb.5:11-6:3
The carnal mind of man. Ro.8:5-8
The natural, fleshly nature of man.
Ro.7:14-17
The struggle within fighting against
what one should do. Ro.7:14-25;
Gal.5:16-18;1 Th.4:3-5; Jas.4:2; 4:4
Mind of.
Discussed. Ro.8:5-8
Fate of. Ro.8:5-8
Focus of. Ro.8:5-8
Meaning. Ro.8:5-8
Vs. the spiritual **s.** Lk.12:13-21
Nature Works - Shortcomings of.
Cannot inherit the kingdom of God.
1 Cor.15:50
Cannot make a person perfect. Gal.3:3
Cannot please God. Ro.8:8
Causes man to die. Ro.8:13
Does not justify a person before God.
Ro.3:20; Gal.2:16
Dreams filthy dreams that defiles a
person. Jude 8
Is as grass, withers ever so quickly.
1 Pt.1:24
Is not a part of spiritual beings. Lk.24:39
Is so corrupted that it even spots the
garments worn by a person. Jude 23
Money, silver & gold can consume the
f. Jas.5:3, cp. Mt.6:19-20
No good thing dwells within the **f.**
Ro.7:18
Profits nothing. Jn.6:63
Reaps corruption. Gal.6:8
Serves the law of sin & death.
Ro.7:25; 8:1-4
Stirs a fleshly, carnal commitment.
Jn.13:36-38
Stirs lust. 1 Pt.2:11
Struggles against prayer. Mt.26:41;
Mk.14:38
The carnal vs. the spiritual view of the
f. Lk.22:33-37

The lust of the **f.** is not of God.
1 Jn.2:15-16
Wars against the soul & spirit.
Mt.26:41; Mk.14:38; 1 Pt.2:11
Withers & falls away. 1 Pt.1:24-25
Works of the **f.**
Seventeen works. Gal.5:19-21
Twenty-three works. Ro.1:29-32
Results. (See **CARNAL**, Traits of)
A divided church. 1 Cor.1:10-16, cp.
1 Cor.1:10-4:21
A struggling soul. Ro.7:14-25
Death. Ro.6:23; 8:5-8; 8:12-13
Deforms & stymies growth. One remains
only a babe in Christ. 1 Cor.3:1-2
Dullness of hearing. Heb.5:11
Falling & failing. Lk.22:33-37;
Heb.6:9-20
Grieving the Lord. Mk.9:19-22
Has to be treated as a babe in Christ.
Can receive only the milk of the
Word, not the meat of the Word.
1 Cor.3:1-2; Heb.5:11-6:3
Hurting & cutting a minister.
2 Cor.2:3-4
Self-deception. 1 Cor.3:18-23
Works shall be burned up in the judg-
ment. 1 Cor.3:13-15
Sin of.
A life spent in lusts, cravings. Eph.2:3
Discussed. Acts of the sinful nature.
1 Jn.2:15-17
Lists of fleshly sins. Ro.1:24-32; 3:9-20;
1 Cor.6:9-11;10:6-10; Gal.5:19-21;
Eph.4:25-32; Col.3:8-9; 1 Tim.1:9-10;
2 Tim.3:1-5; 1 Pt.2:1; 4:3
Traits of.
A struggling soul. Ro.7:14-25
Allowing the leaven of sin in one's
life. 1 Cor.5:6-8
Being complacent toward sin.
1 Cor.5:1-2; 5:6-13; Rev.3:1-6
Being contentious & divisive.
1 Cor.1:11; 3:3-4
Being enemies of the cross. Ph.3:18-19
Being weak. Ro.15:1-3
Boasting about one's flesh. Gal.6:12-13
Compromising. Gal.2:11-14
Engaging in legal disputes. 1 Cor.6:1-8
Exalting some ministers over others.
1 Cor.3:3-4; 3:5-9; 3:21-23
Faithlessness. Mk.9:19-22
False security. Ro.13:11-14
False teachers. 2 Pt.2:10; Jude 19
Having double standards. Gal.2:11-14
Immaturity. Mt.17:14-21; Mk.9:14-29;
1 Cor.3:1-2
Immorality. 1 Cor.5:1-13
Indulgence. 1 Cor.6:12-20
Judging others. Mt.7:1-5; Ro.2:1;
1 Cor.4:1-5; 4:6-13
Living unrighteously. 1 Cor.6:9-11
Looking progressive, but being dead.
Rev.3:1
Losing one's first love. Rev.2:4
Misusing one's spiritual gifts.
1 Cor.12:1-14:40
Powerlessness. Lk.9:37-45
Prayerlessness. Mk.9:28-29
Rebelling against God. Ro.8:5-8
Unbelief. Mt.17:19-21
Worldly wisdom. 1 Cor.3:18-20; Jas.3:15
Verses. List of. Mk.8:32-33; Jn.6:26-27
Vs. the Spirit. Discussed. Ro.8:1-17
Vs. the spiritual man. Ro.8:1-17;
1 Cor.2:14-3:4

SING - SINGING
By believers.
At the gathering of believers.
Mt.26:20
In the midst of joy. Jas.5:13
In the midst of trial. Acts 16:25
To admonish one another through **s.**
Col.3:16
To admonish oneself in one's heart by
s. to the Lord. Eph.5:19
To **s.** in the Spirit. 1 Cor.14:15
Discussed. Eph.5:18-21
In heaven.
By the heavenly host. Rev.5:8-10
By the redeemed. Rev.14:3

SINGLENESS OF EYE
Meaning. Mt.6:22

SINGLES - UNMARRIED (See AGE; WIDOWS; UNMARRIED)
Discussed. 1 Cor.7:8-9

SINNER - SINNERS (See MAN; SIN)
And Christ.
Christ associated with. Mk.2:15;
Lk.5:27-32
Christ is a friend of **s.** Lk.7:34
Jesus came to save **s.** Lk.5:27-32
S. can come to Christ. Lk.5:1-2
S. were comfortable with Christ. Mt.9:10-11
Attitude toward.
By society. Mk.2:16-17
By the church. Mk.2:15
Many neglect **s.** Will not touch them. Mt.8:3
Some feel that they are more accept-
able than **s.** Mt.9:12-13
Deliverance. (See **SIN**, Deliverance)
A sinner saved. Lk.7:36-50
By the death of Christ. Ro.5:8
Must pray. Lk.8:13-14
Must repent. Lk.5:30-32
The attitude necessary for deliverance.
Lk.18:13
There is hope for the **s.**, even for the
most wild & mean. Mk.5:1-20
What it takes for a **s.** to enter heaven.
Mt.21:28-32
Duty.
To draw near God & to cleanse one's
hands & purify one's heart. Jas.4:8
To seek cleansing. Mk.1:40; 1:43
Judgment of.
Will be disowned by God & Christ.
Mt.7:21-23; 25:1-12, esp. 12;
Lk.12:8-9; 13:24-27, esp. 27
Will face judgment for all the ungodly
things done against Christ. Jude 14-15
Will suffer tribulation & anguish. Ro.2:8-9
State of. (See **MAN**, State of, Present)
All men are **s.** Lk.13:1-9
One's pleasure in sin needs to be turned
into mourning. Jas.4:8-9, esp. 9
S. are under law. The law was made
for the **s.** 1 Tim.1:8-11
S. leave behind a path of destruction &
misery. Ro.3:16
S. need to be turned from sin. Jas.5:19-20
State of **s.** Are spiritually sick. Mt.9:12-13
The power to reach **s.** Discussed. Mk.2:13-17

SINS AGAINST
Discussed. Eph.2:1-2
Meaning. Mt.6:14; Eph.2:1-2

SIX-SIX-SIX (666) OF ANTICHRIST
Meaning. Rev.13:18

SKEPTIC - SKEPTICISM (See AGNOSTIC; UNBELIEF)

SLANDER - SLANDERER - SLANDERING SLANDEROUS (See BLASPHEMY; JESUS CHRIST, Accusations Against; MALICIOUS TALKER; MINISTER; Accusations against; TONGUE)
Against the Holy Spirit. Mt.12:31-32;
Mk.3:29-30; Lk.12:4-12
Caused by.
Backsliding - a shipwrecked faith.
1 Tim.1:19-20
Claiming deity. 2 Th.2:4
Covetousness & worldliness. Jas.2:6-7
False religion. Rev.2:9
Natural & physical difficulties & cir-
cumstances. Rev.16:9-11, 21
Not doing to others as we should.
1 Tim.6:1
Not living responsibly & righteously before
the world. 1 Tim.6:1; Tit.2:1-5, esp. 5
Persecution. Acts 26:11
Professing Christ, but living a hypo-
critical life. Ro.2:24, cp. 17-29
Rejection & hatred of Christ. Jn.8:48-59;
Acts 18:5-6
The antichrist. Rev.13:1, 6
The dragon, Satan. Rev.13:4-6
Charged against. Christ. Mt.9:3; Mk.2:6-7;
Jn.10:36
Discussed. Tit.3:3; Jas.4:11-12
Duty.
Not to be a **s.** 1 Cor.6:9-11
Not to fellowship with a railer.
1 Cor.5:11
Not to partake of the Lord's Supper
with **s.** in one's heart. 1 Cor.5:7-8
Not to rail, even when railed against.
1 Pt.3:9
Not to speak evil of any person, not a
single person. Tit.3:2
Not to use Christian liberty as a cloak,
an excuse to hold **s** against someone.
1 Pt.2:16
To be as children in **s.**, having nothing
to with **s.** 1 Cor.14:20
To bless when **s.** 1 Cor.4:11-13
To have such a good conscience that
those who **s.** will be put to shame.
1 Pt.3:16, cp. 15
To know that people watch to find ac-
cusations. Lk.6:7
To lay aside all **s.** 1 Pt.2:1
To live a righteous life, not giving the
world any reason for **s.** 1 Pt.2:12
To prepare for the end time: a terrible period
of world-wide **s.** 2 Tim.3:1-5, esp. 3
To put away all evil or **s.** speaking.
Eph.4:31
To put away **s.**, all **s.** Eph.4:31; Col.3:8
To put off **s.** Col.3:8
To rejoice & endure **s.** for the sake of
Christ. Mt.5:11-12
To suffer being reviled even as Christ
did. 1 Pt.2:21-24
Is forgiven. Mk.3:28
Meaning. Mt.9:3; Mk.7:22; Ro.1:29-30;
1 Cor.5:11; 6:10; 2 Cor.12:19-21; Col.3:8-11;
Eph.4:31; Col.3:8-11; 2 Tim.3:2-4; Tit.2:3,
1 Pt.2:1

Of what.
Believers. Mt.5:11-12; 1 Pt.2:21-24
Christ upon the cross. Mt.27:39-44;
1 Pt.2:21-24, esp. 23
Results.
Judgment of. Death. Ro.1:29-32, esp. 32
The **s.** shall not inherit the kingdom of
God. 1 Cor.6:9-10
Sin of.
Religion can be guilty of **b.** Rev.2:8-11
Will be a trait of the last days.
2 Tim.3:1-2; Rev.6:9-11, 21
Will be committed by the antichrist.
Rev.13:4-8
The promise to believers when slandered. To
be blessed & greatly rewarded. Mt.5:11-12
Trait - Characteristic of.
False leaders & teachers within the
church. 2 Pet.2:10-12; 3 Jn.10
The ungodly & unrighteous. Ro.1:18, 29-32
Unbelievers. Mk.15:29-32; Lk.23:39;
Tit.3:3
Who is often **s.**
Believers. 1 Pt.2:12; 3:16; Acts 2:1-13,
esp. 13; 24:5-6; Rev.2:9
Christ. (See **JESUS CHRIST**, Ac-
cused - Accusation against)
Ministers & church leaders. Lk.7:33;
Acts 6:13; 3 Jn.9-10
Who it is that **s.**
A whole generation of unbelievers
who stand against true righteousness.
Mt.11:16-19
Corrupt political & religious officials.
Lk.22:66-71; 23:1-5
Religious leaders. Acts 6:9-15; 24:1-9
Some church leaders & members who
oppose the minister. 3 Jn.9-10
Some religionists. Mt.9:34
The average citizen who mocks spiri-
tual things. Acts 2:1-13, esp. 13

SLAVE - SLAVES - SLAVERY
Discussed. 1 Tim.6:1-2; 1 Pt.2:18-20
Different kinds of **s.** Acts 16:16-17
Duty.
To masters. Discussed. Col.3:22-25
To submit to masters. 1 Pt.2:18-20
Toward a Christian supervisor.
1 Tim.6:1-2
Eliminated by Christianity. Eph.6:5-9
Enforced labor. Discussed. Mt.5:41
In the Roman Empire. Discussed.
Eph.6:5-9
Instructions to. Eph.6:5-9
The only record of a **s.** brought to Christ
by another person. Mt.8:8
Treatment of. Phile.1:8-21

SLEEP - SLEPT
Reasons for. Mt.26:40-41
Symbol - Type.
Jesus **s.** in the midst of a storm.
Mt.8:24
Of death. Meaning. Lk.8:50; Jn.11:13
Spiritual slumber. Mt.25:5

SLEEP, SPIRITUAL (See SLOTHFUL; SLUMBER, SPIRITUAL)
Duty.
Must not **s.** as others, but watch & be
sober. 1 Th.5:6
Must not **s.** but be prepared for the
Lord's return. Mt.25:1-13, esp. 5;
Mk.13:35-36
Meaning. Mt.25:5

SLEEPINESS (See SLEEP, SPIRITUAL; SLOTHFUL)
Example. Reluctant to obey because of
being tired & sleepy. Lk.5:4-5
Result. Secures little if anything. Lk.8:18
Verses. List of. Lk.8:18

SLEEPLESS NIGHTS
Meaning. 2 Cor.6:5

SLOTHFUL - SLOTHFULNESS (See LAZY; SLEEP, SPIRITUAL; ZEAL, LACKING)
Discussed. Ro.13:11-14
Work & employment. 2 Th.3:6-18
Duty.
Not to lack zeal. Ro.12:11
To awaken out of sleep & **s.** Ro.13:11-12
To be diligent & not **s.** Heb.6:11-12
To stay awake, always working &
preparing for the Lord's return.
Mt.25:1-13, esp. 5
Example. Reluctant to obey. Lk.5:4-5
Meaning. A **s.** servant. Mt.25:24-30, cp.
14-30; Ro.12:11
Result. Secures little if anything. Lk.8:18
Verses. List of. Lk.8:18

SLOW
Caused by.
Closing one's heart to the truth. Acts
28:27
Failure to be rooted in the Word of
God. Heb.5:11-14
Failure to hear the Word of Christ. Jn.8:43
Failure to recognize & discern that
Christ is the Savior of the world.
Lk.12:56
Failure to seek after God. Ro.3:11
Sin, the love of sin. 2 Tim.3:1-7, esp. 7
Spiritual insensitivity. Lk.9:44-45
Unbelief. Not believing all of the
Word of God. Lk.24:25
Describes. Depraved nature. Ro.3:10-12
Meaning. Heb.5:11
Verses. List of. Lk.9:44-45

SLUGGARD (See SLOTHFULNESS)

SLUMBER - SLUMBERED-- DROWSINESS (See SLEEP, SPIRI- TUAL; SLOTHFULNESS)
Reasons for. Mt.26:40-41
Symbol - Type.
Jesus **s.** in the midst of a storm. Mt.8:24
Of death. Meaning. Lk.8:50; Jn.11:13
Spiritual slumber. Mt.25:5

SMYRNA
Church of.
Discussed. Rev.2:8
One of the seven churches of Revela-
tion. Rev.2:8-11
Represents the persecuted church.
Rev.2:8-11
City of. Discussed. Rev.2:8

SNAKES
Discussed. Mt.10:16
Paul healed of a **s.** bite. Acts 28:1-6
Symbolized - Type of.
Jesus' death. Lifted up by Moses.
Jn.3:14-15
Satan. Rev.20:2
Wisdom. To be wise or shrewd as a **s.**
Mt.10:16

SNARE - SNARES
Fact.
Money is a **s.** Will drown one in destruction & perdition. 1 Tim.6:9
The Lord's return is coming upon earth
as a snare. One must, therefore, watch
in order to escape. Lk.21:34-36
Unbelievers are caught in the **s.** of the
devil. Believers must, therefore,
reach them.
2 Tim.2:24-26
Meaning. Lk.21:34-35

SOBER - SOBRIETY (See DRUNKEN- NESS; MIND; SELF-CONTROLLED; TEMPERATE)
Duty.
Believers are not to be drunk but so-
ber. 1 Th.5:6-8
Believers are to live **s.** lives, that is,
self-controlled, disciplined, & tem-
perate lives. Tit.2:12-13; 1 Pt.1:13
Ministers & their wives are to be
blameless, **s.**, & never drunk.
1 Tim.3:2, 11; Tit.1:8
The aged are to be **s.** & never drunk.
Tit.2:2-3, 5
Women are to be **s.** minded. 1 Tim.2:9
Young men & women are to be **s.**
minded. Tit.2:4-7
Warning.
Must be **s.** & guard against pride, not
thinking too highly of oneself &
one's gifts. Ro.12:3
Must be **s.** & pray & watch for the end
of all things. 1 Pt.4:7
Must be **s.**, watching for the Lord's
return. 1 Th.5:1-9, esp. 6-8. Cp.
Tit.2:12-13

SOCIAL ACTIVITIES - SOCIAL LIFE
Discussed. 1 Cor.6:12; 8:1-13; 10:14-
11:1
Limits of freedom. 1 Cor.10:14-11:1
Questionable functions. Ro.14:1-23
Questionable pleasures. 1 Cor.8:9-11;
10:14-11:1
Duty. To fellowship & be sociable.
Jn.2:1-2

SOCIAL CONCERNS
Of mankind. Vs. spiritual concerns.
Jn.2:3-5

SOCIAL JUSTICE
Preached. By John the Baptist. Lk.3:10-14

SOCIAL LADDER
Climbing. An illustration. Rev.2:8-9

SOCIAL NEEDS
Duty. To meet as world evangelism goes
forth. Ro.15:22-33

SOCIAL RESPONSIBILITIES
Discussed. Acts 2:42

SOCIETY (See CITIZENSHIP; WORLD)
Attitude of **s.** Toward the sinner.
Mk.2:16-17
Corrupt **s.**
Discussed. Acts 17:11
In the end time. Will be godless & de-
stroyed. Rev.14:8; 16:17-21; 18:2-7
Of the ancient world. Corrupt. Acts
16:14

Cradle of. Changed to Europe. Acts 16:6-11
Duty. To evangelize. Acts 16:6-11
Errors of. Opposes the righteousness & morality of Christianity. Acts 19:21-41
Hope of. New principles of life. Lk.6:27-38

SODOM AND GOMORRHA
Destroyed by God. 2 Pt.2:6
Discussed. Mt.10:15; 11:23
Illustrates - Symbolizes.
    Jerusalem. Rev.11:8
    Judgment. The judgment of God. Mk.6:11; Lk.10:12; 2 Pt.2:6; Jude 5-7

SOJOURN - SOJOURNER
Describes. Believers upon earth. 1 Pt.1:17
Duty.
    To pass the time of one's **s.** upon earth in fear. 1 Pt.1:17
    To **s.** upon earth looking for the heavenly city. Heb.11:9-10
Meaning. 1 Pt.1:17

SOLDIER
Duty.
    Must not mock & mistreat Christ as the **s.** did at the cross. Mt.27:26-38
    Not to accept bribes & transgress the law. Mt.28:12-15
    Not to fear, act rashly, & violate the law. Acts 27:42-44, esp. 42
    To be a sincere worshipper & seeker after God. Acts 10:1-48
    To believe Christ & to seek Christ in behalf of others. Mt.8:5-13
    To carry out one's duty in true justice despite the people's wishes & violence. Acts 21:31-40
    To seek how to escape the judgment of God. Lk.3:14, cp. 1-14
Great faith found in a **s.** Lk.7:1-10
Treatment of Christ by soldiers before & during His death. Mt.27:26-38
Type - Symbol of. The believer's spiritual warfare.
    Must not become entangled in the world. 2 Tim.2:4
    Must put on the breastplate of faith & love. 1 Th.5:8
    Must put on the whole armor of God. Eph.6:10-20

SOLOMON
Illustrates. How a person must seek Christ above all else. Lk.11:30-32

SON OF GOD (See **JESUS CHRIST**, Claims; Deity)

SON OF MAN (See **JESUS CHRIST**, Claims, Deity; Names - Titles; Son of Man)

SON OF PERDITION (See **MAN DOOMED TO DESTRUCTION**)

SONS OF GOD (See **CHILDREN OF GOD**)

SONS, TWO
Parable.
    Of the prodigal son. Lk.15:11-32
    Of two **s.** What it takes to enter heaven. Mt.21:28-32
Why God so often chose the younger **s.** to receive the inheritance in the O.T. Ro.9:13

SONS--CHILDREN OF GOD (See **ADOPTION**)

SOOTHSAYER (See **SORCERY**)
Discussed. The misuse of human life. The power of sin & money vs. the power of Jesus' name. Acts 16:16-24

SOPATER
Believer from Berea who traveled with Paul. Acts 20:4

SORCERER - SORCERY (See **ASTROLOGY; SUPERSTITION**)
Discussed.
    Sins & judgment of. Acts 13:7-11; 16:16-17; Rev.21:8
    The false profession of a **s.** Acts 8:5-25
Error of.
    Men fear & respect supernatural forces other than God. Jn.19:8-11
    Men seek destiny in superstition. Jn.5:2-4
    To sweep the earth in the end time. Rev.9:20-21
Verses. List of. Jn.19:8-11

SORROW - SORROWFUL-- TROUBLED (See **GRIEF**)
Caused by.
    Knowing that loved ones are lost. Ro.9:1-3
    Making foolish & rash promises. Mt.14:9, cp. 1-12
    Rejecting Christ. Mt.19:22, cp. 16-22
    The death of loved ones. Jn.11:33-35; 1 Th.4:13-14
Danger of. Often becomes self-centered; wallowing around in **s.** Jn.16:5-6
Deliverance from.
    By focusing upon the resurrection of Christ. Jn.16:5-6, 20-22
    By not becoming wrapped up in covetousness, in money. 1 Tim.6:10
    By repentance, a true godly sorrow. (See **SORROW, GODLY**) 2 Cor.7:10
    By understanding & hoping for the return of Christ. 1 Th.4:13-18

Meaning. Mt.26:37; Lk.6:20-23

SORROW, GODLY (See **CONTRITION**)
Is a brokenhearted sorrow over sin. Lk.15:20-21; 22:61-62
Leads to conviction. Acts 2:37
Vs. worldly sorrow. 2 Cor.7:10

SOSIPATER
Relative of Paul. Ro.16:21

SOSTHENES
A Christian. Acts 18:17; 1 Cor.1:1

SOUJOURNER (See **STRANGERS**)

SOUL
And spirit. Meaning. Jn.4:23; 4:23-24
Attitude toward the **s.** Mk.8:36-37
Discussed. Struggled against by the flesh. 1 Pt.2:11
Duty.
    To abstain from fleshly lusts, for they war against the **s.** 1 Pt.2:11
    To be cleansed & purified in **s.** 1 Pt.1:22

To believe in Christ & save one's **s.** Heb.10:39, cp. 37-39
To beware of covetousness, for one's **s.** can be required this night. Lk.12:15-21
To fear Him who can destroy both body & soul in hell. Mt.10:28
To live separated from the world, for the world grieves the **s.** of the righteous. 2 Pt.2:7-8
To love God with all of one's **s.** Lk.10:25-28, esp. 27
To purify one's **s.** by obeying the truth. 1 Pt.1:22
To save souls from death through conversion. Jas.5:20
To save the **s.** Vs. gaining the world. Mk.8:36-37
To see above all else that one's **s.** prospers & grows. 3 Jn.2
Fact.
    S. are ripe for harvest. Jn.4:35
    The ungodliness of the world grieves the **s.** of the righteous. 2 Pt.2:8
Judgment of evil souls.
    Destroyed in hell. Mt.10:28
    Eternal death. Jas.5:20
    Punishment. 2 Pt.2:8-9
    Tribulation & anguish. Ro.2:8-9
Meaning. Mt.16:25-28; 22:37; Mk.8:36-37; 12:29-31
Value of.
    Is immortal. Mt.10:28
    Is priceless. Giving up all to save one's **s.** Mt.13:45-46
    Is worth more than the world. Reasons. Mt.16:25-28

SOUL-WINNING (See **PREACHING; WITNESSING**)

SOUL-WINNING, CROWN OF
Meaning. 1 Th.2:19-20

SOUND DOCTRINE
Meaning. Tit.2:1

SOUNDNESS--MADE WHOLE (See **COMPLETE HEALING**)

SOVEREIGNTY (See **GOD; JESUS CHRIST**)

SOWER OR FARMER, PARABLE OF THE
How men receive the gospel. Mt.13:1-9; Mk.4:1-20
Illustrates.
    Patience needed to combat temptation & trials & to wait for the Lord's return. Jas.5:7-9
Traits. Discussed. 2 Tim.2:6

SOW - SOWING (See **WITNESSING**)
Duty.
    To sow the gospel. Mt.13:1-9; Mk.4:1-20; Jn.4:35-37
    To sow to the spirit. Gal.6:7-9, esp. 8
Law of. Whatever one **s.** one shall reap. Jn.12:39-41; 2 Cor.9:6; Gal.6:7-9

SPAIN
Paul wanted to reach & evangelize Spain. Ro.15:24, 28

SPEAK - SPEECH (See **TONGUE; WARNS**)
Duty.
To be seasoned with salt. Col.4:6
To reflect one's testimony for Christ. Mt.26:73-74
To talk about the Lord all day long. Col.3:17
What the believer is to **s.** & talk about.
Sound doctrine. Tit.2:1
The mystery of Christ. Eph.6:19-20
The things that cannot be condemned. Tit.2:8
The truth, not lies. Eph.4:25
Wisdom, the wisdom of God. 1 Cor.2:6-7

SPEAKING
Spiritual gift of. Meaning. 1 Cor.1:5-7

SPEAKING EVIL (See **SLANDER; SPEAKS AGAINST; TONGUE**)
Trait of divisive people. Ro.16:17-18

SPEAKS AGAINST; TONGUE
Discussed. Jas.4:11-12
Meaning. Jas.4:11-12; 1 Pt.2:1
Trait of divisive people. Ro.16:17-18

SPECK IN THE EYE
Parable of. Watch hypocrisy & criticism. Lk.6:41-42

SPECTACULAR, THE (See **SENSATIONALISM**)

SPECULATIONS (See **PHILOSOPHY; RATIONALISM; REASONING; TEACHERS, FALSE**)
Discussed. 1 Tim.4:7; 6:20-21; 2 Tim.2:14; 2:16-18; 2:23

SPIRIT (See **MAN**, Depravity, Spiritually Dead; State, Present; **SALVATION**)
Blind **s.** Defiles a man. Mt.15:12-14
Duty.
Must worship God in **s.** Jn.4:23-24; 4:23
To keep one's spiritual fervor. Ro.12:11
Fact.
Angels are **s.** Heb.1:7, 14
God is **s.** Jn.4:23-24; 4:23
Man's **s.** is housed by a body, a tent. 2 Cor.5:1-4
Material vs. spiritual approach to God. Heb.8:1-13; 9:1-14; 9:23-28;10:1-18
Meaning. Jn.4:23-24; 4:23
The **s.** is the basic part of a man's being.
It is the **s.** that is to be saved in the day of Jesus Christ. 1 Cor.5:5
It is the **s.** that is to worship God. Jn.4:23; 4:23-24
It is the **s.** that knows all about man. 1 Cor.2:11
Value of.
Can live forever. Ro.8:10-11
Is more important than the physical. 1 Tim.4:8
Shall live in heaven with God. Heb.12:23; 1 Pt.3:19

SPIRITISM
Discussed. Col.2:18-19

SPIRITS - SPIRITUAL BEINGS
Duty. To test the spirits of teachers. 1 Jn.4:1-6
False - evil - unclean. (See **SPIRITS, EVIL**)
Discussed. 1 Jn.4:1-6
Vs. true **s.** 1 Jn.4:1-6

True. (See **ANGELS**)
Discussed. 1 Jn.4:1-6
Vs. false **s.** 1 Jn.4:1-6

SPIRITS, EVIL (See **EVIL SPIRITS**)

SPIRITUAL
Things said to be **s.**
S. believers.
Spiritual believers are able to discern all things. 1 Cor.2:15
Spiritual believers are to restore backsliders. Gal.6:1
Spiritual believers vs. carnal believers. 1 Cor.3:1
S. blessings. God blesses believers with all **s.** blessings. Listed & discussed. Eph.1:3
S. food & drink. Are to eat & drink of the **s.** food & drink just as Israel did. 1 Cor.10:3-4
S. forces of wickedness (evil spirits). Believers struggle against all forces of wickedness. Eph.6:12
S. gifts.
Are to desire **s.** gifts. 1 Cor.14:1
Are to share some **s.** gift in order to build up believers. Ro.1:11
Are to use **s.** gifts to edify the church. 1 Cor.14:12
Must not be ignorant about **s.** gifts. 1 Cor.12:1
S. sacrifices. The very purpose of believers is to offer up **s.** sacrifices to God. 1 Pt.2:5
S. songs. Are to sing **s.** songs within one's own heart & among believers. Eph.5:19; Col.3:16
S. things.
Are to be shared. Ro.15:27
Are to compare **s** things with **s.** things. 1 Cor.2:13
Are to sow **s.** things within the world & among believers. 1 Cor.9:11
S. understanding. Are to pray for & to be filled with **s.** understanding. Col.1:9
The believer's resurrected body. It is raised a **s.** body. 1 Cor.15:44-46
The **s.** law. Ro.7:14
The **s.** house, the church. Believers are being built into a **s.** house, into the true church of God. 1 Pt.2:5
The **s.** Rock (Christ). We are to partake of the **s.** Rock, of Christ. 1 Cor.10:3-4
Things that lead away from the **s.** Mt.16:17
Vs. the physical. Discussed. 2 Cor.4:17-18

SPIRITUAL ABANDONMENT (See **JUDGMENT**)
A judgment of God. Jn.12:39-41; Ro.1:24-32; 1:24;11:7-10; 2 Th.2:11; Jas.2:12-13

SPIRITUAL ADULTERY (See **ADULTERY, SPIRITUAL**)

SPIRITUAL BLESSINGS (See **BLESSINGS**)

SPIRITUAL BLINDNESS (See **UNBELIEF**)
Caused by.
Discussed. Ro.1:21
Spiritual dullness. Lk.9:44-45
Deliverance from. By Christ. Jn.9:1-7

Discussed. Lk.11:45-46; Ro.13:11-12; 2 Pt.1:8-11
Fact. The lost are blind. Mt.9:27-31
Faults of the spiritually blind.
Blind to God's purpose. Mt.11:25-27
Blind to the Messiah. Mt.11:25-27
Blind to the truth. Mt.11:25-27
Discussed. Mk.8:10-13
Meaning. Rev.3:16-17
Parable of. The blind leading the blind. Lk.6:39
Results.
Causes others to be blind (followers, children). Lk.6:39
Fail to see the truth. Mk.6:52
Is of the world, worldly wisdom. 1 Cor.2:6-13
Warning against. Mt.16:1-4
Is inexcusable. Motive for. Mk.8:11; 8:12
Will suffer judicial **b.** Reasons. Mt.13:13-15

SPIRITUAL BONDAGE (See **BONDAGE, SPIRITUAL; ENSLAVEMENT, SPIRITUAL; SIN**, Results)

SPIRITUAL DEATH (See **DEATH, SPIRITUAL**)

SPIRITUAL EXPERIENCE (See **GLORY**)
Described. Mt.17:2; 17:3; 17:4; 17:5-8; 17:5
God knows exactly what spiritual experience a believer needs. Mt.17:4
Results. Humility vs. being puffed up. Acts 4:23-24

SPIRITUAL FAMILY (See **FAMILY OF GOD**)

SPIRITUAL FOOD (See **HUNGER, SPIRITUAL; SATISFACTION, SPIRITUAL**)

SPIRITUAL FOUNDATION (See **FOUNDATION, SPIRITUAL**)

SPIRITUAL GIFTS (See **GIFTS, SPIRITUAL**)

SPIRITUAL GROWTH - MATURITY (See **GROWTH, SPIRITUAL**)

SPIRITUAL HISTORY (See **HISTORY, SPIRITUAL**)

SPIRITUAL HUNGER (See **HUNGER & THIRST**)

SPIRITUAL IMMATURITY (See **IMMATURITY, SPIRITUAL**)

SPIRITUAL INHERITANCE (See **INHERITANCE; REWARD**)

SPIRITUAL INSENSITIVITY (See **SPIRITUAL BLINDNESS; DULLNESS, SPIRITUAL**)

SPIRITUAL INSIGHT (See **SPIRITUAL SIGHT; UNDERSTANDING**)

SPIRITUAL INVESTMENTS - TREASURES (See **SEEK - SEEKING**) **SPIRITUAL MIND** (See **MIND**)

SPIRITUAL REBIRTH (See **BORN AGAIN; NEW BIRTH; NEW CREA-TION;NEW MAN; REGENERATION; SALVATION**)

SPIRITUAL SATISFACTION (See **SAT-ISFACTION, SPIRITUAL**)

SPIRITUAL SENSES
Natural vs. spiritual **s.** Mt.16:2-4

SPIRITUAL SIGHT - SPIRITUAL UN-DERSTANDING (See **KNOWLEDGE; UNDERSTANDING**)
Focus is to be Christ & Christ alone.
Jn.9:1-41
Meaning. Jn.20:20
Stages of spiritual sight. Jn.9:8-41
The promise of spiritual sight.
Insight into the truth. Given to believ-ers only. Lk.10:21
To those who abide in Christ. Jn.1:38-39

SPIRITUAL STRUGGLE - WARFARE
Caused by.
An inward battle. The very nature of man himself: flesh & spirit.
Ro.7:14-25; Gal.5:17
Division within one's very family.
Mt.10:34-38
Friendship with the world. Jas.4:1-4
Indecision. Choosing other things be-fore God. Lk.9:57-62; 11:23;
14:18-20; 16:13
The devil. 1 Pt.5:8-9
The flesh. 1 Pt.4:1-5
The invisible forces & evil spirits.
Eph.6:12
Trying to serve two masters. Lk.16:13
Deliverance from - Victory - Triumph Over.
All creation shall be delivered.
Ro.8:18-27
By arming oneself with the mind of Christ. 1 Pt.4:1-2
By Christ. He feels for man's spiritual struggle. Heb.2:17-18; 4:14-16
By faith. 1 Jn.5:4-5
By fighting to lay hold on eternal life.
1 Tim.6:12
By God. He assures deliverance for the believer. Ro.8:28-39
By the armor of God. Eph.6:10-24;
1 Th.5:8
By the peace of Christ. Jn.14:27;
16:33
By the power of the Spirit. Ro.8:1-17
By three things. Ro.8:23-27
By using the spiritual weapons of God.
2 Cor.10:3-5
By watching & staying alert.
1 Cor.16:13
How a struggling soul conquers its turmoil. Ro.7:14-25
Discussed. Mt.11:28-30; Ro.6:14-15;
7:14-25;8:18; 8:23-27; 8:28-39;2
Cor.10:1-6; 10:3-5; Eph.6:10-24
The warrior for Christ. 1 Tim.1:18-20
Duty.
To cast down imaginations & every high thing & to captivate every thought for Christ. 2 Cor.10:5, cp.
Ro.8:5-7; Ph.4:8
To discipline & control & fight with all of one's might. 1 Cor.9:26-27,
cp. 24-27

To endure hardness & not become en-tangled with the world. 2 Tim.2:3-4
To fight the good fight. 1 Tim.1:18
To put on the armor of God.
Eph.6:10-24
To put on the breastplate of faith & love & the helmet of salvation.
1 Th.5:8
To struggle against sin. 1 Jn.2:1
Glimpse into the spiritual struggle be-tween Satan & God. Lk.22:31
Nature - Where it occurs.
In creation. Ro.8:18-23
In the carnal mind. Vs. the spiritual mind. Ro.8:5-8
In the flesh. Vs. the spirit. Gal.5:16-21;
5:22-26
In the mind & imagination.
2 Cor.10:3-5; 11:3
Lust that is within one's body. Jas.4:1-4
Within man - groaning for deliverance.
Ro.7:14-25; 8:18-27; 2 Cor.5:1-4
Purpose.
To attain to the resurrection from the dead. Ph.3:11
To conquer the forces of evil in the world. Eph.6:10-24
To control one's thoughts imagina-tions & arguments. 2 Cor.10:3-5
To guard one's mind. 2 Cor.11:3
To secure immortality. 2 Cor.5:1-10
Weapons of.
Armor of God. Eph.6:10-24
Faith & a good conscience. 1 Tim.1:18
Faith & love & hope. 1 Th.5:8

SPIRITUAL THIRST (See **HUNGER & THIRST; HUNGER, SPIRITUAL; SATISFACTION, SPIRITUAL**)

SPIRITUAL TREASURES (See **BLESS-INGS; INHERITANCE; REWARD**)
Meaning. Mt.6:19-20

SPIRITUAL TRUTH (See **TRUTH,** Spiritual)

SPIRITUAL WORLD - SPIRITUAL DIMENSION (See **ETERNAL LIFE; HEAVEN**)
Conflict - Struggle within.
Between the forces of good & evil.
Rev.12:1-17
Controls the affairs of earth. Rev.12:1-17
The last great war within the heavenly world. Rev.12:1-17
Misconception. Misunderstood by natural man. Mk.12:24
Origin of. Christ. Jn.8:42-43
Nature - Reality of. (See **HEAVEN,** Characteristics - Nature) Mt.22:29
Cannot be known by man or worldly wisdom. 1 Cor.2:6-13; 3:18-20
Discussed. Mt.22:29; Mk.12:25
Is another dimension of being, another world, the spiritual world. Mt.19:16;
Jn.3:31
Unknown to man. Must be revealed.
Lk.10:22; Jn.3:13; 3:31; 8:14; 8:15-16;
8:19; 8:23; 8:42-43; 11:7-10
Relationships in. Discussed. Mk.12:25
Revealed. By God alone. Mk.12:24
Unbelief in.
By false teachers. Jude 8-10
Denied. Mt.22:23-33; 22:29
Discussed. 2 Pt.2:10-12

Reasons for man's unbelief. Minimize & ignore the spiritual world.
Mk.8:11
Vs. the physical world, dimension.
Discussed. Lk.10:22; Jn.8:14; 8:15-16;
8:23
Five differences. Lk.20:27-38

SPIT - SPITTING
Sign of utter contempt. Mk.14:65

SPITE
Reasons. Threefold. Mt.13:53-54

SPLENDOR
Meaning. 2 Th.2:8

SPOIL (See **CAPTIVE**)

SPORTS
Described as.
Exercise. 1 Tim.4:7
Fighting. 1 Cor.9:26
Running & pressing. 1 Cor.9:24-27;
Ph.3:14; Heb.12:1
Walking. Eph.4:1; Ph.3:16; Col.2:6;
1 Jn.2:6
Weights. Heb.12:1
Wrestling. Eph.6:12
Exhortations.
To discipline & control oneself.
1 Cor.9:24-27
To exercise for godliness. 1 Tim.4:8
To fight the good fight. 2 Tim.4:7
To finish the race of life. 2 Tim.4:7
To lay aside every weight. Heb.12:1
To mind the things learned. Ph.3:16
To press for the prize. Ph.3:14
To run the race - enduring. Heb.12:1
To subject one's body. Heb.12:2
To walk by the rules. Ph.3:16
Reward.
Receives a crown. 2 Tim.4:8
Receives the high calling of God. Ph.3:14
Receives the joy of the reward.
Heb.12:2
Receives the prize. 1 Cor.9:24-25

SPOT - SPOTLESS
Christ gave Himself so that the church might be **s.** Eph.5:27
Christ lived a **s.** life. 1 Pt.1:19
Duty.
To be diligent & live a **s.** life.
2 Pt.3:14
To keep oneself unspotted from the world. Jas.1:27
To keep the commandments of God without spot. 1 Tim.6:14
Fact. False teachers are spots & blem-ishes on the church. 2 Pt.2:13
Meaning. 2 Pt.3:14

STABLISH - STABILITY (See **STAND FIRM; STRENGTHEN; STRONG**)
Duty. To be established in the faith. Col.2:7
Meaning. Col.2:7; 1 Th.3:13
Source - Comes from
Christ. 1 Th.3:13
God. 1 Pt.5:10
God & Christ. 2 Th.2:17

STAFF - STAFFING (See **LEADERS**)
Of a church. Seeking. Discussed. Acts 11:25

STAND FIRM (See **ENDURANCE; PERSEVERANCE; STEADFAST-NESS**)
Discussed. Ph.4:1
Duty. To be established in the faith. Col.2:7
Meaning. 1 Cor.16:13-14; 2 Cor.1:21-22; Col.2:7; 1 Th.3:13;2 Th.2:16-17; 1 Pt.5:10
Source - Comes from
Christ. 1 Th.3:13
God. 1 Pt.5:10
God & Christ. 2 Th.2:17

STAR - STARS (See **SORCERY; SU-PERSTITION**)
Men seek destiny in the **s**. Jn.5:2-4
Of the Magi. Discussed. Mt.2:2

STAR, DAY - MORNING STAR
Title of Christ. 2 Pt.1:19; Rev.2:28; 22:16

STARS, THE SEVEN OF REVELATION
The ministers of the seven churches of Revelation. Rev.1:16, 20

STARVATION
Fact. To be severe in the last days. Rev.6:7-8

STATE (See **CITIZENSHIP; GOV-ERNMENT**)

STATE, CIVIL
Duty.
To respect civil authorities. 1 Pt.2:16-17
To submit to **s**. Reasons. 1 Pt.2:13-17
When disobedience is permitted. 1 Pt.2:13-14

STATUS
Duty. To be content with one's **s**. in life. Jas.1:9-11
Facts. **S**. does not matter to God. 1 Cor.7:17-24

STEALING
Discussed. Ro.13:9; Eph.4:28
S. from God. Acts 5:1-11
Duty.
Are not to steal. Ro.13:9; Eph.4:18
Are not to **s**. but to show good faith in every respect. Tit.2:10
Example of. Judas embezzled the funds of the Lord. Mt.26:15
Fact. Men steal earthly riches from others. Mt.6:19
Kinds of. Three kinds. Ro.13:9
Meaning. Mk.7:22; 1 Cor.6:10
Result - Judgment. Shall not inherit the kingdom of God. 1 Cor.6:9-10

STEADFAST
Meaning. 1 Pt.5:10

STEADFASTNESS (See **ENDURANCE; PERSEVERANCE**)
Duty.
Not to fall from one's **s**. 2 Pt.3:17
The minister is to be **s**. 2 Cor.4:1
To be **s**. in laboring for the Lord. 1 Cor.15:58
To be **s**. in one's faith in Christ. 1 Cor.16:13; Col.2:5

To be **s**. To endure & hope for salvation. Mt.24:13; Mk.13:13
To stand fast & hold to the Word of God. 2 Th.2:15, cp. Ph.2:16
To stand fast against the devil. 1 Pt.5:8-9
To stand fast in the liberty of Christ. Gal.5:1
To stand fast in the Lord. Ph.4:1
To stand fast in unity with other believers. Ph.1:27
Essential.
For God's leadership. Mt.2:12
Must be steadfast to the end. Heb.3:14
Meaning. Acts 2:42; Col.2:5
Results - Reward of.
Salvation. If endure to the end. Mt.10:22
The crown of life. Jas.1:12
Source of strength to endure. God's compassion & tender mercy. Jas.5:11

STEPHANAS
Christian believer in the early church. 1 Cor.16:15-18
Discussed. 1 Cor.1:16

STEPHEN THE DEACON, THE FIRST CHRISTIAN MARTYR
Discussed. Acts 6:8-15; 7:1-53; 7:54-60
Message of. Acts 6:9-10
The Defender. Acts 7:1-53

STEWARD (See **MANAGER; STEW-ARDSHIP; THOSE ENTRUSTED**)
Discussed. Lk.19:11-27
Parable of the faithful & unfaithful steward. A strong warning - be prepared. Lk.12:41-48
Parable of the laborers in the vineyard. God's glorious grace. Mt.20:1-16
Parable of the pounds. Every man is tested. Lk.19:11-27
Parable of the talents: the steward's duty to work for the Lord. Mt.25:14-30
Parable of the unjust steward: man & money. Lk.16:1-13
Parable of the unmerciful steward. The spirit of forgiveness. Mt.18:21-35
Parable of the wicked tenant: Israel's rejection of Jesus' Messiahship. Mt.21:33-46
Duty. (See **STEWARDSHIP**)
To be a faithful & wise **s**. Lk.12:42
To be faithful. Lk.12:42-48; 1 Cor.4:2
To be forgiving. Mt.18:21-35
To give & support the ministry of Christ. Lk.8:3
To labor diligently in the Lord's vineyard. Mt.20:1-16
To manage & look after God's vineyard. Mt.21:33-46
To use one's gifts & minister to others. 1 Pt.4:10
To use one's talents & increase them. Mt.25:14-30
Essential. Must be faithful or face severe consequences. Mt.21:44; 25:30
Fact. Cannot serve God & money or possessions. Lk.16:13
Judgment of the unfaithful **s**.
To be delivered to the tormentors. Mt.18:34
To be destroyed & have his possessions given to another. Mt.21:41
To be separated from the Lord. Lk.12:46-48

To be stripped of everything & cast into outer darkness. Mt.25:30
To be stripped of everything & slain. Lk.19:20-27
To lose all true riches. Lk.16:11
To lose what was rightfully his own. Lk.16:12
Parable of. Faithful & unfaithful **s**. A warning: be prepared. Lk.12:41-48
Reward of the faithful **s**.
To be given a great reward. Lk.19:24-26
To be given just payment. Mt.20:9-10
To be made ruler of the Lord's household. Lk.12:42-44
To be made ruler over many things. Mt.25:21, 23
Who the steward is.
Discussed. Lk.12:41-48; 1 Cor.4:1-2
The manager of the Lord's property. Lk.16:2-3 cp. 16:1-12
The supervisor of laborers. Mt.20:8, cp. 1-16

STEWARDSHIP (See **GIVE - GIVING; STEWARD; TITHE**)
Attitude toward.
Basic questions asked about **s**. 1 Cor.16:1-4
Distrusting God. Acts 5:1-4
Fivefold attitude. Mk.6:35-44
Keeping back. Acts 5:1-4
The world's need & resources. Mk.6:35-44
Described. As a grace. 2 Cor.8:6-7
Discussed. Mk.12:41-44; 1 Cor.16:1-4; 2 Cor.8:1-15; 9:1-7; 9:8-15;Heb.7:1-10
Believers & money. Lk.16:1-13
Instructions on receiving offerings. 1 Cor.16:2-4
Question of. The widow's mite. Lk.21:1-4
Worldly men are examples of **s**. Lk.16:8
Duty.
Not to misuse money, but to meet the needs of people. Lk.11:42
To accept compensation. Lk.10:7
To be committed to helping the needy. Acts 4:32
To examine one's motive in **s**. Lk.14:12-14; 2 Cor.9:8-15
To faithfully use what one has, both gifts & possessions. Lk.16:1-13
To give all one is & has above personal necessities. Lk.9:16-17; Acts 4:34-37; 5:1-4
To give generously. Meet needs unselfishly. Ro.12:13
To give sacrificially, out of need. Mk.10:21-22; 12:41-44; Lk.21:4Ph.4:10-19
To meet the needs of the poor & oppressed. Lk.11:42
To meet the needs of the minister. Ph.4:10-19
To revive giving to missions. Ph.4:10-19
To support ministers. Lk.10:7; 1 Cor.9:1-15; 16:5-9
Double honor. 1 Tim.5:17-20
To trust God & set an example. Lk.9:16-17; 10:4
To trust God, not money. Lk.21:2
To work so that one will have to give & meet the needs of others. Lk.12:31-34; Eph.4:28
Verses. List of. Mk.10:21-22; 10:23; 10:29-30

Must be **s.** in order to bear up under suffering & death. 1 Pt.5:10

Must be **s.** in the faith. Ro.1:4-12; Col.2:6-7; 1 Th.3:1-2

Must be **s.** time & again in the truth. 2 Pt.1:12

Must be **s.** with believers. 2 Cor.1:21

Must have one's heart **s.** with grace & not with rituals, ceremonies, & religious rules. Heb.13:9

Meaning. Ro.1:11; 1 Th.3:1-2; 2 Th.3:3-5

Source.

Christ. 1 Th.3:12-13; 2 Th.3:3

God. Through the gospel & the preaching of Jesus Christ. Ro.16:25; 1 Pt.5:10

God & Christ together. 2 Th.2:16-17

Ministers & preachers. Ro.1:18

Oneself. One's own determination & commitment to be **s.** Jas.5:8

STRUCK DOWN

Duty. To cast down imaginations & subject every thought to Christ. Cor.10:3-5

Meaning. 2 Cor.4:7-9

STRUGGLING

Meaning. Col.2:1

STUBBORN (See **HARD - HARDNESS; SELF-WILL**)

Discussed. Ro.2:6-10

A person can be **s.** & self-willed in heart & hearing. Acts 7:51

Meaning. Ro.2:8

Verses. List of. Lk.15:11-13; Ro.2:8

STUDENTS

Argue & oppose Stephen. Acts 6:9-10

Duty. Toward their teachers. Gal.6:6-10

STUDY (See **DEVOTION; MEDITATION; WORD OF GOD**)

Challenge to. Devotion essential. Three essentials. Mt.13:52

Duty.

Not to be lazy & complacent in **s.** Heb.5:11-12

To meditate & **s.** Lk.10:41-42

To move on beyond elementary teachings & grow. Heb.5:11-12

To **s.** for comfort & hope. Ro.15:4

To **s.** for doctrine, reproof, correction, & instruction in righteousness. 2 Tim.3:16

To **s.** for eternal life & to learn the truth about Christ. Jn.5:39

To **s.** for God's approval. 2 Tim.2:15

To **s.** with a readiness of mind, to see if the gospel is true. Acts 17:11

Verses. List of. Lk.10:41-42

STUMBLE - STUMBLING - STUMBLING BLOCK

Caused by.

Abusing one's liberty in Christ. 1 Cor.8:9

Disobeying the Word of God. 1 Pt.2:8

Misleading others. Mt.23:13; Lk.11:44

Not accepting that Christ Had to be crucified for one's sins. 1 Cor.1:23

Seeking God & righteousness by some way other than by Christ. Ro.9:31-33; 10:1-4

The ways one offends others. Mt.18:15; Mk.9:42

Discussed. Mt.18:5-10; Lk.11:44; 17:1-2

Duty.

Not to **s.** by persecution & ridicule. Mt.13:21; Mk.4:17; Jn.16:1-4

Not to do anything that will be a **s.** to a brother. Ro.14:21

Not to offend in questionable activities. Ro.14:1-23; 1 Cor.8:1-13

Not to **s.** in anything. 1 Cor.10:32; 2 Cor.6:3

Not to **s.** in questionable activities. Ro.14:1-23; 1 Cor.8:1-13

Not to **s.** others. 1 Cor.8:9-11; 10:23-28; 10:29-11:1

To be without **s.** until the day of Christ. Ph.1:10

To correct offending brothers. Mt.18:15-20

To cut out of one's life all that **s.** Mt.5:29-30; 18:7-9; Mk.9:43-48

To focus upon not putting a stumbling block in a brother's way. Ro.14:13

To guard against being a stumbling block. 1 Cor.8:9-11; 10:23-28; 10:30-11:1

To keep from being a stumbling block. Three ways. Ro.14:13-15

To love, for love keeps one from being a stumbling block. 1 Jn.2:10

To mark those who cause division & **s.** Ro.16:17-18

Example.

Causing a whole church to stumble. Rev.2:14

Christ keeps one from becoming a stumbling block. Mt.17:27

Fact.

Christ died for our **s.** Ro.4:25

Many will be **s.** because of Christ in the end time. Mt.24:9-10

The gift of Christ justifies us from many **s.** Ro.5:16

We all **s.** in many things, especially in word & tongue. Jas.3:2

How. Six ways. Mk.9:42

Judgment of those who **s.** Shall be cast into a furnace of fire. Mt.13:37-42

Meaning. Mt.5:29; 17:27; Ro.14:13-15; 2 Cor.6:3; Ph.1:9-10

Steps to correcting. Mt.18:15-20

Verses. List of. Mk.9:42

Warning against. Mt.18:5-10, 15

Warning against **s.** others. Mt.18:5-10; Lk.17:1-2

If one **s.** in one point, he is guilty of all the law. Jas.2:10

Ways one causes others to sin. Mt.18:15

What **s.** men about Christ.

Four things **s.** Jn.6:59-71

His claims. Jn.6:61

His cross, blood. Jn.6:61; 1 Cor.1:23; Gal.5:11

His Lordship. Jn.6:62

His Person & claims. 1 Pt.2:7-8

His works. Mt.11:1-6, esp. 6; Mt.13:53-58

SUBJECTION - SUBMIT - SUBMISSION

Believers are to be subject to God.

To be **s.** to God's will. Lk.1:26-38; 1:38

To pray for God's will to be done. Mt.6:10

To **s.** so totally that God's Word can be fulfilled in their lives. Lk.1:38

To **s.** to God & resist the devil. Jas.4:7

To yield themselves & their body parts totally to the Lord. Ro.6:13

Duty.

Believers are to be **s.** to church leaders. Heb.13:17

Believers are to be **s.** to the elders. 1 Pt.5:5-7

Believers are to be **s.** to other believers. Eph.5:21; 1 Pt.5:5-7

Believers are to be **s.** to the minister. 1 Cor.16:16

Children are to be **s.** to their parents. Eph.6:1-2; Col.3:20

Citizens are to be **s.** to the government. Ro.13:1-7; 1 Pt.2:13

Employees are to be **s.** to their employers. Discussed. 1 Pt.1:18-20

Servants are to be **s.** to their masters; employees are to be **s.** to their employers. Eph.6:5-8; Col.3:22-25;1 Pt.2:18-19

The church is to be **s.** to Christ. Eph.5:24

The younger are to be **s.** to the elder. 1 Pt.5:5-6

Wives are to be **s.** to their husbands. Eph.5:22-24; Col.3:18; 1 Pt.3:1

Fact. Creation is subject to the curse & corruption of sin. Ro.8:20

Meaning. Jas.4:7

SUBMISSIVE; WISDOM, Of Men

Errors - Failures of.

Cannot save man. 1 Cor.2:5; 2:6; 2:7-9; Col.2:8. Cp. Ro.1:18-32

Is sometimes based upon false beliefs. Mk.2:6-12

Is used by men to escape the truth. Mk.11:29-33

Essential.

In life. Must do the only reasonable thing: commit one's body & service as a living sacrifice to God. Ro.12:1-2

In preaching & witnessing. Must be sound, logical. Acts 18:4, 19; 24:25, cp. Acts 17:2

Meaning. Jas.3:17-18

Proves. God's existence. Ro.1:19

SUBSTITUTION

The death of Christ. (See **JESUS CHRIST**, Death, Substitutionary)

SUCCESS

Formula for **s.**; laws of **s.**

Believing & abiding in Christ. Jn.15:5, cp. Jn.3:16; 10:10;Col.2:9-10

Continuing on, enduring to the end. Mt.10:22

Discussed. Mt.13:12

Forgetting past failures & pressing on toward the goal. Ph.3:13-14

Magnifying Christ in one's body. Ph.1:20-21

Not giving in to weariness & never fainting. Gal.6:9

Obeying the rules already learned. Ph.3:16

Praying according to God's will. 1 Jn.5:14-15

Running & controlling oneself & subjecting one's body in order to obtain **s.** 1 Cor.9:24-27
The world's view of **s.** vs. the Lord's view of **s.** Mk.10:42-43

SUFFER GRIEF
Meaning. 1 Pt.1:6

SUFFERING (See **DISEASE; PERSECUTION; SICKNESS; TRIALS - TRIBULATION**)
Caused by.
 Not because of sin. Lk.13:1-9; Jn.9:1-3; 11:4
 The sovereign will of God. Jn.9:1-3; 11:1-16, esp. 11:4; 2 Cor.12:7-10
 The ultimate cause. Mt.8:17
Deliverance.
 By being armed with the attitude of Christ. 1 Pt.4:1-6
 By enduring. Heb.11:32-40
 By following Christ's great **s.** 1 Pt.2:21-25
 By God's power. Sustains through **s.** 2 Cor.1:3-11; 4:7-18
 By Jesus. He bore our diseases & **s.** Mt.8:17
 By not fearing **s.** Rev.2:10
 By prayer. Prayer that saves the sick. Jas.5:14-15
 Creation shall be delivered from **s.** Ro.8:18-27
 How to handle **s.** 1 Pt.3:3-4:19
 Is assured by God. Ro.8:28-39
 The provision for. 1 Pt.5:10-11
Described. As a reward. Mk.10:30
Discussed. Lk.13:1-9; Ro.8:28-39; 2 Cor.1:3-11; 1 Pt.5:10-11
 How the church is to stand up under **s.** 1 Pt.5:1-11
 Of the early believers. Heb.11:32-34; 11:35-40
 Of the early church. 1 Pt.4:12
 Of the minister. 1 Cor.4:9-10; 4:11-13
Duty.
 S. should not keep one from worshipping. Mt.12:9-10
 To participate in Christ's **s.** 1 Pt.4:12-19
 To count **s.** for Christ a privilege. Acts 5:41
 To endure. 2 Cor.6:3-10
 To follow the example of Christ in **s.** 1 Pt.1:21
 To minister to those who have need & are in adversity. Mt.25:34-40; Heb.13:3; Jas.1:27
 To put on the mind of Christ. 1 Pt.4:1-6
 To stand up under the painful trial of **s.** 1 Pt.4:12-19
 To suffer before violating one's conscience. 1 Pt.2:18-20
Example. Christ. (See **JESUS CHRIST**, Death, Sufferings of)
Fact.
 Are sharing in the **s.** of Christ. 1 Pt.4:12
 God gives a glow of His glory to the **s.** believer. 1 Pt.4:14
Meaning. Ro.8:18
Purpose.
 Discussed. Jn.9:1-3; 11:4
 God's glory. Jn.11:4
 To make one a testimony. 2 Cor.1:3-4
 To teach prayer. Jas.5:14-15
 To test & prove one's faith. 1 Pt.1:7

What **s.** does. Ro.5:3-5; 2 Cor.1:3-11
Why God allows suffering. Mt.8:1-4; 1 Pt.4:12
Why God does not always heal. Mt.8:1-4
Why people **s.** Lk.13:1-9
Results.
 Assures great reward. Mt.19:29
 Assures salvation. Mt.10:22
 Assures that one shall reign with Christ. 2 Tim.2:12
 Assures that one shall be glorified with Christ. Ro.8:16-18
 Fills up & completes the **s.** of Christ. Mk.10:30
 Reflects the life of Christ in one's body. 2 Cor.4:11
 Self-pity, bitterness, apathy. 2 Cor.1:6
 Will be perfected, established, strengthened & settled. 1 Pt.5:10
Suffering & sin. Discussed. Jn.9:1-3
Verses. List of. Ro.8:16-17

SUNDAY (See **SABBATH - SUNDAY**)

SUPER-SPIRITUALITY
Discussed. 1 Cor.1:12; 4:7; 4:8
Meaning. Gal.5:26

SUPERSTITION (See **ASTROLOGY; SOOTHSAYER; SORCERY**)
Astrological charts, fortune telling. Jn.19:8-11
Caused by.
 Twisting the teachings of God's Word (the resurrection). Mt.14:1-2
 Worshipping God in ignorance in the wrong way. Acts 17:22-34; 18:1-6
Discussed. Acts 14:8-20
Error of.
 Men fear & respect forces other than God. Jn.19:8-11
 Men seek destiny in forces other than God. Jn.5:2-4
Fact. Modern man is **s.** Acts 28:4-9
Nature of. Acts 14:8-13

SUPPER OF GOD, THE GREAT (See **BANQUET OF GOD, GREAT**)
Discussed. Lk.14:15-24; Rev.19:17-21
Parable of. Jesus' invitation--man's excuses. Lk.14:15-24

SUPPLICATION (See **PETITION; REQUESTS**)

SUPPLY (See **NEEDS - NECESSITIES; SATISFACTION, SPIRITUAL**)

SUPPLY, DIVINE (See **SATISFACTION, SPIRITUAL**)
Source of. God. Verses. List of. Jn.6:10-13

SURETY (See **ASSURANCE; SECURITY**)

SURFEITING (See **DISSIPATION**)
Meaning. Lk.21:34-35

SURRENDER TO GOD (See **COMMITMENT; CROSS, DAILY; DEDICATION; HEART**)
Absolute **s.** The arrest of Jesus. Jn.18:1-11
Cost of. Discussed. Mk.1:9
Duty.
 To be so **s.** that one becomes an instrument in the Lord's hands. Acts 14:3
 To heed & **s.** to the chastisement of God. Heb.12:5-13

To **s.** all for the knowledge of Christ. Ph.3:7-8
To **s.** one's life totally to God. Ro.12:1
To **s.** to God & not sin. Ro.6:16
To yield oneself & one's body members to God. Ro.6:13
Essential.
 Five **e.** Jn.18:1-11
 Must live the crucified life with Christ. Lk.9:23; Ro.6:2; 8:36; 2 Cor.4:11Gal.2:20
 Must **s.** all that one is & has. Mk.10:21
 To follow Christ. Mt.8:19-20
Fact. The believer is not his own. Has been bought with a price. 1 Cor.6:20
Of resources. Essential to meet the world's needs. Mt.14:18-21
Of the minister. To give himself continually to prayer & to the ministry of the Word. Acts 6:4
What is to be **s.** Mt.6:9

SUSANNA
Discussed. Supported Jesus. Lk.8:3

SWAYING
Answer to. Mt.11:7
Sign of weakness. Mt.11:7

SWEARING (See **CURSING; OATHS**)
Discussed. Mt.5:33-37; 23:16-22; Jas.5:12
Law governing. Mt.5:33-37
Results. Weak self-image & spiritual destruction. Mt.5:44
Wrong of. Jas.5:12

SWELLINGS (See **ARROGANCE**)

SWINDLERS
Duty.
 Must face the fact & repent if we are guilty of **s.** Mt.23:25
 Not to take more than what is due one. Lk.3:13-14
Meaning. 1 Cor.5:9-10; 6:10
Verses. List of. 1 Cor.5:9-10

SYMPATHIZE
Communicates two things. Mt.8:14-15
Duty.
 Not to allow Satan to touch us, but to keep ourselves from sin. 1 Jn.5:18
 Not to touch a woman sexually, not immorally. 1 Cor.7:1-2
 To know that Christ is touch by the feelings of our infirmities. Heb.4:15-16
 To seek the touch of Jesus. Mt.9:29; 20:34; Heb.4:15-16
 To touch Jesus to meet our needs. Mt.9:20-22; Mk.3:10; Lk.6:19
 To touch no unclean thing. 2 Cor.6:16-17
Meaning. Heb.4:15-16

SYMPATHY - EMPATHY (See **CARE; COMPASSION; LOVE**)
Duty.
 To be sympathetic. 1 Pt.3:8
 To bear the infirmities of the weak. Ro.15:1
 To labor & support the weak. Acts 20:35

To remember & help those who suffer. Mt.25:34-40; Heb.13:3; Jas.1:27

To sacrificially minister to all--no matter who they are. Lk.10:33-35, cp. 30-36

To show compassion for all men, even enemies. Lk.10:33-37

To show genuine interest & care. Ro.12:15

To show s. & to help the backslider. Gal.6:1-3

To show s. to those who have lost loved ones. Jn.11:35-36

Of Jesus Christ.
Discussed. Heb.4:14-16
Feels for man. Feels with every trial & hurt. Heb.4:14-16
Identified with every conceivable experience of men. Lk.2:40

SYNAGOGUE
Discussed. Mt.4:23; Mk.1:21
Fact.
Christ preached in the s. despite formal religion. Mk.1:39; Jn.18:20
Christ worshipped in the s. Mt.12:9; 13:54; Lk.4:16
Position in the s. was coveted by the religionists. Mt.23:6
The s. was always the first place Paul preached the gospel. Acts 13:14-16; 13:46-47
The last time Jesus was in the s. Lk.13:10
The ruler of the s. Discussed. Mt.9:18-19

SYNTYCHE
Discussed. Ph.4:2-3

SYRIA
Discussed. Mt.4:24
Paul's home province. Acts 15:39-41
Visited by Paul on his second mission. Acts 15:41

SYROPHENICIAN WOMAN
Daughter was healed of a demon. Caring for the rejected. Mk.7:24-30

T

TABERNACLE (See TEMPLE)
Abused by Israel. Acts 7:42-53
Dedicated by blood. Heb.9:21-22
Discussed. Heb.9:1-28
A picture of the t. Its structure & furnishings. Heb.9:11-14
Picture. Heb.9:11-14
Sanctuaries of. The Holy Place & Most Holy Place. Heb.9:1-10
Spiritual, heavenly t.
Contrasted with the earthly t. Heb.9:1-14
Discussed. Heb.9:1-14
Minister of. Is Jesus Christ. Heb.8:2; 8:3; 8:4-5; 9:1-14
The building & structure plans were given by God. Heb.8:5
Was the pattern for the earthly t. Heb.8:2; 8:3; 8:4-5; 9:8-10; 9:11-14; 9:23-24
Type - Symbol of.
Christ. How each part of the t. symbolized & pictured Christ. Heb.9:11-14
Discussed. Heb.9:11-14
Heaven. Heb.9:23-24
The presence of God. Rev.21:3

TABERNACLES, FEAST OF (See FEASTS) Jn.7:37-39

TAKE HEED (See BE CAREFUL; BEWARE; HEED, TAKE; WATCH - WATCHING)
Meaning. Mk.8:15; Lk.21:34-35

TALENTED, THE
How the t. enter heaven. Mt.19:16-22

TALENTS (See AMBITION - GIFTS)
Duty. To surrender to Christ. Mt.14:18-21
Parable of the Talents. Watch & work for judgment is coming. Mt.25:14-30

TALK (See CONVERSATION; CURSING; TONGUE)
Sins of. Foolish t. Eph.5:4

TALKERS, MERE

TALKERS, VAIN & EMPTY (See TALKERS, MERE)

TARES (See WEEDS)
Meaning. Parable of the Wheat & the T. Why evil exists. Mt.13:24-30

TARSUS
Birthplace of Paul the apostle. Acts 9:11; 21:39; 22:3
Paul fled to T. from Damascus--fled a plot to kill him. Acts 9:23-31
Paul was in T. when Barnabas recruited him to be one of the ministers in Antioch. Acts 11:25-26

TASTE - TASTED
Meaning. Heb.6:4-5

TAX COLLECTOR
Discussed. Mt.9:9-13; Mk.2:14; Lk.5:27; 19:1-2
Rejected by the people. Lk.7:29-31

TAXES
A particular taxation was used by God to cause Jesus' birth in Bethlehem. Lk.2:1-6
Duty. To pay t. Ro.13:6
Good citizenship. Mt.17:24-27
Kind of t.
Poll tax. Mt.22:17; Mk.12:14
T. of Rome. Ro.13:6
Temple t. Mt.17:24
State vs. God. Mk.12:13-17
Why Christ paid t. Six reasons. Mt.17:27

TEACH - TEACHER - TEACHING
Appointed - Called to t.
Are called by Christ. Mt.28:19-20; Eph.4:11, cp. 7-11; 1 Tim.1:12
Are called by God. 1 Cor.12:8; 1 Tim.2:3-7; 2 Tim.1:12
Are gifted to t. Acts 13:1; Ro.12:6-8; 1 Cor.12:28; Eph.4:11; 1 Tim.2:7; 2 Tim.1:11-12
Are given a special anointing. 1 Jn.2:20; 2:27
Duty.
Behavior of. Tit.2:7-8
Fivefold duty. 2 Tim.1:6-12
Not to teach with the wrong motive-- for money & gain. Tit.1:11
Of ministers. Must be able & ready to t. 1 Tim.3:2

Of the church. To have many t. carrying on its ministry. Acts 13:1; 15:35
Of young t. Tit.2:7-8
To avoid petty arguments & speculations. 2 Tim.2:14-21
To be ready to teach. 2 Tim.2:24-26
To be responsible in teaching the truth. Mt.23:2
To be strong. 2 Tim.2:1-7
To consistently t. the church. Acts 11:25-26; 18:11
To develop disciples & other teachers, so that they can t. others. 2 Tim.2:2
To endure abuse for the gospel. 2 Tim.1:6-12
To exhort daily. Heb.3:13-19
To flee lusts & follow after the Lord. 2 Tim.2:22-26
To fulfill one's ministry--fill up the brim. 2 Tim.4:5
To go & t. all nations. The great commission. Mt.28:19-20
To have a clear conscience. 2 Tim.1:3
To hold fast in three areas. 2 Tim.1:13-18
To hold fast sound words, that is, the Word of God. 2 Tim.1:13
To live a consistent life--to live what one teaches. Ro.2:21-24; Jas.3:13-18; 3:14-16
To make sure that one's t. is clear & easy to understand. 1 Cor.14:19
To pray for disciples. 2 Tim.1:3
To preach sound doctrine. 2 Tim.4:2
To preach the Word. 2 Tim.4:1-5
To reason & persuade. Acts 18:4
To remember the resurrected Lord. 2 Tim.4:16-18
To sense the urgency of t. Acts 18:4
To t. & admonish one another. Col.3:16
To t. & preach Jesus Christ daily, in the church & from house to house. Acts 5:42
To t. about the antichrist. 2 Th.2:5
To t. both publicly & house to house. Acts 20:20-21
To t. if called. Jas.3:1
To t. new believers. Acts 11:22-26; 14:22-23; 15:32; 19:9-10
To t. no other doctrine than that of Christ. 1 Tim.1:3; 6:3-5
To t. the things which concern Christ, no matter where one is. Acts 28:30-31
To t. the way of the Lord diligently. Acts 18:25
To t. with authority. Mk.1:22
To warn & t. every man. Col.1:28
Duty toward.
Discussed. Gal.6:6-10
To test t. To test what they teach. 1 Jn.4:1-6
Elementary t. ABC's of t. Heb.6:1-2
Fact.
A t. can teach only so many students. Ratio needs to be limited. Mt.10:2
A t. either accepts or rejects the law. Mt.5:19
A t. influences others. For good or bad. Mt.5:19
Is not enough by itself. Rev.2:1-7
Speech is the major tool for t. Jas.3:1
How to t. Discussed. Tit.2:7-8
In the early church. Many hungered to learn. Acts 11:26

Meaning. Acts 2:42; 11:19-30; 13:1;
Eph.4:11; 1 Tim.2:7; 2 Tim.1:11-12
Message. (See **MESSAGE**)
The doctrine & teachings of Christ.
2 Jn.9-11
To be the Word of God. 2 Tim.3:10-13
Of Christ.
Are to guard. 2 Jn.7-11
Discussed. 2 Jn.7-13
Position.
Highly esteemed. **T**. sit in Moses'
seat. Mt.23:2
Some well know **t**. in Jesus' day.
Lk.2:46-47
Rejected. In the last days people will re-
ject sound **t**. 2 Tim.4:3-4
Source. To be the Word of God.
2 Tim.3:14-17
Temptations of.
Misusing the tongue. Jas.3:1-12
Temptations common to teachers.
Jas.3:1-18
Testimony of a **t**. 1 Tim.1:12-17
The message of sound **t**. Tit.2:1-3:11
Theological basis of. The grace of God.
Tit.2:11-15
Traits.
Discussed. 2 Tim.2:2
Must be appointed & qualified to **t**.
1 Tim.2:3-7
Warning. Must guard against a threefold
danger. Mt.9:35
When to teach.
Every day. In the temple daily. Acts
5:42
For a solid year. Acts 11:25-26
For two whole years. Acts 19:10
Long enough to teach, warn, & present
every man perfect in Christ Jesus.
Col.1:28

TEACHERS, FALSE (See **APOSTASY;
DECEIVE; RELIGIONISTS**)
Behavior - Characteristics - Traits.
Are deceptive. Ro.16:18; Col.2:4;
Eph.4:14
Are not saved. Jude 17-19
Are prideful. What false **t**. take pride
in. 1 Tim.6:4
Are servants of corruption. 2 Pt.2:10-22
Are to wax worse & worse. 2 Tim.3:13
Are troublemakers. Gal.1:6-7
Are worldly minded & sensual: follow
mere natural instincts. Jude 17-19
Cause division. Three ways. Jude 17-19
Deny Christ. 2 Pt.2:1
Discussed. Mt.7:15; 7:16; 1 Tim.6:3-5;
2 Tim.3:1-3; 3:13; 2 Pt.2:10-22; Jude
4-16, 17-19
Character & conduct. 2 Pt.2:10-22
Do not understand what they teach.
1 Tim.1:6-7
Enslave others. Gal.2:3-5
Enter the church hypocritically.
Gal.2:3-5
Follow false messiahs & saviors.
Jn.5:43
Follow the way of rebellion against
God & reject authority. Jude 11
Follow the way that forsakes the life of
God. Jude 11
Lead people to reject Christ. Jn.11:49-53
Lead sheep to destruction, away from
life. Jn.10:10
Make a good impression, outwardly.
Gal.6:12-13

Persecute & criticize true believers.
Gal.4:29
Pervert the gospel. Gal.1:6-9
Preach & **t**. fables. 2 Tim.4:3-4
Preach & **t**. myths & speculations &
controversies. 1 Tim.1:3-4
Preach & **t**. tradition. Mt.15:9
Resist the truth. 2 Tim.3:8
Seduce & deceive. 2 Cor.11:13-15
Serve their own desires & appetites.
Ro.16:17-18
Spirit of. Is evil. 1 Jn.4:1
Turn people away from the truth.
2 Tim.3:3-4
Described as.
Antichrist. Many antichrists.
1 Jn.2:18; 4:2-3; 2 Jn.7
Boasters in the flesh. Gal.6:12-13
Deceivers. 2 Jn.7
Dogs, evil workers, mutilators of the
flesh. Ph.3:2
Enslavers of followers. Gal.2:3-5
False apostles & ministers.
2 Cor.11:13-15
False prophets. 1 Jn.4:1-6
Of the world. 1 Jn.4:5
Persecutors of believers. Gal.4:29
Perverters of the gospel. Gal.1:6-9
Servants of corruption. 2 Pt.2:19
Spirits. 1 Jn.4:1-6
They who went out from the church.
1 Jn.2:19
Troublemakers. Gal.1:6-7
Wolves in sheep clothing. Mt.7:15
Discussed.
A sign of the end time is the coming of
false **t**. 2 Tim.3:6-9; 1 Jn.4:1-6
Danger of false **t**. 1 Tim.1:3-11
False **t**. are corrupt. 2 Tim.3:6-9
False **t**. will come into the church.
Acts 20:29-30
Guarding against antichrists or false **t**.
1 Jn.2:18-23
Guarding against strange teaching.
Heb.13:9-11
How to tell if a person is a false **t**.
1 Jn.4:2-3
Nine accusations against false religion.
Mt.23:13-36
Protection against. By fearing false **t**.
because they are messengers of Sa-
tan. 2 Cor.11:13-15
Testing the spirits of false **t**. 1 Jn.4:1-6
The contrasting false **t**. Tit.1:10-16
The danger of the leaven, the false
doctrine of religionists. Mk.8:15
The description of false **t**. & their
apostasy. 1 Tim.4:1-5; 6:3-5; 6:20-21;
2 Pt.2:1-9; 2:10-22
The irresponsible shepherd or false **t**.
Jn.10:11-13
The traits & judgment of false teach-
ers. Jude 3-16
The warning against false prophets.
Mt.7:15-20; Ph.3:2
The warning against false religion.
Mt.23:1-12
The warning to reject a heretic.
Tit.3:10-11
Error.
Are deceived & seduced by an evil
spirit. 1 Tim.4:1-2; 1 Jn.4:1-6
Discussed. 1 Tim.4:1-5; 6:20-21;
Tit.1:10-16; 2 Pt.2:1-9; 2:10-22;
1 Jn.2:18-23; 4:1-6; Jude 3-16

Do not understand what they say nor
what they teach. 1 Tim.1:7
Follow the false wisdom & teaching of
this world. Jas.3:14-16
Fourfold error. Mt.7:15
Have seared consciences. 1 Tim.4:1-2
Pervert the gospel. Gal.1:6-9
Sins of. Discussed. Acts 13:7-11
Example of.
Bar-jesus or Elymas. Acts 13:7-11
Hymenaeus & Philetus. 2 Tim.2:17
Fact.
Are used by evil spirits. 1 Jn.4:1-6
Experience four things. Mt.10:5
Judgment of.
Discussed. Ordained to judgment.
2 Pt.2:1; 2:3-9; 2:20-22; Jude 4-7,
11, 14-15
To be cursed, anathema. Jude 4
To be the least in the kingdom of
heaven. Mt.5:19
Why false **t**. shall be judged.
Gal.5:10-12
Motive.
Discussed. Gal.6:12-13
Job, money, livelihood, recognition.
Mt.23:1-12
To make a good showing by adding
numbers. Gal.6:12-13
Nature.
Appear as messengers of light, but are
deceivers. 2 Cor.11:13-15; Eph.6:11
Blind. Lk.6:39
Deceptive. Mt.7:15
Discussed. Mt.7:17
Fourfold nature. Mt.7:17
Known by their fruit. Mt.7:16
Protection against.
By an anointing from Christ. 1 Jn.2:20
By contending for the faith. Jude 3-16
By fearing false **t**. because they are
messengers of Satan. 2 Cor.11:13-15
By guarding oneself. Mk.8:15;
Ph.3:1-3; Heb.13:9-16; 2 Pt.3:17;
1 Jn.2:18-22
By knowing their danger. 1 Tim.1:3-11
By marking & watching out for false **t**.
Ro.16:17-20
By not welcoming false **t**. in one's
home. 2 Jn.10-11
By remembering that there are false **t**.
Jude 17-19
By testing the spirits. 1 Jn.4:1-6
By the Holy Spirit & the truth.
1 Jn.2:20-21
By turning away from false **t**.
1 Tim.6:20-21
Discussed. Jude 17-25
Results.
Cause followers to be blind. Lk.6:39
Enslaves people. 2 Pt.2:19
Source - Where false **t**. are.
From within & without the church.
Acts 20:29-30
In the church, hypocritically. Gal.2:3-5;
1 Tim.1:3-20; 2 Pt.2:1; 1 Jn.2:19;
Jude 4-16
Teaching of.(See **TEACHING, FALSE**,
Message of)
Verses. List of. Mk.8:15; Lk.21:8
Warning against - Danger of.
Are actually the messengers of Satan.
2 Cor.11:13-15
Discussed. 2 Pt.2:1; 2:3-9; 2:20-22
Disturb & overthrow some.
2 Tim.2:14; 2:16-18

Not to be welcomed in one's home.
2 Jn.10-11
Teaches others to break the commandments of God. Mt.5:19-20
Why false **t.** teach false doctrine. Discussed. 2 Pt.2:3

TEACHERS OF THE LAW

Accusations against.
Nine **t**. Mt.23:13-36
Seven charges. Lk.11:37-54
Authority of. Discussed. Mt.7:29
Beliefs of. Strong, steeped in. Mt.12:10
Described. Mt.22:35
Described as.
Fools. Lk.11:39-41
Self-righteous. Lk.11:39-41; 15:25-32
"Vipers." Meaning. Mt.3:7
Discussed. Mk.12:28; Lk.6:2; 6:7;
Ro.2:17-29; Gal.2:3-5; 2:4; 2:11-13;
Jas.2:14-26
The wisdom of the world's scribes is
destroyed by the cross. 1 Cor.1:19-20
Fact.
Are prospects for the gospel. Reasons.
Acts 17:17
Object to God's judgment. Ro.3:1-8
Some are converted. Acts 6:7; 18:8, 17
Jesus accused lawyers of burdening men
down with laws & rules. Lk.11:45-52
Meaning. Ro.2:17-29
Need.
Spirit needed by **t**. Lk.18:9-14
To become a true **t**. Ro.2:28-29
Opposed Christ.
Discussed. Mt.12:10; 16:21; 17:22
How the **r.** opposed Christ.
Accused Christ.
Of being demon possessed.
Mk.3:22-30; Lk.11:14-16
Of opposing religion. Reasons.
Jn.7:20-24
Arrested Christ. Four pictures of
commitment. Mt.26:47-56
Hunted Christ down. Jn.11:57
Initiated Christ's death. Jn.18:28-
19:15
Mocked Christ upon the cross.
Mt.27:42-43
Murmured against Christ's claim.
Jn.6:41-43
Persecuted Christ. Jn.5:16
Plotted against Christ. Jn.12:19
Plotted the death of Christ.
Mt.16:21; 26:3-5; Jn.5:16, 17-18;
7:1-2; 8:39-40; 8:54-59; 10:31-33,39
Plotted to kill Lazarus, the evidence
of Christ's deity. Jn.12:10
Put Christ on trial. (See **JESUS
CHRIST**, Trials)
Questioned Christ. (See **JESUS
CHRIST**, Challenged)
His source of power. Lk.11:14-16
Rejected Christ. Reasons. Mk.11:33
Sent an investigating committee to
observe Christ. Lk.5:17
Sought to kill Christ even as they had
killed the prophets. Lk.11:47-51
Tried to discredit Christ. Mk.10:1-4;
11:27-33
Response of Christ to **r.** opposition.
Mt.22:41-46; 23:13-36
Why the **t.** opposed Christ.
Considered Christ a rabble-rouser.
Jn.7:32-36

Feared the loss of their position,
esteem & livelihood. Mt.12:1-8;
12:10; 16:12;21:23; 22:15-22;
22:23-33;22:34-40; 23:1-12
For allowing His disciples to work
on the Sabbath. Mk.3:1-6
For associating with outcasts & sinners. Mk.2:13-17
For breaking ceremonial law. Mk.3:4
For breaking tradition. The Scribal
law. Mt.12:1-8; 12:9-13; 12:10;
15:1-20;15:6-9; 16:1-12; Mk.2:23-
24; 3:1-6; 7:1-13; Lk.6:1-5
For driving out demons. Mk.3:22-30
For forgiving sins. Mk.3:6-7
For healing on the Sabbath.
Mk.3:1-6
For not fasting, not keeping the ritual of **f**. Mk.2:18-22
Four reasons why the **t**. opposed
Christ. Mk.14:1-2
Reasons. Lk.13:14; 22:2; Jn.5:16
Several events of the last week of
Christ's life. Mk.3:22; 11:27
Were confused over Christ. Jn.6:52-53
Were insanely angry & vengeful
against Him. Lk.6:1-11
Opposed the early church.
Feared the church. Reasons. Acts 4:2-4
Feared the loss of position, livelihood.
Acts 4:2-4
Opposed the gospel. Reasons. Envy, jealousy, fear. Acts 17:5
Privileges of. Lk.15:31-32
Have the Word of God. Ro.3:1-2
Problem with.
Charges against. Lk.11:37-54
Had a condemnatory, critical spirit.
Jn.8:3-6
Had an empty worship. Mt.15:7-9
Misused the ministry for money &
livelihood. Mt.23:14; Lk.20:46-47,
esp. 47
Possessed the wrong kind of righteousness. Mt.5:20
Put tradition before God's commandments. Mt.15:1-6
Questioned the authority of Christ.
Lk.6:7; 20:1-2
Sought recognition, attention, & position. Lk.20:46
Taught without authority. Mt.7:29
Were hypocritical religionists, false
teachers. Mk.7:1-13
Were spiritually blind. Mt.15:12-14
Problem with - Errors of.
Fact.
Some cared for Jesus. Lk.13:31
Five problems. Lk.14:1-6; 15:25-32
Four problems. Mt.12:10; Mk.14:1-2
In relation to God & Christ & Scripture.
Are confused & perplexed over
Christ. Jn.6:52-53
Are ignorant of Christ's coming.
Mt.2:3-6
Are in the church, but not planted
by God. Mt.15:12-14
Are not of God. Mt.15:12-14
Corrupt God's Word. Mt.12:1-2;
Lk.11:52; 13:14
Misinterpret the words of Christ.
Jn.6:52-53
Miss the truth of Christ. Reasons.
Mk.12:36-37
Plunder the way of God. Lk.11:39-41

Seek signs for proof. Mk.8:10-13
In relation to life & behavior.
Are greedy. Lk.16:14-15
Are hypocritical. Cp. leaven. Lk.12:1-3
Can fail & fall. Jn.7:20-24
Change their appearance & seek
recognition & position. Mt.23:5
Commit sins. Common to leaders.
Listed. Acts 4:5-10
Do not understand repentance.
Lk.15:28
Love the praise of men more than
the **t**. of God. Jn.12:42-43
Oppose Christ. "Sat by"; critical;
refused to participate. Lk.5:17
Their life is warped. Lk.13:14
Their prayer is a prayer of religion.
Lk.18:9-14
In relation to others.
Often become witch hunters. Acts
21:20-26
Persecute believers. Jn.16:1-6
Place form & ritual before people in
need. Mk.2:23-24; Lk.6:1-11;
10:29-37;13:14-16; 14:3
Seek to destroy the ministry of
those who differ. Lk.19:47-48
Their attitude toward the sinner &
outcast. Mk.2:16-17
In relation to righteousness & salvation & religion.
Are in the field of religion, but not
in the house of salvation.
Lk.15:25
Are incorrectly thought to be
genuine. Lk.20:45-47
Are self-righteous. Lk.16:14-15;
18:9-14
Five faults. Lk.7:36-50; 15:25-32
Many faults. Lk.11:37-54
Not acceptable to God.
Lk.11:39-41
Resting in false security.
Ro.11:6-10
Are social **t**. Mt.6:14-15
Argue against a heart religion.
Ro.3:1-8
Have an inadequate religion. Example of. Herod. Mk.6:20
Have some righteousness, but not
enough for heaven. Mt.5:20
Honor the past & its heritage, but
neglect the present. Lk.11:47-51
Know the truth but fail to confess it.
Jn.12:42-43
Lack one central thing: faith.
Lk.15:29
Mistakes of. In seeking acceptance
with God. Mt.5:20; Ro.10:1-3
Stress ritual. Gal.5:1-6
Stress rules & regulations. Lk.5:30-35
Strict vs. loose religion. Mt.5:17-18
Several problems. Lk.20:45-47
Ten problems. Ro.2:17-29
Questioned Jesus about the great law.
Heart touched. Mt.22:34-40;
Mk.12:28-34
Seek to discredit Jesus. Lk.10:25-37
Teaching of. (See **TEACHING, FALSE**)
Errors of. Mt.16:12
Evil & dangers of. Mk.8:14-21
Vs. Jesus. (See **RELIGIONISTS**, Opposed Christ, above)
Accused Christ of devil possession.
Mk.3:22-30

Opposed Christ. (See **JESUS
CHRIST**, Opposed; Response to;
RELIGIONISTS, Opposed Christ)
Lk.5:17; 6:7; 20:1-8
Plotted Christ's death. Lk.22:1-2;
23:10
Warned - Fate of.
Beware of some things. Mk.12:38-40
Dangers confronting. Mt.3:7-10
God's case against. Ro.2:17-29
Nine accusations made by Christ
against **t**. Mt.23:13-36
Seven charges made by Christ against
t. Lk.11:37-54
Who **t**. were. Discussed. Jn.5:10; 5:15-16
Zenas, a **t**. who was a committed be-
liever. Tit.3:13

TEACHING, FALSE (See **APOSTASY;
TEACHERS, FALSE**)
Discussed. How to deal with. Tit.2:10-11
Duty.
To guard against strange teaching.
Mk.8:15; Heb.13:9-16; 2 Pt.3:17;
1 Jn.2:18-22
To reject heretics. Tit.2:10-11
To turn away from. Tit.2:9
Error of.
Baalim: worldliness. Rev.2:14-15
Jezebel: seduction into false **t**.
Rev.2:20-21
Nicolaitans: license & worldliness.
Rev.25-7
Message - Teaching of.
Denies the incarnation. 1 Jn.2:18;
2:22-23; 4:2-3; 2 Jn.7
Denies the Lord. The most tragic
teaching of all. 2 Pt.2:1
Denies the supernatural - scoffs at.
2 Pt.3:1-7
Discussed. 1 Tim.1:3-11; 4:3-5;
1 Jn.2:18;2:22-23
Does not preach or teach the words of
the Lord Jesus Christ. 1 Tim.6:3
Focuses upon self-help, self-esteem,
humanism. 1 Tim.6:5
Hinders a person from obeying the
truth. Gal.5:7-12
Involves four errors, four gospels.
Mt.7:18; Ph.3:1
Involves three major teachings.
Gal.1:6-7
Is a story, a creation of their own
mind. Acts 17:29; 19:24-26;
Ro.1:22-23; 1:24-25; 1 Cor.8:4-8;
Gal.4:8; 4:9-11; Col.2:20-23;
2 Pt.1:16
Is against Christ.
Discussed. Col.2:8-10; 2:11-12;
2:13-15; 2:16-19; 2:20-23;
2 Pt.2:1
Rail against Christ & spiritual
things even when angels would
never dare do such. 2 Pt.2:10-12
Is contrary to God's Word. 2 Pt.2:1
Is effective, but only half true.
Mt.7:17
Is empty words. Col.2:4
Is enticing, seducing words. Col.2:4
Is false science & knowledge.
1 Tim.6:20-21
Is godless chatter.
1 Tim.6:20-21
Is heresy. 2 Pt.2:1
Is a godless myth & old wives tales.
1 Tim.4:7

Is to be tested. 1 Jn.4:1-6
Perverts the gospel. Gal.1:6-9
Preaches & teaches fables. 2 Tim.4:3-4
Preaches & teaches myths & specula-
tions & controversies. 1 Tim.1:3-4
Preaches & teaches traditions.
Mt.15:9
Teaches the ideas of men as the doc-
trine of God. Mt.15:9
Teaches things that should not be
taught. Tit.1:10-12
Vs. true teaching. 1 Tim.1:3-20; 6:3-
5; Jas.3:13-18
Warning against - Dangers of.
Discussed. Jude 3-6, 17-25
Fourfold. Heb.13:9-11
Is a deceptive message, of evil spirits.
1 Tim.4:1-2; 1 Jn.4:1-6
Is a lie, a lie from a person who does
not even know God. 1 Jn.2:22-23
Is the teaching of a messenger of Sa-
tan, not of God. 2 Cor.11:13-15
Teaches people to break God's com-
mandments & keeps them out of
God's kingdom. Mt.5:19-20

TECHNOLOGY
Weakness of. 2 Tim.3:6-9

TEMPERANCE - TEMPERATE (See
DISCIPLINE; SELF-CONTROL)
Discussed. 1 Cor.6:12
Duty.
Ministers must be **t**. Tit.1:8
The aged must be **t**. Tit.2:2
To be **t**. in all things. 1 Cor.9:24-27,
esp. 25
Meaning. Gal.5:22-23; Tit.2:2
The power to be **t**.
Comes from one's own discipline &
effort. 2 Pt.1:5-7
Comes from the Holy Spirit. Gal.5:22-23
Verses. List of. 1 Cor.6:12

TEMPLE, THE
Abuse of. By Israel. Acts 7:42-53
Administration - Supervision of. The cap-
tain or administrator of the **t**. Acts 4:1
Building - Structure of.
Arcades. Mk.11:27
Collection boxes of. Mk.12:41
Court of Women. Treasury in.
Lk.21:1
Courts of the **t**. Mt.21:12-16
Parts, buildings of. Discussed.
Mk.11:15
Treasury of. Mk.12:41
Care - Treatment of.
Abusing, misusing. Lk.19:45-48
Blasphemed by the antichrist.
Rev.13:5-6
Cleansed by Christ. Mt.21:12-16;
Lk.19:45-48; Jn.2:12-22
Cleansed of commercialism.
Mt.21:12-16
Desecrated. Ways **d**. Jn.2:14
Warning to those who abuse.
Mk.11:15-19; 1 Cor.3:16-17, cp.10-17
What the **t**. is to be. Mt.21:12-16
Discussed. Jn.2:14
T. tax. Mt.17:24
The heavenly temple. Rev.11:19;
15:5-8
Fact.
Jesus has the power to erect the new **t**.
Jn.2:18-21

The **t**. of God will be the reward of
believers. Rev.3:12
The **t**. was supported by Christ. Three
reasons why. Mt.17:25
In the last days.
The door to the **t**. is to be closed in the
last days. No one will be allowed in.
Rev.15:8
The **t**. is to be blasphemed by the anti-
christ. Rev.13:5-6
The **t**. is to be marked for judgment.
Rev.11:1-2
Names - Titles.
The believer's body is called the tem-
ple of the Holy Spirit. 1 Cor.6:19-20
The church is called the temple of the
Holy Spirit. 1 Cor.3:16-17
Nature - Described as.
God's house. Jn.2:15-17
Jesus' body. Becomes the **t**. of men.
Jn.2:18-21
The house of prayer. Mt.21:13;
Mk.11:15-17
Prophecy. Of the **t**. destruction.
Mt.24:1-4; Lk.21:5-8
Who is cast out of the **t**. Five persons.
Mk.11:15-17

TEMPLE, SPIRITUAL
Identified as - Refers to.
Christ indwelling believers. Eph.2:19-21
Christ's body. Jn.2:18-21
God indwelling the believer.
2 Cor.6:16
The believer's body. 1 Cor.6:19-20
The church. All believers together. 1
Cor.3:16-17; Eph.2:22; Heb.3:6; 1
Pt.2:5

TEMPORAL
Vs. the eternal. 2 Cor.4:17-18

TEMPERATE
Discussed. 1 Cor.6:12; 1 Pt.1:13
Duty.
Believers are not to be drunk but self-
controlled. 1 Th.5:6-8
Believers are to live **s**. lives, that is,
disciplined, & temperate lives.
Tit.2:12-13; 1 Pt.1:13
Ministers & their wives are to be
blameless, **s**., & never drunk.
1 Tim.3:2, 11; Tit.1:8
The aged are to be **s**. & never drunk.
Tit.2:2-3, 5
The elderly in particular are to give
special attention to self-control.
Tit.2:2
To add temperance, self-control to
one's faith & life. 2 Pt.1:5-7, esp. 6
To control one's words & tongue.
Jas.3:2
To control oneself. 1 Cor.9:25
To control sin & lust. Ro.6:12
To fight with determination.
1 Cor.9:26
To guard against disqualification.
1 Cor.9:27
To run, to press for the prize.
1 Cor.9:24
To run with certainty. 1 Cor.9:26
To strive for the mastery. 1 Cor.9:25
To subject one's body. 1 Cor.9:27
Women's minds are to be **s**. 1 Tim.2:9
Young men & women's minds are to
be **s**. Tit.2:4-7

Essential. Great control required.
1 Cor.9:23-27
Fact.
Preaching self-control convicts people.
Acts 24:25
The disciplined & self-controlled are
prospects for the gospel. Acts 17:18
Meaning. Gal.5:22-23; 1 Tim.3:2-3; 1
Pt.1:13; 4:7; 5:8-9; 2 Pt.1:5-7; 8-9
Verses. List of. 1 Cor.6:12
Warning.
Must be **s.** & guard against pride, not
thinking too highly of oneself &
one's gifts. Ro.12:3
Must be **s.** & pray & watch for the end
of all things. 1 Pt.4:7
Must be **s.**, watching for the Lord's re-
turn. 1 Th.5:1-9, esp. 6-8. Cp. Tit.2:12-13
Without self-control. Meaning.
2 Tim.3:2-4

TEMPTATION
Basic facts. Discussed. Jas.1:2-27
Caused by - Source of. Jas.4:1-6
Discussed. Jas.1:13-15; 1:13-18; 4:1-
3; 4:5
Lust, envy, pride. Jas.4:14-15; 4:1-3;
4:5
Not of God. Mt.4:1
Not of the nature of God. Jas.1:13-18
Satan.
Begs God for permission to tempt
man. Lk.22:31
Buffets & harasses the believer.
2 Cor.12:9
Fills the heart of man with evil.
Acts 5:3
His purpose. To hurt & cut the heart
of God. Lk.11:17-18; 22:31;
Jn.12:31; 1 Pt.5:8; Rev.12:3-4; 12:9
Seeks to corrupt the mind & to turn
it from the simplicity of the gos-
pel. 2 Cor.11:3
Seeks to get an advantage. 2 Cor.2:11
Seeks to sift people back & forth.
Lk.22:31
Tempts the husband & wife when
they neglect each other sexually.
1 Cor.7:5
Certainty of.
Is inevitable. Lk.17:1-2
Pull after pull. Mk.9:42-50
Described as.
A wilderness experience. Mk.1:13
List of temptations. 1 Pt.1:6
Discussed. Lk.4:2; Jas.1:2; 4:1-6; Pt.1:6-9
Duty.
Not to tempt God. Mt.4:7
To persevere until Jesus returns.
Jas.5:7-11
To prepare & conquer. Three prepara-
tions. Jas.1:19-27
Essential - Warning against **t.**
Must be vigilant & resist the devil.
1 Pt.5:8-9
Must flee the very appearance of evil.
1 Th.5:22
Must watch & pray that one does not
enter **t.** Mt.26:40-41
How to overcome & conquer **t.**
By avoiding every kind of evil.
1 Th.5:22
By combatting step by step. Jas.5:7-20
By guarding against two dangers.
Mt.4:5-7

By having an attitude of joy during **t.**
Jas.1:2-4
By learning & knowing the Scriptures
& standing fast in them. 1 Pt.3:17,
cp. 15-18
By prayer. Mt.6:13; Mt.26:41;
Lk.22:39-46
By putting on the armor of God.
Eph.6:10-18
By quoting, recalling & using Scrip-
ture. Mt.4:2-4, cp., 4, 7, 10
By resisting the devil & drawing nigh
to God. Jas.4:7-8
By resisting to the point of blood.
Heb.12:3-4
By turning to Christ.
He helps, succors us. Heb.2:18
He keeps, protects us in the hour of
t. Rev.3:10
By turning to God.
God knows how to deliver out of **t.**
2 Pt.2:9; Rev.3:10
God's control & making a way to
escape. 1 Cor.10:13
God's grace. 2 Cor.12:9, cp. 7-9
God's help. Mk.1:13
Discussed. Lk.4:2; 1 Cor.10:13
How to meet. Mt.4:1-11
Verses. List of. Mk.1:12
Kinds of **t.**
Discussed. Mt.4:2-4
T. common to all believers. Jas.2:1-26
T. common to teachers. Jas.3:1-18
T. common to the gifted. Jas.4:11-5:6
T. to be self-centered. Mt.4:2-4
T. to be self-confident & to boast in
self. Jas.4:13-17
T. to by-pass God. Lk.4:9-12
T. to compromise. Mt.4:8-10
T. to hoard wealth. Jas.5:1-6
T. to judge others. Jas.4:11-12
T. to love the world. 1 Jn.2:15-16
T. to meet one's needs in one's own
strength. Mt.4:2-4
T. to misunderstand true wisdom.
Jas.3:13-18
T. to misuse the tongue. Jas.3:1-12
T. to profess faith without works,
deeds. Jas.2:14-26
T. to seek after riches. 1 Tim.6:9-10
T. to show partiality & favoritism.
Jas.2:1-13
T. to test Christ.
By asking Him to prove Himself
time & again. Mt.16:1
By trying His patience, seeing how
far one can go. 1 Cor.10:9
T. to test God. Mt.4:5-7
By returning to one's dead religion.
Acts 15:10
By challenging Him to prove Him-
self time & again. Heb.3:9
T. to think one is above falling into
sin. Gal.6:1
T. to use the spectacular. Mt.4:5-7
Meaning of **t.** Heb.3:7-11
Of Jesus Christ. Mt.4:1-11; Mk.1:12-13;
Lk.4:1-15
Purpose of **t.** Mt.4:1
Discussed. 1 Pt.1:7; 4:12
To bring greater joy & rejoicing to the
believer. 1 Pt.4:12-13
To bring praise, honor, & glory to
Christ. 1 Pt.1:7
To experience the very special pres-
ence of God. 1 Pt.4:12-14, esp. 14

To honor & glorify Christ. 1 Pt.1:7
To prepare for service. Lk.4:1-2
To prove that a person truly accepts
Jesus as the true Messiah. Mk.7:27
To prove that one believes God's
promise of the eternal inheritance.
Heb.11:8-10, cp. 11:1-40
To prove that one believes the power
of Christ. Mt.9:28
To prove the believer's patience & en-
durance. Jas.1:3, cp. 3-5
To strengthen the believer. Mk.1:12
To teach one patience & endurance.
Jas.1:2-4
To test & prove the believer. Jas.1:2; 1:7
Results.
If one sins. Death. Jas.1:14-16
If the believer conquers **t.**
He is made perfect & complete.
Jas.1:4
He is to be blessed. Lk.4:13-15
He is to receive the crown of life.
Jas.1:12
When is a person tempted.
After making a major decision.
Mk.1:12
Discussed. Mt.4:1-11
During the common affairs of day to
day life. 1 Cor.10:13
When a person does not have some-
thing & desires it. Jas.4:1-5, cp.
Mt.6:24-34
When the heart is drawn by an inner
lust toward something. Jas.1:12-13

TENANTS, WICKED
Parable of. Lk.20:9-18

TEMPTED (See TESTED)

TEN COMMANDMENTS (See COM-
MANDMENTS)

TENDER - TENDERHEARTED (See
COMPASSION-COMPASSIONATE;
MERCY; MINISTERING; SYMPA-
THY)
Discussed. 1 Pt.3:8
The Lord is full of tender mercy. Jas.5:11

TERRIBLE TIMES
Meaning. 2 Tim.3:1

TERROR
Duty. Believers are not to fear the terror
of persecutors. 1 Pt.3:14
In the end time. Discussed. Rev.6:12-17
The **t.** of the Lord. To stir us to witness.
2 Cor.5:11

TERTIUS
Secretary who wrote Romans for Paul.
Ro.16:22

TERTULLUS
The lawyer who represented the religionists against Paul. Acts 24:1-9

TEST - TESTING (See TEMPTATION,
Purpose; TRIAL)
Discussed. Every person is being **t.**
Lk.19:11-27; 20:9-18
Duty.
To be proven before being ordained as
a deacon. 1 Tim.3:10

To examine & **t**. oneself, whether one be in the faith. 2 Cor.13:5

To **t**. all things. 1 Th.5:21

To **t**. one's own work. Gal.6:4

To **t**. the good will of God. Ro.12:1-2, esp. 2

To **t**. the sincerity of one's love. 2 Cor.8:8-9

To test all things. 1 Th.5:21

Meaning. Heb.3:7-11

Results - Reward.

To receive a great reward of joy & rejoicing in the great day of redemption. 1 Pt.4:12-13

To receive an eternal inheritance. Heb.11:8-10; 11:16; 11:26

To rule & reign with Christ forever. Lk.22:28-30

Will receive the answer to one's need & prayer. Lk.17:14

The purpose of **t**.

Discussed. 1 Pt.4:12

To bring greater joy & rejoicing to the believer. 1 Pt.4:12-13

To bring praise, honor, & glory to Christ. 1 Pt.1:7

To experience the very special presence of God. 1 Pt.4:12-14, esp. 14

To prove one's patience & endurance. Jas.1:3, cp. 3-4

To prove that one accepts Jesus as the true Messiah. Mk.7:27

To prove that one believes God's promise of the eternal inheritance. Heb.11:8-10, cp. 11:1-40

To prove that one believes the power of Christ. Mt.9:28

The **t**. of a man is the fruit he bears.

Reveals if a person is a disciple of Christ. Jn.15:8

Reveals if a person is a false teacher. Mt.7:16-20, esp. 16, 20

Reveals if a person truly repents. Mt.3:8

Reveals if a tree is to be cut down & destroyed. Lk.13:7

TESTAMENT, NEW (See COVENANT, NEW)

Discussed. 2 Cor.3:6-18; Heb.8:6-13; 9:15-22

Established between God & man. Mt.26:26-30

Meaning. 2 Cor.3:6

TESTAMENT, OLD (See COVENANT, OLD)

Vs. the new order, the new testament. Lk.16:16; 16:17-18; 2 Cor.3:16-18; Heb.8:6-13; 9:15-22

TESTED

Meaning. Heb.3:7-11

TESTIMONY (See WITNESS - WITNESSING)

Discussed. 1 Pt.2:11-12

The great eyewitness account of salvation. 2 Pt.1:16-18

Duty.

Not to be ashamed of the **t**. of our Lord. 2 Tim.1:8

Not to quit. Ph.2:25-30

To be a **t**. by approaching God like He says--through the sacrifice of blood. Heb.11:4

To be a **t**. to one's spouse, seeking to save him or her. 1 Cor.7:13-16; 1 Pt.3:1-3

To be examples to all in sharing the Word. 1 Th.1:7-8

To be faithful in stewardship, for it stirs many to faithfulness. 2 Cor.9:2

To be so close to Christ that one cannot help but testify. Acts 4:20

To be the light of the world. Mt.5:14-16; Ph.2:15

To be the salt of the earth. Mt.5:13

To behave righteously so that those who slander us now will glorify God in the day of judgment. 1 Pt.2:11-12

To believe in Christ so strongly that one testifies. 2 Cor.4:13

To have a strong **t**. Ro.1:8; 3 Jn.3-4, 5-8

To honor employers & supervisors lest the name of God be blasphemed. 1 Tim.6:1

To live above criticism. Ro.14:15-16; 1 Cor.8:9-13

To live what we preach lest the name of God be blasphemed. Ro.2:23-24

To mark good examples. Ph.3:17-21

To testify to every person who asks about our hope in Christ. 1 Pt.3:15

To walk wisely before the lost. Col.4:5

To watch social activities. Ro.14:1-23; 1 Cor.8:1-13; 10:14-11:1

Essential.

For believers to have a good **t**. Mt.28:19-20; Acts 1:8; Ro.1:8; 1 Pt.3:15; 3 Jn.3-4, 5-8

For deacons to have a good **t**. Acts 6:3; 1 Tim.3:8-13

For elders, bishops, & ministers. 1 Tim.3:1-7; Tit.1:5-9

Example.

A devout man, one who obeyed God's commandment - Ananias. Acts 22:12

A good **t**. among all. Stood in the truth - Demetrius. 3 Jn.12

A great believer - Philemon. Phile.1:1-7

A just & God-fearing man - Cornelius. Acts 10:22

A lady full of good works - Dorcas. Acts 9:36-43

A man greatly changed. Phile.1:8-21

A messenger with a good report. 3 Jn.12

A strong faith. Heb.11:32-40

A strong **t**. Boldness & power. Acts 4:13-14

A young man with a dynamic **t**. - Timothy. 16:1-3

Marks of a godly **t**. 2 Tim.3:10-13

Of hope & perseverance. Heb.11:32-40

Of John. God is revealed. 1 Jn.1:1-5; 5:13-15

Of Paul.

Before a crazed mob. Acts 22:1-21

Triumphant **t**. of Paul. 2 Tim.4:6-8

Of serving in second place. Ph.2:19-22

Reasons for following. Ph.3:17-21

Some early believers. Tit.3:12-15; Phile.1:22-24

The believers' great Hall of Fame. Heb.11:1-40

Power to testify. The Holy Spirit. Acts 1:8; 2:4

Purpose.

To declare the death & resurrection & coming judgment of Christ. Acts 10:42

To lead people to repentance & faith in Christ. Acts 20:21

To prove that Jesus is the Messiah. Acts 18:5

To reconcile men to God. 2 Cor.5:19-20

To tell people what great things Christ has done for the believer. Mk.5:18-20

TETRARCH

Meaning. Mt.14:1-14

THADDAEUS - LABBEUS - JUDAS, THE APOSTLE, SON OF JAMES

Discussed. Mk.3:18

THAMAR

Saved by God. Mt.1:3

THANKFUL - THANKFULNESS - THANKSGIVING (See GRATITUDE; WORSHIP)

Duty.

To give **t**. after healing. Only one of ten lepers. Lk.17:15-19

To give **t**. in all circumstances. Eph.5:18-21; 1 Th.5:18

To give **t**. publicly after blessing. Lk.13:11-13

To give **t**. to God for His blessings. Jn.5:13-14

To pray with thanksgiving. Ph.4:6-7

To receive all things with thanksgiving. 1 Tim.4:3-4

To thank God for always giving us victory through Christ. 2 Cor.2:14

To thank God for answered prayer. Jn.11:41

To thank God for believers always. Eph.1:15-16; Ph.1:3; 1 Th.1:2

To thank God for Christ, God's unspeakable gift. 2 Cor.9:15

To thank God for food. Jn.6:11

To thank God for His inheritance. Col.1:12

To thank God for His peace. Col.3:15

To thank God for people receiving the Word of God as the Word of God. 1 Th.2:13

To thank God for the death of Christ. 1 Cor.11:24

To thank God for the privilege of doing all things for Him. Col.3:17

To thank God for the salvation of believers. 2 Th.2:13

To thank God for victory over death. 1 Cor.15:57

Meaning. 1 Tim.2:1

Trait of men. Lk.17:15-19

THEOLOGIANS

Impact of Jesus upon. Mk.2:18-22

THEOPHILUS

Discussed. Acts 1:1

Man to whom Luke writes his gospel & the Book of Acts. Lk.1:3

Recipient of the Book of Acts. Acts 1:1

THESSALONICA

Discussed. Acts 17:1-9

Visited by Paul on his second mission. Acts 17:1-9

THEUDAS, THE REVOLUTIONARY
Discussed. Acts 5:36-37

THIEVES - THEFTS (See **STEALING**)
Behavior - Traits.
Enter & steal from houses. Lk.12:39
Enter houses by some way other than
the door. Jn.10:1
Seek money & possessions instead of
Christ. Mk.14:10-11; Jn.12:6
Steal from travelers. Lk.10:30
Steal, kill, & destroy. Jn.10:10
Caused by - Source of **t**. The heart.
Mk.7:20-23
Duty.
Not to steal, but to work & give to
meet the needs of the world.
Eph.4:28
Not to steal from masters & em-
ployers, but to show that one can be
trusted. Tit.2:9-10
Not to suffer as a thief.
1 Pt.4:15
Fact. Two **t**. Crucified with Christ.
Lk.23:32, 39-43
Meaning. Mk.7:22; 1 Cor.6:9-10
Results.
Defiles a man, greatly so. Mk.7:20-23
Shall not inherit the Kingdom of God.
1 Cor.6:9-10

THINKING
Described. As vain, empty. Ro.1:21
Duty. To cast down. 2 Cor.10:5
Fact.
God scatters the proud in the **t**. of their
heart. Lk.1:51
People imagine empty things against
God. Acts 4:25
Meaning. 2 Cor.10:5

THINKING, POSITIVE (See
THOUGHTS; MIND)

THIRST
Duty.
To give food & water to those who **t**.
Mt.25:33-40
To serve Christ so diligently that one
sometimes goes without food & wa-
ter. 2 Cor.11:27, cp. 23-28
Fact.
Christ thirsted upon the cross.
Jn.19:28
People **t**. in hell. Lk.16:24
For righteousness. Mt.5:6

THIRST, SPIRITUAL (See **FOOD,
SPIRITUAL; HUNGER, SPIRITUAL;
WATER, LIVING**)
Duty.
To come to Christ & take of the water
of life freely. Rev.22:17
To fill one's **t**. by coming to Christ.
Jn.7:37-38
To **t**. after righteousness. Mt.5:6
Results.
One shall be a citizen of heaven &
never **t**. again. Rev.7:15-17
One's heart shall overflow with rivers
of living water. Jn.7:37-38
Source of satisfaction.
Discussed. Jn.4:10; 4:13-14; 7:37-39
Jesus Christ. Jn.4:10; 4:13-14; 6:34-35;
7:37-39
Vs. physical **t**. Jn.4:13; 7:37-39

THOMAS, THE APOSTLE
Confrontation with Christ. Great convic-
tion & confession. Jn.20:24-29
Discussed. Mk.3:18
Questioned where Jesus was going. Jn.14:4-7

THORNS
Described as. The world. Mt.13:7, 22
Symbol. Of the curse upon the earth.
Mt.27:29

THOSE ENTRUSTED
Discussed. Lk.19:11-27
Parable of the faithful & unfaithful
steward. A strong warning - be pre-
pared. Lk.12:41-48
Parable of the laborers in the vineyard.
God's glorious grace. Mt.20:1-16
Parable of the pounds. Every man is
tested. Lk.19:11-27
Parable of the talents: the steward's
duty to work for the Lord. Mt.25:14-30
Parable of the unjust steward: man &
money. Lk.16:1-13
Parable of the unmerciful steward. The
spirit of forgiveness. Mt.18:21-35
Parable of the wicked tenant: Israel's
rejection of Jesus' Messiahship.
Mt.21:33-46
Duty. (See **STEWARDSHIP**)
To be a faithful & wise **t**. Lk.12:42
To be faithful. Lk.12:42-48; 1 Cor.4:2
To be forgiving. Mt.18:21-35
To give & support the ministry of
Christ. Lk.8:3
To labor diligently in the Lord's vine-
yard. Mt.20:1-16
To manage & look after God's vine-
yard. Mt.21:33-46
To use one's gifts & minister to others.
1 Pt.4:10
To use one's talents & increase them.
Mt.25:14-30
Essential. Must be faithful or face severe
consequences. Mt.21:44; 25:30
Fact. Cannot serve God & money or pos-
sessions. Lk.16:13
Judgment of the unfaithful **t**.
To be delivered to the tormentors.
Mt.18:34
To be destroyed & have his posses-
sions given to another. Mt.21:41
To be separated from the Lord.
Lk.12:46-48
To be stripped of everything & cast
into outer darkness. Mt.25:30
To be stripped of everything & slain.
Lk.19:20-27
To lose all true riches. Lk.16:11
To lose what was rightfully his own.
Lk.16:12
Parable of. Faithful & unfaithful **t**. A
warning: be prepared. Lk.12:41-48
Reward of the faithful **t**.
To be given a great reward. Lk.19:24-26
To be given just payment. Mt.20:9-10
To be made ruler of the Lord's house-
hold. Lk.12:42-44
To be made ruler over many things.
Mt.25:21, 23
Who the steward is.
Discussed. Lk.12:41-48; 1 Cor.4:1-2
The manager of the Lord's property.
Lk.16:2-3 cp. 16:1-12
The supervisor of laborers. Mt.20:8,
cp. 1-16

THOUGHT - THOUGHTS (See **MIND;
WISDOM; WRONGS, RECORD OF**)
Duty.
Not to focus upon the necessities of
life but upon God & His righteous-
ness. Mt.6:28-34
To cast down imaginations & subject
every **t**. to Christ. 2 Cor.10:5
To focus upon Christ & not faint. Heb.12:3
To let the Word of God discern one's
t. Heb.4:12
To meditate upon the Word of God.
1 Tim.4:15
To think soberly, wisely. Ro.12:3
What to think upon. Is clearly spelled
out. Ph.4:8; 2 Cor.10:3-5
Essential.
Must think before building a tower, a
life. Lk.14:28-32
Positive thinking. Discussed. Ph.4:8-9
Source - power to think positively.
1 Cor.2:16; Ph.2:5
Evil thoughts.
Caused by - source. The heart.
Mt.15:9, cp. Mt.9:4
Creates false gods. Jn.8:54-59
Meaning. Mt.7:21
Prevented. By guarding self around the
opposite sex. Jn.4:27
Fact. Are known by God. 1 Cor.3:20
Of the natural man. Vain, empty, futile.
Ro.1:21; 1 Cor.3:20, cp. 18-20
Worldly **t**. (See **WISDOM,
WORLDLY**)
Are illogical. Exposed. Mt.12:11
Are opposed by God. 1 Cor.3:18-20
Must repent of worldly **t**. Acts 8:22

THOUGHTLESS (See **MINDLESS**)

THRONE
Of Christ.
Fact.
Has been exalted to rule & reign
over all beings of all worlds &
dimensions. Eph.1:19-23; 2 Pt.3:22
Has been given the throne of David.
Lk.1:31-33
Has been seated at the right hand of
the **t**. of God. Heb.8:1; 12:2
Is to be worshipped & praised as the
exalted Lord upon the throne.
Rev.5:11-14, esp. 13
Shall judge from the **t**. of His glory.
Mt.25:31-46, esp., 31
Promised. Believers shall rule upon the
t. with Christ. Rev.3:21
Of God.
Discussed. Rev.4:1-11
Throne of judgment. Rev.20:11
Who stands before. Rev.7:11-12

THROW OFF
Meaning. Heb.12:1; 1 Pet.2:1

THYATIRA
Church of.
Discussed. Rev.2:18-22
One of the seven churches of Revela-
tion. Rev.2:18-22
Represents the compromising or per-
missive church. Rev.2:18-22
City of. Rev.2:18

MASTER SUBJECT INDEX

TIME - TIMING
Abuse of. Five ways. Mk.1:21
Discussed.
 Hebrew & Roman t. Mk.6:48
 Jewish t. Mk.1:32
 The threat of t. Four threats. Ro.13:11-14
Duty - Essential.
 The believer & the threat of t.
  Ro.13:11-14
 To grasp the opportunity while one
  can. Jn.2:3-5; 11:7-10
 To know that t. is short. 1 Cor.7:29-31
 To make the most of every opportu-
  nity. Eph.5:16; Col.4:5
 To point out the world's sin. It is t. to
  do so. Jn.7:6-9
 To seize t. Mk.1:21
 To use t. wisely. Ro.13:11-14
Facts.
 God knows the exact, the best time to
  act. Jn.11:6
 T. is short. Lk.9:59-60
 T. is to end, cease. Rev.10:6
 The end of time is at hand. 1 Pt.4:7
 The hour is urgent. Lk.10:1-4;
  Heb.3:13
 The t. of the Gentiles will end & Israel
  will be restored. Lk.21:24
Fullness of. (See **FULNESS OF TIME**)
 Began with the times of the Gentiles.
  Lk.21:24
 Discussed. Gal.4:4
Jesus - the pivotal point of history. (See
 HISTORY) Lk.7:28; 11:23

TIME, FULLNESS OF (See **FULLNESS OF TIME**)

TIME HAS COME, THE
Discussed. Gal.4:4; Eph.1:10
Fulfilled by Christ. Discussed. Lk.3:1-6;
 3:1-2
Meaning. Mk.1:15; Ro.5:6-7
World prepared by a forerunner. Three
 ways. Jn.1:23

TIME, THE LAST
Discussed. 2 Pt.3:3; Jude 17-19
Measured differently by God & man.
 Two ways. 2 Pt.3:8

TIMES & DATES, THE
Meaning. 1 Th.5:1-3

TIMES & SEASONS, THE (See **TIMES & DATES, THE**)

TIMOTHY
Call of. To the ministry. 1 Tim.1:18
Discussed. Acts 16:1-3; Ro.16:21;
 Ph.2:22; 1 Tim.1:2
Epistles written to. 1 Tim. & 2 Tim.
Life & ministry.
 A resident of Lystra. Acts 14:20
 Disciple of Paul. Discussed. Ph.2:22
 Release from prison. Heb.13:23
 Served in second place. Ph.2:19-22
 The beginnings of his ministry. Acts 16:1-3
Paul's concern for Timothy's welfare.
 1 Cor.16:10-12

TIRED - TIREDNESS (See **BURDENED; WEARY - WEARINESS; PRESSURE; YOKE**)
Discussed. Mt.11:28-30
Duty. To rest. The danger of too much
 rest. Mk.6:30-34

TITHE - TITHING (See **STEWARDSHIP**)
Duty. Not to misuse money, but to use
 money to meet the needs of people.
 Lk.11:42
Fact.
 Judged by the amount kept back, not
  the amount given. Lk.21:3
 T. was essential to the Jews. Mt.23:23
 The religionists were strict tithers.
  Lk.11:42
Warning. Against t. for attention.
 Mt.23:5; Mk.12:38; Lk.11:43

TITLES
Seeking. Discussed. Mt.23:5-7; Lk.11:43

TITUS
Delivered the severe letter of Paul to
 Corinth. 2 Cor.7:6
Discussed. Tit.3:12
Sent by Paul to minister. 2 Tim.4:10
Used by God to bring revival to Corinth.
 2 Cor.7:13-16
Was a disciple of Paul. 2 Cor.8:16-24;
 Tit.1:4
Was a Gentile believer. Made a test case
 for salvation by grace. Gal.2:3-5
Was the leader of a delegation overseeing
 the churches. 2 Cor.8:16-17

TOLERANCE - TOLERANT
Conditions of. Discussed. Mk.9:38-41
Discussed. Lk.9:49-50
Of ministers. Of those who differ from
 us. Ph.1:17-18
When one is not to be t.
 In dealing with fellowship with unbe-
  lievers. 1 Cor.6:14-18
 In dealing with shameful sin in the
  church. 1 Cor.5:1-5; 5:6-13
 In dealing with those who deny the
  deity & teaching of Christ. 2 Jn.7-11

TOMB
Discussed. Mt.27:65-66; Mk.5:3

TONGUE (See **WORDS**)
Described as.
 A world of evil. Jas.3:6
 An open grave. Ro.3:13-14
 A restless evil. Jas.3:8
 Corruptible. Ro.3:13-14
 Double tongued. 1 Tim.3:8; Jas.1:8
 Fire. Jas.3:6
 Speaking evil. Discussed. Jas.4:11-12
Discussed. Eph.4:25; 4:29; 4:30;
 Jas.1:19-27; 3:1-12
Duty.
 Not to be mere talkers & deceivers.
  Tit.1:10-12; 1:16; 3:9
 Not to lie. Eph.4:25
 Not to offend others in word. Jas.3:2
 Not to speak evil of people. Tit.3:2;
  Jas.4:11
 To avoid petty arguments & specula-
  tions. 2 Tim.2:14-21
 To be clean-mouthed. Eph.5:4
 To be controlled. Jn.4:27
 To confess Jesus Christ, that He is
  Lord. Ph.2:9-11
 To control the tongue. Jas.3:6
 To guard against worthless talk. Eph.4:29
 To keep a tight rein on. Jas.1:26
 To lay aside all evil speaking. 1 Pt.2:1
 To love in deed & truth, not in word
  only. 1 Jn.3:18

To put away all evil speaking. Eph.4:31
To shun useless chatter. 2 Tim.2:16-18
To speak to ourselves in psalms &
 hymns & spiritual songs. Eph.5:19
To speak with grace. Col.4:5-6
To stop one's tongue. 1 Pt.3:10
To talk about Christ all day long.
 Col.3:17
To use sound speech that cannot be
 condemned. Tit.2:8
To waste no time in needless chatter.
 Lk.10:4
Fact.
 Can be tamed only by Christ. Jas.3:8
 Every t. shall confess Christ to be Lord
  in the day of judgment. Ph.2:9-11
Sins of.
 A world of iniquity. Jas.3:6
 Boasting. Jas.3:5
 Discussed. Ro.3:13-14; Col.3:8-11
 Evil & deceptive speaking. 1 Pt.3:10
 Idle words. Meaning. Mt.12:36
 Misusing the t. Jas.3:1-12
 Slander. Jas.4:11-12; 1 Pt.2:1
 Speaking vs. listening. Jas.1:19-27
 Swearing. Jas.5:12
 Unruly, full of deadly poison. Jas.3:8
What the t. does.
 Defiles a man. Mt.15:10-11
 Determines man's destiny. Mt.12:31-37
 Exposes the kind of person a man is.
  Threefold. Mt.12:34-35

TONGUES, GIFT OF
Discussed. Acts 2:4; 10:46; 1 Cor.12:8-10
 Contrasted with prophecy.
  1 Cor.14:1-5; 14:1-25
 Paul & tongues. 1 Cor.14:15-20
 Problems with. 1 Cor.14:6-14
 The place of t. in the early church
  services. 1 Cor.14:26-40
Interpreting t. Gift of. Discussed.
 1 Cor.12:8-10

TORCHES OF BURNING FIRE, SEVEN (See **BLAZING LAMPS, SEVEN**)

TORMENT (See **FIRE, EVERLASTING; HELL; LAKE OF FIRE**)
Of hell. Discussed. Lk.16:24

TOUCH - TOUCHED (See **SYMPA-THIZE**)
Communicates two things. Mt.8:14-15
Duty.
 Not to allow Satan to t. us, but to keep
  ourselves from sin. 1 Jn.5:18
 Not to t. a woman sexually, not im-
  morally. 1 Cor.7:1-2
 To know that Christ is t. by the feel-
  ings of our infirmities. Heb.4:15-16
 To seek the t. of Jesus. Mt.9:29;
  20:34; Heb.4:15-16
 To t. Jesus to meet our needs.
  Mt.9:20-22; Mk.3:10; Lk.6:19
 To t. no unclean thing. 2 Cor.6:16-17
Meaning. Heb.4:15-16

TRADE GUILDS - UNIONS
Corrupt. Persecute the church. Rev.2:18-19

TRADITION (See **RELIGION - RITUAL**)
Discussed. 1 Cor.11:2-16
Duty.
  To hold fast to the **t.** & instructions taught in Scripture. 1 Cor.11:2; 2 Th.2:15
  To withdraw from all who do not walk after the **t.** of Scripture. 2 Th.3:6-7
Error - Problem with.
  Are but the commandments of men. Mt.15:9
  Can become hypocritical. Mt.15:1-9, esp. 7; 23:13
  Can enslave people in false teaching & lead them away from Christ. Col.2:8
  Emptiness of. Mk.7:1-13
  Placed above God's Word. Mk.7:8; 7:9-12; 7:13
  Placed before man. Lk.13:14-16; 14:1-6
  Religionists often rank **t.** above the needs of man. Mt.15:2; Mk.7:5
  Teaches empty, vain behavior. 1 Pt.1:18-19
Of the church. When to be followed. 1 Cor.11:2-16
Of the Jews.
  Caused rejection of some. Mt.9:20
  Sabbath. **T.**, rules & regulations. Mt.12:1-8
  Stressed **t.** Mt.15:1-20; 15:6-9
Old vs. new. Mt.9:16-17

TRAINING (See **DISCIPLES**, Training of; **TEACHERS - TEACHING**)
Of the disciples. Intensified. Launched a new phase. Mt.16:13-20; 16:21-28
To precede service. Mt.10:1-4; 10:1

TRAITORS (See **APOSTASY; DENY - DENIAL; TREACHEROUS**)

TRANCE
Discussed. Acts 10:9-22

TRANSFIGURED - TRANSFIGURATION (See **JESUS CHRIST**, Transfiguration)
Meaning. Mt.17:2; Mk.9:2-3
Of Christ. Strengthened to bear the cross. Mt.17:1-13; Mk.9:2-13; Lk.9:28-36
Witnessed by Peter & the other apostles. 2 Pt.1:16-18

TRANSFORM - TRANSFORMED - TRANSFORMATION (See **CONVERSION; RENEW - RENEWAL**)
Hope of. To be conformed to Christ. 1 Jn.3:2
Meaning. Ro.12:2
Source.
  By the Holy Spirit. Changes believers into the image of Christ. 2 Cor.3:18
  By the power of the gospel. Mt.13:33
  How the gospel **t.** Lk.13:21

TRANSGRESSION (See **LAW-BREAKING; LAWLESSNESS; SIN; VIOLATION**)
Caused by.
  Adam's sin. Ro.5:13-14
  Being deceived. 1 Tim.2:14
  Breaking the law. Ro.4:14-15
  Committing sin. 1 Jn.3:4
Counteracted - Delivered from. By Christ.
  He was counted among the transgressors. Lk.22:37
  He died to redeem us from our **t.** Heb.9:15

Discussed. Ro.4:14-15; Eph.2:1-2
Meaning. Mt.6:14; Eph.2:1-2; Heb.2:2; 1 Jn.3:4

TREACHEROUS
Discussed. 2 Tim.3:2-4

TREASURE, SPIRITUAL (See **RICHES**)
Duty.
  To buy the gold possessed by Christ. Rev.3:18
  To esteem Christ greater riches than the riches of the world. Heb.11:26
  To give up all for the knowledge of Christ. Ph.3:8
  To have one's understanding enlightened. Eph.1:18-19
  To preach the unsearchable riches of Christ. Eph.3:8
  To seek spiritual **t.** Mt.6:19-20; Lk.12:31-34; 16:9; 18:18-23
Parable of the Hidden **T.** Giving all for Christ. Mt.13:44; Ph.3:8
Vs. earthly **t.** Lk.12:31-34; 18:18-23
Vs. evil **t.** Mt.12:34-37, esp. 35
What is the spiritual **t.**
  Believers are considered a **t.** Mt.13:44
  Christ is a **t.** Mt.13:44; Ph.3:8
  God is a **t.** 2 Cor.4:7
  The good **t.** of the heart. It bears good things. Mt.12:35
  The kingdom of heaven. Mt.13:44
  The **t.** of heaven. Mt.6:19-20
  Wisdom & knowledge are **t.** The **t.** of all things is hid in Christ. Col.2:3

TREE
Parable of a good & corrupt **t.** Lk.6:43-45

TREE OF LIFE, THE
Meaning. Rev.2:7
Purpose of. To give an abundant & fruitful life. Rev.22:2
Who has the right to the tree of life.
  Not those who tamper with the Word of God. Rev.22:19
  The obedient. Rev.22:14
  The overcomers. Rev.2:7

TRESPASS (See **SIN AGAINST; TRANSGRESSIONS**)
Meaning. Mt.6:14

TRIALS - TRIBULATION (See **LIFE**, Storms of; **SUFFERING; TEMPTATION**)
Attitude toward.
  To glory in. Ro.5:3
  To have an attitude of joy. Jas.1:2-4
Basic facts. Discussed. Jas.1:2-27
Deliverance through **t.** - How to conquer.
  By a sure foundation. Lk.6:46-49
  By Christ.
    His love. Ro.8:35-39
    His power over fear & **t.** Mt.8:23-27
  By enduring. A call to endurance. 2 Cor.6:3-10
  By four things. 1 Pt.1:8-9
  By God.
    He conquers fear for us. 2 Tim.1:7
    He knows how to deliver. 2 Pt.2:9
    He prepares a way to escape. 1 Cor.10:13
    He protects the believer. Acts 28:1-15
    His power sustains. 2 Cor.4:7-18
    His purpose in delivering from **t.** Acts 5:19-21

By standing up under the painful **t.** 1 Pt.4:12-19
By trusting & praising the Lord through circumstances. Lk.1:39-42
Discussed. Ph.4:11-14; Jas.1:12; 1 Pt.5:10-11
  God's part & man's part in conquering **t.** Ph.4:11-14
How the church progresses under **t.** 2 Th.1:4-5
Verses. List of. Mk.1:12
Discussed.
  God & suffering. 2 Cor.1:3-11
  How to act in **t.** 1 Pt.4:12-19
  Purpose for **t.** & suffering. 2 Cor.1:3-11; 4:7-18; 6:3-10
Duty. (See **TRIALS**, Deliverance through)
  Not to question **t.** Mt.2:13-18
  To enter the kingdom of God through many **t.** Acts 14:22
Listed. Many fold. Mt.7:24-25; 7:26-27
Meaning. Ro.2:9; 2 Cor.1:4
Of Christ.
  Bearing unbelievable **t.** & weight. Mk.14:32-42; Lk.22:39-46
  Confronting terrible **t.** & death. Mt.26:36-46
  Described. Unbearable. Lk.22:41-44; Ro.5:3-5
  He experienced & suffered every trial of man. Lk.2:40
Purpose for trials.
  Discussed. Ro.5:3-5; 2 Cor.1:3-11; 4:7-18; 6:3-10; 1 Pt.1:7
  To stir endurance. Ro.5:3-5; Jas.1:2
  To test & prove our faith. 1 Pt.1:7
  To test & prove us. Jas.1:2
Results.
  Fear. Jn.16:17-19
  Twofold. Jas.1:3-4
Rewards for conquering.
  Discussed. Jas.1:12
  To be great. Mt.5:10-12
Verses. List of. Jn.6:17-19

TRIALS, POLITICAL (See **JESUS CHRIST**, Trials, Legal)

TRIBULATION--DISTRESS, THE GREAT (See **END TIME**, Antichrist)
A chart of the great **t.** Discussed. Mt.24:1-31; Mk.13:1-37; Rev.13:2
A picture of the very end. Rev.11:14-19
Book of Destiny. Rev.4:1-5:14
Deliverance from. (See **TRIBULATION, THE GREAT**, Who Escapes)
Discussed. Mt.24:1-31; 24:15-28; 24:29-31; Mk.13:1-37; Lk.21:5-38
Events of.
  Antichrist. (See **ANTICHRIST**). Lk.21:16
    Rise of the antichrist. Rev.6:1-8; 11:7-10; 13:1-10;17:7-14
    Rise of the false prophet. Rev.13:11-18
  Armageddon, Battle of. Rev.11:18; 14:20; 16:12-16;19:17-21
  Babylon, capital of the world.
    Discussed. Rev.17:1-24; 19:1-4
    Is destroyed. Rev.14:8; 16:17-21; 18:1-24
  Events during the Great Tribulation. Rev.8:1-21:8
  Events preceding the Great Tribulation. (See Outlines and footnotes) Rev.6:1-7:17

Gaining control of the economy.
Rev.6:5-6; 13:16-17
Gaining control of the energy - oil.
Rev.6:6
Gaining control of the food. Rev.6:5-6
Gaining control of the military.
Rev.6:1-8; 9:12-21; 13:7
God & Magog. Rev.20:7-10
Israel's conversion. (See **JEWS; ISRAEL**)
Marriage supper of the Lamb.
Rev.19:1-10
Persecution by the antichrist.
Deception. Rev.13:13-17
Discussed. Mt.24:9; Mk.13:9;
Lk.21:12-19
Martyrs - martyrdom. Rev.6:9-11; 7:9-
17; 11:1; 11:2; 12:11; 17:6; 18:24
Of believers. Rev.6:1-11; 7:14;
11:7-10;12:10-17; 13:7-10;
13:15-18; 17:6; 18:24
Revival during. Rev.19:1-10
Spiritual struggle behind world events.
Rev.12:1-17
Supernatural power - miraculous signs.
Rev.13:11-18
The final triumph of Christ.
Rev.11:14-19; 19:11-20:15
The mark & number of the antichrist.
Discussed. Rev.13:16-18; 14:9-12
Number 666. Rev.13:18
Rejected by believers. Rev.14:9-
12; 15:1-3
Two witnesses. Rev.11:3-13
World's final rebellion. The final re-
bellion of men. Rev.11:18; 14:20;
16:12-16;19:17-21
Fate of believers.
144,000 Jews saved. Rev.7:1-8
Countless multitude of Gentiles saved.
Rev.7:9-17
Sealed, protected from the judgments
of God. Rev.7:2-3; 9:3-6
Governments of.
A confederation of states - a world
government. Rev.13:1-2; 13:8-10;
16:12-16;17:7-18; 19:17-21
A false prophet. Rev.13:11-18
A political ruler. Rev.13:1-10
Capital of the world - Babylon.
Rev.14:8; 18:1-24
Man's behavior pictured. Rev.6:15-17
Origin of the term "the great tribulation."
Mk.13:19
Overall view of. Rev.11:14-19
Prophecy of. By Daniel.
Prophecies - Predicted.
The antichrist. Mk.13:1-37
The seventieth week of the end time.
Mt.24:15; Mk.13:1-37; 13:14
Prophecies of the antichrist. Chart of the
prophecies of Daniel & Revelation.
Rev.13:2
Satan. (See **SATAN**)
Signs of.
Discussed. Mt.24:1-31; Mk.13:1-37;
Lk.21:5-28; Rev.6:1-7:17
Mockers. Jude 18
Persecution - the tragic sign. Mt.24:9;
Mk.13:9; Lk.21:12-19
Time of. Three & one half years.
Rev.11:1-2; 12:6, 14; 13:5
Warning.
To believers. Mt.25:1-46; Mk.13:28-37;
Lk.21:34-36
Watchfulness essential. Mt.24:42-51;
25:1-46; Mk.13:28-37; Lk.21:34-36

World to be destroyed. Mt.24:29
Who escapes God's judgments in the
tribulation.
Believers. Rev.3:10
Those sealed & protected by God in
their foreheads. Rev.7:2-3; 9:3-6
Those who obey God's command &
loyal to the faith of Jesus.
Rev.13:10; 14:12
Those who remain loyal & steadfast.
Rev.13:8-10; 14:12
Those who reject the beast's mark.
Rev.14:9-12; 15:2-4
Who is victorious through the persecu-
tion of the antichrist.
A countless multitude of martyrs.
Rev.7:9-17
A Jewish remnant - 144,000. Rev.
7:1-8; 14:1-5
God's servants, the prophets.
Rev.11:18
Overcoming brothers. Rev.12:11
The loyal & steadfast. Rev.13:7-10;
14:12
The martyrs who are slain for the
Word of God. Rev.6:9-11
The saints. Rev.11:18; 13:10; 14:12
Those harvested by Christ. Rev.14:14-16
Those who die in the Lord. Rev.14:31
Those who "fear...and give glory to
God." Rev.11:11-13
Those who fear God's name.
Rev.11:18
Those written in the book of life.
Rev.13:8-10; 14:12; 14:13
Victors over the beast. Rev.15:2-4

TRIED
Duty.
To be proven before being ordained as
a deacon. 1 Tim.3:10
To examine & **p.** oneself, whether one
be in the faith. 2 Cor.13:5
To **p.** all things. 1 Th.5:21
To **p.** one's own work. Gal.6:4
To **p.** the good will of God. Ro.12:1-2,
esp. 2
To **p.** the sincerity of one's love.
2 Cor.8:8-9
Meaning. Heb.3:7-11

TRINITY, THE (See **GOD; HOLY
SPIRIT; JESUS CHRIST**)
Nature. Perfect unity in the Godhead.
Jn.16:14-15
Revelation of.
In Paul's great benediction.
2 Cor.13:14
In the baptism of Christ. Mt.3:16
In the coming of the Holy Spirit & in
His witness to Christ. Jn.15:26-27
In the great work of salvation. 1 Pt.1:2
In the statement of faith at baptism.
Mt.28:19-20
In the teaching ministry of the Holy
Spirit. Conforms perfectly with the
teaching of Christ. Jn.14:25-26
In the work of adoption as sons of
God. Gal.4:4-7

TRIUMPH (See **VICTORY - VICTORI-
OUS LIVING**)

TRIUMPHAL ENTRY (See **JESUS
CHRIST**, Triumphal Entry)

TROAS
City where Paul received the vision to
evangelize Europe. Acts 16:8-11
Paul revisited. Acts 20:4-6

TROPHIMUS
A believer. Discussed. Acts 20:4-6
Became sick & had to be left behind by
Paul. 2 Tim.4:20

TROUBLE (See **HARDPRESSED**)
Deliverance from. Jn.14:1-3

TROUBLEMAKER
Vs. peacemaker. Mt.5:9

TRUCEBREAKERS (See **FAITHLESS;
UNFORGIVING PERSONS**)

TRUMPET JUDGMENT
Events during the great tribulation.
Rev.8:1-11:19
Fifth **t.** Demonic-like locusts. Rev.8:13-9:11
First four **t.** Natural catastrophes.
Rev.8:6-12
Of Revelation. Blasted forth by seven
angels. Rev.8:2-5
Seventh **t.**
An overall picture of things to come.
Rev.11:14-19
Demonic-like military horsemen.
Rev.9:12-21

TRUMPET OF THE LORD
At the return of the Lord. To sound when
He returns. Mt.24:31; 1 Cor.15:51-52;
1 Th.4:16

TRUST - TRUSTED - TRUSTWORTHY
(See **BELIEVE; FAITH**)
Believers **t.** by Christ. Lk.8:23;
2 Tim.1:12-14
Duty.
To **t.** & commit one's soul to God.
1 Pt.4:19
To **t.** God to take care of one's needs
& necessities. Mt.6:25-34; Lk.10:4;
12:22-23
To **t.** the Lord to keep that which one
commits to Him. 2 Tim.1:12
Meaning. 1 Tim.6:20
Object of. Trust God, not money. Lk.21:2
Reasons to **t.**
Christ set a dynamic example for us.
Trusted & committed His spirit to
God who judges righteously.
Lk.23:46; 1 Pt.2:23
Other believers have set a dynamic ex-
ample for us. Stephen. Acts 7:59
Two reasons. Mt.6:8
Results.
Stirs a willingness to suffer for Christ,
an unashamed willingness.
2 Tim.1:12
Stirs diligent labor. 1 Tim.4:10
Verses. List of. Lk.10:4
Vs. fear. Lk.8:25

TRUSTS, FALSE
Problem with. False basis. Building a life
upon. Lk.6:49

TRUTH - TRUTHFULNESS
Abuse of. 2 Pt.2:10-22
Discussed. Jn.8:32; Eph.6:11; 2 Jn.1-2
The **t.** is Jesus Christ. Jn.14:6; Rev.3:7
The **t.** is the protection against false
teaching. 1 Jn.2:20-21

Duty.
To be established in the **t**. 2 Pt.1:12
To be open to the **t**. Jn.4:25
To bear witness to the **t**. Acts 26:25
To come to the knowledge of the **t**. 1 Tim.2:3-6, esp. 4
To gird oneself with **t**. Eph.6:14
To handle the **t**. in the right way. 2 Tim.2:15
To know the **t**. 1 Jn.2:20-21
To obey the **t**. Reasons. Gal.5:7-12; 1 Pt.1:22
To share & mark the **t**. Mk.4:21-25
To speak **t**. with one's neighbor. Eph.4:25
To walk in the **t**. 2 Jn.4; 3 Jn.3-4
Fact.
God created all things for those who believe & know the **t**. 1 Tim.4:3-5, esp. 3
T. cannot be hid. Mk.4:21
T. is concealed. Reason. Lk.8:9-10
T. must be revealed by God. 1 Cor.3:18-20
The **t**. will be known someday. Mt.10:26-27
Meaning. Eph.5:9
Jesus Christ is truth & the Word of God is truth. 2 Jn.1-2; 3 Jn.3-4
The **t**. is Christ. Jn.14:6
The **t**. is the Word of God. Jn.8:32; 17:17-19
True vs. false; real vs. unreal. Jn.1:9
Nature of t. **T**. is very narrow. Lk.8:18
Parable of. Mk.4:21-25
Power of.
Grows the believer. Eph.4:15, cp. Acts 20:32; 1 Tim.3:16; 1 Pt.2:2-3
Liberates & sets man free. Jn.8:32
Purifies the soul. 1 Pt.1:22
Sanctifies the believer. Jn.17:17-19
Problems.
Blindness to. Mk.6:52
Counterfeit **t**. The "seemingly true." Lk.8:18
T. is hid to natural man. The reason why. Lk.10:21
Reward of. Seekers & achievers receive more. Lk.8:18
Seek - seeking.
Bias against Biblical truth, against Christ & the Bible. Acts 17:11
How one is to seek **t**. Lk.11:31
To diligently seek **t**. Lk.11:31
Source.
God. 1 Jn.4:6
Jesus Christ. Jn.1:14; 14:6; 15:26; 16:13; 18:37; Col.2:9-10;
The gospel. Gal.2:5; 2:14
The Holy Spirit. Jn.14:17, cp. 1 Cor.2:13
The Word of God. Jn.17:17-19
Spiritual t.
Hid from the wise & self-sufficient. Mt.11:25-27
Many are blind & ignorant to the **t**. Mt.12:11
Those who reject the t.
Are often deceived because they do not love the **t**. 2 Th.2:10
Do not obey the **t**. Ro.2:8-9
Follow after the flesh & resist the **t**. 2 Tim.3:6-9
Often disobey the **t**. because they are deceived. Gal.3:1
Seek after the world & are destitute of the **t**. 1 Tim.6:5

Serve & worship creation more than the Creator. Ro.1:25
Will be damned. 2 Th.2:12
Will turn away from the **t**. in the end time. 2 Tim.4:3-4

TRYPHENA & TRYPHOSA
Two Christian ladies of the early church. Ro.16:12

TUMULTS (See **DISORDER**)

TURN
Discussed.
A strong **t**. 1 Th.1:5-10
Dramatic **t**. Does not last & lacks depth. Mt.13:5-6, 20-21; Lk.8:11-15
Experience of **t**. 2 Cor.4:6
Various types of **t**. Lk.8:4-15
Duty - Essential.
Must be willing to be changed. Mk.3:16-19
To be **t**. & become as little children. Mt.18:3
To be **t**. before preaching the gospel. 2 Cor.4:6
To strengthen fellow believers once **t**. Lk.22:32
How a person is t.
By a stirred heart. What happens. Jn.8:31
By believers bearing witness. Jas.5:19-20
By repentance. Acts 3:19
By turning to God. 1 Th.1:9-10
Steps to. Discussed. Lk.19:1-10
Illustrated.
Centurion's confession at the cross. Mk.15:39
Ethiopian eunuch. Acts 8:37-38
Onesimus' change of life. Phile.1:10-16
Matthew **c**. was dramatic. Mt.9:9; 9:9-13
Paul's **c**. was to show God's mercy for great sinners. 1 Tim.1:15-16
Zacchaeus new life. Lk.19:1-10
Many sought to know the Lord. Acts 13:42-45
Marks of. Gal.1:13-16; 1 Th.1:5-10
Meaning. Mt.18:3; Acts 3:19
A complete change. Gal.1:13-16
A convulsive experience. Mk.1:25-26
A repentance. Lk.19:8-10
A returning after failing. Lk.22:31-34
A shining of God in one's heart. 2 Cor.4:6
A turning away from error. Jas.5:19-20
A turning from one's own way. Jas.5:19-20
A washing, a sanctification, a justifying. 1 Cor.6:11
An awakening from sleep or death. Eph.5:14
Becoming as a little child. Mt.18:1-4
Results.
Given light. Eph.5:14
Hides a multitude of sins. Jas.5:19-20
One's sins are blotted out. Acts 3:19; Jas.5:19-20
One's soul is saved. Jas.5:19-20
Proves the deity of Christ. Lk.20:6
The refreshing presence of the Lord. Acts 3:19
To Judaism. Discussed. Mt.23:15
Warning.
Can be ignored and forgotten. 2 Pt.1:9

Can be snatched away by the devil. Lk.8:5, 12
Can blind one's eyes to the need for **t**. Mt.13:15; Mk.4:12; Jn.12:40; Acts 28:27

TYCHICUS
A believer & disciple of Paul who served others. Col.4:7-8
Discussed. Acts 20:4; Eph.6:21-22; Tit.3:12
Sent by Paul to minister. 2 Tim.4:12

TYRE
City of. Discussed. Mk.7:24; Acts 21:1-3
Jesus visited the coasts of Tyre. Mt.15:21
Paul's seven day mission in Tyre. Acts 21:1-16

U

UNASHAMED (See **GUILT; SHAME - SHAMEFUL**)
Duty.
To be **u**. of the gospel. Ro.1:16-17; 1:16
To have one great hope. To be **u**. Ph.1:20
Meaning. 1 Jn.2:28

UNBELIEF (See **REJECTION**)
Answer to - Deliverance from.
God's faithfulness. He is faithful despite **u**. 2 Tim.2:13
Overcome by evidence. Jn.20:26-28; 20:29
The rebuke & reproof of Jesus. Mk.16:14
Caused by.
An evil heart. Heb.3:12
Being inconsistent & illogical. Mt.12:22-30; 12:26-28; Jn.12:37-41
Being obstinate despite the evidence. Acts 4:15-18
Being offended by Christ. Offended by four things. Jn.6:59-71
Being spiritually blind. Mk.8:10-13
Claiming to be too wise to believe in God. Ro.1:22-23
Deliberate, wilful unbelief. Mt.13:10-17; 13:13-15
Error & misconception. Thinking that one's **u**. voids Christ & God's Word. If a person disbelieves something, he thinks it will not be so. Ro.3:3
Failing to hear the voice of Jesus & to follow Him. Jn.10:25-27
False teachers who walk after the way of rebellion & unbelief. Jude 11
Fearing the loss of one's position, esteem, & livelihood. Mt.12:1-8; 12:10; 16:12; 21:23; 21:25-27; 22:15-22; 22:23-33; 22:34-40; 23:1-12
Following after the lusts of Satan. Jn.8:44-45
Greed & self-confidence & self-righteousness. Lk.19:47-48
Holding a false concept about Jesus. Jn.20:26
Is not predestinated or determined by God. Jn.12:39-41
Israel's fall. Ro.11:19-24
Living a fleshly, sensual life. Mt.13:13-15
Loving the darkness of sin. Jn.3:18-20

By being born again by the Word of the Lord. 1 Pt.1:23-25

By believing God & developing a strong faith in God's promises. Ro.4:20-21

By following after Christ with strict discipline & control. 1 Cor.9:24-27, esp. 26

By placing the anchor of one's hope in Christ. Heb.6:19-21

By trusting & hoping in God for eternal life. 2 Cor.5:1-10, esp.1

By trusting the love of Christ. Ro.8:35-39

What is **u**.
Attractiveness, beauty, glory, position, riches. Lk.12:15-21; Jas.1:10; 1 Pt.1:24
Life. Jas.4:13-15

UNCHANGEABLE (See **GOD**, Nature; **JESUS CHRIST**, Nature)

UNCLEAN - UNCLEANNESS (See **DE-FILE - DEFILEMENT; IMPURITY; SIN; FILTHINESS; SEXUAL IMPU-RITY**)
Attitude toward. By the church. Mk.2:15
Deliverance - Cleansing. Discussed. Mk.1:40-45
Duty.
Not to touch any **u**. thing, but to live a separated life. 2 Cor.6:17-18
To guard against doing the things that people consider **u**. Ro.14:13-15, esp. 14
To live a moral & clean life. 1 Th.4:6-8
Meaning. Ro.1:24-25

UNCONCERN
Results. Prevents compassion. Lk.10:29-37

UNCTION (See **ANOINTING**)

UNDEFILED (See **CLEAN; MORAL-ITY; PURITY; SPOTLESS**)
Duty.
To keep the bed **u**. Heb.13:4
To practice a pure & **u**. religion. Jas.1:27
Fact.
Christ was **u**., that is, perfect. Heb.7:26
The believer's inheritance is eternal & **u**, that is, perfect. 1 Pt.1:3-4

UNDERSTANDING (See **KNOWL-EDGE; SENSLESSNESS; SPIRITUAL SIGHT; WISDOM**)
Duty.
To be filled with all spiritual **u**. Col.1:9
To be fully assured of one's **u**. Col.2:2
To have one's **u**. enlightened, quickened by God. Eph.1:18
To know & experience the peace of God that passes all **u**. Ph.4:7
To love God with all of one's **u**. Mk.12:33
To pray & sing with **u**. 1 Cor.14:15
To **u**. what one preaches & teaches. 1 Cor.14:19
To **u**. what the will of the Lord is. Eph.5:17
Fact.

False teachers do not **u**. what they say. 1 Tim.1:7
Some things in Scripture are hard to **u**. 2 Pt.3:16
Hindrances to.
Being blind to the works of Christ. Mk.6:52
Being ignorant & unstable. 2 Pt.3:16
Having a blind & dark heart. Eph.4:17-19
Not understanding the Word of God. Mt.13:19
Sin. Ro.1:28-32, esp. 31
Spiritual dullness. Lk.9:44-45
Unbelief. Jn.8:43, cp. 42-47
Meaning. Eph.1:18; Col.1:9
Of the world. Truth hid from. Lk.10:21
Source of - Comes by.
Christ. Lk.24:45; 2 Tim.2:7; 1 Jn.5:20
Creation & faith. Heb.11:3
Creation & nature. Ro.1:20
God quickening the mind. Eph.1:17-21, esp. 17-18
Ministers, preachers, teachers. Acts 26:18, cp. 15-18

UNEASY - UNEASINESS (See **ANXI-ETY; IMPATIENCE**)

UNEQUALLY YOKED (See **YOKED TOGETHER**)

UNFAITHFUL - UNFAITHFULNESS (See **FAITHFULNESS; UNBELIEF**)
Caused by.
Ignoring the Lord's return. Lk.12:41-48
Misusing one's gifts & possessions. Lk.16:1-13, cp. Mt.25:24-30
Failure of. Discussed. Lk.19:15-23
Parable of. Warning. Be prepared. Lk.12:35-48

UNFAITHFUL AND FAITHFUL MAN-AGER
Parable of. Lk.12:35-48

UNFORGIVABLE SIN (See **SIN**)

UNFORGIVENESS (See **FORGIVE-NESS**)
Caused by.
Bad feelings. Mt.6:15
Not forgiving others. Mt.6:14-15
Described. Mt.18:22
The spirit & practice of forgiveness. Mt.18:21-35

UNFORGIVING PERSONS
Meaning. Ro.1:31; 2 Tim.3:2-4

UNFRUITFUL - UNFRUITFULNESS (See **UNPRODUCTIVE**)
Caused by.
False teachers. Jude 12
Loving this world & its life. Jn.12:24-25
Not abiding in the vine. Jn.15:1-8
Sin. Ro.7:5
Worldliness & covetousness & deceitfulness of riches. Mt.13:22; Lk.8:14
Discussed. Mk.11:12-14; 2 Pt.1:8-11
Warning against.
False teachers. Are like trees whose fruit withers. Jude 12
Shall be cut down & burned. Mt.3:10; 7:19; Lk.3:9; Jn.15:6

Shall be judged & condemned. Mt.21:19; Mk.11:12-14; Lk.13:6-9
Shall be rejected & burned. Heb.6:8
Shall disappoint God & stir His condemnation. Lk.13:6
Shall end in death. Ro.6:21; 7:5

UNGODLY - UNGODLINESS (See **GODLESS; LOST, THE; UNBELIEV-ERS**)
Judgment of. (See **JUDGMENT**)

UNHOLY
Meaning. 2 Tim.3:2-4

UNGRATEFUL
Meaning. 2 Tim.3:2-4
Trait of men.
After being blessed. Lk.17:15-19
Is seen in rejecting God despite all the evidence that God exists. Ro.1:21

UNION WITH CHRIST (See **ABIDE - ABIDING; INDWELLING PRES-ENCE**)
Based upon.
The body of Christ.
Believers are members of Christ's body, of His flesh & of His bones. Eph.5:30
Believers are the body; Christ is the head. Eph.4:15-16
Believers comprise, make up the body of Christ upon earth. 1 Cor.12:12-13; 12:27
The death & resurrection of Christ. Believers are counted dead & risen with Christ. Ro.6:3-10
The exaltation of Christ. Believers sit with Christ in heavenly places. Eph.2:6, cp. 4-7
The inheritance & glory of Christ. Believers are joint heirs with Christ. Ro.8:16-17
The mind of Christ. Believers have the mind of Christ. 1 Cor.2:16
The righteousness of Christ. Believers are made righteous in Him. 2 Cor.5:21
The rule & reign of Christ. Believers are to rule & reign with Christ. 2 Tim.2:12
The spirit of Christ. Believers are joined to the Lord in one spirit. 1 Cor.6:17, cp. 15-18
Duty.
To abide in Christ & to let Christ abide in us. Jn.15:4-6
To bring forth fruit unto God. This is the very reason why we are married, joined to Christ. Ro.7:4
To flee immorality, for our bodies are the members of Christ. 1 Cor.6:15-18
To know Christ, the power of His resurrection & the fellowship (union) of His sufferings. Ph.3:10
To let the gospel abide in us. We continue in Christ if the gospel abides in us. 1 Jn.2:24
To partake of Christ, the bread of life. Jn.6:56

UNIONS - TRADE GUILDS
Illustration. Corrupt trade **u.** persecute the church. Rev.2:18; 2:20-21

UNITED
In marriage. Meaning. Mk.10:7-8
Meaning. Mt.19:5

UNITY (See **BROTHERHOOD; DIVISION**)
Discussed. Jn.17:11; 17:21-22; 17:23; 1 Cor.1:10; Eph.4:1-3; 4:4-6
Duty.
  Not to argue or strive over words & false doctrine. 2 Tim.2:14-26
  To accept others--not to show any discrimination. Ro.15:5-6
  To be of one accord, of one mind. Ph.2:2
  To be of one mind & show compassion. 1 Pt.3:8
  To be of one mind & to live in peace. 2 Cor.13:11; 1 Pt.3:8
  To be perfectly joined together in one mind. 1 Cor.1:10
  To live in harmony. 1 Pt. 3:8
  To seek unity & peace. Eph.4:3
  To seek **u.** & to associate with the lowly. Ro.12:16
  To share with all who have need. Acts 4:32
  To strive for togetherness. Lk.9:1
  To strive for **u.**, to stand fast in one spirit. Ph.1:27
  To work for harmony. Ro.15:5-6
Nature of the believers' unity.
  All barriers are broken down. Gal.3:28
  Believers are one body in Christ. Jn.17:11, 20-23; Ro.12:4-5; 1 Cor.12:12-3; Eph.3:6; Col.3:8-11
  Believers are one fold & have only one Shepherd. Jn.10:16
  Believers are one in spirit even as God & Christ are one. Jn.17:21
  Believers possess one heart & one soul. Acts 4:32
  Is based upon love. Jn.17:23
  Is based upon the peace wrought by Christ. Eph.2:14
  Threefold nature. Jn.17:11
Purpose for.
  Discussed. Jn.17:21-22
  Reasons why we should keep the **u.** Seven reasons. Eph.4:4-6
  To grow into a perfect body of believers. Eph.4:13
Source - Comes by - Believers are unified by.
  A binding force. Jn.17:11
  A forgiving spirit. Mt.18:22
  A true spiritual kinship. Mk.3:34-35
  Becoming one of the sheep of God's flock. Jn.10:14-16
  Being gentle to all men. 2 Tim.2:24
  Being placed into the body of Christ by the Spirit. 1 Cor.12:12-13
  Christ. Gal.3:28; Eph.2:13-18; Col.2:19;3:11
    His life in the believer. Jn.17:23; Ph.2:1-2
    His prayer. Jn.17:11-12
    Letting His life flow in & through us. Ph.2:1-4
  Compromising for unity. Acts 21:17-26

Concern for one another. 1 Cor.12:25-26
Discussed. Acts 4:32; Ph.2:1-18; 4:2-3
Esteeming others better than oneself. Ph.2:3
Fellowship. Acts 2:42
God Himself. Jn.17:11, 15, 17, 24
Humbling one's self. Ph.2:5-11
Letting God mesh hearts together. Lk.8:21
Looking to one's rewards. Ph.2:9-11
Not by flesh, heritage, or will. Lk.8:20
Partaking of Christ, of the same bread of life. 1 Cor.10:17
Prayer. Mt.18:19
Standing firm in one spirit. Ph.1:27
The great prayer of Jesus. Jn.17:11, 20-23
The new creation. Eph.3:1-13
The Spirit of God. 1 Cor.12:13
The Word of God. Lk.8:21
Why & how to walk in unity. Eph.4:1-6
Steps to correcting divisiveness. Mt.18:15-20
Unity of ministers. Source. Fivefold. Acts 14:1
Verses. List of. Mk.3:34-35

UNIVERSE
Fact. Injustices shall be rectified. 2 Th.1:6
Misconceptions about the **u.** Many think it is self-creating & self-sufficient. 2 Pt.3:4; 3:5-7

UNJUST JUDGE
Parable of. Secret of prayer. Perseverance. Lk.18:1-8

UNJUST MANAGER
Parable of. The Christian & money. Lk.16:1-13

UNJUST, THE
Fact.
  Believers are not to have legal disputes settled by the **u.** 1 Cor.6:1
  God blesses the **u.** as well as the just in this life. Mt.5:45
  He that is **u.** in little is **u.** in much. Lk.16:10
  The self-righteous think that they are not as **u.** as other men are. Lk.18:11
Judgment of.
  Are preserved by God until the day of judgment. 2 Pt.2:9
  Some **u.** will wait too late to repent & face the judgment of God. Rev.22:10-11
  The **u.** will be resurrected from the dead & judged. Acts 24:15
Salvation of. Christ died for the **u.** 1 Pt.3:18

UNKINDNESS
Duty. To put off **u.** Eph.4:31

UNLEAVENED BREAD, FEAST OF
(See **FEASTS**) Mt.26:17; Lk.22:1

UNLOVED, THE
Fact. Are loved by Jesus Christ & by genuine believers. 2 Jn.1-2

UNMARRIED
Discussed. 1 Cor.7:8-9; 7:25-40

UNMERCIFUL (See **RUTHLESS**)

UNMERCIFUL SERVANT
Parable of. The spirit & practice of forgiveness. Mt.18:21-35

UNNATURAL AFFECTIONS (See **HOMOSEXUALITY**)

UNPARDONABLE SIN
Discussed. Mt.12:31-32; Lk.12:10

UNPRODUCTIVE
Discussed. Mk.11:12-14; 2 Pt.1:8-11

UNREADINESS
Duty. To watch for the Lord's return. Lk.12:35-48

UNREPROVABLE (See **ACCUSATION**)

UNREST (See **ANXIETY**)

UNRIGHTEOUSNESS - UNRIGHTEOUS, THE (See **SIN; UNGODLY; WICKEDNESS; WRONGDOING**)
Deliverance.
  By Christ & His righteous life. There was no **u.** whatsoever in Christ. Jn.7:18
  God cleanses us from all **u.** if we confess our sins. 1 Jn.1:9
  God is not **u.** to forget our work & labor of love. Heb.6:10
  God will be merciful to a man's **u.** & forgive his sins. Heb.8:12
Duty.
  Are not to be yoked, not to have fellowship with **u.** 2 Cor.6:14
  Are not to yield our body members to **u.** Ro.6:13
Fact.
  False teachers love the wages of **u.** 2 Pt.2:15
  Men are filled with all **u.** Ro.1:29
  Unbelievers are deceived by **u.** 2 Th.2:10
Warning.
  False teachers shall receive the reward for **u.** 2 Pt.2:15
  God is not **u.** if he takes vengeance. Ro.3:5
  Shall be damned. 2 Th.2:12
  Shall be judged, severely condemned. Ro.1:18; 2:8
  Shall not inherit the kingdom of God. 1 Cor.6:9

UNRULY
Meaning. Tit.1:10

UNSAVED (See **LOST, THE; UNBELIEVERS**)
Duty. To reclaim the **u.** Jude 22-23
Fact. Being saved is not assured. Mt.14:1-14; 18:13
Message preached to. Acts 17:22-34
Why men are unsaved. Mt.6:31-32; 19:22

UNSEEMLY BEHAVIOR
(See **RUDE**)

UNSELFISH - UNSELFISHNESS (See **CROSS, DAILY - SELF-DENIAL; HUMILITY**)
Duty.
To be **u.** in all things. 1 Cor.10:23-28; 10:29-11:1
To give up whatever social functions are necessary to keep from being a stumbling block. 1 Cor.10:23-28; 10:29-11:1
To seek the welfare of others, not one's own welfare. 1 Cor.10:33

UNTHANKFULNESS (See **THANK-FULNESS; UNGRATEFUL**)

UNTOUCHABLE
Cleansed. By Jesus. The **u.** must seek Jesus in humility. Lk.5:12-16

UNWORLDLINESS (See **WORLDLY - WORLDLINESS**, Deliverance from)

UNWORTHY - UNWORTHINESS
Caused by.
Humility. Knowing one's place & lot in life. Jn.1:27; Jas.1:9-11
Realizing one's insignificance before Christ. Mt.25:37; Lk.5:8; Jn.13:8
Realizing one's terrible sin. 1 Cor.15:9
Sin. Lk.15:17-19
Sense of. Example of. Centurion soldier. Mt.8:8; Lk.7:3
Who is **u.**
The person who puts Christ second in his life. Mt.10:37
Those who reject the invitation of God to attend the wedding of His Son, the Lord Jesus Christ. Mt.22:8
Those who reject the Word of God. Acts 13:46

UPPER ROOM
Disciples argued over positions in Christ's government. Lk.22:24-30
The room where Jesus spent the last night with the disciples before His death. Mt.26:17-35; Mk.14:12-25; Lk.22:7-38; Jn.13:1-16:26

URGE
Duty.
Must **u.** Eight reasons. Heb.3:13-19
To receive the word of **u.** Heb.13:22
Gift of. Discussed. Ro.12:6-8
How **u.** is to be given.
By prophesying, proclaiming the message of God. 1 Cor.14:3
Not wrongfully, in deceit; but in truth, **u.** people in the Word of God. 1 Th.2:3-13, esp. 3-6, 11-13
With all longsuffering & doctrine. 2 Tim.4:2
Meaning. Acts 11:19-30; 1 Tim.2:1; 2 Tim.4:2; Heb.3:13-19
The message of **u.**
Employment.
To be quiet & to work diligently. 2 Th.3:12
To honor & obey employees. 1 Tim.6:1-2; Tit.2:9-10
Prayer. To pray for all men. 1 Tim.2:1
Salvation. To be saved from this crooked generation. Acts 2:40
The Christian walk. To walk so as to please God. 1 Th.4:1

The faith.
To continue in the faith. Acts 14:22
To earnestly contend for the faith. Jude 3
The promises & deliverance of God. Acts 27:22-25
The true grace of God. 1 Pt.5:12
Witnessing & ministering. 1 Th.5:14
When **u.** is to be given.
Constantly, always. 1 Tim.4:13
On a daily basis. Heb.3:13; 10:25
When churches experience a revival. Acts 11:23, cp. 19-30
When churches need help. Acts 18:27
When people request a word of **u.** Acts 13:15
When preaching. Lk.3:18, cp. 1-18
When traveling about from church to church. Acts 20:1-2
Who is to be **u.**
All believers. Acts 14:22
All men, everyone. Tit.2:15, cp. 1-15
Believers who are being chastened by the Word. Heb.12:5
Elders & ministers. 1 Pt.5:1
Those who oppose the minister. Tit.1:9
Young men. Tit.2:6

URGENT - URGENCY (See **OPPORTUNITY; TIME**)
Duty.
To go forth & minister. The hour is urgent. Lk.9:59-60; 10:1-4
To grasp the opportunity while one can. Mt.26:10-11
Essential. To follow Christ. Mt.8:21-22

USELESS
Result. Of a depraved nature. Ro.3:10-12

USHERS
Discussed. 2 Cor.8:16-24

UTOPIA
Described. As four things. Jn.8:21
False concept - Misunderstood. Man's concept vs. God's concept. Mk.8:27-9:50
Seeking - Searching for.
By men. Is a search for a great Deliverer. Ro.10:6-7
Man's futile search for **u.** - an earthly deliverer & heaven. Jn.8:21-24
Source. Found in Christ alone. Jn.10:7-10; Ro.10:8-10

UTTERANCE (See **SPEAKING; TONGUES, GIFT OF**)

V

VAIN
Meaning. Acts 4:25-28
Things that can be **v.**, empty.
Appreciation of fellow believers. 2 Cor.9:3
Belief. 1 Cor.15:2
Christ's death & its effect upon us. Gal.2:21
Discussions, talk, speculations. 2 Tim.2:16
Faith. 1 Cor.15:17
Imaginations. Ro.1:21
Labor. 1 Cor.15:58
Mind. Eph.4:17

Religion. Jas.1:26
Suffering for Christ. Gal.3:4
The Christian race. Gal.2:2
The grace of God. 1 Cor.15:10; 2 Cor.6:1
The ministry & labor of ministers. Gal.4:11; Ph.2:16; 1 Th.2:1; 3:5
Words. Eph.5:6
Worship. Mt.15:9; Mk.7:7

VALUED HIGHLY
Meaning. Lk.7:2; Ro.1:29; 2 Cor.12:19-21

VARIANCE (See **DISCORD**)

VAUNT - VAUNTING OF SELF (See **BOAST**)

VEIL OF THE TEMPLE, THE INNER--CURTAIN (See **CURTAIN**)
A chart showing the tabernacle & the inner veil. Heb.9:11-14
Christ was man's forerunner through the inner veil. Heb.6:18-20
Discussed. Heb.9:11-14
The High Priest entered the inner veil only once a year. Heb.9:1-10, esp. 3, 7
Was torn from top to bottom during Christ's crucifixion. Mt.27:51; Lk.23:45

VENGEANCE (See **PUNISHMENT; RETALIATION; REVENGE**)
Caused by.
A desire to live as one wishes. Mk.6:24-25
Being hurt by the sin of a loved one. Jn.8:3-6
Duty. Not to take **v.** Three reasons. Ro.12:19-21
Meaning. Lk.21:22; 2 Th.1:9
Of judgment. Described. Ro.2:6-10
Of the wicked. In eternity. Ro.2:6-10
Results.
God takes **v.** on the persecutors of His followers. Lk.18:6-7
Verses. List of. Lk.21:22
Warning.
Evil men will suffer the **v.** of eternal fire. Jude 7
God will take **v.** Ro.12:19; 2 Th.1:8

VICARIOUS SUFFERINGS AND DEATH OF CHRIST (See **JESUS CHRIST**, Death, Substitutionary)

VICTORY - VICTORIOUS LIVING
How to live victoriously.
By Christ. Ph.4:13
By resisting the devil Jas.4:7
By the keeping power of God. Jude 24-25
By the Spirit of God. Ro.8:1-17; Gal.5:16, 23-25
What conquers the world.
Christ. Lk.9:1; 9:42-43; 10:18
Faith. 1 Jn.5:4-5
The fruit of the Spirit. Gal.5:22-26
The love of Christ. Ro.8:34-39
The new birth. 1 Jn.5:4-5
The power of the Holy Spirit. Ro.8:1-17
Walking in the Spirit. Gal.5:16-21
What does man need victory over.
Death. Jn.8:21-24; Ro.5:12
Judgment. Mt.12:20; Heb.9:27
Evil rule, authority & power, both human & spiritual. 1 Cor.15:24

Satan. Jas.4:7; 1 Pt.5:9-10
Severe circumstances & extreme experiences & forces. Ro.8:35-37; 8:38-39
Sin. Ro.3:23; 5:12; Eph.2:1-3
Spiritual evil & forces. Lk.10:19
The antichrist. Rev.15:2
The flesh. Gal.5:16-21
The world. 1 Jn.2:15-16; 5:4-5
Tribulation, trials, war. Jn.16:33

VIGILANT - VIGILANCE (See **ALERT; READINESS; TEMPERATE; WATCHFULNESS**)

VILE AFFECTIONS (See **SHAMEFUL LUSTS**)

VINDICTIVE (See **RETALIATION; REVENGE; VENGEANCE**)

VINE
Symbol - Type of.
God's kingdom. Mt.20:1-16
Jesus Christ. Relationship of Christ to the people of the world. Jn.15:1-8

VINEGAR--WINE (with gall)
Offered to Jesus on the cross. To deaden pain. Drugged **w**. Mt.27:26-38; Lk.23:36

VIOLATION
Caused by.
Adam's sin. Ro.5:13-14
Being deceived. 1 Tim.2:14
Breaking the law. Ro.4:14-15
Committing sin. 1 Jn.3:4
Counteracted - Delivered from. By Christ.
He was counted among the transgressors. Lk.22:37
He died to redeem us from our **v**. Heb.9:15
Discussed. Ro.4:14-15; Eph.2:1-2
Meaning. Mt.6:14; Eph.2:1-2; Heb.2:2; 1 Jn.3:4
Of the law. Breaking one law makes a person guilty of breaking all the laws. Jas.2:8-11

VIOLENCE
Predicted.
In the last days. Intensified. Lk.21:9-10
Wars & rumors of wars. Mk.13:7-8

VIOLENT
Meaning. 1 Tim.3:2-3

VIRGIN BIRTH (See **JESUS CHRIST**, Birth)
Of Christ.
By the Holy Spirit. Meaning. Lk.1:27; 1:34-35
Discussed. Mt.1:16; 1:23
Necessary. Eight reasons. Lk.1:27

VIRGINS
Parable of ten virgins. A warning to watch for the Lord's return. Mt.25:1-13
When should virgins marry. 1 Cor.7:25-40

VIRTUE (See **GOODNESS**)
Duty. To dress in a modest & virtuous way. 1 Tim.2:9-10; 1 Pt.3:3-5

VISION, WORLD-WIDE
Duty. To have a world-wide **v**. Acts 11:1-18; Ro.1:10-13
Equals success. Formula for success. Mt.13:12
Essential. To follow Christ. Mk.1:16
Greatest challenge known to man. Mt.9:37-38
Need for a world-wide vision.
Discussed. Ro.15:22-33
To pray for laborers. Lk.10:2
To see people who need God's Word. Lk.8:1
To see the fields of souls ready for harvest. Jn.4:35
The harvest of a needful world. Ready for reaping. Mt.9:37-38
Verses. List of. Lk.9:11

VISIONS
Errors - Misconceptions of **v**.
A false approach to God. Col.2:18-19
Seeking God through visions. Col.2:18-19
Example of **v**. By Cornelius. Acts 10:1-8
Gift of. From the Holy Spirit. Acts 2:17-21
Of Christ.
In heaven. Rev.1:9-20
John's vision of Christ. Rev.1:9-20
Of Revelation. Rev.1:9-3:22; 4;1-16:21; 17:1-21:8;21:9-22:21
Purpose of.
To convert & call men to the ministry. Acts 26:19, cp. 26:1-18
To encourage believers. Acts 18:9-11; 2 Cor.12:1-7
To guide & direct believers. Acts 9:10-16; 10:17, cp. 1-48; 16:8-11
To reveal spiritual things to believers. Rev.1:10
To reveal the truth of Christ. Lk.24:23
To show men that they are living in the last days. Acts 2:17-21

VISITATION, DAY OF (See **DAY GOD VISITS US**)
God's Son. Lk.19:44
The day of redemption. Lk.1:68-75, esp. 68

VOCATION
A man can be saved regardless of **v**. 1 Cor.7:17-24

VOICE
Of Christ.
Described. Rev.1:13-16
Known by believers. Jn.20:14-16
Of God.
Spoke to a multitude who were listening to Jesus. Jn.12:28-30
Spoke to Christ. Mt.3:17; Mk.1:11; Lk.3:22
Spoke to John. Rev.1:12
Spoke to Peter, James, & John. Mt.17:5; Mk.9:7; Lk.9:35-36; 2 Pt.1:17

VOW - VOWS
Discussed. Mt.5:33-37; Acts 18:18
Paul takes a vow. Acts 18:18; 21:22-26

VULTURES
Meaning. Lk.17:37
Symbol of judgment. Mt.24:25-28

W

WAGES (See **EMPLOYEE; EMPLOYER; EMPLOYMENT**)
Duty.
Must give a just **w**. Col.4:1, cp. Mt.20:1-16; 1 Cor.9:14, cp. 1-14
Must not cheat or withhold **w**. from laborers. Jas.5:4
Must pay ministers who preach & teach the Word. Gal.6:6-7
Fact. The laborer is worthy of his hire. Lk.10:7

WAGES OF SIN
Fact. False teachers love the wages of unrighteousness. 2 Pt.2:15
Warning.
False teachers shall receive the **w**. of unrighteousness. 2 Pt.2:13
The **w**. of sin is death. Ro.6:23
Those who neglect salvation shall receive a just wage just as transgressors always have. Heb.2:2-3

WAITING UPON THE LORD (See **PRAYER**)
Duty - Essential.
In great crises. Mt.26:36-46
To **w**. for the coming of the Lord. Lk.12:35-36; 1 Cor.1:5-7, esp. 5; 1 Th.1:10
To **w**. for the coming of the Spirit. Acts 1:4
To **w**. for the kingdom of God. Mk.15:43

WAKEFULNESS, SPIRITUAL (See **WATCH - WATCHFULNESS**)
Duty.
To awake & arise from the dead & receive Christ. Eph.5:14
To awake to righteousness & not sin. 1 Cor.15:34

WALK, BELIEVER'S (See **BELIEVER**, Walk)
Discussed. Acts 9:31

WALK, SPIRITUAL (See **ABIDE - ABIDING; BELIEVER**, Life - Walk)
Duty.
Not to **w**. after the flesh but after the Spirit. Ro.8:1, 4
Not to **w**. as unbelievers walk. Eph.4:17
Not to **w**. disorderly, being a busybody. 2 Th.3:11
Not to **w**. mishandling & abusing the Word of God. 2 Cor.4:2
To separate oneself from those who walk disorderly. 2 Th.3:6
To **w**. after the Lord's commandments. 2 Jn.6
To **w**. as children of light. Eph.5:8
To **w**. as Christ walked. 1 Jn.2:6
To **w**. as one has been taught by the Scripture. 1 Th.4:1
To **w**. by faith. 2 Cor.5:7
To **w**. by the rules one has already learned. Ph.3:16
To **w**. carefully, not as fools. Eph.5:15
To **w**. decently & honorably, not in partying, drunkenness, & immorality. Ro.13:13
To **w**. following good examples. Ph.3:17

To **w.** in Christ. Col.2:6
To **w.** in love just as Christ did. Eph.5:2
To **w.** in newness of life. Ro.6:4
To **w.** in the light as Christ is in the light. 1 Jn.1:7
To **w.** in the light of Christ lest darkness overcome one. Jn.12:35
To **w.** in the Spirit & not in the lusts of the flesh. Gal.5:16-18
To **w.** in truth. 3 Jn.4
To **w.** in wisdom toward unbelievers. Col.4:5
To **w.** worthy of one's vocation & call. Eph.4:1
To **w.** worthy of the Lord. Col.1:10; 1 Th.2:12
Fact.
   Believers have been saved to **w.** in good works. Eph.2:8-10, esp. 10
   Believers **w.** in the flesh but they do not war after the flesh. 2 Cor.10:3-5
   False teachers **w.** after the flesh. 2 Pt.2:10
   If one professes God & **w.** in darkness, he lies. 1 Jn.1:6
   Mockers **w.** after their own ungodly lusts. Jude 18

WAKE-UP
Discussed. Mt.24:42
Duty.
   To **w.** Rev.3:2
   To **w.** & be sober. 1 Th.5:6; 1 Pt.4:7
   To **w.** & keep one's clothing lest one be found naked. Rev.16:15
   To **w.** & stand fast in the faith. 1 Cor.16:13
   To **w.** against false teachers. Acts 20:28-31, esp. 31
   To **w.** because history's climax is at hand. 1 Pt.4:7-11
   To **w.** for the Lord's return. Mt.24:42-51; 25:13; Mk.13:35; Lk.12:35-40; 21:36; Acts 20:31
   To **w.** in all things. 2 Tim.4:5
   To **w.** in prayer. Eph.6:18; 1 Pt.4:7
      To **w.** & pray for the end time. Lk.21:34-36
      To **w.** & pray in great trials. Lk.21:34-36, esp. 36
      To **w.** & pray not to enter into temptation. Mt.26:41; Mk.13:33; 14:38; Lk.22:45-46; Col.4:2
Meaning. Mt.24:42; 1 Cor.16:13-14
Need to. Rules for discipleship. Fourfold. Lk.6:39-45
Warning.
   Danger in failing to **w.** Mt.26:40-41
   Must **w.** or one will fall short of God's grace. Heb.12:15-17

WALKING ON THE WATER
By Jesus. Jn.6:19-21

WANDERERS (See APOSTASY; BACKSLIDING; DENIAL)
Caused by.
   False teachers. 2 Pt.2:15-16; Jude 13
   Turning aside to empty discussions, speculations, arguments. 1 Tim.1:5-6, esp. 6
Describes.
   Believers who go astray. 1 Pt.2:25
   The depraved nature. Ro.3:10-12

WANT (See NEEDS - NECESSITIES)

WANTONNESS (See DEBAUCHERY)

WAR (See DIVISION; MURDER; STRIFE)
Believers' attitude in **w.** Mk.13:7-8
Caused by.
   The antichrist. Rev.6:3-4; 6:7-8
   The lust of man. Jas.4:1-3
   The nature of man. Ro.3:15-18
Discussed. Jas.4:1-3
Duty.
   Not to allow license & injustice. Ro.12:18
   To live in peace if possible. Ro.12:18
In the end time.
   Armageddon. Last war upon earth. Rev.19:17-21
   Predicted.
      Rumors of **w.** Mk.13:7-8
      To intensify in the last days. Lk.21:9-10
Sin of. Great **s.** of man. Ro.3:15-18

WARFARE, SPIRITUAL (See SPIRITUAL STRUGGLE - WARFARE)

WARN - WARNING - WARNS
Against apostasy & drifting away from Christ & other believers. Heb.10:26-39
Against being a castaway. 1 Cor.9:27
Against being lukewarm & half-committed. Rev.3:14-22
Against casting away one's assurance. Heb.10:32-39
Against compromise, seduction, immorality, & false teaching. Rev.2:22-23
Against falling away. Heb.6:4-8
   Precautions against. Heb.6:9-20
Against false doctrine & worldliness. Rev.2:14-16
Against forgetting what one has learned & not holding fast. Rev.3:3
Against four dangers. Heb.12:15-17
Against losing one's first love. Rev.2:4-5
Against missing God's rest. Five reasons. Heb.4:1-13
Against neglecting & drifting away from salvation. Heb.2:1-4; 12:15-17
Against refusing to hear Jesus Christ-- shutting one's ear to the cry of His blood. Heb.12:25-29
Against ruining life. The picture of a ruined life. Mt.26:14-16
Against spiritual immaturity or falling away. Heb.5:11-6:20
Against strange teaching. Heb.13:9-16
Against unbelief--against hardening one's heart. Heb.3:7-19
Duty.
   To be seasoned with salt. Col.4:6
   To reflect one's testimony for Christ. Mt.26:73-74
   To talk about the Lord all day long. Col.3:17
   To warn against criticizing & judging ministers. 1 Cor.4:14-15
   To warn every man & to teach every man. Col.1:28
   To warn everyone night & day. Acts 20:31
   To warn the unruly. 1 Th.5:14

In Revelation.
   To remain faithful - to hold fast. Rev.2:10; 3:3; 3:11
   To repent from compromise & idolatry. Rev.2:22-25
   To repent from deadness. Rev.3:3
   To repent from worldliness & corruption. Rev.2:16
Meaning. Heb.12:25
What the believer is to speak & talk about.
   Sound doctrine. Tit.2:1
   The mystery of Christ. Eph.6:19-20
   The things that cannot be condemned. Tit.2:8
   The truth, not lies. Eph.4:25
   Wisdom, the wisdom of God. 1 Cor.2:6-7
   To repent of being lukewarm. Rev.3:15-16
   To repent - to return to one's first love. Rev.2:5
Meaning of "woe." Lk.10:13
The warning of Israel. Israel stands as a warning example to believers. 1 Cor.10:10-13
The warning of the Book of Hebrews. Four interpretations of. Heb.6:4-8
The warning to believers. Sin will cause God to reject a person. 1 Cor.6:9-11
Who warns.
   God. Mt.2:12, 22; Acts 10:22; Heb.11:7
   Ministers. Mt.3:7; Lk.3:7

WASHED - WASHING, SPIRITUAL (See CLEAN - CLEANSING; PURE - PURITY)
Discussed. Jn.13:6-11
Duty.
   Not to return to one's unwashed, sinful condition. 2 Pt.2:20-22, esp. 22
   To have our hearts & bodies washed with pure water. Heb.10:22
   To **w.** away one's sins, calling on the Lord. Acts 22:16
   To **w.** the saints feet--willingly serve them in a spirit of humility. 1 Tim.5:10
How one is **w.**
   By drawing near God. Heb.10:22
   By the blood of Christ. Rev.1:5
   By the mercy of God, the **w.** of regeneration. Tit.3:4-7
   By the name of the Lord Jesus. 1 Cor.6:11
   By the Word of God. Eph.5:26
   Not by physical & ceremonial washings. Heb.9:8-10, esp. 10
   Not by self-effort, declaring that one is **w.**, innocent of sin. Mt.27:24
Meaning. 1 Cor.6:11
Spiritual **w.** Essential before service. Jn.13:6-11

WASHING, CEREMONIAL
Law of. Ceremonial law. Emptiness of. Mk.7:1-13

WASTE - WASTING
Duty. Not to waste food. Jn.6:12
Warning against.
   Wasting one's possessions in riotous living. Lk.15:11-24, esp. 13
   Wasting the Lord's gifts & goods. Lk.16:1-13, esp. 1

WATCH - WATCHFULNESS (See GUARD; WAKE-UP)
Discussed. Mt.24:42
Duty.
To **w.** & be sober. 1 Th.5:6; 1 Pt.4:7
To **w.** & keep one's clothing lest one be found naked. Rev.16:15
To **w.** & stand fast in the faith. 1 Cor.16:13
To **w.** against false teachers. Acts 20:28-31, esp. 31
To **w.** because history's climax is at hand. 1 Pt.4:7-11
To **w.** for the Lord's return. Mt.24:42-51; 25:13; Mk.13:35; Lk.12:35-40; 21:36; Acts 20:31
To **w.** in all things. 2 Tim.4:5
To **w.** in prayer. Eph.6:18; 1 Pt.4:7
To **w.** & pray for the end time. Lk.21:34-36
To **w.** & pray in great trials. Lk.21:34-36, esp. 36
To **w.** & pray not to enter into temptation. Mt.26:41; Mk.13:33; 14:38; Lk.22:45-46; Col.4:2
Meaning. Mt.24:42
Need to. Rules for discipleship. Fourfold. Lk.6:39-45
Warning.
Danger in failing to **w.** Mt.26:40-41
Must **w.** or one will fall short of God's grace. Heb.12:15-17

WATCH OUT
Meaning. Mk.8:15

WATCHINGS (See SLEEPLESS NIGHTS)

WATER (See THIRST, SPIRITUAL)
Discussed.
Christ turned **w.** into wine. Jn.2:1-11
Christ walked upon **w.** Mt.14:22-33; Mk.6:45-52; Jn.6:16-21
Symbol - Type.
Of Christ. Jn.4:1-14; 7:37-39
Of the Holy Spirit. Jn.7:37-39
What **w.** does. Jn.7:37

WATER, LIVING
Discussed. Jn.4:1-14
Duty.
To ask for living water. Jn.4:10
To come to Christ & believe on Him. Jn.7:37-38; Rev.22:17
To take of the **w.** of life. Rev.22:17
Fountains of. Rev.7:17
Is Christ or the Holy Spirit. Discussed. Jn.4:1-14; 7:37-39
Verses. List of. Jn.4:13-14
Results of drinking living water.
Shall be led to living fountains of water. Rev.7:17
Shall experience rivers of living water. Jn.7:38
Shall have one's thirst for fulfillment & satisfaction satisfied. Rev.22:17
Shall partake of the tree of life sitting by the river of living water in heaven. Rev.22:1-2
Shall receive everlasting life. Jn.4:14
Rivers of. Rev.22:1-2
Source.
Christ. Jn.4:1-14, esp. 14; Rev.21:6
Holy Spirit. Jn.7:37-39
The new birth. Jn.3:5
Verses. List of. Jn.4:13-14

WAVER - WAVERING (See BELIEVE AND NOT DOUBT; INSTABILITY; STEADFASTNESS)
Answer to. Discussed. Mt.11:7
Duty.
Not to be carried away with strange doctrines. Heb.13:9
Not to be tossed to & fro by every doctrine. Eph.4:14
To hold fast without **w.** Heb.10:23
Fact. Wavering is a sign of weakness. Mt.11:17

WAY - WAYS
W. of God.
Are just & true. Rev.15:3
Are past finding out. Ro.11:33
Are the **w.** of life. Acts 2:28
Must be prepared before men. Lk.1:76
W. of man.
Are unstable. Jas.1:8
Fade away. Jas.1:11
Follows the sensual & immoral **w.** of false teachers. 2 Pt.2:2
Man walks in his own **w.** Acts 14:16
Misery is in the **w.** of man. Ro.3:16

WAY, THE
Discussed. Acts 9:2
Disturbed a city. Acts 19:21-41
Identified. As Jesus Christ. Verses. List of. Jn.14:6

WAYSIDE--PATH
Some sit by the **w.** Mt.13:4, 19

WEAK - WEAKNESS (See POWER)
Borne by Jesus. Mt.8:16-17
Christ & man's **w.**
Christ bore our **w.** Mt.8:17
Christ healed the **w.** of people. Lk.5:15; 7:21; 8:2; 13:11-13; Jn.5:5-9
Christ is touched with the feelings of our **w.** Heb.4:15-16
Deliverance from.
By Christ. 2 Cor.13:4
His love. Ro.8:35-39, esp. 37
His power. 2 Cor.12:9-10
By faith. Ro.4:19-20; Heb.11:7; 11:8-10; 11:11-12; 11:17-19; 11:23-29; 11:30-40
By standing fast & proving ourselves through the most severe trials. 2 Cor.6:1-10
Duty.
Are not to be **w.** in faith, but to believe God. Ro.4:19-20
Must not be a stumbling block & make others **w.** Ro.14:21
Must realize & acknowledge our **w.** 1 Cor.4:10
Not to despise the **w.** in others. Gal.5:14-15
To bear the infirmities of the **w.** Ro.15:1
To bear the **w.** of the weak. Ro.15:1, cp. Gal.6:1-2
To come boldly to Jesus for help with our **w.** Heb.4:15-16
To glory in our **w.** 2 Cor.11:30; 12:5; 12:7-10
To identify with the **w.** in order to reach them. 1 Cor.9:22; 2 Cor.11:29
To preach the gospel despite **w.** & sickness. Gal.4:13-14
To rejoice in **w.** 2 Cor.12:7-10
To support the **w.** 1 Th.5:14
To take medicine for our **w.** 1 Tim.5:23

Fact.
All men, including priests & ministers, have **w.** & weaknesses & sin. Heb.5:2; 7:28
The Holy Spirit helps our **w.** in prayer. Ro.8:26
Fact. Man is **w.**
He cannot save himself. Ro.5:6-7
Some are misused by men for gain. Lk.20:45-47; Acts 16:16-24
Things that are **w.**
Rituals & ceremonies. Gal.4:9
Some believers. Ro.14:1-2
Some bodies. 2 Cor.10:10
Some consciences. 1 Cor.8:7, 10, 12
The law. Ro.8:3
Those whom God chooses. 1 Cor.1:27

WEALTHY, THE--WEALTH (See RICH - RICHES)
Discussed. Jas.1:9-11
How a rich man enters heaven. Mt.19:16-22
The conditions for seeking power & **w.** Mt.18:1-4
The danger of riches. Mt.19:23-26
The Parable of the Rich Fool. The man of wealth. Lk.12:13-21
The passion for **w.** 1 Tim.6:6-10
The reward for believers. Mt.19:27-30
The Rich Man & Lazarus. The self-indulgent vs. the man of faith. Lk.16:19-31
The root of all evil. 1 Tim.6:10
The secret to contentment. 1 Tim.6:6-10
Duty.
Must be totally committed to helping the needy. Acts 4:32
Must be used to meet needs. Lk.18:18-23
Must fear death even if **w.** Lk.12:20
Must give all beyond necessities to meet the needs of the world. Acts 4:32
Must give all one is & *has*. Lk.14:28-33
Must repent of hoarding. Acts 4:34-37
Must trust God, not money. Lk.21:2
Not to lay up treasures upon earth. Mt.6:19
Not to trust in **w.**, but in the living God. 1 Tim.6:17
Fact.
A person brought nothing into this world & carries nothing out. 1 Tim.6:7
A rich man can know God. Jas.1:9-10
Rich men tend to trust in riches. Mk.10:24
The **w.** will die. Lk.12:20
W. is determined by God. Lk.16:12
Judgment of.
Discussed. Lk.6:24-26; 12:20-21
How the **w.** are to be judged. Mk.10:27
Why the **w.** shall be judged so severely. Lk.16:19-21
Meaning. Mk.10:23
Misunderstanding of - Misconceptions.
One of three great **m.** Lk.16:14-15
Popular view of. Mk.10:26
Thought to be a sign of God's blessings. Mt.19:25; Mk.10:26; Lk.16:14-15
Purpose for **w.** To help others. Lk.16:9

Sin of.
Discussed. Lk.16:19-21
Using weak persons for one's own
ends & urges. Acts 16:16-17;
Jas.5:4-6
Verses. List of. Lk.6:24-26; 8:11-15;
12:15;12:20-21
View of.
Christian's perspective of.
Jas.1:7-11
Jewish view. Mk.10:26
Vs. true spiritual **w.** Lk.12:31-34
Warning - Danger of.
Can lead one to trust in **w.** instead of
God. Lk.12:15-19
Deceives. Four ways. Mt.13:7, 22
Discussed. Mt.19:23-26;
Mk.10:23-27
Greed - selfishness. Lk.12:13-21
Hoarding condemns one. Mt.19:21-22
Is difficult to handle. Lk.18:18-30
Is not a permanent possession. Some-
one else gets it. Lk.12:20-21
Leads men into many temptations &
drowns them in destruction & perdi-
tion. 1 Tim.6:9-10
Leads to a barren & unfruitful life.
Mk.4:19
Will be a witness against one in the
day of judgment. Jas.5:3
Will most likely keep one out of God's
kingdom. Mk.10:17-22; 10:23-27;
10:28
Will most likely lead one to reject
Christ. Lk.18:18-30

WEARY - WEARINESS
Conquered - Overcome by.
Being steadfast in good works & not
fainting. Gal.6:9
Considering the endurance of Christ.
Heb.12:1-4, esp. 3
The rest of Christ. Mt.11:28-30
Discussed. Mt.11:28-30
Verses. List of. Jn.5:2-4

WEDDING
Ceremony.
Honored by Christ. Jn.2:1-2
Jewish **w.** Discussed. Jn.2:1-2

WEDDING FEAST OF CHRIST
God's great invitation to. Mt.22:1-14
The garment of righteousness is essential
to attend. Mt.22:11-14

WEEDS
Meaning. Parable of the Wheat & the **T.**
Why evil exists. Mt.13:24-30

WEEPING (See REMORSE)
Caused by.
Failure & sin. Mk.14:66-72, esp. 72
Worldliness, laughing it up in the
world. Lk.6:24-26, esp. 25
Meaning. Mt.8:12; Lk.13:28
Will be **w.** & gnashing of teeth in judg-
ment. Mt.8:12; Lk.13:28

WEIGHT (See EVERYTHING THAT HINDERS)

WELCOME - WELCOMING
Duty.
Not to **w.** false teachers. 2 Jn.9-11
Not to **w.** the grace of God in vain.
2 Cor.6:1
Not to touch any unclean thing & God
will **w.** one. 2 Cor.6:17-18
To be faithful in feeding the people of
God & one shall **w.** a crown of glory.
1 Pt.5:2-4
To be open & receptive. Acts 17:11
To do the will of God that one might
w. the promise. Heb.10:36
To endure temptation that one may **w.**
the promise of life. Jas.1:12
To humbly **w.** the Word which is able
to save one's soul. Jas.1:21
To keep God's commandments so that
we can **w.** the answers to our pray-
ers. 1 Jn.3:22
To **w.** a spiritual inheritance. Acts
26:18
To **w.** Christ Jesus the Lord. Col.2:6
To **w.** forgiveness of sins. Acts 10:43;
26:18
To **w.** one another even as Christ re-
ceived us. Ro.15:7
To **w.** one's reward. Through diligent
labor. 1 Cor.3:8; 3:13-15; 2 Jn.8
To **w.** others. Lk.9:49-50
To **w.** the answer to prayer. Through
asking, believing, & living an obedi-
ent life. Mt.21:22; Mk.11:24;
Jn.16:24; 1 Jn.3:22
To **w.** the Holy Spirit. Through faith &
baptism. Acts 2:38
To **w.** the Word of God & bring forth
fruit for God. Mk.4:20
To **w.** the Word of God which is able
to save our soul. Jas.1:21
To **w.** those weak in the faith. Ro.14:1
To watch & examine ourselves that we
w. a full reward. 2 Jn.8
Facts.
A doubleminded person shall not **w.**
anything of the Lord. Jas.1:5-8, esp. 7
A person can **w.** nothing unless it is
given by God. Jn.3:27; 1 Cor.4:7
A person prays & asks & does not **w.**
because he asks amiss; he asks to
consume it upon his lusts. Jas.4:2-3
Believers **w.** power after the Holy
Spirit is come upon them. Acts 1:8
Believers who forsake all for Christ
shall **w.** a hundredfold from God.
Mt.19:28-29; Mk.10:29-30
Christ is coming again to **w.** all believ-
ers to Himself. Jn.14:2-3
Faithful believers shall **w.** the reward
of the inheritance. Col.3:23-24
False teachers shall **w.** the reward of
their unrighteousness. 2 Pt.2:13
God sent His Son to redeem us that we
might **w.** the adoption of sons.
Gal.4:3-5
Hypocritical religionists shall **w.** the
greater damnation. Mt.23:14;
Mk.12:40; Lk.20:49
In the day of judgment everyone shall
w. the things done in his body,
whether good or bad.
2 Cor.5:10

It is more blessed to give than to **w.**
Acts 20:35
The heavens have **w.** Christ until the
restoration of all things. Acts 3:19-21
The Lord alone is worthy to **w.** all
power, glory & honor. Rev.4:11;
5:12
The world cannot **w.** the Holy Spirit of
God. Jn.14:16-17
Those who do wrong shall **w.** for the
wrong they have done, & there is no
respect of persons with God. Col.3:25
Those who **w.** God's ministers &
people shall receive an equal reward
with them. Mt.10:40-42
Unbelievers **w.** more & more enslave-
ment to sin. Ro.1:26-27
Whatever good thing a person does, the
same shall be **w.** of the Lord.
Eph.6:8
Wrong-doers shall **w.** for the wrong
they have done. Col.3:24-25
Meaning. Ro.15:7-12
Reward for. Discussed. Mt.10:40-42

WHEAT & WEEDS
Parable of the **w.** & the tares. Mt.13:24-30;
13:36-43
Symbol - Picture of.
Believers. Will be gathered in by
Christ, but the chaff will be burned.
Mt.3:11-12; 13:30; Lk.3:17
Christ. His death. Jn.12:24

WHISPERERS (See GOSSIPS)

WHOEVER - WHOSOEVER
The w., the persons who displease God.
The **w.** of anger. Mt.5:22
The **w.** of denial. 1 Jn.2:23
The **w.** of false teaching. Gal.5:10-12,
esp. 10; 2 Jn.9-11
The **w.** of hate. 1 Jn.3:15
The **w.** of judging others. Ro.2:1
The **w.** of sin. Jn.8:34
The **w.** of transgression. 1 Jn.3:4;
2 Jn.9
The **w.** of unrighteousness. 1 Jn.3:10
The **w.** of unworthiness. 1 Cor.11:27
The w., the persons who please God.
The **w.** of belief. 1 Jn.5:1
The **w.** of blessing. Mt.11:6
The **w.** of confession. Lk.12:8
The **w.** of forgiveness. Acts 10:43
The **w.** of labor. Lk.8:18
The **w.** of thirst. Jn.4:13-14;
Rev.22:17
The **w.** of witnessing. Jn.20:23

WHOLE - WHOLENESS (See HEAL)
Meaning.
Being made **w.** Lk.17:15-19; Acts 4:9
Of both soul & body. Mt.14:36; Acts
3:16
Source of wholeness.
Christ. The name of the risen Lord.
Acts 4:9-10
Faith. Mk.10:51-52

WHOREMONGER (See ADULTERY)

WICKED - WICKEDNESS (See **IM-MORAL PERSON; LOST; MALICE; UNSAVED**)

Behavior of - Error.
    Fall from their stedfastness. 2 Pt.3:17
    Hypocrisy. Mt.22:15-18, esp. 18; Acts 8:18-24, esp. 22
    Immoral, unprincipled behavior. 2 Pt.2:7
    Sin & take pleasure in those who sin. Ro.1:32
    Twist the Scriptures. 2 Pt.3:16-17
Deliverance from.
    By Christ & His righteous life. There was no **w**. whatsoever in Christ. Jn.7:18
    By Christ, His redemption. Tit.2:14
    By God, His mercy & promise not to remember our sins & **w**. any more. Heb.8:12
    God cleanses us from all **w**. if we confess our sins. 1 Jn.1:9
    God is not **w**. to forget our work & labor of love. Heb.6:10
    God will be merciful to a man's **w**. & forgive his sins. Heb.8:12
Described as.
    A sin of omission. Lk.19:15-23
    Being short of God's glory. Mt.18:32-34
    Sin. All **w**. is sin. 1 Jn.5:17-18
Duty.
    Are not to be yoked, not to have fellowship with **w**. 2 Cor.6:14
    Are not to yield our body members to **w**. Ro.6:13
    Not to rejoice in **w**. 1 Cor.13:6
    To depart from **w**. 2 Tim.2:19
    To rebuke those who do **w**. 2 Pt.2:16
Fact.
    False teachers love the wages of **u**. 2 Pt.2:15
    Men are filled with all **u**. Ro.1:29
    Unbelievers are deceived by **u**. 2 Th.2:10
Facts about - Traits.
    Abounds & causes love to become cold. Mt.24:12
    Enslaves & binds a person. Acts 8:23; Ro.6:19
    Is at work in the world now. 2 Th.2:7
    Is hated by Christ. Heb.1:9
    Is not of love. 1 Cor.13:4-7, esp. 6
    The tongue is a world of **w**. Jas.3:6
    Will be a trait of the end time. Mt.24:12
Judgment of those who do wickedness (See **JUDGMENT; PUNISHMENT**)
    Are worthy of death. Ro.1:28-32, esp. 29, 32
    Excluded from God's kingdom. Gal.5:19-21
    Shall be put away from Christ. Mt.7:21-23
    Shall be put out of Christ's kingdom & cast into a furnace of fire. Mt.13:41-42
Meaning. Mk.7:22, 23; 24:12; Ro.1:18, 29; 2:8
Source of. The heart within man. Mt. 23.28; Mk.7:20-23, esp. 22
Warning.
    False teachers shall receive the reward for **w**. 2 Pt.2:15
    God is not **w**. if he takes vengeance. Ro.3:5
    God's case against. Ro.1:18-23
    Shall be damned. 2 Th.2:12
    Shall be judged, severely condemned. Ro.1:18; 2:8
    Shall not inherit the kingdom of God. 1 Cor.6:9
Who is **w**.

Evil spirits & forces. Eph.6:12
Hypocritical religionists. Lk.11:37-39
Immoral persons. 1 Cor.5:1, 13
Satan. Mt.13:19; Eph.6:16
The antichrist. 2 Th.2:8-9
The ungodly & unrighteous. Ro.1:29
The unsaved, those alienated from God. Col.1:21
The whole world. 1 Jn.5:19
This generation. Mt.12:43-45, esp. 45; 16;4
Those who crucified Christ. Acts 2:23
Unfaithful men. Mt.25:14-30, esp. 26-27; Lk.19:12-27, esp. 22-23
Unjust men. Mt.18:23-35, esp. 32-33
Unreasonable & **w**. men. 2 Th.3:2

WICKED HUSBANDMAN, PARABLE OF THE (See **WICKED TENANTS**)

Parable of.
    An overview of world history. Lk.20:9-18
    God & Israel. Mk.12:1-12
    Israel's rejection of Christ. Mt.21:33-46

WICKED TENANTS

Parable of.
    An overview of world history. Lk.20:9-18
    God & Israel. Mk.12:1-12
    Israel's rejection of Christ. Mt.21:33-46

WIDE GATE VS. THE NARROW GATE

Discussed. Mt.7:12-14

WIDOWS

And remarriage. 1 Cor.7:8-9; 7:39-40
Discussed. Treatment of. 1 Tim.5:3-16
Duty.
    To be cared for by children. 1 Tim.5:3-8; 5:16
    To be cared for by the church. Acts 6:1
    To be faithful to God. Lk.2:36
    To honor **w**. that are true widows. 1 Tim.5:3
Fact.
    Christ is touched by the plight of the **w**. Lk.7:12-13;
    True religion is visiting **w**. & fatherless children. Jas.1:27
Sins against the **w**.
    Deceived & cheated by some. Mk.12:40
    Misused for gain. Lk.20:45-47; Acts 16:16-24
Traits. Are often gossipers, idle, busybodies. 1 Tim.5:13

WIDOW'S MITE (See **WIDOW'S OFFERING**)

The question of giving. Lk.21:1-4

WIDOW'S OFFERING

Real giving. Mk.12:41-44
The question of giving. Lk.21:1-4

WIDOW'S SON

Raised from the dead. Great compassion & power. Lk.7:11-17

WIFE - WIVES (See **WOMEN**)

Described as. Weaker vessel. 1 Pt.3:7
Discussed. Eph.5:22-24; Col.3:18; Tit.2:4-5
Dress of. Discussed. 1 Pt.3:3; 3:4-6
Duty.

Fivefold. 1 Pt.3:1-6
Not to commit adultery. Heb.13:4, cp. Mt.5:28
Not to deprive her husband--physically. 1 Cor.7:4-6; Heb.13:4
Of the deacon's **w**. Discussed. 1 Tim.3:11
To be chaste, pure. Tit.2:5
To be discreet, temperate & controlled. Tit.2:5
To be keeper of her home. Tit.2:5, cp. 1 Tim.5:13
To learn & control her tongue. 1 Tim.2:11-12
To love her children. Tit.2:4
To love her husband. Tit.2:4
To obey her husband. 1 Pt.3:5-6
To reverence her husband. Eph.5:33
To submit to her own husband. Eph.5:22; Col.3:18-21

WILD LIVING

Defined. Lk.15:12-13
Duty. Not to walk in **r**., drunkenness & immorality. Ro.13:13

WILDERNESS

Man wandering about in the **w**. of life. Mt.18:11

WILES (See **SCHEMES**)

WILL - WILLS

Four **w**. struggle for man. Mt.6:10
Meaning. Mt.16:24
Of Christ.
    Distinct, separate from God. Jn.6:38
    Subjection of. Absolute submission. Mk.14:41-42
    Supreme subjection to God. Jn.10:11; 10:17-18; 12:27-30;14:30-31; 15:9; 16:11
Of God. (See **WILL OF GOD**)
Of man. (See **PREDESTINATION**)
    Deliberately **w**. to reject Christ. Reason. Jn.5:40-41; 5:42
    Vs. predestination. Discussed. Jn.12:39-41
    W. to distort the truth. 2 Pt.3:5-7

WILL, LAST WILL & TESTAMENT

Discussed. Heb.8:6-13; 9:15-22
Fact.
    Are sometimes misused by religionists. Mk.7:11
    Cannot be changed or annulled. Gal.3:15

WILL OF GOD

Duty - Essential.
    Must do the **w**. of God to be a brother of Christ. Mk.3:35
    To abstain from fornication, immorality. This is the **w**. of God. 1 Th.4:3
    To do the **w**. of God from the heart. Eph.6:6
    To entrust others to the **w**. of God. Acts 21:14
    To give thanks in everything. This is the **w**. of God. 1 Th.5:18
    To journey by the **w**. of God. Ro.1:10; 15:32
    To live the rest of one's life after the **w**. of God, not after the lusts of the flesh. 1 Pt.4:2
    To prove the perfect **w**. of God. Ro.12:2

To silence one's critics by doing good. This is the **w.** of God. 1 Pt.2:15

To stand complete in all the **w.** of God. Col.4:12

Fact.

Christ makes intercession for believers by the **w.** of God. Ro.8:27

Christ sacrificed Himself to do the **w.** of God perfectly. Mt.26:42

It is sometimes God's **w.** for believers to suffer persecution. 1 Pt.3:17; 4:19

Power of God's **w.**

To answer prayers made according to His **w.** 1 Jn.5:14-15

To bring about His **w.** upon earth. Mt.6:10; Lk.11:2

To call & set people apart for service. 1 Cor.1:1; 2 Cor.1:1; Eph.1:1; Col.1:1; 2 Tim.1:1

To cause a person to be born again & to become a child of God. Jn.1:12-13

To deliver us from this present evil world. Gal.1:4

To determine whether a person lives or dies. Jas.4:13-15

To give a spiritual birth to a person by the Word of God. Jas.1:18

To make a person live forever. 1 Jn.2:17

To predestinate. Ro.8:28-30

To reveal that the claims of Christ are true, that he is of God. Jn.7:17

To reward those who endure in doing the **w.** of God. Heb.10:36

To sanctify believers through the offering of the body of Christ. Heb.10:10

To save man. 1 Tim.2:4; 2 Pt.3:9

To secure the believer & to give him everlasting life. Jn.6:39-40

WINE

Duty.

Aged women are not to be addicted to **w.** Tit.2:3

Deacons are not to be addicted to **w.** 1 Tim.3:8

Ministers are not to be addicted to **w.** 1 Tim.3:3; Tit.1:7

No one is to be drunk with wine. Eph.5:18

Fact.

Jesus Christ was charged with being a gluttonous man, a winebibber, & a friend of sinners. Mt.11:19

Jesus provided **w.** for a wedding. Jn.2:1-11; Jn.4:46

John the Baptist never drank **w.** Lk.7:33

The apostles were charged with being drunk with **w.** at Pentecost. Acts 2:13

The **w.** is used as a picture of God's wrath. Rev.14;10-11, cp. 14:18-19

Parable. New wine put in old wine skins. Old vs. new life. Mk.2:22

Uses of wine.

Used as a drug. Mk.15:23

Used as a medicine. Lk.10:34; 1 Tim.5:23

Used at social functions. Jn.2:1-11

Used to symbolize Christ's death in the Passover & in the Lord's Supper. Lk.22:7; 22:15-20

WINESKINS

Parable. New wine put in old **ws.** Old vs. new life. Mk.2:22

WISDOM

Discussed. Difference between **w.** & knowledge. Eph.1:17-18

Duty.

To be wise by declaring that Jesus Christ is of God. Lk.7:35, cp. 33-34

To build one's life upon the rock just as any wise person would do. Mt.7:24-27

To know that it is the holy Scriptures that makes one wise unto salvation. 2 Tim.3:15

To pray for **w.** Eph.1:17; Col.1:9; Jas.1:5

To seek **w.** despite all difficulties. Lk.11:30-32

To seek **w.** diligently. Mt.12:42; Eph.1:17-18

To show that one is wise by good behavior. Jas.3:13-18, esp. 13

To teach every man in all **w.** Col.1:28

Error - Mistake of. Thinking that one can be secure by dedicating oneself to the **w.** of this world. Lk.16:1-7, cp. 1 Cor.1:17-25, 26-31; 2:6-13

Meaning. Eph.1:8; Col.1:9; 2:3; Jas.1:5-8; 3:13-18; 3:13

Of God. (See **KNOWLEDGE**, Of God)

Discussed. 1 Cor.2:6-13

Embodied His wisdom in Christ. 1 Cor.1:24

Is infinite, unsearchable. Ro.11:33

Is revealed to the angelic beings through God's plan of salvation for man. Eph.3:10-12

Knows all His works. Acts 15:18

Vs. the wisdom of the world. 1 Cor.1:17-25, 26-31; 2:6-13

What God's **w.** is. Eight things. Jas.3:17-18

Of Jesus Christ.

Is the very embodiment of God's wisdom. 1 Cor.1:24

Possessed so much **w.** as a man that He astounded men. Mt.13:54

Possesses all the treasures of wisdom & knowledge. Col.2:3

Was filled with wisdom as a child. Lk.2:40

Of man.

Dedication of man to **w.** Is an example for believers. Lk.16:8-13

Described. As wise in his own eyes. Self-sufficient. Mt.11:25-27; 11:25

Discussed. 1 Cor.2:6-13; 3:18-20

Error - Weakness of.

Counts the cross as foolishness. 1 Cor.1:17-25

Is blinded to the truth. Mt.11:25-27; 11:25

Is earthly, sensual, & devilish. Jas.3:15

Is false **w.** Jas.3:14-16

Uses worldly **w.** to deny God. Ro.1:21-23

Errors - Failures of.

Cannot save man. 1 Cor.2:5; 2:6; 2:7-9; Col.2:8. Cp. Ro.1:18-32

Is sometimes based upon false beliefs. Mk.2:6-12

Is used by men to escape the truth. Mk.11:29-33

Is destroyed by God & the cross. Three ways. 1 Cor.1:19-20

Is empty & foolish with God. 1 Cor.3:19

Is to be renounced. 1 Cor.3:18-20

Truth is hid from man. Lk.10:21

Vs. the wisdom of God & the cross. 1 Cor.1:17-25

Vs. true **w.** Jas.3:13-18

Essential.

In life. Must do the only reasonable thing: commit one's body & service as a living sacrifice to God. Ro.12:1-2

In preaching & witnessing. Must be sound, logical. Acts 18:4, 19; 24:25, cp. Acts 17:2

Meaning. Jas.3:17-18

Proves. God's existence. Ro.1:19

Source.

Christ. Lk.21:15

Discussed. Jas.1:5-8

God. Eph.1:17; Jas.1:5

The Holy Spirit. 1 Cor.12:8

True **w.**

Discussed. Jas.3:17-18

Vs. false **w.** Jas.3:13-18

Value & Preciousness of. Wisdom bears a full & abundant life. Eight precious things. Jas.3:17-18

WISDOM, MESSAGE OF

Gift of. Discussed. 1 Cor.12:8-10

WISE MEN (See **MAGI**)

Discussed. Mt.2:1

Worshipped Jesus as King. Mt.2:1-11

WISE VS. FOOLISH BUILDER

Parable of. Describes life. Mt.7:24-27

WITCHCRAFT (See **ASTROLOGY; SOOTHSAYER; SORCERY; SUPERSTITION**)

Discussed. Acts 16:16-17

Meaning. Gal.5:19-21

WITHOUT FAULT

Meaning. Jude 24-25

WITHOUT STRENGTH (See **POWERLESS**)

WITNESS - WITNESSES OF MAN (See **LYING**)

Duty.

Not to bear false **w.** Mt.19:18; Ro.13:9

Not to receive a charge against a person unless there are two or more **w.** 1 Tim.5:19

To present two or three **w.** to one's character or position. 2 Cor.13:1

To take one or two **w.** in seeking reconciliation with a person. Mt.18:15-17

Example of.

Soldiers who were bribed to bear false **w.** about Christ's resurrection. Mt.28:15

The religionists against Paul. Acts 25:7-8

The religionists who bore false **w.** against Stephen. Acts 6:9-15

The religionists who sought false **w.** against Jesus to put Him to death. Mt.26:59-60; Mk.14:53-64

Fact. The law of Moses required two or three **w.** Heb.10:28

WITNESSES, CLOUD OF

Meaning. Heb.12:1

WITNESSES OF REVELATION

Discussed. Rev.11:3-13

WITNESSING TO GOD & CHRIST
Call to. (See **WITNESSING TO CHRIST**, Essential)
    Discussed. Mt.4:18-20
    Must be saved to **w**. Mk.1:25
Challenge.
    It is impossible not to **w**. if one is truly saved. Jn.15:26-27
    Laborers are needed. The harvest is plentiful. Mt.9:37-38
    Neglected. Believers must not be cloistered in the church. Mt.5:13; 5:14
    One must know about Christ before one can be saved. Mt.14:35
    One must see fields of souls ripe for harvest. Jn.4:35
    Preparation for **w**. Threefold. Mt.16:20
    Silence fails; therefore, we must **w**. Jn.12:42-43
    The Pharisees were strong in witnessing to their religion. How much more should believers be. Mt.23:15
Commission.
    Great **C**. Mt.28:16-20; Mk.16:15; Jn.20:19-23
    Sent forth. Mt.10:5-15
    To be witnesses is the very reason why believers are saved. Jn.15:16; Acts 10:39-43, esp. 41-42
    To go as Jesus went. Jn.20:21
    To minister. Mt.20:27-28
    To **w**. to the death & resurrection of Christ. Jn.21:24
Discussed.
    Four Greek words for **w**. Acts 11:19-30
    How men receive the gospel. Mt.13:1-9
    Lessons for **w**. Acts 1:8
    Marks of. Ph.1:12-20
    The Word of God & of John the Apostle. 1 Jn.5:9-15
    The Word of heaven & earth. 1 Jn.5:6-8
Duty.
    Are obligated, indebted to **w**. Ro.1:14-15
    Must not be ashamed to **w**. 2 Tim.1:8; 1:8-10
    Must **w**. because of the importance of the individual to God. Acts 8:26-40
    Must **w**. because the blood of all the lost is upon our hands. Ro.9:1-3
    Must **w**. because there is a great cloud of heavenly believers watching our performance. Heb.12:1
    Not to be ashamed of our Lord. 2 Tim.1:8
    Not to fear **w**. for the Lord is with us. Acts 18:9-10
    To answer & defend the hope of salvation. 1 Pt.13:15
    To be a mature **w**. Ph.1:12-20
    To be diligent & zealous in **w**. Lk.15:4; Ro.10:1-3
    To be ready to **w**.--always. 1 Pt.13:15
    To bear **w**. of Christ. Jn.15:27
    To confess Christ, not deny Him. Mt.10:32-33
    To evaluate one's efforts in **w**. Lk.9:10
    To hold out the Word of life. Ph.2:16
    To live a life that will win people to Christ. 1 Pt.2:11
    To obey God & bear **w**. to His Son. Acts 16:6-11
    To prepare to **w**. 1 Pt.3:15
    To proclaim Christ. 1 Tim.3:16

To share what one has seen & heard. Acts 4:19-20
To sow the seed, the Word of God. Mk.4:1-20; 4:26
To use trials for **w**. Acts 28:4-9
To **w**. & not cloister together. Acts 1:8
To **w**. after one's conversion. Jn.4:28-29
To **w**. in meekness & quietness. Lk.13:21
To **w**. in these places.
    To go into the highways & hedges. Lk.14:21-24
    To go to one's hometown. Lk.8:38-39
    To **w**. in large cities. Strategy for. Acts 28:16-31
    To **w**. in the home. Mt.9:4-7; 9:10-11
    To **w**. in the temple, the church. Acts 5:20
    To **w**. in three places. Mt.5:14-15
    To **w**. to one's neighbors & city. Jn.4:28-29
    To **w**. to one's own church. Acts 11:25-26; 19:10
    To **w**. to the world. Mt.5:14; Jn.17:17-19; Acts 1:8
    To **w**. wherever one's feet are. Eph.6:14-17
To **w**. to God's grace. Tit.2:11-15, esp. 15
To **w**. to the great things God has done for us. Mk.5:18-19
To **w**. to these people.
    To give an answer to every man. 1 Pt.3:15
    To go to sinners. Mk.2:16-17
    To go to the lost until they are found. Lk.15:1-7; 15:8-10
    To go to the rejected. Mk.2:16-17
    To reach our families & friends for Christ. Gal.1:18-20; 1:21
    To reach out to false teachers. Jude 22-23
    To reclaim doubters & the lost. Jude 22-23
    To **w**. to all men--to bear **w**. to what one has seen & heard. Acts 22:14-15
    To **w**. to all who look for redemption. Lk.2:38
    To **w**. to government officials. Ph.1:13; 4:22
    To **w**. to individuals. Acts 8:26-40
    To **w**. to one's brother. Jn.1:35-42
    To **w**. to one's close friend. Jn.1:43-45
    To **w**. to one's family first. Mt.9:4-7; 10:5-6; Lk.8:38-39
    To **w**. to one's friends. Mt.9:10-11; Lk.5:27-29
    To **w**. to one's home & family. Jn.4:53-54
    To **w**. to one's neighbors & city. Jn.4:28-29
    To **w**. to the most unclean. Mk.1:44
    To **w**. to the world. Mt.5:14; Jn.17:17-19; Acts 1:8
To win souls. Reason. 1 Th.2:19-20
Essential.
    Being with Jesus. Acts 4:13-14
    Boldness & power. Source of. Acts 4:13-14
    Faith in Christ. 2 Cor.4:13
    Fourfold. Acts 9:31
    Must be compelled to **w**. Acts 4:20
    Must be led by the Holy Spirit. Acts 8:29
    Must live an honest life. 1 Pt.2:11

Must refuse to be silenced, to compromise. Acts 4:19-20
Example.
    A new convert. People prepared for the message. Mk.8:1-2
    A secret disciple. Stirred to stand by the cross. Lk.23:50-56
    Anna. After seeing God's redemption. Lk.2:38
    First **w**. to Judaea & Samaria. Laymen scattered. Acts 8:1-9:31 Peter. Acts 9:32-35; 9:36-43
    Lay believers. How God uses laymen. Acts 8:1-4
    Men going out & bringing others. Cleansing the most defiled. Mt.14:35
    Of Matthew. Right after his conversion. Mk.2:15
    Paul's **w**.
        A dynamic example in prison. Ph.1:12-19
        His personal method. Acts 20:19-27; Ro.10:1-3
        Immediately upon his conversion. Acts 9:19-22, 29
    Philip to the Ethiopian eunuch. A study of **w**. Acts 8:26-40
    Seventy sent forth. Great purpose. Lk.10:1-16
    The supreme example of **w**. Mt.18:11-14
    W. in one's church for one whole year. Acts 11:25-26
    W. in one's church for two whole years. Acts 19:10
How to go - Method.
    As an evangelist. 2 Tim.4:1-5
    Beginning where a person is. Mk.8:23
    By one's life. Col.4:5
    By one's words & speech. Col.4:5
    Discussed. Lk.10:1-16; Acts 14:1
    Following the rules that govern **w**. Mt.10:5-15
    If one's **w**. is rejected, to turn to willing hearers. Acts 13:46-52; 14:6-7
    Marking out, following strong examples. Ph.3:17-19
    Not falling away because of Christ. Lk.7:23; 9:26
    Preaching the Word. 2 Tim.4:1-5
    Proclaiming Jesus to be the Messiah. Jn.4:31-42
    Sharing one's testimony. Mk.5:18-20; Lk.8:38-39
    Shrewd as snakes; innocent as doves. Mt.10:16
    To be centered in the homes. Lk.9:4; 10:5-6
    Two by two. Reasons. Mk.6:7
    Unashamed. 2 Tim.1:6-12
Meaning. Lk.8:1
Power to **w**.
    Discussed. Mk.16:17-18
    Equipped for **w**. by the Holy Spirit & power. Lk.24:44-49; Jn.15:26-27; 16:7-11; Acts 1:8
    Promised. Lk.24:44-49; Jn.15:26-27; 16:7-11; Acts 1:8
    Source.
        God's grace. Acts 4:33
        God's presence bearing **w**. through signs & miracles. Heb.2:3-4
        The Holy Spirit. Acts 1:8
Predicted. The whole world will be evangelized. Mk.13:10
Problems confronting **w**.

WORD OF CHRIST

Facts about.
 Are gracious. Lk.4:22
 Are powerful. Lk.4:32
 Are spirit & life. Jn.6:63
 Are the Words of eternal life. Jn.6:68
 Are the Words of God. Jn.17:8
 Shall judge men in the last day.
  Jn.12:48
 Shall not pass away. Mk.13:31;
  Lk.21:33
 Were spoken as no man had ever spoken before. Jn.7:46
 Were the **W**. of God. Jn.14:24
Promises to the person who keeps the **W**.
 of Christ.
 Shall never die. Jn.8:51
 Shall receive the abiding presence & care of God. Jn.14:23
 Shall receive the Holy Spirit of God.
  Jn.14:15-16
 Will have God revealed to him.
  Jn.17:6
 Will have the assurance that one knows God. 1 Jn.2:3
 Will receive an open door for evangelism & ministry. Rev.3:8
 Will receive answers to his prayers.
  Jn.15:7

WORD OF GOD (See BIBLE - SCRIPTURE; TRUTH)

Adding to - Abuse of.
 Adding to & taking away from the **W**.
  Rev.22:18-19
 Bias against. By humanists. Acts
  17:11
 Corrupted by religionists. Lk.13:14
 Corrupted. In two ways. Mt.12:1-2;
  2 Cor.2:17
 Distorting. 2 Pt.3:16
 Handling deceitfully. 2 Cor.4:2
 Perverting & twisting. Gal.1:6-7
 Rejecting the **W**. & following tradition. Mk.7:9-13
 Turning people to one's own ideas & positions. Lk.11:52
 Twisting & corrupting. Lk.11:52;
  2 Cor.2:17
Described as.
 A double-edged sword in Christ's mouth. Rev.2:12
 How the term "the Word" is used in Scripture. Nineteen ways. Mk.4:33
 Instructions for building. Mt.7:24-27
 Seed. Mt.13:1-9, cp. 13:18-23
 Spirit & life. Jn.6:63
 The sword of the Spirit. Eph.6:17
 The truth. Jn.17:17; 2 Jn.1-2
 The Word of God. Jn.14:24;
  1 Th.2:13
 The word of reconciliation.
  2 Cor.5:19
 The words of Christ. Jn.14:24;
  Col.3:16
Discussed. 1 Th.2:1-13; 1 Pt.1:22-25;
 2:1-3
 Elementary principles of. Heb.6:1-2
 Milk of. Heb.5:12; 6:1-2
 Must be carried forth by men.
  1 Th.2:1-13
 Not the word of men, but of God.
  1 Th.2:13
 Power of. Heb.4:12
 To dwell, make a home in the heart.
  Col.3:16

Duty.
 A warning against adding to & taking away from the **W**. Rev.22:18-19
 Must allow the **W**. to abide within.
  Jn.5:38
 Must depend upon the Holy Spirit to understand the **W**. Verses. List of.
  Jn.12:16
 Must hear the **W**. to be saved.
  Jn.10:4-5
 Not to be a spiritual babe, unskillful in the **W**. Heb.5:13
 Not to be lazy & lethargic in studying the **W**. Heb.5:11
 Not to be unskillful in using the **W**.
  Heb.5;13
 Not to fall away after tasting the **W**. of God. Heb.6:1-6, esp. 5-6
 Not to forsake Christ when persecution arises against the **W**. Mt.13:21;
  Mk.4:17
 Not to mishandle the **W**. 2 Cor.4:2
 Not to neglect the **W**. Heb.2:1
 Not to stumble at the **W**. 1 Pt.2:8
 To be willing to suffer martyrdom for the **W**. of God. Rev.6:9; 20:4
 To bear & heed the **W**. of exhortation.
  Heb.13:22
 To believe the **W**. Lk.1:45
 To crave the pure spiritual milk of the **W**. 1 Pt.2:1-3
 To desire the **W**. Mk.6:35-44; 8:1-2
 To desire, hunger for & study the **W**.
  1 Pt.2:1-3; Jude 20-21
 To digest & assimilate the **W**.
  Rev.10:8-11
 To endure persecution for the **W**.
  Rev.1:9
 To fulfill the **W**. of God. Col.1:25-29,
  esp. 25
 To glorify the **W**. of the Lord. Acts
  13:48; Jas.1:22
 To handle & teach the **W**. of God accurately. 2 Tim.2:15
 To have a vision of peoples' need for the **W**. Lk.5:1
 To hear & keep the **W**. Lk.11:27-28
 To hear the **W**. of Christ. Lk.9:35;
  Jas.1:19-21
 To hold fast to the **W**. Tit.1:9
 To hold forth the **W**. of life. Ph.2:16
 To keep God's **W**. Jn.17:6; 1 Jn.2:5;
  Rev.3:8
 To labor in the **W**. & doctrine.
  1 Tim.5:17
 To let the **W**. of Christ dwell in us.
  Col.3:16; 1 Jn.2:14
 To live by every **W**. of God. Lk.4:4
 To live righteously so the **W**. of God will not be blasphemed. Tit.2:5
 To make sure that what one claims & experiences agrees with the **W**. of God. Acts 15:13-15, esp. 15
 To memorize the Word of God.
  Col.3:16
 To not merely listen to the Word. Do what it says. Jas.1:22-25
 To obey & keep the **W**. Jas.1:22;
  Rev.3:8
 To place the **W**. before tradition.
  Mk.7:8; 7:9-12; 7:13
 To pray that the message of the Lord may spread rapidly & be honored.
  2 Th.3:1-2
 To preach the **W**. Acts 8:25; Ro.10:8,
  cp. 9-10; 2 Tim.4:2; Tit.1:3

 To press, seek to hear the **W**. of God.
  Lk.5:1; Acts 13:7, 44
 To proclaim the **W**. of God. Col.1:25
 To receive as God's **W**. 1 Th.2:13
 To receive the **W**. Acts 2:41; 11:1;
  1 Th.1:5-6
 To receive the **W**. with meekness.
  Jas.1:21
 To search the **W**. Acts 17:11
 To send the **W**.
  The door is opened to the Gentiles.
   Acts 10:1-33; 10:34-35; 10:36-48
  To the Gentiles first. Acts 10:34-35
 To sow the **W**. Mk.4:14
 To speak the **W**. of God boldly. Acts
  4:31
 To study & correctly handle the **W**.
  2 Tim.2:15
 To study--move on beyond the basic teachings of the **W**. & grow.
  Heb.5:11-6:3
 To teach the **W**. Acts 18:11
 To teach the **W**. to a child. 2 Tim.1:5;
  3:15
 To test preaching by the **W**. Acts
  17:11
Fact.
 Is not a fable. 2 Pt.1:16
 Man's heart craves God & His Word.
  1 Tim.6:4
Fulfilled. (See **PROPHECY**, Fulfilled)
Meaning.
 Is seventeen things. Mk.4:33
 Is truth. Jn.17:17-19
Milk of. Grows a believer. 1 Pt.2:2-3
Nature of.
 Cannot be bound. 2 Tim.2:9
 Endures forever. 1 Pt.1:23
 Is alive & powerful. Heb.4:12
 Is God's **W**. 1 Th.2:13
 Is imperishable. 1 Pt.1:23
 Is inspired. 2 Tim.3:16; 2 Pt.1:19-21
 Is of God, not of men. 1 Th.2:13
 Is taught to believers by the Holy Spirit. 1 Cor.2:13
 Is truth. An historical, orderly, accurate account. Lk.1:1-4; Jn.17:17
 Predicts the world's end. 2 Pt.3:1-8
 The great Book of Revelation. Is said to be the **W**. of God. Rev.1:1-3
 The message of preaching. Tit.1:2-3
Power of - Work of.
 Assures & secures the believer.
  Jn.6:37
 Breaks Satan's power. Mt.17:17-18
 Causes one to be born again. Jas.1:18;
  1 Pt.1:23
 Cleanses a person. Jn.15:3; Eph.5:26
 Convicts - pierces the heart. Heb.4:12;
  Tit.1:9
 Delivers from anxiety, pressure, & stress. Lk.10:38-42
 Destroyed the world in ages past.
  2 Pt.2:5
 Eleven stirring facts about. Rev.22:6-21
 Gives a knowledge of Christ.
  Jn.20:14-16; 2 Tim.3:15
 Grows & builds up believers. Acts
  20:32; 1 Pt.2:1-3
 Grows & matures people. Heb.5:11-6:2
 Imparts the Holy Spirit. Acts 10:44
 Proves salvation & the deity of Christ.
  2 Pt.1:19-21

Sanctifies the believer. Jn.17:17;
Eph.5:26
Shall never pass away. Mt.24:35
Stirs belief that Jesus is the Christ.
Jn.20:31; Acts 17:2-3; 18:28
To arouse & produce faith. Ro.10:17
To bless. Lk.11:28
To create a new man. 1 Pt.1:23
To create the world. Heb.11:3
To destroy the world. 2 Pt.3:5-7; 3:8-10
To free men. Jn.8:31-32
To give hope. Col.1:5
To increase & grow people. Acts 6:7;
12:24; 19:20; 20:28
To make one wise unto salvation.
2 Tim.3:15
To save. Is not bound. Acts 13:26;
2 Pt.2:9
Works effectively in all who believe.
1 Th.2:13
Privilege of. Great privilege to have ac-
cess to the W. Ro.3:1-2
Purpose of. Discussed. 2 Tim.3:16-17
Rejected - Unbelief in.
Leads to unbelief in Christ. Jn.5:45-46;
5:47; 8:37
Some seek for a symbolic, mystical
meaning in the W. Jn.18:19-24
Verses. List of. Jn.5:45-46; 8:37
Response to.
Different ways the W. is received.
Mt.13:1-9
False vs. true response. Lk.8:4-15
How men receive the W. Mk.4:1-20
Surety of.
Christ confirms the W. with signs.
Mk.16:20
Guaranteed. Lk.18:31
Never voided or broken. Ro.3:3-5; 9:6
Nothing can stop the W. & its work.
2 Tim.2:9
Will not return void. Is not bound.
Acts 4:2-4

WORDS (See **TONGUE**)
Duty.
Not to be ashamed of Christ & His **w.**
Mk.8:38; Lk.9:26
Not to preach the gospel with wisdom
of **w.** but in the Spirit & power.
1 Cor.1:17; 2:4; 2:13
Not to preach with flattering, flowery
w. 1 Th.2:3-6
Not to strive over **w.**, speculations &
arguments that do not profit a person.
2 Tim.2:14
Not to take away from the **w.** of
Revelation. Rev.22:18-19
To be nourished in the **w.** of faith &
doctrine. 1 Tim.4:6
To comfort one another with the **w.** of
the Lord's return. 1 Th.4:18, cp. 13-18
To consent to & teach the **W.** of
Christ. 1 Tim.6:3
To guard against being deceived with
vain, empty **w.** Eph.5:6
To guard against the fair **w.** of false
teachers. Ro.16:18
To hear the **w.** of the gospel. Acts
2:22-24
To hold fast sound & healthy teaching.
2 Tim.1:13
To long to hear the **w.** of the gospel.
Acts 13:42, cp. 38-42
To proclaim all the **w.** of the Christian
life. Acts 5:20

To remember the **w.** of the prophets &
the commandments of Christ.
2 Pt.3:2
To speak simple **w.** in church, words
easily understood. 1 Cor.14:9, 19
To turn away from those who reject
the **w.** of our witness. Mt.10:14
Facts.
Heaven is so wonderful that **w.** are in-
adequate to describe it. 2 Cor.12:4
The **w.** of a new heaven & earth are
true. 2 Pt.3:10-18; Rev.21:5, cp.
Rev.21:1-5
Idle. Meaning. Mt.12:36
Warning - Danger of.
Being ashamed of Christ & His **w.** de-
termine a man's destiny. Mk.8:38;
Lk.9:26
Discussed. 2 Tim.2:14-21
Exposes one's heart. Mt.12:34-35
If a person rejects Christ & His **w.**, he
shall be judged. Jn.12:47-50, esp.
47-48
Man's words determine his destiny.
Mt.12:31-37
Unbelief in the O.T. leads to unbelief
in Christ's **w.** Jn.5:46-47

WORK
Meaning. Until Jesus returns. Lk.19:13

WORK OF CHRIST (See **JESUS CHRIST**, Work of - Ministry)
Christ's works.
Christ completed the work God sent
Him to do. Jn.17:4
Christ did greater **w.** than any other
man. Jn.15:24
Christ was compelled to do the **w.** of
God. Jn.9:4
The very purpose of Christ was to do
God's will & to finish God's work.
Jn.4:34-38, esp. 34
The **w.** of Christ convict men.
Jn.15:24
The **w.** of Christ prove that He is the
Son of God. Jn.5:17-47; 5:36, cp.
Jn.10:25
The **w.** of Christ were empowered,
done by God Himself. Jn.14:10
Discussed. Mt.11:4-6
Duty.
To believe in Christ. If one believes,
he shall do the works of Christ &
even greater **w.** Jn.14:12
To believe in Christ because of His
works. Jn.14:10-11
To believe the **w.** of Christ. Jn.10:37-38
Fact.
Christ revealed & did the **W.** of God.
Jn.5:20; 5:36; 9:4
The **w.** of Christ stirred people to
praise God. Lk.19:37
The **w.** of Christ stirs people to wonder
who He is. Mk.6:14-17
Warning.
Christ is not able to do many **w.** where
questions & unbelief reign. Mt.13:58,
cp. 54-58; Mk.6:5-6, cp. 1-6
Failure to repent at the **w.** of Christ
will bring severe judgment.
Mt.11:20-24

WORK OF GOD (See **GOD**, Works Of)
Duty.
Must not destroy the **w.** of God in a
person's life by being a stumbling
block. Ro.14:20-21
To do the **w.** of God - believe on
Christ. Jn.6:29
To speak forth, bear witness to the **w.**
of God. Acts 2:11, cp. 1-13
To work & manifest the **w.** of God in
our lives. Jn.9:1-5
Fact.
Creation is the **w.** of God's hand.
Heb.1:10
God sent Christ to finish God's **w.**
Jn.4:34
God set man over the **w.** of His hand.
Heb.2:7
God showed Israel His **w.** for forty
years in the wilderness. Heb.3:9
God's great **w.** is the forgiveness of
sins through His Son, the Lord Jesus
Christ. Acts 13:38-41
God's **w.** are great & marvelous.
Rev.15:3
The great **w.** of God is to believe on
Christ whom God sent. Jn.6:28-29
Warning.
The night is coming when no man can
work the **w.** of God. Jn.9:4
Will finish His **w.** upon earth & make
it a short **w.** Ro.9:28
Will not be believed by men. Acts
13:41, cp. 38-41

WORK, PHYSICAL OR SECULAR (See **EMPLOYEE; EMPLOYER; EMPLOYMENT**)
Discussed. Col.3:22-4:1
Duty.
To do necessary **w.** Mt.12:5
To **w.** with one's one hands.
1 Th.4:11-12
Why God demands that we **w.** Rea-
sons. 1 Th.4:11-12

WORKING ALL THINGS OUT FOR GOOD (See **ASSURANCE; SECURITY**)
Fact. God works all things out for good to
those who love Him. Ro.8:28

WORKMAN
Discussed. Eph.6:5-8; 6:9

WORKS (See **DEEDS**)

WORKS, DEAD AND EVIL
Discussed. **W.** of the flesh. Gal.5:19-21,
cp. 16-21
Duty.
Are not to fellowship with the unfruit-
ful **w.** of darkness. Eph.5:11
Are to cast off the **w.** of darkness.
Ro.13:12
Fact.
A person is saved from wicked **w.** by
the death of Christ. Col.1:20-22
A person's **w.** expose his false profes-
sion. Shows that he truly denies God.
Tit.1:16
Evil & lawless **w.** disturb the souls of
believers. 2 Pt.2:8
W. of men are dead **w.**, unacceptable
to God. Heb.9:14

W. of the devil are destroyed by Christ. 1 Jn.3:8

W. of the world are evil. Jn.7:7

W. of the world are of the devil. Jn.8:39-47

Warning.

Envy & strife will stir every evil work. Jas.3:16

Evil w. will bring the judgment of the Lord upon a person. Jude 15

Wicked w. alienate & make us enemies of God. Col.1:21

W. can be dead despite one's profession. Heb.6:1; Rev.3:1

WORKS, GOOD (See **FRUIT, GOOD; MAN; PERFECT - PERFECTION**)

Basis. Good w. will be the basis of judgment. Mt.25:31-46

Described as. Dead w. Heb.6:1

Discussed.

Of the church. Rev.2:19

Right vs. wrong motives for good w. Mt.6:1; 6:1-4

What it takes to enter the kingdom of God. Good w. Mt.21:28-32

Duty.

To be a pattern, an example of good w. Tit.2:7

To be rich in good w. 1 Tim.6:18

To cease from working for salvation. Heb.4:10

To do good to all men. Gal.6:10

To do good to one's enemies. Mt.5:44

To do good w. Jn.3:21; 1 Pt.3:11

To do good w. quietly & in secret. Mt.6:3-4

To do good w. that stir people to glorify God. 1 Pt.2:12

To do greater w. than Jesus. Jn.14:12

To do the w. of God, to believe in Christ. Jn.6:29; 1 Jn.3:23

To give good w. precedence over religious law. Mt.12:5

To give to all who ask or take. Mt.5:40; 5:41; 5:42

To have a faith that does good w. Jas.2:14; 2:17-18, 20, 26

To keep on doing good w. Tit.3:8

To know that a man is not justified by w. Gal.3:1-4:7

To let our good works be seen by men. Mt.5:16

To love one's enemies & do good. Lk.6:35

To move on from the foundation of repentance from dead w. Heb.6:1

To purge one's conscience from dead w. Heb.9:14

To repent from dead w. Heb.6:1

To stir others to love & do good w. Heb.10:24

To w. tirelessly for the Lord. 1 Cor.15:58

Essential.

To follow Christ in doing good w. Mk.1:16

To have a faith that does good w. Jas.2:14; 2:17-18, 20, 26

Meaning. Mt.16:25-28; Jas.2:14-26

Nature of w.

Is a law, a principle. Ro.3:27

The w. of the world are evil. Jn.7:7

Purpose.

Are redeemed to be a special people, zealous of good w. Tit.2:13-14

The very reason we are saved is to do good w. Eph.2:10

To lead men to believe. Jn.2:9-11; 2:23

To lead men to glorify God. Mt.5:16

To silence critics by one's good w. 1 Pt.2:15

Results.

Are good, beneficial, & fruitful to men. Tit.3:8

Good w. follow believers to heaven. Rev.14:13

Secures the acceptance & approval of God. Acts 10:34-35; Heb.13:16

Secures the esteem of other believers. 1 Th.5:12

Secures the praise of rulers & leaders. Ro.13:3

W. lead some to believe. Jn.2:23-25

W. make faith perfect. Jas.2:22

W. plus faith justify a man. Jn.2:24

W. prove that one follows God. Jn.3:21

W. prove the believer's faith. Mt.25:34-40

Will be given power to rule. Rev.2:26-27

Vs. faith.

Discussed. Jn.6:28-29; Ro.4:1-8; 4:9-12; Gal.2:1-21; 2:15-16; 2:16; 2:17-18; 3:1-5; Eph.2:8-9; Jas.2:14-26

Faith apart from w. Jn.4:50

Illust. in Abraham. Ro.4:1-3

Obedience & love tied together. Jn.14:23

Vs. love. Mk.12:31

Vs. salvation.

Discussed. Acts 15:1-35; 2 Tim.1:9

The issue of w. vs. faith was answered in the Great Jerusalem Council. Acts 15:1-35

Vs. self-denial. Lk.6:32-34

Weakness of. (See **PERFECT - PERFECTION**)

Believing one is saved because of w. 2 Tim.1:9

Discussed. Col.2:20-23; 2:23

Emptiness of w. Mk.7:1-13

Man cannot do enough good w. to become perfect. Gal.2:15-16

W. are opposed to the believer's rest. Heb.3:7-19; 4:1-13

W. are unacceptable for salvation. Mt.5:20

W. cannot justify a person before God. Ro.3:20; Gal.2:15-16; 2:16; 3:1-4:7

W. cannot make a person acceptable to God. Ro.4:1-8

W. cannot make one acceptable to Christ. Mt.7:22-23

W. cannot make one righteous. Ro.4:1-8, esp. 4-7; 9:30-32; Gal.2:15-16; 3:19-22, esp. 21-22

W. cannot save a person. Gal.3:1-5; Eph.2:8-9; 2 Tim.1:9; Tit.3:4-5

W. cannot void the boastings of men. Ro.3:27

W. give man reason to glory, but not before God. Ro.4:2

W. lead to pride & false humility. Col.2:23

W. put a man under the curse. Gal.3:10-12

WORLD (See **CORRUPTION; INCORRUPTION**)

Attitudes of. Toward the outcast. Mk.2:13-17

Before the flood. Heb.11:7

Blessed. By God. (See **WORLD**, Created)

Ways blessed. Jn.1:9; 1:10-11

Case against. (See **WORLD**, Vs. Christ)

God's c. against all men. Ro.3:9-20

God's c. against all ungodliness & wickedness. Ro.1:18-23; 1:24-32

God's c. against the moralist. Ro.2:1-16

God's c. against the religionists. Ro.2:17-29

Objection of the religionist against God's rejection. Ro.3:1-8

Climax of the w. (See **WORLD**, Judgment of)

Has come. 1 Cor.10:11

How to live under. 1 Pt.4:7-11

The climactic consummation. Ro.8:18-27; 8:28-39; Eph.1:9-10; 2 Pt.3:1-18; Rev.19:11-16

Created - Creation.

Blessed by God.

Given everything needed. Mk.12:1

How God blessed the w. Jn.1:9; 1:10-11

By God. Leased out to men. Lk.20:9

Discussed. Col.1:16-17

God has given all provision for care. Mt.21:33

Scoffed at - not understood. 2 Pt.3:1-7

Deliverance from - How to overcome.

By being born again of God through faith in Christ. 1 Jn.5:4-5

By believers themselves. (See **WORLD**, Duty)

By believing that Jesus Christ is the Son of God. 1 Jn.5:4-5

By Christ.

He came to save the w. Jn.12:47

He gave His flesh for the w. Jn.6:51, cp. 6:52-58

He gives life to the world. Jn.6:33

He is the light of the w. Jn.8:12

He reconciles the w. 2 Cor.5:19-21

He takes away the sin of the w. Jn.1:29

His death. Gal.1:4; 4:1-7; Eph.2:13-18

His peace overcomes the w. Jn.16:33

By faith. 1 Jn.5:4-5

By forsaking the w. Mt.16:25-28

By God. He has loved the w. & given His Son to save the world. Jn.3:16

By guarding against the evil & dangers of religionists & world leaders. Mk.8:14-21

By not being entangled with the w. 2 Tim.2:3-4

By seeking a continuing city & world. Heb.11:10; 11:13-16; 12:22; 13:14

By the Holy Spirit. He convicts the w. of sin. Jn.16:8-11

By the Word of God. A strong witness. Mk.4:30-32

Discussed.

An event for all the w. Lk.1:57-66

Gaining the w. vs. saving the soul. Mk.8:36-37

God's glorious purpose for the w. Ro.11:33-36

How the w. is saved. Ro.10:12-17

Vs. Christ.
Blind to the Messiah. Mt.11:25-27
Christ ushered in a new age. Mt.9:14-17
Christ warns the **w**. Mk.11:1-11
Christ's vision of the **w**. Mt.9:36-38
Cries to be left alone. Mk.1:23-24
Denies Christ. Jn.18:19-24
Guilty of Christ's death. Mk.10:33
Ignores Christ. Reasons. Mk.3:20
Judged by the cross of Christ. Discussed. Jn.12:31-33; 12:31
Not approved by Christ. Mt.10:34-37
Opinion of Christ. Mt.16:13-14
Rebels against Christ. Mk.12:6-8
Rejects Christ.
Difficult to understand. Jn.1:10-11
Reasons. Mk.8:38; Lk.13:31-35
Treatment of Christ. Mt.26:55-56; 26:57-68
Treatment of God's Son. Death of Christ. Mt.27:26-44
Was prepared by God for Christ's coming. Jn.1:23
What life is like since Christ came. Eph.2:13-18
What life was like before Christ came. Eph.2:11-12
Vs. heaven. Discussed. 2 Cor.4:17-18
Vs. the soul. Attitude toward. Mk.8:36-37
Vs. the spiritual **w**. (See **SPIRITUAL WORLD**)
Five differences between the two **w**. Lk.20:27-38
Worldly minded vs. godly minded. Mt.6:19-24
Warning.
Against becoming entangled in the **w**. 2 Tim.2:3-4; 2 Pt.2:10-22
Cannot be saved apart from the gospel. Lk.15:1-7
Causes a man to be empty. Lk.15:16
Christ's return in the end time. Mt.24:30
Discussed. Mk.11:1-11
Fate of. Predicted. Lk.21:5-11
Rebuke of. Three reasons. Lk.9:37-45
Satan's wrath in the last days. Rev.12:12-17
There is a book of destiny. Rev.5:1-4
Wisdom of.
Discussed. 1 Cor.1:17-25; 1:26-31; 2:1-5; 2:6-13; 2:14-16; 3:18-20
To renounce. 1 Cor.3:18-20

WORLD, END OF (See **END TIMES; TRIBULATION, THE GREAT**)

WORLD HISTORY (See **HISTORY**)

WORLD, KINGDOMS OF THE
Victory over. By God & Christ in the end time. Rev.11:14-19

WORLD, SPIRITUAL (See **SPIRITUAL WORLD**)

WORLD ORGANIZATION
A confederation of states in the end time. Rev.13:1-2; 13:8-10; 16:12-16;17:2; 17:7-18; 19:17-21

WORLDLY - WORLDLINESS (See **COMPROMISE; SEPARATION**)
Caused by.
Greed & selfishness. Lk.12:13-21, cp. 12:31-34
List of ten causes. Judgment of. Lk.9:26
Man being wrapped up in **w**. Mt.6:31-32

Selfishness; godless independence. Lk.15:11-13
Dedication of the **w**. To their pursuits. Great dedication. Lk.16:13
Defined.
Love for the **w**. 1 Jn.2:15-17
What **w**. is. 1 Jn.2:15-17
Deliverance from.
By Christ.
By condemning sin in the **w**. Ro.8:3
By His conquest of the **w**. Jn.1:14
By His death. Eph.2:14-18, esp. 15-16; Col.1:22; Heb.2:14-16; 9:13-14; 10:19-20; 1 Pt.3:18
By His giving His **w**. for the life of the world. Jn.6:51
By His power over all **w**. Jn.17:2
By His reconciliation. Eph.2:11-18; Col.1:22
By His resurrection. Acts 2:30-31; Ro.1:3-4
By His suffering in the **w**. for us. 1 Pt.4:1
By condemning sin in the **w**. Ro.8:3
By confessing that Christ has come to earth in the **w**. 1 Jn.4:2-3; 2 Jn.7
By God.
By His being manifested, revealed in the flesh. 1 Tim.3:16
By His power over all **w**. Jn.17:2
By partaking of the **w**., of the life of Christ. Jn.6:54-56
By the Holy Spirit. By walking in Him. Gal.5:16
Deliverance from. (See **WORLD**, Deliverance From)
By being crucified with Christ. Gal.2:20; 6:14
By choosing God instead of the pleasures of sin. Heb.11:24
By keeping oneself unspotted from the world. Jas.1:27
By knowing what the body is designed for. 1 Cor.6:12-20
By living a godly life & looking for Christ's return. Tit.2:12-13
By not becoming entangled with the affairs of this world. 2 Tim.2:3-4
By not being a friend to the **w**. Jas.4:4
By not being caught up in a false sense of security. Mt.24:38-39; 1 Th.5:1-3
By not being conformed to this world. Ro.12:2
By not being deceived with the riches of the world. Mt.13:22
By not loving the world. 1 Jn.2:15-17
By not walking after the world. Eph.2:1-2
By participating in the divine nature. 2 Pt.1:4
By rejecting all who do not confess that Christ has come in the flesh. 1 Jn.2:22-23; 4:2-6; 2 Jn.7
By separating from the world. 1 Cor.5:1-13; 2 Cor.6:17-18
By setting one's affection above & not on the earth. Col.3:2
By taking heed & guarding against the world. Lk.21:34
By testing teachers & not following after false teachers. 1 Jn.4:1
By the Holy Spirit. He convicts one of sin. Jn.16:8-11
How to conquer. Jas.4:4-5; 1 Jn.5:4-5
Time for sin to be pointed out. Jn.7:6-9

Described as.
A master. Mt.6:24
A wilderness. Lk.15:3-4
Being adulteresses & adulterers. Jas.4:4
Cares of the world. (See **CARES OF THE WORLD**)
Climbing the social ladder. Rev.2:20-21
Compromising to save one's job. Rev.2:20
Evil. Mt.6:21-23
Five things. Mt.6:21-23
Following at a distance; sitting down among the crowd. Lk.22:54-55
"Give me" philosophy. Lk.15:11-13
Materialism. Lk.15:11-13
Pleasure-seeking. Acts 17:18
Returning to the world. Lk.15:11-13
Selfish independence. Lk.15:11-13
The disorderly, the idle, the loafers. Acts 17:5
Thorns. Mt.13:7, 22
Discussed. Mt.13:7, 22; Ro.7:14-17; 7:18-20; 12:2; 1 Cor.3:1-4; Gal.5:16-21; 1 Pt.2:11; Jas.4:4
Saving one's life in this world vs. losing one's life for Christ. Lk.9:23-27
Social functions. 1 Cor.6:12; 8:1-13; 10:14-11:1
The prodigal son. Lk.15:11-13
Duty.
Not to be unequally yoked together with the world. 2 Cor.6:14-16
Not to fulfill the lusts of the **w**. Gal.5:16-21
Not to give ourselves over to immorality & strange **w**. (unnatural sexual acts). Jude 7
Not to judge people by the **w**. Jn.8:15
Not to live after the flesh. Ro.8:12
Not to live any longer after the lusts of the **w**. 1 Pt.4:2
Not to set one's mind on the **w**. Ro.8:5
Not to sow to our **w**. Gal.6:8
Not to use our liberty in Christ as an opportunity for the **w**. to sin. Gal.5:13
Not to use the weapons of the **w**. in the spiritual struggle of life. 2 Cor.10:3-5
Not to walk after the flesh. Ro.8:1-4
To abstain from the **w**. 1 Pt.2:11-12; 4:3
To be cleansed from all filthiness of the **w**. 2 Cor.7:1
To combat the desires of the sinful nature. Gal.5:16-21
To complete the sufferings of Christ in our **w**. Col.1:24
To control the **w**.
By having no confidence in. Ph.3:3
By seeking reconciliation when offended. Mt.18:15-17
By struggling against. Ro.8:23-27
To crucify the sinful nature with its affections & desires. Gal.5:24
To hate even the garments spotted by the **w**. Jude 23
To have no confidence in the **w**. Ph.3:3
To live a crucified & sacrificial life in the **w**. Gal.2:20
To make no provision for the **w**. Ro.13:14
To manifest the life of Jesus in our **w**. 2 Cor.4:11
To mortify, put to death, the **w**. Ro.8:12-13
To purify the **w**. by the blood of Christ. Heb.9:13-14
To put away the filth of the **w**. 1 Pt.3:21
To put off the old garment of the **w**. Mk.2:22

To put off the sins of the **w**. Col.2:11
To resist the temptation of the world.
Lk.4:5-8
To seek heavenly treasure not worldly
treasures. Lk.12:31-34
To turn away from the sinful nature &
turn to Christ. Gal.5:24
Effects of. A destressed spirit. 2 Pt.2:6-8
Example of.
Demas. Loved this present **w**. 2 Tim.4:10
Herod's lavish party. Mk.6:14-29
Pilate. Mk.15:15
Judgment of. (See **WORLD**, Judgment
of; **JUDGMENT**) Lk.6:24-26
Meaning. Jn.1:14; Ro.7:5; 8:5-8;
Eph.2:3; 1 Pt.2:11
The struggle within fighting against
what one should do. Ro.7:14-25;
Gal.5:16-18;1 Th.4:3-5; Jas.4:2; 4:4
Nature Works - Shortcomings of.
Cannot inherit the kingdom of God.
1 Cor.15:50
Cannot make a person perfect. Gal.3:3
Cannot please God. Ro.8:8
Causes man to die. Ro.8:13
Does not justify a person before God.
Ro.3:20; Gal.2:16
Dreams filthy dreams that defiles a
person. Jude 8
Evil. 1 Jn.5:19
Is as grass, withers ever so quickly.
1 Pt.1:24
Is not a part of spiritual beings. Lk.24:39
Is so corrupted that it even spots the
garments worn by a person. Jude 23
Money, silver & gold can consume the
w. Jas.5:3, cp. Mt.6:19-20
No good thing dwells within the **w**. Ro.7:18
Pride. 1 Jn.2:15-16
Profits nothing. Jn.6:63
Reaps corruption. Gal.6:8
Serves the law of sin & death.
Ro.7:25; 8:1-4
Sinful. 1 Jn.2:2
Stirs a fleshly, carnal commitment.
Jn.13:36-38
Stirs lust. 1 Pt.2:11
Struggles against man. 1 Jn.5:4-5
Struggles against prayer. Mt.26:41;
Mk.14:38
The carnal vs. the spiritual view of the
w. Lk.22:33-37
The lust of the **w**. is not of God.
1 Jn.2:15-16
Wars against the soul & spirit.
Mt.26:41; Mk.14:38; 1 Pt.2:11
Withers & falls away. 1 Pt.1:24-25
Works of the **w**.
Seventeen works. Gal.5:19-21
Twenty-three works. Ro.1:29-32
Principles governing.
Discussed. Ro.14:1-23; 1 Cor.5:6-13;
6:12-20
Limits of freedom. Ro.14:1-23;
1 Cor.10:14-11:1
Questionable pleasures. Ro.14:1-23;
1 Cor.8:1-13
Problems of - Dangers of.
Discussed. Mt.19:23-26; Mk.10:23-27
Does not satisfy or feed the heart.
Jn.6:26-27
Opposes Christ. Reason. A threat to
one's own desires. Jn.7:32
Things that lead away from Christ.
Mt.16:17
Results - Effects of.

Causes one to lose his soul. Lk.16:19-21
Causes temptations & trials. Jas.4:4
Causes the loss of life. Mt.6:19-20
Causes the loss of meaning & purpose.
Mt.6:19-20
Chokes the life out of men. Three
things. Lk.8:11-15
Chokes the Word & spiritual growth.
Mt.13:7, 22; Mk.4:18-19
Corrupts the church. Rev.2:12-17; 2:18-29
Deceives. Reasons. Mt.6:21-23
Discussed. Mt.6:19-20; Mk.6:14-29
Enslaves. Lk.15:14-16
Makes one an enemy of God. Jas.4:4
Sin of.
A life spent in lusts, cravings. Eph.2:3
Attached to, pre-occupied with the
world. Mk.8:16-20
Discussed. Lust of the flesh.
Lk.12:13-19; 1 Jn.2:15-17
Dress. (See **CLOTHING - DRESS**)
Exposing the human body.
Lk.20:45-47
Evil associations. Lk.22:54-62
Lists of fleshly sins. Ro.1:24-32; 3:9-20;
1 Cor.6:9-11;10:6-10; Gal.5:19-21;
Eph.4:25-32; Col.3:8-9; 1 Tim.1:9-10;
2 Tim.3:1-5; 1 Pt.2:1; 4:3
Seeking position, wealth, honor--
greatness. Lk.22:54-55
Seeking **w**. Lk.9:46
Symbolized.
In Balaam. Rev.2:14
In Demas. 2 Tim.4:10
In Jezebel. Rev.2:20-23
In Nicolaitans. Rev.2:15
Verses. List of. Lk.8:11-15
Vs. being spiritually minded. (See
MIND) Mt.6:19-24; Lk.12:13-21
Vs. God.
Cannot serve two masters. Lk.16:13
Vs. trusting God. Lk.12:29-30
Vs. the Spirit. Discussed. Ro.8:1-17
Warning against.
Discussed. Lk.9:24
Not watching for the Lord's return.
Lk.17:26-30

WORLDLY MINDED (See **MIND;
WORLDLINESS**)

WORLDLY SORROW (See **REPENTANCE**)
Vs. godly sorrow. 2 Cor.7:7-12; 7:10

WORLDLY WISE
Meaning. Mt.11:25

WORRY (See **ANXIETY**)

WORSHIP (See CHURCH, Faithfulness;
PRAISE; PRAYER; THANKSGIVING)
Customs of. When customs are to be fol-
lowed. 1 Cor.11:2-16
Danger - Problems.
Abusing tongues & prophecy in **w**.
1 Cor.14:26-35
Disorderly services. 1 Cor.14:26-40
True **w**. vs. false **w**. Lk.8:4-15
Warning to those who abuse. Mk.11:15-19
Was & can be corrupted. Ro.1:24-25
Withdrawing from **w**. Heb.10:26-31
Worshipping false sacrifices. Heb.10:1-4
Worshipping man-made gods, the dead
& false gods of this world. (See
IDOLATRY) Gal.4:8-11
Discussed. Jn.4:19-24

Duty.
Not to forsake **w**. Heb.10:25
Not to let strife hinder **w**. Mt.12:9-13
Not to neglect public **w**. despite afflic-
tion. Lk.13:11-13
To be faithful to **w**. Mk.1:21;
Lk.13:11-13; Acts 9:26-28
To govern worship services.
1 Cor.14:26-40
To seek God in **w**. Prepares one's
heart for receiving Christ. Jn.4:45
To **w**. continually in the church. Lk.24:53
To **w**. God & God alone. Rev.22:9
To **w**. God after He has blessed one.
Jn.5:13-14
To **w**. in spirit & truth. Jn.4:23-24
Essential.
Christ's glory in the believer. 2 Cor.3:18
God's presence. 2 Cor.3:7
Evaluated by God. God knows man's
heart. Jn.1:46-49
Example of.
By a woman severely diseased.
Lk.13:11-13
Faithfulness. Lk.2:37; 2:41-42
Heavenly **w**. Rev.19:1-6
Failure - Weakness of. (See **RELIGION;
RELIGIONISTS**)
Can be empty, worthless, useless. Mk.7:7
Sitting in the church, but failing to **w**.
Mk.1:23-24
False approach to **w**.
Astrology. Col.2:8-10
Spirits. Col.2:18-19
Visions. Col.2:18-19
How to **w**. (See **JESUS CHRIST**, Media-
tor)
Through Christ alone. Jn.4:22
Meaning. Mt.8:2
Nature.
Earthly **w**. is a shadow of heavenly
things. Heb.8:1-5
Is of the Jews. Jn.4:22
Not by earthly or personal sacrifices.
Heb.10:1-4
Of Christ.
As Lord. Mt.15:25
By all creatures of the universe, both
of heaven & earth. Rev.5:8-14
By angels. Heb.1:6
By believers. Mt.28:17
By the desperate. Mt.9:18; 15:25
By the wise men. Mt.2:1-11
Stressed. Mt.12:9-10
To be a day of universal worship in the
future. Jn.7:6-9
Of idols. (See **IDOLATRY**)
Of the early church.
Discussed. 1 Cor.14:26-40
Rules governing services. 1 Cor.14:16-20
Services. Described. Acts 20:6-12;
1 Tim.4:13
Of the earth. Earthly **w**. is inadequate.
Heb.9:1-10
Reasons. For **w**. Jesus. Lk.24:52
Results. Brings Christ into the home.
Mk.1:29
True **w**.
Discussed. Ro.9:4
What real **w**. is. Acts 24:14-16

WORSHIP, IMPERIAL
Discussed. Rev.2:12; 13:4-8; 13:13-17

WORTHY OF RESPECT)
Meaning. Acts 2:27; 1 Tim.3:8; Tit.2:2

PURPOSE STATEMENT

LEADERSHIP MINISTRIES WORLDWIDE

exists to equip ministers, teachers, and laymen in their
understanding, preaching, and teaching of God's Word
by publishing and distributing worldwide
The Preacher's Outline & Sermon Bible®
and related *Outline* Bible materials,
to reach & disciple men, women, boys, and girls for Jesus Christ.

•MISSION STATEMENT•

1. To make the Bible so understandable - its truth so clear and plain - that men
   and women everywhere, whether teacher or student, preacher or hearer,
   can grasp its Message and receive Jesus Christ as Savior; and...
2. To place the Bible in the hands of all who will preach and teach God's Holy
   Word, verse by verse, precept by precept, regardless of the individual's
   ability to purchase it.

The *Outline* Bible materials have been given to LMW for printing and especially
distribution worldwide at/below cost, by those who remain anonymous. One fact,
however, is as true today as it was in the time of Christ:

• The Gospel is free, but the cost of taking it is not •

LMW depends on the generous gifts of Believers with a heart for Him and a love and
burden for the lost. They help pay for the printing, translating, and placing *Outline*
Bible materials in the hands and hearts of those worldwide who will present God's
message with clarity, authority and understanding beyond their own.

LMW was incorporated in the state of Tennessee in July 1992 and received IRS 501(c) 3 nonprofit status in March 1994. LMW is an international, nondenominational mission organization.
All proceeds from USA sales, along with donations from donor partners, go 100% into under-
writing our translation and distribution projects of *Outline* Bible materials to preachers,
church & lay leaders, and Bible students around the world.

9/98   © 1998. Leadership Ministries Worldwide

Box 21310 - Chattanooga, TN 37424 • (423) 855-2181 • FAX (423) 855-8616
• E-Mail - outlinebible@compuserve.com — www.outlinebible.org •

Equipping God's Servants Worldwide

1. **PAYMENT PLANS.** Convenient and affordable ways to get/use your FullSet with easy payments.

2. **NEW TESTAMENT.** In 14 volumes. Deluxe version 3-ring binders. Also: SoftBound Set, 3 volume set, and NIV edition. All on 1 CD-ROM disc.

3. **OLD TESTAMENT.** In process; 1 volume releases about every 6-8 months, in sequence.

4. **THE MINISTERS HANDBOOK.** Acclaimed as a "must-have" for every minister or Christian worker. Outlines more than 400 verses into topics like Power, Victory, Encouragement, Security, Restoration, etc. Discount for quantities.

5. **THE TEACHER'S OUTLINE & STUDY BIBLE™.** Verse-by-verse study & teaching; 45 minute lesson or session. Ideal for study, small groups, classes, even home schooling. Each book also offers a STUDENT JOURNAL for study members.

6. **OUTLINE BIBLE CD-ROM.** Includes all current volumes and books; Preacher, Teacher, and Minister Handbook. 1 disc. WORDsearch STEP format. Also 50+ Bible study tools unlockable on same disc. **FREE Downloads - www.outlinebible.org**

7. **THE OUTLINE.** Quarterly newsletter to all users and owners of *POSB*. Complimentary.

8. **LMW AGENT PLAN.** An exciting way any user sells *OUTLINE* materials & earns a second income.

9. **DISTRIBUTION.** Our ultimate mission is to provide *POSB* volumes & materials to preachers, pastors, national church leaders around the world. This is especially for those unable to purchase at U.S. price. USA sales gain goes 100% to provide volumes at affordable prices within the local economy.

10. **TRANSLATIONS.** Korean, Russian, & Spanish are shipping first volumes — Others in-process: Hindi, Tamil, Telugu, Chinese, French, German, Finnish.

11. **FUNDING PARTNERS.** To cover the cost of all the translations, plus print, publish, and distribute around the world is a multi million dollar project.

    Church-to-Church Partners send *Outline* Bible books to their missionaries, overseas church leaders, Bible Institues and seminaries...at special prices.

12. **REFERRALS.** Literally thousands (perhaps even you!) first heard of *POSB* from a friend. Now Referral Credit pays $16.00 for each new person who orders from a customer's Referral.

13. **CURRICULUM & COPYRIGHT.** Permission may be given to copy specific portions of *POSB* for special group situations. Write/FAX for details.

9/98

For Information about any of the above, kindly FAX, E-Mail, Call, or Write

Please PRAY 1 Minute/Day for LMW!

PO Box 21310, Chattanooga, TN 37424 • (423) 855-2181 • FAX (423) 855-8616
• E-Mail - outlinebible@compuserve.com — www.outlinebible.org •

OUTLINE BIBLE RESOURCES

This material, like similar works, has come from imperfect man and is thus susceptible to human error. We are nevertheless grateful to God for both calling us and empowering us through His Holy Spirit to undertake this task. Because of His goodness and grace **The Preacher's Outline & Sermon Bible®** - New Testament is complete in 14 volumes, and the Old Testament volumes release periodically. **The Minister's Handbook** is available and *OUTLINE* Bible materials are releasing electonically on **POSB-CD** and our **Web site**.

God has given the strength and stamina to bring us this far. Our confidence is that, as we keep our eyes on Him and grounded in the undeniable truths of the Word, we will continue working through the Old Testament volumes and the second series known as **The Teacher's Outline & Study Bible.** The future includes helpful *Outline Bible* books and **Handbook** materials for God's dear servants.

To everyone everywhere who preaches and teaches the Word, we offer this material firstly to Him in whose name we labor and serve, and for whose glory it has been produced.

Our daily prayer is that each volume will lead thousands, millions, yes even billions, into a better understanding of the Holy Scriptures and a fuller knowledge of Jesus Christ the incarnate Word, of whom the Scriptures so faithfully testify.

As you have purchased this volume, you will be pleased to know that a small portion of the price you have paid has gone to underwrite and provide similar volumes in other languages (Russian, Korean, Spanish and others yet to come) — To a preacher, pastor, lay leader, or Bible student somewhere around the world, who will present God's message with clarity, authority, and understanding beyond their own. *Amen*.

For information and prices, kindly contact your *OUTLINE* Bible bookseller or:

LEADERSHIP
MINISTRIES
WORLDWIDE

P.O. Box 21310, 515 Airport Road, Suite 107
Chattanooga, TN 37424-0310
(423) 855-2181 FAX (423) 855-8616
E-Mail - outlinebible@compuserve.com
www.outlinebible.org — *FREE* download materials

9/98